Derivations and Constraints
in Phonology

Edited by
IGGY ROCA

CLARENDON PRESS · OXFORD
1997

Oxford University Press, Great Clarendon Street, Oxford OX2 6DP
Oxford New York
Athens Auckland Bangkok Bogota Bombay
Buenos Aires Calcutta Cape Town Dar es Salaam
Delhi Florence Hong Kong Istanbul Karachi
Kuala Lumpur Madras Madrid Melbourne
Mexico City Nairobi Paris Singapore
Taipei Tokyo Toronto Warsaw
and associated companies in
Berlin Ibadan

Oxford is a trade mark of Oxford University Press

Published in the United States
by Oxford University Press Inc., New York

British Library Cataloguing in Publication Data
Data available

Library of Congress Cataloguing in Publication Data
Derivations and constraints in phonology/edited by Iggy Roca.
Based on a workshop organized by the editor, held at the
University of Essex in 1995.
Includes bibliographical references and indexes.
1. Grammar, Comparative and general—Phonology.   I. Roca, Iggy.
P217.D47   1997   414—dc21   96–53307
ISBN 0–19–823689–1
ISBN 0–19–823690–5 *(pbk.)*

1 3 5 7 9 10 8 6 4 2

Typeset by J&L Composition Ltd, Filey, North Yorkshire
Printed in Great Britain on acid-free paper by
Biddles Ltd., Guildford and King's Lynn

I dedicate this volume to

MORRIS HALLE

on the occasion of his retirement
and in celebration of his life.

Preface

The present collection grew out of a three-day workshop on derivations and constraints in phonology organized by the editor at the University of Essex in the autumn of 1995. The purpose of the workshop, like that of the collection, was to bring to the fore and thrash out the differences that separate traditional rule-and-derivation generative phonology from its current competitor, Optimality Theory, manifestly growing in vogue by the day. The rationale underpinning this endeavour is that a principled decision about the adequacy of the theories can only be taken when such differences are clearly understood and rigorously stated. The workshop was fruitful in exchange and discussion, and conveniently laid the ground for the written work that is now presented to a wider audience.

The papers in the volume have been written by some of the participants in the Essex workshop and by other leading specialists specifically brought in for the task. The focus has been strictly respected, sometimes against difficult odds. Each paper was submitted to a rigorous review procedure by a team of experts, which included a number of readers anonymous to the authors. The result is, I hope, a valuable contribution to the debate, one in particular that can short-circuit wasteful developments and bring us a little closer to the phonological truth we are all anxious to achieve.

The work is organized in three parts. The first part, Preliminaries, introduces the volume, and will be of particular use to those readers not fully conversant with Optimality Theory in general or with some specific aspect of it. I am confident that the induction to optimality in the first two sections of Chapter 1 and most of Chapter 2 (which deliberately grows harder as it goes on) can be read and understood by anyone familiar with the contents of such recent state-of-the-art surveys of traditional generative phonology as those by M. Kenstowicz (*Phonology in Generative Grammar*, Oxford: Blackwell, 1994) or I. Roca (*Generative Phonology*, London: Routledge, 1994). I am hopeful, therefore, that the inclusion of this induction will foster the unity of the field by ensuring that colleagues who, for some reason or other, have not kept up with the developments of the past three years are not left behind and excluded. The second part of the volume, Theoretical Investigations, contains three chapters aimed at a level of theoretical generality above the rest, dealing respectively with the logical commensurability of classical generative theory with Optimality Theory, the justification of these two theories in the context of phonetic reality, and the bearing of the theories on the learnability issue. The longer third section, Empirical Studies, includes the remainder of the eighteen chapters. Some of the writers take sides for one or the other theory right from the start, while others steer a middle course for as long as allowed by the facts they discuss. A common, if not absolutely universal, finding is that a strictly orthodox Optimality Theory is empirically unworkable. Authors, however, differ in their reactions to this fact, and, while some simply propose the outright dismissal of the theory, others carve out several extensions and modifications in their endeavor to preserve it.

I am grateful to the participants in the Essex workshop for three hard-working days of good-humoured enthusiasm and high phonological acumen, and to the volume's contributors for their commitment and dedication, and their patience and resoluteness in the face of more or less continuous onslaughts by the readers and the editor. I thank the readers for their generosity, the British Academy and the University of Essex for financial assistance, and the Department of Language and Linguistics at Essex for structural and additional financial support. Last but not least, Frances Morphy has proven a most skilful and constructive editor, Leonie Hayler a very humane and helpful assistant editor, and Rosemary Cox a particularly competent PA, and I thank them appreciatively.

Note on transcription: Contributors have been actively encouraged to adhere to IPA conventions, but it is an empirical fact of life that old habits die hard, and some variation has inevitably made it through to the final version.

Contents

Notes on Contributors

DIANA ARCHANGELI, Professor, Department of Linguistics, University of Arizona

JULIETTE BLEVINS, Associate Professor, Centre for Linguistics, University of Western Australia

GEERT BOOIJ, Professor of General Linguistics, Vrije Universiteit Amsterdam and Holland Institute of Generative Linguistics

SYLVAIN BROMBERGER, Emeritus Professor, Department of Linguistics and Philosophy, Massachusetts Institute of Technology

NICK CLEMENTS, Research Director, Centre National de la Recherche Scientifique (CNRS), Paris

MORRIS HALLE, Emeritus Professor, Department of Linguistics and Philosophy, Massachusetts Institute of Technology

MICHAEL HAMMOND, Associate Professor, Department of Linguistics, University of Arizona

WILLIAM J. IDSARDI, Assistant Professor of Linguistics, University of Delaware

SHARON INKELAS, Associate Professor of Linguistics, Department of Linguistics, University of California, Berkeley

JUNKO ITÔ, Associate Professor of Linguistics, Department of Linguistics, University of California at Santa Cruz

RENÉ KAGER, Fellow of the Royal Netherlands Academy of Sciences at the University of Utrecht

ARMIN MESTER, Associate Professor of Linguistics, Department of Linguistics, University of California at Santa Cruz

SCOTT MYERS, Assistant Professor, Department of Linguistics, University of Texas at Austin

ROLF NOYER, Assistant Professor, Department of Linguistics, University of Pennsylvania

ORHAN ORGUN, graduate student, Department of Linguistics, University of California, Berkeley

CAROLE PARADIS, Professor, Department of Linguistics, Laval University

DOUGLAS PULLEYBLANK, Professor, University of British Columbia

Iggy Roca, Reader in Linguistics, Department of Language and Linguistics, University of Essex

Jerzy Rubach, Professor, University of Iowa & University of Warsaw

Nicholas Sherrard, graduate student, Department of Language and Linguistics, University of Essex

Keiichiro Suzuki, graduate student, Department of Linguistics, University of Arizona

William Turkel, graduate student, University of British Columbia

Cheryl Zoll, Assistant Professor, Department of Linguistics and Philosophy, Massachusetts Institute of Technology

PART I
PRELIMINARIES

✦

1

Derivations or Constraints, or Derivations and Constraints?

IGGY ROCA

1. Optimality Theory

Revolutionary change appears to have moved in on phonology, the rule-and-derivation tradition of the past thirty-odd years now seemingly being discarded for constraint-based approaches, Optimality Theory notable among them. Indeed, both the speed of transmission of OT and the explosion in research it has triggered in a short time-span are remarkable by any standards in the field of phonology, and probably in the whole of linguistics.

The basic theoretical dichotomy we are facing can be summed up in the following question: Does the grammar contain (orderable) rules, or only (surface) constraints? Thus, suppose we want to derive the surface string [AC] from the underlying representation /AB/ (justified, say, by its occurrence in [ABZ]). Traditional generative phonology will postulate a rule B → C /__], for] = end of string, from which the derivation in (1) will ensue:

(1) Traditional derivation
   /AB/   underlying form
   C   rule: B → C /__]
   [AC]   surface form

In Optimality Theory, the same regularity will be expressed by means of a two-layered machinery. On the one hand, a (universal and automatic) procedure (named GEN, for generator) provides the target form [AC] from the source /AB/. GEN, however, also supplies a large (possibly infinite) number of competitors, among them [AB], [AD], [AF], [ABZ], [FGHIJK], etc., all from the same source. We obviously want these impostors banned as surface representations of /AB/. This ban is enforced by a team of (in principle also universal) constraints, each of which inhibits one aspect of any surface manifestation of /AB/ that is not precisely the desired target [AC]. A stylized display ('tableau') of both the action and the dramatis personae implicated in the plot just described is given in (2) (the substance of each constraint 'C_n' is, of course, immaterial to the point being made):

(2) OT tableau (unranked constraints)

/AB/	C_1	C_2	C_3	C_4	...
[AB]	*				
☞ [AC]					
[AD]		*			
[AF]			*		
[ABZ]				*	
etc.					

In this simplified example we are assuming that each of the illegitimate forms violates only one constraint (cf. the asterisk in the corresponding intersections), and that the winning output [AC] (marked in the tableau by a pointing hand) violates none. One of the crucial differences between Optimality Theory and other constraint-based theories is, however, that OT constraints can be (and frequently are) violated. What happens is that, like the animals in Orwell's farm, the constraints are not all equal in rank, and consequently compliance with higher-ranked constraints has priority over compliance with their lower-ranked comrades. A more realistic (if still hypothetical) alternative to tableau (2) will therefore be (3) (>> = 'higher-ranked than').

(3) OT tableau (ranked constraints)

/AB/	C_1	>>	C_2	>>	C_3	>>	C_4	...
[AB]	*							
☞ [AC]					*			
[AD]			*					
[AF]	*		*					
[ABZ]			*				*	
etc.								

Here, the violation of C_3 by [AC], the winning candidate, is offset by the violation of C_1 by [AB] and [AF], and of C_2 by [AD] and [ABZ] (also by [AF], irrelevantly, since this form already violates C_1). As can be seen, therefore, a (surface) form is optimal when it enjoys the best obedience score for the hierarchized constraints, respect for higher constraints naturally taking precedence.

This thumbnail summary of Optimality Theory should be sufficient to give the uninitiated reader a flavor of the mechanics of the theory, and allow us to proceed (a fuller, more technical presentation of OT is given in Chapter 2).

What are the advantages of this new way of looking at phonology that phonologists appear to find so enticing? Here are some, combed from the OT literature:

It captures legitimate *surface* regularities, thus providing a formalism for the phenomenon of conspiracy (cf. Kisseberth 1970).

It uniformizes the grammar, since constraints are also necessary under rule-and-derivation approaches (cf., e.g., Lexical Phonology; Paradis 1988–9; Myers 1991).

It provides a direct formal framework for representing universality and markedness, because both GEN and the constraints are assumed to be universal and related to markedness.

It accounts for the emergence of unmarked patterns in the face of structural odds.

It provides a fertile ground for explaining the learnability of the system, because:

GEN is included in UG;
each constraint is (ideally) also included in UG; and
the learnability burden then reduces to constraint ranking (and establishment of lexical representations, in common with traditional generative theory).

It dispenses with the power inherent in rule interaction.

It allows parallel operation of the constraints, and thus a declarative (as against procedural) formulation of them.

If this were the end of the story, it would be well-nigh inevitable to agree that OT represents genuine phonological progress (in the way, for instance, of Autosegmental Phonology earlier), and the field would accordingly have little choice but to move forward in unison (as indeed happened with Autosegmental Phonology). As many of the papers in this volume bear witness, however, this target has still not been quite achieved. The ensuing discussion explores some of the reasons for this state of affairs.

2. OPACITY

One problematic area for OT concerns opaque surface forms. In traditional generative phonology, rules can of course be extrinsically ordered (cf. Bromberger and Halle 1988). Among the relations enabled by this extrinsic ordering are counterfeeding and counterbleeding (Kiparsky 1968). A set of abstract examples will clarify this, in preparation for the real-language data to be discussed in subsequent sections.

2.1 *Feeding and counterfeeding*

Suppose that our input representation AB in derivation (1) above is in fact not lexical, but in turn derived from lexical /AA/ by the rule in (4):

(4) A → B /A__

A feeding relationship between this rule and its predecessor in (1) (B→ C/__]
= 'rule (1)') will yield the desired surface form [AC], as follows:

(5) Feeding relationship
    /AA/
      B   rule (4)
      C   rule (1)
    [AC]

In this derivation, rule (4) feeds rule (1), in that, by changing lexical A into B, rule (4) has increased the number of forms to which rule (1) can apply (B can input rule (1), but its predecessor A cannot).

   Suppose we now give these two rules the converse order:

(6) Counterfeeding relationship
    /AA/
      –   rule (1)
      B   rule (4)
    [AB]

The rules now stand in a counterfeeding relation, since rule (4) is externally prevented from feeding rule (1), which consequently fails to apply. The resulting output, [AB], is therefore opaque in the context of our grammar, because such an output meets the structural description of one of the rules of this grammar (rule (1)) to which none the less it has not been subjected. A counterfeeding ordering, therefore, enforces rule under-application.

   The situation just described seems problematic for a theory such as the one I have been sketching, where constraints act exclusively on surface representations. I offer a demonstration in tableau (7), where I have sought comparability between the two accounts by translating our two rules (1) and (4) into the two (negative) surface constraints *B] and *AA, respectively (other constraints are responsible for the rejection of such obviously unwanted candidates as [ZY], [EFGHIJ], etc., all respectful of our two stated constraints, but these additional constraints can simply be presupposed here):

(7) Seeking a counterfeeding candidate selection in OT

a.	/AA/	*B]	*AA	b.	/AA/	*B] >> *AA		c.	/AA/	*AA >> *B]	
	[AB]	*			[AB]	*			[AB]		*
	[AA]		*		[AA]		*		[AA]	*	
☞	[AC]			☞	[AC]			☞	[AC]		

As can be seen, of the three plausible candidates included in these tableaux, only [AC] emerges unviolated, irrespective of the ranking of the two constraints, and therefore this form will always be selected: [AC] by definition complies with the requirements of both constraints (which we are adopting as functionally equivalent to our previous rules). By contrast, the true surface form in the language we are considering, [AB], invariably violates *B], therefore always scoring lower than [AC]. This demonstration illustrates the difficulties faced by OT as described above in handling traditional counterfeeding relationships such as that displayed in (6).

2.2 Bleeding and counterbleeding

Let us now imagine that our standard grammar again contains the lexical form /AA/, and the rules A → B /A__ (our familiar rule (4)) and A → Y / [__ (= 'rule (8)'; [= string initial). Suppose first that these two rules apply in the order just given:

(8) Counterbleeding relationship
    /AA/
      B   rule (4)
    Y   rule (8)
    [YB]

In (8) both rules have applied, maximizing the change from /AA/ to [YB]. Suppose, however, that we (extrinsically) invert the ordering:

(9) Bleeding relationship
    /AA/
    Y   rule (8)
    –   rule (4)
    [YA]

Now rule (4) has been 'bled' by rule (8), because the replacement of the first A with Y by (8) has destroyed the environment required by rule (4) (A__), which consequently cannot apply. A bleeding ordering, therefore, decreases the number of forms that undergo a rule. Contrariwise, counterbleeding, exemplified in (8) above, maintains this number unaltered.

It is clear that, by inducing apparent rule over-application, a counterbleeding ordering also gives rise to opacity, since it generates surface forms that exhibit no motivation for some change they have undergone. For instance, in derivation (8), the surface form [YB] cannot be entirely traced back to its underlying ancestor /AA/, since the second A can only change to B in the presence of a preceding A (rule (4)), but no such A is visible in the surface, having been changed to Y by rule (8).

The difficulties posed for OT by counterbleeding are displayed in the tableaux in (10), where I have translated rule (8) by the constraint *[A. Note, in addition, that these tableaux accommodate a further constraint (more precisely, family of constraints), 'Faithfulness' (abbreviated 'F'), standard in OT, and which promotes identity of input and output, as will be seen in more detail in Chapter 2 (clearly, for our purposes here F may not outrank our two other constraints, or else such constraints would be nullified):

(10) Seeking a counterbleeding candidate selection in OT

a. /AA/	*AA	*[A	F
[AA]	*	*	
☞ [YA]			*
[YB]			**

b. /AA/	*AA >>	*[A >>	F
[AA]	*	*	
☞ [YA]			*
[YB]			**

c. /AA/	*[A >>	*AA >>	F
[AA]	*	*	
☞ [YA]			*
[YB]			**

The question that obviously arises at this point is whether these problematic results for OT are an artefact of our simplifications (remember, for instance, that we have simply translated our rules (1) and (4) into constraints) or whether they hold as a matter of theory-internal logic. The answer is 'both'. On the one hand the tableaux in (7) and (10) show that the derivational effects of counterfeeding and counterbleeding relations are mathematically inexpressible in Optimality Theory. From this perspective, therefore, the attestation of opaque forms in languages would pose a serious problem for OT, since such forms represent precisely what OT predicts not to exist. The source of opacity, however, is not located in the forms themselves, but in the rules that generate them. Consequently, a salvaging move is available: if the rules are changed, the opacity will disappear. This strategy was already adopted by Koutsoudas et al. (1974), in a different context, in their attempt to do away with ordered rules. Now, in OT it is a matter of changing, not the rules (OT programmatically has no rules!), but rather the substance of the constraints or the representations. It is in this light that we must interpret Kager's injunction in Chapter 15 below that 'one cannot, and should not, directly transfer the conceptual categories of rule-based theory into OT', a piece of advice he takes up in earnest in his reanalysis of South Eastern Tepehuan data. Likewise, Rubach (Chapter 18 below) provides a successful OT account of opaque Polish data through an alternative analysis of their prosodic structure, although eventually he runs into an insurmountable problem, the test-piece of his discussion. A reasonable bottom line is, therefore, that opacity does present a strong challenge to Optimality Theory, one which needs to be attended to urgently if we want to make sure that we are not building our castles in sand (see McCarthy 1995 for discussion from an OT perspective). Most appropriately, a number of papers in this collection take up this issue with data from an assortment of languages. Interestingly, we will see that different writers respond differently to the challenge, some purposely turning their backs on the theory, while others endeavour to modify it to achieve compatibility with the data.

3. Empirical Need for Ordered Rules

In this section I discuss data from Imdlawn Tashlhiyt Berber, Dutch, Polish, Gere, Hebrew, and Yokuts which attest to the empirical reality of opacity. Some of these data point to the need for morphology-associated strata, while others appear either to require rule ordering and derivations or to call for the re-formation of Optimality Theory.

3.1. *Lexical strata*

Two word-formation processes of IT Berber make reference to pre-surface levels of phonological representation (Clements, Chapter 9 below): imperfective stem formation and a pattern of templatic derivation. In Dutch (Booij, Chapter 8 below), there is evidence for the assignment of both phonological rules and morphological processes to different strata (lexical and postlexical, cyclic and postcyclic).

Some minimal background on IT Berber phonology is needed in order to understand the data. As is well known since Dell and Elmedlaoui (1985), *all* ITB segments qualify in principle for syllable nuclearity, nucleus formation taking place in stages that start off with the most sonorous segment (/a/) and wind up with the least sonorous ones (voiceless plosives). At each such stage, the goal is the creation of CV syllables.

Imperfective stem formation (ISF) involves gemination of the one consonant which is parsed as an onset in the input (perfective) verb stem at a representational level that precedes the subsequent annexation of the consonant to the adjacent syllable in the perfective forms. The result of ISF is given in (11) (syllables are bracketed and nuclei underlined):

(11) ITB imperfective stem formation

Input	Imperfective stem	
(r̲) (ʃq)	rʃʃq	'be happy'
(b̲) (xl̲)	bxxl	'be stingy'
(mr̲z)	mmrz	'wound in the head'
(xn̲g)	xxng	'choke'

As mentioned, the onset that is input to imperfective stem formation is not always retrievable from the surface form of the perfective, where it can become integrated in the neighboring syllable (the reason for this annexation is orthogonal to our present discussion; see Chapter 9 below for details):

(12) ITB perfective surface forms
   (rʃq)
   (bxl̲)
   (mr̲z)
   (xn̲g)

A straightforward analysis of these facts allots CV syllabification ('Core Syllabification') to the lexical stratum, and annexation to the postlexical stratum (the domains of annexation are the Phonological Phrase and the Prosodic Utterance, both clearly postlexical). Imperfective stem formation is instrumental to the creation of words, and therefore it must be lexical. The resulting stratal organization is summarized in (13):

(13) ITB stratal organization (1st attempt)
   Lexical
   Core Syllabification
   Imperfective Stem Formation
   Postlexical
   Annexation

The 'Tirrugza' pattern of templatic derivation also examined by Clements supports the postulation of an additional lexical stratum. The data are given in (14):

(14) ITB Tirrugza templatic derivation

Base	Templatic derivative	
a-rgaz	t-i-rrugza	'man'
a-!nttajfu	t-i-!nttujfa	'dummy'
ʃʃrif	t-i-ʃʃurfa	'sharif'
wurga	t-i-wwurga	'to dream'

The template (C)CCuCCa obviously needs to tell Cs from Vs in the input. This would be a straightforward matter in most languages, but not so in IT Berber, where *all* segments but /a/ are syllabically ambiguous in underlying representation. The problem is that the derivative template must select all the base consonants ([+cons] segments), but only the vowels ([−cons]) that end up as non-nuclear. In surface representation, however, consonants are also split into nuclear and non-nuclear, and therefore the procedure is seemingly in need of a conjunction ('select [+cons] segments and non-nuclear [−cons] segments'), descriptively awkward and explanatorily vacuous. This conjunction is avoided if we make reference to a level of syllabification at which all vowels (maximum sonority segments) have been tested for nuclearity, but consonants still have not. All we have to say then is that the Cs of the template exclusively select input non-nuclear segments (hence the preservation of /i/ in the form for 'dummy' but not in the form for 'sharif' in (14) above). This analysis leads to the enriched stratal system in (15):

(15) ITB stratal organization (final)
   Lexical
   S1: Core Syllabification 1 (for /a, i, u/)
       Templatic Derivation
   S2: Core Syllabification 2 (for remainder)
       Imperfective Stem Formation

   Postlexical
   Annexation

The derivational analyses we have proposed are obviously satisfactory. In OT the facts inevitably impose stratum-bound evaluations. This strategy was adopted by McCarthy and Prince (1993) in their analysis of Axininca Campa, and by others since, the obvious implication being that strata in the style of Lexical Phonology are not incompatible with OT in the eyes of its practitioners.

   In the two ITB cases we have examined, the need for pre-surface phonological structure stems from processes of word-formation, not from the phonology itself. As Clements suggests, this fact might weaken the bearing of this evidence on the issue of multi-level phonology (word formation may, after all, be disjoint with the phonology; cf., e.g., Halle and Vergnaud 1987 and Halle and Marantz 1993). The Dutch data discussed by Booij in Chapter 8 below make available precisely this phonological evidence.

   The first class of Dutch data we will discuss supports the organization of the phonology into a lexical and a postlexical stratum. The relevant rules, Coda Devoicing and Schwa Onset, stand in a counterbleeding relationship, as follows (NB '.' = syllable boundary):

(16) a. Coda devoicing: $[-son] \rightarrow [-voice] / \_\_$.
   b. Schwa onset: syllables headed by schwa must have an onset

The effects of (16a) and (16b) are illustrated in (17):

(17) a. hel[t]   'hero'   cf. hel.[d]in   'heroine'
     b. ik heb 't   'I have it'   cf. wij hebben   'we have'
         .[pət].   .[bə].
         hij had 't   'he had it'   cf. wij hadden   'we had'
         .[tət].   .[də].

In (17a) Coda Devoicing is bled in the derivative by the prior assignment of the obstruent to the onset. This result is still attainable without phonological strata by simply ordering the phonology (including in particular Coda Devoicing) after all the morphology (as in SPE, Halle and Vergnaud 1987, or Halle and Marantz 1993). Consider, however, the forms in (17b), where the verb's final consonant has undergone devoicing ([hɛ.pət], etc.), despite being in the onset (we know that it is in the onset because Schwa Onset (16b) prohibits onsetless schwas). This shows that Coda Devoicing counterbleeds Schwa Onset:

(18)   A fragment of Dutch grammar
       Suffixation   (e.g. *-in* in *heldin* 'heroine'; *-en* in *hebben* '(we) have')
       Coda Devoicing   (e.g. *hel*[t] 'hero'; *he*[p]; '(I) have')
       cliticization   (e.g. [ət] '*t* 'it' attachment)
       Schwa Onset   (e.g. *he.*[pət] in *heb* '*t* 'have it')

On the reasonable assumption that cliticization operates syntactically, the counterbleeding ordering Coda Devoicing > Schwa Onset will correlate with a lexical/postlexical stratal division:

(19) Counterbleeding in Dutch

/hɛld/	/hɛld/	/hɛb/	/hɛb/	
				Lexical
	-in			Suffixation
hɛld	hɛl.din	hɛb	hɛb	(Re)syllabification
t	NA	p	p	Coda Devoicing
				Postlexical
			-ət	Cliticization
NA	NA	NA	hɛ.pət	Schwa Onset

It could be thought at this point that this stratal division can be obviated if the /b/ of *heb* is parsed ambisyllabically in *heb*[ət], since such a /b/ would then automatically meet the structural description of Coda Devoicing because of its coda constituency. Such syllable restructuring would, of course, be nothing but a repair strategy aimed at achieving compatibility of opaque data with OT by a reanalysis of the input structure along the lines discussed in section 2 above. In the present case, however, this solution is not available, because demonstrably ambisyllabic Dutch obstruents do not undergo Coda Devoicing (cf. *adder* [adər] 'snake', where [d] remains voiced in spite of its ambisyllabicity, attested by the shortness of [a], Dutch rimes being minimally bipositional).

A second case of stratal ordering in Dutch implicates stress. Consider the following forms:

(20) a. proféssor → proféssors 'professor(s)'
　　　 béz[ə]m → béz[ə]ms 'broom(s)'
　　　 kánon → kánons 'canon(s)'
　　 b. kanáal → kanálen 'canal(s)'
　　　 ólifànt → ólifànten 'elephant(s)'
　　　 kanón → kanónnen 'gun(s)'

(20) shows that the pattern of plural allomorphy is determined by stress (*-en* after a stressed syllable; *-s* otherwise), while the stress pattern is not affected by pluralization, irrespective of allomorphy.

Derivationally, we can get these results by ordering the stress rules before pluralization. In this way, stress information is available to the plural rule for allomorph selection, while at the same time leaving the stress of the singular unaffected:

(21) Stratal ordering in Dutch (1st version)
　　 Cyclic
　　 Main stress　　　　　 (e.g. *kanáal, absúrd, béz[ə]m*)
　　 Secondary stress　　 (e.g. *ólifànt*)
　　 Postcyclic
　　 Pluralization　　　　 (e.g. *béz[ə]ms, ólifànten*)

The need for stratum ordering carries over to OT. Thus, suppose we try to account for stress invariance by a constraint HEADIDENT requiring perfect matching between the prosodic heads of related words (e.g. between the prosodic heads of the singular and the plural). This type of constraint is the lynchpin of Correspondence Theory, the most recent embodiment of OT (Correspondence Theory will be briefly referred to in passing; for a fuller presentation, see Chapter 2, and McCarthy and Prince 1995). However, such HEADIDENT constraint is not always complied with in Dutch:

(22) absúrd → absurditéit 'absurd(ity)'

The non-native derivational suffix *-iteit* triggers stress movement, in direct contrast to the plural suffix. Such a difference in behavior can be accommodated straightforwardly in standard LP, simply by including non-native suffixation in the cyclic stratum that precedes the postcyclic stratum containing pluralization:

(23) Stratal ordering in Dutch (final version)
　　 Cyclic
　　 Main stress　　　　　　　　　 (e.g. *kanáal, absúrd, béz[ə]m*)
　　 Secondary stress　　　　　　 (e.g. *ólifànt*)
　　 (non-native) Suffixation　 (e.g. *absúrd-iteit*)
　　 Main stress (NB cyclic)　 (e.g. *absurditéit*)
　　 Postcyclic
　　 Pluralization　　　　　　　　 (e.g. *béz[ə]ms, ólifànten*)

Booij suggests that an OT analysis will need two opposing constraint rankings, associated with plural and non-native derivational suffixes (HEADIDENT >> MSR versus MSR >> HEADIDENT, respectively). These alternative rankings amount to two different co-phonologies, here equivalent to level ordering (Inkelas, Orgun and Zoll discuss the issue of co-phonologies in Chapter 13 below). Whatever way we look at it, therefore, multi-level phonology appears inevitable in OT. As mentioned above, however, this result is commonly assumed to be compatible with this theory.

3.2 *Irreducible rule-ordering*

Rule orderings unsupported by the morphology are a more serious embarrassment for OT. Several such cases arise in Yokuts, Hebrew, Gere, and Polish, discussed in Chapters 6, 12, 17, and 18, respectively. I shall briefly review these cases here.

The West African language Gere, discussed by Paradis in Chapter 17 below, has a nine–vowel system (i, ɪ, e, ɛ, a, ɔ, o, ʊ, u) and four tones (H´, MH ', M ¯, L `).

The key data are given in (24):

(24) a. /wɔ́ - CAUS - ɪ - '/   → [wɔ̰́.ḭ] '(I) make them shout'
     b. /wɔ́ - ɪ - '/   → [gṵ́.ḭ] '(I) shout them'

It can be seen that practically identical inputs puzzlingly give significantly divergent outputs.

Some further background on the language is necessary before offering a solution. First, the Gere CAUS(ative) suffix is purely skeletal, X, whereas the 3pl suffix /ɪ/ has no skeletal slot. In turn, the intransitive suffix consists of a floating MH tone.

Paradis's Theory of Constraints and Repair Strategies (see e.g. LaCharité and Paradis 1993) includes both rules and constraints. When constraint violations are created by the morphology, they are immediately (and minimally) repaired by rules at the lowest prosodic level referred to by the violated constraint.

The specific constraints proposed by Paradis for Gere are:

(25) Gere constraints

SONCON: sonority-rising diphthongs only (NB The first high vowel of such diphthongs is assumed by Paradis automatically to become a glide, concomitantly lowering its sonority)

HEIGHTCON: no sequences of non-high vowels

TONECON: no tautosyllabic falling-tone sequences (unless the last tone is L)

OCP: *[round][round] (ɔ excepted)

Let us in this light consider the derivation of [wɔ̰́.ḭ] '(I) make them shout':

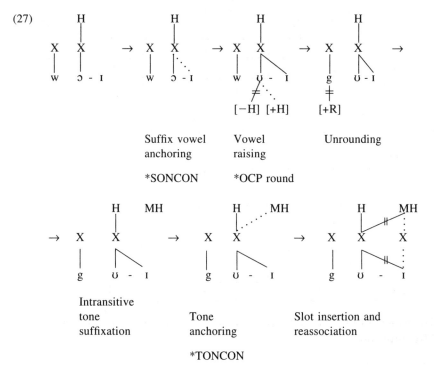

(26)

Suffix vowel anchoring   Tone suffixation   Tone anchoring

As can be seen, nothing exceptional has happened. In particular, no constraint is violated in the course of the derivation, and no need for repair strategies consequently arises. The result is a surface form as close to the underlying form as is consistent with the autosegmental conventions.

Let us now turn to [gʊ́.ì] '(I) shout them', which differs considerably from the underlying form /wɔ́ - ɪ - ⁱ/. The derivation proposed by Paradis is as follows (constraint violations are starred):

(27)

[−H] [+H]   [+R]

Suffix vowel anchoring   Vowel raising   Unrounding

*SONCON   *OCP round

Intransitive tone suffixation   Tone anchoring   Slot insertion and reassociation

*TONCON

The crucial step is the second one, where a violation of SONCON triggers raising of the underlying /ɔ/ to ʊ (which in turn triggers /w/ unrounding to comply with OCP). The motivation for this rising, however, is lost on the way to the surface, with the introduction of the additional skeletal slot repairing the subsequent violation of TONCON. In particular, this new slot destroys the intermediate diphthong that had caused /ɔ/ rising. Slot-insertion is therefore in a counterbleeding relation with Vowel Rising.

Paradis goes on to show that a one-step OT evaluation systematically selects the incorrect output *[wɔ́. ɨ], as is shown in (28). Note that the mutual ranking of some of the constraints is irrelevant to this outcome: from now on, ranked constraints will be separated by solid lines in tableaux, and unranked constraints by broken lines, the standard convention (! after an asterix indicates a fatal violation, the remainder of that candidates's evaluation being shaded to signal its irrelevance).

(28)

/wɔ́ - ɪ - '/	☞ wɔ́ .ɨ	wɔ́ɪ	wʊ́ɪ	gɔ́ɪ	gʊ́ɪ	wɔ́ wɪ́	wɔ́.ɪ	gʊɪ	gʊ́.ɪ	gʊ́.ɨ
TONECON								*!		
PARSE (NON-FEAT)		*!	*!	*!	*!	*!*	*!		*!	
SONCON		*		*						
OCP		*								
FILL (SLOT)	*						*			*
PARSE (FEAT)		*	*	**				**	**	*!*

As in the cases considered in the previous section, the solution involves a two-step evaluation, each step with its own constraint ranking:

(29) 1st cycle

/wɔ́ - ɪ/	gʊ́.ɪ	wɔ́ɪ	wʊ́ɪ	gɔ́ɪ	wɔ́ wɪ́	wɔ́.ɪ	☞ gʊ́ɪ
FILL (SLOT)	*!					*!	
PARSE (NON-FEAT)					*!		
SONCON		*!		*!			
OCP		*!					
PARSE (FEAT)	**		*	*			**

The winner of the first cycle, gʊ́ɪ, is input to the second cycle, associated with MH suffixation:

(30) 2nd cycle

/gʊ́ɪ - '/	gʊ́ɪ	gʊ́ɪ	☞ gʊ́. ɨ
TONECON	*!		
PARSE (NON-FEAT)		*!	
FILL (SLOT)			*

The desired candidate has now emerged victorious. The obvious challenge for OT concerns the need for the evaluation to be carried out in two steps (each with its own constraint ranking) which Paradis contends are assigned to the same stratum, an important point of difference from the Dutch cases examined above.

Polish has an abundance of extrasyllabic consonants (in all word positions) and two remarkably active processes of voice assimilation (regressive and progressive, respectively), often impervious to the presence of (*ex hypothesi*) extrasyllabic sonorants. Rubach proposes in Chapter 18 below that all sonorants (vowels and consonants) are unspecified for voice underlyingly, and that, derivationally, the phonology of Polish contains the following set of stratified ordered rules:

(31) A set of Polish rules
   Lexical Postcyclic
   Initial extrasyllabic sonorant adjunction
   Sonorant default (assigns [+ voice] to prosodified sonorants)

   Postlexical
   Voice assimilation
   Default extrasyllabic sonorant adjunction

The procedure is illustrated in (32) for /krvi/ (the +/− line below the melodies corresponds to the [voice] tier):

(32)

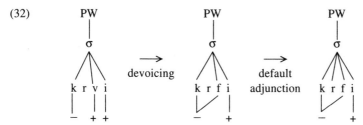

In the input, /r/ is unspecified for voice and unprosodified. Devoicing (v → f) involving progressive assimilation takes place in the first step of the derivation, following which *r* gets prosodified by default adjunction (Rubach assumes that the *r* attaches to the syllable node, rather than to the PW node, because is it trapped in the onset).

Rubach proposes the constraints in (33) for the corresponding OT analysis:

(33) Polish OT constraints
   ALIGN-L(eft): (Align: left edge of stem, left edge of syllable)
   PARSE$_{cons}$: parse consonants into *prosodic* structure
   SON(orant)DEF(ault): all and only *syllabified* sonorants are [+voice]
   SSG = Sonority Sequencing Generalization
   STRICT LAYER = Strict Layer Hypothesis

The orderings in (31) above include counterfeeding (Sonorant Default > Default Adjunction) and counterbleeding (Voice Assimilation > Default Adjunction), inevitably leading to surface opacity, which we know is problematic for OT. Forms such as *mędrka* [mentrka] 'crafty person-gen.sg.' are however accounted for satisfactorily under OT if the ranking in (34) is assumed:

(34) ALIGN-L, PARSE$_{cons}$, SONDEF, SSG >> STRICT LAYER

The tableau in (35) illustrates the approach at work (segments italicized in the underlying form are assumed to be underspecified for voice):

(35)

/mendrka/	ALIGN-L	PARSE$_{cons}$	SONDEF	SSG	STRICT LAYER
☞ PW (mentr ka; + + + − +)					*
PW (mentr ka; + + + − +)		*!			
PW (mendr ka; + + + + + − +)				*!	
PW (mendr ka; + + + + + − +)				*!	
PW (mendr ka; + + + + + − +)			*!		*

The success of this proposal in overcoming the difficulties associated with opacity is due to the wise formulation of the constraints, with structural effects that forestall opacity. Indeed, Rubach argues that the OT analysis has an edge over its derivational alternative on the grounds that it is rooted in simple and independent generalizations (Myers makes a similar point at a more general level in Chapter 4 below; see section 6 below).

The procedure, however, becomes problematic in cases of progressive devoicing such as those in (36) (accounted for derivationally in (32) above):

(36) kr[f]i 'blood (gen.sg.)'   (cf. kre[v]ni 'relative')
    pl[f]ać 'spit (fig.)'   (cf. splu[v]ać 'spit')
    tr[f]ać 'last'
    tr[f]oga 'fright'

(37)

/krvi/	ALIGN-L	PARSE$_{cons}$	SONDEF	SSG	STRICT LAYER
PW | σ /|\ k r v i, − + + +				*!	
PW | σ /|\ k r v i, − + +		*!			
PW | σ /\ k r f i, − +		*!			
PW | σ /\ k r f i, − +			*!	*	
☞ PW | σ / k r f i, − +					*

Note that the (correct) winning candidate, in the last row, complies with the presupposed no-crossing of lines, because the attachment of *r* to the prosodic word node takes place on a separate plane. On the other hand, Rubach suggests that this configuration violates a further constraint which must be brought in to ban split syllables:

(38) CON(stituent) CONTIG(uity): Split phonological constituents are not permitted.

This development creates a serious difficulty for the OT account, which Rubach proposes to answer by means of a two-level constraint evaluation, with each level defined by its own constraint ranking. The ranking for the first level will be as in (39) (rankings crucial to the issue are printed bold):

(39) ALIGN-L, CONCONTIG, **SONDEF, SSG** >> **PARSE$_{con}$**, STRICT LAYER

This ranking carries out the selection in (40) (NB crucially, syllabified sonorants must be filled in for voice at this stage since they are not transparent to voice assimilation):

(40)

/krvi/	ALIGN-L	CONCONTIG	**SONDEF**	SSG	**PARSE**$_{cons}$	STRICT LAYER
☞ PW [σ: k r f i, − +]					*	
PW [σ: k r v i, − + + +]			*!		*	
PW [σ: k r f i, − +]	*!				*	*
PW [σ: k r f i, − +]		*!				*
PW [σ: k r f i, − +]			*!	*		
PW [σ: k r v i, − + + +]				*!		

The (incomplete) winning candidate, in the first row, constitutes the input to level-2 evaluation, with a new constraint ranking (rankings crucial to the issue are again printed bold; note that (41) incorporates the constraints NO-CROSS(ing) and PROG(ressive)-DEV(oicing), with the obvious meanings):

(41) NO-CROSS, PROGDEV, ALIGN-L, CONCONTIG, **PARSE$_{con}$** >>
     >> **SSG, SONDEF**, STRICT LAYER

The complete surface form we are seeking, *kr*[f]*i*, indeed emerges at the end of the procedure (NB *r* finally gets parsed):

(42)

/krvi/	NO-CROSS	PROGDEV	ALIGN-L	CON-CONTIG	**PARSE$_{cons}$**	SSG	SONDEF	STRICT LAYER
☞ PW [σ: k r f i]						*	*	
PW [σ: k r v i]		*!				*	*	
PW [σ: k r f i]	*!					*		
PW [σ: k r f i]					*!			
PW [σ: k r f i]				*!				*
PW [σ: k r f i]			*!		*			*

We must conclude, then, that an OT analysis of the Polish data requires multi-level evaluation, like the previous analyses of ITB and Dutch. The difference is that, while in ITB and Dutch the levels are motivated morphologically, in Polish they are exclusively phonological, a situation inconsistent with consensual OT practice.

Hebrew offers an important testing-ground for the viability of surface-true constraints on two accounts. First, both Tiberian Hebrew and Modern Hebrew are rich in opacity (cf. Chomsky 1951; 1995; Idsardi 1996). Second, the transition from TH to MH opens a useful window into the diachronic dimension of opacity.

Tiberian Hebrew postvocalic spirantization is transparently illustrated by the following data:

(43) TH Transparent Postvocalic Spirantization
      ka:θáv 'write-3ms perf'   yixtó:v 'write-3ms imperf'
      ga:ðlú 'be great-3p perf'   yiɣdá:lu 'be great-3p imperf'

As can be seen, (non-geminate) stops become fricatives after a vowel (k → x, g → ɣ, examining the data from left to right, and t → θ, d → ð, from right to left).

The effects of postvocalic spirantization can, however, become opaque as a result of vowel deletion, as shown in (44):

(44) Opaque postvocalic spirantization
      /katab+u/ → ka:θvú 'write-3p perf'
      cf. /katab/ → ka:θáv 'write-3ms perf'

The focus of Idsardi's discussion is on the changes from TH to MH and their repercussions for the predictions made by both theories. In particular, rule-based theories view phonological change as resulting from the addition of new rules at the end of the grammar (Halle 1962; Kiparsky 1970), an ordering that can obviously bring about surface opacity. By contrast, Idsardi points out that 'in contrast to the rule approach, which has no direct measure of opacity, there is explicit representation of opacity in the OT constraint parameters, and the default state for these parameters is for true surface (transparent) evaluation. Therefore, with OT we would not expect increases in grammar opacity to be favored occurrences in language change'.

For simplicity, we shall only look at the repercussions on opacity of changes in the Hebrew phonemic system. The relevant parts of the inventories of both stages of the language are as follows:

(45)
    TH: p b t d ṭ s z ṣ (ś) ʃ k g q   phonemes
           f v θ ð   x ɣ   allophones only
    MH: p b t d   s z t͡s ʃ k g ⎫
          f v   x ⎬ all phonemes
                                 ⎭

The key fact concerns the restriction of postvocalic spirantization in MH to stops which have a corresponding fricative *phoneme*. A rule-based approach can derive this situation simply by marking the rule of postvocalic spirantization as structure-preserving. It is crucial to realize that what is structure-preserving is the operation of the rule itself, hence the impossibility of a chain */g/ → ɣ → [x] (the last step by fast speech Voicing Assimilation), even though the surface [x] *is* structure-preserving (Structure Preservation is in any event suspended in fast speech, where voice assimilation does derive [ɣ] from x ← /k/).

By contrast, the surface-structure evaluation required by OT makes the analysis of these facts considerably awkward. Consider, for instance, the difficulties faced by OT in obtaining the correct fast speech ouput [jiksos] from the underlying form /ja-gasos/ (the constraint responsible for the deletion of the first stem vowel is assumed):

(46)

/ja-gasos/	Voicing assimilation	Structure preservation	Spirantization
√ jiksos			*!
☞*jixsos			
jiɣsos	*!	*	
jigsos	*!		*

Idsardi discusses several strategies that must unconvincingly be called upon in order to attain the correct result in an Optimality framework, in contrast to the principled and straightforward nature of the rule-based analysis.

More generally, the change from Tiberian to Modern Hebrew involves a considerable increase in opacity—a problematic outcome for OT, which is explicitly built on surface transparency. Substantial changes in constraint parameter setting (cf. McCarthy 1995) or in constraint ranking would therefore be necessary to accommodate the Hebrew facts in this framework. By contrast, a diachronic increase in opacity is a normal state of affairs from the perspective of rule-based theories, which formalize historical change as the addition of rules at the end of the grammar, as already mentioned.

Rich surface opacity is also present in Yokuts (Archangeli and Suzuki, Chapter 6 below). In this language, all lexical long vowels are non-high in the surface (/miik'-it/ → [meek'it] 'was swallowed'). Yokuts also has left-to-right rounding harmony between vowels with the same underlying height (/hud-hin/ → [hudhun] 'recognizes'). Finally, compliance with the surface syllabic template CV(X) can cause shortening of lexical vowels (/laan-hin/ → [lanhin] 'hears') or epenthesis (/lihm-hin/ → [lihimhin] 'runs').

On this backdrop, let us consider the derivational account of the lexical form /c'uum-hin/ 'destroyed':

(47) /c'uum-hin/
	NA	Epenthesis
	u	Harmony
	oo	Lowering
	o	Shortening

The form [c'omhun] is doubly opaque, since it contains no motivation for either Lowering (the surface vowel is short) or Harmony (the harmonized surface vowels do not agree in height). This outcome betrays counterbleeding of Harmony on Lowering, and of Lowering on Shortening. Indeed, if the orderings in (47) are reversed (Shortening > Lowering > Harmony), the surface forms will be transparent (and counterfactual in Yokuts): Shortening will now bleed Lowering (/c'uum-hin/ > *[c'umhun], and Lowering will bleed Harmony (/c'uum-it/ → *[c'oomit] 'was destroyed').

As expected, patterns like those of Yokuts strain the descriptive power of OT, whether in its original formulation or in its newer version, Correspondence Theory. Let us consider Lowering first. Imposing the LOW constraint in (48) on surface forms is obviously insufficient:

(48) LOW (1st version)
      $\mu\mu = [-\text{high}]$

The reason for the insufficiency of (48) is, of course, that Lowering competes with Shortening, which bleeds it if unchecked. Archangeli and Suzuki circumvent this problem with a correspondence reformulation of (48), as in (49):

(49) LOW (final version)
      $\mu\mu \, _{I}R_{o} \, [-\text{high}]$

Constraint (49) inhibits *input* long vowels from surfacing as high (cf. the subscripts on the relational operator R). Correspondence constraints are, however, standardly geared to imposing *identity* between the two correspondents (input–surface or surface–surface identity). Accordingly, constraints like that in (49) represent a new type, 'disparate correspondence constraints', which Archangeli and Suzuki point out is anticipated in McCarthy and Prince (1995).

On the plausible assumption that the standard faithfulness constraints are also operative in Yokuts (under whatever formalization), a problem connected with Lowering still remains. In particular, while the (common) surface vowel inventory of Yokuts corresponds to the unmarked five–vowel system [i, e, a, o, u], its underlying inventory only contains four vowels: /i, a, o, u/ (there is abundant evidence for this mismatch). The problem, therefore, is that, given a surface form like [meek'it] 'was swallowed', there is no motivation for the desired underlying representation /miik'-it/ over the more faithful one

*/meek'-it/. Archangeli and Suzuki's answer to this challenge involves, again, an extension of the general scope of correspondence constraints, which they now allow to refer exclusively to the input. Thus they propose the breakdown of the constraint V=[+ high] (which partly accounts for the materialization of the Yokuts epenthetic vowel as [i]) into the two constraints in (50):

(50) a. {V=[+ high]}$_I$
     b. {V=[+ high]}$_O$

As can be seen, (50a) is exclusively an input constraint. By targeting under-lying high vowels, this constraint will favor /miik'-it/ over */meek'-it/, as desired. Clearly, though, the inclusion of input constraints runs counter to the spirit (and the standard letter) of OT, purposely set up as a theory of *surface* well-formedness: 'Phonological constraints apply to outputs alone or govern input-output relations' (Prince and Smolensky 1993). Input constraints are also investigated by Hammond in Chapter 11 below.

As was mentioned above, Yokuts Harmony is parasitic on [high] agreement (Harmony predictably fails, for instance, in /doos-it/ → [doosit] 'was reported'). A preliminary constraint aimed at capturing this fact is given in (51):

(51) {RD/αHI}
     = every path including [round] includes [αhigh]

However, because the operation of Lowering can render underlying height opaque, (51) clearly cannot account for all the data. What we obviously need is to restrict the scope of the constraint to lexical representation:

(52) {RD/αHI^I}
     = every path including [round] includes [αhigh] in the input

(52) gives the desired result for forms like [c'omhun], from underlying /c'uumhin/, as we know. However, it will fall short of predicting the full harmonized shape of [ʔugunhun] 'drank' (from /ʔugn-hin/), which exhibits epenthesis of /i/ (the default vowel of Yokuts), subsequently rounded by Harmony:

(53)
/ʔug n-hin/		/log wʔ-as/ 'pulverize'
i	Epenthesis	i
u u	Harmony	NA
NA	Lowering	NA
NA	Shortening	NA
[ʔugunhun]		[logiwʔas]

Constraint (52) cannot apply to the epenthesized /i/ (eventually [u] by Harmony), since this /i/ is not present in lexical representation, to which constraint (52) refers.

This problem leads to Archangeli and Suzuki's third extension of standard OT. In particular, they propose the introduction of a new category of 'input-else' constraints:

(54) {RD, αHI^{IE}} (RD/αHI^{IE})
   = every path including [round] includes [αhigh] in the input or, lacking input, in the output

As can be seen in (54), input-else constraints (which Archangeli and Suzuki point out are anticipated in Cole and Kisseberth 1995) make reference to both the lexical and the surface form. This property ensures compatibility of the Yokuts data with Optimality Theory, by circumventing the need for intermediate levels of representation. Arguably, however, some of the changes introduced by Archangeli and Suzuki stretch OT in ways which, if nothing else, are not obviously congenial to its spirit.

4. EXPLANATORY ADEQUACY UNDER OT

The OT difficulties reported on in the previous section will be offset in this section with two accounts of success, involving the phenomena of voiced velar nasalization in Japanese and vowel deletion in South Eastern Tepehuan. In both cases it will be argued that, although derivational analyses are possible, the OT account is superior in that it achieves a higher level of explanation.

The effects on bound morphemes of Voiced Velar Nasalization (a rule of conservative Tokyo Japanese: g → ŋ) are illustrated in (55):

(55) VVN in bound morphemes

gai+jin	'foreigner'	koku+ŋai	'abroad'
go+zeN	'morning'	shoo+ŋo	'noon'
gam+peki	'quay'	kai+ŋaN	'sea shore'
gi+kai	'parliament'	shiŋ+ŋi	'deliberations'
gen+zai	'currently'	sai+ŋeN	'reappearance'

VVN also has a distributional reflection in monomorphemic forms:

(56) VVN morpheme-internally

geta	'clogs'	kaŋi	'key'
giri	'duty'	kaŋo	'basket'
guchi	'complaint'	kaŋŋae	'thought'
go	'game of Go'	sasaŋeru	'give'
garasu	'glass'	tokaŋe	'lizzard'

By contrast, in ordinary compounds VVN is only optional:

(57) VVN in ordinary compounds

geta	'clogs'	niwa+g/ŋeta	'garden clogs'
gara	'pattern'	shima+g/ŋara	'striped pattern'
gei	'craft, art'	shirooto+g/ŋei	'amateur's skill'
go	'Go game'	oki+g/ŋo	'Go played with a handicap'

The simplest account of these facts would correlate the obligatory/optional distinction with the lexical/postlexical application of VVN, the former word-internally and the latter at internal junctures in compounds. Puzzlingly, however, VVN is obligatory in compounds that have undergone Rendaku, a process involving the voicing of the initial obstruent in the second element of the compound (e.g. *ama* 'nun' + *tera* 'temple' → *amadera* 'nunnery'):

(58) VVN in Rendaku compounds:

kuchi	'mouth'	doku+ŋuchi	'abusive language'
kuni	'country'	yuki+ŋuni	'snow country'
kami	'paper'	ori+ŋami	'origami paper'
kaki	'writing'	yoko+ŋaki	'horizontal writing'
kusuri	'medicine'	nuri+ŋusuri	'medical cream'
kirai	'dislike'	onna+ŋirai	'misogynist'

This development obviously throws a spanner in the works of the cyclic account, since the structure of Rendaku and non-Rendaku compounds is identical (in particular, they both have identical junctures). Itô and Mester (1989; 1990) proposed to overcome this difficulty with the following set of assumptions:

(i)   velars are underspecified for [nasal]
(ii) VVN is feature-filling lexically
(iii) VVN is feature-changing postlexically
(iv) [-nasal] is filled in by a cyclic default rule lexically

While the analysis works, Itô and Mester suggest in Chapter 14 below that it is conceptually problematic. First, under the approach, lexical applications of VVN are restricted to underspecified velars. Such underspecification is only preserved in the absence of a previous cycle in which either VVN (→ [+ nasal]) or the cyclic default rule (→ [− nasal]) would have applied. Consequently, the analysis is effectively encoding morphological structure as feature structure, i.e. using the F-element [− nasal] as a diacritic. Second, the analysis requires the stipulation that non-independent stems (e.g. the Sino-Japanese stems in (55) above) do not constitute cyclic domains, since otherwise their underlying initial /G/ would have become /k/ by default (→ [− nasal]) at that earlier cycle, thus blocking any subsequent lexical application of VVN (in Rendaku compounds, by contrast, the /G/ is created in the compound cycle, thereby becoming available for VVN). Third, the need to apply VVN as a cyclic lexical rule conflicts with the (semi-)allophonic nature of the rule, which is clearly not structure-preserving. Fourth, the cyclic default rule (→ [− nasal]) must be *ordered* after VVN.

Let us compare the Optimality analysis, for which Itô and Mester claim undisputed superiority. The constraints and their ranking are given in (59). As can be seen, we are crucially assuming that in the VVN dialect the ranking of *g and Ident$_{SS}$ can go either way, optionally:

(59) VVN Japanese constraints and ranking
  Constraints
  *[ŋ = no initial ŋ
  Rendaku =]$_{X°}$ [$_{X°}$ X
  $\quad\quad\quad\quad\quad\quad$ |
  $\quad\quad\quad\quad\quad\quad$ [+voice]
  *g = no g
  Ident$_{SS}$ = segmental identity between a bound stem and its correspondent free form
  Ident$_{LS}$ = segmental identity between surface and lexical form for [nasal]
  Ranking

  $$*[\eta, \text{Rendaku} \gg \begin{Bmatrix} \text{Ident}_{SS} \gg {}^*g \\ {}^*g \gg \text{Ident}_{SS} \end{Bmatrix} \gg \text{Ident}_{LS}$$

Let us in this light consider the evaluations of *yuki-ŋuni*, with obligatory VVN, and *niwa-g/ŋeta*, where VVN is only optional:

(60)
a.

/yuki-kuni/	*[ŋ	REND	IDENT-SS	*g	IDENT-LS
yuki-guni			*	*!	
☞yuki-ŋuni			*		*
yuki-kuni		*!			

b.

/yuki-kuni/	*[ŋ	REND	*g	IDENT-SS	IDENT-LS
yuki-guni			*!	*	
☞yuki-ŋuni				*	*
yuki-kuni		*!			

(61)

a.

/niwa-geta/	*[ŋ	REND	IDENT-SS	*g	IDENT-LS
☞niwa-geta				*	
niwa-ŋeta			*!		*

b.

/niwa-geta/	*[ŋ	REND	*g	IDENT-SS	IDENT-LS
niwa-geta			*!		
☞niwa-ŋeta				*	*

Straight derivational forms such as *doku* - [ŋ]*a* 'poison fang' exhibit, of course, a behavior similar to Rendaku compounds:

(62)

a.

/doku-ga/	*[ŋ	REND	IDENT-SS	*g	IDENT-LS
doku-ga				*!	
☞doku-ŋa					*

b.

/doku-ga/	*[ŋ	REND	*g	IDENT-SS	IDENT-LS
doku-ga			*!		
☞doku-ŋa					*

As we have seen, the only special machinery required by the OT analysis concerns the free ranking of the constraints IDENT-SS and *g. This, Itô and Mester suggest, compares very favorably with the awkwardness associated with the derivational analysis, noted above.

A similar pledge for OT superiority is made in Chapter 15 by Kager, who argues that the derivational rhythmic analysis of vowel deletion in South-Eastern Tepehuan, although feasible, is inferior to its OT counterpart, crucially grounded in exhaustivity of parsing.

The derivational account proposed in Rice (1992) needs the set of rules listed and illustrated in (63) (see Chapter 15 below for further details):

(63) A metrical derivation in SET

	'pestles' /to-topaa/	'scorpions' /naa-nakasiɾi/
L-R QS trochees	(to.to).(paa)	(naa.na).(ka.si̇).(ɾi)
destressing	———————	—————————
End Rule Left	(tó.to).(paa)	(náa.na).(ka.si̇).(ɾi)
apocope	———————	(náa.na).(ka.si̇ɾ)
syncope	(tót).(paa)	(náan).(ka.si̇ɾ)
de-obstruentization	———————	—————————
stress conflation	(tót).paa	(náan).ka.si̇ɾ
shortening	(tót).pa	—————————
	[tótpa]	[náan.ka.si̇ɾ]

Under this analysis, surface forms can exhibit considerable opacity, the motivation for syncope often being obliterated by stress conflation. This opacity makes the analysis very abstract, a situation that ought to have repercussions on learnability, contrary to fact.

A second source of difficulty for the derivational analysis relates to the destressing pattern, affecting the second in a HH pair of initial syllables but the first in its LH counterpart (this rule is therefore inapplicable to the forms in (63) above):

(64) A metrical derivation in SET

	/ka-karvaʃ/	/gaa-gaaga?/
L-R QS trochees	(ka).(kar).(vaʃ)	(gaa).(gaa).(ga?)
destressing	ka.(kar).(vaʃ)	(gaa).gaa.(ga?)
End Rule Left	ka.(kár).(vaʃ)	(gáa).gaa.(ga?)
apocope	———————	—————————
syncope	———————	(gáag).(ga?)
de-obstruentization	———————	(gáa?ŋ).(ga?)
stress conflation	ka.(kár).vaʃ	(gáa?ŋ).ga?
shortening	———————	—————————
	[kakárvaʃ]	[gáa?ŋga?]

In Rice (1992) the destressing rule is made sensitive to weight. However, besides its powerfulness, such a quantity-sensitive analysis misses the fact that destressing and syncope engage in a conspiracy to obtain initial iambs, i.e. (H) or (LH).

The main intuition behind the OT alternative is that the vowel-deletion processes follow from a conspiracy to maximize exhaustivity of metrical parsing, on the assumption that single-footedness is a priority requirement in SET. In addition, the alternative deletion patterns in word-initial syllables just noted will be readily accounted for if we assume that syncope aims for the selection of a heavy syllable as the metrical head.

The substance and ranking of the SET constraints are as follows:

(65) SET constraints and ranking
      Constraints
      ALL-FT-L: Align (Ft, L, PrWd, L)
      FT-FRM: feet are (moraically) binary and right-headed; heavy syllables are
      prominent; more prominent peaks are preferred
      DEP: every segment in the output has an input correspondent
      MAX-C: every consonant in the input has an output correspondent
      PARSE-σ: all syllables must be parsed into feet
      DISYLL: the PrWd is minimally disyllabic
      STEM CLOSURE: all stems end in C
      MAX-V: every vowel in the input has an output correspondent
      Ranking
      ALL-FT-L, FT-FRM, DEP, MAX-C >> PARSE-σ >> DISYLL >> STEM CLOS.
      >> MAX-V

The following tableau illustrates the workings of this machinery for the simple
form /novi/ ([nóv]):

(66)

/novi/	ALL-FTM, FT-FRM, DEP, MAX-C	PARSE σ	DISYLL	STEM CLOS.	MAX-V
☞(nóv)			*		*
(no.ví)	FT-FRM(PK-PROM)!			*	
(no.víi)	DEP!			*	

A more complex example is given in (67) below, where the WSP included in
FT-FORM has been split to overcome a ranking paradox into a more specific
WSP-FT (= 'bimoraic syllables must not occur in weak positions in feet'), still
under FT-FORM, and a more general independent WSP (= 'heavy syllables are
prominent in foot structure and on the grid'), ranked between STEM CLO-
SURE and MAX-V (the additional constraint RED = NUCμμ enforces bimor-
aicness in the reduplicated syllable):

(67)

/RED-takarui?/	ALL-FT-L	FT FRM	RED=NUCμμ	PARSE-σ	STEM CL	WSP	MAX-V
☞ (táat).ka.rui?				**		*	aa
(táat).kaa.rui?				**		**!	a
(táa).tak.rui?				**		**!	aa
(ta.ták).rui?			*!	*		*	aa
(taat.kaá).rui?		WSP-FT!		*		**	a
(táa).(ta.kàa).(rùi?)	*!***						

As can be seen, the procedure works handsomely. A question, however, arises at this juncture. If the whole drive of the phenomenon concerns the minimization of the number of unfooted syllables, why do some unfooted vowels (and thus the corresponding syllables) make it to the surface? The answer is straightforward in the overall context of Optimality Theory, where condoned constraint violations are always justified by compliance with higher ranked constraints. In the case at hand, the constraints in question have obviously not been formulated, but must be assumed to outrank ALL-FT-L, the designated exterminator of syllables. These are constraints governing syllable phonotactics, which aim for a CV(V)(C) syllable.

We must conclude that the analysis of the SET facts (only partially presented here for simplicity) can be carried out as satisfactorily under OT as under its derivational counterpart. The derivational analysis is, however, suspect at a higher level of explanation. In the first place, it requires a very considerable degree of abstractness. Second, and more importantly, it provides no account for the fact that all syllable-sensitive rules in SET refer to surface syllabification (NB not to pre-surface syllabification), an outcome that Kager takes as a direct indictment of such intermediate levels of representation.

Curiously, it is precisely these pre-surface syllabification levels that Noyer in Chapter 16 below argues are necessary for the analysis of tonal accent placement in ancient Attic Greek, which he claims makes reference to syllable and foot pre-surface (non-stratal) structure. These facts are obviously of utmost importance for the derivation/surface constraint debate, but their complexity makes it advisable simply to refer the reader to Noyer's text.

5. RULES AND OT

One of the strengths of the OT programme already referred to concerns the declared universality of the constraints, which clearly contrasts with the parochialism of standard rules. This is particularly relevant in the context of learnability, which by common consent defines the boundaries of the enterprise of linguistics, and which will be discussed in the next section.

Rule parochialism aside, rule-and-derivation theory has been found also to need constraints. This obviously gives a constraint-only theory like OT a formal edge over standard derivational theory. If it can really do without rules, at least this aspect of its formal superiority will have been substantiated. The analysis of the non-rhotic dialect of Eastern Massachusetts in McCarthy (1993), however, deliberately includes a parochial rule of *r*-insertion.

The basic facts are as follows. Eastern Massachusetts English (like some other varieties of English, including RP) has two contradictory processes of *r*-deletion and *r*-insertion, illustrated in (68):

(68) a. Homer arrived   Home*t* left
     b. Wanda[r] arrived   Wanda left

The form *Homer* in (a) is assumed to end in /r/ underlyingly, as suggested by the spelling and, more to the point, by such derivatives as *Homeric*, whereas *Wanda*, in (b), is assumed not to (cf. the alternation of the parallel *algebra* with the *r*-less *algebraic*). As can be seen, however, the surface distribution of [r] is identical in both forms. The obvious implication is that coda *r* is dropped in some contexts (*Homet*), and inserted in others (*Wanda*[r] *and Wendy*). In a third class set of contexts, underlying /r/ is simply preserved (NB not dropped: *Homer and Jason*), thus dispensing with the need for [r] insertion. Preserved *r*s are traditionally referred to as 'linking', and inserted *r*s as 'intrusive'.

McCarthy (1993) argues that such [r]s have ambisyllabic constituency. He then accounts for the alternations in (68) above by means of the constraints CODA$_R$-CONDITION, which prohibits *r*s in codas (crucially subject to Hayes's 1986 Linking Constraint or Itô and Mester's 1994 'crisp' interpretation of ALIGN), and FINAL-C, which favors C-ending prosodic words (similarly to Kager's STEM CLOSURE, mentioned above):

(69)

a.

	CODA-COND	FINAL-C
☞ Wanda left Home*t*		*
Wanda[r] left Homer	*!	

b.

	CODA-COND	FINAL-C
Wanda arrived Home*t*		*!
☞ Wanda[r]. ra.rrived Homer.		

The universality of these constraints is defended by McCarthy (1993) (FINAL-C) and Blevins (Chapter 7 below) (CODA$_R$-COND). The choice of [r] as an epenthetic consonant in English is, however, highly idiosyncratic, since, as Blevins points out, 'we would not expect a labialized pharyngealized retroflex central dorso-palatal approximant as a default or unmarked segment type within the grammar of any language'. Faced with this situation, McCarthy grabs the bull by the horns and proposes that a phonological rule 'Ø → r' needs to be countenanced in the grammar of the dialect(s) in question. The inclusion of this rule will clearly yield the desired results, but, in the words of Halle and Idsardi in Chapter 10 below, 'reliance on "an arbitrary stipulation that is outside the system of Optimality [McCarthy 1993: 190]" is equivalent to giving up on the enterprise. Data that cannot be dealt with by OT without recourse to rules are fatal counter-examples to the OT research program.'

In fairness to Optimality Theory, Halle and Idsardi explore several alternatives to McCarthy's analysis making use of correspondence constraints, but they come to the conclusion that these are equally unsuccessful. Without dismissing the possibility that an adequate OT solution may one day be found, Halle and Idsardi proceed to provide a standard rule-based account of the Eastern Massachusetts facts, for which they claim not only feasibility but clear superiority, since it can avail itself of the universal Elsewhere Condition to predict the interaction between the rules.

The rules in question are as follows (Schwa Epenthesis accounts for the pre-liquid appearance of schwa in such forms as *fearing* and *feeling* in the dialect being described):

(70) Schwa Epenthesis:

(71) *r*-Deletion:

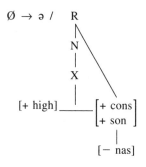

(72) *r*-Epenthesis:

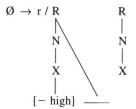

R-Deletion and *r*-Epenthesis are potentially mutually feeding (the deletion of *r* will trigger *r*-Epenthesis in the appropriate context, and conversely). Consequently, it is imperative that the correct order between these two rules be established. Halle and Idsardi's suggestion is that *r*-Epenthesis is made to precede *r*-Deletion by the Elsewhere Condition. Likewise, Schwa-Epenthesis will be ordered before *r*-Deletion (a counterbleeding relationship) by the condition. Moreover, they see the addition of *r*-Epenthesis to the grammar as motivated by hypercorrection, and suggest that the greater specificity of the added rule can be attributed to the pressure imposed by the Elsewhere Condition (a less specific rule would simply be obliterated by its counterpart; cf. Roca 1994: 49–50).

Blevins (Chapter 7 below) takes a different tack in response to the challenge posed by McCarthy's (1993) English-specific rule of *r*-insertion. In particular, like McCarthy, Blevins grasps the empirical nettle and accepts the need for parochial rules in the phonologies of languages, which she suggests are the product of historical debris. Rather than seeing this development as an indictment of the OT program, however, she goes on to develop a model that integrates such rules in the formalism of Optimality Theory.

Blevins adopts a twofold strategy. On the one hand, she contends that some blatantly unnatural phonological constraints (e.g. the notorious 'FREE-V (IN THE NOMINATIVE)' of Lardil in Prince and Smolensky 1993) are not such, but simply morphological rules. The English rule of *r*-insertion obviously does not fall in this category, however, and thus calls for a different provision.

Blevins builds her model on the 'harmonic serialism' mentioned, but not adopted, in Prince and Smolensky (1993:5):

Gen provides a set of candidate analyses for an input, which are harmonically evaluated; the optimal form is then fed back into Gen, which produces another set of analyses, which are then evaluated; and so on until no further improvement in representational Harmony is possible. Here Gen might mean 'do any *one* thing: advance all candidates which differ in one respect from the input'. The Gen ↔ H-eval loop would iterate until there was nothing left to be done, or better, until nothing that could be done would result in increased harmony.

In Blevins's proposal, parochial rules are linked to some constraint, in such a way that the rule is automatically triggered as a repair strategy upon violation of the constraint (this procedure is obviously reminiscent of Paradis's constraints and repair strategies). This new form is then evaluated by the constraint set. If no constraint violation is found, the algorithm comes to a halt. If there is a new violation, the form will re-enter the loop, with similar results. In the event that the violated constraint is not co-indexed with any rule, GEN provides an input for a new evaluation by moving on minimally (cf. the Prince and Smolensky instruction from the quotation above: 'do any *one* thing: advance all candidates which differ in one respect from the input'). And so on.

Let us apply this procedure to the specific case of English *r*-deletion/insertion. First, the phonology of English will contain the machinery specified in (73):

(73) a. CODA$_R$-CON   >>   FINAL-C[r-insertion rule]

$$R$$
$$|$$

   b. *r*-Insertion rule: $\emptyset \rightarrow r /\underline{\quad}$

The complementary forms *Wanda[r.r]arrived and Homer̸ left* will be processed as follows (cf. Fig. 1 in Chapter 7 below):

(74)

Step 1		
CURRENT INPUT	Wanda arrived	Homer left
(NB given)		
EVALUATION:	*FINAL-C	*CODA-CON
Step 2		
CO-INDEXED RULE:	Wandar.rarrived	NA
(NB /r/ is parsed ambisyllabically by convention)		
EVALUATION:	OK → END	———
Step 3		
GEN-1:		
(NB minimally distinct new input)	———	Homer̸ left
EVALUATION	———	OK → END

The bulk of Blevins's paper contains an analysis of nasal-driven sandhi in Gilbertese, which she approaches along similar lines. Her conclusion is that, while language-specific phonological rules are widely attested in the world's languages, their existence does no particular harm to the OT system. Nor are they, she claims, in any way awkward from the perspective of learnability, their exceptionless nature and productivity greatly facilitating the learning task, which Blevins suggests is akin to the learning of the sound inventory.

6. LEARNABILITY, COMPARABILITY, AND CLOSE

I have just referred to learnability once more, and we must now focus on this matter, which is of course commonly given a central role in the evaluation of linguistic theories.

   I have already mentioned that the learning task in the context of Optimality Theory is reduced to underlying representations (an inevitable burden under any theory that looks beyond the surface) and constraint ranking. Two early statements on learnability under OT (Prince and Smolensky 1993: ch. 9 and Tesar and Smolenksy 1993) end on the optimistic note that the learning of both constraint ranking (Tesar and Smolensky) and underlying forms (Prince and Smolensky) is deterministic. Tesar and Smolensky's and Prince and Smolensky's algorithms are, however, mutually supporting, and on closer scrutiny the overall procedure broaches circularity (Roca 1995), Prince and Smolensky's Lexicon Optimization presupposing ranked constraints, while Tesar and Smolensky's algorithm assumes that underlying forms are already available. Pulleyblank and Turkel's proposal in Chapter 5 below attempts to overcome this paradox, and to circumvent such learning traps as local maxima and superset grammars, known to stand in the way of successful convergence in the standard learnability account based on parameter setting.

Reduced to its essentials, the story goes as follows. Suppose that we assume that morphophonological alternations play no role in the early stages of acquisition. Suppose, moreover, that constraints are ranked from the outset (*contra* Tesar and Smolensky), but only randomly to begin with. Learning can now proceed on this simple basis. In particular, the learner will analyse the first datum with the initial (random) ranking. If the analysis succeeds, the ranking will remain (NB the learning device is attributed the property of 'conservatism'), and the procedure will be repeated with the second datum, and so on. Upon encountering data unanalyzable by the existing ranking, however, the learner will introduce minimal changes in this ranking until the analysis is successful (this procedure has obvious connections with Blevins's evaluation algorithm discussed above).

The learning traps mentioned above are overcome by a mechanism Pulleyblank and Turkel name 'gradient retreat'. The claim is that the minimal changes in the ranking are triggered, not just by analysis failures, but also by the learner's search for economy of constraint violation even when the data have been analysed successfully. In the rule-driven theory the implementation of any such strategy would obviously necessitate an additional evaluation metric. Optimality Theory, by contrast, provides a direct measure of this economy, and thus a formal basis for gradient retreat: as Pulleyblank and Turkel put it, 'within Optimality Theory, the metric is the theory itself'.

A related argument for OT superiority is made by Myers in Chapter 4. Myers bases his argument on the claimed universal phonetic grounding of the constraints, in turn rooted on the speaker's awareness of bodily limitations (i.e. the knowledge that certain sounds are difficult to discriminate, to articulate, etc.). Crucially, in OT the phonetic motivation of the phonological patterns is encoded directly (in Myers's words, 'the phonetic observation *is* the constraint'), in contrast with derivational theories (e.g. Grounded Phonology), which necessitate a metatheory. Myers suggests that this inherent weakness of the standard theory stems from the fact that standard rules are not formulated declaratively, and therefore cannot capture phonetic observations directly.

Such meta-empirical confrontations between the two theories as in Pulleyblank and Turkel's or Myers's papers presuppose that the theories are indeed comparable. In Chapter 3 below, Bromberger and Halle specifically address the comparability issue from a logical perspective.

Bromberger and Halle build their argument on the following assumptions: (i) phonological symbols stand for predicates; (ii) phonology is about real things in the real world; (iii) phonological symbols are unambiguous theory-internally, but not necessarily so across theories; and (iv) the phonetic properties of sentences are not overdetermined (i.e. are not brought about by more processes than would be sufficient). Their line of reasoning is as follows. Contrary to first appearances (the phonetic symbols of both theories indeed have different satisfaction conditions), rule-and-derivation phonology and Optimality Theory are not incommensurable, because the satisfaction conditions of their predicates converge when they occur in descriptions of surface representations. From this common ground, Bromberger and Halle suggest that a key question that both (indeed all) phonological theories have to answer is, in their own words: 'what is the sequence of the stages traversed (the set of predicates satisfied) by a speaker in the course of producing utterances satisfying e.g. "$\lambda x[\Omega x]$" [= a certain phonetic realization; IMR] from mnemonic elements merged and structured by the syntax of that speaker?' Underpinning this question is, of course, Bromberger and Halle's assumption (ii) above that phonology (not just phonetic realization) is about real things, not simply a set of convenient analytic abstractions.

In rule-and-derivation theory the answer to the question just posed is contained in any standard derivation, with an underlying and a surface representation, and a number of intermediate representations between them (cf. (1) above). In OT, however, it is clear that the tableaux include no information about how the optimal form has been obtained. For this Bromberger and Halle suggest we must turn to Tesar-like algorithms (Tesar 1995), which they maintain score low as psychological accounts, since they contain a much larger number of intervening stages—ironically, when we consider that one of the forces motivating OT in the first place was precisely dissatisfaction with such intermediate representations.

Bromberger and Halle's conclusion is, therefore, that derivational phonology can be proven superior to Optimality Theory, subject of course to the inevitable caveats about the assumptions built into the argument, some of them at least a matter of personal conviction. Approaching the evaluation task from the opposite end, the case studies reported on here indicate that both theories tend to converge as their empirical coverage increases. Indeed, I have already mentioned that derivational theory has undergone enrichment with (inviolable) constraints through the years. It now looks as if its young constraint-based competitor, OT, has already openly admitted to the need for rules. OT is also stretching its original formal fabric in ways that closer scrutiny may reveal are nothing but covert rules, and perhaps even derivations. It is far from inconceivable, therefore, that at the end of the day we may have to settle for a phonological theory that includes rules alongside constraints, or constraints alongside rules, whichever our favorite notation may happen to be.

ACKNOWLEDGEMENTS

I thank Zaharani Ahmed, Faisal Al-Mohanna, Shu-Ming Chen, Wyn Johnson, Russell Norton, and Nick Sherrard for their valuable contributions to the elaboration of this paper, and I am also deeply indebted to Wyn for word-processing help. Several volume contributors kindly checked on the accuracy of my reporting of their papers. Nick Clements and Mike Hammond sent me very helpful and useful comments on the whole chapter, and Mike Hammond, Bill Idsardi, René Kager, and Marc van Oostendorp were instrumental in the solution of a last minute problem. Many thanks to them all, and of course I accept full responsibility for any remaining flaws.

REFERENCES

Bromberger, S., and Halle, M. (1988). 'Why phonology is different', *Linguistic Inquiry* **20**: 51–70.
Chomsky, N. (1951). 'Morphophonemics of Modern Hebrew'. Master's thesis, University of Pennsylvania. Published by Garland Press (New York) in 1979.
—— (1995). *The Minimalist Program*. Cambridge, Mass.: MIT Press.
—— and Halle, M. (1968). *The Sound Pattern of English*. New York: Harper & Row.
Cole, J., and Kisseberth, C. (1995). 'An Optimal Domains Theory of Harmony'. MS, University of Illinois. ROA-22.
Dell, F., and Elmedlaoui M. (1985). 'Syllabic consonants and syllabification in Imdlawn Tashlhiyt Berber', *Journal of African Linguistics* **7**: 105–30.
Halle, M. (1962). 'Phonology in Generative Grammar', *Word* **18**: 54–72.
—— and Marantz, A. (1993). 'Distributed morphology and the pieces of inflection', in K. Hale and S. J. Keyser (eds.), *The View from Building 20*. Cambridge, Mass.: MIT Press, 111-76.
—— and Vergnaud, J.-R. (1987). *An Essay on Stress*. Cambridge, Mass.: MIT Press.
Hayes, B. (1986). 'Inalterability in CV phonology', *Language* **48**: 525–40.
Idsardi, W. (forthcoming). 'Tiberian Hebrew spirantization and phonological derivatons', *Linguistic Inquiry*.
Itô, J., and Mester, A. (1989). 'Gagyoo: Featural and Prosodic Characteristics'. MS, University of California at Santa Cruz.
—— —— (1990). 'Proper containment and phonological domains'. Handout distributed at KATL, Osaka University, Dec. 1990.
—— —— (1994). 'Reflections on CodaCond and Alignment', in J. Merchant, J. Padgett, and R. Walker (eds.), *Phonology at Santa Cruz*, 3. Dept. of Linguistics, University of California at Santa Cruz, 27–46. ROA-1.
Kiparsky, P (1968). 'Linguistic universals and language change', in E. Bach and R.

Harms (eds.) *Universals in Linguistic Theory*. New York: Holt, Rinehart & Winston, 191–212.

—— (1970). 'Historical linguistics', in J. Lyons (ed.), *New Horizons in Linguistics*. New York: Penguin, 302–15.

Kisseberth, C. (1970). 'On the functional unity of phonological rules', *Linguistic Inquiry* **1**: 291–306.

Koutsoudas, A., Sanders, G., and Noll, C. (1974). 'On the application of phonological rules', *Language* **50**: 1–28.

LaCharité, D., and Paradis, C. (1993). 'The emergence of constraints in generative phonology and a comparison of three current constraint-based models', in C. Paradis and D. LaCharité (eds.), *Constraint-Based Theories in Multilinear Phonology, Canadian Journal of Linguistics* **38**: 127–53.

McCarthy, J. (1993). 'A case of surface constraint violation', in C. Paradis and D. LaCharité (eds.), *Constraint-Based Theories in Multilinear Phonology, Canadian Journal of Linguistics* **38**: 169–95.

—— (1995). 'Remarks on phonological opacity in Optimality Theory', to appear in J. Lecarme, J. Lowenstamm, and Ur Shlonsky (eds.), *Proceedings of the Second Colloquium of Afro-Asiatic Linguistics*. ROA-79.

—— and Prince, A. (1993). *Prosodic Morphology I. Constraint Interaction and Satisfaction*. Forthcoming, MIT Press.

—— —— (1995). 'Faithfulness and reduplicative identity', in J. N. Beckman, L. W. Dickey, and S. Urbanczyk (eds.), *Papers in Optimality Theory*, (University of Massachusetts Papers in Linguistics 18), Amherst, GSLA, 249–384. ROA-60.

Myers, S. (1991). 'Persistent rules', *Linguistic Inquiry* **22**: 315–44.

Paradis, C. (1988–9). 'On constraints and repair strategies', *The Linguistic Review* **6**: 71–97.

Prince, A., and Smolensky, P. (1993). *Optimality Theory: Constraint Interaction in Generative Grammar*. Forthcoming, MIT Press.

Rice, C. (1992). 'Binary and Ternary in Metrical Theory: Parametric Extensions'. PhD dissertation, University of Texas at Austin.

Roca, I. (1994). *Generative Phonology*. London: Routledge.

—— (1995). 'Learnability under Optimality Theory', in *Essex Research Papers in Linguistics* **5**: 1–22; and *FAS Working Papers in Linguistics* **2**: 154–75 (Berlin).

SPE: see Chomsky and Halle.

Tesar, B. (1995). *Computing Optimal Forms in Optimality Theory: Basic Syllabification*. Technical report CU-CS-763-95. Department of Computer Science, University of Colorado, Boulder. ROA-52.

—— and Smolensky, P. (1993). 'The Learnability of Optimality Theory: An Algorithm and Some Basic Complexity Results'. MS, University of Colorado at Boulder. ROA-2.

2

Questions of Priorities: An Introductory Overview of Optimality Theory in Phonology

NICHOLAS SHERRARD

Optimality Theory (OT—Prince and Smolensky (P&S) 1993, McCarthy and Prince (M&P) 1993*a*) is an approach to grammar, most notably phonology, based on the parallel evaluation of possible output forms with regard to a ranked system of violable constraints. This chapter aims to provide a brief working introduction to some of the leading current ideas and applications of phonological OT. Concepts and techniques are emphasized, rather than results or detailed argumentation.

The structure of the article is as follows. Section 1 presents an overview of the essential architecture of OT. Section 2 introduces and classifies, for expository purposes, some of the major types of constraint commonly found in OT analyses. The following four sections delve further into constraints of each type, based upon this classification scheme: markedness, alignment, constituency and correspondence. Lastly, section 7 surveys some more advanced applications drawing on much of the earlier discussion, and poses some challenges for the future development of the theory.

1. ARCHITECTURE

This section presents the fundamentals of OT. Following an illustration in Section 1.1 of essential ideas and notation, Section 1.2 introduces the key concepts somewhat more formally.

1.1 *Why Optimality Theory is different*

Constraint-based approaches have been around in phonology for many years. The crucial distinguishing feature of OT, then, is not so much that it is based on constraint satisfaction but that it allows violation of those constraints. The circumstances where constraints may be breached are clearly laid down: a constraint must always be satisfied unless doing so would involve violating a more important constraint. Implicit in this is a notion of priority, implemented by the architectural requirement that constraints are ranked, so that it is possible in general to determine which of two conflicting demands is to prevail. The success of a candidate output in conforming with the ranked body of constraints operating in the language is termed its *harmony* (following Smolensky 1986). The grammatical output is that candidate whose harmony is optimal.

For an illustration, consider the underlying form /iu/ in a language which permits back, but not front, high vowels in the syllable onset and coda. Assuming, for simplicity, that the surface and underlying forms must consist of exactly the same segments, there are several ways this might be analyzed in OT: one possibility is by the differential ranking of two constraints, *M/i and *M/u, the effect of each being to keep the segment in question out of the syllable margins.

(1) a. *M/i
        No *i* in the onset or coda
     b. *M/u
        No *u* in the onset or coda

The following *constraint tableau* depicts how OT might handle this[1]:

(2)	/iu/	*M/i	*M/u
☞ a.	iw		*
b.	ju	*!	

The left-to-right ordering of constraints denotes their ranking, and * signals a violation: the bold line between two constraint columns signifies that *M/i is ranked higher than, or *dominates*, *M/u. The notation >> is also used to signify dominance (thus, *M/i >> *M/u). ☞ fingers the optimal candidate. Once a candidate output has been excluded because it crucially violates a highly ranked constraint (denoted by !), it is out of the game: any further violations are irrelevant, as are those of the optimal candidate once all other contenders have been eliminated (this is often denoted by shading of the irrelevant cells).

Useful though this example may be for illustrating the notation, the analysis is incomplete. What about the disyllabic possibility [i.u], which violates neither *M/i nor *M/u? Granted that this is not the attested surface form for the grammar in question, some other constraint must be better satisfied by [iw] than [i.u]. One obvious possibility is a constraint requiring syllables to have onsets (cf. Itô 1986): [i.u] violates this twice, [iw] only once.

[1] w, j here denote the high vowels, u and i, in marginal syllabic positions of the output.

(3) ONSET
   Syllables have onsets.

Some caution is necessary here: [ju] is not the grammatical output either, but does not breach the new constraint, ONSET, which accordingly must be outranked by a constraint responsible for the non-optimality of [ju], thus suggesting that *M/i >> ONSET. We also need a way to rule out [.iu.], where both segments constitute a diphthong in the nucleus.

(4) NOCOMPLEXNUCLEUS
   Only one segment in the syllable nucleus.

The impact of these refinements is shown by the modified tableau in (5):

(5) /iu/	*M/i	ONSET	NO COMPLEX NUCLEUS	*M/u
☞ a. iw		*		*
b. ju	*!			
c. i.u		**!		
d. .iu.		*	*!	

The only additional notation here is the dotted vertical line, indicating that the constraints immediately on either side are not crucially ranked: interchanging those constraints makes no difference to the outcome. Note, however, that this notation can introduce some (typically unimportant) indeterminacy as to the identity of the crucial violation.

As P&S (1993) point out, the comparison of candidates in OT emphasizes relatives rather than absolutes. Unsuccessful candidates are eliminated, in effect, by a series of sudden-death playoffs where winning or losing depends entirely on relative harmony: the loser loses just because it sustains a crucial constraint violation which its competitor manages to avoid. As seen in (5), this does not mean that the ultimate winner has an unblemished record, merely that it fares better than any other candidate (and here is the key), taking into account the constraint hierarchy in its entirety. M&P 1994*a* dub the misconception that any optimal candidate cannot violate any constraints 'The Fallacy of Perfection'.

Often constraints have no application in particular situations. In that case, they are unviolated by default: if the answer to the question the constraint poses is 'Not Applicable', no violation can occur.

One final but fundamental point concerns the nature of the constraints themselves. These are not arbitrary stipulations plucked from the air to produce the correct results: every constraint should articulate a universal linguistic tendency (cf. Myers in Chapter 4 below), the divergent behavior of individual languages being attributable to the results of ranking constraints in different orders.

In the example just seen, the constraints ONSET and NOCOMPLEXNUCLEUS reflect the cross-linguistically unmarked status of syllables consisting of an onset and a nucleus, each dominating a single segment: every language has such syllables, although many also have syllables of other shapes (cf. Blevins's 1995 summary of the empirical basis for these assertions; also P&S (1993: ch. 6) for a fuller presentation of CV syllable theory within OT). The constraints *M/i and *M/u, discussed further in 2.1 (but used here largely for ease in presenting the mechanics of OT), also have genuine linguistic motivation: languages, on the whole, prefer consonants for onsets and codas, but vowels for the syllable nucleus.

1.2 *The Optimality engine*

Looking at these ideas more formally, P&S (1993) propose that UG provides a set, *Con*, of constraints from which grammars are constructed, including schemata which may take specific morphemes as arguments. A grammar consists of an ordered ranking of the members of Con. Given an input, a component of UG dubbed *Gen* generates the range of possible candidate linguistic analyses for that input, which the *Eval* module then evaluates by reference to a given ranking of the constraints in Con. The constraint tableau encapsulates these mechanical aspects.

Thus, given any input and any ranking of the *con*straints, a set of candidate outputs is *gen*erated, then *eval*uated with respect to the ranked constraints: this determines the grammatical output associated with the given input. Indeed, Eval creates an ordering of the candidates according to their *relative harmony*, i.e. their performance *vis-à-vis* the ranked body of constraints. The optimal candidate, which will be selected as the output associated with the given input, is the most harmonic in terms of this ordering. Five architectural principles regulate the operation of Con, Gen, and Eval (M&P 1994*a*: 3–6 give a more formal presentation).

- *Universality* demands that all constraints should be present in all grammars, the formal counterpart of the requirement that constraints reflect universal linguistic tendencies. This is not to say that every constraint always plays an active role: constraints involving tones, for instance, may clearly be expected to figure prominently in tone languages, but would typically have no impact in non-tonal languages. In its full form, universality runs into problems of implementation: some constraints proposed in OT analyses appear so language-specific that it is hard to envisage them as being universally present in any useful sense (e.g. the FREE-V constraint in P&S's 1993 analysis of Lardil prevents word-final vowels from surfacing—but only in the nominative case; see Chapter 7 below, however); also, the indefinitely large number of possible constraints is regarded by some as unappealing.

- *Ranking and Violability* formalize the idea of hierarchical ranking of violable constraints, subject to the requirement that any violation should be the minimum needed to secure compliance with higher-ranked constraints. It does not follow from violability that all constraints will be violated in all grammars (e.g. numerous languages completely lack onsetless syllables, which may be equated with inviolability of ONSET in those languages); because no violation of an inviolable constraint can be forced by a superior constraint, such constraints are said to be *undominated* within the language in question. Schematically, constraints within a grammar are organized as in (6):

(6) Inviolable constraints >> Ranked violable constraints >> Inactive constraints

Ranking among the inviolable constraints has no relevance (alternatively, identical grammaticality judgements flow from any ranking of these constraints); the same goes for the inactive constraints. Moreover, some individual pairs of ranked violable constraints fail to conflict, so that little hangs on their relative ranking. Conversely, if two active constraints conflict then they must be ranked, for otherwise optimal harmony will not be uniquely defined[2]: thus, no pair of conflicting constraints can both be undominated within the same grammar.

If harmony, which measures compliance with constraints in the grammar, is to be optimized, then the optimal candidate must sustain a less damaging list of violations than any of its competitors. This means, in addition to the aim of confining violations to constraints as far down the ranking as possible, that any constraint which is violated should be violated with minimal severity.

- *Inclusiveness* prevents Gen from being unduly selective in producing candidate outputs.[3] It is responsible for the need to augment the list of candidates in (2) to include the further reasonable possibilities added in (5).
- It is because of *Parallelism* that OT analyses are generally concerned with surface forms. Parallelism requires optimal satisfaction of the constraint hierarchy to be determined by reference to all the constraints and all the candidate outputs, with no serial derivation. P&S (1993) note that, strictly, parallelism is logically independent of OT (such approaches as the Theory of Constraints and Repair Strategies of Paradis (1988) and Goldsmith's (1993) Harmonic Phonology have much in common with non-parallelist

---

[2] This assertion strictly presupposes that each input gives rise to a single output and would require slight modification for situations where a single grammar permits more than one output (see Section 7.4 below for more on this).

[3] Inclusiveness results in the output of Gen being potentially infinite, which is seen by some as problematical. The influence of undominated constraints in paring down the output of Gen may bear on this—the boundary between Gen and the undominated constraints is blurred, but this does not seem to matter enormously in practice: for a given language, little tends to hang on whether a constraint undominated in that language is also inviolable universally.

OT). None the less, Parallelism lies at the heart of OT's distinctiveness and affords it much of its strength; in practice, it is an integral part of OT (although some latitude is occasionally needed in interpreting the ban on serial derivation; cf. the use of multiple levels in M&P's (1993*a*) analysis of Axininca Campa; also Booij and Clements in Chapters 8 and 9 below [Editor]). The literature contains numerous analyses of phenomena which have proved more or less intractable to conventional derivational approaches (particularly via lexical phonology), but are argued to be elegantly and effectively catered for by a parallel approach.

2. CLASSIFICATION OF CONSTRAINTS

The examples considered so far take little account of the relationship between input and output, either ignoring it or assuming that the two are in some sense identical. This is a huge oversimplification.

With /iu/ as input, the tableau in (5) evaluated various candidates against a selection of constraints, all essentially structural. Among the possibilities not considered were outputs involving deletion (e.g. [i], [u]) or epenthesis (e.g. [iju], [titu]), each transgressing a *faithfulness* constraint aimed at keeping input and output identical. Such constraints are rankable in the normal way and violations need not be fatal (for reasons of learnability, though, they tend universally to be ranked fairly high).

The following tableau revises (5) so as to bring faithfulness into play, looking at [iw], the erstwhile optimal candidate, and two of its closest competitors. (Here and throughout this article, constraints and candidates not bearing directly on the matter in focus are omitted; e.g. in Tableau (8) below, an alternative valid candidate would be *u*.)

(7)[4]   a. MAX-IO: Every element of the input is an element of the output ('No deletion')

      b. DEP-IO: Every element of the output is an element of the input ('No epenthesis')

(8) /iu/	*M/u	DEP-IO	MAX-IO
a. iw	*!		
b. i.tu		*!	
☞ c. i			*

---

[4] The names MAX and DEP derive from 'maximal' and 'dependency' respectively: thus, MAX-IO requires the input to appear maximally in the output, while DEP-IO requires everything in the output to depend on the input. P&S (1993) originally captured the effect of these constraints (under foundational assumptions no longer current) by the constraints PARSE and FILL (see section 2.3).

Although (c) is optimal here, obvious rearrangements of the constraint ranking could give either of the other candidates as optimal. Much work in OT involves balancing the demands of structural and faithfulness constraints along similar lines. For expository purposes, a classification of constraints into two categories, *structural* and *matching*, is adopted, each again subdivided into two classes. Structural constraints are split between *markedness* and *alignment* constraints. Matching constraints may similarly be divided between *constituency* and *correspondence* constraints (including faithfulness constraints such as those just seen). Some overlap inevitably exists between the classes described here, but it creates a natural enough functional split to be helpful.

2.1 *Markedness constraints*

Among the constraints seen so far, ONSET mirrors the cross-linguistic preference for syllables with onsets. The *M/X constraints reflect the preference for certain types of segment to be kept out of syllable margins. P&S (1993) propose that constraints of the form *M/X are universally ranked in a margin hierarchy according to their relative sonority.

(9)[5] *M/a >> *M/i >> *M/l >> *M/n >> *M/t

This scale reflects the universal order of preference whereby obstruents make the best onsets and codas, and non-high vowels the worst.[6] P&S (1993) also suggest a similar *peak hierarchy* ordered the other way around, indicating which segments make the most harmonic nuclei.

(10) *P/X
　　No X in the syllable peak (nucleus)

(11) *P/t >> *P/n >> *P/l >> *P/i >> *P/a

Further up the prosodic hierarchy, a key markedness constraint is FTBIN, requiring foot binarity under either syllabic or moraic analysis[7] (cf. Prince 1980; M&P 1986). Interactions of FTBIN with alignment and constituency constraints figure prominently in OT analyses of metrical phenomena.

　　Each of these constraints reflects a cross-linguistic *preference law* of some kind (cf. Vennemann 1988), consistent with the stance that constraints in OT form part of UG and are present in all languages. While the universal nature of

---

[5] The members of this simplified scale represent, respectively, non-high vowels, high vowels, liquids, nasals, and obstruents. *M/i and *M/u, being on the same sonority level, are freely rankable relative to one another.

[6] It is debatable whether a constraint like *M/t is appropriate: a more positive statement to the effect that t is a good margin (not merely the least bad) might serve better, particularly as we know from ONSET that it is preferable to have a non-empty onset; (cf. Clements in Chapter 9 below [Editor]).

[7] Hewitt (1994) argues that this formulation is too broad and that the constraint should be deconstructed into a larger number of smaller constraints. He also contends that FTBIN should require simultaneous compliance with both syllabic and moraic binarity, not just one or the other.

a few constraints found in the OT literature may be less than obvious, it is generally considered desirable for constraints introduced in OT analyses to be supportable by data from more than a single language (albeit not always practicable; cf. FREE-V mentioned earlier).

It may reasonably be argued that, inasmuch as all constraints other than those regulating the fidelity of output to input reflect cross-linguistic preferences, almost all constraints are markedness constraints; the term is here used as a negative catch-all—members of the other categories in the classification proposed here will be seen to have distinctive unifying characteristics.

2.2 *Alignment constraints*

The essence of Alignment is the idea that many observed linguistic phenomena are by-products of the way natural languages aim to make relevant linguistic objects either coincide or, alternatively, abut cleanly. The Generalized Alignment schema (M&P 1993*b*) encapsulates this insight.

(12) ALIGN(Cat1, Edge1, Cat2, Edge 2) is defined to mean:
For every Cat1 there is a Cat2 such that Edge1 of Cat1 and Edge2 of Cat2 coincide. Cat1, Cat2 can be any prosodic, morphological, or syntactic category. Edge1, Edge2 can be either left or right.

The quantifier order is crucial: in particular, ALIGN(Cat1, Edge1, Cat2, Edge2) and ALIGN(Cat2, Edge2, Cat1, Edge1) typically have very different significance. For example, ALIGN(Ft, L, σ, L) requires all feet to begin at the start of some syllable and is probably undominated in any language. Reversing the arguments has an entirely different result: ALIGN(σ, L, Ft, L) says that every syllable must begin some foot—and is violated by every disyllabic foot.

Of special importance is the means of assessing violations of alignment constraints. The *binary* constraints considered up to now are relatively straightforward—a syllable either does or does not have an onset. Alignment, by contrast, involves *gradient constraint violation*: [σ(σσ)σ] and [σσ(σσ)] both contain one foot which violates ALIGN(PrWd, L, Ft, L), but the former is more harmonic (in terms of that constraint), missing out by only one syllable, rather than two. Such considerations are crucial for assessing minimality of violation.

Alignment phenomena fall quite naturally into two classes according to whether or not the two edge parameters are the same. If both edges are left (or right), the categories are intended to begin (or end) together. The abbreviations ALIGNL/ALIGNR(Cat1, Cat2) will be used henceforth for such instances of ALIGN; indeed, even the arguments may be suppressed if they are clear from the context. When different edges are involved, the constraint may be viewed as about linear concatenation (in a broad sense—alignment constraints of this type may be used to capture extrametrical behavior; e.g. ALIGN(Ft, R, σ, L) encourages final syllables to remain unfooted).

2.3 *Constituency constraints*

Implicit in the discussion of alignment is a notion of prosodic hierarchy, whereby (as one possibility) prosodic words dominate feet, which dominate syllables, which dominate (morae or) segments. The constituency constraints govern the extent to which syllables are dominated (or *parsed*) by feet, feet by prosodic words, and so forth. Acting in concert with alignment and constraints such as FTBIN, constituency is largely responsible for a wide range of metrical phenomena.

Reverting briefly to the remark about extrametricality, the interaction of a parsing constraint with ALIGN(Ft, R, σ, L) can be seen.

(13) PARSE-σ (PARSE-SYLL of M&P 1993*a*; b)
   All syllables are parsed by feet.

As M&P remark, PARSE-σ 'is a familiar aspect of stress theory . . . corresponding broadly to the requirement that foot-parsing be "exhaustive" in rule-based metrical phonology'. Consider, then, a trisyllabic input: the 'extrametrical' candidate (σσ)σ with its unfooted syllable violates PARSE-σ but not ALIGN(Ft, R, σ, L); for the fully footed (σσ)(σ) the opposite holds, as there is no syllable beyond the right edge of the degenerate foot.[8] Thus, *ceteris paribus*, the output exhibits extrametricality only if ALIGN(Ft, R, σ, L) >> PARSE-σ.

It is appropriate to remark on the absence of counterparts whereby segments are parsed by syllables. P&S's (1993) formulation of OT included a *containment* principle requiring all the input to be literally present in the output, segments unparsed by a syllable being unrealized phonetically: PARSE, requiring every input segment to be syllabified, thus had an overall effect similar to the anti-deletion constraint, MAX-IO, with FILL (the prohibition on epenthesis) achieving much the same as DEP-IO. Following M&P (1994*a* et seq.) this PARSE/FILL terminology and the containment principle are no longer current, having been superseded by Correspondence Theory (with which M&P (1994*b*) acknowledge containment is inconsistent).[9]

2.4 *Correspondence constraints*

Most current work in OT uses Correspondence Theory (CT), an approach to faithfulness that makes direct use of the identity ideally existing between input

---

[8] The possibility of a FTBIN violation for the latter candidate also arises, but is not directly relevant here: for definiteness and to avoid this, we may assume the final syllable is bimoraic.

[9] While the outmoded PARSE/FILL terminology still occasionally appears even in current literature where the distinction is not crucial, the policy has here been adopted of reserving PARSE terminology for constituency constraints, updating the earlier nomenclature where appropriate.

and output and generalizes it to other circumstances in which a substantially similar relationship exists. CT develops an approach originally proposed for modelling the identity relationships involved in reduplicative morphology. M&P (1995*a*) argue that this is conceptually equivalent to input/output faithfulness and, accordingly, that a single theory should cover both.

The essence of faithfulness, between input and output, base and reduplicant or whatever, is that both members should be identical. CT uses MAX, DEP, and IDENT to capture these essentials with generality.

Formally, CT involves a pair of representations, generically S_1/S_2 (e.g. input/output, base/reduplicant), related by a *correspondence relation*, regulated by a network of violable constraints (M&P 1995*a*). The most important are stated here in both general and I/O-specific formulations, cf. (7).

(14) MAX
    a. Every segment of S_1 has a correspondent in S_2.
    b. Every input segment has a correspondent in the output.

(15) DEP
    a. Every segment of S_2 has a correspondent in S_1.
    b. Every output segment has a correspondent in the input.

For input/output, the functional equivalence of PARSE and MAX and of FILL and DEP is readily apparent. Like their precursors, MAX and DEP are violable: a transgression of MAX will cause the output to lack a segment present in the input; violating DEP will typically add a segment.

It is debatable whether the segment, rather than the feature, is the appropriate level for correspondence: M&P (1995*a*) propose dealing with featural correspondence with a parametrized family of constraints, one for each distinctive feature.

(16) IDENT (F)
    a. Correspondent segments have identical values for the feature F.
    b. Output correspondents of an input segment have the same value for the
       feature F.

Whilst MAX and DEP each deal with one-way correspondence, IDENT handles both directions in a single constraint. Numerous authors implicitly decompose IDENT by extending the ambit of MAX and DEP to individual distinctive features; arguments in favor of such an approach are given by Lombardi (1995) and Pater (1995).

Strictly, these faithfulness constraints are insufficient to ensure that correspondence is indeed in the nature of identity: nothing so far would prevent the output being, say, the reverse of the input. CT duly includes further constraints to guarantee the good behavior of the correspondence relation (see Section 6.1 below).

The remainder of this chapter surveys a selection of phonological applications of OT, using the groundwork now in place. Because an essential characteristic of OT is the interaction of ranked violable constraints of various kinds, no single analysis involves solely constraints of any one of the categories introduced above—at the very least, basic faithfulness constraints are always likely to be involved. That said, it is usually clear which specific constraints occupy the key roles for any given application of OT, and the discussion below is organized accordingly. The material covered is weighted in favor of analyses whose most interesting aspects are alignment or correspondence theoretically based: typically, markedness and constituency considerations play a supporting, albeit very necessary, part. This reflects a tendency throughout the literature, the observed bias almost certainly being attributable to the pivotal role of parallelism in OT, most potently displayed through alignment and correspondence.

3. On Markedness

This section looks briefly at the role of markedness within OT. Section 3.1 introduces the factorial typology. Section 3.2 then presents some fundamental results on constraint ranking, which have close affinities with the Elsewhere Condition.

3.1 *Factorial typology*

Because n objects can be arranged in $n!$ ($= 1 \times 2 \times \ldots \times n$) different orders, that number of possible grammars may, in principle, arise from ordering a system of n constraints. Although such factorial numbers rapidly become unmanageably large (e.g. $5! = 120$, but $10!$ exceeds 36 million), the notion of *factorial typology* is useful in examining the linguistic consequences of differential ranking of small numbers of constraints. Moreover, the number of distinct combinations one actually has to consider is seldom as large as the factorial figure. This is borne out by the following simple example, based on constraints already introduced.

P&S (1993: ch. 6) present a (necessarily idealized) analysis of CV syllable typology. They show that onsets are optional in a language if ONSET is dominated by both the faithfulness constraints, MAX and DEP. Otherwise, onsets are required: if MAX is lowest-ranked, compliance with ONSET is enforced by phonetic deletion; if DEP is lowest-ranked, epenthesis is used instead. Similar results apply for codas, with NOCODA rather than ONSET as the relevant markedness constraint.

(17) NOCODA (-COD of P&S 1993: 85)
    Syllables do not have a coda.

This example also bears out the observation that the full factorial number of permutations is seldom achieved in practice. The typology described above includes only three alternative patterns of behavior, whereas there are 6 (= 3!) possible rankings of the constraints involved. Here, the apparent reduction in the number of possibilities occurs because the constraints fail to conflict pairwise: for instance, given that MAX is lowest-ranked, any potential problem in satisfying DEP or ONSET can easily be avoided by deleting as much input material as is needed to sidestep the difficulty.

3.2 *Constraining constraint ranking*

The frequent failure to realize the full factorial number of constraint rankings is only partly attributable to the absence of conflict between constraints: the figure may also be reduced because of universal restrictions on the freedom of ordering of constraints. For instance, as already seen, the members of the peak and margin hierarchies are subject to universal restrictions on their relative ranking.

One constraint may be masked by another so that its effect is nullified. A key result, Pāṇini's Theorem (P&S 1993: 81–2, 106–8, 221), essentially requires that in order for both *specific* and *general* versions of a constraint to operate actively within a grammar, the more specific must dominate the more general; conversely, if the more general is dominant, then its specific counterpart cannot have any effect in the grammar and, in particular, will not serve to eliminate any candidate outputs from consideration.

This principle enjoys a close affinity with the Elsewhere Condition (Kiparsky 1973 and elsewhere). The Elsewhere Condition and Pāṇini's Theorem might be argued to be necessary in linguistics for similar reasons: without something like the Elsewhere Condition, the application of a more general rule before a more specific one could bleed the latter out of existence (cf. Roca 1994: 49–50). Rule-ordering does not arise for Pāṇini's Theorem, but much the same considerations apply.

For example, cross-linguistically, codas are absent in the unmarked case, as reflected in NoCODA. The total absence of codas in a given language depends on whether NoCODA is undominated. Following Itô (1986), some languages are analysed as allowing codas only in given (typically language-specific) circumstances. Various alternatives are possible (see 7.3), but all have similar effects. For the present purpose, the original OT formulation suffices:

(18) CODACOND (Lardil: P&S 1993: 99)

    A coda consonant has only Coronal place or else no place specification of its own at all.

Pāṇini's Theorem (or something along the same lines) is needed in order for a constraint like CODACOND to be active—for, if NoCODA is obeyed, CODACOND trivially must be as well; this suggests that CODACOND >> NOCODA. Actually, its status is marginally less clear-cut: conceivably, two candidates, both violating NOCODA, might be distinguished solely by the fact that only one breaches CODACOND, in which case the relative ranking would not matter.

In Sherrard (1995), however, it is argued that when one constraint logically implies another, the stronger constraint must be ranked higher in order to be active. *Local conjunction* (Smolensky 1993; 1995) may be seen as a special case of this: the idea here is that two constraint violations are more severe when they occur in the same location—or, more accurately, within a common domain. The local conjunction of two constraints dominates them both. For a simplified illustration, consider the following three constraints in which (c) is the local conjunction of (a) and (b):

(19) a. NOOBSTRUENTCODA: No obstruents in the coda
      b. NOVOICEDOBSTRUENT: No voiced obstruents
      c. NOVOICEDOBSTRUENTCODA: No voiced obstruents in the coda

(20) NOVOICEDOBSTRUENTCODA >> NOOBSTRUENTCODA, NOVOICEDOBSTRUENT

For *local* conjunction, it is essential in (c) that the voiced obstruent and the obstruent coda coincide i.e. the voicing must be in the coda: having a voiced obstruent onset and a separate voiceless obstruent coda would violate both (a) and (b) but not their *local* conjunction.

Local self-conjunction of constraints is possible. NOCOMPLEX furnishes a good example: while NOCOMPLEX seeks to disallow syllable nodes with more than one segment, its local conjunction with itself disallows syllable nodes dominating more than two segments. This process may be iterated: thus, defining NOCOMPLEX(n) to be a ban on syllable nodes with more than n segments:

(21) ... >> NOCOMPLEX(3) >> NOCOMPLEX(2) >> NOCOMPLEX(1) = NOCOMPLEX

It is worth emphasizing that the notion of local conjunction is applicable in any phonological or morphological domain. In (19) that domain is a syllable position. Itô & Mester (1996) show how the combination of local self-conjunctions within the stem and within the morpheme may be used to capture derived environment effects (in the parlance of cyclic and lexical phonology). There are two essential points involved here. The first is that, as a direct consequence of Pāṇini's Theorem, if one domain properly includes another then the local conjunction of constraints in the narrow domain will necessarily dominate the same conjunction for the broader domain: as a particular case of this, the self-conjunction of any constraint local to a morpheme outranks that same self-conjunction local to a stem, except when the stem and the morpheme coincide. Itô & Mester's key insight, that this is precisely the distinguishing characteristic of non-derived environments, enables them to account for the Japanese phenomenon of *rendaku* within OT: it seems likely that similar arguments may be brought to bear on the numerous other situations where derived and non-derived environments exhibit different phonological behavior (cf. Kiparsky 1993).

3.3 *Universal hierarchies*

Reference has already been made to the use of constraint sub-hierarchies in P&S (1993) to capture sonority effects in syllabification. A similar technique can account for segmental inventories within individual languages (P&S 1993: ch. 9). P&S reflect the fundamental insight that, cross-linguistically, Coronal enjoys special status as the unmarked place of articulation (cf. Paradis and Prunet (1991) and references therein) in two ways: coronal place is more harmonic than labial place; equivalently, the constraint against labial place outranks that against coronal place.[10]

(22) Coronal unmarkedness
    a. Harmony scale   Cor $\succ$ Lab[11]
    b. Dominance hierarchy   *Lab >> *Cor

P&S (1993: ch. 9) use this observation to explain why the only complex articulations found in the consonant inventory of the Australian language, Yidiɲ, are those involving coronal. Crucially, they rank the featural faithfulness constraint, Max^{feature}, above *Cor but below both *Lab and a ban on totally placeless segments. It follows from this ranking that any segment underlyingly specified for, say, both coronal and labial place (irrespective of which articulation is primary and which secondary) will be realized as a coronal because deletion of the Labial feature (in breach of Max^{feature}) is a more harmonic alternative than preserving it (at the expense of violating *Lab).

It follows that a variety of possible inputs all lead to an output with only coronal place. A question naturally arising from this observation is how the learner is to identify the appropriate input. P&S propose a principle of *Lexicon Optimization*, the thrust of which is that the learner chooses the input relative to which the observed output is most harmonic.

Here, a purely Coronal input yields a Coronal output, violating only low ranked *Cor; but any of the other possible inputs with the same output (e.g. an input with labial C-place and coronal V-place) would incur that same markedness violation plus, at the very least, one for the higher-ranked Max^{feature}. This leads to the conclusion that Yidiɲ has no underlying mixed place consonants.

Some interesting observations arise from this analysis:

---

[10] Here and throughout this discussion, labial is to be taken as a generic non-coronal place: the same analysis would apply, *mutatis mutandis*, to other non-coronal places of articulation.

[11] $\succ$ denotes relative harmony. Thus, coronal place is more harmonic than labial. This notation also appears in connection with candidate outputs.

- The argument presupposes that the learner has already acquired the constraint ranking of the language in question, a topic addressed by Tesar and Smolensky (1993) (see also Pulleyblank and Turkel, Chapter 5 below, for consideration of related issues).
- It would perhaps be more accurate to say that Coronal is the unmarked supra-glottal place of articulation. Lombardi (1995) argues that pharyngeal place is yet more unmarked than coronal. She contends, following McCarthy (1994), that both ʔ and h have Pharyngeal place (and are specified for a dependent feature [+glottal]); Lombardi accounts for the relative rarity of such undisputed pharyngeals as ʕ and ħ by a cross-linguistically high-ranking constraint, *Phar/-glottal, against [-glottal] pharyngeals. Such a constraint is redolent of the *grounding conditions* of Archangeli and Pulleyblank (1994), which seek to reflect phonetically based implicational relationships (cf. Pulleyblank et al. (forthcoming), where such grounded constraints are used in an OT-based typological analysis of tongue root harmony—see Section 4.3 below).

Kiparsky (1994) proposes an alternative way of looking at essentially the same issues (see Alderete et al. (1996) for discussion of the relative merits of this and other approaches). He proposes that, rather than constraints proscribing particular values for various phonological categories (e.g. place of articulation), there are faithfulness constraints operating to ensure that underlying featural specifications are preserved. Kiparsky achieves this, essentially, by requiring separate MAX and DEP constraints for each marked value and for the category itself.

Thus, adopting the stance of Lombardi (1995) on Pharyngeal, Kiparsky's counterpart of the dominance hierarchy for coronal unmarkedness would proceed along the following lines:

(23) a. MAX(Labial), MAX(Dorsal) >> MAX(Coronal) >> MAX(Place)
    b. DEP(Labial), DEP(Dorsal) >> DEP(Coronal) >> DEP(Place)

If Coronal is taken as the unmarked Place, then MAX/DEP(Coronal) are not needed.

Pāṇini's Theorem, of course, demands that if all these 'specific' constraints are to be active then each of the respective hierarchies must dominate the constraint which is its 'general' counterpart (i.e. MAX(Place)/DEP(Place)).

4. ALIGNMENT APPLICATIONS

Alignment is highly versatile, as might be hoped of a formalism that permits general combinations of any pair of prosodic or grammatical constituents. Much phonological (indeed, much linguistic) analysis involves processes of linear decomposition or combination, concatenation, or edge coincidence: each may be analysed as an instance of alignment, and such analyses form the core of this section.

4.1 *Problems in syllabification*

The Arabic dialects of Iraq and Cairo use different sites for otherwise substantially identical epenthesis processes. The usual generative approach (cf. Itô 1986) assigns to Arabic a CV(C) syllabic template, attributing the divergent epenthesis patterns to directional syllabification (Cairene: left to right; Iraqi: right to left). The standard example reduces to an exercise in matching /CVCCCV/with that template: CVC.CV.CV. for Cairene versus CV.CVC.CV. for Iraqi.

(24) a. Cairene   /ʔul+t+lu/→ʔul.t*i*.lu

   b. Iraqi   /gil+t+la/→gi.l*i*t.la,   } 'I said to him'

Mester and Padgett (1994) note that the (seemingly) inherently procedural nature of such directionality had been seen as a serious challenge for constraint-based theories like OT—but show that OT is equal to the task: they explain the observed variation by differentially ranking ALIGNL(σ, PrWd) and ALIGNR(σ, PrWd). Here, ALIGNL, ALIGNR are primarily about syllables; violations are denominated in the next prosodic unit down, morae.[12]

Evaluating both candidates with reference to the input /CVCCCV/, the 'Iraqi' candidate, CV.CVC.CV, violates ALIGNL by four morae altogether: the first syllable is perfectly aligned, the second is misaligned by one mora (CV) and the third by three morae (CV.CVC). The 'Cairene' candidate, CVC.CV.CV, incurs five morae of ALIGNL violation (two for the second syllable, three for the third). So, in terms of ALIGNL, the Iraqi candidate is more harmonic than the Cairene.

Similar analysis applies for ALIGNR: the Iraqi candidate sustains four morae of violation (three for the first syllable, one for the middle, but none for the last), the Cairene only three morae (2/1/0). When ALIGNR is crucial, the Cairene output wins. Thus, ALIGNL>>ALIGNR leads to the surfacing of the Iraqi form, and ALIGNR>>ALIGNL to the Cairene. The final step is to conclude that these two Align constraints are ranked differently in the respective dialects.

Kenstowicz (1994) analyzes the more complex epenthetic behavior of Chukchee (cf. Spencer 1994 for a similar approach). Chukchee, too, has a CV(C) syllable template, handling stray consonants by schwa epenthesis; unlike in Arabic, however, such schwas usually occupy gaps between mor-

---

[12] Mester and Padgett (1994) attribute to McCarthy the suggestion that alignment violations should usually be measured in units of the next prosodic level down from the category the constraint is mainly about.

phemes. Kenstowicz uses CONTIGUITY to confine epenthetic schwas to inter-morpheme gaps.

(25) CONTIGUITY (Kenstowicz 1994)
   'If / . . . xyz . . . / are contiguous in lexical structure, then
      (i)   *[xəy] (i.e. do not epenthesize between adjacent lexical elements)
      (ii) *[x<y>z] (i.e. do not underparse underlying lexical material)'

The first clause bans epenthesis, but evidently applies only within a morpheme (alternatively, morpheme boundaries block 'lexical adjacency'):

(26) /miml + qaca+n/ → mimləqacan (*miməlqacan)   'place near water'

CONTIGUITY explains the location of epenthetic segments between morphemes, but cannot be undominated in Chukchee: there are instances where the epenthesis site does lie within a morpheme and not, as CONTIGUITY would predict, at the word edge.

(27) a. /pne + k/ → pənek (*əpnek)   'to grind'
     b. /tnut + k/ → tənutək (*ətnutək)   'to swell'
     c. /miml/ → miməl (*mimlə)   (cf. 26)   'water'

The key to the lack of epenthesis sites at word margins appears to be for a constraint along the limits of Lx≈PR of P&S (1993) to dominate CONTIGU-ITY.[13] Lx≈PR is a double-edged alignment constraint requiring coincidence of (both edges) of lexical and prosodic words, so that epenthesis avoids word edges even at the expense of a CONTIGUITY violation.

(28) /pne + k/		Lx≈PR	CONTIGUITY	DEP
☞	a. pənek		*	*
	b. əpnek	*!		*

4.4 *Word stress*

The usual approaches to stress in generative phonology involve some variation on the theme of grouping syllables into higher levels of structure, primary stress being equated with the head of the highest level and secondary stresses with heads of intermediate levels (Halle and Vergnaud 1987, Halle and Idsardi 1995, and Hayes 1995 all present comprehensive treatments along these lines).

We already have constraints like PARSE-σ available to ensure that, as far as may be, parsing can occur: the mechanics are driven by an alignment exercise similar to that seen in Arabic syllabification. For example, Hayes (1995: 62–4)

---

[13] Kenstowicz (1994) reviews other constraints that might have accounted for the observed phenomena, but don't—e.g. (27) a/b, but not c, could be explained by ONSET and/or NOCODA.

analyzes the stress pattern of Pintupi: main stress is on the initial syllable of the word, with secondary stresses on every other syllable thereafter, except the final syllable.

Hayes groups Pintupi syllables into left-headed binary feet ($\acute{\sigma}\sigma$) from left to right, before collecting all the feet, along with any unfooted final syllable, into a higher Word Layer, which he argues is left-headed. He accounts for the stresslessness of the final syllable by positing that unfooted syllables cannot be stressed. (29) illustrates how this algorithm produces the attested stress profile.

(29)
[x				]	Word Layer
(x)	(x)	(x)	(x)		Foot Layer
(σ σ)	(σ σ)	(σ σ)	(σ σ)	σ	
[(yúma)	(ɹ̀ŋka)	(màra)	(tʲù̠ɹa)	ka]	'because of mother-in-law'

Key contributions come from the following constraints (restated to underscore the variants used in this application).

(30) a. FTBIN
       All feet dominate two syllables.
     b. PARSE-σ (Cohn and McCarthy 1994)
       All syllables are parsed by feet, or else by Prosodic Words.[14]
     c. FT-FORM (Trochaic) (Cohn and McCarthy 1994)
       Feet are trochaic (i.e. $(\acute{\sigma}\sigma)_{Ft}$)

The binary footing is driven by FTBIN, the presence of an unfooted syllable being evidence for the following ranking.

(31) FTBIN, FT-FORM (Trochaic) >> PARSE-σ

These alone do not identify the unfooted syllable: ALIGNL(Ft, PrWd) is needed to resolve the issue. For a five-syllable word, we must consider the possible footings in (32).[15] The argument closely resembles that employed in determining the Arabic syllabifications.

(32)	ALIGNL(Ft, PrWd)	
	1st Foot	2nd Foot
☞ a. [(σ σ) (σ σ) σ]		σσ
b. [(σ σ) σ (σ σ)]		σσσ!
c. [σ (σ σ) (σ σ)]	σ	σσ!σ

---

[14] This differs from the formulation (13) of M&P (1993a). For further discussion, see section 5 below.

[15] The constraints Lx≈Pr and PARSE-FT ('All feet are parsed by Prosodic Words') are here assumed undominated.

Candidate (a) triumphs because its first foot is perfectly left-aligned with the prosodic word, while its second foot is as close to such alignment as it possibly could be, given that the first foot is in the way.

It is worth highlighting a slightly different type of alignment that arises quite naturally in this context. The situations seen so far all aim to have the edges of two prosodic constituents coincide. Essentially identical considerations apply where one of the items to be aligned is a morphosyntactic category.

A simple example is ALIGN-ROOT-FT = ALIGNR(Root, Foot), used by Cohn and McCarthy (1994) to explain the distinct stress patterns in Indonesian for monomorphemic and bimorphemic words: for instance, the bimorphemic form *bicarákan* ('speak about something') is not stressed as **bìcarákan* with secondary stress on the initial syllable, as would happen if it were monomorphemic. The next tableau provides part of the answer:[16] but for ALIGN-ROOT-FT, the violations of PARSE-σ and ALIGNL(PrWd/Ft) would exclude the attested form (a); the opposite result ensues because both are crucially dominated by a constraint that only (b) violates.

(33)	ALIGN-ROOT-FT	PARSE-σ	ALIGNL (PrWd/Ft)
☞ a. [bi(caral)kan]		**	*
b. [(bica) (ralkan)]	*!		

This vividly illustrates an important insight running through much of the Generalized Alignment work in M&P (1993*b*) (and other research based thereon), enabling OT to handle the ability of morphology to contribute directly to the determination of metrical structure.

It remains to explain why the attested form is not **bi(cára)kan* but bi(cará)-kan: bearing in mind that Indonesian metrical feet are trochaic, the opposite result might have been expected. The answer lies in the domination of FT-FORM(Trochaic) by yet another alignment constraint, RIGHTMOST(σ́) = ALIGNR(σ́, PrWd), requiring the stressed syllable to be the last in the word. Although only **[bi(cára)kan]* satisfies FT-FORM, it transgresses dominant RIGHTMOST(σ́) by two syllables, *bi(cará)kan* prevailing because its infringement of RIGHTMOST(σ́) is limited to a single syllable.

Similar arguments characterize much OT-based work in metrical phonology. Obviously, additional constraints need to be brought into play to account for some of the more interesting effects, and these sometimes present new analytical challenges. The essentials, though, often remain along similar lines.

Crowhurst and Hewitt (1994) derive interesting typological conclusions

---

[16] Cohn and McCarthy (1994) also use a further dominated constraint, ALL-FT-R = ALIGNR(Ft, PrWd). While this plays an important role in Indonesian stress allocation, it is not needed for our limited purposes.

from an examination of this sort of analysis, arguing that, while conventional parametric approaches to metrical phonology proceed on the basis that iterativity and directionality of footing are independent both of one another and of the permissibility of degenerate feet, implicational relations exist between the constraints used to produce the same results under OT. This has potentially major consequences for the dialectal and diachronic variations predicted by the respective theories.

4.3 *Autosegmental associations*

Pulleyblank et al. (forthcoming) make crucial use of featural alignment techniques (cf. Kirchner 1993; Akinlabi 1995) to explain tongue-root harmony patterns in various African languages. The alignment constraints involved are ALIGNL/R(ATR, Word)) requiring coincidence of the ATR featural span with the word edges. A grounding constraint is also important here: LO/TR combines LO/RTR and *LO/ATR which, respectively, demand that low vowels be produced with tongue-root retraction and ban low vowels with tongue-root advancement. Also in point are featural correspondence constraints, notably MAXATR, DEPATR connecting the underlying form and surface realizations of tongue-root specifications, and a faithfulness requirement for autosegmental associations (DEPPATHATR).

Tongue-root advancement in Degema is dominant/recessive, the result that any underlying ATR feature spreads throughout the word being achieved by having DEPPATHATR dominated by each of the other constraints. ATR cannot be unrealized on the surface (which would violate MAXATR) and, granted that there must therefore be an ATR featural span, the alignment constraints require it to occupy the entire word. Although additional association lines may be needed to bring this about, the low ranking of DEPPATHATR ensures that the most harmonic outcome is indeed to insert them.

Emalhe, by contrast, exhibits an asymmetric harmony pattern. Here, the non-low vowels harmonize in that ATR vowels co-occur with other ATR vowels, and similarly for RTR. This does extend to the low vowels, which are always retracted and may be preceded or followed by retracted non-low vowels. However, while low vowels may follow ATR vowels, they cannot precede them. This pattern is captured by the ranking in (34):

(34) MAXATR >> ALIGNL(ATR, Word), LO/TR >> MAXLO >> ALIGNR(ATR, Word)

The following tableaux illustrate how this ranking accounts for the behavior of final and initial low vowels respectively.

Questions of Priorities 63

(35) ATR sImA LO 'dance'	MAXATR	ALIGNL (ATR,Wd)	LO/TR	MAXLO	ALIGNR (ATR,Wd)
a. ATR sima LO	*!				
☞ b. ATR sima LO					*
c. ATR ∧ simə LO			*!		
d. ATR ∧ sime LO				*!	*

In (35), failure of right ATR alignment is the price of satisfying the grounding condition while also retaining the underlying low and ATR specifications.

(36) ATR zArI LO 'be long'	MAXATR	ALIGNL (ATR,Wd)	LO/TR	MAXLO	ALIGNR (ATR,Wd)
a. ATR zarı LO	*!				
b. ATR zari LO		*!			
c. ATR ∧ zəri LO			*!		
☞ d. ATR ∧ zeri LO				*	

Here, on the other hand, even if the initial vowel is posited to be underlyingly low (perhaps improbably, having regard to the Lexicon Optimization principle), that featural association would have to be sacrificed in order to comply with the dominant constraints. The ATR span must cover the initial low vowel, which duly raises so as to meet the grounding condition.

4.4 *Affixation*

Having already noted extrametricality as an interesting consequence of aligning different edges, let us examine a further application: positioning of affixes.
Simple cases, involving prefixation or suffixation, may be explained by constraints aligning affixes with roots or stems.

(37) inform-<u>ed</u>, inform-<u>ation</u>, <u>mis</u>-inform, <u>mis</u>-inform-<u>ed</u>, <u>mis</u>-inform-<u>ation</u>

(38) a. ALIGNPFXROOT = ALIGN(PREFIX, R, ROOT, L)   Prefixes immediately precede a
                                                    root.
     b. ALIGNSFXROOT = ALIGN(SUFFIX, L, ROOT, R)   Suffixes immediately follow a
                                                    root.
     c. ALIGNPFXSTEM = ALIGNL(PREFIX, STEM)   Prefixes come first.
     d. ALIGNSFXSTEM = ALIGNR(SUFFIX, STEM)   Suffixes come last.

All these are violable in English, as (39) shows. (a/b) both violate ALIGNSFX-
ROOT and ALIGNSFXSTEM; (c) violates ALIGNPFXROOT and ALIGNPFXSTEM.

(39) a. form-<u>al</u>-<u>iz</u>-<u>ation</u>
     b. organ-<u>iz</u>-<u>ation</u>-<u>al</u>
     c. <u>un</u>-<u>re</u>-construct-<u>ed</u>

The hypothesis that individual sets of 'lexical' constraints exist for each affix
is opposed by (a/b), where the same suffixes appear, with different orderings.
(39) resembles the footing arguments, where a constraint requiring something
to appear in final or initial position has to be broken because another object,
similarly constrained, is already there. But there are other possible reasons for
violating constraints like those in (38): phonotactic considerations might take
priority, as in regular English plural formation, where ALIGNSFXROOT is rou-
tinely infringed, an OCP-based constraint forcing the failure of the plural
suffix *[-z]* to perfectly abut the root in sibilant-final forms.

   Similar considerations arise in connection with the third person singular
suffix */-i/* in Axininca Campa (AC; see M&P (1993*a*; 1993*b*) for more extensive presentations).

(40) a. iñčʰiki   /i + N + čʰik + i/   'he will cut'
     b. iñčʰikaati   /i + N + čʰik + aa + i/   'he will cut again'

(a) shows the suffix without allophonic variation. In (b), epenthetic *t* is inserted
to avoid direct contact between heteromorphemic vowels. This might be
explained by high ranking of ONSET: although ONSET cannot be undominated
as words can begin with *iñ-*, a ranking such as (41) would cater for this.

(41) ALIGNL(Stem, PrWd) >> ONSET >> DEP

ONSET >> DEP holds because (b) surfaces as *iñ.čʰi.kaa.ti* (violating DEP), not
*iñ.čʰi.kaa.i (infringing ONSET); the ONSET violation in the optimal form for

(a), coupled with the ungrammaticality of *tiñ.čʰi.ki (due to DEP and ALIGNL), ensures ALIGNL>>ONSET.

A third conceivable candidate in (40b) is *iñ.čʰi.kaai*, where the vowels of the final two morphemes fall within one syllable. Although a constraint banning multiply complex nuclei would cover this, it would not cater for (42).

(42) iŋkomati (*iŋkomai)   /i + N + ko + ma + i/   'he will cut'

Complex nuclei appear in the AC data, and the tie between *iŋkomati* and *iŋkomai* cannot be broken by fitting, say, NOCOMPLEXNUCLEUS into the ranking already established. However, M&P note that vowels at the stem/suffix juncture never surface in the same AC syllable; this focus on adjoining vowels in different morphemes brings a morphological dimension to what has hitherto appeared to be a purely phonological problem. ALIGN-STEM-σ, requiring the stem to be coterminous with a syllable, does the trick, both in accounting for (42) and in eliminating *iñ.čʰi.kaai* in the earlier example: without such a constraint dominating DEP, the output in (42) would indeed have been *iŋ.ko.mai*.

(43) /i + N + ko + ma + i/	ALIGN-STEM-σ	ONSET	DEP
☞ a. iŋ.ko.ma.ti			*
b. iŋ.ko.mai	*!		
c. iŋ.ko.ma.i		*!	

Alignment plays a part in many other varieties of affixation too. M&P (1993*b*) discuss the case of the affix *-um-* in Tagalog.[17] *-um-* comes as close to the left edge of the stem as possible, subject to the overriding requirement that its *m* should not be syllabified as a coda.

(44) a. /um + iyák/→u.mi.yák   'cry'
     b. /um + káin/→ku.má.in.   'eat'
     c. /um + gradwet/→gru.mad.wet   'graduate'

This pattern may be accounted for by having NOCODA>>ALIGNPFXSTEM: NOCODA is plainly violable in Tagalog (cf. the three word final codas in (44)) and must, in turn, be dominated: ALIGNSTEM = ALIGNR(Stem, OUTPUT) duly avoids final coda deletion or vowel epenthesis.

---

[17] According to Aspillera (1993: 43), verbs with the affix *um* emphasize the doer of the action or the act itself, typically either where no object is needed to complete the meaning or where there is an object which is not being emphasized.

(45) /um + káin/	ALIGNSTEM	NOCODA	ALIGNPFXSTEM
a. um.ká.in		**!	
☞ b. ku.má.in		*	k
c. ká.um.in.		**!	ká
d. ku.má.i	*!		k

5. ELABORATING ON CONSTITUENCY

Let us now look more closely at some constituency constraints that have already cropped up. Two formulations of PARSE-σ have been used, repeated here for convenience.

(46) PARSE-σ
    a. (= 13) All syllables are parsed by feet (M&P 1993*a*; 1993*b*)
    b. (= 30b) All syllables are parsed by feet, or else by Prosodic Words (Cohn and McCarthy 1994)

It is not instantly clear how compliance with the latter version is to be gauged. Presumably, it is not intended that a syllable parsed by a PrWd, but not by a foot, should incur no violation; more probably, Cohn and McCarthy's aim is to emphasize that, even if the first clause is infringed, the proviso will not be. This might be expressed by decomposing their constraint into two sections: (46a) and a higher ranked (perhaps undominated) requirement that any syllable not parsed by a foot must be dominated by a PrWd.

    This interpretation is inconsistent with the Strict Layer Hypothesis (SLH) of Selkirk (1984) to the effect that units of the prosodic hierarchy are composed of units of the next layer down and, conversely, any unit of the hierarchy is exhaustively contained within the dominating unit of the next layer up. Selkirk (1995) weakens the earlier categorical statement of the SLH, which she now proposes replacing by four constraints, two apparently universally inviolable (47) and two violable (48); these remain equivalent to the SLH in the weak sense that the SLH is satisfied if and only if each of the individual constraints is satisfied.

(47) a. LAYEREDNESS
        No prosodic category dominates a higher prosodic category.
        (e.g. No syllable dominates a foot)
    b. HEADEDNESS
        Any prosodic category (other than one in the bottom level of the prosodic hierarchy) must dominate a member of the next layer down.
        (e.g. A PrWd immediately dominates a foot)

(48) a. EXHAUSTIVITY

No prosodic category immediately dominates a constituent below the next layer down.

(e.g. No PrWd immediately dominates a syllable)

b. NONRECURSIVITY

No prosodic category immediately dominates a constituent of the same layer.

(e.g. No PrWd immediately dominates a PrWd)

As Selkirk (1995) notes, the constraints in (47) together embody the essence of the SLH. The refinements in (48) are needed to deal with various challenges to the rigidity of the hierarchy[18] (e.g. Inkelas 1989; M&P 1993*a*; 1993*b*—see Selkirk 1995: 190 for fuller references).

For instance, the alternative formulations of PARSE-σ may be reconciled by appeal to EXHAUSTIVITY; Selkirk (1995) presents additional evidence for the violability of EXHAUSTIVITY in arguing that such English functional phrases as in (49) should be analysed as a phonological phrase (PhPh) immediately dominating both a (free clitic) syllable, in breach of EXHAUSTIVITY, as well as a PrWd.

(49) a. $((\text{to})\sigma \ (\text{London})_{\text{PrWd}})_{\text{PhPh}}$

b. $((\text{her})\sigma \ (\text{portrait})_{\text{PrWd}})_{\text{PhPh}}$

She further contends that the violability of NONRECURSIVITY is borne out by the behavior of affixal clitics, as in (50a). Here, we see the weak form of the English pronoun *him* giving rise to a nested PrWd structure headed by the host; note, by contrast, that using the strong form of the pronoun (50b) complies with NONRECURSIVITY.

(50) a. $((\text{need})_{\text{PrWd}} \ (\text{'m})_{\sigma})_{\text{PrWd}}$

b. $((\text{need})_{\text{PrWd}} \ (\text{him})_{\text{PrWd}}) \ _{\text{PhPh}}$

Peperkamp (forthcoming) offers further evidence for the violability of NON-RECURSIVITY. In her analysis of Italian stem + word compounds, such as in (51), she argues that some speakers lexicalize such compounds, thereby subjecting them to a requirement that both the compound and its head be analysed as prosodic words.

(51) $(\text{euro}(\text{parlamento})_{\text{PrWd}}) \ _{\text{PrWd}}$ 'euro-parliament'

---

[18] Hayes (1995: 109–10) comments in his justification for moving away from the 'exhaustive' approach taken in his own earlier work: 'For foot structure, there does seem to be some pressure for all syllables to be incorporated into feet, but this is hardly the pervasive phenomenon found in syllabification . . . The upshot seems to be that in our present state of knowledge, it would be aprioristic to adhere firmly to a rigid principle of exhaustive prosodic parsing . . .' Whilst not couched in OT terms, Hayes's empirically based remarks support the use of violable constraints in analyzing metrical phenomena. Indeed, as Kager (1995: 462) notes, the manuscript of Hayes (1995) helped shape OT stress theory.

Peperkamp's analysis of the constraints involved effectively illustrates the interaction between constituency and other constraints regulating the phonology/syntax interface. She contends that the two main competitors to the analysis in (51), which violates NONRECURSIVITY, fall foul of higher ranked constraints: $(europarlamento)_{PrWd}$ would infringe an alignment constraint requiring each lexical word (here, *parlamento*) to be left-aligned with a prosodic word; $(euro)_{PrWd}(parlamento)_{PrWd}$, however, transgresses the requirement that the entire compound should itself be dominated by a prosodic word.

This last constraint is a variant of the WRAP family, introduced by Truckenbrodt (1995) to handle issues involving the syntax/phonology interface. In its general formulation (Selkirk 1996), WRAP(GCat, PCat) requires the elements of a morphosyntactic constituent (GCat) in the input to be contained within a prosodic constituent of type PCat in the output. For Peperkamp's problem, the relevant member of the family is WRAP(Lex, PrWd), where Lex is a lexical item.

Truckenbrodt's own prototype, WRAP-XP (= WRAP(LexP, PhPh)), requires lexical phrases to be contained within phonological phrases. He derives a factorial typology involving WRAP-XP, NONRECURSIVITY, ALIGN-XP (= ALIGNL/R(LexP, PhPh)). Much as for the compounding question, the differences boil down to a question of what happens when a lexical phrase dominates two phrasal complements (e.g. [V NP NP]). Is this to be parsed phonologically as a single phonological phrase, two such phrases side by side, or one with another nested inside it? The first alternative will typically violate ALIGN-XP, which must accordingly be bottom-ranked if that parsing is to prevail (as in Chichewa). For the second case, Wrap-XP must likewise come last (as in Chi Mwiini). Finally, the recursive pattern—similar to (51)—involves low ranking of NONRECURSIVITY, as in Kimatuumbi.

6. CORRESPONDENCE THEORY IN ACTION

After considering in Section 6.1 extensions to the correspondence constraints already introduced (following M&P 1995*a*: appendix A, the source of all constraints unless otherwise indicated), illustrations are given of the strength of an approach based on Correspondence Theory. The initial motivation for CT came from M&P's programme on Prosodic Morphology, of which Section 6.2 gives highlights. Section 6.3 describes Urbanczyk's (1994) illustration that double reduplications can be explained in CT by parallel ranking of separate correspondences for each reduplication. Section 6.4 introduces the arguments of Benua (1995) and Kenstowicz (1995) that correspondence ideas also apply in derivational morphology. Finally, Section 6.5 presents proposals concerning the special status of morphological and prosodic heads in CT.

6.1 *Basic constraints: expansion and elaboration*

For ease of reference, the general forms of the key faithfulness constraints introduced previously are repeated. Recall that CT posits a pair of representations, S_1/S_2, linked by a *correspondence*, Ω (so that the correspondent of the segment X is $\Omega(X)$—see footnote 23).

(52) MAX   Every segment of S_1 has a correspondent in S_2.

(53) DEP   Every segment of S_2 has a correspondent in S_1.

(54) IDENT(F)   Correspondent segments have identical values for the feature F.

MAX and DEP respectively deal with under- and over-parsing, while the IDENT family imposes featural identity between correspondents. Further constraints ensure correspondence is well-behaved. CONTIGUITY has already been seen in the context of Chukchee epenthesis. Much as MAX and DEP are needed as distinct constraints, it is appropriate to decompose CONTIGUITY.

(55) a. I-CONTIG ('No skipping')
      The portion of S_1 standing in correspondence forms a contiguous string.
    b. O-CONTIG ('No intrusion')
      The portion of S_2 standing in correspondence forms a contiguous string.[19]

M&P (1995*a*) attribute Chukchee's preference for morpheme-edge epenthesis to high ranking of O-CONTIG, but for which the output string would be broken up by a segment having no correspondent.[20] For I-CONTIG, they cite Diyari, where high-ranked NOCODA causes deletion of all word-final consonants but I-CONTIG >> NOCODA blocks similar deletions word-medially. Diyari word-final deletion violates Right Anchoring.

(56) ANCHORING
    Any element of the right(left) edge of S_1 has a correspondent at the same edge of
    S_2.

ANCHORING enjoys close affinities with the theory of Generalized Alignment, so much so that much of the latter may be recast in terms of anchoring (M&P 1994*b*; 1995*a*; Alderete et al. 1996). Alignment of morphological and prosodic categories is tantamount to edge-anchoring in input/output correspondence.

LINEARITY prohibits metathesis, while UNIFORMITY and INTEGRITY seek to ensure that the relation of correspondence is one-to-one in both directions.

---

[19] There is arguably an infelicity of notation here, in that specific choices of S_1 and S_2 are implicitly made in naming the subconstraints of CONTIGUITY; that said, it is acknowledged that I(nput) and O(utput) are the archetypal values of S_1 and S_2.

[20] This seems to beg a question about the nature of the Chukchee I/O correspondence. For both the attested and unattested outputs in /miml + qaca + n/ → *mimləqacan* (*miməlqacan), epenthesis breaks up the correspondent portion of the output string. If, however, individual correspondences exist for each morpheme, then *mimləqacan* would satisfy O-CONTIG(*miml*) whereas *miməlqacan would violate it.

(57) LINEARITY
Correspondence respects the precedence structure of S_1/S_2.

(58) UNIFORMITY
No element of S_2 has multiple correspondents in S_1.

(59) INTEGRITY
No element of S_1 has multiple correspondents in S_2.

UNIFORMITY aims to outlaw *coalescence* (or *fusion*). Pater (1995) discusses the well-known Indonesian case (cf. Halle and Clements 1983: 125) where the coda nasal in the prefix /meN/ is forced by, chiefly, a ban (*NC) on nasal + unvoiced obstruent sequences to merge with the ensuing onset, in violation of UNIFORMITY. The main justification for analysing this as fusion is that the surface consonant combines the nasality of the (placeless) N with the place of the following unvoiced obstruent. In /meN + tulis/→*menulis* ('to write'), the surface form violates UNIFORMITY[21] but wins because its main challengers each break one of the higher ranked MAX, DEP, *NC, IDENT(Nasal), or IDENT(Exp).[22]

INTEGRITY discourages situations where one input segment surfaces in two output segments.[23] To distinguish an INTEGRITY violation from the more common epenthesis, it is necessary to establish that the 'first' and 'second' output segments actually correspond to the same input segment, rather than one or other merely being unpaired.

Integrity violations are observable in the Spanish data (Cole 1995: 94), where underlying mid-vowels surface as diphthongs under stress.

(60) a. cont-á-ba   'he counted'   c[ué]nt-a   'he counts'
     b. neg-á-ba   'he denied'   n[ié]g-a   'he denies'
     c. solt-ámos   'we release'   s[ué]lto   'I release'

The final constraint is not peculiar to CT, but fits quite naturally here.

(61) STROLE (Structural Role, adapted from M&P 1993a: 134)
     Correspondents have identical syllabic roles.

STROLE requires onsets to correspond with onsets, and codas with codas. Gafos (1995) notes that it is undominated in Temiar. Thus, if a reduplicative morpheme requires a consonant in onset position, the onset of the base is chosen; however, where the reduplicant demands a coda consonant, the coda of the base is used instead. Reducing the intricacies of Temiar

---

[21] The default surface form of the prefix is *meŋ*, supporting the view that its realization as *men* reflects the combination of nasality with the place of the initial onset of *tulis*.

[22] Pater (1995) uses IDENT(Exp) to preclude the addition of voicing. Following Steriade (1995: 155f.), voiced obstruents are specified for a feature [pharyngeally *exp*anded] as well as [voice] for which both obstruents and sonorants are specified.

[23] Strictly, it has to be presupposed that Integrity is unviolated in order for the notation, $\Omega(x)$, to be well defined. That said, integrity violations are few and far between, and for most practical purposes (including those of this chapter) this point can safely be set aside.

morphology to the strict minimum needed here, the semelfactive form of the active voice and the continuative form of the causative voice are both formed from the same base (the perfective form of the active voice) by the rules in (62).

(62) a. Semelfactive: $C_1VC_2 \rightarrow C_1a.C_1VC_2$
     b. Continuative: $C_1VC_2 \rightarrow t.rC_2.C_1VC_2$

The semelfactive copies the onset of the base, while the continuative copies its coda.

(63) kɔɔw   'call' (PERFECTIVE ACTIVE)
     ka.kɔɔw   'call' (SEMELFACTIVE ACTIVE)
     t.rw.kɔɔw   'call' (CONTINUATIVE CAUSATIVE)

6.2 *Reduplication and prosodic morphology*

The leading works in Correspondence Theory, M&P (1994*a*; 1995*a*), both build on the programme of Prosodic Morphology (PM) begun in M&P (1986) and transferred to OT as from M&P (1993*a*) (M&P 1995*b* gives a recent general overview of PM). They are primarily concerned with reduplicative phenomena in PM, especially the considerations which cause divergence between the exponent of a reduplicative morpheme and its base. Reduplicants and bases are argued to correspond in essentially the same way outputs correspond to inputs: that is, CT applies to the Base/Reduplicant pair (B/R) exactly as it applies to Input/Output (I/O).

Let us look at some examples, drawn from M&P (1995*a*), of the kind of question PM seeks to address.

(64) In Balangao why should the reduplicated form of *taynan* be *ma-tayna-taynan* ('repeatedly be left behind') rather than, say, **ma-taynan-taynan* or **ma-tayna-tayna* (see also M&P 1994*a*)?

(65) What is the reason for the asymmetry in Indonesian reduplicated forms such as *t*ari-me*n*ari ('dance' + RECIPROCAL)? Why should the affix *meN* yield a reduplicated form of *tulis* like *menulisnulis* ('write' + INTENSITY + REPETITIVE)?

(66) Given that Chumash has a process deleting *l* before a coronal consonant, why should this not have any effect in such reduplicative situations as the realization of */s + RED + tal'ik'/* as *ʃtaltal'ik'* ('his wives'), rather than either *ʃtatal'ik'* or *ʃtata'ik'*?

The core of the answer is essentially the same every time: deviations from expected identities occur to satisfy a more pressing constraint. Here is the basic framework: separate correspondence relations are posited, between input and output in the non-reduplicative morphology, and between base and reduplicant: it is vital to note that the base of the reduplicative morphology is also the output of the non-reduplicative part of the grammar. The diagram in (67) illustrates the strategy.

(67) Input: Stem

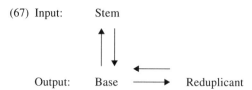

      Output: Base   ⟶   Reduplicant

The arrows denote a correspondence. It is natural to ask why none appear between stem and reduplicant: although such a direct correspondence is possible (and theoretically exists), its effects are very uncommon cross-linguistically and so almost always come so far down the constraint hierarchy as to be completely masked.[24] This may be expressed schematically:

(68) Input/Output Faithfulness, Base/Reduplicant Faithfulness
     >> Input/Reduplicant Faithfulness

In (64) the base of the reduplication, *taynan*, is totally faithful to the input, but violates NoCODA (twice, in fact, but only the word-final occurrence concerns us here). Thus, for Balangao, I/O-Faithfulness >> NoCODA. The reduplicative prefix *tayna-* lacks that coda, which in turn suggests that NoCODA >> B/R-Faithfulness.[25] Between them, these dispose of the other candidates.

    Schematically:

(69) Input/Output Faithfulness >> Phono-Constraint >> Base/Reduplicant Faithfulness

This does not assert that *every* Balangao 'phono-constraint' lies between these two extremes, but it is precisely those constraints which do fall in that range that give rise to most of the interesting asymmetries. This phenomenon exemplifies the eponymous Emergence of the Unmarked, the subject of M&P (1994*a*) and a recurring theme of subsequent work: a markedness principle (here NoCODA) suppressed in the normal (i.e. non-reduplicative) operation of the grammar becomes effective in reduplication.[26]

We have already seen how Indonesian NC fusion causes results like /*meN* + *tulis*/→*menulis*. Against this background, a result like that in (70) is not unexpected.

---

[24] The exception that proves this rule is Klamath (M&P 1995*a*: Section 6).

[25] This is a slight oversimplification. B/R contiguity evidently dominates NoCODA: were this not so, the medial coda, *y*, in *taynan* would not surface. However, it is valid to say that NoCODA outranks the key components of B/R Correspondence.

[26] The derived environment effects noted in Section 3.2 also exemplify emergence of the unmarked in relation to constraints ranked above the stem-local and below the morpheme-local self-conjunction of any pertinent constraint: see Itô and Mester (1996) for further discussion.

(70) tari + meN + tari   → tarimenari
      Base + *meN* + Reduplicant

But what of (71)?

(71) meN + tulis + tulis   → menulisnulis
      meN + Base + Reduplicant

One can see readily enough why the influence of *meN* might cause the *t* of the Base to fuse with the nasal, but there is not even a neighbouring nasal for the reduplicant *t* to coalesce with! In this tableau the all-embracing term 'phono-constraint' may, for definiteness, be taken as the constraint *NC against sequences of nasal + voiceless obstruent.[27] Here and in subsequent tableaux dealing with reduplication, the base of the reduplication is underlined for each candidate, faithfulness violations being counted in terms of the number of segments involved.

(72)	/meN-tulis-RED/	Phono-constraint (*NC)	I/O Faithfulness	B/R Faithfulness
a.	men<u>tulis</u> tulis	*!		
☞ b.	me<u>nulis</u> nulis		*	
c.	me<u>nulis</u> tulis		*	*!

What is intriguing here is that B/R Faithfulness makes the crucial difference despite being dominated by both the phono-constraint and I/O Faithfulness. (a) is immediately ruled out because the phonotactic constraint is dominant. Once the grammar has recognized the inevitability of an I/O violation, it has to cut its losses by avoiding the B/R infringement. This example incidentally bears out the low ranking of Input/Reduplicant faithfulness, satisfied by (c), but not by the optimal output. It is worth emphasizing that the reversion to *t* in the reduplicant in (c) makes matters worse, not better: it results in two faithfulness infringements—one between input (*tulis*) and base (*nulis*), the other—fatally—between base (*nulis*) and reduplicant (*tulis*).

M&P call situations like this 'overapplication': here, nasal fusion over-applies. It comes as no surprise that 'underapplication' phenomena are also found: indeed in Chumash,[28] the same phonological process in the same language is responsible for both underapplication and overapplication (or, at least, something very close to it).

(73) a. Underapplication: /s + RED + tal'ik'/ → ʃtaltal'ik'   'his wives'
      b. Overapplication: /s + RED + pil + tap/ → spitpi<l>tap   'it is falling in'

---

[27] Pater (1995) shows that *NC >> I/O Faithfulness, strictly not established by the earlier analysis.
[28] Chumash is perhaps better known for its leftwards sibilant harmony phenomena involving the [anterior] value of coronal affricates and fricatives. Although the process is seen here in the realization of *s* as ʃ in (66), this has no bearing on the matters at hand.

Denoting the ban on 1 + coronal sequences by *l[cor]; M&P argue that Chumash has a high-ranking constraint $R = \sigma_{\mu\mu}$, forcing the reduplicant to be a heavy syllable (CVC, as the language has no long vowels). This templatic constraint forces underapplication; it simultaneously prevents the overapplication which would occur if $R = \sigma_{\mu\mu}$ were not present (as may be confirmed by ignoring the first constraint column in (74) and noting that the overapplied (c) would prevail).

(74)	/s + RED + tal'ik'/	$R = \sigma_{\mu\mu}$	MAX (B/R)	*1[cor]	MAX (I/O)
☞ a.	ʃ tal tal'ik'		**	*	
b.	ʃ ta tal'ik'	*!	***		
c.	ʃ ta taik'	*!	**		*

The very fact that $R = \sigma_{\mu\mu}$ has no key part to play in the second situation (/s + RED + pil-tap/ 'it is falling in') is exactly what leads to overapplication: even if $R = \sigma_{\mu\mu}$ were removed, the winner would still be (a).

(75)	/s + RED + pil-tap/	$R = \sigma_{\mu\mu}$	MAX (B/R)	DEP (B/R)	*1[cor]	MAX (I/O)
☞ a.	s pit pi tap		**			*
b.	s pi pi tap	*!	***			*
c.	s pil pi tap		***!	*		*
d.	s pil pil tap		***!		*	

M&P contend that this qualifies as overapplication, an issue on which there may be room for more than one view (bearing in mind that the winning candidate could be argued to replace the offending *l* with a *t* rather than deleting it). However, the credentials of (74) seem more firmly established and the over- and underapplication effects exhibited there may be captured by the following broad rankings.

(76) a. Underapplication:
   Phono-Constraint ($R = \sigma_{\mu\mu}$) >> B/R Faithfulness >>I/O Faithfulness
   b. Overapplication:
   B/R Faithfulness >> Phono-Constraint (*l[cor]) >>I/O Faithfulness

It is not possible to do more here than provide a taster of the power of CT as applied to Prosodic Morphology. In particular, the notion of Emergence of the Unmarked is likely to prove a cornerstone of much future work in OT: essentially it says that, while basic considerations of (I/O) faithfulness may cause the needs of structural phonological considerations to take a back seat from time to time, they are still there, just waiting for the right moment to assert their presence.

6.3 *Double reduplication*

Urbanczyk (1994) gives a striking example of the independence of correspondences, simultaneously demonstrating the applicability of a parallel approach to an ostensibly serial situation in Northern Lushootseed, where two reduplicative prefixes can apply to the same word at the same time. Specifically, she considers the diminutive prefix DIM ($= C_1\text{í}$) with a fixed segment in its nucleus, and the distributive prefix DIST ($= C_1V_1C_2$). The situation of immediate interest is (77c): when DIST precedes DIM, DIST is not realized in its usual CVC form, but appears instead to copy DIM.[29]

(77) a. bəda?   'child'
      b. bí-bəd-bəda? /DIM + DIST + bəda?/   'dolls, 'litter'
      c. bí-bi-bəda? /DIST + DIM + bəda?/   'young children'

Urbanczyk accounts for this with distinct correspondences for DIM and DIST, proposing the following ranking to deal with these data:

(78) OCP/NoLink >> MAX-DIST >> NoCODA >> MAX-DIM

OCP/NoLink, a hybrid constraint aimed at disposing of candidates with geminates or adjacent identical consonants, immediately rules out the 'obvious' $C_1V_1C_1$-C_1V_1-$C_1V_1C_2V_2C_3$ form, *bíb-bi-bəda?*, where both DIM and DIST take their usual shape. Removing the offending coda *b* from the first prefix mends the OCP breach (and is better in terms of NoCODA), but sustains an additional MAX-DIST violation.

Although MAX-DIST >> MAX-DIM, varying the exponent of DIM cannot produce a more harmonic candidate: for instance, realizing DIM as $C_1\text{í}C_2$, instead of $C_1\text{í}$, immediately violates NoCODA as well as the dominated MAX-DEP; when DIST is added, either a further NoCODA violation or a higher-ranking MAX-DIST mark arises—each is fatal.

A noteworthy characteristic of these affix-specific correspondences is that both require total reduplication: that one affix tends to be realized as CV and the other as CVC may be seen as a by-product of the constraint ranking. For instance, the usual CVC and CV forms of DIST and DIM are due largely to interaction of the ranking MAX-DIST >> NoCODA >> MAX-DIM with a dominant constraint, AFX≤σ (M&P 1994*b*), placing an upper limit on the size of an affix.

---

[29] Hammond (1991) gives an alternative analysis of the same phenomenon in pre-optimality Prosodic Morphology.

6.4 *Correspondence between surface forms*

Benua (1995) applies the ideas of CT to morphological truncation. She argues that in English, for example, the abbreviations to *H*[æ]*r*, *L*[æ]*r*, *G*[æ]*r* of such personal names as Harry, Larry, and Gary involves a correspondence between base and truncated forms where the latter systematically violate a constraint of English banning *ær* sequences before a pause or another consonant. This may be rendered schematically as in (79), which has a form similar to that used earlier to characterize Emergence of the Unmarked, save that here the unmarked form might be said to have been submerged by truncation.

(79) Base/Truncated (B/T) faithfulness >> Phono-Constraint
        >> Input/Output Faithfulness

Benua notes that the parallels between B/T and Base/Reduplicant corre-spondences are not total. A particularly crucial difference is that B/T correspondence relates two distinct words, while B/R correspondence involves only one. This rules out the kind of two-way interdependence seen in situations like *menulisnulis* (71), where the surface form of the base is directly influenced by that of the reduplicant. In particular, it rules out such possibilities as changing the pronunciation of an unabbreviated base so as to enable the truncated form to satisfy simultaneously both the phonotactic constraint and B/T faithfulness.

Kenstowicz (1995) takes a similar approach to Benua's, applying it more widely; he contends that a correspondence relation exists wherever a consti-tuent of a derivative structure is also a word in its own right (see Peperkamp, forthcoming, for an examination of the interaction of this proposal with some of the constituency-based considerations discussed in section 5). Kenstowicz also seeks to extend the idea still further, proposing a family of *Uniform Exponence* constraints operating to minimize allomorphic differences in reali-zations of lexical items. Chapter 14 below also deals with surface–surface correspondences within OT.

6.5 *Head Faithfulness*

Alderete (1995) contends that prosodic heads enjoy a special status which can be reflected by separate faithfulness constraints in CT. The thrust of his argument is that all faithfulness constraints have counterparts restricted to prosodic heads: by Pāṇini's Theorem, the restricted version must dominate its more general fellow.

A pattern inverse to Emergence of the Unmarked arises in situations like (80):

(80) Head Faithfulness >> Phono-Constraint >> I/O Faithfulness

Russian vowel-lowering exemplifies this: here the relevant phono-constraint,

*Mɪᴅ, militates against mid-vowels. The surface form of *stól* ('table') retains the underlying mid-vowel, o, because it is stressed and head faithfulness (specifically, Hᴇᴀᴅ(σ)-Iᴅᴇɴᴛ(Height)) dominates *Mɪᴅ. In some inflected forms, however—including all those of *stól*—the desinences, not the roots, are stressed: the unstressed root is now not a prosodic head, and head-faithfulness is no longer in point. Thus, in *stalý* (*stól* + Gᴇɴɪᴛɪᴠᴇ), the root vowel lowers because *Mɪᴅ>>Iᴅᴇɴᴛ(Height).

Similar constraint families correspond to each prosodic category: moreover, these are in principle freely rankable among each other because no Pāṇinian specific-to-general relationship exists between, say, Head(σ)-Faithfulness and Head(Ft)-Faithfulness, although both stand in such a relation to plain I/O-Faithfulness. Alderete (1995) gives a cross-linguistic analysis of the metrical status of epenthetic vowels using the factorial typology generated by orderings of Hᴇᴀᴅ(σ)-Dᴇᴘ, Hᴇᴀᴅ(Ft)-Dᴇᴘ and canonical stress constraints.

In similar vein, M&P (1994*b*; 1995*a*) accord preferred status to roots (i.e. morphological heads). Observing that, cross-linguistically, affixes tend to be more 'unmarked' than roots in the sense of being simpler both syllabically and segmentally and involving smaller segmental inventories, M&P propose a universal faithfulness metaconstraint.

(81) Root Faithfulness >> Affix Faithfulness

For an example of this universal ranking in action, Sanskrit roots, but not affixes, contain onset clusters. This may be accounted for by ranking the structural constraint, NᴏCᴏᴍᴘʟᴇxOɴsᴇᴛ, below root faithfulness but above affix faithfulness. Similar reasoning yields the Turkish harmony patterns whereby vowels may be distinctively specified for the feature [back] in roots only, vowels in affixes taking their [back] value from the root. As M&P (1995*a*) emphasize, the universal nature of the metaconstraint means there can be no languages in which these patterns are reversed. Thus, for instance, no language could permit onset clusters in affixes but not in roots.

7. Vᴀʀɪᴀᴛɪᴏɴs

This section surveys some advanced applications which, for one reason or another, it seems inappropriate to pigeon-hole. In this closing section, the common thread is that the scholars concerned have sought to refine some of the fundamental ideas underlying parts of what we have seen so far.

Section 7.1 briefly draws attention to the existence of some foundational controversies. Section 7.2 then gives an overview of Buckley's *constraint domains* proposal. Section 7.3 looks at Itô & Mester's *non-crisp alignment*. Lastly, Section 7.4 takes a step beyond the largely synchronic issues considered elsewhere in this article.

7.1 *Difficulties and dissenters*

Some authors (e.g. Hammond 1995; Chapter 11 below [Editor]; Russell 1995) have sought to dispense altogether with inputs, supplementing the output constraints from 'standard' OT with separate constraints characterizing individual underlying forms. Golston (1996) takes a subtly different line, proposing instead that an input may be characterized in terms of the structural constraint violations a faithful output would incur; he argues that this essentially renders the input form superfluous.

As for the controversy over universality of constraints, Green (1993) has proposed that it is not constraints, but *metaconstraints* that are universal, each constraint being a (typically) parametrized instance of a much smaller collection of metaconstraints: the generalized alignment schema is perhaps the archetypal instance of such a metaconstraint. This approach has the dual advantage of dealing in a principled manner with a range of apparently idiosyncratic constraints, as well as rationalizing (and so reducing) the load on the learner.

The requirement that all constraints be ranked is not accepted by everyone. In particular, there are differing views on whether the simultaneous presence of alternative forms within a given language reflects indeterminacy of ranking or the coexistence of similar but non-identical grammars (see also Chapter 13). Also of concern is the possibility of multiple grammars being present at different levels of a single language (e.g. M&P's 1993*a* analysis of Axininca Campa; cf. 7.2 below); the constraint re-ranking involved in such situations is unappealing from a parallelist perspective. It remains for further research to determine whether such multiple levels are genuinely necessary.

7.2 *Domain-specific constraints*

In many situations, proponents of OT argue that it does as well as, or better than, cyclical approaches. Buckley (1995*a*; 1995*b*; 1996) contends that OT needs refinement in order to handle some particularly intricate derivations. An impressive example comes from Kashaya, where Buckley's (1994) cyclical approach requires five levels of representation and temporary extrametricality, which his subsequent work seeks to obviate through a parallel approach restricting constraints to particular domains.

The main phonological point of interest here is Kashaya's selective iambic lengthening (IL) whereby a light syllable heading a bisyllabic iambic foot sometimes becomes heavy. IL applies to roots and to some suffixes, but not others—the problem is how to deal with this divergent behavior. The critical fact about Kashaya IL is that the 'lengthening' suffixes always lie nearer the root, so enabling the word to be partitioned into contiguous lengthening and non-lengthening domains.

The pattern of footing in Kashaya is achieved in OT by the ranking in (82).

ASYM, requiring the strong branch of a branching iamb to be heavy, is in focus here: it bears much of the responsibility for both IL and the related phenomenon of foot-flipping, where initial CV: CV sequences usually have their vowel lengths interchanged so as to form a perfect CVCVV iamb.

(82) FTFORM(Iambic) >> PARSE-σ >> ALIGNR(Ft, Word)[30] >> FTBIN, ASYM

Such a ranking accounts for the footing of something like /mo-mac-ed–ela/[31] ('I keep running in there'), but fails to explain the vowel lengths in (momá:) (cede) (la). The incidence of IL relies crucially on the ranking of ASYM relative to an I/O faithfulness constraint, Q-IDENT, requiring the quantities of input and output vowels to be identical: IL occurs only when ASYM >> Q-IDENT. This is where the idea of constraint domain comes into play. Buckley observes that the input falls naturally into two sections (separated by –), according to whether or not IL applies; labelling the domain of IL application {1} and the non-lengthening domain {2}, he considers the restrictions of Q-IDENT to the respective domains.

(83)	/mo-mac-ed–ela/	Q-IDENT$^{\{2\}}$	ASYM	Q-IDENT$^{\{1\}}$
a.	(moma)(cede)(la)		**!	
b.	(moma)(cede:)(la)	*!	*	
☞ c.	(moma:)(cede)(la)		*	*
d.	(moma:)(cede:)(la)	*!		*

Essentially the same analysis also caters for foot flipping, as in /qá:-cid–u/ ('keep leaving')

(84)	/qá:-cid–u/	Q-IDENT$^{\{2\}}$	ASYM	Q-IDENT$^{\{1\}}$
a.	(qá:)(cidu)		*!	
b.	(qáci)(du)		*!	*
☞ c.	(qáci:)(du)	*!		**

Buckley (1996) seeks to deal with further side-effects, such as the stress reallocations attendant on foot-flipping, and similar issues by marrying his constraint domain technique with considerations of paradigm uniformity like those of Kenstowicz (1995). As mentioned earlier, the treatment of Axininca Campa in M&P (1993*a*), arguably the centrepiece of early work in OT, suffers from the shortcoming (so far as concerns parallelism) that sequential level ordering and re-ranking are required for different affixation processes. Super-

---

[30] Kashaya stress is actually based on the phonological phrase rather than the word, but the distinction is not relevant in the one-word examples Buckley considers, nor essential to the purpose of the exercise.

[31] Notation: - denotes suffix boundaries; – indicates the demarcation between lengthening and non-lengthening suffixes.

ficial similarities, at least, seem to exist with the Kashaya problem, and it may be that the existing analysis of Axininca Campa could be refined in a similar fashion.

7.3 *Non-crisp alignment*

Coda conditions have been briefly mentioned already, the focus there being on their logical relationship with NoCoda. Itô & Mester (1994) propose an alignment formulation of coda conditions like that which we have mentioned in relation to Lardil (also found in e.g. Japanese and Finnish; see Yip 1991; Blevins 1995: 227ff. for discussion of some phonological considerations).

(85) shows a typical coda condition, restating P&S's coda condition (altered to exclude the possibility of coronal place) alongside two (potentially) equivalent formulations due to Itô & Mester (1994); the equivalence of the first two versions is not problematical but, at least on a naïve view of alignment, (c) seems to be saying simply that all consonants are syllable-initial. In order for this to amount to a coda condition, rather than a mere ban on codas and syllabic consonants, the interpretation of alignment needs refinement.

(85) CodaCond
    a. *Feature geometric version (P&S 1993: 99 modified)*
       A coda consonant can have no place specification of its own at all.
    b. *Linking version (Itô and Mester 1994: 27)*
       Codas are disallowed unless linked to a following onset
    c. *Alignment formulation (Itô and Mester 1994: 31)*
       AlignL(Consonant, σ)

In Japanese, a coda can only occur when:

(86) a. the coda consists of the moraic nasal; or
    b. the coda consists of a nasal homorganic with the onset of the following syllable; or
    c. the coda is the first half of a geminate consonant (usually voiceless—Vance 1987: 42).

This situation is close but not identical to that above. Itô and Mester's analysis (in which a notion of feature geometry is implicit; see e.g. Clements and Hume 1995) is as follows: the moraic nasal is placeless (or has coronal place); the homorganic nasals are underlyingly placeless, taking their place from the succeeding onset; the geminates share a root node. With this interpretation, Japanese satisfies the feature geometric statement of the coda condition (with a rider permitting coronal nasals).

The following diagrams (based on Itô and Mester 1994: 34) illustrate this.

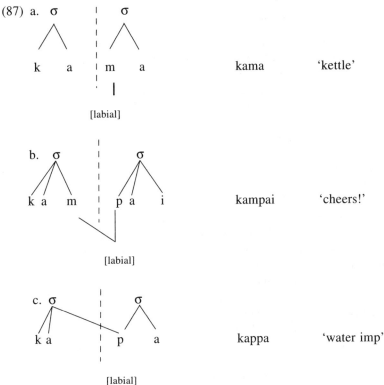

(87) a.   σ   σ   kama   'kettle'

k   a   m   a

[labial]

b.   σ   σ   kampai   'cheers!'

k a   m   p a   i

[labial]

c.   σ   σ   kappa   'water imp'

k a   p   a

[labial]

All the examples in (87) obey the feature geometric coda condition. In (a) it is met vacuously because there is no coda to consider; in (b) the coda consonant *m* shares the place of the following onset *p*; in (c) the coda consonant does not even have a root node of its own, let alone a place node: it shares those of the onset *p*.

Itô and Mester square these observations with their alignment formulation by extending the notion of alignment. Naïvely, neither of the coda consonants in *kampai* or *kappa* would be said to be left aligned with the beginning of a syllable. If, however, each consonant is identified with its place node, the difficulty goes away: the place nodes of the coda consonants fall at the start of the following syllable and so are indeed properly aligned.

To distinguish between these two interpretations, Itô and Mester term the modified situation where alignment is brought about by equating the consonant with its place node 'non-crisp alignment'. It is important to note that such alignment is not disrupted by having links to the place node straddle the syllable boundary.

7.4 *Beyond synchronic phonology*

So far the discussion has been essentially synchronically orientated. However, it is natural to want to go beyond asking what grammars are possible in OT, and consider the more dynamic question of how diachronic language change, dialectal variation, and the like are reflected within the theory.

A reasonable initial working hypothesis is that languages which evolve directly from one another typically involve similar constraint rankings: although ideally such developments might be supposed to involve something like re-ranking one pair of constraints at a time, the unfeasibility of taking snapshots at any given point in the evolutionary process renders this hard to establish. However, the effort is still probably worthwhile: rule-based phonology typically tells us *what* happens in a language, but OT arguably places greater emphasis on *why what happens happens* by supplying priorities and objectives for the grammar. If research can reveal patterns in how these develop, that may in turn shed additional light on the structure of UG.

Conversely, OT's success (or otherwise) in dealing with such issues may be seen as a testing-ground for the theory as a whole: at the least, it will establish how happily OT, a fundamentally static theory, can cope in an evolutionary context which is, by its very nature, dynamic. In many situations seen so far, the apparent serial nature of phonological processes has been made to seem illusory—language change presents a real challenge for such argumentation.

Cho (1995) gives a diachronic account of an alternation between n-ø in Korean. The essential facts are that some 200 years ago *n* began to delete in word-initial position before either *i* or *y*, and *ni* is nowadays completely neutralized in word-initial position (apart from a few recent loanwords); word-medially, however, /n/ surfaces even in some cases where it was not present historically. We thus have cases of both insertion and deletion of nasals.

Cho proposes that the following four constraints deal with both these alternations and, through reranking, their historical development.

(88) a. J(s)   (= *Son][i)
        'Sonorant Juncture': no sonorant consonant followed by a high front vocoid
        (*i/y*) across a prosodic word boundary
    b. J   (= *C][i)
        'Juncture': no consonant followed by *i/y* across a prosodic word boundary
    c. *[ni
        No /ni/ or /ny/ at the start of a prosodic word
    d. *Obs Son
        'Sonorant Agreement': No obstruent + sonorant sequences

She presents a historical picture of how the ranking of these constraints has developed over time (Sonorant Agreement, being undominated at all stages, is omitted from this profile).

(89) Stage   Ranking
   (i)   Pre-17c.   Faithfulness >> J(s), *[ni >> J
   (ii)   18c.   Faithfulness, J(s), *[ni >> J
   (iii) 19/early 20c.   J(s), *[ni >> Faithfulness >> J
   (iv) Current Standard   J(s), *[ni >> Faithfulness, J
   (iv') Current Variant   J(s), *[ni >> J >> Faithfulness

Let us examine how a selection of particular forms have evolved over the years in accordance with this re-ranking pattern (blank boxes indicate no change, doubly occupied boxes that alternative forms exist at a given stage of the language).

(90) Stage	/nip/ 'leaf'	/il/ 'work'	/man + nip/ '10,000'	/cipan + il/ 'house work'	/sek + yuli/ 'colored glass'
(i)	nip	il	man + nip	cipan + il	sek + yuli
(ii)	nip ip			cipan + il cipan + nil	
(iii)	ip			cipan + nil	
(iv)					sek + yuli seŋ + nyuli
(iv')					seŋ + nyuli

One point borne out by the Korean diachronic data is that, where change occurs, it is a two-stage process: the thin edge of the wedge is admission of an alternative (ip, cipan + nil, seŋ + nyuli), which takes over at the next stage of evolution. This supports Cho's stance on change in constraint ranking: first the neutralization of an existing ranking, e.g.

(91) *Faithfulness >> *[ni >> J*
     ↓
  *Faithfulness, *[ni >> J*

followed by the instatement of a new order:

(92) *Faithfulness, *[ni >> J*
     ↓
  [ni >> Faithfulness >> J

It is implicit in Cho's analysis that a common underlying form exists throughout the historical evolution of a given word, but alternative views are possible: Hutton (1996) advances a *Synchronic Base Hypothesis* that all input candidates produced by Gen are based on the current output form, earlier forms of the language no longer being available as underlying representations for Gen to operate upon. Hutton argues that speakers of Modern English might otherwise use the Proto-Germanic *stainaz*, the Old English *stān*, or the Middle English *stoon* as underlying form for 'stone'. While the thrust of this view seems reasonable, clarification of the exact mechanics of Gen and the nature of underlying forms may be needed before this hypothesis can be fully assessed.

Plainly there is likely to be a practical difference between the variations involved in Cho's Korean analysis (which appear relatively minor) and those of Hutton's example (which are comparatively substantial). An alternative proposal, which might cover both Cho's approach and Hutton's objections, would be for Gen to produce candidates based on historical as well as current forms, but to expect faithfulness to such earlier forms to become progressively lower-ranked as the sources go further back in time; we have, of course, already seen numerous situations involving simultaneous faithfulness to multiple inputs. Reynolds and Sheffer (1994) discuss similar issues in the context of dialectal variation.

The final strand concerns first language acquisition. Gnanadesikan (1995) expresses the view that a child's phonology initially has constraints against phonological markedness outranking faithfulness, with the result that outputs are unmarked: she further contends that constraints in child phonology are essentially the same as in an adult grammar, as are the lexical inputs. On these issues, the views of Smolensky (1996) are broadly supportive. Hale and Reiss (1997) advance a contrary view: for them, faithfulness initially outranks constraints against marked structure. Essentially, they call into question both Gnanadesikan's assumptions that the child's input forms and constraints are the same as those of the adult phonology.

These OT approaches to language change and acquisition all depend on assumptions regarding underlying forms and constraint ranking. In Sherrard (1995) the device of *adjacency* was introduced to characterize pairs of grammars whose constraint rankings differ minimally; this notion also extends to the output forms optimal under adjacent grammars. The topics discussed in this subsection all involve a similar duality between constraint rankings and candidate forms optimal under those rankings, and may prove amenable to an analysis based on adjacency: today's second best may be tomorrow's optimal output, or even a neighbour's preferred form today. Similar ideas arise in Chapter 5 of this volume, and in Pulleyblank et al. (forthcoming)

Whilst OT analyses have been advanced for all the issues raised here, there may yet be some cause for concern. The diverse approaches we have seen in relation to these topics go directly to the heart of OT. Consider some of the questions that have arisen here.

- What is in the lexicon?
- How constant are input forms?
- How are we to deal with multiple outputs?
- What is the significance, if any, of 'almost optimal' forms?

- Must all conflicting constraints be ranked?
- . . . and what happens if they aren't?

Fundamental questions, every one: and although seen here in relation to situations involving changing grammars, each will need to be addressed satisfactorily if Optimality Theory is to achieve the status and credibility that its success with synchronic questions suggests it merits.

ACKNOWLEDGEMENTS

Thanks to Chris Golston, Heather Hughes, Russell Norton, Iggy Roca, and three anonymous reviewers for helpful comments and/or discussions. Thanks also to the Rutgers Optimality Archive (ROA—http: //ruccs.rutgers.edu/ roa.html) and its contributors for making available much otherwise unpublished material. All remaining errors, misinterpretations, and infelicities are my responsibility.

REFERENCES

Akinlabi, A. (1995). 'Featural affixation', in A. Akinlabi (ed.), *Theoretical Approaches to African Linguistics*. Trenton, NJ: Africa World Press.

Alderete, J. (1995). 'Faithfulness to Prosodic Heads'. MS, University of Massachusetts, Amherst. ROA-94.

——, Beckman, J., Benua, L., Gnanadesikan, A., McCarthy, J., and Urbanczyk, S. (1996). 'Reduplication and Segmental Unmarkedness'. MS, University of Massachusetts, Amherst. ROA-134.

Archangeli, D., and Pulleyblank, D. (1994). *Grounded Phonology*. Cambridge, Mass.: MIT Press.

Aspillera, P. (1993). *Basic Tagalog for Foreigners and Non-Tagalogs*. Rutland, Vt.: Tuttle.

Beckman, J. N., Dickey, L. W., and Urbanczyk, S. (eds.) (1995) (University of Massachusetts Occasional Papers in Linguistics 18) *Papers in Optimality Theory*. Amherst: Graduate Linguistic Student Association.

Benua, L. (1995). 'Identity effects in morphological truncation', in Beckman et al. (1995: 77–136). ROA-74.

Blevins, J. (1995). 'The syllable in phonological theory', in Goldsmith (1995: 206–44).

Buckley, E. (1994). *Theoretical Aspects of Kashaya Phonology and Morphology* (revision of 1992 thesis, University of California at Berkeley). Stanford: CSLI.

—— (1995a). 'Optimal iambs in Kashaya', to appear in *Rivista di Linguistica*.

—— (1995b). 'Alignment and Constraint Domains in Manam Stress'. MS, University of Pennsylvania. ROA-56.

—— (1996). 'Uniformity in Extended Paradigms'. MS, University of Pennsylvania.

Cho, Y. Y. (1995). 'Language change as reranking of constraints', paper given at the 12th International Conference on Historical Linguistics, University of Manchester.

Clements, G. N., and Hume, E. (1995). 'The internal organization of speech sounds', in Goldsmith (1995: 245–306).

Cohn, A., and McCarthy, J. (1994). 'Alignment and Parallelism in Indonesian Phonology'. MS, Cornell University and University of Massachusetts, Amherst. ROA-25.

Cole, J. (1995). 'The cycle in phonology', in Goldsmith (1995: 70–113).

Crowhurst, M., and Hewitt, M. (1994). 'Directional Footing, Degeneracy and Alignment'. MS, University of North Carolina, Chapel Hill, and Brandeis University. ROA-65.

Gafos, A. (1995). 'On the Proper Characterization of "Nonconcatenative" Languages'. MS, Johns Hopkins University, Baltimore. ROA-106.

Gnanadesikan, A. (1995). 'Markedness and Faithfulness Constraints in Child Phonology'. MS, University of Massachusetts, Amherst. ROA-67.

Goldsmith, J. (1993). 'Harmonic phonology,' in J. Goldsmith (ed.), *The Last Phonological Rule: Reflections on Constraints and Derivations*. Chicago: University of Chicago Press, 21–60.

—— (ed.) (1995). *The Handbook of Phonological Theory*. Oxford: Blackwell.

Golston, C. (1996). 'Direct Optimality Theory: representation as pure markedness', *Language* 72: 713–748.

Green, T. (1993). 'The Conspiracy of Completeness'. MS. MIT. ROA-8

Hale, M. and Reiss, C. (1997). 'Formal and empirical arguments concerning phonological acquisition'. MS, Concordia University, Montreal. ROA-104.

—— (1996). 'The Comprehension/Production Dilemma in Child Language: A Response to Smolensky'. MS, Concordia University, Montreal. ROA-132

Halle, M. and Clements, G. N. (1983). *Problem Book in Phonology*. Cambridge, Mass.: MIT Press.

—— and Idsardi, W. (1995). 'General properties of stress and metrical structure', in Goldsmith (1995: 403–43).

—— and Vergnaud, J.-R. (1987). *An Essay on Stress*. Cambridge, Mass.: MIT Press.

Hammond, M. (1991). 'Morphemic circumscription', in G. Booij and J. van Marle (eds.), *Yearbook of Morphology 1990*. Dordrecht: Kluwer, 195–210.

—— (1995). 'There Is No Lexicon!' MS, University of Arizona. ROA-43.

Hayes, B. (1995). *Metrical Stress Theory: Principles and Case Studies*. Chicago: University of Chicago Press.

Hewitt, M. (1994). 'Deconstructing Foot Binarity in Koniag Alutiiq'. MS, University of British Columbia.

Hutton, J. (1996). 'Optimality Theory and historical language change', paper presented at the 4th Phonology Workshop, University of Manchester.

Inkelas, S. (1989). 'Prosodic Constituency in the Lexicon'. Thesis, Stanford University (New York: Garland 1990).

Itô, J. (1986). 'Syllable Theory in Prosodic Phonology'. Thesis, University of Massachusetts, Amherst.

—— and Mester, A. (1994). 'Reflections on CodaCond and Alignment', in Merchant et al. (1994: 27–46).

—— (1996) *Rendaku I: Constraint Conjunction and the OCP*. Handout of talk given at the Kobe Phonology Forum. ROA-144.

Kager, R. (1995). Review article: Hayes (1995). *Phonology* **12**: 437–64.

Kenstowicz, M. (1994). 'Syllabification in Chukchee: a constraints based analysis', in A. Davison, N. Maier, G. Silva, and S. Y. Wan (eds.), *Proceedings of the Formal Linguistics Society of Mid-America* iv. University of Iowa. ROA-30.

—— (1995). 'Base-identity and uniform exponence: alternatives to cyclicity', in J. Durand and B. Laks (eds.), *Current Trends in Phonology: Models and Methods*. Paris: CNRS and Salford: Salford University Press, 1996, pp. 363–93. ROA-103.

Kiparsky, P. (1973). ' "Elsewhere" in phonology', in S. Anderson and P. Kiparsky (eds.), *A Festschrift for Morris Halle*. New York: Holt Rinehart & Winston, 93–106.

—— (1993). 'Blocking in Nonderived Environments', in S. Hargus & E. Kaisse, eds., *Studies in Lexical Phonology*. San Diego: Academic Press.

—— (1994). 'Remarks on markedness,' handout of talk given at Trilateral Phonology Weekend 2.

Kirchner, R. (1993). 'Turkish vowel harmony and disharmony: an Optimality Theoretic account', paper presented at Rutgers Optimality Workshop 1. ROA-4.

Lombardi, L. (1995). 'Why Place and Voice Are Different: Constraint Interactions and Featural Faithfulness in Optimality Theory'. MS, University of Maryland, College Park. ROA-105.

McCarthy, J. (1994). 'The phonetics and phonology of Semitic pharyngeals', in P. Keating (ed.), *Papers in Laboratory Phonology, III*. Cambridge: Cambridge University Press.

—— and Prince, A. (1986). 'Prosodic Morphology'. MS, University of Massachusetts, Amherst, and Brandeis University.

—— —— (1993*a*). *Prosodic Morphology I: Constraint Interaction and Satisfaction*. Technical Report 3, Rutgers University Center for Cognitive Science. To appear, MIT Press.

—— —— (1993*b*). 'Generalized alignment', in G. Booij and J. van Marle (eds.), *Yearbook of Morphology 1993*. Dordrecht: Kluwer, 79–153. ROA-7.

—— —— (1994*a*). 'The emergence of the unmarked: optimality in prosodic morphology', in M. Gonzàlez (ed.), *Proceedings of the North-East Linguistics Society* 24. Amherst, Mass.: Graduate Linguistic Student Association, 333–79. ROA-13.

—— —— (1994*b*). 'Two lectures on prosodic morphology', talks presented at the OTS/HIL Workshop on Prosodic Morphology, University of Utrecht. ROA-59.

—— —— (1995*a*). 'Faithfulness and reduplicative identity', in Beckman et al. (1995: 249–384). ROA-60.

—— —— (1995*b*). 'Prosodic morphology', in Goldsmith (1995: 318–66).

Merchant, J. Padgett, J., and Walker, R. (eds.) (1994). *Phonology at Santa Cruz*, iii. University of California at Santa Cruz, Linguistics Research Center.

Mester, A., and Padgett, J. (1994). 'Directional syllabification in generalized alignment' in Merchant et al. (1994: 79–87). ROA-1.

Paradis, C. (1988). 'On constraints and repair strategies', *Linguistic Review* **6**: 71–97.

—— and Prunet, J.-F. (eds.) (1991) *The Special Status of Coronals: Internal and External Evidence*. San Diego, Calif.: Academic Press.

Pater, J. (1995). 'Austronesian Nasal Substitution and other NÇ effects'. (revised 1996).

MS, McGill University. To appear in R. Kager, H. van der Hulst, and W. Zonneveld (eds.), *The Prosody Morphology Interface*. ROA-160.

Peperkamp, S. (forthcoming). 'The prosodic structure of compounds', in *Proceedings of the International Conference on Interfaces in Linguistics*, Oporto, Nov. 1995.

Prince, A. (1980). 'A metrical theory for Estonian quantity', *Linguistic Inquiry* **11**: 511–62.

—— and Smolensky, P. (1993). *Optimality Theory: Constraint Interaction in Generative Grammar*. Technical Report 2, Rutgers University Center for Cognitive Science. To appear, MIT Press.

Pulleyblank, D., Ping J.-K., Leitch, M., and Ola, N. (forthcoming), 'Typological variation through constraint rankings: low vowels in tongue root harmony', in *Proceedings of the Arizona Phonology Conference, Workshop on Features in Optimality Theory*, University of Arizona.

Reynolds, B. and Sheffer, H. (1994). 'Variation and optimality', *Penn Working Papers in Linguistcs* **1**: 103–10.

Roca, I. (1994). *Generative Phonology*. London: Routledge.

Russell, K. (1995). 'Morphemes and Candidates in Optimality Theory'. MS, University of Manitoba. ROA-44.

Selkirk, E. (1984). *Phonology and Syntax: The Relation between Sound and Structure*. Cambridge, Mass.: MIT Press.

—— (1995). 'The prosodic structure of function words', in J. Morgan and K. Demuth (eds.), *Signal to Syntax: Bootstrapping from Speech to Grammar in Early Acquisition*. Hillsdale, NJ: Lawrence Erlbaum 187–213.

—— (1996). 'Phonological and interface constraints on prosodic phrasing', handout of talk given at the Utrecht Workshop on Phrasal Phonology.

Sherrard, N. (1995). 'Adjacency and Freedom of Ordering in Optimality Theory'. Dissertation, University of Essex.

Smolensky, P. (1986). 'Information processing in dynamical systems: foundations of harmony theory', in D. E. Rumelhart, J. L. McClelland, and the PDP Research Group, *Parallel Distributed Processing: Explorations in the Microstructure of Cognition*, i: *Foundations*. Cambridge, Mass: MIT Press/Bradford Books, 194–281

—— (1993). 'Harmony, markedness, and phonological activity', handout from talk given at Rutgers Optimality Workshop 1 (revised 1995). ROA-87.

—— (1995). 'On the internal structure of the constraint component Con of UG', handout from talk given at UCLA. ROA-86.

—— (1996). 'On the Comprehension/Production Dilemma in Child Language'. MS, Johns Hopkins University, Baltimore. ROA-118.

Spencer, A. (1994). 'Syllabification in Chukchee: Optimality Theory vs. Lexical Phonology', in R. Wiese (ed.), *Recent Developments in Lexical Phonology*. Düsseldorf: Heinrich Heine Universität, 205–26

Steriade, D. (1995). 'Underspecification and markedness', in Goldsmith (1995: 114–74).

Tesar, B., and Smolensky, P. (1993). 'The Learnability of Optimality Theory: An Algorithm and Some Basic Complexity Results'. MS, University of Colorado at Boulder. ROA-2.

Truckenbrodt, H. (1995). 'Phonological Phrases: Their Relation to Syntax, Focus and Prominence'. Thesis, MIT

Urbanczyk, S. (1994). 'Double reduplications in parallel', in Beckman et al. (1995: 499–532).

Vance, T. (1987). *An Introduction to Japanese Phonology*. Albany: SUNY Press.

Vennemann, T. (1988). *Preference Laws for Syllable Structure and the Explanation of Sound Change*. Berlin: Mouton de Gruyter.

Yip, M. (1991) 'Coronals, consonant clusters and the coda condition', in Paradis and Prunet (1991: 61–78).

PART II
THEORETICAL INVESTIGATIONS

✦

3

The Contents of Phonological Signs: A Comparison Between Their Use in Derivational Theories and in Optimality Theories

SYLVAIN BROMBERGER and MORRIS HALLE

1. INTRODUCTION

In all the exchanges that we are aware of between proponents of Rule-based Derivational phonology (DT, from here on) and proponents of Optimality phonology (OT from here on), the participants seem to take for granted that the phonological symbols on which both sides rely mean the same thing in both kinds of theories. In other words, they seem to take for granted that switching between OT and DT analyses has no effect on the semantic values that attach to such symbols as 'æ', 'œ', '[+ voice]', '[labial]', and so on: that these and other phonemic and feature symbols carry the same information, have the same semantic content, regardless of whether they occur in the context of a derivation or in the context of a tableau. In this chapter we want to question this presumption of semantic invariance between OT and DT. We will, in fact, argue that many—perhaps all—such symbols mean different things in the two kinds of contexts.

Questioning the presumption of semantic invariance between DT and OT is not an innocuous move. It has deep consequences for how we should go about gauging the relative merits of contributions to the two approaches. To see why, we need but imagine a world much like this one, but in which proponents of DT and proponents of OT use symbols that not only have different meanings but also look different. In such a world we wouldn't begin to compare their contributions without first finding out whether their respective predicates were designed to cover the same sorts of entity and, if so, whether on the basis of similar or different aspects. We would need that knowledge to determine whether the two approaches are in conflict, and if so on what points, or whether they are compatible—and if so whether because they supplement each other, or because their assumptions are mutually irrelevant. In other words, in such a world, we would have to become explicit about how the meanings of their

symbols are related before embarking on a critical comparison or even deciding on appropriate grounds for comparison: truth, plausibility, simplicity,
generality, convenience, explanatory depth, all of these, some of these? But
questioning the presumption of semantic invariance is tantamount to looking at
the real world as differing from that imaginary one in only a superficial
respect, namely in that the proponents of the two approaches happen—perhaps
for historical reasons—to use symbols of the same shape. They might as well
have used symbols of different shapes. In fact that might have been less
misleading. And so, in this the real world as in our imaginary one, we have
to determine how the meanings that attach to their symbols are related before
engaging in critical comparison or even deciding on what grounds they should
be compared. Of course, even if the symbols have different meanings in the
two approaches, it does not follow that these meanings must be totally unrelated or that the two approaches cannot stand in any kind of conflict. In the last
part of the chapter we will, in fact, bring out points of contact between these
semantic values and give a reason why a DT approach might be preferred to an
OT one. It does follow that any critical comparisons should take into consideration the difference between the semantic values that each assigns to the
same signs as well as the range of phenomena they appear to be covering at
any particular time.

This chapter differs thus from others in this collection in that it focuses on
the symbols used in the analysis of linguistic facts rather than on specific
analyses. Phonological theories, as usually presented are—from a philosophical perspective at least—frustratingly unspecific about the semantics of their
notation and hence about what exactly they describe. That is—up to a point—a
good thing: issues about the meanings and references of the terms one uses can
be tedious, elusive, suspect, divisive, inhibiting, and empirically unproductive,
to say the least. And since one can achieve much in phonology, as in other
sciences, while ignoring such issues, they can also seem pointless. There is,
furthermore, the danger of addressing them prematurely, while the discipline
and its connection to neighboring ones is still in too much flux. But ignoring
such issues also has a downside: it leaves the *truth conditions* of phonological
claims unspecified, that is, what the world must contain and be like if these
claims are true, and what it might not contain or not be like, if they are false.
That is a loss. At best it leaves us with only a partial understanding of these
claims, at worst it invites confusion about their relationship to each other and
to the evidence that allegedly supports them. Thus to see clearly what, if
anything, about our understanding of reality is at stake in a debate such as
the debate between the proponents of DT and OT, we need to know as
explicitly as we can how their symbols relate to that reality, and not just
how their adherents analyse representations whose links with it are left in
the dark. And what could be of more interest in such a debate than its bearing
on our understanding of what is real? So this chapter should be read—like

other papers on which the two of us have collaborated—with foundational rather than empirical questions in mind. The two families of questions must obviously be brought together eventually. But much preliminary work needs to be done first. This chapter belongs to the too often neglected foundational side.

In what follows we first present certain assumptions which need to be made explicit and justified; we next examine consequences of these assumptions for the semantics of DT; we then examine corresponding consequences for OT and bring out that the semantic values of similar phonological symbols are not the same in both contexts. We end with a discussion of how the two approaches might nevertheless be critically compared. Throughout the discussion we rely on extremely simplified versions of DT and OT, on the ground that these already contain all the elements needed to make our point. We limit ourselves to phonemic and feature symbols for the same reason.

2. Assumptions

We begin by putting forth three assumptions on which our discussion depends. We think that these assumptions are unproblematic and, in principle at least, widely accepted. But since they are seldom openly stated, and are often disregarded in practice, they may be more controversial than we think.

I. Our *first assumption* is that phonological symbols, that is, phoneme symbols, feature symbols, prosodic segmentation brackets, stress diacritics, and so on, can be replaced without loss of meaning by *predicates*, can be thought of as abbreviations for, as convenient stand-ins for, predicates. We will limit our attention here to phonemic and feature symbols, but we think that this assumption can eventually cover other symbols as well.

The term 'predicate' is used with different connotations in different theoretical settings. We use the term as it is used in predicate logic. In predicate logic, expressions called predicates are characterized principally by two traits that matter to us. (*a*) Predicates do not denote individual objects or events, but are *true of* them. So, for instance, the predicate 'hot' does not denote anything but is true of each hot thing, and fails to be true of cold things. (*b*) Predicates are associated with *satisfaction conditions*, conditions that define what they are true of. So, for instance, the predicate 'hot' is associated with the condition or property of being hot and is true of all and only objects that satisfy that condition. In short, the predicate 'hot' is true of objects that are hot.

Predicates, as we use the term, are thus to be distinguished from so-called *individual constants*, that is, from names or singular terms like 'Hillary Rodham Clinton', or '5', from expressions that, unlike predicates, purport to denote, to name individual objects, rather than to be true of them. The difference becomes obvious when we think of what is involved in specifying the semantics of the two classes of expressions. Giving the semantics of an individual constant requires one to specify its reference, if any, whereas giving the semantics of a predicate requires one to specify its satisfaction conditions.

In canonical notation—when their syntax is made explicit—predicates combine with two other kinds of expressions to form statements: individual constants and quantifiers. So if, in accordance with a well-known notational system, we let 'H' stand for the predicate 'hot' and 'a' stand for the name of some object a, then 'Ha' states that a is hot, and '$(\forall x)Hx$' states that everything is hot.

In what follows we will not use the notational system used in the example above, but will use *lambda notation* instead. Though this notation may seem rebarbative at first, it is actually quite easy to decode and will be much easier to relate to standard phonological symbols than other notations. So, instead of using 'hot' or 'H' as above, we use '$\lambda x[\text{hot } x]$' to write the predicate, and '$\lambda x[\text{hot } x](a)$' to state that a is hot, and '$(\forall y)\{\lambda x[\text{hot } x](y)\}$' to state that everything is hot.[1]

As can be seen from this example, the lambda notation lets one incorporate familiar terms (e.g. 'hot') in more formal symbols. This turns out to be very helpful when we want to display the predicate nature of phonological terms. So instead of the equivocal symbol 'æ' in isolation—which underspecifies whether it stands for an individual constant or a predicate—we will use '$\lambda x[\text{æ } x]$'; and instead of '[+round]'—whose logical form is totally obscure—we will use '$\lambda x[+\text{round } x]$'.[2] Thus to say of something called 'α' (we postpone for the time being saying what α might be) that it is [+round], we will write '$\lambda x[+\text{round } x](\alpha)$', and to state that something is [+round] we will write '$(\exists y)\{\lambda x[+\text{round } x](y)\}$'.

The reasons for holding that phonological symbols are stand-ins for predicates in the above senses are straightforward. The alternative is to hold that they are singular terms, that is, names. But what could they be names of? Not of particular fragments of individual utterances produced at some specific time and specific place by some specific person. Even if one could make sense of that idea—for instance, of the idea that '[+round]' or even 'æ' is the name of a part of an utterance, which utterance among the zillion that have been produced or that will some day be produced would it be the name of? Nor can they plausibly be names of abstract objects, of objects located neither in space nor in time. That would not be compatible with the fact that phonology is an empirical science and thus dependent on causal interactions between observers and what is under investigation. Abstract objects cannot stand in any such

---

[1] Predicates in lambda notation combine with quantifiers and other logical operators in the same way as predicates in the standard predicate notation.

[2] In this system of notation, variables can be freely substituted for each other. Thus '$\lambda x[+\text{round } x]$' and '$\lambda y[+\text{round } y]$' are synonymous. It is also best, to avoid confusion, not to use the same variables after quantifiers and after lambdas.

relation to observers. They are, by definition, causally inert. Other objects may come to mind, but none of those that we are aware of seems to survive close scrutiny. Furthermore, the symbols we need must express something that distinct actual utterances can have in common, that can be aspects shared by distinct utterances. Unless one is willing to indulge in weird metaphysical ontologies, predicates seem best suited for that function.

Phonologists, obviously, do not display their symbols in ways that commit them to a predicate interpretation. Nor do they manipulate their symbols in ways that look like any of the known predicate calculi. But that by itself does not entail that the predicate interpretation is unwarranted. There are historical reasons for their reliance on a more neutral system of notation. And there is also a good rationale for this practice: using and manipulating predicate notation would greatly complicate their presentations and their computations. Using predicate notation—and paying the cost in complexity—is useful when we need to be forthcoming about the truth conditions of phonological claims, that is, when we need to be *explicit* about their semantic value. On most other occasions one need not be so finicky, and other notational devices are more effective.

II. Our *second assumption* may seem self-evident, but will turn out to have rather surprising consequences. It is that *within any theoretical approach to phonology*, be it DT or OT—or any other approach for that matter—any particular phonological symbol stands for the same predicate in *all* contexts. By 'same predicate' we mean predicate having the *same defining satisfaction conditions*. Phonological symbols such as 'æ' and '[+round]' occur standardly in the description of underlying representations, in the descriptions of surface representations, in the descriptions of items in the lexicon, in the statement of rules, in the formulation of constraints, and so on. Our second assumption is that the semantic content—the satisfaction conditions—of any given symbol (now thought of as predicates) must be the same in all these contexts *within any single theoretical approach*, and a fortiori within any given analysis adopting that approach. In other words, we assume that within DT and within OT phonological symbols are used unambiguously.[3]

On the other hand, we do *not* assume that similar phonological symbols stand for the same predicates *across theoretical approaches*, across DT analyses and OT analyses. That, obviously, is the very assumption that we intend to deny. And there is no a priori reason to assume that it is true, even if it may have gone unquestioned in the literature. The assumption about unambiguity that we are making, on the other hand, follows from the presumption that DT and OT analyses, whatever their shortcomings, are both at least semantically

---

[3] This assumption should actually be slightly modified for descriptions of items in the lexicon. But this modification would not crucially affect our present discussion, and will be ignored here. We will come back to it on some other occasion.

coherent. Derivational analyses are committed to semantic unambiguity, by the nature of rules, which are blind to the derivational history of their inputs and outputs and must apply whatever that history. The symbols in the statements of rules and the symbols in the formulation of the various levels of a derivation must thus be taken to have the same meaning. Optimality analyses are committed to semantic unambiguity if by nothing else, at least by the prominence they give to faithfulness constraints. Symbols in the statements of these constraints and in the formulations of the inputs and outputs of GEN must be taken to have the same meaning.

III. Our *third assumption, this-worldly realism,* is trickier to state succinctly without getting lost in labyrinthine philosophical questions and qualifications. Its basic tenet is, however, clear. We assume that the statements[4] of a plausible phonological theory—and we deem both OT and DT to be plausible—*purport to be true*, and furthermore purport to be about *things in this our actual spatio-temporal world.* This double assumption, note, in turn entails the further assumption that phonological predicates, insofar as they are ever true of anything, are true of datable, placeable things such as, for instance, individual actions, or events, or mind/brain phases, or specific people at specific times—in short, true of things in this the actual world.

One way of making clear the point of that assumption, and of bringing out, perhaps, its controversial nature, is by contrasting it with two alternatives which some may deem plausible.

One alternative—which is sometimes labelled *instrumentalism*—would flatly deny that all the statements of DT and OT purport to be true. It would hold instead that DT and OT provide essentially symbol-manipulating recipes that put *linguists* in a position to compute certain outputs from certain inputs in more or less economical ways but without purporting to contain information beyond that contained in these inputs and outputs.[5]

Instrumentalists would look, for instance, at a DT derivation as a computation performed by *a linguist* (qua theoretician, not qua speaker) who, by manipulating certain symbols in accordance with certain rules, was able to calculate in a more or less efficient way the description of a surface representation from the description of an underlying representation. Such instrumentalists would deny that anything could be claimed for the derivation itself beyond the fact that it enabled a practitioner to pair the right descriptions. They would deny that any truth claim need be warranted on behalf of intervening representations, or on behalf of their ordering, or on behalf of the rules, and so on. For such instrumentalists it would make sense to ask whether the description of the underlying representation in a derivation was true or warranted; it would

---

[4] Except perhaps certain conditionals. But those should be irrelevant for the rest of the discussion.

[5] There are some who would even hold that not even the inputs but only the outputs purport to be true.

also make sense to ask whether the description of the surface representation was true or warranted; but it would make no sense to ask whether the steps in the derivation represented anything real. And such instrumentalists would, in turn, look at a derivational *theory*—that is, at any specific version of DT—as simply a recipe, or set of recipes, for constructing derivations. They would deny that the statements of the theory had more than instrumental value, were either true or false. They would interpret the DT agenda as that of providing computational recipes. Instrumentalists expect efficiency of phonological theories, not truth or insight.

Similarly, such instrumentalists would look at an OT tableau as no more than a device that a linguist (again, qua theoretician, not qua speaker) might use to calculate the description of a surface representation from the description of an underlying representation; they would deny that any truth claim about the tableau would be warranted beyond the fact that it enables *linguists* to pair the right descriptions. And such instrumentalists would look at any specific version of OT as a recipe, or set of recipes, for constructing tableaux with no more than instrumental value, and they would interpret the OT agenda as that of providing such recipes.

Instrumentalism has many attractions. Like many related forms of empiricism, it has the attraction of seeming to minimize what one needs to claim on behalf of a theory to deem it acceptable. That is the point of exempting statements of a theory from the demand that they be true. An instrumentalist is someone who asks only that a theory 'work', never mind whether it is true, false, probable, or meets other controversial demands.

Although we think that instrumentalism is ultimately incoherent and untenable, we cannot make the case here on the basis of the rough sketch we have just given. Suffice it then to say that instrumentalism would turn phonology into something that we—and many others—would find of little interest. The fact that many proponents both of DT and of OT aspire to rules or constraints that have psychological reality—that represent something real and not just computationally useful—indicates that our attitude is widely shared.

A second alternative to this-worldly realism is the view that phonology is not about things in the actual spatio-temporal world, but is about abstract, non-spatio-temporal objects, a version of a more general view often called *Platonism*, according to which there are abstract particulars, abstract individuals. One version of phonological Platonism would hold that the symbols of phonology are names of abstract objects, the sort of things often called *types*.[6] We have

---

[6] In contrast to *tokens*. Tokens are actual utterances produced at specific times at specific places by specific speakers. They are datable and placeable. Types, if there are types, are not. Tokens are said to *realize* or *instantiate* types by those who hold that there are types, though they also allow for types that are not instantiated by any tokens. It is important, in this connection, not to confuse the notion of an *occurrence* of a type within another type and the notion of a token *instantiating* a type. Suppose that there are such things as types, then the sentence type (1), *Joe's cat hates Mary's*

already mentioned and dismissed that version when arguing that phonological symbols are stand-ins for predicates and not for names. But another form of Platonism might hold that these symbols, though stand-ins for predicates, stand in for predicates that are *true of* abstract types, not of concrete particulars. So, for instance, Platonists of the sort we have in mind would hold that '[+round]' can indeed be rendered as '$\lambda x[+\text{round } x]$' without semantic loss, but would hold further that the sort of things of which '$\lambda x[+\text{round } x]$' is true are abstract types, not particular utterances produced at a specific time, at a specific place, by a specific speaker, or some other spatio-temporal thing, but by which they would mean some non-spatio-temporal things residing perhaps where infinite widthless Euclidean lines and pure numbers reside. We do not wish to deny here that there are abstract objects. There may well be such things. Maybe some branches of mathematics and of metaphysics study some of them. We just don't think that phonology can be about any of them. As we mentioned before, that would be incompatible with the fact that phonology is an empirical science.

Admittedly, phonologists seldom mention specific concrete entities. But, as we shall see, that does not entail that their theory must countenance abstract types.

3. Derivational Theory

We now turn to some of the consequences of these assumptions for Derivational Theory. As we mentioned earlier, we will limit ourselves to a very simplified version of DT that already contains the elements we need for our discussion. Our focus will be on the consequences of our assumptions for the meaning, the semantic content, of the phonological symbols in the context of that simplified version of DT. These consequences should carry over to more sophisticated versions. Since we assume that these symbols are stand-ins for predicates, our focus will be on the *satisfaction conditions* of these predicates. What are these satisfaction conditions like? Our worldly realism requires that

cat, contains two occurrences of the type (2), *Cat*, but contains no tokens of (2), no instantiations of the type (2), since such instantiations must be in space and time but types cannot be. On the other hand, if you now produce a token of (i.e. an instantiation of) (1), then that token will contain two tokens (two instantiations of) (2), but no occurrences of it.

The type/token distinction was first named by C. S. Peirce (1958:iv., 423): 'there is but one word "the" in the English language; and it is impossible that this word should lie visibly on a page or be heard in any voice, for the reason that it is not a Single thing or Single event. It does not exist; it only determines things that do exist. Such a definitely significant Form, I propose to term a *Type*. A single event which happens once and whose identity is limited to that one happening or a Single object or thing which is in some single place at any one instant of time, such event or thing being significant only as occurring just when and where it does, such as this or that word on a single line of a single page of a single copy of a book, I will venture to call *Token*.'

For further discussions, see Bromberger (1989), Bromberger and Halle (1992), Hutton (1990), Katz (1990), Peirce (1958), and references therein.

they be met by spatio-temporal things. Since actual utterances produced by actual people at actual places and actual times are crucially pertinent aspects of that reality, let us look at them first. And, to fix ideas, let us concentrate on one such utterance, one produced by SB in Colchester on 1 September 1995 around 3 p.m. local time, which we transcribe here in standard English orthography:

(1) Canadians live in houses.

Because this chapter is being written in 1996, that utterance is now history, is now gone and beyond our perception. But DT can nevertheless still associate a derivation with it. In rough outlines, that derivation would look like (2):

(2) {[kænæd-i-æn], Noun . . . } + {[z], Pl . . . }+{[liv], Verb . . . } + {[in] Prep
    . . . } + {[hɪːs] Noun . . . } + {[z] Pl . . . }
    . . . .
    . . . .
    kənéydiyənzlɪvɪnháwzəz

A fuller exposition would, of course, contain more steps and additional details, and might contain references to rules, and so on. We set all that aside for a longer discussion at another time, and as not essential to our current topic.

Let us first turn to the phonological symbols in the *last* line, which is presumably closest to the noises and articulatory gestures that SB actually produced that day in Colchester, and let us begin with the first of these symbols, 'k'. Most phonologists view 'k' itself as an abbreviation rendered roughly as

(3) k = $_{df}$ dorsal [−continuant, −voiced, −nasal]

Putting (3) in lambda notation—to make explicit that 'k' is a predicate—yields

(4) $\lambda x[kx]$ = $_{df}$ $\lambda x[$dorsal x & −continuant x & −voiced x & −nasal x]

where (4), setting some technicalities aside, will be represented somewhat loosely as the conjunction of predicate (5), which has the virtue of bringing out that the feature symbols in isolation are also stand-ins for predicates

(5) $\lambda x[kx]$ = $_{df}$ $\lambda x[$dorsal x] & $\lambda x[$−continuant x] & $\lambda x[$−voiced x] & $\lambda x[$−nasal x]

In other words, if we call A the thing at Colchester to which k applies, then the following statement is true:

(6) $\lambda x[$dorsal x](A) & $\lambda x[$−continuant x](A) & $\lambda x[$−voiced x](A) & $\lambda x[$−nasal x](A)

Two questions now arise. What sort of thing does 'A' refer to in (6)? And how did A meet the satisfaction conditions of the predicate defined by (5) so as to make (6) true?

The first of these questions we will answer very simply for present purposes: 'A' refers to SB at the time of the utterance of the first segment. In other words, think of SB as a sequence of stages that make up his lifeline as an organism, and think of one of these stages as the stage he was in when he produced that initial segment in Colchester. For present purposes, these stages should be thought of as forming mereological combinations, that is, as combining with each other as parts to form larger wholes that can in turn combine with other parts or other wholes to form still more encompassing wholes. This is no doubt crude, but it will have to do for the present. Any refinement would take us far afield—and require that we greatly complicate our notation—without affecting our main point, which concerns the semantic value of the predicates. And in any case, we will eventually have to drop references to that specific event in Colchester, and generalize. So 'A' in (6) designates SB-at-a-stage-during-the-time-of-the-utterance. In what follows, instead of 'A' we will use the mnemonically more helpful 'SB', and we will use it as short for 'SB-at-a-stage-during-the-time-of-the-utterance', counting on context to foil any confusion and, in particular, any confusion due to the fact that different occurrences of 'SB' will have to refer to different stages of SB. Sometimes we will have to distinguish explicitly among different stages of SB. We will do so by using subscripts.

The second question is open to two answers.

When SB produced the first segment of that utterance, he performed a certain articulatory gymnastic: he closed his oral cavity completely with the dorsum of his tongue, he put his vocal cords in a configuration that prevented them from vibrating, he raised his velum. But that gymnastic was preceded by an 'intentional' mind/brain condition,[7] by a mental set, an impulse (it is unlikely that an exact word is available) to move these articulators through these gymnastics, a state that presupposed knowledge of English, that was expressed in the gymnastic of the articulators—was executed so to say—but needn't have been.

According to the first answer (6), or equivalently, (7),

(7) $\lambda x[kx](SB)$

is true because SB actually performed the gymnastics, and the conjuncts in (6) are predicates that describe various linguistically relevant features of the gymnastic. Thus, according to that first answer, the predicate defined by (5) was satisfied because SB performed the gymnastic, and would not have been satisfied if SB had not performed that gymnastic.

According to the second answer, (6) (and *ipso facto* (7)) is true because SB

---

[7] That such intentional conditions must occur was pointed out long ago by Lenneberg (1967), in his work on the synchronies of speech production. The neural paths to the various articulators being of different lengths, instructions to move them must leave the brain at different times, thus requiring that the effect be 'intended' before being accomplished.

was in the intentional mind/brain state that preceded the gymnastics, and the conjuncts in (6) describe relevant features of that state by alluding to how it would be executed, if and when executed. Thus, according to the second answer, the predicate defined by (5) was satisfied, *not* because SB performed the gymnastic, but because SB had the "intention" to perform the gymnastic.[8] The fact that he performed the gymnastic is good evidence that he had the intention, but the predicate would have been satisfied even if he had stopped short of performing the gymnastic.

The second answer is clearly more in accordance with the practice of phonology than the first. The predicates of phonology should be satisfiable even on some occasions when no gestures are produced, as in subvocal speech, mullings, silent writing, silent reading, and so on. And they should be satisfied sometimes even when the gestures that a speaker produces are not the ones that the predicate describes according to the first answer, as when that speaker makes adjustments for impediments in the mouth or noise in the environment. Thus (6) and (7) should be readable as true regardless of whether SB produced his utterance 'normally' or subvocally or read it silently, or even produced it in a slightly distorted way. Finally, as we shall see in a moment, this answer, after some modification, turns out to be compatible with our assumption that phonological symbols must be unambiguous, must have the same meaning wherever they occur in a derivation, whereas the first answer is not. So we adopt that second answer.

A similar answer is clearly forthcoming for each of the other symbols in the last line of (2). So, for instance 'ə' stands in for a predicate defined *grosso modo* as

(8) $\lambda x[\text{ə}x] = _{df} \lambda x[-\text{round } x \ \& \ -\text{high } x \ \& \ -\text{low } x + \text{back } x \ \& \ -\text{ATR } x]$

and represented for present purposes somewhat loosely as

(9) $\lambda x[\text{ə}x] = _{df} \lambda x[-\text{round } x] \ \& \ \lambda x[-\text{high } x] \ \& \ \lambda x[-\text{low } x] \ \& \ \lambda x[+\text{back } x] \ \& \ \lambda x[-\text{ATR } x]$

and

(10) $\lambda x[\text{ə}x](\text{SB})$

that is,

(11) $\lambda x[-\text{round } x](\text{SB}) \ \& \ \lambda x[-\text{high } x](\text{SB}) \ \& \ \lambda x[-\text{low } x](\text{SB}) \ \& \ \lambda x[+\text{back } x](\text{SB}) \ \& \ \lambda x[-\text{ATR } x](\text{SB})$

---

[8] In what follows we will continue to use the word 'intention', but the reader should understand that we use the term in a somewhat technical sense, without all the usual connotations. 'Impulse' might be less misleading, but not much. We assume that as the discipline progresses it will be possible to replace such infelicitous talk with talk that is about states which supervene on brain states.

is true because SB in Colchester had the articulatory intention predicated by the conjuncts in (11). And similarly, for the other symbols in that last line. So far, then, so good.

But let us now turn to the phonological symbols in the *first* line. They require that we modify these definitions. The modification will seem minor, but everything that follows hinges on it.

The first of these phonological symbols, 'k', could plausibly stand for the predicate with the satisfaction conditions assigned so far in the last line, that is, those specified in (5) and (4). On such a reading, SB met the defining satisfaction conditions of that predicate in Colchester twice: once by having the right articulatory 'intentions' (by meeting the satisfaction conditions of each of the predicates in the right-hand conjunction of (5)) *immediately* before performing the actual uttering; and once *at an earlier stage*, as part of his intention to use certain morphemes retrieved from memory in an order fixed by his syntax and his semantics. We know that he had those 'intentions' at some stage, since he carried them out eventually, so why not impute them to him from the start, so to say? But the same cannot be said about the first 'æ', or about the second one, or about the third one (nor about the 's' in the middle). The 'æ' defined on the model of (5) would be

(12) $\lambda x[\text{æ } x] =_{df} \lambda x[-\text{back } x] \ \& \ \lambda x[-\text{high } x] \ \& \ \lambda x[+\text{low } x] \ \& \ \lambda x[-\text{round } x]$

and thus for

(13) $\lambda x[\text{æ } x](\text{SB})$

to be true, there would have had to be a stage of SB at which he intended to front the dorsum of his tongue, to lower it, to unround his lips, and so on. But there is no reason at all to believe that there ever was such an SB stage in Colchester: he definitely did not execute the corresponding gymnastics there when he produced (1).

It is true that we characterized satisfaction conditions above so as to allow for unexecuted intentions in subvocal speech, and for modifications when required to overcome physical impediments. But what we are dealing with here is, from a linguistic perspective, importantly different. SB did not intend æ subvocally at all as when reading or mulling, and though he, in a sense, produced schwa sounds *instead* of æ sounds, he did not do so deliberately or because of some accidental impediment, but he did so automatically, in a way driven by the implicitly cognized rules of his acquired phonology.

So (12) won't do as a definition of the 'æ's that occur in the first line.

We now face a dilemma. 'k' appears in the last line and in the first line; 'æ' appears in the first line only. We have said that 'k' in the last line is a stand-in for a predicate pertaining to articulatory intentions—in other words, a predicate that was satisfied by an SB stage because, at that stage, SB had certain articulatory intentions. The same cannot be said about the 'æ's in the first line.

So we must either deny that 'k' in the *last* line and 'k' in the *first* line stand for the same predicate—have the same satisfaction conditions attached to them; or we must deny that 'k' and 'æ' in the *first* line stand for the same *sort* of predicates, since the predicate represented by 'æ' cannot pertain to articulatory intentions. Or we must revise our view that 'k' in the *last line* is a stand-in for a predicate pertaining to articulatory intentions.

The first option is ruled out by our second assumption: that within a given theory each phonological symbol has the same meaning wherever it occurs. The second option is not only counterintuitive, but it too is ruled out by that second assumption, since 'æ' can appear in the description of surface representations, that is, in last lines of derivations, as well as in first lines; a different example, such as 'Canada is beautiful', would have had an 'æ' in the last line as well as in the first line. That leaves us with the last option.

Fortunately, there is an obvious way of effecting that last option without drastically revising what we have said so far about the predicates in the last line. It is to hold that at *all* the stages at which SB undertook to produce the utterance in Colchester, he had the intention to perform certain gymnastics *unless* some rule or rules precluded them. (This sentence must be read carefully, giving 'intention' scope over 'unless'). On this revised view of things, 'k' is a stand-in not for the predicate defined by (5) but for the predicate defined by (14):

(14) $\lambda x[\underline{k}x] = {}_{df} \lambda x[\text{upsr dorsal } x]$ & $\lambda x[\text{upsr } -\text{continuant } x]$ & $\lambda x[\text{upsr } -\text{voiced } x]$ & $\lambda x[\text{upsr } -\text{nasal } x]$

in which 'upsr' abbreviates the clause 'unless precluded by some rule'. (Note that it occurs as part of, as inside, the predicate.) And similarly (12) is replaced by (15)

(15) $\lambda x[\underline{æ} x] = {}_{df} \lambda x[\text{upsr } -\text{back } x]$ & $\lambda x[\text{upsr } -\text{high } x]$ & $\lambda x[\text{upsr } +\text{low } x]$ & $\lambda x[\text{upsr } - \text{round } x]$

From here on, we will underline defined phonological symbols wherever their expanded definitions contain 'upsr' clauses, as we did in the case of (14) and (15).

So, on this new reading, the 'k' in the first line of (2) records that at an initial stage SB intended[9] to perform-certain-gymnastics-unless-some-rule-or-rules-precluded-this, and the 'k' in the last line records that at a final stage SB had a similar intention. The 'upsr' clauses in the more explicit versions of these occurrences happen to carry no consequences—are, so to say, barren. On the other hand, the 'æ's in the first line record that at some initial stage SB intended to perform-certain-gymnastics-unless-some-rule-or-rules-precluded-this, but the 'upsr' in the more explicit versions of these occurrences do

---

[9] In our quasi-technical sense of 'intend'.

have consequences, since, according to the theory, rules did intervene, and this is reflected by the absence of 'æ's in the last line.

Though we have not spelled out the lines between the first and the last line, we can safely assume that phonological symbols would occur in them as well. Some of these symbols may be identical to some appearing in the first line or in the last line, some may not. The latter possibility is, in fact, crucial to DT. But whatever the case, these symbols will all be open to the same kind of inter-pretation as those in the first and last line, as being stand-ins for predicates with 'upsr' clauses in the feature predicates connoting articulatory intentions.

But our account still needs to be reconciled with three other facts about (2) essential to DT: first, the fact that each phonemic symbol in (2) occurs, not in isolation, but ordered with other symbols in whole lines; second, the fact that each of these lines in turn occurs, not in isolation, but in a derivation, that is, ordered with other lines; and third, the fact that that derivation as a whole pertains not only to the utterance produced by SB in Colchester but to indefi-nitely many other actual and conceivable utterances.

We now turn to those three facts.

On the analysis that we are proposing, the last line of (2) as a whole—like its phonological constituent symbols—stands for a predicate, but a more complex one. The occurrence of the phonological symbols in the line signifies that the predicates they stand in for are part of the expansion of that more complex predicate—are part of its definition. And the order in which these symbols occur in the line signifies the order in which the things of which the predicates are true occurred in time.

More specifically, the last line stands in for the predicate that we abbreviate as (16),

(16) $\lambda x[\underline{\Omega}x]$

and that is defined by (17),

(17) $\lambda x[\underline{\Omega}x] =_{df} \lambda x[(\exists r)(\exists s)(\exists t) \ldots (\exists u)(\exists v)\{r < s \,\&\, s < t \,\&\, \ldots \,\&\, u < v \,\&\, \lambda y[\underline{ky}](r) \,\&\, \lambda y[\underline{əy}](s) \,\&\, \lambda y[\underline{ny}](t) \,\&\, \ldots \,\&\, \lambda y[\underline{əy}](u) \,\&\, \lambda y[\underline{zy}](v) \,\&\, \Sigma\{r,s,t, \ldots, u,v\} = x\}]$

Those not fully comfortable with lambda notation can get an intuitive grasp of (17)—of the satisfaction conditions it describes—by looking at a very rough paraphrase of what statement (18), built on it, asserts:

(18) $\lambda x[\underline{\Omega}x](SB)$.

(18) asserts of a stage of SB (*a*) that it was made up (i.e. was the mereo-logical sum, the Σ) of subsidiary stages (r,s,t, . . . u,v); (*b*) that these subsidiary stages occurred chronologically so that r came before s, s before t, . . . u before v; and (*c*) that the first of these stages, r, was a k̲, in other words, met the satisfaction conditions of '$\lambda x[\underline{kx}]$' given above, that the second of the stages, s, was a ə̲, in other words, met the satisfaction conditions of '$\lambda x[\underline{əx}]$' (which

we have not bothered to spell out), . . . and that the last of these stages was a z̲, in other words, met the satisfaction conditions of '$\lambda x[\underline{z}x]$'.

Turning now to the first line, it too stands for a complex predicate, and the significance of the phonological symbols in it is the same as that of the phonological symbols in the last line. In other words, each phonological symbol signifies that the predicate for which it stands occurs in the expansion (or definition) of that more complex predicate; and the order of these phonological symbols signifies the order[10] of the elements of which these phonological predicates are predicated.

However, the claim that the first line as a whole stands for a predicate requires either a long investigation into the semantics of syntactic/morphological symbols or a leap of faith to the belief that syntactic/morphological symbols—or at least those that survive to the inputs of DT phonology—are also stand-ins for predicates—predicates, moreover, that can combine with phonological predicates to form more complex predicates. We opt for faith, because at this point we have but the dimmest ideas about the satisfaction conditions of syntactic/morphological predicates. Still, without that faith, it is difficult to see how our third assumption—that the theory is a 'this-worldly' theory—can be maintained. But we leave that discussion for another occasion.

Abbreviating the predicate corresponding to the first line as (19),

(19) $\lambda x[\underline{\Gamma}x]$

we can define it in terms of syntactic and phonological predicates as (20),

(20) $\lambda x[\underline{\Gamma}x] =_{df} \lambda x[(\exists l)(\exists m) \ldots (\exists n)(\exists o)\{l \prec m \ldots \& \ldots \& n \prec o \&$
    $\lambda y[\{[\underline{kænæd\text{-}i\text{-}æ}], \text{Noun} \ldots \}y](l) \& \lambda y[\{\underline{z}, \text{Pl} \ldots \}y](m) \& \ldots \&$
    $\lambda y[\{[\underline{h\dot{i}s}],\text{Noun}\}y](n) \& \lambda y[\{\underline{z}, \text{Pl} \ldots \}y](o) \& \Sigma(l,m, \ldots n,o) = x\}]$

In a more explicit definition, (20) would, of course, be expanded into a still more complex definition in which the phonological symbols would be replaced by their own explicit definitions, described above, and exemplified by (14) and (15).

Here, as before, those who are not comfortable with lambda notation can get an intuitive grasp of the satisfaction conditions that the definition connotes by looking at the paraphrase of a statement about SB built on it.

(21) $\lambda x[\underline{\Gamma}x](SB)$

(21) asserts of a stage of SB (*a*) that it was made up (was the mereological sum, the Σ) of a number of subsidiary stages (l,m, . . ., n,o); (*b*) that these subsidiary stages were ordered so that l was prior to m, . . . n prior to o; (*c*) that the first of these stages was a stage of which the predicate 'being the intention

---

[10] We leave in abeyance here whether that ordering is temporal ordering or some other sort of ordering. That is why we use '$\prec$' instead of '$<$' in (20).

of uttering the noun pronounced [kænædiæn] unless rules or rules require modification' . . . that the last of these stages was a stage of which the predicate 'being the intention of uttering the plural morpheme pronounced z unless some rule or rules require modification'.

Let us now turn to the derivation as a whole, still read as about that utterance produced by SB in Colchester, and see what the order of the lines signifies.

Though we have not even sketched the lines that intervene between the first and last lines, if we are right so far about those two, then it is safe to assume that these other lines too are stand-ins for predicates true of SB and expandable on the model of (17) and (20). So without going into the details of such expansion, let us abbreviate these predicates as '$\lambda x[\underline{\Delta}x]$', . . . , '$\lambda x[\underline{\Lambda}x]$'. The fact that the first line precedes the second line, the second the third, . . . until we finally reach the last line, signifies two things: (*a*) that SB went through a series of stages in Colchester: first a stage that met the satisfaction conditions of '$\lambda x[\underline{\Gamma}x]$', then one that met those of '$\lambda x[\underline{\Delta}x]$', then . . ., then one that met those of '$\lambda x[\underline{\Lambda}x]$', and finally a stage that met the satisfaction conditions of '$\lambda x[\underline{\Omega}x]$'; (*b*) that each of these stages brought its successor about through a process modulated by phonological rules internalized by SB. Thus what the derivation as a whole expresses about the utterance in Colchester (we will see in a moment how to construe it more broadly)—is also expressed by the conjunction[11]

(22) $\lambda x[\underline{\Gamma}x](SB_1)$ & $\lambda x[\underline{\Delta}x](SB_2)$ & $\lambda xy[\underline{\text{motivate }}xy](SB_1\ SB_2)$ & . . . . $\lambda x[\underline{\Lambda}x](SB_m)$
    & $\lambda x[\underline{\Omega}x](SB_n)$ & $\lambda xy[\underline{\text{motivate }}xy](SB_m\ SB_n)$ & ¬ $(\exists t)\{\lambda xy[\underline{\text{motivate }}xy](SB_n t)\}$

In (22) '$\lambda xy[\underline{\text{motivate }}xy]$' is a dyadic predicate whose satisfaction conditions are met by a pair of speaker-stages if and only if the first member of that pair brings about the second member, and does this through a causal process modulated by internalized phonological rules. Note that this characterization implies that the predicate is transitive, and therefore that (22) entails (23):

(23) $\lambda x[\underline{\Gamma}x](SB_1)$ & $\lambda x[\underline{\Omega}x](SB_m)$ & $\lambda xy[\underline{\text{motivate }}xy](SB_1\ SB_n)$

in other words, that the stage described by the first line 'motivated' the stage described by the last line.

Let us now finally turn to the third fact about (2) with which our account has to be reconciled, the fact that (2) pertains to indefinitely many actual and conceivable utterances beyond the one produced by SB in Colchester.

One way of accommodating our account so far to this third fact would make (2) true but uninteresting. It consists in interpreting (2) as expressing a statement with underspecified arguments. On this interpretation, (2) can signify what (22) signifies, but it can also signify what (22) would have signified had it

---

[11] We remarked above that we would use 'SB' ambiguously to refer to different stages of SB. In (22) we use subscripts to flag that different stages of SB are mentioned. Without some such device (22) would make no sense.

contained different arguments, that is, had 'SB$_1$' and 'SB$_2$' been replaced by references to other stages—either other stages of SB, or stages of some other English speaker—that brought about an utterance transcribable as (1). On this interpretation (2) is not only systematically ambiguous and vague but could not be true unless someone on some occasion had had the intention of uttering (1).

Fortunately there is another way of accommodating this third fact, a way that makes (2) unambiguous, not vague, and—importantly—more interesting because capable of being true regardless of whether anyone ever intended to utter (1). It interprets (2) as not referring explicitly or implicitly to any individual stages at all, but as signifying a *law*, a *nomological generalization*, that happens to have been instantiated by SB in Colchester, but need never have been instantiated to be true (if true). Any theory worth its salt entails indefinitely many laws over and above those that have instantiations, and this should be true of any acceptable interpretation of DT. The law expressed in our notation is

(24) $\Delta(\forall z)\{\lambda x[\Gamma x](z) \rightarrow (\exists u)\{\lambda x[\Delta x](u) \,\&\, \lambda xy[\underline{\text{motivate}} \; xy](zu)\} \,\&\, \ldots$
$(\exists v)\{\lambda x[\underline{\Delta}x](v) \,\&\, (\exists w)\lambda x[\underline{\Omega}x](w) \,\&\, \lambda xy[\underline{\text{motivate}} \; xy](vw) \,\&\,$
$\neg\,(\exists t)\{\lambda xy[\underline{\text{motivate}}\,xy](wt)\}\}\}$

Informally, (24) states that to *any* stage satisfying the predicate of the first line, i.e. (20) there must correspond a stage satisfying the predicate of the second line and motivated by the former . . . and a stage satisfying the predicate of the last line that is motivated by a stage satisfying the predicate of the penultimate line, but motivates no further stage. The initial symbol Δ marks the modality of what follows, namely that it is a law,[12] and not an ordinary accidental generalization, and thus that it entails counterfactual conditionals.

Since motivation, as we have defined it, is transitive, (24) entails

(25) $\Delta(\forall z)\{\lambda x[\underline{\Gamma}x](z) \rightarrow (\exists w)\{\lambda x[\underline{\Omega}x](w) \,\&\, \lambda xy[\underline{\text{motivate}} \; xy](zw) \,\&\,$
$\neg\,(\exists t)\{\lambda xy[\underline{\text{motivate}}\,xy](wt)\}\}\}$

which, roughly speaking, states that any stage satisfying the predicate of the first line must motivate a stage satisfying the predicate of the last line.

A proposition such as (25) can, without harm, be paraphrased as describing a relationship between an underlying representation and a surface representation. However, we must be careful not to interpret 'representation' in such a paraphrase as referring to abstract entities of some sort, or, in fact, to any entities. (25), like the law of universal gravitation, or for that matter the law of supply and demand, does not refer to any particular entity or entities, abstract or concrete. The law has a domain of spatio-temporal entities (speaker stages),

---

[12] It is the statement of a very idealized law, but in that respect it is very much like the statement of laws provided by other natural sciences.

but it can be true even if, by happenstance, no entity in that domain ever meets its antecedent conditions.

Before leaving DT, we should point out that generalizations such as (24) (and (25)) are not to be confused with rules. They are not rules. Rules are, in the term sometimes used by Chomsky, 'cognized' by speaker-hearers. Not so these generalizations. They are not part of a speaker-hearer's mind/brain endowment. Furthermore, unlike rules, they express truths (or falsities): if (24) is true, then our spatio-temporal world is subject to a nomological generalization about some speaker-hearers (speakers who share SB's idiolect), to which it is not subject if (24) is false. However, *the truth conditions* of (24) require that there be speakers capable of cognizing rules. But note that this requirement follows from the *meaning*, from the satisfaction conditions, of the phonological symbols in (2).

4. OPTIMALITY THEORY

We now turn to Optimality Theory. OT would presumably also offer an analysis of the utterance token that SB produced in Colchester, but that analysis would be in the form of a tableau, not of a derivation. The tableau would have an input, which we will assume would be given either in a form identical to the first line of (2) or in a form that at least contains the same phonological symbols as that first line; that is, it would assign the same phonological 'underlying' structure to the utterance. The tableau would contain a set of GEN outputs, one of which—the 'winner'—would, we will assume, be identical to the last line of (2), the others of which would differ from that winner in ways that do not matter for this discussion.[13] The tableau would also contain a set of constraints the details and order of which do not matter for this discussion either.

Let us now look at the 'k' that would occur at the initial position of the 'winner'. Following reasoning similar to our reasoning about the last line of (2), we take that 'k' to be a stand-in for a predicate true of a stage of SB at Colchester, and true of that stage because it was a stage of 'intending' to move articulators in certain specific ways.

But the predicate for which 'k' is a stand-in in the tableau cannot have exactly the same satisfaction conditions as the 'k' in the derivation, the satisfaction conditions given in the definition (14). That definition presupposes the possible intervention of rules, and OT does not admit rules.

On the other hand, the satisfaction conditions of the 'k' in the tableau cannot

---

[13] Our assumptions that the input of GEN would be identical to the first line of the derivation (2) and that the 'winner' would be identical to the last line are not crucial to establish our claim that the symbols shared by DT and OT that share the same shape do not share the same meaning, but enable us to simplify the discussion considerably.

be those given by definition (5) either, and this for reasons similar to those that led us to reject (5) as inappropriate for the 'k' in the DT derivation. 'k' happens to occur in the 'winner' and in the input to GEN; 'æ', however, though it occurs in the input to GEN, and in some of the outputs of GEN, it does not occur in the 'winner' at all. We cannot deny that the 'k' in the 'winner' and the 'k' in the input to GEN are stand-ins for the same predicate: that is ruled out by our second assumption, the assumption that within a theory each phonological symbol has the same meaning, wherever it occurs. We cannot deny that 'k' and 'æ' are stand-ins for similar predicates, since that is not only counterintuitive but open to the same objection: in other tableaux 'æ' can appear in the description of 'winners' even if it does not happen to do so in this one.

The solution of the dilemma here is analogous to the solution of the corresponding dilemma raised by DT: the predicate for which 'k' is a stand-in in the tableau is in every respect identical to the predicate for which it is a stand-in in the derivation, except for one crucial difference: the 'unless' clauses in (14) get replaced by a different one, roughly 'unless not optimal according to the UG constraints as ranked for the language of the speaker', a clause that we will abbreviate as 'uno'. In other words, in OT the predicate for which 'k' is a stand-in is defined by (26). (From here on, we will use double underlining for OT predicates, to distinguish them from DT predicates.)

(26) $\lambda x[\underline{\underline{k}}x] =_{df} \lambda x[\text{uno dorsal } x]$ & $\lambda x[\text{uno} -\text{continuant } x]$ & $\lambda x[\text{uno} -\text{voiced } x]$ & $\lambda x[\underline{\underline{\text{uno}}} -\text{nasal } x]$

By parity of reasoning, the 'æ's in the tableau stand not for (15) but for

(27) $\lambda x[\underline{\underline{æ}} \ x] =_{df} \lambda x[\text{uno} -\text{back } x]$ & $\lambda x[\text{uno} -\text{high } x]$ & $\lambda x[\text{uno} +\text{low } x]$ & $\lambda x[\text{uno} -\text{round } x]$

These definitions will obviously do for the occurrences in the 'losers' as well. And similar ones, which we will not bother to spell out, are forthcoming for the other phonological symbols.

So, on the reading proposed here, the 'k' in the input to GEN records that at some initial stage SB intended to perform-a-certain-gymnastics-unless-this-would-not-be-optimal-etc. and the same letter in the 'winner' records that at a final stage SB had the identical intention. The 'uno' clauses in the definition happen to carry no consequences in these occurrences. On the other hand, the 'æ's in the input to GEN record that at some initial stage SB intended to perform-a-certain-(different)-gymnastics-unless-this-would-not-be-optimal-etc. but the 'uno' clause in the definition did carry consequences. We leave aside for the moment what the occurrence of the phonological symbols in the 'losers' signify.

The account so far—like the account at a similar stage of our discussion of the phonemic symbols in DT—still needs to be reconciled with three other important aspects of phonological symbols: first, the fact that these symbols do not occur in isolation, but occur in an ordered sequence with other symbols in whole lines; second, the fact that each of these lines occurs not in isolation but in a tableau; third, the fact that the tableau as a whole pertains not only to the utterance produced by SB in Colchester but to indefinitely many other actual and conceivable utterances. But we can be relatively brief since we can repeat—though with a few *crucial* modifications—much of the discussion on the analogous points about (2) and DT.

The 'winner' as a whole stands for a predicate similar in every respect to the one defined by (17), but with the constituents in that definition replaced by the corresponding predicates belonging to OT, that is, defined with 'uno' clauses instead of 'upsr' clauses. Using double underlining to mirror the similarities and differences, the definition becomes

(28) $\lambda x[\underline{\underline{\Omega}}x]$ = $_{df}$ $\lambda x[(\exists r)(\exists s)(\exists t) \ldots (\exists u)(\exists v)\{r < s \ \& \ s < t \ \& \ldots \& \ u < v \ \& \ \lambda y[\underline{ky}](r)$
     & $\lambda \underline{\underline{y[\partial y}}](s) \ \& \ \lambda y[\underline{ny}](t) \ \& \ldots \& \ \lambda y[\underline{\partial y}](u) \ \& \ \lambda y[\underline{zy}](v) \ \& \ \Sigma\{r,s,t, \ldots, u,v\}=x\}]$

The informal gloss on the statement corresponding to (18), namely

(29) $\lambda x[\underline{\underline{\Omega}}x](SB)$

is similar to the informal gloss for (18), except, again, that the mentions of DT predicates must be replaced by mentions of OT predicates. We refer the readers to that previous gloss and let them make the substitutions.

The input to GEN as a whole stands for a predicate very similar to the one defined by (20), but again with the phonological constituents replaced by the corresponding phonological predicates of OT, defined with 'uno' clauses instead of 'upsr' ones. Using double underlining to mark the difference, the definition of that predicate is (30):

(30) $\lambda x[\underline{\underline{\Gamma}}x]$ = $_{df}$ $\lambda x[(\exists l)(\exists m) \ldots (\exists n)(\exists o)\{1 \prec m \ldots \& \ldots \& \ n \prec o \ \& \ \lambda y[\{[\underline{k\text{æ}n\text{æ}d\text{-}i\text{-}}$
     $\text{æ}], \overline{\overline{N}}oun \ldots \}y](l) \ \& \ \lambda y[\{\underline{z}, Pl \ldots \}y](m) \ \& \ldots \& \ \lambda y[\{[\underline{h\textit{ɨ}s}],Noun\}\overline{y](n)} \ \&$
     $\overline{\lambda}y[\{\underline{z}, Pl \ldots \}y](o) \ \& \ \Sigma(l,\overline{m}, \ldots n,o) = x\}]$

And the informal gloss for

(31) $\lambda x[\underline{\underline{\Gamma}}x](SB)$

is similar to the informal gloss for (21), except that the mention of DT predicates must be replaced by mentions of OT predicates. The structural similarities between these OT and DT definitions and their glosses, however, should not blind us to the differences. These differences raise an important question that we will take up later, namely whether (21) and (31) could be true together. Standard notation implies that they must be true together. We will argue that they can't be.

We turn now to the relationship between (31) and (29) expressed by the fact that the former corresponds to the input and the latter to the winning output of

GEN. That relationship is reminiscent of the relationship between the first and the last line of the derivation, a relationship between something describable as an underlying representation and something describable as a surface representation. But it cannot be the relationship expressed by the dyadic predicate 'motivate' in (23). That relationship is a transitive relation whose occurrence is modulated by phonological rules. The relationship expressed by the positioning of inputs and winning outputs of a tableau is neither transitive nor modulated by phonological rules. Furthermore, the relation expressed by the dyadic predicate 'motivate' holds only between stages that satisfy DT predicates. Not so the relationship that concerns us now. So let us introduce a new dyadic predicate. To flag its similarity with '$\lambda xy[\underline{\text{motivate}}\ xy]$' we will use a similar notation, and to flag its roots in OT, we will use double underlining:

(32) $\lambda xy[\underline{\underline{\text{motivate}}}\ xy](SB_1\ SB_2)$

In short, then, the tableau asserts the analogue of (23), namely (33):

(33) $\lambda x[\underline{\Gamma}x](SB_1)$ & $\lambda x[\underline{\Omega}x](SB_2)$ & $\lambda xy[\underline{\underline{\text{motivate}}}\ xy](SB_1\ SB_2)$

We can now account for the fact that the tableau is relevant beyond the event in Colchester in a very straightforward way. It—like the derivation of DT—can be construed as expressing a law, a nomological generalization, that happens to have been instantiated in Colchester, that may have been instantiated on many other occasions, but that might never have been instantiated while still being true. That nomological generalization in lambda notation is

(34) $\Delta(\forall z)\{\lambda x[\underline{\Gamma}x](z) \rightarrow (\exists w)\{\lambda x[\underline{\Omega}x](w)$ & $\lambda xy[\underline{\underline{\text{motivate}}}\ xy](z\ w)\}\}$

We have not said anything so far about the 'losing' outputs of the tableau, but it is easy to see what the tableau—interpreted as significant beyond Colchester—asserts through them. If we let '$\lambda x[\underline{\Delta}x]$' abbreviate one of the predicates expressed by one of these outputs, then the tableau also expresses not only (34), but also (35):

(35) $\Delta(\forall z)\{\lambda x[\underline{\Gamma}x](z) \rightarrow \neg\ (\exists w)\{\lambda x[\underline{\Delta}x](w)$ & $\lambda xy[\underline{\underline{\text{motivate}}}\ xy](z\ w)\}\}$

which essentially states that stages which satisfy the conditions of the input predicate never bring about stages satisfying the conditions of the 'losing' predicates.

The DT derivation (2)—interpreted as expressing a family of generalizations—expresses no generalization analogous to (35). On the other hand, the OT tableau—interpreted as expressing a family of generalizations which includes the single positive (34) and many negative ones like (35)—expresses nothing analogous to (24). That difference, in many eyes, is at the heart of what differentiates DT and OT. But it should not make us overlook the less openly displayed difference on which we have dwelt so far: that the predicates even in generalizations that look similar, such as (34) and (25), do not have the same satisfaction conditions, and thus that the truth conditions of even similar-looking generalizations are deeply different.

5. Comparing DT and OT

If what we have said so far is right, one might conclude that contributions to DT phonology and contributions to OT phonology are what has come to be called in some circles 'incommensurable', and that the switch from DT to OT by many linguists constitutes what has been called a 'paradigm shift', a kind of switch that is said to mark many so-called 'revolutions' in the history of the natural sciences.

The notion of incommensurability was introduced in contemporary philosophy of science by Thomas Kuhn and Paul Feyerabend. Roughly speaking, two theories are said to be incommensurable when no logical contradictions or entailments can exist between their respective statements, and thus when it is in principle impossible to establish that if one is right the other must *ipso facto* be wrong. This will happen, according to Kuhn and Feyerabend and others—as we read them—when the terms used by the two theories differ in meaning so that the satisfaction conditions of the predicates of one theory can be met independently of the satisfaction conditions of the predicates of the other theory. In other words, two theories T_1 and T_2 are incommensurable, on the view we are describing, if it is possible for something to meet the satisfaction conditions of any predicate belonging to T_1 without it following that something (the same thing, or something else) meets, or fails to meet, the satisfaction conditions of any of the predicates belonging to T_2. In such a situation the generalizations couched in the vocabulary of T_1 and those couched in the vocabulary of T_2 would clearly be logically independent, would neither logically entail nor logically exclude each other.

It is of course easy to come up with plausible examples of theories that stand in such a relationship of incommensurability: Keynesian economics and quantum mechanics, for instance. The interest in the notion is generated, however, not by such boring examples of theories that don't even seem to share terminology, but rather by Kuhn's, Feyerabend's, and other people's claim that certain historical theories which *seem* to share terminology, and which *seem prima facie* commensurable and even mutually exclusive, actually do not share terminology and are incommensurable, are, in principle, actually compatible. A frequently alleged instance is that of Aristotelian and Copernican astronomy. Both rely on the term 'planet' and thus seem to say mutually contradictory things about a same set of objects. Closer scrutiny allegedly shows that these theories use the term with different meanings to denote a different range of objects, and thus link the term 'planet' with distinct and independent satisfaction conditions. Other examples involve theories using such terms as 'atom' and 'energy' and 'gravitation'. Those are the sort of examples implicated in what Kuhn and others after him have called 'paradigm shifts' in the history of science.

We have argued in the two previous sections that in spite of appearances to the contrary, DT and OT do not share terminology, except at a very superficial notational level. Admittedly, we have limited ourselves to a few terms in that terminology, but the considerations we have put forth can obviously be expanded to reach beyond these examples. And nothing we have said implies that relations of mutual implications or exclusions exist across the terminologies. So there is no reason to hold that if, for instance, '$\lambda x[\underline{\Gamma}x]$' is true of anything, then '$\lambda x[\underline{\Gamma}x]$' must *ipso facto* also be true of something, perhaps the same thing. For all we have said so far, there is a possible world in which the first is true of some SB stage but the second one is not, and there is another possible world in which the second is true of some stage of SB but the first one is not. And there is a third possible world in which both are true of some SB stages, possibly, though not necessarily, the same stage.

There is nevertheless a strongly felt conviction abroad that the two theories could not be true together, or, more narrowly, that the laws implicit in a derivation such as (2), namely law (24) or even (25), and laws implicit in the corresponding tableaux, such as (34), cannot be true together. There could conceivably be a plausible theory that combines aspects of OT and DT, that is, that uses both sets of predicates, but there will never be a plausible theory that entails both (24) and (34). And this not because these two laws are *logically* incompatible, could not 'in principle' both be true. Nor even because such an ecumenical theory would be uneconomical. The felt conviction—which we share—goes deeper. We now want briefly to describe the ground of that conviction.

To do this we need a third set of predicates, predicates that belong to neither DT nor OT as we have described these so far. Fortunately, we can describe their satisfaction conditions very quickly: their satisfaction conditions are exactly the same as the satisfaction conditions of predicates belonging to DT and exactly the same as the satisfaction conditions of predicates belonging to OT, but without any 'unless' clauses. In fact, we have already defined some of them. So, for instance, this set of predicates includes (5), repeated here as (36),

(36) $\lambda x[kx] =_{df} \lambda x[\text{dorsal } x]$ & $\lambda x[-\text{continuant } x]$ & $\lambda x[-\text{voiced } x]$ & $\lambda x[-\text{nasal } x]$

and it includes (9), repeated here as (37),

(37) $\lambda x[\text{ə}x] =_{df} \lambda x[-\text{round } x]$ & $\lambda x[-\text{high } x]$ & $\lambda x[-\text{low } x]$ & $\lambda x[+\text{back } x]$ & $\lambda x[-\text{ATR } x]$

and so on. To mark that a predicate belongs to this third set, we will write it with *no* underlining, as above. And though this may be somewhat misleading, we will refer to such predicates as 'phonetic' predicates. They include defined ones as well, and in particular (38):

(38) λx[Ωx] = $_{df}$ λx[(∃r)(∃s)(∃t) . . . (∃u)(∃v){r < s & s < t & . . . & u < v & λy[ky](r)
& λy[əy](s) & λy[ny](t) & . . . & λy[əy](u) & λy[zy](v) & Σ{r,s,t, . . ., u,v}=x}]

Note that no underlining occurs in either the definiendum or the definiens.
To get an intuitive grasp of the satisfaction conditions sketched in (38), simply
go back to the gloss for (17) and make the obvious adjustment by mentally
deleting all underlinings.

With the help of these predicates we can state a set of laws entailed by DT
laws and by OT laws. To fix ideas, let us look at two specific ones.

The first entailed by (25) of DT, namely (39):

(39) Δ(∀z){λx[Γx](z) → (∃w){λx[Ωx](w) & λxy[motivate xy](zw) &
¬ (∃u)(λxy[motivate xy](wu)) & λ[Ωx](w)}}

states that any stage that satisfies the predicate of the first line of the derivation
(2) motivates (in the DT sense) a stage that satisfies the predicate of the last
line (and thus is a stage that does not motivate further stages) and that *also*
satisfies the 'corresponding' *phonetic* predicate 'λx[Ωx]'.

The second one, entailed by (34) of OT,

(40) Δ(∀z){λx[Γx](z) → (∃w){λx[Ωx](w) & λxy[motivate xy](z w) & λx[Ωx](w)}}

states that any stage that satisfies the predicate of the input of the tableau
motivates a stage that satisfies the predicate of the winner and that *also*
satisfies the 'corresponding' *phonetic* predicate 'λx[Ωx]'.

But if it is possible for both (39) and (40) to be true—if the derivation and
the tableau on which they are grounded can both be valid—that would mean
that stages satisfying 'λx[Ωx]' can be explained in three different ways. They
can be explained as brought about through a process that is an instantiation of
law (39), or as brought about through a process that is an instantiation of law
(40), and through a process (or processes) that is the instantiation of both laws
more or less simultaneously. More concretely, it would mean that the utterance
by SB in Colchester could have been brought about by one of two independent
processes, either of which would have been sufficient to bring the utterance
about, or that it was brought about through the joint operation of both, though
either would have been sufficient. But that seems highly implausible. Not
logically impossible. But implausible. We would have a theory that allows
for 'overdetermination'. Overdetermination is rare and implausible in the
absence of strong evidence, but is, admittedly, not impossible.[14]

---

[14] Scepticism about overdetermination has deep roots and a long history. Thus we find that Sir
Isaac Newton gave the following rule in his 'Rules of Reasoning in Philosophy': 'Rule I: We are to
admit no more causes of natural things that such are both true and sufficient to explain their
appearance' (Newton 1934: 398). Contemporary philosophers discuss the notion mostly in connection with issues in the philosophy of mind (the rationality of allowing mental causation as well
as physical causation to account for human behavior and attitudes). For references to the relevant
literature, see e.g. Yablo (1992), who summarizes the relevant principle succinctly: 'If an event x is
causally sufficient for an event y, then no event x* distinct from x is causally relevant . . . ', or Kim
(1979).

What has been said about this pair of derivation and tableau can, obviously, be repeated and generalized for any pair of derivations and tableaux with superficially (i.e. when put in standard notation) identical last line and 'winner'. So, if there are such pairs, anyone sceptical about overdetermination (and most scientists are) must conclude that DT and OT cannot both be right.

We can, of course, envisage things unfolding in such a way that DT and OT somehow end up entailing only distinct phonetic predictions, and thus avoid the issue of overdetermination. But this is very improbable and at most of abstract speculative interest—and, in any case, would make it even less likely that they could both be right. Such a situation could theoretically take two forms.

In the first form, DT and OT would entail *only* laws whose formats are respectively like those of (39) and (40), with phonological predicates in the antecedent that look identical when translated in standard phonological symbols, but with *phonetic* predicates in the consequent that exclude each other— that cannot be simultaneously satisfied by anything—that look very different when translated in standard phonological symbols. In other words, DT would yield only derivations with first lines identical (in standard notation) to the input of tableaux that OT generates, but with last lines that are different (in standard notation or in phonetic predicate notation) from the winners in the tableaux. In such an unlikely eventuality, DT and OT would essentially be making conflicting predictions about what speakers can intend to pronounce. Very strictly speaking, they could still be *logically* compatible, but any sensible linguist would judge that one of them, *at most*, could be right.

In the second form, DT and OT would entail only laws whose formats are again respectively like (39) and (40), but this time not only with phonetic predicates that look different when translated in standard symbols but also with phonological predicates in the antecedent that look different when translated in standard phonological symbols. In other words, DT would yield only derivations whose first lines are unlike the input of any tableau provided by OT, and whose last line is unlike the winner of any tableau provided by OT. In this imaginary situation DT and OT would neither be redundant nor make conflicting predictions. But—assuming that each made at least some verified predictions, and neither made disconfirmed ones—they would then at best each be demonstrably incomplete, and neither could be right.

In short, then, unless one is willing to countenance overdetermination, it would be a mistake to argue that DT and OT could both be simultaneously right, both give us a correct view of reality—from the fact that they rely on predicates with entirely different satisfaction conditions.[15]

But if DT and OT cannot both be right, it may now look as if the debate

---

[15] We had to rely on a third set of predicates, *predicates belonging to neither DT nor OT*, to make this point about incommensurability. Whether analogous devices are available in the case of other scientific theories that have been alleged to be incommensurable is an interesting question that we can obviously not pursue here.

between their respective proponents should—in principle at least—be decided in a fairly obvious way, eventually, though not immediately. Proponents of DT will continue for a while to come up with derivations that entail laws like (39), proponents of OT will continue for a while to come up with tableaux that entail laws like (40), and the group that eventually comes up with the largest number of confirmed laws (while being charged with no disconfirmed ones)—and seems likely to continue to do so—will carry the day. Along the way, quibbles may arise about what counts as confirmation and disconfirmation of this or that law (in its guise of derivation in the case of laws like (39) or in its guise of tableaux in the case of laws like (40)) and how much weight should be attached to this or that case, but these can be settled in the way scientists usually settle such questions. Note, by the way, that the phonetic predicates (in their guise of last line of derivations and of 'winners' in tableaux) in these laws would play an indispensable role in this way of conducting the debate.

However, as scientists, we not only seek theories that beget large numbers of confirmed generalizations, we also want them to beget explanations.

These two objectives can—up to a point—be met in one fell swoop, since by providing generalizations one often also provides grounds for answers to why-questions. When and how is a complicated matter, but without going into it we can see that, in the instances that interest us, this will often be the case. So, for example, in the situation that we have envisaged above, DT and OT would each provide an answer to

(41) Why do English speakers say 'kənéydiyənzlɪvɪnháwzəz', that is, get to a stage satisfying '$\lambda x[\Omega x]$' and not 'kænæydiænzlivinhɪ:səz', a stage satisfying some other predicate?

DT would do so by subsuming the fact in the question under (39) and OT by subsuming it under (40). The two answers would be different, and what we said above about overdetermination also means that they could not both be true. Nevertheless, OT and DT would each be able to come up with an answer simply because each is able to come up with an appropriate generalization. And so the theory that eventually yields the largest number of confirmed generalizations will also be the one that eventually yields answers to the largest number of why-questions like (41).

However, why-questions like (41) are not the only explanatory questions we expect phonology to answer. We also expect it to answer explanatory *what*-questions, and in particular questions like (42):

(42) What is the sequence of the stages traversed (the set of predicates satisfied) by a speaker in the course of producing utterances satisfying e.g. '$\lambda x[\Omega x]$' from mnemonic elements merged and structured by the syntax of that speaker?

DT provides such answers, and is designed to provide further ones since it is designed to yield laws like (24) which predict sequences of stages. OT, on the other hand, does not provide such answers, and is designed not to do so, since it is explicitly designed not to yield laws about sequences of stages, but instead to yield only laws like (34) which, like (25), concern 'motivation' relations between underlying stages and surface ones, and are silent about intervening ones. OT therefore, no matter how successful in providing generalizations like (34), will forever leave us in the dark about a family of questions to which DT can, at least in principle, yield answers. That is a good reason for pursuing DT rather than OT. And since a good reason for pursuing DT rather than OT is also a good reason for accepting the presumptions of DT over the presumptions of OT, it is a good reason for deciding the debate between them immediately in favor of DT without waiting to see which one is likely to accumulate the largest number of generalizations.

Two rejoinders will no doubt come to mind. The first rejoinder allows that DT is designed to answer questions such as (42) that OT cannot, even in principle, answer, but insists that the situation is symmetrical, since no theory can answer every question and OT, for its part, is designed to answer a type of question that DT cannot answer, of which an example, somewhat roughly put, would be

(43) In what respect is an utterance satisfying '$\lambda x[\Omega x]$' optimal?

However, there is an important difference between (43) and (42). All phonologists must admit that (42) is a legitimate question, whatever their views about specific derivational accounts of this or that surface representation. That is, all phonologists who are realists and who agree that so-called underlying representations and surface representations are actually implicated in real time in the production of utterances—whether proponents of DT or OT—implicitly accept the presuppositions of questions like (42): that there are stages of the sort assumed by that question. But the same is not true of (43). From the point of view of DT, the notion of optimality is at best suspect, and the fact that creative and gifted linguists have come up with tableaux should eventually turn out to rest on aesthetically intriguing, but ultimately accidental, epiphenomena that need to be explained but that have little if any explanatory depth themselves. One can think of analogies in other disciplines. So, for instance, the predictive power of the laws of geometric optics is explainable ultimately in terms of the mechanisms and laws of the wave theory of light, but not vice versa.

The second rejoinder denies that OT cannot offer answers to questions like (42). It can, though these answers have to supplement the information contained in tableaux and be built with the help of algorithms such as those proposed by Tesar—or certain variations thereof. But if one allows that such algorithms may be—and for all we know actually are—implemented in the brain of speakers and could actually be invoked in speech performance, then, the second rejoinder goes, OT offers answers to questions like (42) that are at least as cogent as the answers offered by DT.

This is not the place for a detailed discussion of Tesar's and Tesar-like algorithms. The pertinent facts about them, for what concerns us here, are certain overall characteristics that—as far as we understand them—these algorithms all share. They all describe computational processes that build in a finite—though normally very large—number of steps the 'winner' output for any given input to a tableau; in other words, these computational processes halt after a finite interval with the description of the 'winner' when started with an appropriate set of ordered constraints and an appropriate 'underlying' string. Such a process typically begins operating at the left edge of the input 'underlying' string, and produces a finite number of new strings, say, n new strings, after scanning that left edge and performing on it whatever operations the phonology allows. The process then 'selects' from among these n new strings one in particular as a temporary 'winner', the one that is optimal so far according to the ranked constraints. It can do so in a finite number of steps, since n is finite and the number of constraints is finite. It then takes that temporary 'winner' as input, turns to the next segment, and performs on that segment whatever operations are allowed by the phonology, thereby producing a set of, say, m new strings, all alike at the left edge, but different at the second segment. It then selects from among these m strings as new temporary 'winner' the one that is optimal, so far again, according to the constraints. It then compares that tentative 'winner' with the previous 'losers' to determine whether one of the latter might not be 'better' because, for instance, the constraint it violates has a lower weight than the combination of constraints violated by the new tentative winner. If so, it takes the latter as new input for operations on the second segment and discards that second tentative 'winner'. If not, it proceeds to the next segment of the second tentative 'winner', and repeats the process of selecting, going back, perhaps discarding and starting all over again, or going on, until it reaches the right edge, where it will eventually come to a halt. In short, any system, whether a brain or an artefact, that implements such an algorithm must go through a very large number of stages, each satisfying OT predicates, but most of which will be of no consequence, before settling on what it will articulate.

Whether or not Tesar-type algorithms can equip OT with search procedures that do the work of tableaux depends on the nature of the constraints that OT eventually adopts. But let us assume for the sake of this discussion that there are such algorithms. In other words, let us assume that OT can, in principle, and could eventually, in fact, come up with an answer to questions like (42) built by applying such algorithms. That should not end the matter. We still have to compare the tenor of such putative answers with that of the putative answers provided by DT. And for this we must compare DT derivations, for plausibility and simplicity, not with tableaux, but with descriptions of Tesar-type productions that generate the 'winner' of tableaux from inputs to GEN.

Plausibility is a matter about which people can, of course, disagree. But Tesar-type accounts are prima facie much less plausible as psychological accounts than derivations. Off-hand, we can think of no other non-volitional psychological system that proceeds along such searches, that massively assumes, stores, discards, re-assumes, re-discards states along the way to action, all this without new inputs ever intervening.

When it comes to simplicity, it seems obvious that DT accounts will always be simpler than accounts based on Tesar-type procedures. Tesar-type procedures require a much larger number of intervening stages and operations than do the derivations of DT, and involve greater amounts of redundancy and detours. This is somewhat ironical, since it was misgivings about intermediate representations that motivated much of the interest in OT to begin with.

CONCLUSION

We want to stress that our comparison of DT and OT, and our reason for viewing DT as more promising than OT, were based on a number of essentially non-empirical considerations. We started from three assumptions. The first was that phonological symbols stand for predicates. The second was that phonology is about things in this our spatio-temporal world, and more specifically about speaker–hearer stages. The third was that phonological symbols are used unambiguously within any theory, within DT and within OT, though not necessarily across them. We argued—not from specific empirical considerations but from considerations about the character of the theories—that the predicates on which DT and OT rely come with distinct satisfaction conditions that converge at some points but not at all points. It is *only* because of this convergence that the two theories can be compared along empirical lines at all. In the course of our discussion we added a fourth assumption: that the phonetic characteristics of utterances are not 'overdetermined', are not brought about by two or more independent processes any one of which would have been sufficient. That was an assumption based on admittedly somewhat inchoate considerations which we—and presumably others—find compelling and which justify the view that the competition between DT and OT is real and is about what we believe about the actual world. The debate between DT and OT will have to be settled—if it is ever settled—by appeal to how well they predict and answer legitimate questions about specific empirical evidence. But it will never be settled cleanly until and unless we become more explicit about the validity of these non-empirical considerations and, in particular, about their consequences for the meaning each theory implicitly assigns to the phonological symbols they both share.

ACKNOWLEDGEMENTS

We are grateful to Thomas Green, Ned Hall, Jim Harris, Bill Idsardi, Michael Kenstowicz, Russell Norton, Iggy Roca, Philippe Schlenker, and the participants in the Essex Workshop on Derivations and Constraints in Phonology in September 1995 for comments on previous versions of this chapter and other forms of help. Morris Halle gratefully acknowledges the assistance of the British Academy for support towards his travel expenses.

REFERENCES

Bromberger, S. (1989). 'Types and tokens in linguistics', in A. George (ed.), *Reflections on Chomsky* (Oxford: Blackwell), 58–89. Also in Bromberger (1992).

—— and Halle, M. (1986). 'Why phonology is different', *Linguistic Inquiry* **20**(1): 51–70.

—— —— (1992). 'The ontology of phonology', in Bromberger, *On What We Know We Don't Know*. Chicago: University of Chicago Press/Stanford: Center for Study of Language and Information, 209–28.

Feyerabend, P. K. (1962). 'Explanation, reduction, and empiricism', in H. Feigl and G. Maxwell (eds.), *Minnesota Studies in the Philosophy of Science 3*. Minneapolis: University of Minnesota Press, 28–97.

—— (1975). *Against Method*. London: New Left Books.

Hutton, C. M. (1990). *Abstraction and Instance: The Type–Token Relation in Linguistic Theory*, Oxford: Pergamon.

Katz, J. J. (1990). *The Metaphysics of Meaning*. Cambridge, Mass.: MIT Press.

Kim, J. (1979). 'Causality, Identity, and Supervenience in the Mind–Body Problem', *Midwest Studies in Philosophy 4*. Minneapolis: University of Minnesota Press 31–50.

Kuhn, T. S. (1970). *The Structure of Scientific Revolutions*, 2nd edn. Chicago: University of Chicago Press.

—— (1983*a*) 'Commensurability, comparability, communicability', in P. D. Asquith and T. Nickles (eds.), *Proceedings of the 1982 Biennial Meeting of the Philosophy of Science Association* vol. ii. East Lansing, Mich.: PSA, 669–88.

—— (1983*b*). 'Rationality and theory choice, *Journal of Philosophy* **80**: 563–70.

—— (1990). 'Dubbing and redubbing: the vulnerability of rigid designation, in C. W. Savage (ed.), *Scientific Theories*. Minnesota Studies in the Philosophy of Science 14. Minneapolis: University of Minnesota Press, 298–318.

Lenneberg, E. H. (1967). *Biological Foundations of Language*. New York: Wiley.

McCarthy, J., and Prince, A. (1995). 'Faithfulness and Reduplicative Identity', in J. N. Beckman, L. W. Dickey, and S Urbanczyk (eds.), *Papers in Optimality Theory* (University of Massachusetts Occasional Papers 18). Amherst: GLSA, 249–384. Also to appear in R. Kager, H. van der Hulst, and W. Zonnereld (eds.), *The Prosodic Morphology Interface*. Cambridge: Cambridge University Press. Also in Rutgers Optimality Archive, http: //ruccs.rutgers.edn/roa.html.

Newton, I. (1934). *Mathematical Principles of Natural Philosophy*, trans. A. Motte and F. Cajori. Berkeley, Calif.: University of California Press.

Peirce, C. S. (1958). *Collected Papers of Charles Sanders Peirce*, iv, ed. C. Hartshorne and P. Weiss. Cambridge, Mass.: Harvard University Press.

Prince, A., and Smolensky P. (1993). 'Optimality Theory: Constraint Interaction in Generative Grammar'. MS, Rutgers University and the University of Colorado. Rutgers Center for Cognitive Sciences RUCCS-TR-2. To appear, Cambridge, MA: MIT Press.

Smolensky, P. (1995). 'On the explanatory adequacy of Optimality Theory', talk at the conference on Current Trends in Phonology, Abbaye de Royaumont, France, June 1995.

Tesar, B. (1995a). *Computing Optimal Forms in Optimality Theory: Basic Syllabification*. Technical Report CU-CS-763-95, Feb. 1995. Dept. of Computer Science, University of Colorado, Boulder. Also in Rutgers Optimality Archives ROA-52, http: // ruccs.rutgers.edu/roa.html.

—— (1995b). 'Computational Optimality Theory'. Dissertation, Dept. of Computer Science, University of Colorado at Boulder. Also in Rutgers Optimality Archive ROA-90, http: //rucs.rutgers.edu/roa.html.

Yablo, S. (1992). 'Mental causation', *Philosophical Review* **101** (2): 245–80.

4

Expressing Phonetic Naturalness in Phonology

SCOTT MYERS

In comparing sound patterns across languages, a phonologist develops a sense of what patterns are 'natural', in that they occur frequently in the world's languages, and what patterns are 'unnatural', in that they are unlikely to occur. In many cases, we would agree that what distinguishes a natural pattern from an unnatural one is that the former is phonetically natural, in that it corresponds to a phonetic pattern. In this chapter I will argue that Optimality Theory (OT: Prince and Smolensky 1993) is better able than traditional derivational models to express the correspondence between phonetically natural phonological patterns and their phonetic counterparts. This makes OT better suited than derivational models to distinguish natural phonological patterns from unnatural ones.

Consider, for example, the process of nasal place assimilation, in which a nasal must match a following consonant in place of articulation. This is one of the most widespread sound patterns in the world's languages. It occurs, for example, in English, as in (1), and in the Bantu language Chichewa, as in (2):

(1) English: Negative *in-* ~ *im-*
    in-ordinate **in**-direct **im**-possible **im**-balance

(2) Chichewa: Class 9/10 *n-* ~ *m-* ~ *ŋ-*
    n-seko 'laughter (Class 9/10)' cf. -seka 'laugh'
    m-badwá 'native (Class 9/10)' cf. -badwa 'be born'
    ŋ-gwázi 'fighter (Class 9/10)' cf. -gwaza 'stab'

In English, the Level 1 negative prefix *in-* ~ *im-* is produced with a labial nasal when it occurs before a labial consonant, and otherwise with an alveolar nasal (Borowsky 1986).[1] In Chichewa, any sequence of a nasal and a following tautosyllabic consonant must be homorganic.

---

[1] The categorical pattern of nasal place assimilation discussed here is to be distinguished from the gestural overlap that in faster speech rate leads frequently to perceived assimilation, e.g. the *n* in *seven plus seven* being heard as *m* (Browman and Goldstein 1990). The gestural overlap is optional, gradient, rate-dependent, and insensitive to morphological categories. The place assimilation illustrated in (1), on the other hand is obligatory, categorical, independent of rate, and restricted to Level 1 forms.

In a derivational framework, this pattern can be represented with a rule that spreads Place, as in (3). But while this rule adequately derives the appropriate forms, it does not tell us anything about what a natural pattern of place assimilation looks like.

There are strong tendencies in place assimilation across languages (cf. Mohanan 1993). First, *place assimilation tends to be regressive*. It is the first consonant that assimilates to the second, as in (3), rather than vice versa, as in (4a). Second, *nasal is the unmarked target for place assimilation*. If a non-nasal consonant assimilates in place to a following consonant, then a nasal consonant in such a position does so as well. Thus we would not expect to find place assimilation requiring the target to be non-nasal, as in (4b), and it is relatively rare for the target to be unrestricted, as in (4c). Third, *coronal consonants are more likely targets than non-coronals* (Mohanan 1993; Kim 1995). Generally, if the target is restricted to one place of articulation, it will be coronal. Fourth, *nasal place assimilation is unmarked*. A language that allows nasal + consonant clusters generally has some form of nasal place assimilation.

As Mohanan (1993) points out, it is impossible just by examining rules such as those in (3) and (4) to distinguish the natural from the unnatural. The unnatural processes in (4a) and (4b) are no more formally complex than the natural and common process in (3). Nor do these unnatural processes violate any general constraints on rule application or rule formulation. Examination of the rules and representations, then, cannot explain the typological trends in nasal place assimilation. Furthermore, it cannot answer the basic question as to why there should be such a process in the first place. McCarthy (1988: 86) suggests that nasal place assimilation is common because it is formally simple:

(3)

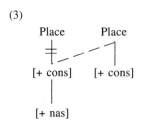

(4)

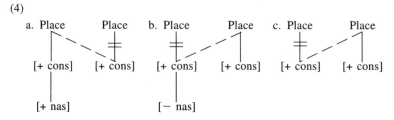

the insertion of a single association line. But a grammar without any such rule is yet simpler.

We can, on the other hand, explain a lot about nasal place assimilation by looking at it as a phonetically natural process. From this perspective, nasal place assimilation is common because it reflects the pervasive phonetic phenomenon of coarticulation (i.e. gestural overlap). Browman and Goldstein (1990) demonstrate some of the effects of gestural overlap in consonant clusters in X-ray data for the phrase *seven plus seven*. They show that in faster speech the labial closure for the /p/ in *plus* can overlap the tongue-tip closure for the /n/ in *seven* to the extent that acoustic cues for the /n/ are masked and it is perceived as labial [m̩]. Gestural overlap leads in this case to a perceived assimilation, which could lead language learners to posit a regular assimilation process. The perceptual confusion brought about by gestural overlap accounts for the existence of place assimilation.

The typological tendencies in nasal place assimilation discussed above can also be seen to reflect phonetic tendencies. Take, for example, the tendency for the first consonant to lose its place specification, rather than the second. Kohler (1990) and Ohala (1990) suggest that this is related to the fact that place cues are more robust in the CV transition than in the VC transition. Fujimura et al. (1978) and Ohala (1990) show that errors in the identification of place are more common for the first consonant in a cluster than for the second. The first consonant in a cluster tends to lose its place specification because listeners are often confused as to what its place specification is.

Next, consider the fact that a nasal is the most common target for place assimilation. Kohler (1990) suggests that the targets of place assimilation generally belong to consonant classes that have highly confusable place cues. The place of articulation of nasals is particularly difficult to identify, as evidenced by the fact that listeners tend to confuse the nasals with each other (Miller and Nicely 1955). Hura et al. (1992) found that errors in the identification of place in the first consonant of a consonant cluster are most frequent when that consonant is nasal.

The target of nasal place assimilation is also frequently restricted to coronals (Mohanan 1993; Kim 1995). Browman and Goldstein (1990: 362) point out that because coronal gestures are quick, they are the most likely gestures to be hidden when overlapped by adjacent gestures. Byrd (1994) found in an electropalatographic study of consonant clusters that coronal stops in the first position in a cluster tended to be overlapped for their entire duration, a significantly higher percentage of overlap than with non-coronal gestures in the same position. Byrd (1992) and Kim (1995) show that this susceptibility to overlap leads to greater confusion with respect to place if the first consonant in a cluster is coronal.

We see, then, that the natural phonological pattern of nasal place assimilation corresponds in detail to phonetic patterns. Such correspondences account for the existence of the pattern, as well as the cross-linguistically common conditions on its application. The natural patterns of place assimilation are the ones that correspond to phonetic patterns.

Phonetic explanations are available for many natural phonological patterns (Stampe 1979; Lindblom 1983; Ohala 1983; Archangeli and Pulleyblank 1994). Phonological nasalization of a vowel next to a nasal, for example, corresponds to the phonetic pattern of velic coarticulation (Cohn 1993). Phonological closed-syllable shortening corresponds to the phonetic fact that vowels are shorter in closed syllables than in open syllables (Maddieson 1985). Phonological palatalization in English (e.g. *confess* vs. *confession*) corresponds to gradient postlexical palatalization as in *confess your* (Zsiga 1995). Phonological vowel reduction corresponds to phonetic undershoot (Lindblom 1963). In all these cases, understanding why the phonological pattern is the way it is involves looking outside the grammar into the areas of speech production, perception, and processing.

However, there have been some fundamental problems with such phonetic explanations of phonological patterns. Phonetic explanations can explain why phonological patterns are the way they are, but they cannot account for the *regularity*, *categoriality*, or *language-specificity* of those patterns.

Consider first the issue of regularity. Phonetic explanations of sound patterns are based on statistical tendencies. There tend to be more errors of identification of place in nasals and in codas than in other contexts, but of course there are also many cases in which listeners correctly identify place in these contexts. Phonological nasal place assimilation, on the other hand, is often absolutely obligatory and exceptionless, as in the case of Chichewa. It is automatically applied to novel forms by Chichewa speakers, and forms that violate the assimilatory pattern are not considered to be Chichewa. The perceptual tendencies by themselves do not suffice to account for this.

Second, phonetic explanations are based on gradient phenomena, while phonological patterns are categorical. The gestural overlap that is the basis of the phonetic account of nasal place assimilation is gradient, but the assimilation itself is categorical. The coronal gesture of /n/ in *seven plus seven* can be more or less overlapped, depending mainly on speech rate. The assimilated labial nasal in *impossible*, on the other hand, is not partly labial, but rather is fully labial at all speech rates, just like any underlying labial. The assimilation cannot be reduced to gestural overlap.

Third, phonetic explanations of sound patterns are based on universal generalizations about human articulation and perception, but phonological patterns vary from language to language. In Chichewa, for example, the nasal + consonant cluster in nasal place assimilation must be tautosyllabic, and in English it must be within a Level 1 construction (cf. the unassimilated clusters in *non-professional* and *nine people*). These details clearly do not follow from any general phonetic considerations, yet they are essential aspects of these nasal place assimilation patterns.

In general, phonetic explanations of phonological patterns fail to the extent that they fail to recognize a distinction between phonetics and phonology (Pierrehumbert and Beckman 1988; Cohn 1993; Sproat and Fujimura 1993). A phonological pattern is a pattern in the distribution of phonetic targets in a language, while a phonetic pattern is a pattern in the ranges of realizations associated with a target. There is often a strong correspondence between the two sorts of pattern, but they are not the same.

In this chapter I will argue that Optimality Theory provides a way to bridge this gap between phonetic explanations and phonetically natural phonological patterns. Derivational models cannot capture this relation, and therefore cannot provide an adequate model of phonetically natural patterns in phonology.

My proposal is that in OT it is possible to incorporate phonetic general-izations directly into the phonological constraint hierarchy. In Section 1, I discuss some crucial assumptions about the nature of phonological representa-tions and constraints. In Section 2, I introduce the notion of a phonetic constraint, and show how it can be used in the evaluation of phonological representations. I illustrate the approach by applying it to two phonetically natural phonological patterns: nasal place assimilation and tonal dissimilation. I compare this approach to other accounts in Section 3.

For the body of the chapter, I will be discussing how to express the correspondence between phonetic patterns and phonological patterns in the case of phonetically natural rules such as nasal place assimilation. I will postpone until Section 4 the controversial issue of how much of phonology is phonetically natural.

1. BACKGROUND ASSUMPTIONS

1.1 *Phonological representations as phonetic objects*

The pervasive assumption in generative phonology (whether derivational or constraint-based) is that phonological representations are objects of the gram-mar which must be translated into phonetic events. The feature [voice], for example, is assumed to be an element of the formal language of representa-tions. The phonological grammar of a language generates outputs that include specifications of [voice], which are then the input to phonetic implementation: a mapping from phonological representations to articulatory and/or acoustic events. According to this view, phonological representations are relatable to phonetic events, but they are not themselves phonetic.

Such an assumption, though, makes it difficult to account for the extensive correspondences between phonetic and phonological patterns, since it means that the two domains have little formal vocabulary in common. An alternative view, which I will adopt, is that a phonological representation is a phonetic object, and the elements of a phonological representation are phonetic *targets* (Lindblom 1963; Lindblom et al. 1979; Browman and Goldstein 1990; Perkell et al. 1995). A target is an articulatory configuration (or auditory state) that is the goal of articulatory movements, corresponding to the configuration (or state) that would be reached if sufficient time is allowed and sufficient effort is expended. The target value for a voiced sound, for example, is vocal-fold vibration (or low-frequency pulsing). Achievement of this goal in an oral stop often requires expansion of the supraglottal vocal tract through lowering of the larynx and advancement of the tongue root (Westbury 1983). In a vowel, on the other hand, these supraglottal gestures are unnecessary. The goal is the same in both cases, but the means differ.

A great deal of evidence has accumulated that articulatory gestures are defined in terms of targets. Lindblom et al. (1979) had speakers produce vowels while holding small wooden blocks between their teeth, preventing normal jaw movement. Speakers normally distinguish low vowel from high vowels mainly through the degree of jaw opening (Johnson et al. 1993). But in the bite-block condition, with immobilized jaw, speakers were able to produce the same distinction easily by raising and lowering the tongue body with respect to the jaw. This yielded an acoustically normal vowel, produced in an abnormal way. What was constant between the normal and the bite-block vowels was the vocal-tract area function (i.e. place and degree of constriction) for each vowel. The articulatory movements used to produce that configuration were quite different in the two conditions.

Studies of undershoot (Lindblom 1963) have shown that under some conditions the target value is not reached. According to Lindblom (1990), there need only be as much movement toward the target value as to allow discrimination of the lexical item being produced from other possible lexical items. The target value for a low vowel, for example, is approximated by the high value of F1 that is approached asymptotically in realizations of low vowels as speech gets slower and more careful. Johnson et al. (1993) suggest that the target values for vowels are never actually attained in production, and are directly measurable only in perception tasks.

The assumption that the phonological representation consists of phonetic targets makes it easier to make connections between phonetics and phonology, since they now share the same basic vocabulary. Lexical items are represented in memory in terms of arrays of targets for various phonetic dimensions. The business of phonology, then, is the selection of the appropriate array of phonetic targets for each utterance.

1.2 *Constraints in optimality theory*

In Optimality Theory (Prince and Smolensky 1993; McCarthy and Prince 1994; 1995), a set of universal operations (GEN) maps a given input representation to a large set of potential outputs. These candidate outputs are evaluated against a ranked set of constraints, and the one that best satisfies the constraints is selected as the actual output.

A crucial interaction is between the constraints on output representations and the *Faithfulness* constraints (McCarthy and Prince 1995). These constraints express the conservative tendency for phonological forms to remain constant from context to context. Two critical Faithfulness constraints are MAX-IO and DEP-IO, which govern the relation between input (I) and output (O):

(5) a. MAX-IO (X): An element X in the input must have a correspondent in the output.

b. DEP-IO (X): An element X in the output must have a correspondent in the input.

MAX-IO forbids deletion, while DEP-IO forbids insertion. Deletion or insertion occurs only if one of these constraints is crucially dominated by a constraint on output representations.

A constraint in OT is a function from phonological representations to violations. In actual practice, constraints are often formulated as prose statements to the effect that a representation must or must not have a certain property. The constraint ONS (Prince and Smolensky 1993), for example, is stated as 'Syllables must have onsets'. The Obligatory Contour Principle (McCarthy 1986) is stated as 'Adjacent identical elements are prohibited'. These are not obviously functions, but rather are statements about representations.

How do we derive violations from such statements? Each such statement can be reduced to a statement that some configuration X is bad, or that X has a cost. The implicit convention is that for each instance of X in a representation being evaluated there is a violation of the constraint. The Obligatory Contour Principle, for example, is violated by each pair of elements that are adjacent and identical. The positively formulated ONS is violated by every syllable that lacks an onset.

The consequences of a constraint violation are not built into the statement, but are determined by constraint ranking. Moreover, it is irrelevant to the function of the constraint '*X*' *why* X has a cost, i.e. what the problem with X is. All that we need to know is that there is a statement that X for some reason or other is undesirable.

Given the assumption that phonological representations consist of phonetic targets (Section 1.1.), a constraint in OT can be seen as a statement that a given array of phonetic targets is undesirable for some reason. Conversely, any such statement has a coherent interpretation as an OT constraint. This equivalence is the basis of my analysis of correspondences between phonetic and phonological patterns.

2. MODELLING CORRESPONDENCES BETWEEN PHONETICS AND PHONOLOGY

We have been considering statements that a given sort of phonetic target has a cost. Such statements are not limited to phonology, but also play an important role in phonetics, especially in the 'H&H' (Hypo- and Hyper-) model of Lindblom (1990). Lindblom characterizes a scale of speech situations according to the relative importance of the discriminability of the message versus the expenditure of effort by the speaker. These two criteria are opposed to each other in that discriminability can only be enhanced by expending more effort on careful and forceful articulation, while articulatory effort can only be reduced at the cost of some loss of discriminability. Lindblom's proposal is that speakers continually monitor just how clear they must be, in view of the information assumed to be shared by the speaker and the listener, and that they expend the minimal articulatory effort to attain that sufficient level of clarity.

Such a strategy is typical of goal-directed behavior. To pick up an object on a table, for example, we move the hand that is closest to the object, unless that hand is full or less suited than the other hand. By the time we are adults, we have become quite efficient at subconsciously calculating the most efficient way to move toward our habitual goals.

To act in this way in producing speech, a speaker must be aware of the relative physiological costs of various articulatory gestures. Willerman (1994) provides a model of the physiological factors that make up 'articulatory cost' (see also Lindblom 1990; Lindblom and Maddieson 1988). Willerman points out that there is a physiological cost to (*a*) displacements of the articulators from neutral position, (*b*) fine temporal or spatial control, or (*c*) fractionation of an articulator into independent areas. Willerman uses such factors to derive patterns of markedness in segment inventories. We can express this knowledge in the form of statements that 'X is difficult to produce', where X is a target vocal-tract configuration.

Speakers have a corresponding knowledge of the relative discriminability of speech sounds. Moon (1991) shows that speakers asked to speak carefully reorganize their articulations so as to maximize the auditory distance among their different vowels, by minimizing undershoot and gestural overlap. Guion (1995) finds that vowels in more frequently occurring words are more reduced and less distinct from other vowels than in less frequently used words. More frequent items are known to be more discriminable than less frequent items, as evidenced by the fact that listeners access more frequent lexical items more quickly and with fewer errors than they do less frequent items. Guion argues that speakers adjust the level of effort in their productions to reflect the difference that frequency of occurrence makes in the listener's ability to discriminate items.To do this, the speaker must know which targets are less discriminable than others. This knowledge can be expressed in the form of statements that 'target configuration X is difficult to discriminate from other target configurations'.

Statements of the form 'X is difficult to articulate' or 'X is difficult to discriminate' are extralinguistic statements about the limitations of one's body. Statements about the difficulty of a speech-oriented gesture are part of the same body of knowledge that allows one to judge that it would be wiser to walk across the room than to try to leap across it. Statements about the difficulty of perceiving a speech sound are part of the same body of knowledge that convinces one that one's stereo speakers need repair.

But such statements also have exactly the same form as the OT constraints discussed in Section 1.2. Both these phonetic statements and the conventional OT constraints are statements that a given target configuration has a cost. Thus, given the interpretive convention for constraints in the form of a statement, discussed in Section 1.2, the phonetic statements are straightforwardly interpretable as OT constraints. If such a phonetic statement is incorporated into the hierarchy of constraints, it can have a role in determining target configurations and inducing phonological patterns. Phonetic factors can be included among the criteria according to which targets are selected. Phonological patterns can correspond to phonetic patterns because some constraints on phonological representations are drawn directly from phonetic knowledge.

I will now illustrate how this approach works by applying it to two phonetically natural phonological patterns: nasal place assimilation (Section 2.1) and tonal dissimilation (Section 2.2). The approach involves interpreting phonetic generalizations as OT constraints, and ranking them with respect to the Faithfulness constraints.

2.1. *An analysis of nasal-place assimilation*

The first phonetic generalization mentioned in the introduction with respect to nasal-place assimilation was that in a consonant cluster the place cues of the first consonant are harder to discriminate than those of the second consonant. Another way of putting this is to say that place cues are relatively difficult to discriminate if they are on an unreleased consonant, i.e. a consonant that is not immediately followed by a sound with a more open articulation, such as a vowel:

(6) ALIGN-CV: Place of a consonant that isn't immediately before a more open articulation is difficult (to distinguish).

It is more difficult to identify place of articulation in nasals than in other consonant classes. Monitoring one's own performance in speech perception, one could make the following observation:

(7) *PL/NAS: Place exclusively associated with nasal is difficult (to distinguish).

It is important that place of articulation is not difficult to identify if it is shared between a nasal and a following consonant. Listeners will take a cue wherever they find it, and if the same place is distributed over more than one segment, that just gives the listener more chances to find a usable acoustic cue.

The target consonant in place assimilation must be *both* nasal *and* in coda position. In other words, to be bad enough to warrant changing the representation, a form must combine both perceptual disadvantages. A nasal in onset position or a non-nasal in coda position each has just one perceptual problem and remains unchanged. To capture the fact that it is only the combination that is fatal, we use the notion of local constraint conjunction (Smolensky 1994: 8).

(8) If there is a constraint *X and a constraint *Y, then the conjoined constraint *X-&^{A}- *Y is violated only if the same element A violates both *X and *Y.

ALIGN-CV is violated by coda-place specifications, and *PL/NAS by nasal-place specifications. Thus the conjoined constraint ALIGN-CV-&*PL/NAS is violated only by place specifications in coda nasals, but not by those in non-nasal codas or in onset nasals.

In nasal-place assimilation, the place specification of the first consonant is lost.[2] This is a violation of the Faithfulness condition MAX-IO (Pl):

(9) MAX-IO (Pl): A place target in the input must have a correspondent in the output.

This constraint forbids deletion of place specifications. The actual output in cases of nasal place assimilation has deletion of a place specification, so ALIGN-CV-&*PL/NAS must dominate MAX-IO (Pl). It is a higher priority to avoid exclusive nasal coda place specifications than it is to keep all place specifications.

We must account for the fact that the nasal not only loses its own place specification but also gains that of the following consonant. This means that an output with a place specification is preferred over one that lacks a specification. One reason for this could be that such a placeless nasal would be difficult to distinguish from other nasals. This can be formulated as in (10):[3]

(10) SPECIFY (Pl): A segment without a Place target is difficult (to distinguish).

---

[2] We assume a fully specified input. In some analyses, the nasal in this position is said to be systematically underspecified for place, so that place assimilation is always feature-filling. The principle that ensures this context-sensitive underspecification will be equivalent in effect to a neutralization process.
[3] There would not be any articulatory problem with a placeless nasal. The positions of the articulators would be determined by coarticulation with neighbouring sounds, as in the case of placeless /h/.

This constraint dominates the Faithfulness constraint DEP-IO (A), which forbids the insertion of an association line.

(11) DEP-IO (A): An association in the output must correspond to an association in the input.

Thus Place specifications do not spread except to fill the Place of a consonant that would otherwise be placeless. DEP-IO (A) must be dominated by DEP-IO (Pl), which forbids the insertion of a place specification, to ensure that the best way to get a place specification is by spread rather than insertion.

The neutralization of place in coda position is due to the ranking ALIGN-CV-&*Pl/Nas >> MAX-IO (Pl), while the assimilation is due to the ranking SPECIFY (Pl) >> DEP-IO (A). This is illustrated in tableau (12), which shows the evaluation of an input $n + pV$, as in *impossible*, or $n + bV$, as in (2).[4]

(12) Input: Cor Lab

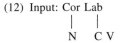

Candidates	ALIGN-CV & *PL/NAS	SPECIFY (Pl)	DEP-IO (A)	MAX-IO (Pl)
a. Cor Lab | | N C V	* (Cor) *! * (Cor)			
b. Lab | N C V		*!		*
c. ☞ Lab /\ N C V			*	*

Candidate (12a) is identical to the input, so it is the one that best obeys the Faithfulness constraints DEP-IO (A) and MAX-IO (Pl). But the coronal node

---

[4] In OT tableaux, candidate representations are listed in random order in the leftmost column, while constraints are arranged left to right in order of dominance. An asterix in the i-th row and the j-th column indicates a violation of the j-th constraint in the i-th candidate. The pointing finger indicates the optimal candidate. An exclamation point indicates a fatal violation, and shading indicates that the violations in that box are irrelevant, the choice of candidate having been decided by a higher constraint. In the case of conjoined constraints, the violations of the individual conjunct constraints are shown below the name of the conjunct (e.g. ALIGN-CV in (12)), in the bottom half of the box. Violations of the conjoined constraint (e.g. ALIGN-CV-&-*PL/NAS) are shown in the top half of the box below the ampersand.

in this candidate violates *both* ALIGN-CV (since it is not before a more open articulation) *and* *PL/NAS (since it is exclusively associated with a nasal). It therefore violates the conjoined constraint ALIGN-CV-&*PL/NAS, the highest-ranked constraint, and is less optimal than (12c), which does not violate this constraint. Candidate (12b) violates SPECIFY (Pl), because it has a consonant with no place specification. It is therefore less optimal than candidate (12c), which obeys this constraint. The optimal candidate, then, is (12c), with assimilation of the nasal to the following consonant.[5]

The optimal output for a nasal + consonant cluster in the input is a cluster in which one place specification is shared between the two consonants. This satisfies ALIGN-CV, *PL/NAS, and SPECIFY (Pl). However, so far no constraint ensures that it is the place of the second consonant that endures rather than the first. Thus the incorrect output *nt in (12), e.g. *intossible, would satisfy the constraints as well as the actual *mp*. ALIGN-CV establishes that it is the second consonant in a cluster that is easier to perceive, but we have to capture the fact that it is the more easily perceived place specification that is preserved. To express this, we link ALIGN-CV to a Faithfulness constraint of the CONTIGUITY family (Kenstowicz 1994; McCarthy and Prince 1995), which requires that adjacency relations be preserved.

(13) CONTIGUITY-OI: If two elements a and b are adjacent in the output, then their input correspondents f(a) and f(b) are also adjacent.

This constraint is violated if two elements are juxtaposed in the output which were not juxtaposed in the input. The constraint needs to be linked with ALIGN-CV because the sequence that is preserved is exactly the one specified by ALIGN-CV: a consonantal place specification followed by a more open articulation.

We link the two constraints through a relation proposed and motivated by Hewitt and Crowhurst (forthcoming), which we will refer to as disjunction.[6] A disjoined constraint is violated if either of the disjunct constraints is violated by a designated class of elements.

(14) If there is a constraint *X and a constraint *Y, then the disjoined constraint *X-$\vee^A$-*Y is violated iff the set of elements A violates either *X or *Y.

---

[5] These constraints apply to a nasal + consonant cluster in phrase-final position only if it is systematically released. There are presumably further constraints reflecting the specific perceptual challenges of utterance-final unreleased consonants (Householder 1956), which are involved in cases of place assimilation in utterance-final clusters.

[6] Hewitt and Crowhurst refer to the relation as conjunction. Whether you call the relation conjunction or disjunction depends on what you treat as being analogous to truth in a logical truth table: constraint violation or constraint satisfaction. I am taking the statement in a constraint to be true if it corresponds to the evaluated representation, i.e. if there is a violation. Given this assumption, Hewitt and Crowhurst's relation is disjunctive.

(15) Input: Cor Lab
     | |
    N C V

Candidates	CONTIGUITY-OI-√^{CV}-ALIGN-CV &*Pl/Nas	DEP-IO (A)	MAX-IO (Pl)
a. ☞ Lab /\ N C V	*	*	*
b. Cor /\ N C V	*! *	*	*

The disjoined constraint CONTIGUITY-OI-√^{CV}-ALIGN-CV is violated if *either* the place specification of a consonant isn't followed by a more open articulation (ALIGN-CV) *or* the place specification wasn't adjacent to that articulation in the input (CONTIGUITY-OI) (see (15)). In both candidates, one of the place specifications has been deleted and the other place specification has spread to replace it. In both cases, then, the spread place specification is adjacent to an element that it was not adjacent to in the input. The labial specification in (15a) is adjacent to whatever precedes the nasal, and the coronal in (15b) is adjacent to the V following the second consonant. Therefore both candidates violate CONTIGUITY-OI. For the disjoined constraint CONTIGUITY-OI-√^{CV}-ALIGN-CV, however, the only violations that are relevant are those that involve the elements involved in ALIGN-CV, i.e. a consonantal place specification and a more open articulation that follows it. In candidate (15a), the contiguity of these two elements is preserved in the mapping from input to output, while in (15b) it is not. In (15b), the consonantal place specification that immediately precedes the following V is not the specification that was in that position in the input. This candidate therefore violates CONTIGUITY-OI-√^{CV}-ALIGN-CV, while (15a) does not. Candidate (15a) is therefore the optimal candidate.

This is a conventional OT analysis in terms of how the constraints are used to evaluate candidates (though less so in its use of constraint disjunction and conjunction). The innovative aspect of the analysis is in the origin of the constraints. The constraints on feature configurations are not taken from an a priori set of constraints on phonological representations, but rather are extralinguistic statements that are imported into the constraint hierarchy.

The core of the analysis is the set of statements about difficulties of perception. It is difficult to perceive the place of articulation of a nasal (*PL/NAS), particularly in coda position (ALIGN-CV). It is difficult to identify a consonant with no place of articulation (SPECIFY (Pl)). In a language with nasal place assimilation, these perceptual considerations outweigh the general tendency to maintain inputs as they are—a tendency represented in this case by the Faithfulness constraints MAX-IO (Pl), DEP-IO (A) and CONTIGUITY-OI. Nasal-place assimilation results from this ranking.

Itô and Mester (1994) provide an account of such neutralization of place contrasts in coda position, using the alignment constraint ALIGN-L (C-Place, σ). This elegant analysis derives the correct results, but one has to wonder why there is not a corresponding constraint ALIGN-R (C-Place, σ), which would have the opposite effect. In the phonetic constraint account, such a constraint could not exist because it would have no phonetic basis.

We can now address the problems pointed out earlier in previous phonetic explanations of phonological patterns. The first one was that nasal-place assimilation is obligatory (within the appropriate domain), although the phonetic patterns it is based on are optional tendencies. The second problem was that the phonological patterns are categorical, while their phonetic counterparts are gradient. The third problem was that different languages can have different nasal-place assimilation patterns, even though the same articulatory and perceptual factors are present in all languages.

In the OT analysis, the phonetically natural phonological patterns are obligatory, categorical, and language-specific because these are the properties of phonological patterns. Phonological patterns are obligatory in OT because each form in a language is evaluated with regard to the same constraint hierarchy, and that evaluation always selects a unique optimal form. The patterns are categorical because it is categorical targets that are evaluated, not gradient realizations. Phonological patterns vary from language to language because the constraint ranking can vary from language to language. These are general properties of phonological constraint evaluation and interaction, and they determine how a phonetic constraint is interpreted when it is imported into the phonological constraint hierarchy.

I would maintain, therefore, that this is a formalization of phonetic explanations that successfully takes into account the distinction between phonetic and phonological patterns, while allowing us to capture the correspondence between them.

2.2 *The Obligatory Contour Principle as a perceptual constraint*

The Obligatory Contour Principle (OCP: Leben 1973; 1978; McCarthy 1986) is a constraint on nonlinear representations:

(16) OCP: Adjacent identical elements are prohibited.

The OCP forbids sequences of identical elements. In the domain of tone, for example, it requires that a sequence of high-toned syllables be represented with a single high tone, as in (17b), rather than with two, as in (17a) (Kenstowicz and Kidda 1987, Hyman 1987).

(17) a. *H   H   b. H
        | | / \
        σ   σ   σ   σ

In segmental phonology, the OCP requires that a geminate stop be represented as a single consonant distributed over two timing units, rather than as a sequence of two identical stops (Prince 1984; McCarthy 1986). Phonological processes are blocked if their output would violate the OCP (McCarthy 1986; Borowsky 1986; Myers 1995).

Dissimilation can be seen as a process that takes an input that violates the OCP and turns it into an output that obeys the OCP. In Shona, for example, a sequence of syllables that in isolation is high-toned surfaces as toneless if it immediately follows a high-toned clitic (Myers 1995):

(18) a. í-*banga* cf. *bángá* 'knife'   b. vá-*sekuru* cf. *sékúru* 'grandfather'
        cop-knife   2a-grandfather
        '(it) is a knife'   'grandfather (honorific)'

     c. H   H   H
        | / \ |
        i -banga → i-banga

The input in these cases includes a sequence of two high tones, as in (17a), in violation of the OCP. By deleting the second high tone, the output is brought into conformity with the OCP, as in (18c).

In a derivational analysis, we could account for this pattern with a dissimilatory rule, as in (19).

(19) H → Ø / H ____

But such an analysis makes no connection between this process and the OCP. In such an analysis it is a coincidence that the sequence of high tones that changes in (18) is exactly the sort of sequence that is avoided in underlying representations or the output of phonological rules. Moreover, the derivational account misses the generalization that the juxtaposition of two high tones almost always induces a dissimilatory change in the Bantu languages. In Rimi, it is the left high tone that deletes. In other cases in Shona, the left high tone retracts away from the right one. In Chichewa, the right high tone retracts away to the right. What is common to all of these cases is that the output obeys the OCP.

In OT, dissimilation can be expressed through ranking the OCP above a Faithfulness constraint (Myers 1995). In Shona, we can say that the OCP dominates MAX-IO (T), as in (20):

(20) MAX-IO (T): A tone in the input must have a correspondent in the output.

MAX-IO (T) is violated any time a tone is deleted. Tones are deleted in Shona only if the OCP would otherwise be violated, therefore OCP dominates MAX-IO (T).

We can account for the fact that it is the leftmost tone that survives in Shona by relating it to the general leftward alignment of tones in the language. Floating tones, for example, are associated with the leftmost available syllable in their domain (Myers 1995). This is expressed through the constraint ALIGN-L:

(21) ALIGN-L: Every tone must be associated with the first syllable of the domain.

This constraint is dominated by MAX-IO (T), since one does not delete underlying tones that are associated with non-initial syllables.

The evaluation of example (18a) is illustrated in (22).

Candidate (22a) is less optimal than the other two because it violates the OCP, the highest ranked constraint. Candidates (22b) and (22c) both obey the OCP, and they both violate MAX-IO (T). With respect to these two constraints, then, they are equally optimal. However, the high tone in (22b) is on the leftmost available syllable, which satisfies ALIGN-L. It is therefore more optimal than (22c), with the high tone more to the right, and is the optimal candidate. Other patterns of dissimilation result if other Faithfulness constraints are dominated by the OCP (e.g. MAX-IO (Association)), or if rightward tone alignment dominates leftward tone alignment.

But why should identical adjacent elements be disfavored, i.e. why should there be an OCP? An insightful phonetic account of this dissimilatory tendency

(22) Input: H   H
        | / \
       i banga

Candidates	OCP	MAX-IO (T)	ALIGN-L
a. H H 	/ \ i banga	*!		*
b. ☞H 	 i banga		*	
c. H / \ i banga		*	*!

has been proposed by Ohala (1981; 1993), who notes that listeners compensate in speech perception for the pervasive effects of coarticulation. Dissimilation, he argues, occurs when listeners overextend this perceptual compensation.

For example, F2 of a vowel after a coronal consonant tends to be slightly higher than after a labial or velar consonant—an acoustic effect of consonant–vowel coarticulation. Ohala (1981) reports the results of a vowel-identification experiment in which listeners compensated for this coarticulatory effect: a vowel had to be more fronted to be identified as front when it occurred in the fronting context (after a coronal) than if it occurred in a non-fronting context (after a labial or velar). Ohala suggests that in the fronting context listeners attributed some of the frontness of the vowel to the context. Other evidence of perceptual compensation for coarticulatory effects was found by Mann and Repp (1980) and Kawasaki (1986).[7]

Ohala argues that speakers can make errors in this sort of perceptual compensation. If listeners hear a sequence of elements that share some acoustic property, they could decide that the property really only belongs to one of the elements and that the other has it only by virtue of coarticulation. In some dialects of Shona, for example, labiovelar *w became velar ɣ after a labial (e.g. *bw > bɣ). Ohala suggests that the labiality of the labiovelar w was attributed to the coarticulatory influence of the preceding labial, and listeners reinterpreted the labiovelar as an intended velar. In general, Ohala proposes that dissimilatory sound changes result from hypercorrection—perceptual overcompensation for distortions introduced in production.

Such an account can be applied to the case of tonal dissimilation as in (18). A toneless syllable next to a high-toned syllable has a higher f0, at least in the portion closest to the high-toned syllable, than a toneless syllable next to a toneless syllable. This is an instance of tonal coarticulation (Shen 1990). A listener confronted with a sequence of two high tones, as in (18a), could decide that only one of the syllables bears high tone, and that the other has raised f0 due to coarticulation. The result, if it was generalized and caught on in the speech community, would be a dissimilatory sound change.

One compelling aspect of this explanation of dissimilatory effects is that the proposed factors are all independently motivated. Perceptual compensation accounts not only for dissimilation, but also for other aspects of speech perception that have nothing to do with dissimilation. Indeed, such compensation is a general modality-independent phenomenon of perception. A visual counterpart is the fact that in a scene bathed in red light viewers would attribute all redness to the light, and so would have difficulty distinguishing an object that really was red.

---

[7] Lindblom and Studdert-Kenndey (1967) demonstrated perceptual compensation for undershoot, and Pierrehumbert (1979) found such a effect correcponding to f0 downtrends.

The perceptual account also goes a long way toward explaining what features are subject to dissimilation and across what distance (Ohala 1981; 1993). Generally, the targets and scope of dissimilation correspond to the targets and scope of coarticulation. Ohala notes, for example, that there are cases in a broad variety of languages in which aspiration or breathiness on a consonant is lost if the next consonant is aspirated or breathy, even if a vowel intervenes. The best known case is Grassman's Law in Indo-European, as in Proto-Indo-European *ḇenḏ > Sanskrit banḏ. This is an expected sort of dissimilation in Ohala's theory because aspirated or breathy-voiced consonants have strong coarticulatory effects on a neighbouring vowel, which could then affect the perception of an aspirated or breathy-voiced consonant on the other side of the vowel. On the other hand, there could not be dissimilation of the feature [sonorant] or [continuant] across a vowel, e.g. *bad > ban or bal, since these contrasts have no such coarticulatory effect on the intervening vowel.

The perceptual account of dissimilation is thus quite successful in explaining why dissimilation should occur, as well as some key conditions on the process. The problems with this explanation, however, are the same as in the case of nasal-place assimilation: the explanation cannot account for the fact that phonological dissimilation is obligatory and language-particular. Perceptual compensation is usually very accurate, and errors of overcompensation are only occasional. In Shona, on the other hand, tone deletion as in (18) is not an occasional error, but an obligatory alternation pattern.

I propose the same sort of solution as in the case of nasal-place assimilation: that speakers monitor their own speech and are aware of what configurations present perceptual problems. The OCP can be restated as an observation of this sort:

(23) OCP: A sequence of identical specifications is difficult (to distinguish).

According to this version of the OCP, listeners prefer to assume that identity of successive elements is due to coarticulatory sharing of properties. If this observation is incorporated into the constraint hierarchy in a position dominating MAX-IO (T) (20), then systematic dissimilatory tone deletion will result, as in (22).

The perceptual perspective can shed light on a directional asymmetry in tonal dissimilation: *when one of the two identical tones is deleted, it is usually the second one.* Given the sequence H_1H_2, the process $H_2 \rightarrow \emptyset$ is more common than $H_1 \rightarrow \emptyset$. Within Bantu, for example, H_2 is deleted in Luganda (Stevick 1969), Haya (Hyman and Byarushengo 1984: 64), Makua (Cheng and Kisseberth 1979), Venda (Cassimjee 1983), Tonga (Meeussen 1963: 74), Bemba (Sharman 1963: 101), Kirundi (Goldsmith and Sabimana 1984), CiRuri (Massamba 1984: 241), Jita (Downing 1990: 135), Chichewa (Kanerva 1989: 25), Southern Kipare (Odden 1985: 408), Llogoori (Goldsmith 1992: 77), Kihehe (Odden 1994: 309), Makonde (Odden 1994: 308), and Kikerewe

(Odden 1995). The only case in Bantu in which H_1 is regularly deleted is Rimi (Schadeberg 1979). Apart from Bantu, the second of two like tones is deleted in Moore (Kenstowicz et al. 1988: 86), Arusa (Levergood 1987: 61, 87), Margi (Pulleyblank 1986: 204), Sanskrit (Kiparsky and Halle 1977), Lithuanian (Blevins 1993: 245), Japanese (Poser 1984: 131), and Carrier (Pike 1986: 415).[8]

I would suggest that the explanation for this asymmetry lies in the cross-linguistic tendency towards downtrends in f0. Over the course of a phrase, each successive pitch peak is lower than the previous one. Such a downward trend in f0 seems to occur in some form in all languages, though with language-particular variation in conditioning (Liberman and Pierrehumbert 1984; Poser 1984; Pierrehumbert and Beckman 1988).

The result of this trend is that high tones and low tones are closer to each other in f0 toward the end of the phrase than they are toward the beginning of the phrase. One would therefore expect tonal distinctions to be more difficult to hear the further a tone is from the beginning of the phrase. I am not aware of any experimental evidence to this effect, but it is my experience that tones are easier to transcribe toward the beginning of the phrase than toward the end. In f0 traces of Chichewa, for example, high and low tones toward the end of a longer phrase are often distinguished only by a few Hertz, if at all.

Assuming that these observations do reflect a real perceptual difficulty, we can restate the constraint ALIGN-L (21) as in (24):

(24) ALIGN-L: A high tone is more difficult (to distinguish), the further it is from the beginning of the intonational phrase.

ALIGN-L is independently motivated by the fact that it enforces the left-to-right association of tones, which has generally been taken to be the universal default directionality (Pulleyblank 1986: 11). Interpreting dissimilation as perceptually motivated, then, allows us to account for a directional asymmetry in dissimilation that seems arbitrary from a purely formalist perspective.

The perceptual account can also incorporate the findings of Berkley (1994) and Pierrehumbert (1993; 1994) that there are gradient dissimilatory effects evident in quantitative analyses of lexicons. In these studies, machine-readable dictionaries were surveyed for statistical trends in consonant sequences, comparing the number of attested sequences of a given sort to the frequency expected from the frequency of the constituent consonants. Pierrehumbert (1993) found that in Arabic roots, occurrences of similar consonants in the same root were significantly less than would be expected. Combinations of root consonants were more severely underrepresented the closer they were to

---

[8] In Haya (Hyman and Byarushengo 1984) and Sanskrit (Kiparsky and Halle 1977: 212), a lexicalized set of high-toned morphemes has the property of inducing deletion of preceding high tones. But the general rule in both languages is to delete the right tone.

each other in position, and the more similar they were to each other. Pierre-humbert modelled the effect as a gradient function of these two factors. Pierrehumbert (1994) and Berkley (1994) found similar results in studies of English consonant sequences, and conclude that the OCP, as the expression of the dissimilatory tendency, must be interpreted as a gradient statistical general-ization. But this is difficult to reconcile with the obligatory and categorical effects of dissimilation in cases such as Shona.

I would suggest instead that the trends that Pierrehumbert and Berkley have discovered reflect not the OCP directly, but rather the pattern of perceptual errors that are the source of the OCP. If listeners make sporadic errors over-compensating for coarticulation, as Ohala suggests, then there will be a general diachronic tendency to reanalyse forms with similar targets in close proximity. The result of such a tendency over time would be the skewing of the lexicon that Pierrehumbert and Berkley observe. A general obligatory dissimilation process arises when the avoidance of such perceptual errors, as embodied in (23), is incorporated into the evaluation of categorical targets. Such an account is only available, however, if the OCP is directly related to the gradient pattern of perceptual errors.

3. Comparisons

Having outlined a particular approach within OT to capturing correspondences between phonetic and phonological patterns, I will in this section clarify how it differs from other approaches. In Section 3.1 we will consider derivational models, in 3.2 an alternative constraint-based model, and in 3.3 the pure phonetic approach.

3.1 *Derivational approaches*

A derivational approach is inherently ill-equipped to incorporate phonetic insights because of its input orientation. A phonological rule is defined in derivational generative phonology in terms of a structural description and a structural change. The former defines the sort of non-surface representation that is subject to the operation, and the latter defines how such a representation is to be changed. The surface representation is a product of the set of all such operations, but nothing in a particular rule can refer directly to the surface representation. Only the phonological output has any relevance to production and perception, so the inability of phonological rules to refer to the output renders them incapable of capturing correspondences between phonetic pat-terns and phonological patterns.

Constraints in OT, on the other hand, are output-orientated. They refer to the output of all phonological processes (GEN) and to the representation that is phonetically interpreted. All OT constraints refer to the output, and only the Faithfulness constraints refer to anything else in addition to the output. OT constraints, then, are well suited to expressing phonetic patterns in phonology, since they deal with the representation that is involved in production and perception.

The particular approach to phonetic explanations of phonological patterns exemplified here is, moreover, only possible in an output-oriented model with a *declarative* format for constraints. The approach relies on the equivalence of phonetic observations and OT constraints, which is possible only because both are statements about phonetic targets. There would be no way, on the other hand, to equate a phonetic observation with either the structural description or the structural change of a phonological rule in a derivational model, since these cannot be construed as statements.

3.2 *Grounded Phonology*

Archangeli and Pulleyblank (1994) argue for the following constraint on constraints, a part of what they call the *Grounding Hypothesis*:

(25) A constraint on feature co-occurrence must be grounded. i.e. it must be phonetically motivated.

A constraint against a given combination of features is phonetically motivated if there is a phonetic explanation for why that combination of features would be problematic.

They propose, for example, the HI/ATR Condition, as in (26). This constraint accounts for the fact that high vowels tend to be [+ ATR], and contrasts in [ATR] are more marked in high vowels than in mid vowels.

(26) The HI/ATR Condition: If [+ high], then [+ ATR] and not [− ATR].

The HI/ATR Condition is grounded. They point out that raising the tongue stretches it out vertically and narrows it horizontally, pulling the tongue root forward. Raising the tongue body and advancing the tongue root are therefore an efficient combination of synergetic gestures.

Archangeli and Pulleyblank argue, as I have here, that the explanation for the distinction between natural and unnatural patterns in phonology lies outside the formal representations in the patterns of production and perception. Thus the goals and basic assumptions of their model are shared by my proposal here. But the two models differ in the conception of what a constraint is. In Grounded Phonology, a constraint is a grammatical statement about phonological representations. The connection between the constraint and the phonetic factors that ground it lies, not in the speaker's knowledge of language, but in the metatheoretical explanations as to why there should be such a constraint in Universal Grammar. The HI/ATR Condition, for example, does not itself refer to the articulatory considerations in which it is said to be grounded, and these considerations play no role in the phonological grammar. There is a systematic redundancy between the phonetic observation and the corresponding phonological constraint—both are represented independently in two separate and autonomous modules of the speaker's knowledge. It cannot be said, therefore, that the phonetic fact accounts for the phonological pattern.

In the approach advocated here, on the other hand, the phonetic observation *is* the constraint. The speaker's knowledge of what is difficult to produce or to perceive is directly incorporated into the grammar as criteria for the evaluation of potential phonological representations. There is no redundancy, since the phonological constraint is simply the phonetic observation as it is used in phonology. In this account, we can really say that the observed phonological patterns are derived from the phonetic observations and their interactions with Faithfulness. Constraints on feature co-occurrence must be phonetically grounded because they are derived from phonetic knowledge.

3.3. *Phonetic approaches*

The present account is based on the phonetic explanations for sound patterns put forward in such work as Ohala (1983) and Lindblom (1983). What this account offers is a way to extend these explanations to synchronic phonological patterns. The proposed model provides a bridge for these phonetic explanations to cross over from the domain of gradient and statistical generalizations into the domain of categorical well-formedness.

One crucial step in this account is speakers' knowledge of their physical limitations. It is statements of this sort of knowledge that are imported into the phonology and which derive phonological patterns. Of course, the physical limitations are in turn explainable in terms of physics and physiology. Listeners find it hard to identify the place of articulation of nasals because of the intensity of the resonances of the nasal cavity, and the concomitant damping of the resonances of the oral cavity. But listeners in observing the difficulty of perception in such a case are unaware of this physical background. They are only aware of their confusion in this situation.

4. FORMALISM VERSUS FUNCTIONALISM: HOW NATURAL IS PHONOLOGY?

I have proposed a means to express phonetically natural phonological patterns in a way that captures their correspondence with phonetic patterns. The argument is based on the uncontroversial presupposition that there are such phonetically natural patterns. But I have left open the broader issue of just how pervasive such phonetically natural phonology is. Are all cross-linguistically common phonological patterns phonetically natural? Or is there a residue of widespread processes for which there is no phonetic explanation?

I would hold with those who answer that all cross-linguistically common phonological patterns reflect phonetic patterns (Stampe 1979; Lindblom 1983; Ohala 1983; Archangeli and Pulleyblank 1994). According to this perspective, which we can refer to as *phonetic functionalism*, the explanation for all recurring sound patterns lies outside the grammar, in the domains of vocal tract physiology, auditory perception, and memory organization.

Within generative phonology, however, the usual approach to sound patterns has been one that can be characterized as *formalism*: the idea that the principles that shape sound patterns have to do with the structure of representations, and that the physical realization of the phonological categories is largely irrelevant to their patterning. A formalist approach is assumed in most work in both derivational and constraint-based models of generative phonology, and was the distinguishing characteristic of the structuralist school before that.

Formalist accounts are fundamentally incapable of dealing insightfully with the kind of phonetically natural patterns we have been discussing in this paper. But Anderson (1981) argues that not all phonology is phonetically natural, and that there is a significant residue of phonetically unnatural phonological patterns. He argues that the theory of phonology is concerned precisely with the phonetically unnatural residue, since it is there that one will find the specifically linguistic principles that govern sound patterns. He does not succeed, however, in delineating any such principles. He does not offer a formalist explanation for sound patterns that have no phonetic explanation. Rather, he simply establishes that some sound patterns currently have no known explanation.

We can draw no conclusion from our present ignorance—the fact that there are many sound patterns that we do not understand. In seeking insight into why phonological patterns are the way they are, it makes sense to adopt the general strategy in science of maximizing the generality of our explanations and seeking explanations based on independently motivated factors. This is the basis of phonetic functionalism—to seek non-ad hoc explanations for phonological patterns, by looking for factors that also explain other things as well as the patterns we are focusing on. As Lindblom (forthcoming) expresses it: 'Derive language from non-language!'

Consider the Faithfulness constraints, for example. These have been treated here as being formal axioms. Yet they can be conceived of as governing the correspondence between different memory representations, for example, between related lexical items (McCarthy 1995; Benua 1995). Under this interpretation, the Faithfulness constraints require that related items resemble each other as much as possible. These constraints are violable, so that *in-* and *im-* in English can be recognized as being instances of the same negative morpheme. But the general rule is that, if there is not a strong resemblance between two forms, they can't be instances of the same morpheme.

Such a requirement that there be a correspondence among the various instantiations of a category is not limited to phonology, but is crucial to the formation and maintenance of *any* cognitive category. We accept all sorts of different creatures as belonging to the category 'bird', for example, on the basis of certain correspondences among them in anatomy and behavior. Such correspondences are violable, in that not all birds fly and not all birds have feathers, but generally we will not classify something as a bird unless it has strong resemblances to previous birds we have encountered. Faithfulness can be seen as a special case of this general principle of correspondence of tokens within a type.

Hayes (1995) appeals to grammar-external factors in his discussion of the Iambic–Trochaic Law. According to this principle, iambic feet (unstressed— STRESSED) are canonically uneven in quantity, with the stressed syllable longer and heavier than the unstressed syllable. Trochaic feet (STRESSED— unstressed), on the other hand, are canonically even in quantity. This asymmetry is supported both by stress typology and by quantity alternations (Prince 1990; Hayes 1995). Hayes relates this tendency in the grouping of syllables to general tendencies in rhythmic grouping, extending beyond language. He notes, for example, that, in experiments where beats alternate in duration but not intensity, subjects asked to group the beats tended to group them iambically: short–long (Woodrow 1951). But subjects asked to do the same for beats alternating only in intensity group them trochaically: loud–soft. It is not clear at this point what is responsible for this rhythmic tendency, but it is clear that it is not limited to language.

Cases such as these suggest that functionalist approaches to language structure, if they are formalized sufficiently to make precise predictions, can go a long way toward distinguishing possible phonological systems from impossible ones.

REFERENCES

Anderson, S. (1981). 'Why phonology isn't natural', *Linguistic Inquiry* **12**: 493–540.
Archangeli, D., and Pulleyblank, D. (1994). *Grounded Phonology*. Cambridge, Mass.: MIT, Press.
Benua, L. (1995). 'Identity effects in morphological truncation', in J. N. Beckman, L. W. Dickey, and S. Urbanczyk (eds.), *Papers in Optimality Theory* (University of Massachusetts Occasional Papers 18). Amherst: GLSA, 77–136.
Berkley, D. (1994). 'Variability in obligatory contour effects', *Chicago Linguistic Society* **38**(2): 1–12.

Blevins, J. (1993). 'A tonal analysis of Lithuanian nominal accent', *Language* **69**: 237–73.

Borowsky T. (1986). *Topics in the Lexical Phonology of English*. New York: Garland Press.

Browman, C., and Goldstein, L. (1990). 'Tiers in articulatory phonology, with some implications for casual speech', in J. Kingston and M. Beckman (eds.), *Papers in Laboratory Phonology I: Between the Grammar and Physics of Speech*. Cambridge: Cambridge University Press, 341–76.

Byrd, D. (1992). 'Perception of assimilation in consonant clusters: a gestural model', *Phonetica* **49**: 1–24.

—— (1994). *Articulatory Timing in English Consonant Sequences*. UCLA Working Papers in Phonetics 86. Los Angeles: UCLA Phonetics Laboratory.

Cassimjee, F. (1983). 'An autosegmental analysis of Venda nominal tonology', *Studies in the Linguistic Sciences* **13**: 43–72.

Cheng, C.-C., and Kisseberth, C. (1979). 'Ikorovere Makua tonology', *Studies in the Linguistic Sciences* **1**: 31–63.

Cohn, A. (1993). 'Nasalization in English: phonology or phonetics', *Phonology* **10**: 43–82.

Downing, L. (1990). 'Problems in Jita Tonology'. Dissertation, University of Illinois, Urbana.

Fujimura, O., Macchi, M., and Streeter, L. (1978). 'Perception of stop consonants with conflicting transitional cues: a cross-linguistic study', *Language and Speech* **21**: 337–46.

Goldsmith, J. (1992). 'Tone and accent in Llogoori', in D. Brentari, G. Larson, and L. MacLeod (eds.), *The Joy of Grammar*. Amsterdam: John Benjamins, 73–94.

—— and Sabimana, F. (1984). 'The Kirundi verb', in F. Jouannet (ed.), *Modèles en tonologie (Kirundi et Kinyarwanda)*. Paris: Éditions du Centre National de la Recherche Scientifique, 19–62.

Guion, S. (1995). 'Frequency effects among homonyms', *Texas Linguistic Forum* **35**: 103–16.

Hayes, B. (1995). *Metrical Stress Theory: Principles and Case Studies*. Chicago: University of Chicago Press.

Hewitt, M., and Crowhurst, M. (1996) 'Conjunctive Constraints and Templates in Optimality Theory', *North Eastern Linguistics Society* **26**: 101–15.

Householder, F. (1956). 'Unreleased PTK in American English', in M. Halle, H. Lunt, H. McLean, and C. Schooneveld (eds.), *For Roman Jakobson*. The Hague: Mouton, 235–44.

Hura, S., Lindblom, B., and Diehl, R. (1992). 'On the role of perception in shaping phonological assimilation rules'. *Language and Speech* **35**: 59–72.

Hyman, L. (1987). 'Prosodic domains in Kukuya', *Natural Language and Linguistic Theory* **5**: 311–33.

—— and Byarushengo, E. (1984). 'A Model of Haya Tonology', in G. Clements and J. Goldsmith (eds.), *Autosegmental Studies in Bantu Tone*. Dordrecht: Foris, 53–104.

Itô, J., and Mester, A. (1994). 'Realignment', paper presented at the Utrecht Prosodic Morphology Workshop.

Johnson, K., Flemming, E., and Wright, R. (1993). 'The hyperspace effect: phonetic targets are hyperarticulated', *Language* **69**: 505–28.

—— Ladefoged, P., and Lindau, M. (1993). 'Individual differences in vowel production', *Journal of the Acoustical Society of America* **94**: 701–14.

Kanerva, J. (1989). *Focus and Phrasing in Chichewa Phonology*. New York: Garland.

Kawasaki, H. (1986). 'Phonetic explanation for phonological universals: the case of distinctive vowel nasalization', in J. Ohala and J. Jaeger (eds.), *Experimental Phonology*. Orlando, Fla.: Academic Press, 81–103.

Kenstowicz, M. (1994). 'Syllabification in Chukchee: a Constraints-Based Analysis', available by ftp from Rutgers Optimality Archive.

—— and Kidda, M. (1987). 'The obligatory contour principle and Tangale tonology', in D. Odden (ed.), *Current Approaches to African Linguistics*, 4. Dordrecht: Foris.

—— Nikiema, E., and Ourso, M. (1988). 'Tonal polarity in two Gur languages', *Studies in the Linguistic Sciences* **18**: 77–103.

Kim, S. (1995). 'Coronal/non-coronal asymmetry in place assimilation', *Texas Linguistic Forum* **35**: 153–72.

Kiparsky, P., and Halle, M. (1977). 'Towards a Reconstruction of the Indo-European Accent', in L. Hyman (ed.), *Studies in Stress and Accent, Southern California Occasional Papers in Linguistics 4*. Los Angeles: University of Southern California, 209–38.

Kohler, K. (1990). 'Segmental reduction in connected speech in German: phonological facts and phonetic explanation', in W. Hardcastle and A. Marchal (eds.), *Speech Production and Speech Modelling*. Dordrecht: Kluwer, 69–92.

Leben, W. (1973). *Suprasegmental Phonology*. New York: Garland.

—— (1978). 'The representation of tone', in V. Fromkin (ed.), *Tone: A Linguistic Survey*. New York: Academic Press, 177–220.

Levergood, B. (1987). 'Topic in Arusa Phonology and Morphology'. Dissertation, University of Texas at Austin.

Liberman, M., and Pierrehumbert, J. (1984). 'Intonational invariance under changes in pitch range and length', in M. Aronoff and R. Oehrle (eds.), *Language Sound Structure*. Cambridge, Mass: MIT Press, 157–233.

Lindblom, B. (1963). 'Spectrographic study of vowel reduction', *Journal of the Acoustical Society of America* **35**: 1773–81.

—— (1983). 'Economy of speech gestures', in P. MacNeilage (ed.), *The Production of Speech*. New York: Springer, 217–45.

—— (1990). 'Explaining phonetic variation: a sketch of the H&H Theory', in W. Hardcastle and A. Marchal (eds.), *Speech Production and Speech Modelling*. Dordrecht: Kluwer, 403–39.

—— (forthcoming). 'The study of speech sounds', in B. Lindblom, P. MacNeilage, and M. Studdert-Kennedy, (eds.), *Evolution of Spoken Language*. Orlando, Fla.: Academic Press.

—— Lubker, J., and Gay, T. (1979). 'Formant frequencies of some fixed-mandible vowels and a model of speech motor programming by predictive simulation', *Journal of Phonetics* **7**: 147–61.

—— and Maddieson, I. (1988). 'Phonetic universals in consonant systems', in

L. Hyman and C. Li (eds.), *Language, Speech and Mind: Studies in Honor of Victoria A. Fromkin*. London: Routledge, 62–78.

—— and Studdert-Kennedy, M. (1967). 'On the role of formant transitions in vowel recognition', *Journal of the Acoustical Society of America* **42**: 830–43.

McCarthy, J. (1986). 'OCP effects: gemination and antigemination', *Linguistic Inquiry* **17**: 207–64.

—— (1988). 'Feature geometry and dependency: a review'. *Phonetica* **43**: 84–108.

—— (1995). 'Extensions of Faithfulness: Rotuman revisited'. University of Massachusetts, Amherst. Available by ftp from Rutgers Optimality Archive.

—— and Prince, A. (1994). 'The emergence of the unmarked', *North East Linguistic Society* **24**: 333–79.

—— —— (1995). 'Faithfulness and reduplicative identity', in J. Beckman, S. Urbanczyk and L. Walsh (eds.), *Papers in Optimality Theory* (University of Massachusetts Occasional Papers 18). Amherst GLSA,: 249–384.

Maddieson, I. (1985). 'Phonetic cues to syllabification', in Victoria Fromkin (ed.), *Phonetic Linguistics*. Orlando: Academic Press, 203–22

Mann, V., and Repp, B. (1980). 'Influence of vocalic context on perception of the [ʃ]-[s] distinction', *Perception and Psychophysics* **28**: 213–28.

Massamba, D. (1984). 'Tone in Ci-Ruri', in G. Clements and J. Goldsmith (eds.), *Autosegmental Studies in Bantu Tone*. Dordrecht: Foris, 235–54.

Meeussen, A. (1963). 'Morphotonology of the Tonga verb', *Journal of African Linguistics* **2**: 72–92.

Miller, G., and Nicely, P. (1955). 'An analysis of perceptual confusions among some English consonants', *Journal of the Acoustical Society of America* **24**: 338–52.

Mohanan, K. P. (1993). 'Fields of attraction in phonology', in J. Goldsmith (ed.), *The Last Phonological Rule*. Chicago: University of Chicago Press, 61–116.

Moon, S.-J. (1991). 'An Acoustic and Perceptual Study of Undershoot in Clear and Citation-Form Speech'. Dissertation, University of Texas at Austin.

Myers, S. (1995). 'OCP Effects in Optimality Theory', Unpublished paper, University of Texas at Austin.

Odden, D. (1985). 'An accentual approach to tone in Kimatuumbi', in D. Goyvaerts (ed.), *African Linguistics*. Amsterdam: John Benjamins, 345–419.

—— (1994). 'Adjacency parameters in phonology', *Language* **70**: 289–330.

—— (1995). 'Verbal tone melodies in Kikerewe', paper presented at the Annual Conference on African Linguistics 26. Los Angeles: UCLA.

Ohala, J. (1981). 'The listener as a source of sound change', in C. Masek, R. Hendrick, and M. Miller (eds.), *Papers from the Parasession on Language and Behavior*. Chicago: Chicago Linguistics Society, 178–203.

—— (1983). 'The origin of sound patterns in vocal tract constraints'. in P. MacNeilage (ed.), *The Production of Speech*. New York: Springer, 189–216.

—— (1990). 'The phonetics and phonology of aspects of assimilation', in J. Kingston and M. Beckman (eds.), *Papers in Laboratory Phonology*, i: *Between the Grammar and Physics of Speech*. Cambridge: Cambridge University Press, 258–75.

—— (1993). 'The phonetics of sound change', in C. Jones (ed.), *Historical Linguistics: Problems and Perspectives*. London: Longman, 237–78.

Perkell, J., Matthies, M., Svirsky, M., and Jordan, M. (1995). 'Goal-based speech motor control: a theoretical framework and some preliminary data'. *Journal of Phonetics* **23**: 23–36.

Pierrehumbert, J. (1979). 'The perception of fundamental frequency declination', *Journal of the Acoustical Society of America* **66**: 363–9.

—— (1993). 'Dissimilarity in the Arabic verbal roots', *North East Linguistic Society* **23**: 367–81.

—— (1994). 'Syllable structure and word structure: a study of triconsonantal clusters in English', in P. Keating (ed.), *Phonological Structure and Phonetic Form: Papers in Laboratory Phonology III*. Cambridge: Cambridge University Press, 168–88.

—— and Beckman, M. (1988). *Japanese Tone Structure*. Cambridge, Mass.: MIT Press.

Pike, E. (1986). 'Tone contrasts in Central Carrier', *International Journal of American Linguistics* **52**: 411–18.

Poser, W. (1984). 'The Phonetics and Phonology of Tone and Intonation in Japanese'. Dissertation, MIT.

Prince, A. (1984). 'Phonology with tiers', in M. Aronoff and R. Oerle (eds.), *Language Sound Structure*. Cambridge, Mass.: MIT Press, 234–44.

—— (1990). 'Quantitative consequences of rhythmic organization', in *Parasession on the Syllable in Phonetics and Phonology*. Chicago: Chicago Linguistic Society, 355–98.

—— and Smolensky, P. (1993). 'Optimality Theory: Constraint Interaction in Generative Grammar'. To be published by MIT Press.

Pulleyblank, D. (1986). *Tone in Lexical Phonology*. Dordrecht: Reidel.

Schadeberg, T. (1979). 'Über die Töne der verbalen Formen im Rimi;, *Afrika und Übersee* **57**: 288–313.

Sharman, J. (1963). 'Morphology, Morphophonology and Meaning in the Single-Word Verb-Forms in Bemba'. Dissertation, UNISA, Pretoria.

Shen, X. (1990). 'Tonal coarticulation in Mandarin', *Journal of Phonetics* **18**: 281–95.

Smolensky, P. (1994). 'Harmony, Markedness, and Phonological Acitivity'. Available by ftp from Rutgers Optimality Archive.

Sproat, R., and Fujimura, O. (1993). 'Allophonic variation in English /l/and its implications for phonetic implementation', *Journal of Phonetics* **21**: 291–311.

Stampe, D. (1979). *A Dissertation on Natural Phonology*. New York: Garland.

Stevick, E. (1969). 'Pitch and duration in Ganda', *Journal of African Languages* **8**: 1–28.

Westbury, J. (1983). 'Enlargement of the supraglottal cavity and its relation to stop consonant voicing', *Journal of the Acoustical Society of America* **73**: 1322–6.

Willerman, R. (1994). 'The Phonetics of Pronouns: Articulatory Bases of Markedness'. Dissertation, University of Texas at Austin.

Woodrow, H. (1951). 'Time perception', in S. Stevens (ed.), *Handbook of Experimental Psychology*. New York: Wiley, 1224–36.

Zsiga, E. (1995). 'An acoustic and electropalatographic study of lexical and postlexical palatalization in American English', in B. Connell and A. Arvaniti (eds.), *Phonology and Phonetic Evidence: Papers in Laboratory Phonology IV*. Cambridge: Cambridge University Press, 282–302.

5

Gradient Retreat

DOUGLAS PULLEYBLANK and WILLIAM J. TURKEL

1. INTRODUCTION

In Principles and Parameters theory (Chomsky 1981), languages vary along a finite number of finitely valued dimensions known as *parameters*. Under such an account, a significant part of the process of language acquisition is to use evidence from the ambient language to determine the correct setting of each of the parameters. The learning algorithm proceeds via a number of hypothesized grammars, searching through a space of possible languages. The goal of this search is to arrive at a grammar for which all and only the sentences of the ambient language are grammatical. When such a target grammar is reached, the learning process has been successful, and the learner is said to have *converged*. In a variety of cases, however, successful convergence may be prevented by a *trap*, a property of the parametric space which can prevent the convergence of the learning algorithm.

A number of traps have been discussed in the parameter setting literature. We will be concerned here with variants of two: the Subset Problem and Local Maxima. The subset problem (Berwick 1985; Wexler and Manzini 1987) arises when the learner chooses a parameter setting that yields a language which is a superset of the language yielded by another setting of the same parameter. Under the assumption that the learner does not have access to negative evidence (see Marcus 1993 for a review), there will be no evidence that will enable the learner to reset the parameter to the correct setting. A local maximum (Gibson and Wexler 1994; Frank and Kapur 1994) is a grammar which is not the target grammar, but which is better than any other grammar which is near to it in the parametric space. Under the assumptions that the learner is *greedy* and *conservative*, it will be unable to leave the local maximum. Greediness prevents the learner from making a non-optimizing move, and conservatism prevents it from making large scale changes to its current hypothesis.

In Optimality Theory (OT) (Prince and Smolensky 1993) languages are defined by varying the ranking of a set of universal constraints. Part of the acquisition problem is to use ambient language evidence to determine the correct ranking of the constraints. Once again, the learner must search a finite, multidimensional space (the constraint-ranking space) for the target grammar. An important open question is whether or not there are traps in Optimality Theoretic spaces. In this chapter, we demonstrate that even very small constraint-ranking spaces may contain traps for a class of algorithms similar to those discussed in the parameter setting literature.

We show, however, that the problem of traps is inherently different for Optimality Theory. An intrinsic part of OT is the claim that optimality does not entail an absence of constraint violation: the grammar equates 'minimal violation' with grammaticality, and fully grammatical forms will often involve the violation of some class of constraints. The notion of violable constraint has significant consequences for the operation of a learning algorithm. Even though two grammars *A* and *B* may both define some form *G* as grammatical, it does not follow that *G* is equally 'good' for both *A* and *B*: form *G* may violate some constraint or constraints in language *A* which are more highly ranked than the comparable constraints in language *B*. We show that by being sensitive to such degrees of constraint violation, a learner operating in an OT space may avoid or escape from a class of traps that it would otherwise be subject to.

2. OPTIMALITY THEORY AND LEARNING

Language acquisition within OT involves two interacting components. On the one hand, learners must acquire the particular ranking that constitutes the grammar of the language being learned; on the other hand, learners must acquire a lexicon, assigning appropriate morphological and phonological structures to the words of their language. The tight interconnection of these two aspects can be seen by comparing the effects of a pair of constraints such as MAXIO and DEPIO (McCarthy and Prince 1995).

(1) *Faithfulness constraints*
 MAXIO: Every segment of the input has a correspondent segment in the output.
 DEPIO: Every segment of the output has a correspondent segment in the input.

Imagine that the learner encounters two forms, [hɪm] 'hymn' and [wɪmən] 'women'. Imagine, moreover, that the learner posits the underlying forms /hɪm/ and /wɪmən/ for these two forms. Under such an analysis, both MAXIO and DEPIO are satisfied, and the learner is free to adopt either the grammar *MAXIO >> DEPIO*, or *DEPIO >> MAXIO*. (As discussed in the next section, we assume here that constraints are always completely ranked.)

Imagine, however, that the learner posits the input forms /hɪm/ and /wɪmn/ for these two words, the latter based perhaps on knowledge of pairs such as [d͡ʒʌg]/[d͡ʒʌg+z] 'jug/jugs' versus [d͡ʒʌd͡ʒ]/[d͡ʒʌd͡ʒ+əz] 'judge/judges', where a vowel schwa [ə] is inserted to break up the input cluster [. . . d͡ʒ+z . . .].

Given this hypothesis concerning underlying forms, one could ascertain that the correct grammar is *MaxIO* >> *DepIO* through the application of an algorithm such as the Constraint Demotion algorithm (Tesar and Smolensky 1993; Tesar 1995). To see this, consider the violations incurred by the two forms [hɪm] and [wɪmən]. For the input↔output pair /hɪm/↔[hɪm], both MaxIO and DepIO are satisfied since the input and output are identical; for the pair /wɪmn/ ↔[wɪmən], however, there is a violation of DepIO because the schwa that appears on the surface does not appear underlyingly. In order for [wɪmən] to be the optimal surface form (which experience tells us to be the case), it is necessary for the DepIO violation to be less serious than a MaxIO violation. This can be seen by a consideration of the tableau in (2).

(2) *Where the optimal output is analysed as involving epenthesis*

/wɪmn/	Syllable Constraints	MaxIO	DepIO
wɪmn	*!		
wɪm		*!	
☞ wɪmən			*

Imagine, however, that a different hypothesis is entertained concerning underlying forms. Specifically, imagine that the underlying forms of [hɪm] and [wɪmən] are assumed to be /hɪmn/ and /wɪmən/. Postulation of /wɪmən/ is transparently motivated; postulation of /hɪmn/ could be motivated by the observation of pairs such as [hɪm] 'hymn' versus [hɪmnəl] 'hymnal'. Given this hypothesis concerning underlying forms, the constraint demotion algorithm would cause DepIO to be ranked above MaxIO: *DepIO* >> *MaxIO*. To see this, consider again the violations incurred by the forms [hɪm] and [wɪmən]. In this case, [wɪmən] incurs no violations since both DepIO and MaxIO are satisfied. Of interest is the case of [hɪm]. For the input↔output pair /hɪmn/ ↔[hɪm], MaxIO is violated and must, therefore, be ranked below DepIO.

(3) *Where the optimal output is analysed as involving deletion*

/hɪmn/	Syllable Constraints	DepIO	MaxIO
hɪmn	*!		
☞ hɪm			*
hɪmən		*!	

The problem is the interconnectedness of the lexicon and the grammar. The nature of optimal lexical representations depends on the constraint ranking; the ranking of constraints depends on properties of lexical representations. The problem for acquisition is that neither a structured lexicon nor an articulated grammar is supplied to the learner. If the learner makes a wrong move at some point in the acquisition process, it must not be locked into the wrong grammar permanently, but must be able to recover from its error.

As a long-range goal, we seek to develop a learning model that will achieve both the establishment of a grammar and the establishment of a lexicon. As a first step towards this goal, we aim at establishing basic properties of the phonological grammar. This is based on the following consideration. The earliest stages of phonological acquisition involve the identification of patterns that do not involve morphophonemic alternation (see Goad 1993 and references therein). As such, there would be no reason for the learner to establish underlying lexical entries that are not essentially isomorphic with the output representations.[1] Assuming that this premorphological stage persists for some period of time, we must assume that a significant amount of learning goes on before the stage where morpheme alternations are identified and used to construct optimal underlying representations. Hence the stage of acquisition considered here assumes knowledge of surface forms, but does not assume any knowledge of correctly structured underlying forms (see Hale and Reiss 1995). We return to this issue in Section 4.2.

3. Demonstrating the Existence of Traps

Four things are necessary to show that a learner will encounter traps during acquisition: a *space*, a *move operator*, a *distance measure*, and a *learning algorithm*.

A constraint-ranking space arises from permutations of N universal constraints. We can specify an Optimality Theory grammar with a permutation of constraints of length N. Each permutation r corresponds to one of the $N!$ possible languages, and to a point in constraint-ranking space. Each of the permutations is also a possible hypothesis for our learner, which will entertain one of those permutations at a time. We can think of the learner as being at a particular point in the hypothesis space. As the learner changes its hypothesis,

---

[1] If inputs differing from outputs are not stored in the lexicon at the earliest stages of acquisition, then there is little pressure to force constraints to dominate faithfulness. This could be consistent, therefore, with proposals whereby constraints of the faithfulness class are highly ranked at the earliest stages of acquisition (Hale and Reiss 1995) but could also be consistent with proposals where faithfulness conditions are lowly ranked (Gnanadesikan 1995; Smolensky, forthcoming; etc.). Note, however, that nothing in the algorithm developed here requires such initial rankings. In fact, we argue in Section 5.1 that by not making such limiting assumptions on the ranking of faithfulness constraints, the performance of the learner is aided.

it moves through the hypothesis space.[2] For simplicity, we assume that any possible permutation is also a possible hypothesis for the learner. In other words, we assume that there are no rankings that are ruled out a priori by Universal Grammar, and that maturational factors do not prevent certain hypotheses from being entertained (cf. Bertolo 1994). Two issues need to be made explicit concerning rankings themselves. First, the nature of adult grammars needs to be established. Specifically, the default assumption within Optimality Theory is that all constraints are strictly ranked. Modifications of such complete ranking have been proposed in various places, however, whereby certain sets of constraints may be locally conjoined, crucially non-ranked, encapsulated, etc. (Pesetsky 1994, Broihier 1995*b*, Crowhurst and Hewitt 1995, Legendre *et al.* 1995, etc.). We abstract away from such issues of conjoined or nonranked constraints and assume for the purposes of this chapter that all constraints in an adult grammar are strictly ranked. Second, it has been suggested by Tesar and Smolensky (1993) that the learner starts with a completely unranked set of constraints and ranks them. Consistent with the Continuity Hypothesis (see Bloom 1994 for discussion and references), we assume instead that the learner posits fully ranked sets of constraints at all stages.[3] In various places in this chapter, we use the notation *ijk* as shorthand for *i>>j>>k*, where *i*, *j*, and *k* are arbitrary constraints. The hypothesis space for three constraints {*i,j,k*} would therefore be: *ijk, ikj, jik, jki, kij, kji*.

The learner starts by entertaining one of the possible rankings as its initial hypothesis. In general, there are two ways of characterizing this initial ranking. One possibility is that it is the same for every learner. In this case, it may have special properties that aid the learner in converging to any possible target language (as proposed in Gibson and Wexler 1994). Alternatively, the learner may start with any of the rankings as its initial ranking. In general, this tends to make the learning problem more difficult, since at least some of the possible initial states will make it unlikely or impossible for the learner to converge successfully. There are two observations about this latter case, however. The first is that a more powerful learner may be able to converge successfully from problematic initial states (Turkel 1996). The second is that such power appears to be necessary because there are some spaces which do not have any non-problematic initial states. We will consider such a space here, for phonological acquisition in the OT framework. Such a space has also been investigated for phonological acquisition in a parametric framework (Broihier 1995*a*), so the lack of a distinguished initial state is not a special property of Optimality

---

[2] We use the pronoun *it* to refer to the learner because we are describing a learning algorithm; a machine. Such usage underscores the fact that our learner is an abstraction which should not be confused with a human child.

[3] Smolensky (forthcoming) seems to adopt this position as well, since a back-and-forth iterative evaluation of postulated inputs and rankings is envisaged.

Theory. We assume, therefore, that the initial state of the grammar is a full grammar (*ijk*, *ikj*, . . .) randomly selected from the set of possible grammars.

The move operator we use is *Swap*. Each of the permutations *r* is a possible hypothesis for the learning algorithm. Swap exchanges any two constraints in a given constraint ranking to yield another ranking.[4] The distance between two rankings is defined as the minimum number of swaps required to convert one ranking to the other. For example, *ijk* can be converted to *ikj*, *jik*, or *kji* with a single swap (*j* swaps with *k* in the first case, *i* with *j* in the second, *i* with *k* in the third). To convert *ijk* to *jki* or *kij* would require a minimum of two swaps. For example, *jki* can be achieved by first swapping *i* with *j* (*jik*) and then swapping *k* with *i*. The space that we consider here involves only three constraints and is therefore very small—each of the rankings is at a distance of 1 or 2 from all of the rest. As a result, allowing moves of distance 2 is equivalent to allowing any grammar in the space to move to any other grammar. Because of this, conservatism of the learning algorithm plays no significant role in the case examined here, and we assume that movement can be from any grammar to any other grammar for our space. We note, however, that conservatism could play a significant role in constraining movement of the learner in a larger space.

Our learning algorithm is the Constraint Ranking Triggering Learning Algorithm (CRTLA), after Gibson and Wexler (1994):

(4)   *Constraint Ranking Triggering Learning Algorithm*
Given an initial ranking of *N* constraints, the learner attempts to analyze an incoming datum *S*. If *S* can be successfully analyzed, then the learner's hypothesis regarding the target grammar is left unchanged. If, however, the learner cannot analyse *S*, then the learner moves to a new grammar. *S* is reprocessed with the new ranking. If analysis is now possible the new ranking is adopted. Otherwise, the original ranking is retained.

We say that the learner can analyze a datum *S* when that datum is optimal for some postulated input. For discussion, see section 4.1. We assume that the data are uniformly distributed.

The initial version of the CRTLA that we consider is strictly *error-driven*— it will not attempt to change the current hypothesis if the input sentence can be analysed[5] (cf. Wexler and Culicover 1980). We also investigate a version of the CRTLA which is not strictly error-driven, but which attempts to make improving moves whether or not the learner can analyze the input sentence with the current hypothesis. We refer to this second version of the CRTLA as a

---

[4] Nick Sherrard brought to our attention a paper by Cho (1995) arguing that diachronic changes are a two-stage process where initially two ranked constraints become unranked, and then the unranked constraints get reranked. Since we do not consider the possibility of unranked constraints here, we do not address this possibility.

[5] We return to the issue of *analysis* in some detail later in the chapter, laying out exactly how the learner decides that a move constitutes improvement.

gradient retreat learner, demonstrating that it takes direct advantage of inherent properties of Optimality Theory.

The CRTLA is also *memoryless*—it does not retain former settings or input data. Being error-driven, the CRTLA remains in its current grammar unless it fails to analyse a form. To the extent that the learner moves to grammars that allow the analysis of grammatical forms, increasingly large amounts of data should become analysable. That is, as the learner 'ascends' towards a target, it should make gradually fewer numbers of errors. Since the CRTLA is memoryless, however, nothing ensures that the current grammar is consistent with all previously received input data. This in turn means that it is possible for the learner to err and then adjust its learning path on the basis of such errors—the learner does not necessarily follow a flawless path to the target grammar in a deterministic fashion.

4. A SMALL CONSTRAINT-RANKING SPACE WITH TRAPS

Even a very small constraint-ranking space will often contain traps for the CRTLA. To demonstrate this, we make use of three syllable structure constraints adapted from Prince and Smolensky (1993). We focus on the fact that even with such a small number of constraints, there may be situations where the CRTLA encounters the subset problem. Once this is established, we go on to suggest that intrinsic properties of Optimality Theory also provide a partial solution to the subset trap.

The constraint space that we examine in this section is based on the following three constraints:

(5) *Constraints*
    a. MAXIO: Every segment of the input has a correspondent segment in the output.
    b. NoCODA: A syllable does not have a coda.
    c. ONSET: Every syllable has an onset.

MAXIO requires that all material found in an input form also appear in a corresponding output form (McCarthy and Prince 1995). That is, MAXIO prohibits deletion. For the small schematic class of grammars considered here, the MAX constraint family has an equivalent effect to the PARSE family of Prince and Smolensky (1993).

NoCODA prohibits the appearance of a syllabic coda. For the purposes of the demonstration here, no particular assumptions concerning syllable structure are crucial. Whatever the correct nature of the syllable, this constraint rules out a class of postvocalic consonants within the syllable.

ONSET performs the opposite function, requiring the appearance of a prevocalic consonant. Again, the details of a syllabic theory do not bear on the schematic interaction of these constraints that is crucial for the establishment of traps.

In order to focus our attention on a small space of grammars, we assume that all consonants or vowels appearing in a representation are fully syllabified, and we assume that there is no epenthesis. In addition, we assume that there are no syllable-internal consonant clusters, and that all vowels are short. In formal terms, we assume that constraints such as DepIO and *Complex are ranked above the constraints being considered here (Prince and Smolensky 1993; McCarthy and Prince 1993; 1995; etc.).

Consider now the six possible grammars (*3!*) generated by these three constraints.

(6) *Possible grammars*
    LG1: MaxIO >> NoCoda >> Onset
    LG2: MaxIO >> Onset >> NoCoda
    LG3: NoCoda >> MaxIO >> Onset
    LG4: NoCoda >> Onset >> MaxIO
    LG5: Onset >> MaxIO >> NoCoda
    LG6: Onset >> NoCoda >> MaxIO

Under the assumption that the learner begins in one of the six grammars given in (6), the central learning task is to move from the initial state to the state characterizing the ambient language. To examine why a particular move would either be good or bad, we must consider the types of data that are analysed as grammatical or ungrammatical by particular grammars.

4.1 *Analysis of data*

Given the assumption that data are unstructured, the learner can reach only fairly minimal conclusions on the basis of the individual items that are presented. We consider the nature of such conclusions here. Since we are assuming that there are no clusters and no long vowels, the data that the learner receives may contain only four possible surface syllabic forms: *V*, *CV*, *CVC*, *VC*.

When the learner encounters a given form (*CV*, *CVC*, etc.), it knows that the form encountered must be the optimal output for some input in that language, or else the form would not have appeared in the primary linguistic data.[6] The learner does not know, however, what the input corresponding to such a form looks like. The task for the learner at this stage is to reach conclusions about the suitability of a grammar, while provided with information about outputs only and with no information about morphologically induced alternations. Of

---

[6] For the purposes of this chapter, we abstract away from issues of 'noise', bilingual environments, imperfect perception, and so on. We assume, therefore, that all data encountered are correctly identified and optimal according to the grammar being acquired.

crucial importance in this procedure is how to establish when a grammar provides a grammatical analysis for some form, and how to establish that an alternative grammar provides a superior/inferior analysis. To lay out the procedure, we first go through the simple case of a *VC* form, and then consider the three additional forms.

Learner is located in a particular grammar g. As already described, we assume that the learner starts in some fully articulated grammar, and moves from grammar to grammar within the space. For this procedural demonstration, we assume that the initial state is the grammar NOCODA >> MAXIO >> ONSET.

A form f *is encountered by learner.* Some item from the primary linguistic data is encountered by the learner, a form that the learner will attempt to analyse. In this case, let us assume that the learner encounters a *VC* form.

Learner ascertains whether f *is optimal in* g *for some input.* The learner must now attempt to analyse the form encountered. In the case under consideration, the learner must attempt to analyse the form *VC* for the grammar NOCODA >> MAXIO >> ONSET. First, let us assume an input that is identical to the *VC* output, that is, an input that would correspond exactly to the output in terms of its segmental make-up.

(7) *Attempting to analyse a VC surface form*

/VC/	NOCODA	MAXIO	ONSET
VC	*!		*
☞ V		*	*
Ø		**!	

As seen in (7), the output *VC* would not be optimal for a /VC/ input in this language. The violation of NOCODA is fatal because NOCODA is the most highly ranked of the three constraints. It could be the case, of course, that some alternative input could give a different result. An important issue, therefore, is how to establish whether there could or could not be a better input/output pair, one where the observed output would be optimal for the grammar in question.

To examine this issue, the learner must be able to posit additional inputs for any output under consideration. For example, a *VC* output could be related to a *VC* input, it could be related to a *V* or *CVC* input, or it could be related to something more complex. As stated above, we abstract away from issues of clusters here, restricting the scope of the problem by assuming that there are no syllable-internal clusters and that there is no epenthesis: given these simplifying assumptions, an input can only be identical to the output, or related to it via deletion. A full account will have to take both syllable-internal clusters and insertion into consideration. The ranking of the relevant faithfulness constraints will have to be determined, and the learner will need to entertain the sorts of input that would be consistent with more complex surface syllabic structures and more complex input/output mappings.

One issue for the learner is determining when it has encountered the optimal possible input/output relation—how many possibilities should be considered? In a large space, it is clear that the number of possibilities considered by the learner at any stage must be restricted. One way of proceeding would be to examine a faithful input/output pair in addition to some small number of randomly selected additional pairs where the input includes Cs or Vs not found in the output. Because the learning space considered here is so small, we do not examine this issue in detail; for the error-driven version of the CRTLA, we provided the learner with the full set of input/output pairs where the input is related to the output via identity or deletion. This ensured that the learner was able to establish correctly whether a grammar could grammatically analyse any form encountered.[7]

Consider the constraint violations incurred by the *VC* candidate that we are seeking to analyze. First, this candidate violates ONSET. It can be seen, however, that this violation is not fatal, since ONSET is ranked below MAXIO. This violation, therefore, is not an obstacle to having *VC* declared the optimal candidate. In contrast, consider the violation of NOCODA. With respect to NOCODA, a *VC* candidate cannot avoid a violation, whatever the input, and the violation is fatal given the ranking. That is, given the high ranking of NOCODA, no candidate with a coda could ever be optimal. As a result, the grammar under consideration fails to provide an analysis of the *VC* form.

Learner considers a move to a new grammar h. The learner then swaps two constraints, to attempt an analysis of the same form, *VC*, with a different grammar. Since the learner is *error-driven* and *greedy*, it only considers making a move if it has identified an error, and the move is contingent on the new grammar providing an improved analysis. For the case under consideration, let us assume that the learner swaps the two constraints NOCODA and MAXIO, resulting in the grammar: MAXIO >> NOCODA >> ONSET.

Learner ascertains whether the analysis of f *in* h *is better than in* g. For the new grammar, the same form (*VC*) is again analysed. In addition, the learner assumes the same input as was used to analyse the form previously. In this example, therefore, the input again corresponds exactly to the output.

---

[7] This assumption is reexamined and revised within the context of the gradient retreat learner examined in section 5.

(8) *Attempting to analyze a VC surface form with a different grammar*

/VC/	MAXIO	NOCODA	ONSET
☞ VC		*	*
V	*!		*
Ø	*!*		

As can be seen from (8), the occurring surface form *VC* is optimal for the particular input assumed. That is, the new grammar successfully assigns an analysis to a surface *VC* form. Whether or not /VC/ is actually the optimal input for the surface *VC*, this grammar has succeeded in analysing *VC* where the previous grammar failed.

If better in h, *then the learner accepts the contingent move to* h. Since the datum under consideration was nonoptimal in the original grammar (NOCODA >> MAXIO >> ONSET), and is the optimal output for at least one input in the second grammar (MAXIO >> NOCODA >> ONSET), the learner keeps as its new state the second grammar.

If the same or worse in h, *then the learner rejects the contingent move, remaining in* g. If the original grammar had assigned an analysis and the second grammar had not, then the move being considered would have been rejected and the learner would retain its original grammar. For example, if the learner had started in the grammar MAXIO >> NOCODA >> ONSET, then a datum like *VC* would not cause it to accept a contingent move to the grammar NOCODA >> MAXIO >> ONSET.

Note that a class of interesting cases have not yet been examined: those where both grammars correctly assign analyses to the same datum. This type of case is the focus of section 5.

4.2 *Grammaticality of outputs in the six languages*

Given the procedure laid out in the last section, we summarize in (9) the forms that each of the six grammars analyzes as grammatical.

(9) *Grammatical surface forms*

Language	Data	Language	Data
LG1	{CV, V, CVC, VC}	LG4	{CV}
LG2	{CV, V, CVC, VC}	LG5	{CV, CVC}
LG3	{CV, V}	LG6	{CV}

In order for a form to be analyzed as grammatical in a particular language, it must be the case that there is some input for which the observed output would be optimal in that language. The relevant evaluations for the six languages considered here are summarized in Appendix 1.

Crucially, note that in determining whether a form can be analyzed by a particular grammar, the learner only has access to outputs, which underdetermine the inputs. Let us consider this issue in some detail. There are three sorts of possibility that one could envisage for the learner. First, one could imagine that all inputs posited by the learner are strictly faithful to the output. Second, one could posit that all inputs are strictly unfaithful. Third, one could imagine some mixture of faithful and unfaithful inputs; that is, one could imagine some sort of stochastic mechanism whereby the learner postulates inputs in a random or probabilistic fashion. It is important to keep in mind in considering these possibilities that we are considering a stage of learning that *precedes* morphological analysis. The learner does not, therefore, have any plausible way of actually postulating morphologically appropriate input forms.

Considering these three possible ways of positing inputs, we can immediately reject the second one, where inputs are necessarily different from outputs. It is hard to imagine what advantage there could be in assuming a learning principle that so rampantly violates the common property of input/output correspondence in adult grammars.

The choice between the remaining possibilities is less obvious. An initial consideration might lead one to assume input/output identity. This could be motivated on the grounds that the learner has not acquired morphology, and hence has not acquired the sorts of representations that would robustly motivate phonological alternations. But to assume that all inputs are identical to observed outputs is effectively to not assume inputs at all. This is problematic on several counts. With regard to the Continuity Hypothesis, this approach assumes qualitatively different evaluations on the part of the adult speaker and the initial learner. In addition, the failure to postulate inputs, or the postulation of inputs that are strictly identical to outputs, seems inconsistent with certain properties of even the earliest stages of acquisition. It has been demonstrated in work such as Werker and Tees (1984), Werker and Lalonde (1988), etc., that infants of 10 to 12 months of age have tuned their perception of language contrasts to those of the ambient language. Where younger infants display an ability to perceive contrasts found both in the ambient language and in other unfamiliar languages, this ability appears to decrease markedly by the end of the first year of life. Infants are performing linguistic analysis at these early stages, and they are analyzing linguistic surface forms in a way that enables them to extract information about contrastive patterns. Such analysis also involves making distinctions between acoustic properties that serve to contrast a given language's phonemes, and other acoustic properties that may, for example, serve only to identify a particular speaker (see Jusczyk 1993 for a model of early perceptual development). These sorts of consideration suggest that by one year of age children have established that input representations

(representations encoding contrast) are distinct from output representations (representations interpretable phonetically), and that certain types of contrastive information in inputs are appropriate to the language that they are learning, while others are not. This does not necessarily mean that such infants have actively begun word acquisition, but it does suggest that the components necessary for such acquisition are being assembled, and there does not seem to be evidence for equating input forms with output forms.

From a different perspective, one might ask whether assuming input/output identity would help or hinder the acquisition process. The answer to this question seems to depend on the particular language under consideration. For example, the learner might benefit from positing strict input/output identity if confronted with a language allowing complex syllable structures, where input complexities are preserved in the output (a Dutch-type language). On the other hand, if the ambient language contextually simplified underlying complexities by having at least certain outputs conform to a more limited syllable template, then assuming strict input/output identity might hinder the learner (a Catalan-type language). Of course, the learner does not know in advance what type of language it will encounter. We assume, therefore, that inputs may be different from outputs, at a cost in terms of faithfulness constraints.

To summarize: in line with Continuity Hypothesis, we assume that all stages of grammatical development involve the postulation of input representations. In addition, we assume that inputs need not be identical to outputs, although deviations will presumably be of limited types.

Returning to the issue of grammaticality assessments, in order for the learner to conclude that an encountered surface form is grammatically analyzed by the current grammar, there must be some input/output pairing for which the surface form is optimal. If unable to analyze an occurring surface form as optimal, then the learner's current grammar must be incorrect, and it attempts to move to a new grammar. Note that the learner never has direct access to a deductively established class of inputs, and may indeed posit and evaluate an input that is ultimately not correct for the surface form encountered. Since we are examining a stage of learning that precedes morphological analysis, it is hard to see how things could be otherwise. We assume in consequence that at early stages no lexical input forms are retained in memory by the learner. The learner is at a stage where it is attempting early analysis of a grammar, but has not started the long-term development of a lexicon.

4.3 Movement from one grammar to another

From the summary of grammatical surface forms in (9), two types of information can be obtained. First, one can observe which forms the learner will be exposed to during the course of language acquisition. Second, one can ascertain which forms convey information about the target ranking to the learner. The latter forms are known as *triggers*, and are summarized in (10).

(10) *Triggers*

Language	Triggers	Language	Triggers
LG1	{V, CVC, VC}	LG4	*none*
LG2	{V, CVC, VC}	LG5	{CVC}
LG3	{V}	LG6	*none*

The basic difference between the set of syllables that can trigger changes and those that cannot is that the CV syllable is not a trigger. Since all six languages include CV syllables (such syllables can indeed form perfect input/output pairs in all six languages), encountering a CV syllable would never result in a triggered change.

Note that languages LG1 and LG2, and languages LG4 and LG6, define identical sets of data and therefore have identical sets of triggers. Such languages are weakly equivalent—they are indistinguishable with respect to the sets of optimal forms. Since the constraints defining such languages are ranked differently, however, the two pairs of languages are not strongly equivalent, something which we address in the next section.

By inspecting the sets of triggers for our constraint-ranking space, we can see that there are a number of traps for the CRTLA involving subset/superset relations. Consider a learner that starts in language LG1 (or enters LG1 during learning) when the target is language LG3. Under standard assumptions, there will never be any positive evidence to trigger a change from language LG1 to language LG3. Again, we examine this problem in the next section.

(11) *LG1 and LG3: a superset/subset relation*

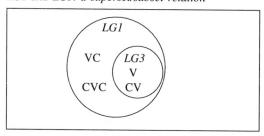

By taking the set difference of the set of triggers for any language A and the set of triggers for any language B, we can determine which forms can trigger a change from language A to language B (provided the form is in the input, of course). For example, the set difference of LG1 and LG3 is {CVC, VC} (*LG1\LG3*: {V, CVC, VC} \ {V} = {CVC, VC}). The (non-empty) sets of such triggers are as follows:

(12) *Triggers that can cause a shift from one language to another*

Endpoint of shift	Shift	Triggers
LG1	LG3→LG1	{CVC, VC}
	LG4→LG1	{V, CVC, VC}
	LG5→LG1	{V, VC}
	LG6→LG1	{V, CVC, VC}
LG2	LG3→LG2	{CVC, VC}
	LG4→LG2	{V, CVC, VC}
	LG5→LG2	{V, VC}
	LG6→LG2	{V, CVC, VC}
LG3	LG4→LG3	{V}
	LG5→LG3	{V}
	LG6→LG3	{V}
LG5	LG3→LG5	{CVC}
	LG4→LG5	{CVC}
	LG6→LG5	{CVC}

From these sets we can determine the possible transitions from one grammar to another, as illustrated in (13).

(13) *Transitions*

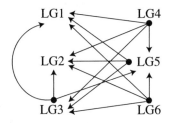

Several points can be observed about possible movement in this space of grammars. Some grammars can be reached directly or indirectly from almost any starting point. For example, LG1 can be reached from all grammars except LG2. Other grammars are not similarly accessible. For example, LG3 can be reached from only three starting-points, and LG4 cannot be reached from any point (other than itself).

On the basis of such possibilities, four learning scenarios can be distinguished, as summarized in (14).

(14) *Learning scenarios*

	Target language	Input to learner	Probability of encountering a particular datum
Scenario 1	LG1 or LG2	{CV, V, CVC, VC}	1/4
Scenario 2	LG3	{CV, V}	1/2
Scenario 3	LG5	{CV, CVC}	1/2
Scenario 4	LG4 or LG6	{CV}	1

Languages LG1 and LG2 both define the full set of {CV, V, CVC, VC} as grammatical. As such, when the target grammar is either LG1 or LG2, the learner's ambient environment will include a full array of data. We assume, moreover, that all four data types occur with equal frequency. This defines scenario 1. With the other scenarios, the particular forms defined as grammatical by a particular target language differ, hence the forms that the learner encounters differ. In all four scenarios, equal frequency of all data is assumed.

To analyze these four scenarios, we use the Markov Chain model of the CRTLA (Niyogi and Berwick 1993). By using Markov Chains, we are able to determine the likelihood of moving from one grammar to the other, where a move must be triggered because of the nature of the CRTLA.

Consider scenario 1, where the target is either LG1 or LG2. If the learner starts in either LG1 or LG2, then all data encountered will be fully grammatical, and the learner will not move to a new grammar.

(15) *Target = LG1 or LG2*

Start point	Grammatical at start point		Target	Grammatical in target
LG1	{CV, V, CVC, VC}	NO	LG1	{CV, V, CVC, VC}
LG2		MOVE	LG2	

If the learner starts in some other grammar, however, then certain data may trigger a shift. For example, imagine that the learner starts in LG3. LG3 defines {V, CV} as grammatical and *{CVC, VC} as ungrammatical (see (9)). Since the target is LG1 or LG2, all of {CV, V, CVC, VC} may be encountered in the primary linguistic data. If *V* or *CV* is encountered, then the learner will remain where it is, namely in LG3; if *CVC* or *VC* is encountered, then the learner will attempt to move, since LG3 cannot analyze either form successfully.

(16) *Target = LG1 or LG2*

Start point	Grammatical at start point		Target	Grammatical in target
LG3	{CV, V}	→	LG1	{CV, V, CVC, VC}
			LG2	

Whether an attempt to move is successful depends on the probability of the triggering forms being grammatical in the language to which the learner attempts a move. From *LG3*, the learner could attempt a move to any of LG1, LG2, LG4, LG5, or LG6—the target grammars are just two of the possibilities. Suppose that the form encountered by the learner is CVC. This form is grammatical in LG1, LG2, and LG5 and is ungrammatical in the other languages. Hence if the learner attempts a move to LG1, LG2, or LG5, the move will be retained, while if it attempts a move to either of LG4 or LG6, the move will be rejected by the learner. Similarly, if the learner encounters the form VC, then a move to either of LG1 or LG2 will be successful, while any other move would fail.

Overall, the probability of moving from one grammar to another involves two factors: (i) the odds of encountering a form that is not optimal in the grammar where the learner is located, and (ii) the odds of moving to a particular alternative grammar where the form under consideration is analyzed as optimal.

Consider a specific case for illustration, schematized in (17). Assuming that the learner starts in LG3, and is attempting to converge on LG1 or LG2, the probabilities are calculated as follows. One half of the time, the learner will receive a datum that is analyzable in LG3 (i.e. CV or V) and it will remain where it is. One half of the time, an error (i.e. a non-optimal analysis) will be signalled because the learner receives a form that it cannot analyze (i.e. VC or CVC).

(17) *Probabilities of making a move from LG3 to LG1 or LG2*

State of learner	Datum	Grammatical?	Move considered	Grammatical?	Probabilities	
					Stay put	Move to
LG3	CV	YES	None		LG3: 1/4	
	V	YES	None		LG3: 1/4	
	VC	NO	→ LG1	YES		LG1: 1/20
			→ LG2	YES		LG2: 1/20
			→ LG4	NO		
			→ LG5	NO	LG3: 3/20	
			→ LG6	NO		
	CVC	NO	→ LG1	YES		LG1: 1/20
			→ LG2	YES		LG2: 1/20
			→ LG4	NO	LG3: 1/20	
			→ LG5	YES		LG5: 1/20
			→ LG6	NO	LG3: 1/20	
			Total probability		LG3: 3/4	LG1: 1/10
						LG2: 1/10
						LG5: 1/20

Encountering an error causes the learner to attempt to move. There are five languages that constitute possible moves. If the form that the learner is considering is VC (which it will be, a quarter of the time), then the learner can successfully complete a move to either LG1 or LG2 because there is an optimal analysis available for VC in those languages; on the other hand, a VC datum could not cause a move to any of languages LG4, LG5, or LG6 because VC is not grammatical in those languages. Hence the learner has a 1/4 chance of encountering a VC datum, and a 2/5 chance of making a successful move triggered by such a datum, giving an overall probability of 1/10 (1/4 × 2/5) of moving when encountering a VC (1/20 chance of moving to LG1 and 1/20 chance of moving to LG2). In addition to a VC, a move could be triggered by encountering a CVC. Like VC, the learner would encounter a CVC form 1/4 of the time. In three of the five languages to which the learner could move, namely LG1, LG2, and LG5, a CVC form is grammatical. Hence the learner has a 3/20 chance of encountering a CVC datum and making a legitimate move (1/4 × 3/5). Overall, after encountering a single form, the probability of remaining in LG3 is 3/4, 1/10 of moving to LG1, 1/10 of moving to LG2, and 1/20 of moving to LG5. The learner would never move to LG4 or LG6 from LG3, since none of the forms that it might encounter is grammatical in LG4 or LG6 but ungrammatical in LG3.

Of course, the state of the learner after encountering a single form is not our main concern. Rather, we are interested in the behavior of the learner as the number of forms increases. We determine the probabilities of being in any particular state as the number of data goes to infinity, a result referred to as *learnability in the limit*. The results for scenario 1 are shown schematically in (18). From any starting grammar, the learner will successfully converge on a target of LG1 or LG2.

(18) *Scenario 1 in the limit*

Success rate (%)		Target grammar
100	LG1	
100	LG2	
100	LG3	→ LG1/LG2
100	LG4	
100	LG5	
100	LG6	

The precise algorithm used for calculating probabilities is laid out in Appendix 2, as are transition matrices for all four scenarios. The point of importance to be retained from these cases is primarily whether or not a target grammar can be reached from any particular starting point.

When we consider the results in scenarios 2, 3, and 4, we find that convergence is not possible from all starting points. For scenario 2, if the learner starts in either LG1 or LG2, it cannot reach the target grammar. Similarly, if the learner starts in any of LG4, LG5, or LG6, then it may successfully move to the correct grammar, but it may also move to LG1 or LG2, in which case it is trapped there.

(19) *Scenario 2 in the limit*

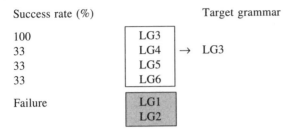

A similar pattern of partial success and partial failure is observed in scenario 3.

(20) *Scenario 3 in the limit*

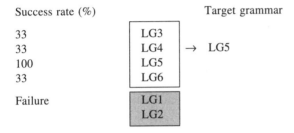

Finally, a pattern of almost complete failure can be observed for scenario 4.

(21) *Scenario 4 in the limit*

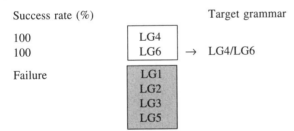

For scenarios 2, 3, and 4, the learner must be lucky enough to start in the target language in order to converge to that language with probability 1. For all three scenarios, languages LG1 and LG2 are traps—if the learner finds itself in such a language, no error-driven move can cause it to change state, since all data are analyzable. In addition, languages LG3 and LG5 are traps with respect to scenario 4. The specific problem is that LG1 and LG2 are supersets of the target languages LG3 and LG5, while all of LG1, LG2, LG3, and LG5 are supersets of the target languages LG4 and LG6. The learner finds itself trapped in a superset, unable to move to a subset grammar on the basis of errors (since there aren't any—all grammars analyze a CV syllable as grammatical).

5. Gradient Retreat

As seen in the last section, a consideration of the behavior of the four scenarios in the limit (18–21) demonstrates both success and failure. When the target is one of the superset languages, the learner can converge to that language or to the weakly equivalent language from any starting grammar. When the target language is LG3 or LG5, however, then LG1 and LG2 are traps. The smallest languages, LG4 and LG6, never act as traps, while the largest languages, LG1 and LG2, frequently do. That the learner can never move from a larger language to a smaller language is an example of the *subset problem*, illustrated with a Venn diagram in (22):

(22) *Subsets and supersets*

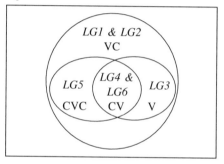

The problem is that if the learner starts in a superset language such as LG1 or LG2, then every datum encountered is analyzable (CV, V, CVC, VC). If the only data encountered are CV and V (as with LG3), CV and CVC (as with LG5), or only CV (as with LG4 and LG6), the learner has no way of recognizing such a pattern and moving to a subset language.

5.1. The mechanism of gradient retreat

The subset problem is a general problem for learnability (see Berwick 1985; Wexler and Manzini 1987). The extent of the problem depends on the nature of the learner, with the problem being acute for error-driven learners. It should be stressed, however, that the problem of subsets relates in no specific way to Optimality Theory. Of interest, however, is the fact that Optimality Theory provides a mechanism for escaping from a significant class of supersets. We call the basic idea *gradient retreat*.

(23) *Gradient retreat*
  i. Whether or not a form is optimal, and therefore grammatical, in two grammars, the analysis of the form in one grammar may incur less costly violations than its analysis in the other.
  ii. The learner may move from a grammar p to a grammar q because a form is analyzed in q with less costly violations than in p.

Since constraints are ranked and violable, the same violation may be lowly ranked in one grammar and more highly ranked in another. By taking such ranking distinctions into consideration, the learner is able to find its way out of a class of traps. Although we demonstrate gradient retreat with grammars that are in a subset/superset relation, the gradient retreat mechanism is a principled solution to the more general problem of local maxima as well. To escape from a local maximum, the learner would need to make a series of retreats to a grammar from which the target grammar was accessible. Whether or not such retreat paths are available to more sophisticated learners operating in larger spaces remains to be investigated.

Two types of move are licensed by gradient retreat. To see this, there are four possible relations to be considered between analyses in a current grammar and analyses in a grammar that is being considered for a move. First, it is possible that the datum encountered by the learner is identified as optimal in both current and potential grammars. Second, it is possible that the datum is optimal in the current grammar but not in the potential grammar. Third, the reverse is possible—the datum is optimal in the potential grammar but not in the current grammar. Fourth, the datum may not be optimally analysed in either grammar. These four possibilities are schematized in (24).

(24) *Possibility of a move by the CRTLA*

	Current grammar	Result of swap	Move?
a.	Datum analyzed as optimal	Datum analyzed as optimal	No
b.	Datum analyzed as optimal	Datum not analyzed as optimal	No
c.	Datum not analyzed as optimal	Datum analyzed as optimal	Yes
d.	Datum not analyzed as optimal	Datum not analyzed as optimal	No

The CRTLA as sketched above would move in only one case: the current grammar fails and the grammar resulting from swap succeeds (24c).

But imagine that we adopt a somewhat different criterion for movement. After the current grammar analyzes a datum, it considers a move if overall violations are lower as a result of swap. That is, if demotion of a violated constraint does not result in an optimal input/output pair being analyzed as non-optimal, then such a demotion is retained by the learner. Essentially, this proposal incorporates a form of constraint demotion (cf. Tesar and Smolensky 1993), but without making any assumptions about knowledge of input forms and without assuming a set of initially unranked constraints.

To see how this works, let us assume that the learner is currently in LG2 and is targeting LG3, and that the datum [V] is encountered (note that LG2 is a superset of LG3). Given the assumptions that we motivated above concerning input forms, there are four possible inputs that could correspond to a [V] output, /V/, /CV/, /VC/, and /CVC/. The learner would select one of the four input/output pairings for evaluation. Consider the possibility of selecting the faithful pairing, /V/ ↔ [V]. Under such an analysis, output [V] is optimal for input /V/ for both LG2 and LG3.

(25) *LG2—violations for a surface V with an underlying /V/*

/V/	MaxIO	Onset	NoCoda
☞ V		*	
∅	*!		

(26) *LG3—violations for a surface V with an underlying /V/*

/V/	NoCoda	MaxIO	Onset
☞ V			*
∅		*!	

Note, however, that the violation of Onset incurred by the optimal candidate [V] in each case is ranked higher in LG2 than in LG3. Hence if LG2 attempts to demote the constraint violated by the optimal candidate, and derives LG3 in so doing, the move will be retained because the output form in the new grammar ranks the offending constraint lower, and continues to analyze the observed [V] as optimal.

Consider a different type of case. All six languages provide a way of successfully analyzing surface [CV] forms as optimal: an input /CV/ will result in a perfect output [CV] in all six languages. Of course, surface [CV] syllables may not in fact correspond to underlying /CV/ sequences. For example, imagine that the target language is either LG4 or LG6, that it defines only CV forms as grammatical. Imagine further that the language has related pairs of words such as ʃa/ʃat+ə 'cat MASCULINE/FEMININE', du/dus+ə 'soft MASCULINE/ FEMININE', pəti/pətit+ə 'small masculine/feminine', and so on. (These pairs are obviously drawn from French, although French is not the type of language illustrated by either LG4 or LG6.) If the learner were to be located in LG1 or LG2, it would successfully analyze all such words—but incorrectly consider [CVC] and [VC] syllables to be possible. In spite of the fact that no [CVC] or [VC] syllables are ever encountered, a strictly error-driven learner could make no progress until the developmental stage where morphological analysis becomes possible. Of course, the conclusion that all surface [CV] outputs correspond to input /CV/ sequences is both incorrect and unnecessary—as already discussed above. Consider what would happen if the learner encountering such forms happened to posit an input sequence other than /CV/, for example, /CVC/. Languages LG2 and LG3 (the same pair just considered for a [V] form) would analyze such a form as follows:

(27) *LG2—violations for a surface CV with underlying /CVC/*

/CVC/	MaxIO	Onset	NoCoda
☞ CVC			*
CV	*!		
VC	*!	*	*
V	*!*	*	
∅	*!**		

(28) *LG3—violations for a surface CV with underlying /CVC/*

/CVC/	NoCoda	MaxIO	Onset
CVC	*!		
☞ CV		*	
VC	*!	*	*
V		**!	*
∅		**!*	

In this case, the particular analysis of a CV datum (/CVC/ ↔ [CV]) is non-optimal in language LG2, but is better, in fact optimal, in LG3. Crucially, movement in this case is from a superset (LG2 generates CV, V, VC, CVC) to a subset (LG3 generates CV).

A third type of movement is possible when an input/output pair is non-optimal in both current and revised grammars. Consider a situation where the learner is located in LG6 and encounters a surface form [VC] (possible if the target is actually LG1 or LG2). A move to LG5 is considered. Note in considering this example that the only syllable that is grammatical in LG6 is CV, while LG5 analyzes both CV and CVC as grammatical. Neither grammar analyzes VC as grammatical, hence no move could be made from LG6 to LG5 according to the conventional CRTLA. Consider the case where the learner happens to postulate an input that is faithful to the observed VC datum, that is, /VC/ ↔ [VC]. Assessment of optimal outputs would be as follows:

(29) *LG6—violations for a surface VC with underlying /VC/*

/VC/	MAXIO	ONSET	NOCODA
VC	*!	*	
V	*!		*
☞ Ø			

(30) *LG5—violations for a surface VC with underlying /VC/*

/VC/	ONSET	MAXIO	NOCODA
VC	*!		*
V	*!	*	
☞ Ø			

In both cases, the optimal output would be null: failing to parse the input would be preferable to incurring an Onset violation. Both grammars, therefore, fail to derive [VC] as a grammatical output. The two grammars differ, however, in that the [VC] candidate violates more highly ranked constraints in LG6 than in LG5. All else being equal, therefore, the LG5 grammar is preferable to that of LG6. For this case, therefore, movement from LG6 to LG5 would be possible, though not vice versa.

Note that the observed datum VC violates both Onset and NoCoda. LG6 does not allow either type of violation, while LG5 allows one but not the other. Movement to LG5, therefore, constitutes improvement, even if LG5 does not analyse VC as grammatical. Such movement is possible under gradient retreat, but impossible by the strictly error-driven CRTLA.

Finally, gradient retreat also allows movement from a language where a form is grammatical to a language where it is not. (We consider how such movement might be avoided in our assessment of gradient retreat in section 5.3.) Consider a case where the learner encounters a V form and is currently in LG2. As seen in (25), V is the optimal output for an underlying /V/ in LG2. Hence V can be successfully analyzed by the learner if it posits an appropriate input form. In contrast, V is nonoptimal in a language such as LG6, where only CV is generated. If the learner has access to the full range of possible inputs, guaranteeing that it will identify an optimal input/output relation if there is one, and if the CRTLA is strictly error-driven, then it would be impossible to move from LG2 to LG6 on the basis of a V, since this form is grammatical in LG2 and ungrammatical in LG6. Consider, however, the possibility of gradient retreat if a V is encountered and if the underlying form /VC/ is postulated by the learner.

In LG2, the output form V is suboptimal for an input /VC/, as seen in (31).

(31) *LG2—violations for a surface V with an underlying /V/*

/VC/	MaxIO	Onset	NoCoda
☞ VC		*	*
V	*	*	
∅	*!*		

Similarly in LG6, an input /VC/ would not give rise to an output V. This can be seen from the tableau in (29) which was just examined for slightly different reasons. Hence if the learner posits a /VC/ input for a surface form V, then neither grammar affords a grammatical analysis of the datum.

A consideration of the violations of /VC/ ↔ [V] shows, however, that more highly ranked constraints are violated in LG2 than in LG6. The gradient retreat learner could therefore make a move from LG2 to LG6, a move that would take it from a grammar where a V is grammatical (though not under the current analysis) to one where a V is ungrammatical.

Overall, the possibilities of movement by the CRTLA with gradient retreat are summarized in (32).

(32) *Possibility of a move by the CRTLA with gradient retreat*

Current grammar	Result of swap	Lower violations?	Move
a. Datum analyzed as optimal for postulated input	Datum analyzed as optimal for postulated input	No / Yes	No / Yes
b. Datum analyzed as optimal for postulated input	Datum not analyzed as optimal for postulated input		No
c. Datum not analyzed as optimal for postulated input	Datum analyzed as optimal for postulated input		Yes
d. Datum not analyzed as optimal for postulated input	Datum not analyzed as optimal for postulated input	No / Yes	No / Yes

As can be seen by comparing (32) with (24), the possibility of movement increases when the learner moves to demote violations, whether or not such a move actually brings about an improvement in grammaticality.

5.2. Changes in transitions

By incorporating the gradient retreat mechanism into the CRTLA, the set of triggered transitions in the space is changed. The learner considers not only the grammaticality of a form but also whether a form is better in one grammar than in another. Gradient retreat adds numerous transitions to the set of triggers that can cause a shift from one language to another, such that the total set of triggers based both on errors and retreat is as in (33) (compare with (12)).

(33) *Triggers based on gradient retreat*

Endpoint of shift	Shift	Triggers
LG1	LG2 → LG1	{V}
{CV, V, CVC, VC}	LG3 → LG1	{CVC, VC}
	LG4 → LG1	{V, CVC, VC}
	LG5 → LG1	{V, VC}
	LG6 → LG1	{V, CVC, VC}
LG2	LG1 → LG2	{CVC}
{CV, V, CVC, VC}	LG3 → LG2	{CVC, VC}
	LG4 → LG2	{V, CVC, VC}
	LG5 → LG2	{V, VC}
	LG6 → LG2	{V, CVC, VC}
LG3	LG1 → LG3	{CV, V}
{CV, V}	LG2 → LG3	{CV, V}
	LG4 → LG3	{V, VC}
	LG5 → LG3	{V}
	LG6 → LG3	{V, VC}
LG4	LG1 → LG4	{CV, V}
{CV}	LG2 → LG4	{CV, V}
	LG3 → LG4	{CV, V}
	LG5 → LG4	{CV, V}
	LG6 → LG4	{V}
LG5	LG1 → LG5	{CV, CVC, V}
{CV, CVC}	LG2 → LG5	{CV, V}
	LG3 → LG5	{CVC}
	LG4 → LG5	{CVC, VC}
	LG6 → LG5	{CVC, VC}
LG6	LG1 → LG6	{CV, V}
{CV}	LG2 → LG6	{CV, V }
	LG3 → LG6	{CV, CVC}
	LG4 → LG6	{CVC}
	LG5 → LG6	{CV, V}

Many of the cases of movement involve examples of retreat from supersets; other examples involve principled movement between weakly equivalent grammars. We assess the behavior of gradient retreat in the next section.

5.3. Performance of gradient retreat

The result of changed transitions is increased ability for the learner to move about the space of grammars. This increased mobility can be observed by comparing possible movements with and without gradient retreat for each of the three scenarios under consideration. We first present the results showing where movement is possible and where it is excluded, and then discuss the issue of probabilities of success for all scenarios. For details of transition matrices, see Appendix 3.

(34) *Scenario 1: gradient retreat in the limit*

Success rate (%)	Error driven	Target	Gradient retreat	Success rate (%)
100	LG1		LG1	51
100	LG2		LG2	51
100	LG3	→LG1←	LG3	51
100	LG4	LG2	LG4	51
100	LG5		LG5	51
100	LG6		LG6	51

For scenario 1, convergence is still possible from all grammars, although the rate of success decreases.

For scenario 2, recall that the strictly error-driven learner fails to converge on the target if it starts in or enters either LG1 or LG2. With gradient retreat, the pattern shifts, with convergence from both LG1 and LG2 becoming possible. Rates of success also increase for all cases where the learner is not in the target to start with.

(35) *Scenario 2: gradient retreat in the limit*

Success rate (%)	Error-driven	Target	Gradient retreat	Success rate (%)
			LG1	47
			LG2	47
100	LG3		LG3	47
33	LG4	→LG3←	LG4	47
33	LG5		LG5	47
33	LG6		LG6	47
failure	LG1			
	LG2			

Finally, for scenario 3, both failures by the strictly error-driven CRTLA are again removed by gradient retreat, with convergence to LG5 possible from all points in the space. Again, rates of success increase except when the learner starts in LG5.

(36) *Scenario 3: gradient retreat in the limit*

Success rate (%)	Error driven	Target	Gradient retreat	Success rate (%)
			LG1	47
			LG2	47
33	LG3		LG3	47
33	LG4	→LG5←	LG4	47
100	LG5		LG5	47
33	LG6		LG6	47
Failure	LG1 LG2			

Finally, recall that convergence to languages LG4 and LG6 was completely impossible in the strictly error-driven CRTLA unless the learner was lucky enough to start in the target language. With gradient retreat, convergence becomes possible from all grammars, achieved 100 per cent of the time.

(37) *Scenario 4: gradient retreat in the limit*

Success rate (%)	Error-driven	Target	Gradient retreat	Success rate (%)
			LG1	100
			LG2	100
100	LG4	→ LG4 ←	LG3	100
100	LG6	LG6	LG4	100
			LG5	100
			LG6	100
Failure	LG1 LG2 LG3 LG5			

5.3. Assessment of gradient retreat

Adding the gradient retreat mechanism to the CRTLA enables it to move to *all* grammars in the space from *all* grammars in the space. There are no longer any absolute traps. Performance is not perfect, however. The learner does not end up in the target grammar with probability 1 for any of the scenarios. In assessing this aspect of the learner's performance, it is important to distinguish between two properties of the learner's performance: (i) ability to move to some grammar *n*, (ii) probability of making such a move.

The strictly error-driven CRTLA performs poorly on the first count. It is able to move to certain grammars and unable to move to others. It falls into two types of trap: it cannot move from a superset language to a subset language, and it cannot move between weakly equivalent languages. As illustrations of the superset/subset problem, it was seen that there was absolute failure to move from LG1 or LG2 (supersets) to either LG3 or LG5 (subsets), and that there was absolute failure to move from languages LG1, LG2, LG3, LG5 (supersets) to LG4 or LG6. In addition, there is no movement possible from LG1 to LG2 in scenario 1, since the two languages are weakly equivalent (see (5) in Appendix 2).

In the cases where the error-driven CRTLA succeeds in moving to the target language, its performance varies. Movement to an overall superset language is perfect (100% convergence in scenario 1), while movement in other cases is quite poor (see the success rate columns of (35–37)); performance is perfect if the learner accidentally starts in the target grammar, but is at 33% otherwise in the space examined. It is unclear that simple changes in the algorithm would alter this performance.

The behavior of the CRTLA with gradient retreat is quite different. Within the space of languages considered, there are no absolute traps. From all starting points, it is possible to reach all target grammars.

In terms of the probability of reaching a target grammar, gradient retreat causes the performance of the learner to increase for convergence to the subset languages (LG3, LG4, LG5, and LG6) at the cost of decreased performance for convergence to the superset languages (LG1 and LG2). This is to be expected, since the gradient retreat mechanism allows the learner to escape from superset languages, even when they are the target language. In terms of percentages (see the success rate columns of (35–37)), the gradient retreat mechanism results in perfect convergence to the absolute subset languages LG4/LG6 (scenario 4), improved convergence in scenarios 3 and 4 (47% success in both), and markedly poorer performance with the superset languages targeted in scenario 1 (51% success).[8]

We suspect, however, that the actual percentages obtained under gradient retreat are less significant than the simple ability to move to all grammars. This is because there are various minimal modifications of the algorithm which should improve the rates of success without affecting basic possibilities of movement through the space.

Consider the effect of a fairly minimal change such as the following: instead of considering a single datum at a time, consider a small set of data, for example, *three* forms. Considering such a set, allow movement only if the move constitutes improvement for some members of this class, and does not

---

[8] The default CRTLA is set up such that the learner will not leave the target grammar once it has entered it. This assumption is not built in with gradient retreat, however. If we do assume that the gradient retreat CRTLA somehow knows the target grammar when it enters it, and will not leave it, then all grammars in our space are learnable in the limit with probability 1. This assumption is somewhat problematic, however, from the standpoint of learnability (cf. Gold 1967; Osherson *et al.* 1986).

constitute decreased performance for any. That is, if all forms result in improvement, move; if some are neutral and some involve improvement, move; if any form involves a worse evaluation, then stay in the current grammar. Consider this change with regard to targeting a subset language such as LG6, a language generating only CV forms. Only CV forms will be observed in the data. If an input CV were posited, then the input/output pairing /CV/ ↔ [CV] would be optimal in all six languages, and such analyses would be neutral with respect to movement. On the other hand, if a /CVC/ input were posited, then the /CVC/ ↔ [CV] pair would fare better in *LG6* than in the superset languages. If all data encountered are of the type CV, then movement towards the subset language ought to be comparable, in terms of probability, to the results given here for gradient retreat. On the other hand, consider a case where the target language is a superset, for example LG1. In this case, even with only three data considered, odds are against all three constituting CV forms (1/4 × 1/4 × 1/4 = 1/64)—but only CV input can consistently result in a neutral or improved analysis in LG6: a V form is neutral (/CV/ ↔ [V], /VC/ ↔ [V]), better (/CVC/ ↔ [V]), or worse (/V/ ↔ [V]) in LG6 (and note that the faithful pair is worse); a VC form is neutral (/CVC/ ↔ [VC]) or worse (/VC/ ↔ [VC]) in LG6 (note again that the faithful pair is worse); a CVC is systematically worse. If a set of data is considered, the probability of moving to LG6 if LG6 is the target should be largely unaffected; the probability of making the same move if LG1 is the target should be markedly reduced.

There are other possibilities that could have comparable effects. For example, a distinction could be made between movement to a grammar where a form is optimal, and movement to a grammar where a form is non-optimal, with movement guaranteed in the former case and only probabilistically occurring in the latter. Such an approach would effectively combine properties of the strictly error-driven learner with the learner allowing for gradient retreat.

In the current context, we simply note that such possibilities exist, and leave their exploration for future work. The significant result here is that gradient retreat allows the learner to move throughout the space of grammars, rather than remaining trapped in supersets.

6. Conclusion

In this chapter, we investigated the use of a simple learner that is comparable to a trigger-based learner from the parameter-setting literature. As with studies of parameter-setting, we demonstrated that there are traps in Optimality Theoretic spaces. Optimality Theory provides a mechanism whereby a simple learner can escape from some of these traps, however. The basic idea is that the notion of gradient violation allows the learner to retreat from a superset when a form that is optimal in both grammars incurs fewer, more lowly ranked violations in the subset grammar. We refer to this as gradient retreat. We have demonstrated the utility of gradient retreat with a triggering learning algorithm, but the relevance for gradient violation for a learner is not dependent on that particular approach to learning. The crucial point is that the central mechanisms of Optimality Theory perform more than a binary evaluation of *grammatical* versus *ungrammatical*. Two grammatical forms may differ in that one violates constraints that the other does not, and the same may be true for a pair of ungrammatical forms. Being sensitive to such differences in constraint violation allows the learner to move in a much more subtle fashion through the space of possible grammars, allowing retreat from a class of traps such as supersets.

Gradient retreat mechanisms will need to be investigated in larger spaces with more realistic and complete learners, but we have shown that Optimality Theory, in principle at least, allows for some solutions to standard learnability problems that are not available under parameter-setting and rule-governed accounts. It might be possible to achieve an effect comparable to gradient retreat within a parametric theory or within a rule-based derivational theory if one were to develop an evaluation metric that could determine how good a form was in a particular grammar. See, for example, Clark (1992) for such an evaluation metric for syntactic structures within a genetic algorithm fitness function. The advantage of Optimality Theory is that the fitness function is built in. It is an inherent part of the theory, central to basic grammatical analysis, rather than being added on solely for the purposes of learning. In rule-based theories, there might be many possibilities for possible evaluation metrics; within Optimality Theory, the metric is the theory itself.

ACKNOWLEDGEMENTS

This article overlaps with papers presented at Maryland Mayfest '95: Formal Approaches to Learnability, and the Essex Workshop on Constraints and Derivations in Phonology. We thank the University of Maryland for travel support to the former and the Humanities Research Board of the British Academy for travel support (Pulleyblank) to the latter. We thank Robert Berwick, Bill Idsardi, Kevin Broihier, Ted Gibson, Partha Niyogi, and Ken Wexler for ideas and discussion related to this paper, and the audiences in Maryland and Essex for helpful comments and questions. We thank in particular Sylvain Bromberger, Russell Norton, Iggy Roca, Nick Sherrard, and an anonymous reviewer who provided detailed comments on earlier drafts. Finally, we acknowledge support to Pulleyblank from the Social Sciences and Humanities Research Council of Canada, the Nederlandse Organisatie voor Wetenschappelijk Onderzoek, and the University of Girona.

REFERENCES

Bertolo, S. (1994). 'General Constraints on Maturational Solutions for the Triggering Learning Algorithm Local Maxima Problem'. MS, Rutgers University.

Berwick, R. C. (1985). *The Acquisition of Syntactic Knowledge*. Cambridge, Mass.: MIT Press.

Bloom, P. (1994). 'Recent controversies in the study of language acquisition', in M. A. Gernsbacher (ed.), *Handbook of Psycholinguistics*. San Diego, Calif.: Academic Press, 741–79.

Broihier, K. (1995*a*). 'Phonological triggers'. Presentation given at Maryland Mayfest '95: Formal Approaches to Learnability.

—— (1995*b*). 'Optimality Theoretic Rankings with Tied Constraints: Slavic Relatives, Resumptive Pronouns and Learnability'. MS, MIT. ROA-46.

Cho, Y.-M. Y. (1995). 'Language change as reranking of constraints'. International Conference on Historical Linguistics, Manchester.

Chomsky, N. (1981). *Lectures on Government and Binding*. Dordrecht: Foris.

Clark, R. (1992). 'The selection of syntactic knowledge', *Language Acquisition* **2**: 85–149.

Crowhurst, M., and Hewitt, M. (1995). 'Directional Footing, Degeneracy, and Alignment'. ROA-65.

Frank, R., and Kapur, S. (1994). 'On the Use of Triggers in Parameter Setting'. MS, University of Delaware and University of Pennsylvania.

Gibson, E., and Wexler, K. (1994). 'Triggers', *Linguistic Inquiry* **25**(3): 407–54.

Gnanadesikan, A. (1995). 'Markedness and Faithfulness Constraints in Child Phonology'. MS, University of Massachusetts, Amherst.

Goad, H. (1993). 'On the Configuration of Height Features'. Dissertation, University of Southern California.

Gold, E. M. (1967). 'Language identification in the limit', *Information and Control* **10**: 447–74.

Hale, M., and Reiss, C. (1995). 'The Initial Ranking of Faithfulness Constraints in UG'. MS, Concordia University. ROA-104.

Jusczyk, P. (1993). 'From general to language-specific capacities: the WRAPSA model of how speech perception develops', *Journal of Phonetics* **21**: 3–28.

Legendre, G., Wilson, C., Smolensky, P., Homer, K., and Raymond, W. (1995). 'Optimality and wh-extraction', in J. N. Beckman, S. Urbanczyk, and L. Walsh Dickey (eds.), *Papers in Optimality Theory* (University of Massachusetts Occasional Papers 18), Amherst: GLSA, 307–36.

Marcus, G. F. (1993). 'Negative evidence in language acquisition', *Cognition* **46**: 53–85.

McCarthy, J. J., and Prince, A. (1993). 'Prosodic Morphology I: Constraint Interaction and Satisfaction'. MS, University of Massachusetts, Amherst, and Rutgers University. RuCCS-TR-3.

—— —— (1995). 'Faithfulness and reduplicative identity', in J. N. Beckman, L. Walsh Dickey, and S. Urbanczyk, (eds.), *Papers in Optimality Theory* (University of Massachusetts Occasional Papers 18). Amherst: GLSA, 249–384.

Niyogi, P., and Berwick, R. C. (1993). 'Formalizing triggers: a learning model for finite spaces'. AI Memo 1449, CBCL Paper 86, MIT.

Osherson, D. N., Stob, M., and Weinstein, S. (1986). *Systems That Learn*. Cambridge, Mass.: MIT Press.

Pesetsky, D. (1994). 'Principles of sentence pronunciation'. Handouts, MIT. ROA-42.

Prince, A., and Smolensky, P. (1993). *Optimality Theory: Constraint Interaction in Generative Grammar*. Rutgers University Center for Cognitive Science Technical Report 2.

Smolensky, P. (forthcoming). 'On the comprehension/production dilemma in child language', *Linguistic Inquiry* 27.

Tesar, B. B. (1995). 'Computational Optimality Theory'. Dissertation, University of Colorado, Boulder.

—— and Smolensky, P. (1993). 'The Learnability of Optimality Theory: An Algorithm and Some Basic Complexity Results'. MS, University of Colorado, Boulder.

Turkel, W. J. (1996). 'Acquisition by a Genetic Algorithm-based model in spaces with local maxima', *Linguistic Inquiry* 27: 350–5.

Werker, J. F., and Lalonde, C. E. (1988). 'Cross-language speech perception: initial capabilities and developmental change', *Developmental Psychology* 24: 672–83.

—— and Tees, R. C. (1984). 'Cross-language speech perception: evidence for perceptual reorganization during the first year of life', *Infant Behavior and Development* 7: 49–63.

Wexler, K., and Culicover, P. (1980). *Formal Principles of Language Acquisition*. Cambridge, Mass.: MIT Press.

—— and Manzini, M. R. (1987). 'Parameters and learnability in Binding Theory', in T. Roeper and E. Williams (eds.), *Parameter Setting*. Boston: Reidel.

APPENDIX 1. *Forms Analysed as Grammatical in Each of the Six Languages*

The tableaux in this appendix organize input/output pairings in a standard fashion, although the goal is slightly different from normal input/output evaluation. The goal of each tableau here is to determine which of the outputs *CV*, *V*, *CVC*, and *VC* can be successfully analysed as grammatical by a given language. Recall from the text that candidates involving complex clusters, long vowels, long consonants, or epenthesis are not considered in this paper.

LG1: MAXIO >> NOCODA >> ONSET

(1) *LG1—Possible surface forms: CV, V, CVC, VC*

LG1			MAXIO	NOCODA	ONSET
/CV/	a. ☞	CV			
	b.	V	*		*
/V/	c. ☞	V			*
	d.	Ø	*!		
/CVC/	e. ☞	CVC		*	
	f.	CV	*!		
/VC/	g. ☞	VC		*	*
	h.	V	*!		*
	i.	Ø	*!*		

For *LG1*, the high ranking of MAXIO makes it possible for all of {CV, V, CVC, VC} to be optimal: retention of all lexically specified segments is more important than obeying either NOCODA or ONSET. The same is true for *LG2*.

LG2: MAXIO >> ONSET >> NOCODA

(2) *LG2—Possible surface forms: CV, V, CVC, VC*

LG2			MAXIO	ONSET	NOCODA
/CV/	a. ☞	CV			
	b.	V	*!	*	
/V/	c. ☞	V		*	
	d.	Ø	*!		
/CVC/	e. ☞	CVC			*
	f.	CV	*!		
/VC/	g. ☞	VC		*	*
	h.	V	*!	*	
	i.	Ø	*!*		

LG3: NoCODA >> MAXIO >> ONSET

(3) *LG3—Possible surface forms: CV, V*

LG3			NoCODA	MAXIO	ONSET
/CV/	a. ☞	CV			
	b.	V		*!	*
/V/	c. ☞	V			*
	d.	Ø		*!	
/CVC/	e.	CVC	*!		
	f. ☞	CV		*	
/VC/	g.	VC	*!		*
	h. ☞	V		*	*
	i.	Ø		**!	

This language exhibits a much more restricted pattern of grammaticality. Because of the high ranking of the NoCODA constraint, an optimal output can never contain a coda. Inputs containing a / . . . VC/ sequence therefore result in outputs without the final C. This can be seen in the ungrammaticality of (3e,g) and the corresponding grammaticality of (3f,h). Overall, *LG3* is incapable of generating either a *CVC* or a *VC* output. Like *LG1* and *LG2*, *LG3* is capable of generating outputs of the *CV* and *V* types. Note, however, that even here there is an interesting difference between *LG3* and the previous languages examined. In *LG3*, there is no unique input-type for a surface *CV* or *V*: a surface *CV* may correspond to either an input /CV/ or /CVC/, while a surface *V* may correspond to either /V/ or /VC/.

LG4: NoCODA >> ONSET >> MAXIO. *LG4* results in an even more restricted system than *LG3*. As can be seen in (4), only a surface *CV* is analysed as grammatical.

(4) *LG4—Possible surface forms: CV*

LG4			NoCODA	ONSET	MAXIO
/CV/	a. ☞	CV			
	b.	V		*!	*
/V/	c.	V		*!	
	d. ☞	Ø			*
/CVC/	e.	CVC	*!		
	f. ☞	CV			*
/VC/	g.	VC	*!	*	
	h.	V		*!	*
	i. ☞	Ø			**

For both /V/ and /VC/ inputs, it is better to not syllabify at all (the Ø case) than to syllabify a form without an onset. For a /CVC/ input, the optimal output retains the initial *CV* but eliminates the final *C*. The low ranking of MAXIO thus results in the deletion of segments in any sequence that would violate the NoCODA and ONSET conditions.

LG5: ONSET >> MAXIO >> NoCODA. *LG5* presents a similar intolerance of onsetless syllables, but tolerates codas.

(5) *LG5—Possible surface forms: CV, CVC*

LG5			ONSET	MAXIO	NoCODA
/CV/	a. ☞	CV			
	b.	V	*!	*	
/V/	c.	V	*!		
	d. ☞	Ø		*	
/CVC/	e. ☞	CVC			*
	f.	CV		*!	
/VC/	g.	VC	*!		*
	h.	V	*!	*	
	i. ☞	Ø		**	

Because of the high ranking of ONSET, syllables like *V* and *VC* are ungrammatical—it is preferable to delete a *V* or a *C* rather than to allow an onsetless syllable to surface.

LG6: ONSET >> NoCODA >> MAXIO. Finally, *LG6* derives a pattern similar to *LG4*: only *CV* syllables are tolerated.

(6) *LG6—Possible surface forms: CV*

LG6			ONSET	NoCODA	MAXIO
/CV/	a. ☞	CV			
	b.	V	*!		*
/V/	c.	V	*!		
	d. ☞	Ø			*
/CVC/	e.	CVC		*!	
	f. ☞	CV			*
/VC/	g.	VC	*!	*	
	h.	V	*!		*
	i. ☞	Ø			**

As with the *LG4*, the impossibility of both onsetless syllables (*V*, *VC*) and syllables with codas (*CVC*, *VC*) results from the ranking of ONSET and NOCODA over MAXIO.

APPENDIX 2. *Transition Matrices for Error-Driven Learner Without Gradient Retreat*

To determine probabilities, we begin by constructing a transition matrix *T* for each scenario, where each cell in the matrix shows the probability that the learner will make a triggered change from one grammar to another in a single step. We assume that the learner may have any grammar as its initial state.

(1) *Transition matrix for scenario 1: target = LG1 or LG2*

Start state	End state					
	LG1	LG2	LG3	LG4	LG5	LG6
LG1	1/1	0	0	0	0	0
LG2	0	1/1	0	0	0	0
LG3	1/10	1/10	3/4	0	1/20	0
LG4	3/20	3/20	1/20	3/5	1/20	0
LG5	1/10	1/10	1/20	0	3/4	0
LG6	3/20	3/20	1/20	0	1/20	3/5

(2) *Transition matrix for scenario 2: target = LG3*

Start state	End state					
	LG1	LG2	LG3	LG4	LG5	LG6
LG1	1/1	0	0	0	0	0
LG2	0	1/1	0	0	0	0
LG3	0	0	1/1	0	0	0
LG4	1/10	1/10	1/10	7/10	0	0
LG5	1/10	1/10	1/10	0	7/10	0
LG6	1/10	1/10	1/10	0	0	7/10

(3) Transition matrix for scenario 3: target = LG5

Start state	End state					
	LG1	LG2	LG3	LG4	LG5	LG6
LG1	1/1	0	0	0	0	0
LG2	0	1/1	0	0	0	0
LG3	1/10	1/10	7/10	0	1/10	0
LG4	1/10	1/10	0	7/10	1/10	0
LG5	0	0	0	0	1/1	0
LG6	1/10	1/10	0	0	1/10	7/10

(4) *Transition matrix for scenario 4: target = LG4 or LG6*

Start state	End state					
	LG1	LG2	LG3	LG4	LG5	LG6
LG1	1/1	0	0	0	0	0
LG2	0	1/1	0	0	0	0
LG3	0	0	1/1	0	0	0
LG4	0	0	0	1/1	0	0
LG5	0	0	0	0	1/1	0
LG6	0	0	0	0	0	1/1

Raising the transition matrix T to a power m yields the probability that the learner will be in a given state after m iterations. This is known as the *finite sample case*. Learnability *in the limit* is established by considering T^m as m goes to infinity. The behavior in the limit for each of the scenarios above is shown in (5–7).

(5) *Scenario 1 in the limit: target = LG1 or LG2*

Start state	End state					
	LG1	LG2	LG3	LG4	LG5	LG6
LG1	1	0	0	0	0	0
LG2	0	1	0	0	0	0
LG3	1/2	1/2	0	0	0	0
LG4	1/2	1/2	0	0	0	0
LG5	1/2	1/2	0	0	0	0
LG6	1/2	1/2	0	0	0	0

(6) *Scenario 2 in the limit: target = LG3*

Start state	End state					
	LG1	LG2	LG3	LG4	LG5	LG6
LG1	1	0	0	0	0	0
LG2	0	1	0	0	0	0
LG3	0	0	1	0	0	0
LG4	1/3	1/3	1/3	0	0	0
LG5	1/3	1/3	1/3	0	0	0
LG6	1/3	1/3	1/3	0	0	0

(7) *Scenario 3 in the limit: target = LG5*

Start state	End state					
	LG1	LG2	LG3	LG4	LG5	LG6
LG1	1	0	0	0	0	0
LG2	0	1	0	0	0	0
LG3	1/3	1/3	0	0	1/3	0
LG4	1/3	1/3	0	0	1/3	0
LG5	0	0	0	0	1	0
LG6	1/3	1/3	0	0	1/3	0

(8) *Scenario 4 in the limit: target = LG4 or LG6*

Start state	End state					
	LG1	LG2	LG3	LG4	LG5	LG6
LG1	1/1	0	0	0	0	0
LG2	0	1/1	0	0	0	0
LG3	0	0	1/1	0	0	0
LG4	0	0	0	1/1	0	0
LG5	0	0	0	0	1/1	0
LG6	0	0	0	0	0	1/1

APPENDIX 3. *Transition Matrices for Error-Driven Learner with Gradient Retreat*

Adding to the set of possible transitions changes the behavior of the CRTLA for each of the scenarios, both when a single form is considered and in the limit. We provide here the transition matrices for the four scenarios considered, first after a single datum and then in the limit.

In the limit, the transition matrices are as follows:

(1) *Gradient Retreat Learner—transition matrix for scenario 1: target = LG1 or LG2*

Start state	End state					
	LG1	LG2	LG3	LG4	LG5	LG6
LG1	56/80	4/80	5/80	5/80	7/80	3/80
LG2	4/80	57/80	6/80	5/80	3/80	5/80
LG3	8/80	8/80	51/80	3/80	4/80	6/80
LG4	15/80	12/80	4/80	39/80	6/80	4/80
LG5	8/80	8/80	4/80	6/80	49/80	5/80
LG6	12/80	12/80	6/80	4/80	6/80	40/80

(2) *Gradient Retreat Learner—transition matrix for scenario 2: target = LG3*

Start state	End state					
	LG1	LG2	LG3	LG4	LG5	LG6
LG1	24/40	0/40	5/40	5/40	3/40	3/40
LG2	4/40	17/40	6/40	5/40	3/40	5/40
LG3	0	0	35/40	3/40	0	2/40
LG4	4/40	4/40	4/40	28/40	0	0
LG5	4/40	4/40	4/40	6/40	17/40	5/40
LG6	4/40	4/40	4/40	4/40	0	24/40

(3) *Gradient Retreat Learner—transition matrix for scenario 3: target = LG5*

| Start state | End state | | | | | |
	LG1	LG2	LG3	LG4	LG5	LG6
LG1	12/20	2/20	1/20	1/20	3/20	1/20
LG2	0	16/20	1/20	1/20	1/20	1/20
LG3	2/20	2/20	10/20	1/20	2/20	3/20
LG4	2/20	2/20	0	12/20	2/20	2/20
LG5	0	0	0	1/20	18/20	1/20
LG6	2/20	2/20	0	0	2/20	14/20

(4) *Gradient Retreat Learner—transition matrix for scenario 4: target = LG4 or LG6*

| Start state | End state | | | | | |
	LG1	LG2	LG3	LG4	LG5	LG6
LG1	6/10	0	1/10	1/10	1/10	1/10
LG2	0	6/10	1/10	1/10	1/10	1/10
LG3	0	0	8/10	1/10	0	1/10
LG4	0	0	0	10/10	0	0
LG5	0	0	0	1/10	8/10	1/10
LG6	0	0	0	0	0	10/10

(5) *Gradient Retreat Learner—scenario 1 in the limit: target = LG1 or LG2*

| Start state | End state | | | | | |
	LG1	LG2	LG3	LG4	LG5	LG6
LG1	0.2537	0.2516	0.1503	0.1030	0.1405	0.1009
LG2	0.2537	0.2516	0.1503	0.1030	0.1405	0.1009
LG3	0.2537	0.2516	0.1503	0.1030	0.1405	0.1009
LG4	0.2537	0.2516	0.1503	0.1030	0.1405	0.1009
LG5	0.2537	0.2516	0.1503	0.1030	0.1405	0.1009
LG6	0.2537	0.2516	0.1503	0.1030	0.1405	0.1009

(6) *Gradient Retreat Learner—scenario 2 in the limit: target = LG3*

| Start state | End state | | | | | |
	LG1	LG2	LG3	LG4	LG5	LG6
LG1	0.1060	0.0628	0.4702	0.2339	0.0220	0.1051
LG2	0.1060	0.0628	0.4702	0.2339	0.0220	0.1051
LG3	0.1060	0.0628	0.4702	0.2339	0.0220	0.1051
LG4	0.1060	0.0628	0.4702	0.2339	0.0220	0.1051
LG5	0.1060	0.0628	0.4702	0.2339	0.0220	0.1051
LG6	0.1060	0.0628	0.4702	0.2339	0.0220	0.1051

(7) *Gradient Retreat Learner—scenario 3 in the limit: target = LG5*

Start state	End state					
	LG1	LG2	LG3	LG4	LG5	LG6
LG1	0.0702	0.1754	0.0246	0.0930	0.4737	0.1632
LG2	0.0702	0.1754	0.0246	0.0930	0.4737	0.1632
LG3	0.0702	0.1754	0.0246	0.0930	0.4737	0.1632
LG4	0.0702	0 .1754	0.0246	0.0930	0.4737	0.1632
LG5	0.0702	0.1754	0.0246	0.0930	0.4737	0.1632
LG6	0.0702	0.1754	0.0246	0.0930	0.4737	0.1632

(8) *Gradient Retreat Learner—scenario 4 in the limit: target = LG4 or LG6*

Start state	End state					
	LG1	LG2	LG3	LG4	LG5	LG6
LG1	0	0	0	0.5000	0	0.5000
LG2	0	0	0	0.5000	0	0.5000
LG3	0	0	0	0.5000	0	0.5000
LG4	0	0	0	1	0	0
LG5	0	0	0	0.5000	0	0.5000
LG6	0	0	0	0	0	1

PART III
EMPIRICAL STUDIES

✦

6

The Yokuts Challenge

DIANA ARCHANGELI and KEIICHIRO SUZUKI

1. INTRODUCTION

A challenge to Optimality Theory (henceforth, OT) (Prince and Smolensky 1993, McCarthy and Prince 1993*a*) comes from certain cases which have been characterized by the interaction of multiple rules. Such cases are problematic if they create a situation in which some linguistically significant generalizations are non-surface true, the property also known as phonological *opacity* (Kiparsky 1971; 1973). Under the serial-derivational model, such a situation is dealt with by the interaction of ordered rules. Since constraints in OT are stated in terms of output well-formedness, however, there is no means of referring to any intermediate stage of derivation.

A classic case of phonological interaction that has been analysed using considerable rule ordering is the pattern observed in Yawelmani Yokuts (e.g Newman 1944; Kuroda 1967; Kisseberth 1969; Kenstowicz and Kisseberth 1977; 1979). Thus the complexity of the data found in Yokuts has served as a testing ground for phonological theories. In this chapter we attempt to give an OT analysis of part of the Yokuts system. In particular, we focus on the featural aspects of Yokuts phonology, the phenomena known as Lowering, Harmony, and Raising.[1] Theoretically, we suggest three extensions to the formulation of constraints: disparate correspondence constraints, input markedness constraints, and Input-Else constraint prioritization. Briefly put, *disparate correspondence constraints* allow correspondence between nonidentical elements; *input markedness constraints* evaluate the relative markedness of input segments; and *Input-Else* constraints impose a specific requirement on the level at which a constraint applies. Conceptually, all of the above extensions are counter-Optimality Theoretic. However, a careful examination of the Yokuts dialects and the modifications themselves reveal that these extensions are not unreasonable.

The rest of this chapter is organized as follows. Section 2 provides the

---

[1] The prosodic properties (Epenthesis and Shortening) are introduced and discussed only as needed. See sources cited for discussion of the prosodic phenomena; see Archangeli and Suzuki (1996*b*) for an OT account of the prosodic properties.

theoretical background, clarifying our assumptions. Section 3 gives an overview of the phonological background of Yokuts. In Section 4 we discuss
Lowering, Harmony, and Raising. A brief sketch of each of these phenomena
under the derivational framework is provided, followed by our OT analysis.
Section 5 concludes the discussion.

2. THEORETICAL BACKGROUND

In this work, we assume a standard view of OT (Prince and Smolensky 1993;
McCarthy and Prince 1993*a*), including Generalized Alignment (McCarthy
and Prince 1993*b*) and Correspondence Theory (McCarthy and Prince 1995;
McCarthy 1996). We do propose a modification of Correspondence Theory,
however.

Correspondence Theory has been introduced to capture formally the similarity between input–output relations and base–reduplicant relations (McCarthy
and Prince 1995). Since then, the notion of correspondence has been explored
mainly in its role with respect to *faithfulness*, where faithfulness refers to
identity between representations. However, by definition,[2] correspondence
itself is simply a relation between two elements: identity of those elements
is not inherent in the correspondence relation, but rather is forced by various
types of faithfulness constraint, such as IDENT, MAX, and DEP, which require
identity of one type or another. Thus, one might imagine constraints requiring
correspondence between *nonidentical* elements. In fact, such a theoretical
move is anticipated in McCarthy and Prince (1995: 270):

> One topic worthy of future investigation is the potential for stating constraints other
> than the faithfulness variety on correspondent pairs in input and output. Developments
> along this line can produce the same general effect as the 'two-level' rules introduced
> by Koskenniemi (1983) and further studied by Karttunen (1993), Lakoff (1993), and
> Goldsmith (1993), and others.

We believe such 'disparate' correspondence is critical to an OT analysis of the
Yokuts featural phenomena; by extension, disparate correspondence may be a
key to resolving other cases which have been used to argue for mediating
levels of representation.

3. LANGUAGE BACKGROUND

There are three points to review about the Yokuts dialects in this background
section: the vowel inventory; the syllable inventory; and alternations in syllable structure that are relevant for the featural alternations.

---

[2] Correspondence (definition): 'Given two strings S_1 and S_2, correspondence is a relation $\Re$ from the elements of S_1 to those of S_2. Segments $\alpha \varepsilon S_1$ and $\beta \varepsilon S_2$ are referred to as correspondents of one another when $\alpha \Re \beta$' (McCarthy and Prince 1995: 262).

First, except for Wikchamni, at the surface, the Yokuts dialects have five vowel qualities; Wikchamni has seven.

(1) Yokuts surface vowels

	all dialects				*Wikchamni only*	
i	e	a	o	u	ü	ö

We assume the features [+high], [−high], [low], [round], and [back] to represent the vowels of the Yokuts dialects, as shown in (2).[3] The features [low] and [back] are necessary for Wikchamni, which has two additional vowels in its inventory.

(2)   How features correspond to segments

	All dialects					:	*Wikchamni only*	
	i	e	a	o	u	:	ü	ö
[high]	+	−	−	−	+	:	+	−
[low]			+			:		
[round]				+	+	:	+	+
[back]			+	+	+	:		

Our assumption is that all Yokuts dialects share the same set of features, including redundant ones. This enables us to distinguish vowel harmony in Wikchamni from that in the other dialects by a simple reranking.[4] The constraint responsible for this distinction is RD/BK, a grounded constraint (Archangeli and Pulleyblank 1994a; Hong 1994). The definition of RD/BK is given in (3).

(3)   RD/BK: If [round], then [back] (after Archangeli and Pulleyblank 1994a; Hong 1994). (If a segment is specified for [round], the segment must be specified for [back].)

In the dialects other than Wikchamni, RD/BK is never violated, since all round vowels are [back]. In Wikchamni, however, RD/BK must be violated to accommodate the two additional central round vowels ([ü] and [ö]). We show later, in

---

[3] This departs from the previously assumed features for Yawelmani Yokuts, by having 3 height specifications ([+ high], [− high], and [low], as opposed to two ([high] and [low], etc.). Isolating [a] as a sole [low] vowel becomes important in our analysis of Wikchamni Raising. Under the non-crucial assumption that all Yokuts dialects share the same set of features, we posit a redundant [low] and [back] in the other dialects of Yokuts as well.

[4] One could, of course, account for the difference by positing different feature sets for different dialects; for example, [+ high], [− high], and [round] for the dialects other than Wikchamni, and additionally [low] and [back] for Wikchamni. However, a significant drawback of such an approach is that vowel harmony must be characterized in two different ways for respective dialects: one is plain [round] harmony (for non-Wikchamni dialects) and the other is [round] and [back] harmony (for Wikchamni). In contrast, the proposed feature set allows a unified treatment of vowel harmony patterns in all Yokuts dialects (for more discussion of Harmony, see sections 4.2 and 4.3).

Section 4.3, that the ranking of RD/BK with respect to the other constraints is the only difference in contrasting vowel-harmony patterns between Wikchamni and the other dialects.

There are length correlations with these vowel qualities. Surface [i, u, ü] typically surface only where they correspond to input short vowels. By contrast, the mid vowels [e, ö] surface only where they correspond to long vowels in the input. We address this asymmetry in section 4.1 on Lowering.

Second, syllables in the Yokuts dialects are quite simple. All syllables have onsets; vowels may be long or short; a single coda is possible. Additionally, there are virtually no long vowels in closed syllables at the surface. The surface syllables are given schematically for easy reference (for an elementary OT analysis of Yokuts syllables, see Archangeli forthcoming).

(4) Yokuts syllables
     CV   CVV   CVC

Finally, inputs do not necessarily conform to the surface syllabification in two ways. First, inputs may include CVVC strings–which look like long vowels in closed syllables. These sequences surface as CVC if they syllabify as a single syllable. Second, inputs may include strings with more than two adjacent consonants, e.g. . . . VCCCV . . .. These sequences surface with an appropriately placed epenthetic high vowel: . . . VCiCCV . . . . or . . . (VCuCCV). . . .

Since the epenthetic vowel is typically a high front vowel, we propose two markedness constraints, given in (5).[5] These constraints preferring vowels to be [+ high] and not [back] are critical in this language family.[6]

(5) a. V≈[+ high]:   vowels are high.
     b. V≈[front]:   vowels are front.

The constraint, V≈[+ high], figures in our analysis of the feature alternations; values for frontness (or backness) are entirely predictable except in Wikchamni, so these feature values figure only in our discussion of that dialect.

Both Shortening and Epenthesis interact with the feature phenomena in these languages. Our focus, however, is on the feature interactions, and we do not give a formal analysis of the syllabification phenomena here.[7]

---

[5] In OT literature, it is normally the case that markedness constraints are expressed in the form of *X where the more marked the X is, the higher the ranking of the constraint *X (e.g. Prince and Smolensky 1993; Smolensky 1993). Since our analysis does not hinge on the issue of whether markedness constrains are negative or positive, we use 'positive' markedness constraints (5) to express the generalization in a more direct manner.

[6] The presence of the feature [front] is not required in our analysis. We include the constraint here for completeness and ignore it elsewhere.

[7] For the purpose of the present discussion, we also assume inputs which include the approporiate prosodic template, rather than developing the set of constraints necessary to select the optimal candidate. For OT discussion of template selection and its interation with other constraints, see Zoll (1994) and Archangeli and Suzuki (1996*b*).

4. DATA AND ANALYSIS

This section presents the three key patterns, *Lowering*, *Harmony*, and *Raising*, each of which affects features in Yokuts. For each phenomenon, we sketch the pattern and the derivational account before presenting our OT analysis. The phenomena and arguments are well known from the classical rule ordering literature (Kuroda 1967; Kisseberth 1969; Kenstowicz and Kisseberth 1977; 1979) so we do not labour the discussion here.[8]

4.1 *Lowering*

One of the intriguing properties of Yokuts is the mismatch in vowel height between input and output: input long vowels are non-high in the output. Our understanding of both this phenomenon and OT lead us to conclude that if correspondence-based OT is to account for the full pattern, then we must refer to the correspondence of non-identical elements. That is, we consider faithfulness constraints to be only a subclass of the correspondence constraints. To demonstrate this, we first lay out the data, then our analysis.

There are numerous alternations in Yokuts supporting the existence of this height mismatch (see e.g. Newman 1944; Kuroda 1967; Kisseberth 1969; Kenstowicz and Kisseberth 1979). One type of evidence is illustrated in (6). The first column shows the surface forms of roots with long vowels; in each case, the long vowel is non-high. The second column shows the same roots with the suffix -aaʔaa-, which requires that the preceding root have a short vowel; where the vowel is intrinsically short, the root vowels in (6c,d) are high. (The difference in length of root vowels is due to the templatic morphology; see Archangeli 1983; 1984; 1991 for derivational analyses; see Zoll 1994 for an OT account.)

(6) Data on Lowering

CVVC-t, e.g. /taan-t/		CVC-aaʔaa- . . . , e.g. /tan-aaʔaa-hin/	
a. taan-it	'was gone'	tanaaʔaahin	'had gone'
b. doos-it	'was reported'	(dosooʔoo. . .)	(constructed form)
c. meek'-it	'was swallowed'	mik'aaʔan	'is swallowing'
d. ʔootʼ-ut	'was stolen'	ʔutʼaaʔaanit	'is going to be stolen'

The pattern can be expressed by a rule which lowers long vowels:

---

[8] See Goldsmith (1993), Lakoff (1993), and Wheeler and Touretzky (1993) for further attempts to address these phenomena in models with 3 levels of representation.

(7) Lowering rule

[+high]→[−high]

In OT terms, of course, we want to express this pattern as a constraint on outputs, requiring that long vowels be nonhigh (see also Cole and Kisseberth 1995; Davis 1995).

(8) Lowering (*preliminary*): μμ≈[−high]
Any long vowel must be [−high].

Ranking this constraint higher than faithfulness to [+high] (given in (9)) forces long vowels to be assigned [−high], regardless of their input values. This is shown in (10) below for the input /ʔuuʈ'-t/ 'was stolen'. The optimal candidate satisfies the lowering constraint μμ≈[−high] because the long vowel is non-high, while violating IDENTI→O[+high] (9), the faithfulness constraint on the feature [+high].[9]

(9) IDENTI→O[+high]
Any output correspondent of an input segment specified for [+high] is [+high].

(10) Lowering

/ʔuuʈ'-t/	μμ≈ [−high]	IDENT→O [=high]
a. ☞ [ʔootʼut]		*
b. [ʔuutʼut]	*!	

This is the crux of our analysis of Lowering. However, there are a number of issues that need to be resolved before the analysis is complete.

4.1.1 *Input–output correspondence*

First, as noted in section 3, input CVVC sequences may correspond to surface CVC sequences, so input long vowels do not necessarily correspond to surface long vowels. However, as the forms in (11) show, lowering occurs none the less. In (11a,c) the intrinsic length of the vowel is revealed because the first syllable is open. In (11b,d,e) these vowels surface as short in closed syllables; the intrinsic length is implicit, however, through both the non-high vowels [e,o] and the odd harmony patterns (disharmonic in (11d): [. . . o . . . a . . .], and harmonic in (11e): [. . . o . . . u . . .]) (see section 4.2 on Harmony).

[9] We follow McCarthy and Prince (1995: 266) and Pater (1995: 15) in separating the symmetric IDENT constraint family into asymmetric constraints, IDENTI→O and IDENTO→I. The arrow appearing in these constraint names represents a 'direction' of mapping between the input and the output.

(11) Lowering in closed syllables
  a. meek'it < miik'-t 'was swallowed'
  b. mek'k'a < miik'-k'a 'swallow!'
  c. ʔoot'ut < ʔuut'-t 'was stolen'
  d. ʔot'k'a < ʔuut'-k'a 'steal!'
  e. ʔot'nut < ʔuut'-nit 'will be stolen'

These facts suggest an amendment to our basic lowering package: the lowering constraint is sensitive to *input* length, not output length.[10]

(12) Lowering: $\mu\mu$ $_I\Re_O$ [−high]

  Any input long vowel must be [−high] in the output.

This constraint is particularly interesting, since it suggests that correspondence constraints extend beyond faithfulness: here, the correspondence is between *length* at one level of representation and *height* at the other, disparate correspondence. This becomes more obvious when the constraint is phrased in the standard format for correspondence constraints:

(13) Lowering (final): $\mu\mu$ $_I\Re_O$ [−high]

  Any output correspondent of an input long vowel must be [−high].

We realize that there are other ways to phrase this constraint. The primary reason we see for using non-correspondence terminology is so that 'correspondence constraints' are restricted to 'faithfulness constraints'. However, the cost of that restriction is the need for a further type of constraint, and would deny the real parallel between constraints like (13) and faithfulness constraints. Thus, we propose the disparate correspondence constraint in (13).

4.1.2 Interaction with constraints on high

First, there are two constraints that prefer surface high vowels. In addition to IDENTI→O[+high] (9), the standard faithfulness constraint, there is also a constraint requiring vowels to be [+high], V≈[+high] (5a), which forces epenthetic vowels to be [+high] (discussed in Section 3). The lowering constraint, $\mu\mu$ $_I\Re_O$ [−high] (13), must outrank both of these height constraints, or lowering will not be preferred. This is shown by the alternative rankings in (14): regardless of which of the [+high] constraints outranks $\mu\mu$ $_I\Re_O$ [−high], the incorrect output is selected (candidates which are erroneously chosen as optimal are indicated by ❽).

[10] In fact, 'input' is a euphemism here, for the length may be the result of some morphologically determined template rather than inherent in the input representation of a vowel. In Archangeli and Suzuki (1996*b*) we address this very issue. In this work, we simply use 'input', with the caveat noted here.

204   *Empirical Studies*

(14) μμ ₁ℜₒ [−high] must outrank V≈[+high] and IDENTI→O[+high]

/ʔuut'-t/	IDENTI→O[+high]	V≈[+high]	μμ ₁ℜₒ [−high]
a. (☞) [ʔoot'ut]	*!	**	
b ❽ [ʔuut'ut]			*

/ʔuuʈ'-t/	V≈[+high]	μμ ₁ℜₒ [−high]	IDENTI→O[+high]
c. (☞) [ʔoot'ut]	*!*		*
d. ❽ [ʔuut'ut]		*	

4.1.3 *Interaction with constraints on non-high*

One problem with the constraints given so far is that they predict that all *short* vowels will surface as [+high]. This is, of course, false: short [a,o] (and [e] by Lowering and Shortening) are also possible in Yokuts. Short [a] is readily dealt with by introducing the faithfulness constraint, IDENTI→O[low] (15), which must be ranked above V≈[+high].

(15) IDENTI→O[low]

   Any output correspondent of an input segment specified as [low] must be [low].

This ranking, as exemplified in the tableau in (16), ensures that input low vowels are low in the output, since [+low, +high] do not combine.

(16) IDENTI→O[low] >> V≈[+ high]

/xat-hin/	μμ ₁ℜₒ [−high]	IDENTI→O [low]	V≈[+ high]	IDENTI→O [+high]
a. ☞ [xathin]			*	
b. [xithin]		*!		

The second vowel of concern is the mid round [o]. By the constraint ranking developed thus far, input /o/ should raise to [u], as shown in (17).

(17) V≈[+ high] forces a short non-high vowel to raise

/bok'-hon/	μμ ₁ℜₒ [−high]	IDENTI→O [low]	V≈[+high]	IDENTI→O [+high]
a. ☞ [bok'hin]			*!	
b. ❽ [buk'hin]				

While this is the case in a limited environment in Wikchamni (see Section 4.4), it is not the general case in the Yokuts dialects. This suggests a special faithfulness constraint requiring identity of [−high]. Another IDENT constraint on [−high], IDENTI→O[−high] (18), must outrank V≈[+high], so that an input /o/ does not undergo raising.

(18) IDENTI→O[−high]

    Any output correspondent of an input segment specified as [−high] must be [−high].

This is illustrated in (19), where only the relevant constraints are included. Were these two constraints ranked in the opposite order, *[buk'hin] would erroneously be selected as the optimal form.

(19) IDENTI→O[−high] >> V≈[+high]

/bok'-hin/	IDENTI→O[−high]	V≈[+high]
a. ☞ [bok'hin]		*
b. [buk'hin]	*!	

Together with the constraint rankings developed above, we have the following constraint hierarchy (20): top-ranked constraints are μμ $_1\Re_O$ [−high], the constraint responsible for lowering, IDENTI→O[low], the faithfulness constraint for input low vowels, and IDENTI→O[−high], the faithfulness constraint for input mid vowels. Ranking V≈[+high] below these three constraints means that the effect of V≈[+high] is visible only in the case of epenthetic vowels.

(20) Ranking Summary: Lowering

    μμ $_1\Re_O$ [−high]
    IDENTI→O[low]   >>   V≈[+high]   ,   IDENTI→O[+high]
    IDENTI→O[−high]

4.1.4 *Remaining issue: What is the optimal input for [e/ee]?*

There is a remaining issue to address, pointed out to us by Bruce Hayes: given that there are five surface Yokuts vowel qualities, [i, e, a, o, u], what restricts the input to the four qualities, /i, a, o, u/? As stated thus far, our constraint hierarchy does not make this restriction. Yet we believe it is an important restriction to make: the asymmetries in the distribution of [e/ee] make it clear that these vowels always correspond to input long high vowels.

There are three empirical problems with selecting an input mid front vowel. First, there is a length asymmetry. All such vowels potentially correspond to long vowels. None is necessarily a short vowel. Yet, if the vowel /e/ is possible, it should appear both short and long. Second, there is a harmony asymmetry. All such vowels harmonize with a preceding high vowel, never with a preceding mid vowel. Yet, if the vowel /e/ is possible, it should harmonize with /o/, since harmony is height dependent (see Section 4). Finally, there is a distributional asymmetry. In roots, vowels alternate in length sufficiently to establish that surface [e] corresponds to input /ii/, giving four input vowels, /i, a, o, u/. The only location for the putative input /e/ is in suffixes (where vowel distribution is restricted to /i/ and /a/ almost exclusively). Yet, if /e/ is a possible input, there is no explanation for this odd skewing.

Lexicon Optimization, developed in Prince and Smolensky (1993) and Itô *et al.* (1995), provides a means to derive an optimal input when multiple inputs converge on a single output form (see Pulleyblank and Turkel, Chapter 5 above, for further elaboration). In tableau (21), the two input–output pairs, having the same output, [ee], are compared in the constraint hierarchy developed above. Our hierarchy produces the same output form, [ee], from the two different inputs: /ii/ and /ee/. Lexicon Optimization singles out the best *input*, by comparing which input–output pair has fewer violations.

(21) Lexicon Optimization: /ee/ is chosen as the better input for [ee]

/ii/ vs. /ee/	$\mu\mu_i\Re_O$ [−high]	IDENTI→O [−high]	V≈[+high]	IDENTI→O [+high]
a. (☞) /ii/ [ee]			*	*!
b. ❽ /ee/ [ee]			*	

In this tableau, /ee/ (21b) is incorrectly chosen as the best *input*, since /ii/ (21a) entails a violation of the faithfulness constraint (IDENTI→O[+high]). Violations between both candidates with respect to the other constraints are the same; thus, the choice must be made by the faithfulness constraint, picking an input completely faithful to the output. As discussed above, however, output [e/ee] must be analysed as the result of Lowering from input /ii/.

The analytic problem is resolved if we acknowledge that the preference for vowels to be [+high], characterized by the markedness constraint, V≈[+high], holds of the *input* as well as the output. These two constraints are given in (22):

(22) a. {V≈[+high]}ᵢ: Input vowels are [+high]
     b. {V≈[+high]}ₒ: Output vowels are [+high].

We assume that this type of *input markedness* constraint must be dominated by its output counterpart, so that it plays no role in the normal input-to-output evaluation.

In (23) we show that this constraint pair, replacing the earlier V≈[+high], results in the correct pairing between input and output vowels.

(23) Lexicon Optimization: [e/ee] cases

/ii/ vs. /ee/	$\mu\mu$ ${}_I\Re_O$ [−high]	IDENTI→O [−high]	{V≈[+high]}$_O$	{V≈[+high]}$_I$	IDENTI→O [+high]
a. ☞ /ii/ [ee]			*		*
b. /ee/ [ee]			*	*!	

The input–output pair (23a) which shows the effect of Lowering is correctly picked, satisfying the proposed {V≈[+high]}$_I$.

The input markedness constraint in (22a) falls foul of one of the most important principles of OT: that there be no restrictions of any kind imposed on the input. It is claimed that the inventory of a given language must derive from the interaction of markedness constraints with faithfulness constraints (Prince and Smolensky 1993; Smolensky 1993). However, if the markedness constraints are sensitive only to the output, it is impossible to account for a case in which output segments exist which are not part of the input inventory. This is what we believe to be the case for the Yokuts dialects.

The Yokuts facts challenge the prohibition against restrictions on inputs which is central to OT. However, there are factors which lead us to believe that our proposal is compatible with OT, and with Correspondence Theory in particular. First, as pointed out by Kevin Russell (p.c.), Correspondence Theory opens the door for input constraints: Correspondence Theory allows constraints on the output, on input–output relations, and on output–input relations. Why not allow them on the input as well? Second, constraints on output–input relations, such as DEP constraints, restrict input options and so are a type of constraint on the input. Third, the saving grace of DEP constraints is that they are rankable and violable constraints, but that is exactly what we are proposing here: rankable, violable constraints referring solely to the input. Finally, we tentatively propose that input markedness constraints are inherently ranked below the corresponding output markedness constraint, and so can figure only in Lexicon Optimization, rather than anywhere at all in a language.

4.2. Harmony

In this section, we consider Harmony from an OT point of view. Harmony in Yokuts is characterized as height-dependent round/back harmony progressing rightward (Newman 1944; Kuroda 1967; Kisseberth 1969; Kenstowicz and Kisseberth 1977; 1979; Archangeli 1984; 1985). In this section, we focus on vowel harmony in the Yokuts dialects other than Wikchamni (we discuss Wikchamni harmony in the following section, 4.3). With respect to Harmony, the underlying Yokuts vowels, /i, u, o, a/, are divided into two height series /i, u/ (high) and /o, a/ (non-high). Thus, an underlying high vowel surfaces as [u] when following /u/, and an underlying non-high vowel surfaces as [o] when following /o/. The examples in (24) show the alternation which takes place in the aorist suffix /-hin/. The suffix surfaces either as [-hun] if it is preceded by a high back round vowel (24a), or as [-hin] if it is preceded by any other vowel (24b).

(24) a.   dubhun   < dub-hin   'led by the hand'
          hudhun   < hud-hin   'recognized'
    b.   xathin   < xat-hin   'ate'
          xilhin   < xil-hin   'tangled'

For the dubitative suffix /-al/, the same pattern holds: it surfaces as [-ol] when preceded by a non-high back round vowel (25a), and as [-al] when preceded by the other vowels (25b).

(25) a.   bok'ol   < bok'-al   'might find'
          k'o?ol   < k'o?-al   'might throw'
    b.   xatal   < xat-al   'might eat'
          hudal   < hud-al   'might recognize'

The iterative nature of round harmony is illustrated by the examples in (26a). Here, harmony takes place in all suffixes, whereas in (26b), the intervening high vowel in the indirective suffix *-sit-* blocks harmony between non-high vowels, giving rise to a surface [-k'a] rather than *[-k'o].

(26) a.   t'ulsuthun   < t'ul-sit-hin   'burns for'
    b.   bok'sitk'a   < bok'-sit-k'a   'find (it) for (him)!'
          *bok'sitk'o
          *bok'sutk'o

These patterns have led to a rightward rule of [round] and [back] spread, schematized below.[11]

(27) Harmony rule

Under OT, however, the emphasis shifts subtly. Rather than focusing on how to determine the output given an input, the focus is largely on whether the output itself is as well-formed as can be. This well-formedness is determined

---

[11] See Archangeli (1985) for the dependency treatment of Harmony in Yokuts under the rule-based approach.

in two ways, by faithfulness to the input representation and by goodness of the output representation. Following much current work in OT, we assume that harmony results from satisfying leftward or rightward alignment of the harmonic features (Kirchner 1993; Pulleyblank 1994; Archangeli and Pulleyblank 1994*b*; Cole and Kisseberth 1995; but see Beckman 1995 against using Alignment to achieve harmony). This suggests our constraint ALIGNCOLOR, a constraint that can be evaluated by examining output representations. We borrow the term 'Color' from Padgett (1995) to denote a class node dominating [back] and [round], which is independently motivated in Odden (1991).[12]

(28) ALIGNCOLOR: ALIGN (Color (= [round], [back]), Right, Wd, Right)
The right edge of every Color (= [round], [back]) is aligned with the right edge of some word.

ALIGNCOLOR is central in defining the goodness of output representations in Yokuts, illustrated in the following tableau. In (29), ALIGNCOLOR is best satisfied if Color features have spread throughout the word to the final vowel.[13] Incomplete harmony, as in candidates (29b,c), incurs ALIGNCOLOR violations.

(29) ALIGNCOLOR induces rightward harmony

/t'ul-sit-hin/	ALIGNCOLOR
a. ☞ [t'ulsuthun]	
b. [t'ulsuthin]	*!
c. [t'ulsithin]	*!*
d. ❽ [t'ilsithun]	

However, the fourth candidate, (29d), *[t'ilsithun], also satisfies ALIGNCOLOR since both [round] and [back] are perfectly aligned at the right edge of the word. The problem in this form is that [round] and [back] have been lost from the initial vowel, which is [round] and [back] in the input. Faithfulness constraints on each of the Color features prevent this candidate from being selected. These constraints are IDENTI→O[round] (30a), which requires that input [round] vowels be [round] in the output, and IDENTI→O[back] (30b), which requires the same for [back].

---

[12] Padgett (1995) proposes Feature Class Theory (FCT), an alternative theory of feature organization, aimed to replace Feature Geometry. In FCT, feature classes, such as PLACE, are defined as sets of features (having no tree-theoretic dependency relation). The direction suggested by Padgett (1995) seems promising; nevertheless, we do not pursue the idea of FCT here. Thus, our use of the term 'color' here should be understood as the Back-Round node within the traditional notion of Feature Geometry, as discussed in Odden (1991).

[13] Candidates containing [ü], such as [t'ul-süt-hün], are immediately eliminated by the undominated constraint RD/BK.

(30) a. IDENTI→O[round]

   Any output correspondent of an input segment specified as [round] must
   be [round].

 b. IDENTI→O[back]

   Any output correspondent of an input segment specified as [back] must
   be [back].

These constraints penalize unround/nonback output vowels corresponding to
input round/back vowels, such as the root vowel of candidate (29d), *[t'il-
sithun]. The O→I counterparts of these constraints, IDENTO→I[round] and
IDENTO→I[back], are necessarily dominated by ALIGNCOLOR. Since the distinction between IDENTI→O[round] and IDENTI→O[back], as well as the one
between IDENTO→I[round] and IDENTO→I[back], is not crucial in the general
harmony pattern, we use combined forms, IDENTI→O[Color] and IDENTO→I
[Color], on the assumption that a single more general constraint is preferred to
multiple more specific constraints.

(31) a. IDENTI→O[Color]

   Any output correspondent of an input segment specified as [Color$_i$] must be
   [Color$_i$].

 b. IDENTO→I[Color]

   Any input correspondent of an output segment specified as [Color$_i$] must be
   [Color$_i$].

The proposed faithfulness constraints correctly pick a winner (32a).

(32) ALIGNCOLOR and two types of IDENT constraints

/t'ul-sit-hin/	IDENTI→O[Color]	ALIGNCOLOR	IDENTO→I[Color]
a. ☞ [t'ulsuthun]			**
b. [t'ulsuthin]		*!	*
c. [t'ulsithin]		*!*	
d. [t'ilsithun]	*!		*

4.2.1 *The height dependence*

The constraints developed thus far do not address the issue of height dependence. We turn to that now. The essence of our proposal is the observation that
each token of [round] is associated to a single value for high, be it [+high] or
[−high], as in [t'ulsuthun] and [bok'ol] respectively. This is expressed by the
constraint below.[14]

---

[14] This constraint is quite similar to grounded feature co-occurrence constraints (Archangeli and
Pulleyblank 1994*a*; 1994*b*), but extends that notion to allow [αhigh]. We assume that inspection of
the physical properties of the features involved in any feature co-occurrence constrains of the type
{F, αG} will show grounding of the sort discussed by Archangeli and Pulleyblank. See discussion
in Hong (1994) of the physical properties of [round] and [high] and problems with the grounding of
[round] and [αhigh].

(33) {ROUND, αHIGH} (RD/αHI)

> Every path including [round$_i$] includes [αhigh].
>
> (Each token of [round] must be linked to vowels of the same height.)

As illustrated in (34), RD/αHI is satisfied if a particular token of [round] is associated only to vowels of one height. If [round] is associated with both high and non-high vowels, then the constraint is violated.

(34) RD/αHI is satisfied   RD/αHI is violated

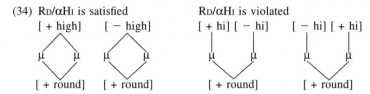

The result of this constraint is height-dependent harmony, as shown in (35). Candidate (35b) crucially violates RD/αHI, and candidate (35c) is eliminated by IDENTI→O constraints. Candidate (35a), while violating ALIGNCOLOR, wins by being faithful to the input.

(35) RD/αHI results in height-dependent harmony

/hud-al/	IDENTI→O [Color]	RD/αHI	ALIGN COLOR	IDENTO→I [Color]
a. ☞ [hudal]			*	**
b. [hudol]		*!		*
c. [hidol]	*!			*

4.2.2 *Preventing transparency: featural correspondence*

The harmony-blocking effect of the height difference is observed in such forms as [bok'sitk'a] 'find (it) for (him)' (*[bok'sitk'o]). However, as the tableau below demonstrates, the constraints developed thus far allow vowels of different heights to be 'transparent' to harmony, rather than forcing them to be 'opaque'. Candidate (36a) is the correct one, but (36c) is chosen.

(36) Nothing prevents transparency!

/bok'-sit-k'a/	IDENTI→O [Color]	RD/αHI	ALIGNCOLOR	IDENTO→I [Color]
a. (☞) [bok'sitk'a]			**!	
b. [bok'sutk'a]		*!	*	*
c. ☻ [bok'sitk'o]			*	*
d. [bak'sitk'o]	*!			*

The difference between the candidates [bok'sitk'a] and *[bok'sitk'o] is that the latter form has an extra, inserted instance of [round], in order to have a final round vowel.[15] Insertion of [round] violates faithfulness; in particular, DEP[round] is violated.

(37) DEP[round] (DEPRD)
   Every output token of [round] corresponds to an input token of [round].

The constraint DEP[round] is a constraint on feature correspondence. This is different from the basic assumption of *segment* correspondence introduced in McCarthy and Prince (1995). We assume, following Pulleyblank (1995), that *features* can correspond without any reference to the segment they associate to.

We suggest generalizing DEP[round] to DEP[Color] (DEPCOLOR), since neither [back] nor [round] may be inserted in these languages. This proposal serves a useful purpose in our discussion of Wikchamni harmony.

Addition of DEPCOLOR as a further constraint dominating ALIGNCOLOR has exactly the necessary effect: candidates in which [round] has been inserted by GEN fatally violate DEPCOLOR, despite [round] being better right-aligned in candidates like (38c,d).

(38) Preventing transparency

/bok'-sit-k'a/	IDENTI→O [Color]	DEP COLOR	RD/αHI	ALIGN COLOR	IDENTO→I [Color]
a. ☞ [bok'sitk'a]				**	
b. [bok'sutk'a]			*!	*	*
c. [bok'sitk'o]		*!		*	*
d. [bak'sitk'o]	*!				*

In sum, we account for the distribution of surface [round] and [back] in the following way. First, the constraints on faithfulness to [round], both featural and segmental, are high-ranked. The feature [round] is not inserted: all surface [round] features result from [round] in the input, subsumed under the undominated DEPCOLOR. Further, all input [round] and [back] vowels remain [round] and [back] in the output, a result of the undominated IDENTI→O[Color] (though the same result can be independently derived by undominated RD/BK). Finally, height-dependent rightward harmony of [round] and [back] is accomplished by best satisfying both RD/αHI and ALIGNCOLOR.

---

[15] An alternative would be to assume that [bok'sitk'o] as a single token of [round] linked to two nonadjacent vowels, [bo$_j$k'sitk'o$_j$], where 'j' co-indexes the round feature. There are two possible resolutions here: (i) NOGAP (Itô et al. 1995); and (ii) Universally ill-formed (Archangeli and Pulleyblank 1994*a*). Under the first resolution, a new constraint prohibiting gapped representations would be necessary, NOGAP. But if we follow Archangeli and Pulleyblank (1994*a*), such gapped representations are universally ill-formed and so not possible results from GEN; therefore, we do not need to introduce a new constraint such as NOGAP.

(39) Ranking summary: Harmony
Rᴅ/Bᴋ
IᴅᴇɴᴛI→O[Color]   >>   AʟɪɢɴCᴏʟᴏʀ   >>   IᴅᴇɴᴛO→I[Color]
Dᴇᴘ[Color],
Rᴅ/αHɪ

The grounded constraint Rᴅ/Bᴋ governs the inventory requirement that all round vowels be [back]. The high-ranked constraint, Rᴅ/αHɪ, requires that [round] be associated to a single value for [high], while the lower-ranked constraint, AʟɪɢɴCᴏʟᴏʀ, is satisfied by rightward harmony. The pattern results when these constraints are both satisfied, even at the cost of violating IᴅᴇɴᴛO→I[Color], which prefers that output [round] and [back] vowels are respectively [round] and [back] in the input. These six constraints constitute our basic analysis of Yokuts harmony.

4.2.3. *Remaining issue: phonological opacity*

There are two complicating factors which we discuss below. First, due to Lowering, input long high vowels are not high at the surface, yet it is the *input* height that is relevant for harmony. Consider the examples in (40).

(40) a. c'omhun   < c'uum-hin   'destroyed'
        *c'omhin
     b. c'oomal   < c'uum-al   'might destroy'
        *c'oomol

The first form in (40) shows the effect of harmony, even though the root vowel and the suffix vowel disagree in height at the surface. In (40b), by contrast, the suffix vowel surfaces as [a], showing no effect of harmony. This is because Lowering renders the effect of the height-dependent Harmony opaque (non-surface true) (Kiparsky 1971; 1973). Thus, evaluating Rᴅ/αHɪ (33) with respect to *outputs* does not account for the patterns. It suggests that {Rᴅ/αHɪ^I} (41) is the necessary constraint.

(41) {Rᴅ/αHɪ^I}
Every path including [round$_i$] includes [αhigh] in the input.

However, epenthesis creates a second complication which contrasts with the case of Lowering. Some output high vowels enter fully into the harmonic system even though they are not present in the input: these vowels are epenthetic; their insertion ensures well-formed syllable structure by preventing complex onsets or codas (see section 3 above). In (42), epenthetic vowels are italicized: in (42a) the epenthetic vowel harmonizes, while in (42b) it interrupts harmony.

(42) a. ʔug*u*nhun   < ʔugn-   'drank'
     b. log*iw*ʔas   < logw-   'pulverize'
        *log*iw*ʔos

In a derivational analysis, these facts have been used to argue that epenthesis necessarily *precedes* harmony, since epenthesis both feeds and bleeds harmony. Under OT, the implication is that $R_D/\alpha H_I$ (33) is evaluated on the output, because an epenthetic segment has no correspondent in the input: evaluating $R_D/\alpha H_I$ solely with respect to *inputs*, using $\{R_D/\alpha H_I{}^I\}$ (41), does not account for the patterns. The result of these two complications is that there is no unique level of representation at which $R_D/\alpha H_I$ may adequately apply.

To resolve this problem, we follow up on an observation made by Cole and Kisseberth (1995): harmony responds to input values for [high] *if there are such values*; otherwise it responds to output values for [high]. Only the epenthetic vowel has no input value for [high]: for all other vowels, the input value is the relevant one. To account for this fact, Cole and Kisseberth (1995) propose a Uniformity constraint which restricts the height requirement to either an input value or, lacking one, an output value (p. 17).[16] This constraint solves the complications introduced by Lowering and Epenthesis. The effect of Lowering, which may produce a conflict between input and output, has no effect on Harmony since the input values are the ones that are considered. By contrast, Epenthesis does have an effect on Harmony since the epenthetic vowels have no input values.

Formally, we propose to do this by specifying the levels of representation with respect to which constraints are evaluated (see McCarthy 1995 for the actual formulation of such restrictions). We characterize the specific requirement for a constraint to refer either to an input or, lacking that, to an output, as 'Input-Else'.[17] The schematic definition of Input-Else is given in (43).

(43) Input-Else (IE)

> In cases where there is a discrepancy between input and output structures, input structure takes precedence over output structure; otherwise, output structure is opted for.

Note that in our analysis Input-Else plays a crucial role not only in Harmony but also in Raising.

Given Input-Else, we now reformulate our $R_D/\alpha H_I$ (33) to accommodate Lowering and Epenthesis.

---

[16] Cole and Kisseberth's (1995) analysis is demonstrated under Optimal Domains Theory (ODT). ODT represents feature domains as the confluence of the bracketing of a phonological string and the expression of a feature within that substring (Cole and Kisseberth 1994). Since features may or may not be expressed within a substring, this provides a means of representing both input and output values in the candidate set. An input [+high] vowel which surfaces as non-high (as in Yokuts Lowering) is represented with both a [+high] and a [−high] domain expressed. Correspondence Theory (McCarthy and Prince 1995; McCarthy 1996) achieves the same end by making correspondences between input and output elements.

[17] Cole and Kisseberth (1995) argue that this characteristic can be naturally motivated if we extend the notion of *faithfulness*.

(44) {Round, αHigh^{IE}} (RD/αHi^{IE})

Every path including [round$_i$] includes [αhigh] in the input or, lacking an input, in the output

(Each token of [round] must be linked to vowels of the same height in the input or, lacking an input, in the output.)

RD/αHi^{IE} is sensitive to input values of the [high] feature, as well as the epenthesized [high]. The tableaux in (45) illustrate how RD/αHi^{IE} accounts for the complex interactions among Harmony, Lowering, and Epenthesis. For comparison, the previous versions of RD/αHi (i.e. RD/αHi (33), evaluated at the output, and RD/αHi^I (41), evaluated at the input) are placed on the right-most column. Cells marked ✂ are where the problem lies with each alternative version of this constraint.

(45) Harmony with Lowering and Epenthesis

/c'uum-al/	RD/αHi^{IE}	Align Color	IdentO→I [Color]	RD/αHi	RD/αHi^I
a. ☞ [c'oomal]		*			
b. [c'oomol]	*!		*	✂	*

/ʔugw-hin/	RD/αHi^{IE}	Align Color	IdentO→I [Color]	RD/αHi	RD/αHi^I
c. [ʔugiwhin]		*!*			
d. ☞ [ʔuguwhun]			*		*✂

In the first tableau in (45), candidate (45b) violates RD/αHi^{IE}, since it is the *input* value of [high] (=[−high] in the root) that counts. Notice that, without Input-Else, RD/αHi cannot eliminate (45b), and the wrong output would have been chosen as the winner. In the second tableau, RD/αHi^{IE} correctly predicts Harmony through the epenthetic high vowel, whose [high] value is not present in the input. The notion of Input-Else is thus vital in accounting for the full range of Harmony phenomena.

4.3 Wikchamni Harmony

In this section, we demonstrate that a reranking of the same set of constraints developed for the Yokuts dialects in the previous section is able to account for Wikchamni Harmony. This reranking is necessitated not by the harmony facts but by a basic characteristic of Wikchamni: that it allows central rounded vowels, [ü] and [ö], in its surface vowel inventory. We account for these facts by ranking RD/BK lower in the hierarchy. But let us examine the pattern and then turn to the details of the analysis.

Wikchamni differs from the other Yokuts dialects in having a high central rounded vowel, [ü], and a mid central rounded vowel, [ö]. Gamble (1978) notes that '/i/ and /ë/ are high and mid, central vowels with some degree of rounding. The degree of lip-rounding varies somewhat depending on environment and speaker, but is usually less than the rounding accompanying the back vowels' (p. 6).[18]

Wikchamni vowel harmony is characterized by the existence of /ü/. It is a case not only of round harmony but also backness harmony. As pointed out in Gamble (1978) and Archangeli (1985), Wikchamni necessitates an additional statement in the condition on harmony: backness, as well as roundness, spreads. This is because a suffix high vowel harmonizes to a high central rounded vowel [ü], as well as to a back rounded vowel [u], as in the dialects like Yawelmani. The examples in (46a,b) show the pattern of alternation which takes place in all Yokuts dialects, whereas the one in (46c) shows the additional harmony which is peculiar to Wikchamni: the suffix /-ši/ surfaces as [-šü] if it is preceded by a high central round vowel. The same-height requirement is also applicable to Wikchamni, as shown in (46d), where an intervening low vowel blocks harmony between two high vowels.

(46) a. p'in'ši   < p'in'-ši   'stung'
     b. hutšu   < hut-ši   'knew'
     c. tü?üššü   < tü?üs-ši   'made'
     d. pʰüwaasitʰ < pʰüwaas-itʰ   'was pounded'
        *pʰüwaasütʰ

A long /üü/ is subject to the Lowering restriction (see section 4.1), resulting in a surface non-high vowel [öö]. This is shown in (47): the lowered [öö] in both forms does not block harmony, even though it is non-high at the surface.

(47) a. tüwöö?üč'   < t'üwüü-(?)ič'   'to wet' Agentive
        *t'üwöö?ič'
     b. ?ütʰöötüč'   < ?ütʰüüt-(?)ič' 'to get angry'
        *?ütʰöötič'

In Wikchamni, RD/BK must be violated in order to allow [ü] and [ö] in its inventory. How low should RD/BK be ranked? As shown in (48), RD/BK must be dominated by ALIGNCOLOR, allowing the suffix high vowel to surface as [ü].

The critical points are (i) that DEPCOLOR outranks RD/BK. This prevents

---

[18] Throughout this chapter, high central round vowels and mid central round vowels are represented as [ü] and [ö] respectively, instead of the original symbols used in Gamble (1978). Odden (1991) characterizes these vowels as back unrounded vowels, based on his own observation. We maintain, however, the view taken in Archangeli (1985) in assuming that these vowels are non-back rounded vowels.

adding any Color features, such as [back], to rule out *[tü?üssu]; and (ii) that
ALIGNCOLOR outranks RD/BK in order that harmony proceed from /ü/, to rule
out *[tü?üsši]. Ranking with respect to IDENTO→I[Color] is irrelevant.

(48) IDENTO→I[Color] >> RD/BK

/tü?üs-ši/	DEPCOLOR	RD/αHI	ALIGN COLOR	RD/BK	IDENTO→I [Color]
a. ☞ [tü?üssü]				***	*
b. [tü?üsši]			*!	**	
c. [tü?üssu]	*!			**	*

Thus, the difference between Wikchamni and the other dialects is the position
of RD/BK in the constraint hierarchy (see (39) for the hierarchy developed for
the other dialects). The Wikchamni ranking accounts both for the existence
of /ü/ and [ü, ö] and for the different harmonic effects, *and is the only
alternative available*: RD/BK can either outrank ALIGNCOLOR (standard Yokuts)
or ALIGNCOLOR can outrank RD/BK (Wikchamni) This reranking constitutes a
single step down in the Yokuts constraint hierarchy, but this small step has
broad effects, simultaneously allowing round non-back vowels and changing
the nature of harmonic effects accordingly.

The real advantage of positing ALIGNCOLOR rather than ALIGNROUND should
now be clear. Characterizing Harmony in Yokuts as both [round] and [back]
harmony enables a unified treatment of both cases of Harmony by a simple
reranking of RD/BK. Lower ranking of RD/BK is independently necessitated by
inventory consideration, as discussed above. A characterization of general
Harmony as [round] harmony alone would entail an additional constraint to
account for the spreading of [back] in Wikchamni Harmony. The proposed OT
analysis accounts for the Wikchamni pattern without any such stipulation.

The significance of DEPCOLOR is more subtle. DEPCOLOR eliminates a
candidate like *[tü?üssu] because such a candidate would require an added
Color node for the third vowel, circled in (49).

(49) A violation of DEPCOLOR

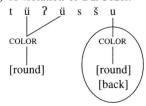

Without DᴇᴘCᴏʟᴏʀ, an incorrect form, (48c) or (49), is selected as optimal. The attested form (48a) is worse than the other contenders with respect to Rᴅ/Bᴋ.

(50) Ranking summary: Wikchamni Harmony
    IᴅᴇɴᴛI→O[Color],
    Dᴇᴘ[Cᴏʟᴏʀ],   >>   AʟɪɢɴCᴏʟᴏʀ   >>   IᴅᴇɴᴛO→I[Color]
    Rᴅ/αHɪ   Rᴅ/Bᴋ

4.4. *Wikchamni Raising*

In this section we discuss vowel-raising, a phenomenon occurring only in the Wikchamni dialect of Yokuts, Wikchamni (Newman 1944; Gamble 1978). In Wikchamni, short /o/ raises to [u] when the following vowel is /i/.[19] The resulting sequence is [u . . . i], not [u . . . u], as Harmony predicts.

The examples in (51a) show raising before the future suffix /-in/. Raised vowels are italicized. The root vowel of both 'doctor' and 'sour' surfaces as [u] when followed by [i]. The underlying /o/ in these roots is revealed in (51b), which shows the effect of harmony with /-at/, the dubitative suffix. In (51c), raising does not take place if the root vowel is not an underlying /o/.

(51) a.   t'*u*yxin   < t'oyx-in   'will doctor'
           p*u*ṭk'in   < poṭk'-in   'will sour'
      b.   t'oyxot   < t'oyx-at   'might doctor'
           poṭk'ot   < poṭk'-at   'might sour'
      c.   tawtin   < tawt-in   'will run'
           *tiwtin

We can characterize this pattern with a Raising Rule, as in (52).

(52) Raising Rule

    [round]
      |
     μ   μ
     f̶ ‒ ‒ ‒ ‒ ‒ ‒_|
   [−high]   [+high]

In terms of OT, however, raising cannot simply be the result of a rewrite rule. We argue that raising is due to the effort to avoid an antagonistic feature combination in sequence, in this case avoiding [− high] followed by the antagonistic [+ high]. This idea is expressed in OT terms, using Sequential Grounding (Smolensky 1993; Suzuki 1996; Archangeli and Suzuki 1996*a*), a syntagmatic extension of Grounding (Archangeli and Pulleyblank 1994*a*; 1994*b*). We assume a paradigmatic constraint preventing the combination of [+high] and [−high], as in (53).

---

[19] Our analysis assumes that raising is triggered by any of the high vowels, including /u/ and /ü/. This does not conflict with Gamble's (1978) description of the phenomenon, since virtually all suffix high vowels are restricted to /i/ in Wikchamni.

(53) *[−Hɪ]/[+Hɪ]:
    If a vowel is [−high], then it is not [+high].

This constraint might be based on the logical impossibility of the feature combination. However, since the combination of [−high] and [+high] is articulatorily impossible as well, such a constraint is phonetically grounded.

    We extend this constraint sequentially, to prohibit a non-high vowel followed by a high vowel.

(54) *[−Hɪ] . . . [+Hɪ] (preliminary)
    If a vowel is [−high], then it must not be followed by a vowel that is [+high].

The tableau in (55) shows that both *[−Hɪ] . . . [+Hɪ] and IDENTI→O[+high] must dominate IDENTI→O[−high] so that the non-high vowel raises rather than lowering the high vowel.

(55) IDENTI→O[+high], *[−Hɪ] . . . [+Hɪ] >> IDENTI→O[−high]

/t'oyx-in/	IDENTI→O[+high]	*[−Hɪ] . . . [+Hɪ]	IDENTI→O[−high]
a. ☞ [t'uyxin]			*
b. [t'oyxin]		*!	
c. [t'oyxen]	*!		

The next tableau shows that *[−Hɪ] . . . [+Hɪ] must be dominated by both IDENTI→O[low] and IDENTI→O[+high], so that only /o/, and not /a/, undergoes raising.

(56) IDENTI→O[low], IDENTI→O[+high] >> *[−Hɪ] . . . [+Hɪ] >> IDENTI→O[−high]

/tawt-in/	IDENTI→O [low]	IDENTI→O [+high]	*[−Hɪ] . . . [+Hɪ]	IDENTI→O [−high]
a. [tiwtin]	*!			*
b. ☞ [tawtin]			*	
c. [tawten]		*!		

Raising is particularly interesting in the way it interacts with the other phenomena, Harmony and Lowering. In considering these interactions below, we show that the basic Sequential Grounding constraint in (54b) must incorporate the notion of Input-Else.

4.4.1 *Interaction with Harmony*

The forms in (51a) show that raised /o/ does not trigger harmony between the root [u] and the suffix vowel [i] (as in *t'uyx-in*). Raising creates the context which could serve as the input to Harmony, but Harmony does not apply. (57) illustrates how this is captured by ordered rules within a derivational model.

(57) a.   t'oyx-in   b.   t'oyx-in
              ↓   Harmony   ↓   Raising
          t'oyx-in   t'uyx-in
              ↓   Raising   ↓   Harmony
          t'uyx-in   *t'uyx-un

In (57a), when Harmony precedes Raising, Harmony is not applicable and only Raising applies to the form *t'oyx-in*, resulting in the correct output *t'uyx-in*. If Raising were to apply before Harmony, however, as shown in (57b), the resulting form would be subject to Harmony, and the final output **t'uyx-un* would be ill-formed. Thus, Raising cannot precede Harmony.

Under OT, the picture is slightly different. Recall that the constraints responsible for harmony are RD/αHI^{IE} and ALIGNCOLOR, whose definitions are repeated below.

(58) a. RD/αHI^{IE}: Every path including [round$_i$] includes [αhigh] in the input or,
          lacking an input, in the output.
      b. ALIGNCOLOR: ALIGN (Color (= [round], [back]), Right, Wd, Right):
          The right edge of every Color (= [round], [back]) is aligned with the right
          edge of some word.

Let us consider a tableau for an input /t'oyx-in/: the constraints proposed already select the attested output if *[− HI] . . . [+ HI] is ranked below RD/αHI^{IE}.

(59) *[− HI] . . . [+ HI] and Harmony

/t'oyx-in/	RD/αHI^{IE}	ALIGNCOLOR	*[− HI] . . . [+ HI]
a. ☞ [t'uyxin]		*	
b. [t'uyxun]	*!		
c. [t'oyxin]		*	*!

Candidate (59b) loses out by violating RD/αHI^{IE}, since the underlying height of the root vowel is [−high]. This is a case where underlying height ([−high]) and surface height ([+high]) conflict, and the height which RD/αHI^{IE} is sensitive to is the underlying one, ([−high]). Thus, *[−HI] . . . [+HI] must be dominated by RD/αHI^{IE} to block harmony.

4.4.2 *Interaction with Epenthesis*

The next set of data, in (60), shows that not only the underlying /i/ but also the epenthetic high-vowel triggers Raising. In each form, a CC-final root undergoes epenthesis and the root /o/ surfaces as [u]. This interaction, too, is explained by rule ordering in the derivational model.

(60) a. t'uyixši   < t'oyx-ši   'doctored'
      puṭik'ši   < poṭk'-ši   'soured'
   b. ʔuṭ'iwhat   < ʔoṭ'w-hat   'hairs'
      tuʔiṭ'hat   < toʔṭ'-hat   'heads'

Thus the epenthetic vowel must be visible to Raising. This is already assured by our constraint, $*[-H_I] \ldots [+H_I]$, since its evaluation considers the *surface* value of [high].

Interaction with Lowering

We now turn to Lowering. The data in (61) shows that Raising can be triggered by a vowel which undergoes Lowering. In (61), the root vowel /o/ is raised by the following long high vowel in the future suffix /-iina/, despite the fact that it surfaces as the non-high [-eena] due to Lowering.

(61)   puk'eena   < pok'-iina   'will find'

What these data show is that the vowel which conditions Raising does not have to be high at the surface. Thus, Raising must refer to the *input* value of [high].

4.4.3 Raising is another case of Input-Else

As in the case of Harmony, it is crucial that Raising be sensitive to the value of [high] in the input, or lacking one, to the output value. This is the property which is exactly captured by Input-Else (43). Thus, we propose that our Sequential Grounding constraint, $*[-H_I] \ldots [+H_I]$, must also be subject to an Input-Else application.

(62) $[-H_I] \ldots [+H_I]^{IE}$ (*final*)
     If a vowel is [−high], then it must not be followed by a vowel that is [+high] *in the input or, lacking an input, in the output.*

Clearly, the Input-Else requirement is enforced only on the consequent [+high], and not on the antecedent [−high]. If Input-Else were to govern the antecedent [−high] vowels, the constraint $(*[-H_I]^{IE} \ldots [+H_I])$ would never produce a correct output, incurring a violation in forms with input /o . . .i/ sequences, such as /pok'-ʔin/ ([puk'ʔin]) without forcing raising.

With this modification, it is now possible for $[-H_I] \ldots [+H_I]^{IE}$ to account for the cases involving Lowering and Epenthesis. The tableaux in (63) show Lowering and Epenthesis.

(63) Lowering and Epenthesis cases

/pok'-iina/	$\mu\mu\ _1\Re_O$ [−high]	IDENTI→O [+high]	*[−HI] . . . [+HI]^{IE}	IDENTI→O [−high]
a. ☞ [puk'eena]		*		*
b. [pok'eena]		*	*!	
c. [pok'iina]	*!		*	

/t'oyx-ši/	$\mu\mu\ _1\Re_O$ [−high]	IDENTI→O [+ high]	*[− HI] . . . [+ HI]^{IE}	IDENTI→O [−high]
d. ☞ [t'uyixši]				*
e. [t'oyixši]			*!	

In the first tableau, candidate (63c) is immediately eliminated, failing $\mu\mu\ _1\Re_O$ [−high] (lowering). Candidate (63b) violates *[−HI] . . . [+HI]^{IE}, since a surface [−high] vowel is followed by an *input* [+high] vowel. Candidate (63a) is correctly picked by satisfying *[−HI] . . . [+HI]^{IE}. In the second tableau, candidate (63d) wins by not violating *[−HI] . . . [+HI]^{IE}, because the epenthetic vowel lacks an input value for [high] and its *output* value is counted.

Furthermore, recall from (56 b,c) that IDENTI→O[+high] crucially outranks *[−HI] . . . [+HI]^{IE}. The discussion of Lowering required that $\mu\mu\ _1\Re_O$ [−high] outrank IDENTI→O[+high]. A prediction of this ranking is that long /oo/ will not be raised, even when preceding a high vowel. This is indeed the case (Gamble 1978:17), as illustrated below. In (64a), the underlying long /oo/ is followed by /i/ in the aorist suffix -*ši*, but it remains unchanged; this is also true with an epenthetic vowel as trigger in (64b).

(64)   a.   hoyooši   < hoyoo-ši   'named'
       b.   toocix   < toocx-ø   'scare!'

As shown above, once again, Input-Else plays a critical role in determining where the relevant information to a particular constraint lies. Finally, we give the Wikchamni constraint hierarchy in (65).

(65) Ranking summary: Wikchamni Raising

$\mu\mu\ _1\Re_O$ >> IDENTI→O >> IDENTI→O >> *[− HI] . . . [+ HI]^{IE} >> IDENTI→O
[−high]   [+high]   [low]   [−high]
RD/αHI   ALIGN
               COLOR

5. CONCLUSION

We have discussed the three central Yokuts featural phenomena, Lowering, Harmony, and Raising, from the perspective of Optimality Theory. Our account of Lowering exploits two extensions to the model. First, we extended correspondence to crucially non-identical elements (i.e. 'disparate' correspondence), along the line suggested in McCarthy and Prince (1995): input length corresponds to output [−high] in these languages. Second, we extended Correspondence Theory to input-only constraints, proposing an input markedness constraint, both violable and rankable, rather than a constraint directly governing the input.

In considering both Harmony and Raising, we made use of Cole and Kisseberth's (1995) notion of an 'Input-Else' designation, evaluating input elements if any and otherwise evaluating output elements. We also exploited a central proposal from McCarthy (1995) that level designations may be restricted to only one part of a constraint, rather than holding true of the entire constraint. These two proposals enable the analysis to account for the data without reference to an interim level of representation.

These are the costs of the analysis. What is gained follows. First, very specifically, we have accounted for why Wikchamni harmony change and inventory change go hand-in-hand: under this analysis, there is no alternative. The inventory change results from reranking a single constraint in the only possible way, and an automatic consequence of this reranking is the harmonic change. Second, more generally, we have offered an OT analysis of height dependent harmony, which might well extend to other parasitic harmony systems. Finally, we have provided an OT account of the complex Yokuts feature phenomena, patterns which involve a fairly high degree of phonological opacity–an issue also raised in McCarthy (1995). We believe that our analysis is more conservative in its theoretical assumptions than are analyses of parts of the same data found in Cole and Kisseberth (1995) and Davis (1995). The ability to characterize such complex patterns of opacity is critical to the success of OT as a theory; it is therefore important that extensions to the model be minimal.

ACKNOWLEDGEMENTS

* Special thanks to Stuart Davis, Dirk Elzinga, Mike Hammond, Bruce Hayes, Jessica Maye, and Iggy Roca for helpful discussion and comments as we prepared this paper. Work by both authors was supported by NSF FAW award no. BNS-9023323 to Diana Archangeli.

REFERENCES

Archangeli, D. (1983) 'The root CV template as a property of the affix: evidence from Yawelmani', *Natural Language and Linguistic Theory* **1**: 347–84.

—— (1984). 'Underspecification in Yawelmani Phonology and Morphology'. Doctoral dissertation, Massachusetts Institute of Technology.

—— (1985). 'Yokuts harmony: evidence for coplanar representations in nonlinear phonology', *Linguistic Inquiry* **16**: 335–72.

—— (1991). 'Syllabification and prosodic templates in Yawelmani', *Natural Language and Linguistic Theory* **9**: 231–83.

—— (forthcoming). 'Optimality theory: an introduction to linguistics in the 1990s', in Archangeli D. and D. T. Langendoen (eds.), *Optimality Theory: An Introduction*. Oxford: Blackwell.

—— Pulleyblank, D. (1994a). *Grounded Phonology*. Cambridge, Mas.: MIT Press.

—— (1994b). 'Kinande Vowel Harmony: Domains, Grounded Conditions, and One-Sided Alignment'. MS, University of Arizona and University of British Columbia.

—— and Suzuki, K. (1996a). 'Menomini vowel harmony: opacity and transparency in OT', in K. Suzuki and D. Elzinga (eds.), *Proceedings of the South Western Optimality Theory Workshop I: Features in OT*.

—— —— (1996b). 'Yokuts templates: correspondence to neither input nor output', in B. Agbayani and N. Harada (eds.), *Proceedings of the South Western Optimality Theory Workshop II*.

Beckman, J. (1995). 'Shona height harmony: markedness and positional identity', in J. Beckman, L. Dickey, and S. Urbanczyk (eds.), *Papers in Optimality Theory*. University of Massachusetts Occasional Papers 18, 53–75.

Cole, J., and Kisseberth, C. (1994). 'An Optimal Domains Theory of Harmony'. MS, University of Illinois. ROA-22.

—— —— (1995). 'Restricting Multi-level Constraint Evaluation: Opaque Rule Interaction in Yawelmani Vowel Harmony'. MS, University of Illinois. ROA-98.

Davis, S. (1995). 'Some matters regarding the derivational residue'. Paper presented at the Tilburg Conference on the Derivational Residue in Phonology.

Gamble, G. (1978). *Wikchamni Grammar*. Berkeley, Calif.: University of California Press.

Goldsmith, J. (1993). 'Harmonic phonology', in Goldsmith (ed.), *The Last Phonological Rule: Reflections on Constraints and Derivations*. Chicago: University of Chicago Press, 21–60.

Hong, S.-H. (1994). 'Issues in Round Harmony: Grounding, Identity and their Interaction'. Doctoral dissertation, University of Arizona.

Itô, J., Mester, A., and Padgett, J. (1995). 'NC: licensing and underspecification in Optimality Theory', *Linguistic Inquiry* **26**.

Karttunen, L. (1993). 'Finite-state constraints', in J. Goldsmith (ed.), *The Last Phonological Rule: Reflections on Constraints and Derivations*. Chicago: University of Chicago Press, 173–94.

Kenstowicz, M., and Kisseberth, C. (1977). *Topics in Phonological Theory*. New York: Academic Press.

—— (1979). *Generative Phonology: Description and Theory*. New York: Academic Press.

Kiparsky, P. (1971). 'Historical linguistics', in W. Dingwall (ed.), *A Survey of Linguistic Science*. College Park, Md.: University of Maryland Press.

—— (1973). 'Phonological representations', in O. Fujimura (ed.), *Three Dimensions of Linguistic Theory*. Tokyo: Taikusha, 1–136.

Kirchner, R. (1993). 'Turkish Vowel Harmony and Disharmony: An Optimality Theoretic Account'. MS, University of California, Los Angeles. ROA-4.

Kisseberth, C. (1969). 'On the abstractness of phonology: the evidence from Yawelmani', *Papers in Linguistics* **1**: 248–82.

Koskenniemi, K. (1983). *Two-Level Morphology: A General Computational Model for Word-Form Recognition and Production*. Department of General Linguistics, University of Helsinki.

Kuroda, S.-Y. (1967). *Yawelmani Phonology*. Cambridge, Mass.: MIT Press.

Lakoff, G. (1993). 'Cognitive phonology', in J. Goldsmith (ed.), *The Last Phonological Rule: Reflections on Constraints and Derivations*. Chicago, University of Chicago Press, 117–45.

McCarthy, J. (1995). 'Remarks on Phonological Opacity in Optimality Theory'. MS, University of Massachusetts, Amherst. ROA-79.

—— (1996). 'Faithfulness in Prosodic Morphology and Phonology: Rotuman Revisited'. MS, ROA-110.

—— and Prince, A. (1993*a*). 'Generalized Alignment'. MS, University of Massachusetts, Amherst, and Rutgers University. ROA-7.

—— —— (1993*b*). 'Prosodic Morphology I: Constraint Interaction and Satisfaction'. MS, University of Massachusetts, Amherst, and Rutgers University.

—— —— (1995). 'Faithfulness and reduplicative identity', (University of Massachusetts Occasional Papers 18) in J. N. Beckman, L. W. Dickey, and S. Urbanczyk (eds.), *Papers in Optimality Theory* Amherst: GLSA, 249–384.

Newman, S. (1944). *Yokuts Language of California*. New York: Viking Fund.

Odden, D. (1991). 'Vowel geometry', *Phonology* **8**: 261–89.

Pater, J. (1995). 'Austronesian Nasal Substitution and Other NC Effects'. MS, ROA-92.

Padgett, J. (1995). 'Feature Classes', in J. N. Beckman, L. W. Dickey, and S. Urbanczyk (eds.), *Papers in Optimality Theory*. (University of Massachusetts Occasional Papers 18). Amherst: GLSA, 385–420.

Prince, A., and Smolensky, P. (1993). 'Optimality Theory: Constraint Interaction in Generative Grammar'. MS, Rutgers University and University of Colorado at Boulder.

Pulleyblank, D. (1994). 'Neutral Vowels in Optimality Theory: A Comparison of Yoruba and Wolof'. MS, University of British Columbia.

—— (1995). 'Featural asymmetries: out from under()specification' *[sic]*, Paper presented at the colloquium, University of Arizona.

Smolensky, P. (1993). 'Harmony, Markedness, and Phonological Activity'. MS, Johns Hopkins University.

Suzuki, K. (1996). 'Double-sided effect in OT: sequential grounding and local conjunction', in K. Suzuki and D. Elzinga (eds.), *Proceedings of the South Western Optimality Theory Workshop I: Features in OT*.

Wheeler, D., and Touretzky, D. (1993). 'A connectionist implementation of cognitive phonology', in J. Goldsmith (ed.), *The Last Phonological Rule: Reflections on Constraints and Derivations*. Chicago,: University of Chicago Press, 146–72.

Zoll, C. (1994). 'Directionless Syllabification in Yawelmani'. MS, University of California, Berkeley. ROA-28.

7

Rules in Optimality Theory:
Two Case Studies

JULIETTE BLEVINS

1. INTRODUCTION

Within Optimality Theory, as formulated by Prince and Smolensky (1993) (P&S) and extended in much subsequent work, surface forms within a language are those which optimally satisfy a sequence of universal violable constraints. What differentiates grammars is the ranking of constraints, and the possibility that a constraint may only hold of a designated morpheme or class of morphemes within a particular grammar. All constraints are claimed to be universal; the failure of a constraint to be evidenced in a particular language is taken as confirmation that the constraint is too low on the constraint hierarchy to be visible.

Derivational models of phonology, following in the tradition of Chomsky and Halle (1968), take surface forms to be the output of an ordered set of language-specific rules applying to underlying forms. Questions of universal markedness or naturalness are stated outside of the language-specific ordered rule system (in *The Sound Pattern of English*, as marking conventions; in autosegmental work, as representational constraints like the Obligatory Contour Principle). Gradually, as derivational models have become more and more concerned with distinguishing universal and language-specific aspects of sound patterns, a wider range of constraints have been imposed on rule systems and some degree of rule-ordering has been eliminated. For instance, in Myers's (1991) model the phonological component consists of filters, which enforce universal restrictions on sound-sequencing, persistent unordered rules, which define the inventory of phonological elements for a given language, and SPE-style ordered language-specific phonological rules, which define the distribution of phonological elements for a given language. Nevertheless, derivational accounts remain distinct from Optimality grammars in recognizing parochial rules which do not reflect universal naturalness or markedness principles.

Given this background, one potential argument against Optimality Theory (OT) as formulated in P&S is that certain sound patterns are the result of language-specific rules. Since OT has no place for such parochial rules, the theory, as it stands, is empirically inadequate. This is essentially the argument I will propose here. However, universal constraint ranking and violability in OT are responsible for the success of the theory in handling apparent rule conspiracies, emergence of the unmarked, and the general property of languages to instantiate certain phonotactic targets again and again by distinct strategies. Given these advantages of the constraint-based model, I suggest that language-specific rules be admitted within OT grammars.

I propose two revisions of current Optimality Theory (OT) based on two case studies detailing the evolution of language particular rules. First, I suggest that, in addition to universal constraints which form the core of the grammar, language-particular phonological rules exist at the periphery. The patterns I refer to as 'phonological rules', exemplified here by Gilbertese nasal sandhi, cannot be viewed as phonologically 'natural' or phonetically 'grounded' but are best understood in terms of historical reanalysis of formerly transparent, phonetically motivated alternations. Phonological rules are indexed to particular constraints, and function as language-particular alternatives to Gen. I suggest that the ubiquity and transparency of phonological rules within individual grammars make them easily learnable. A second language-specific rule type is also recognized: again phonological alternations are neither 'natural' or phonetically 'grounded' but are best understood in terms of historical morphological reanalysis due to opacity under sound change. The particular case I discuss is subtractive V-deletion in Lardil nominatives. The primary contribution of this chapter is to demonstrate that parochial sound patterns are often best understood in terms of their diachrony: each step of a complex diachronic development is well understood phonetically or typologically, but the synchronic result is not, and must be recognized as an aberration within the grammar.

In section 2 I outline differences between universal constraints and language-specific phonological rules as first proposed by McCarthy (1993) in his detailed analysis of alternations involving English /r/ in Eastern Massachusetts dialects.[1] In section 3 I detail a prime example of a phonological rule operative in Gilbertese, and demonstrate how this rule has arisen from historical reanalysis of phonetically well-understood sound changes. In section 4 I suggest factors contributing to the learnability of language specific rules. Section 5 reviews the alternations present in Lardil nominative forms. I argue that, *contra* P&S, V-deletion in Lardil nominatives is not a slightly altered form of a universal phonological constraint. Rather, this word-formation rule is part of Lardil morphology, and has arisen through morphological rule inversion. The morphological component of the grammar is distinct from the phonological constraint-ranking, and includes language-particular rules of word-for-

---

[1] Throughout the discussion of English, 'r' represents the single English rhotic glide phoneme whose phonetic realization is discussed in detail below.

mation, including the rule forming nominative words from Lardil uninflected stems. Section 6 is a brief summary.

2. CONSTRAINTS, UNIVERSALITY, AND PHONOLOGICAL RULES.

Optimality Theory is in its early stages, and yet hundreds of markedness constraints have been proposed to account for sound patterns of the world's languages. Some of these constraints are well motivated in terms of phonological typology, while others instantiate phonetically motivated associations (cf. Myers, this volume, for discussion of the role of phonetics in motivating OT constraints).[2] An example of a typologically motivated constraint is ONSET which states: 'Every syllable has an Onset' (P&S: 25). This constraint is motivated by the fact that no languages lack onsetless syllables, some languages bar onsetless syllables, many languages have diverse strategies for eliminating onsetless syllables, and the unmarked syllabification of VCV strings is V.CV. A constraint with clear phonetic motivation is the Weight-to-Stress Principle which states: 'Heavy syllables are prominent in foot structure and on the grid' (Prince 1990; P&S: 53). Metrical prominence can be instantiated by increased duration, loudness, and/or marked pitch patterns. Since heavy syllables are typically longer than light syllables, this constraint can be viewed as instantiating a well-motivated phonetic principle: all else being equal, longer auditory stimuli are more perceptually salient than shorter ones. Another well-motivated phonetic constraint, *VOICELESS VOWELS ('Voiceless vowels are ill-formed'), treats voiceless vowels as highly marked segment types and accounts for the cross-linguistic rarity of distinctively voiceless vowels. Functionally, we can view this constraint as expressing the perceptual weakness of voiceless vowels.

However, along with well-motivated constraints, phonological systems also appear to incorporate language-specific rules whose historical origins may be well understood phonetically but whose synchronic status can in no way be viewed as resulting from aspects of universal grammar. Phonological rules are particular operations on phonological representations which specify structural descriptions and structural changes. McCarthy (1993) is one of the first to admit that language-specific phonological rules might play a role in Optimality accounts. In his OT analysis of alternations involving /r/ in Eastern Massachusetts English, the distribution of the rhotic shown in (1) and the generalizations stated in (2) are determined by the interaction of the two constraints in (3).

CODA$_R$-COND requires that /r/ be in the onset, and FINAL-C prohibits

---

[2] It is not implausible that all universal phonological constraints be phonetically grounded. However, there are a fair number of phonological constraints, like ONSET, which as yet have no widely accepted phonetic explanation (though see Greenberg 1995; Ohala and Kawasaki-Fukumori (forthcoming)).

vowel-final prosodic words. CODA$_R$-COND bars /r/ from being exclusively in the coda, but allows ambisyllabic /r/, where /r/ is licensed by virtue of its association with the following onset. Assuming that word-final intervocalic /r/ is ambisyllabic, the range of distributional facts falls out from the ranking CODA$_R$-COND >> FINAL-C. In other words, in phrase-final position, or before a consonant, (1a,c), [r] will not surface, due to the impossibility of ambisyllabicity. Vowel-final words followed by vowel-initial words within the phrase will be produced with linking ambisyllabic [r] (1b,e), since this eliminates a FINAL-C violation without violating CODA$_R$-COND. The data in (1e) is of particular interest, since it demonstrates the further empirical coverage gained by reference to prosodic words. As argued in Selkirk (1984) and Selkirk and Shen (1990), the one position where proclitics can be promoted to prosodic word status is phrase-finally. In English, vowel-final phrase-medial proclitics never trigger intrusive *r*. As McCarthy points out, the distribution of intrusive *r* in (1e) is unexplained in any analysis which assumes that it serves to relieve a hiatus violation.

(1) [ɹ]-sandhi in Eastern Massachusetts English (McCarthy, 1993)

a.	c. *r* Loss
The spa seems to be broken	The spaʀ seems to be broken
He put the tuna down	He put the tuneʀ down
The boat tends to yaw some	You'ʀe somewhat older

b. *r* Intrusion	d. *r* Linking
The spar̲ is broken	The spar is broken
He put the tunar̲ away	He put the tuner away
The boat'll yawr̲ a little	You're a little older

e. Intrusive *r* after phrase-final function words only: proclitics promoted to Prosodic Words in phrase-final position (Selkirk 1984; Selkirk and Shen 1990)

I said I was gonnar̲, and I did   but: He shoulda(*r̲) eaten.
If you haftar̲, I'll help   a lotta(*r̲) apples

(2) Generalizations over rhotic distribution in [ɹ]-sandhi dialects

a. Intrusive [ɹ] occurs between a lax word-final vowel and a following word-initial vowel.

b. Linking [ɹ] occurs between a lax word-final vowel and a following word-initial vowel.

c. Elsewhere, word-final /r/ is lost.

(3) A constraint-based analysis (McCarthy, 1993)

CODA$_R$-COND: /r/ is licensed only in syllable onset position.

FINAL-C or *V]PrWd: A prosodic word cannot end in a (short) vowel, though it can end in a consonant or glide. (Alternatively, a prohibition against final non-high vowels, or final lax vowels.)

Assumption: Word-final consonants are ambisyllabic when the next word begins with a vowel (Kahn 1980).

Constraint ranking: $CODA_R$-COND >> FINAL-C

One might already argue that $CODA_R$-COND which bars coda rhotics looks like a language-specific constraint. However, this constraint can be motivated both phonetically and typologically. Postvocalic coda /r/ in English dialects is phonetically a glide with vowel-like formant structure or rhoticization of a preceding vowel (Lindau 1978; 1985). In reviewing Delattre's 1967 cineradiographic data for 46 American English speakers, Lass and Higgs (1984) find significant differences between postvocalic coda /r/ and onset /r/, as summarized in (4). Whereas retroflexion occured in 24% of all onset /r/s, in post-nuclear positions the advanced velar /r/ accounted for 86% of /r/, with only 3% of /r/s showing retroflexion. Lip-rounding of /r/ occured in prenuclear position for all of Delattre's speakers, and was absent for all pronunciations of coda /r/. The only constant in terms of articulation was pharyngeal constriction, which occured in all /r/s, regardless of position. Similarly, Lindau (1978) also found tongue-root retraction to be the only invariant articulatory correlate of *r*-coloring in vowels.

(4)   Review of Delattre's 1967 cineradiographic data for 46 American English speakers
      (Lass and Higgs 1984)

	Onset /r/	Post-vocalic coda /r/
Retroflex	24	3
Apical-alveolar approx.	22	0.3
Palato-velar	50	86
dorsum active	70	66
tongue blade active	30	33
Lip-rounding	100	0
Pharyngeal constriction	100	100
Non-rhotic	0	11

In other words, postvocalic coda /r/s in American English are typically realized as pharyngealized or pharyngealized palatal approximants (the 'bunched' *r* described by Uldall (1958)), while onset /r/s additionally involve lip-rounding and may also involve raised tongue tip and retroflexion. In terms of acoustic effect, constrictions in the palatal region and the lower pharynx produce lowered third formants (Delattre 1951; Fant 1968; Ohala 1985). Lindau (1978) demonstrates that pharyngeal constriction in rhoticized vowels also results in auditory lowering and backing of vowels due to slight raising of F_1. Lip-rounding is also associated with lowering of the third formant (as well as the second), while retroflexion can lower F_4 or F_3 (in palatals), and generally brings F_2, F_3, and F_4 closer together (Ladefoged and Maddieson 1996: 27–8). Summarizing this data, we find that the extreme lowering of the third formant associated with American English /r/ is not so extreme in coda position, where lip-rounding and retroflexion are uncommon. Given this, and the effect of pharyngealization on F_1, it appears that weakly articulated postvocalic /r/s have less extreme lowering of F_3 than onset rhotics, and are perceptually similar to lowered and backed vocalic off-glides of preceding vowels.[3] In sum, the extreme lowering of the third formant associated with American English /r/ is not so extreme in coda position, where lip-rounding and retroflexion are uncommon. Given this, and the effect of pharyngealization on F_1, it appears that weakly articulated postvocalic /r/s have less extreme lowering of F_3 than onset rhotics, and are more perceptually similar to lowered and backed vocalic off-glides of preceding vowels. Difficulty of perceiving weak coda /r/s is expresed by CODA$_R$-COND. R-loss as a sound change is a reinterpretation of the vowel-like rhotic glide as a nuclear vowel, due to the acoustic and perceptual similarities of weak rhoticization and central/back/ round off-glides.

As a phonetically well-motivated constraint, then, we expect to find evidence of McCarthy's CODA$_R$-COND in the form of coda /r/-loss in other languages with rhotic glides, assuming that, as in English, coda rhotics have a less extreme articulation than onset rhotics. One interesting case is the Ngajan dialect of Dyirbal (Dixon 1980; 1990), where syllable-final /ɹ/ (in addition to / l,y/) was reinterpreted as length on a preceding vowel, but the apical rhotic trill /r/, which contrasts with the post-alveolar rhotic glide /ɹ/, was retained. In neighbouring Nyawaygi, which also has two rhotic phonemes /r, ɹ/, the rhotic glide /ɹ/ has been lost word-finally, and in some word-medial codas. Comparative data is shown in (5). Note that the same CODA$_R$-COND is evidenced word-finally in Wargamay, but instead of being resolved by /r/-loss, an epenthetic copy vowel is inserted in (5d,e).

(5) Typological support for CODA$_R$-COND: ɹ-loss in Ngajan Dyirbal and Nyawaygi (south-eastern Queensland; Dixon 1980: 213) N.B. rhotics /r, ɹ/ contrast.

	pre-Dyirbal	Ngajan Dyirbal		
a.	*gubaɹ	gubaa		'scrub wallaby'
b.	*jalguɹ	jaaguu		'meat'
c.	*ŋubirbil	ŋubirbii		'long leech'

	pre-Dyirbal	Nyawaygi	Wargamay	
d.	*jalbaɹ	jalba	jalbaa	'beard'
e.	*ŋamiɹ	ŋami	ŋamiɹi	'hungry'
f.	*gaɹbu	gaabu	gaɹbu	'three'
g.	*guɹga	guuga	guɹga	'back of neck'

In contrast, however, there is no clear phonetic or typological support for English intrusive 'r' as a phonologically natural process. A basic question remains, then, in the synchronic analysis: at the phonological level, why is the

---

[3] Lass and Higgs (1984) propose that the phonetics of American English /r/ are conservative, and that a number of sound changes in Old, Middle, and Early Modern English can be explained by assuming that Old English /r/ was produced with primary palatal and pharyngeal constrictions.

word-final epenthetic consonant in these dialects of English /r/?[4] As McCarthy (1993: 190) demonstrates, /r/ cannot be viewed as the default consonant in English. The argument most relevant to the discussion which follows is that if /r/ is the epenthetic segment in English, then /r/ should be a common and natural unmarked segment type in the the world's languages. But this is not the case. As McCarthy points out, in cases where /r/ epenthesis occurs, it is 'always historically secondary to deletion of *r*, from which it derives by reanalysis' (Vennemann 1972; McCarthy 1991).[5] To this we could add the fact that cross-linguistically the phonetics of the English rhotic glide which, as discussed above, can involve tongue-root retraction, retroflexion, bunching of the dorsum, and lip-rounding, all contribute to a highly marked segment type. On independent grounds, then, we would not expect a labialized pharyngealized retroflex central dorso-palatal approximant as a default or unmarked segment type within the grammar of any language.[6] McCarthy (1993: 190) concludes that /r/ is not the default consonant in English, and suggests that the grammar of Eastern Massachusetts English contains a phonological rule of /r/-insertion:

(6) A rule of English r-insertion (McCarthy 1993: 191, n. 12)[7]

$\emptyset \rightarrow r$ / ___]$_{\text{PrWd}}$

But what does McCarthy mean by 'rule'?

By a 'rule' here I mean a phonologically arbitrary stipulation, one that is outside the system of Optimality. This rule is interpreted as defining a candidate set {*Wanda, Wandar*}, and this candidate set is submitted to the constraint hierarchy. That is, this rule enlarges the candidate set to include non-melody-conserving candidates . . . which are then evaluated by the constraint hierarchy in the familiar way. . . . The role of the

---

[4] Or, in Bristol English, why is the word-final epenthetic consonant [l]?

[5] Vennemann (1972: 216) actually goes further, suggesting that epenthetic segments are never simply the default or least marked segments: 'Hiatus rules are motivated only to the extent that they create the preferred syllable structure . . . but the particular identity of the introduced consonant(s) is synchronically unmotivatable.' Rhotic epenthesis is difficult to motivate phonetically in most languages; /ɹ/ is arguably the epenthetic glide between low vowels in Yukulta (see 24c), but here it could also reflect a historical reanalysis of /r/-loss. A reviewer suggests that perhaps in English rhotics are relatively unmarked in the post-lax-vowel environment. However, even with this context-sensitive notion of markedness, one cannot account for absence of rhotic epenthesis in other languages which have not undergone historical rhotic loss.

[6] McCarthy also points out that if /r/ is a default consonant in the sense of lacking phonological feature specifications in English, then it is difficult to explain the phonological assimilation of vowels to following tautosyllabic /r/ (*fir, tern, car*), which does not occur postlexically in hypocoristics (cf. [sɪɹ] from *Cyril*, [tɛɹ] from *Terry*, [kæɹ] from *Karen*.). However, no lexical alternations are involved here, so it could be the case that what McCarthy refers to as lexical assimilation actually involves lexicalized vowel qualities.

[7] McCarthy first suggests a general rule $\emptyset \rightarrow r$, but acknowledges that /r/ is never inserted to save an onset violation. The context-sensitive rule of /r/-insertion incorporates this observation. I will suggest co-indexing /r/-insertion with FINAL-C, directly incorporating the relationship between this rule and specific constraint violations.

rule . . . is to enlarge the candidate set in a very limited way, stipulating the phonologically unnatural phenomenon of *r* epenthesis. (McCarthy 1993: 190–1)

In other words, McCarthy is suggesting that the phonologically arbitrary
information expressed in (6) be excluded from the class of universal constraints and be incorporated into the Gen function which defines candidate
output strings for evaluation against input. But since Gen, in its current
incarnation will already generate candidates including {*Wanda, Wanda?,
Wandar*} among others, the status of phonological rules within the grammar
and their interaction with Gen must be made more precise.

   Within OT, the grammar defines a pairing of input and output forms. A
function, termed 'Gen' (short for 'generator'), generates a set of candidate
outputs for each given input form. The precise nature of Gen has not been
discussed in the literature. Prince and Smolensky (1993: 4–5) state:

we generate (or admit) a set of candidate outputs, perhaps by very general conditions
. . . Gen contains information about the representational primitives and their universally
irrevocable relations: for example, that the node s may dominate a node Onset or a node
m (implementing some theory of syllable structure), but never vice versa . . . Though
Gen has a role to play, the burden of explanation falls principally on the function H-eval
. . . Optimality Theory abandons two key presuppositions of earlier work. First, that it is
possible for a grammar to narrowly and parochially specify the Structural Description
and Structural Change of rules. In place of this is Gen, which generates for any given
input a large space of candidate analyses by freely exercising the basic structural
resources of representational theory . . .

I propose that phonological rules are language-specific generation strategies
indexed to particular constraints. If a rule-indexed constraint is violated, the
phonological rule applies first, bleeding application of further Gen operations.
In the case of English, r-Insertion will be indexed with FINAL-C. For every
violation of FINAL-C, the input will be subject to *r*-Insertion as a specific
repair strategy. The general insertion/deletion strategies of Gen are blocked by
application of this language-specific rule, presumably an instance of the Elsewhere Principle. Instead of reverting to the position that some constraints are
universal, while others are language-specific, one can remain agnostic on the
universality of constraints by relegating all language-specific phonological
rules to a specific generation block distinct from the constraint hierarchy.

   Gen as defined by P&S above ultimately has to be replaced with some kind
of procedure for determining the optimality of a single candidate. The reason
for this is that, at present, there is no effective means of verifying tableaux.
Current tableaux contain a designated optimal candidate along with several
other candidates chosen essentially at random. We need to know not that the
candidate is better than *some* other candidates, but rather that it is better than
all other candidates. For this verification, we need some way of locating the
particular candidate in the space of possible candidates. One possibility is to

develop the model of harmonic serialism briefly outlined in P&S (p. 5), where there is successive evaluation of alternative candidates:[8]

Among possible developments of the optimality idea, we need to distinguish some basic architectural variants. Perhaps nearest to the familiar derivational conceptions of grammar is what we might call 'harmonic serialism', by which Gen provides a set of candidate analyses for an input, which are harmonically evaluated; the optimal form is then fed back into Gen, which produces another set of analyses, which are then evaluated; and so on until no further improvement in representational Harmony is possible. Here Gen might mean 'do any *one* thing: advance all candidates which differ in one respect from the input.' The Gen´H-eval loop would iterate until there was nothing left to be done, or better, until nothing that could be done would result in increased harmony.

At the point at which a candidate violating a particular constraint C, where C is indexed to a phonological rule, is 'fed back into Gen', the phonological rule would be invoked, pre-empting the more general Gen operations, and returning a new input form. For the purposes of discussion, let us assume the simplest case, where constraints are totally ordered, and where there is a unique optimal form for every instance of H-Eval. In this case, the general control strategy implementing harmonic serialism would look roughly as in Fig. 1, with relevant functions defined in (7).

(7) Functions involved in harmonic serial model of OT
     Gen defines the candidate set including the input, I, and every variant I_{var} resulting from single operations of deletion and insertion (of segments, features, structure, syllables, feet, etc.).

     Eval constructs a tableau for a given input.

     H-Eval constructs tableaux for a given set of candidates and selects the most harmonic candidate.

---

[8] In their discussion of harmonic serialism, P&S include Paradis's (1988*a*; 1988*b*) Theory of Constraints and Repair Strategies, Myers's (1991) model incorporating persistent rules, and Goldsmith's (1990,1993) Harmonic Phonology. However, each of these models differs in other ways from OT. For instance, Paradis's constraints are language-specific and inviolable, and thus differ from the universal and violable constraints of OT. Myers's model divides phonological generalizations into filters, which enforce universal restrictions on sound-sequencing, persistent rules, which define the inventory of phonological elements for a given language, and SPE-style ordered language-specific phonological rules, which define the distribution of phonological elements for a given language. This model is quite different from OT in retaining ordered rules, and in positing non-universal persistent rules, though Myers's filters are clearly the precursors of OT constraints. As in Paradis's model, constraints are inviolable and constraint ordering plays no role. Harmonic Phonology, a form of Three-Level Phonology (Goldsmith 1990; 1993) differs from OT in specifying three distinct levels, and in positing language-specific rules between and within levels. Within levels, rules apply only if they increase the Harmony of a representation, where Harmony is defined by language-specific phonotactics. Harmonic phonology then makes no claims about universal markedness patterns, which are directly instantiated by well-formedness constraints in OT. What I am suggesting is a minimal change in OT which preserves constraint universality, constraint violability, and constraint-ranking.

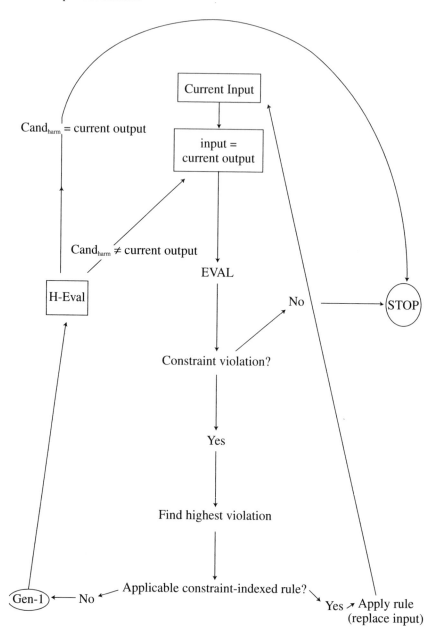

Fig. 1. A model of OT with harmonic serial evaluation

Three important features of Fig. 1 can be emphasized. First, if an input form results in no constraint violation, then nothing happens and the input is the output. Second, when a constraint that is violated is associated with a particular phonological rule, that rule creates a new input form for evaluation. Finally, the effect of the entire control strategy is to circumscribe Gen, first by eliminating its application in cases where no constraint is violated, and second by limiting its application, as suggested by P&S, to 'do any one thing' on each pass in the Gen⟷H-Eval loop.[9]

Consider an English input form / . . . spa is . . . / from (2b). This input form has one violation of FINAL-C, which for the purposes of discussion we shall assume is the only constraint violated. Because rule (6) is indexed with FINAL-C, the rule will apply, replacing the input with / . . . spar̲.is . . . /, where /r/ is in the coda. Now this form will be subject to Eval; $CODA_R$-COND is violated, and let us assume this is the highest and only constraint violation. No phonological rule is associated with this constraint, so the form will be subject to Gen. Gen will supply at least one representation where *r* is ambisyllabic (addition of a single association line), and this form will be chosen as the optimal candidate by H-Eval. Since this form violates no further constraint, the procedure will stop.

In the following section, I attempt to strengthen the argument that language-specific phonological rules are necessary in OT by detailing an additional case of rule inversion in Gilbertese. By examining the origins of Gilbertese nasal sandhi, it is clear how phonological rules can arise out of constraint-based grammars in a regular and principled way. The example of Gilbertese nasal sandhi, like English /r/-insertion, illustrates the extent to which language-specific rule-governed alternations are not amenable to analysis in terms of ranked universal constraints. Like English /r/-insertion, the behavior of Gilbertese final nasals before high vowels can be captured straightforwardly by proposing a constraint-indexed phonological rule which enlarges the candidate set in a restricted way.

3. GILBERTESE NASAL SANDHI: EVIDENCE FOR A PHONOLOGICAL RULE

3.1 *Synchronic description and analysis*

Gilbertese is a Micronesian language spoken in the Gilbert Islands (Kiribati). Descriptions of Gilbertese phonology on which this discussion is based include

---

[9] There are many unresolved questions about the precise nature of Gen, and how Gen might be further optimized to take into account constraint-ranking. For instance, ranking of faithfulness constraints could constrain Gen directly: where instances of MAX or DEP are ranked higher than the particular constraint violated by the input, the Gen operations of insertion and deletion associated with these instances of MAX and DEP would be inhibited, limiting Gen further. But these general issues are well beyond the scope of this chapter. All I intend to show is how language-specific rules can pre-empt Gen within one articulated control strategy.

Cowell (1951), Harrison (1994; 1995; pers. comm. 1995), and Blevins and Harrison (1995).[10] The segmental inventory of Gilbertese is shown in (8).

(8) Gilbertese consonants and vowels[11]

	Bilabial	Apical	Velar	Velarized labial	Front	Central	Back
Stop	p	t	k	p^w	i		u
Nasal	m	n	ŋ	m^w	e		o
Continuants		r		w [$β^w$]		a	

Length is contrastive for vowels and for nasal consonants. Some minimal pairs are shown in (9).

(9) Contrastive length in Gilbertese

ana '3s poss. article'	te pen 'a ripe coconut'	ti '1p subj. marker'
aana 'its underside'	te peen 'a pen'	tii 'only'
on 'full'	te atu 'bundle'	ana '3s poss. article'
oon 'the/some turtles'	te atuu 'head'	anna 'dry land'
tuaŋa 'to tell s-o'		
tuaŋŋa 'to tell him/her'		

Syllable structure is relatively simple: a single consonant is allowed in onset position, though onsets are not obligatory. The syllable nucleus can consist of any number of vocalic elements, provided sonority falls; long vowels are limited to nuclear-initial position. The only licit coda elements are nasals. The bilabial nasals /m, m^w/ have free distribution as codas; other nasals occur word-finally, or word-medially only when followed by a homorganic stop. All vowels are moraic. Moraic nasals (whether geminate or non-geminate) can occur word-initially and are licensed as codas, or, when there is no preceding vowel, by their occurence at the left edge of the syllabification domain. I will refer to these combined constraints on syllable structure in Gilbertese below as SYLLABLE.

(10) Constraints on Gilbertese syllable structure (= SYLLABLE)
  i.   *Complex onset.
  ii. Within complex rhymes, sonority must fall from one segment to the next.
  iii. Long vowels must be rhyme-initial
  iv. *Complex coda.
  v.   Codas must be [+nasal].
  vi. [labial] is the only place feature licensed in domain-medial coda position. (Place features of domain-medial non-labial nasals must be licensed by a following onset position.)
  vii. Moraic segments: all vowels; coda nasals; N/ [$_{PrWd}$_C

---

[10] See Harrison (1994) for a comprehensive bibliography of Gilbertese. Gilbertese data in the text is taken from Harrison (1995). Surface forms marked with double asterisks are predicted by Harrison's rules/descriptions, but unattested in the available data.

[11] Gilbertese /r/ is realized as an apical tap or flap; /w/ is a labiovelar approximant which varies with labiovelar fricative [$β^w$] pronunciation; /t/ is realized as [s] before /i/ in all dialects. Otherwise, all symbols have their IPA values.

All lexical nouns and verbs in Gilbertese are minimally bimoraic, with word-final and word-initial preconsonantal nasals contributing a mora. Examples of bimoraic words include: *koo* 'closed, tight', *ae* 'to drift', *atu* 'bundle', *mka* 'compost', *on* 'turtle'. A unique constraint in Gilbertese demands that phrases (XPs) constitute minimally trimoraic sequences (Blevins and Harrison 1995). Again, there is evidence that coda nasals are moraic: *te atu* 'a/the bundle' and *te on* 'a/the turtle' are well-formed trimoraic sequences, but when these nouns occur in the plural, they lack a determiner. In this case, the bimoraic sequence is bulked up to three moras: *aatu* 'the/some bundles'; *oon* 'the/some turtles.' But a word like *anti* 'the/some spirits' does not undergo initial syllable lengthening, since it is already trimoraic, showing again the moraic status of coda nasals. Further evidence for the moraic status of coda nasals is found in Gilbertese stress patterns, where trimoraic feet are the locus of prominence (Blevins and Harrison 1995). For instance, in the phrase *bwa kamw na akii kookoreai* 'so that you will not cut me up', the foot is parsed into trimoraic feet from right to left with moras italicized: bwa (kam^w na)$_\Sigma$ (akii)$_\Sigma$ (kooko)$_\Sigma$(-reai)$_\Sigma$. The general pattern across moras is . . . sAwsAw] where 's' is a mora with raised pitch, A is a mora with increased loudness, and 'w' is a mora with lower pitch and loudness than the two preceding.

The term 'nasal sandhi' refers to the set of alternations which occur when final (moraic) nasals are rendered nonfinal within the word or phrase. When a morpheme- or word-final nasal is followed by another segment within the phonological word or phrase, three independent strategies, shown in (11) and summarized in (12), serve to preserve the mora contributed by the morpheme final nasal. (The underlying representations in (11) are the isolation forms of individual words.)

Like English /r/-sandhi, Gilbertese nasal sandhi is an exceptionless phonological phenomenon which highlights recurrent problems for the claim that all phonological patterns result from the language-specific ranking of universal constraints alone. To demonstrate this, consider a constraint-based analysis within OT.

(11) Nasal sandhi
   (i) If the final nasal is followed by a non-high vowel, the nasal is realized as a geminate, maintaining the original mora-count by syllabifying as an ambisyllabic coda–onset sequence:

/kan ataa/	/kan orea/	/kan ere/
want know-3s	want hit-3s	want lop
[kan.na.taa]	**[kan.no.re.a]	**[kan.ne.re.a]
'to want to know'	'to want to hit something'	'to want to lop branches'

(ii) If the final nasal is followed by a high vowel, the nasal syllabifies as an onset, and the following high vowel associates to the nasal's floating mora, becoming long on the surface:

/pon iran atuuna/	/kan iria/	/kan uo-ta/
verily hair-of head-3s	want follow-3s	want to carry
[pʷo.nii.ran.na.suu.na]	[ka.nii.ri.a]	**[ka.nuu.o.ta]
'It was his (head) hair.'	'to want to	'to want to
	follow him'	carry something'

(iii) If a final nasal /n ŋ/ is followed by a non-homorganic consonant, and hence cannot be syllabified as a non-final coda, the nasal syllabifies as an onset, and an epenthetic vowel surfaces between the two consonants to carry the nasal's floating mora.

/pon ŋŋai/	/kan moi/
verily 1s	want drink
[pwoniŋŋai]	[kanimoi]
'It was me'	'to want to drink'

(iv) Elsewhere, where a final /n ŋ/ is followed by a homorganic consonant, or where final /m, mw/ is followed by any consonant, the nasal is syllabified as a coda, and no alternations occur.

/pon te kamea/	/kan toka/	/kamw na . . ./
verily art dog	want ride	2sgSUBJ IRR
[pʷontekamea]	[kantoka]	[kamna]
'It was a dog'	'to want to ride'	'you might . . .'

(12) An analysis: nasal sandhi as nasal-mora preservation
   a. When a moraic nasal is followed by a high vowel, the vowel lengthens to preserve the nasal mora.
   b. When a moraic nasal is followed by a non-high vowel, the nasal geminates to preserve its mora.
   c. When a moraic nasal is followed by a consonant but cannot be syllabified as a well-formed coda, an epenthetic vowel is inserted to carry the nasal mora.

The topmost relevant constraints in Gilbertese are MAX-I(nput)O(utput), $MAX-IO_{mora}$, and the constraints on syllable structure outlined above. MAX-IO states that 'Every segment of the input has a correspondent in the output' (McCarthy and Prince 1995(M&P): 264). $MAX-IO_{mora}$ demands the same correspondence at the moraic level: 'Every mora in the input has a correspondent in the output.' This constraint ensures preservation of all moras in correspondent pairs, including morpheme/word-final moras. As far as I am aware, MAX-IO and $MAX-IO_{mora}$ are unviolated in Gilbertese. An additional constraint $MAX_{seg-mora}$ requires that every segment–mora association in the input has a correspondent segment–mora association in the output; this constraint is violated in (11ii,iii). In (11i–ii), where gemination of the nasal occurs before non-high vowels, or lengthening of a high vowel occurs following nasals, INTEGRITY-IO is violated. INTEGRITY (M&P:372) states that 'No element in S_1 has multiple correspondents in S_2'. In examples like (11iii), where an epenthetic vowel surfaces between the nasal and a following consonant, DEP-IO is violated: 'Every segment of the output has a correspondent in the input' (M&P: 264). (Since the correspondences in question are all between input and output, I will omit 'IO' from here on.)

(13) Constraints active in Gilbertese nasal sandhi (in addition to SYLLABLE)

MAX	Every segment of the input has a correspondent in the output.
MAX-$_{mora}$	Every mora in the input has a correspondent in the output. (Floating moras are equivalent to deleted moras.)
MAX$_{seg-mora}$	Every segment-mora association in the input has a correspondent segment–mora association in the output.
INTEGRITY	No element in the input has multiple correspondents in the output. (In order to extend this constraint from copied to doubly associated segments, I assume the following slight modification: 'short segments in the input cannot correspond to long segments in the output.')
DEP	Every segment of the output has a correspondent in the input.

Ranking of these five constraints is evident from the data considered so far. Constraints on syllable structure (SYLLABLE), MAX, and MAX$_{mora}$ are unviolated and therefore are ranked highest. Epenthesis is not used as a mora-saving strategy unless spreading/copying of features is impossible on account of syllabification constraints. For example, in considering the input /kan moi/, *[kan.moi] is ruled out by the coda constraint which requires homorganicity between a non-labial coda and a following segment. However, in this case *[kann.moi] and [*kan.mmoi] are no better, since syllable-final geminates are illicit, and syllable-initial geminates are licensed only at the edge of the syllabification domain. These facts suggest, then, that INTEGRITY dominates DEP: DEP is only violated where melody-spreading is illicit due to higher-ranking syllable structure constraints. The relevant constraints and their rankings are shown in (13).

(13) Constraint ranking relevant to Gilbertese nasal sandhi
{SYLLABLE, MAX, MAX$_{mora}$} >> MAX$_{seg-mora}$ >> INTEGRITY >> DEP

However, the fact that remains to be accounted for is why INTEGRITY violations fall into two different categories: nasal gemination when the following vowel is non-high (11i) and vowel lengthening when the post-nasal vowel is high (11ii). Numerous ad hoc constraints could be formulated to instantiate this bifurcation in the grammar. Consider the constraints in (14).

(14) Parochial (non-universal) constraints

   a. *V V >> *C C >> *V V   b. * C C   V
      \ /   \ /   \ /   \ / |
    [−hi]   [nas] [+hi]   [+nas] [+hi]

(14a) states that, all else being equal, long high vowels are preferred over long (geminate) nasal consonants which in turn are favored over long non-high vowels.[12] I know of no evidence (typological, internal phonological, phonetic, or otherwise) which would support something like (14a). In fact, given that, all else being equal, non-high vowels are intrinsically longer than high vowels (Lehiste 1970), we might expect long non-high segments to be unmarked and favored cross-linguistically. An additional typological fact inconsistent with the markedness ranking in (14a) is that some vowel inventories have short high vowels associated with non-high long vowels (Maddieson 1984). Constraint (14b) bars sequences of geminate nasal followed by high vowel. This constraint could be coupled with a constraint favoring consonant length over vowel length to generate geminate nasals in cases like (11i), but long vowels in (11ii) where otherwise (14b) would be violated. Again, however, it is difficult to view (14b) as part of universal grammar.[13] Why should long nasals but not short nasals be disfavored preceding high vowels (but not before non-high vowels)?

I suggest that, similar to the insertion of English /r/ in sandhi contexts, the distinct strategies for nasal mora preservation in Gilbertese are due to a phonological rule whose origins are ultimately historical. The phonological rule I propose is shown in (15). The floating (i.e. deleted) mora in (15) is assumed to be an automatic consequence of the fact that moras are not licensed within syllable onsets (recall that ONSET is inviolable in CV sequences in Gilbertese):

(15) A phonological rule in Gilbertese: high-vowel mora gain

$$[+hi]$$
$$|\qquad\qquad \text{(Indexed to MAX}_{mora}\text{)}$$
$$N_i\quad V_j$$
$$\cdot \cdot^{\cdot}|$$
$$\mu_i\ \mu_j$$

---

[12] The lowest-ranking constraint against long high vowels could be omitted if we assume that a general constraint preferring long vowels over long consonants is also active. A reviewer notes that vowel quality changes could also result in better output strings if (14a) or (14b) was active. Vowel quality does not change under sandhi, indicating that Faithfulness constraints for vowel quality would outrank the hypothetical constraints in (14).

[13] See below, where the historical phonology of Gilbertese suggests devoicing and subsequent loss of word-final high vowels after nasals. This occured after all nasals, not geminate nasals specifically. An alternative phonological analysis which would also involve ad hoc constraints is one positing abstract [+hi] vowels following all morpheme-final nasals. The necessary constraints under this analysis would be the merger of this abstract vowel with following high vowels (producing surface long high vowels), but the deletion of the abstract high vowel preceding non-high vowels and subsequent compensatory gemination of the preceding consonant. There is no synchronic motivation for the general deletion of a high vowel before a non-high vowel in Gilbertese, where all vowel sequences are freely tolerated provided the vowels are not of the same height (*aiaia* 'their enemies'). Furthermore, the abstract final high vowels which would need to be posited could not be viewed uniformly as the historical remnant of word-final high vowels: nasal final loans like *peen* 'pen' have identical behaviour to proto-Micronesian reflexes of * . . . N{i,u}#; also, some Gilbertese morpheme-final nasals, as in *nim* 'drink something' < pMC *nim* 'drink' derive from nasal-final stems, where no source for the abstract final vowel exists.

Nasal lengthening is the norm due to MAX$_{\text{seg-mora}}$ which demands correspondence at the moraic level, specifically that a segment which is associated to a mora in the input be associated to a mora in the output. Only by lengthening the nasal in pre-vocalic contexts can MAX$_{\text{seg-mora}}$ be adhered to. However, in case the nasal is followed by a high vowel in the input, (15) generates ouput candidates which essentially trump default forms with geminate nasals. As with English r-Insertion, I suggest that rule (15) is indexed to a particular constraint, MAX$_{\text{mora}}$. Violations of MAX$_{\text{mora}}$ will give rise to rule application, as a language-specific alternate to Gen, and this rule application will override other output forms which Gen would normally produce for evaluation. As with English r-Insertion, the origins of rule (15) lie not in universal constraints on sound patterns but rather in the reanalysis of sound change. I turn now to details of this sound change, its relationship to rule (15), and its constraint-based origins.

3.2 *The historical development of nasal sandhi*

As Jackson (1983: 321) observes, short proto-Micronesian *i and *u are systematically lost word-finally after a nasal consonant in Gilbertese (GIL). In (16) proto-Micronesian (pMC) forms from the Proto-Micronesian Wordlist (University of Hawaii at Manoa) are shown with Gilbertese reflexes. Short final high vowels are regularly lost after nasal consonants (16a), but high vowels are not lost after other consonants (16b), and non-high vowels are not lost after nasals (16c). Long high vowels undergo general shortening in word-final position (16d).

(16) Final short high vowel loss: pMC *V > ø / N __ ##
                                 [+hi]

a. pMC		GIL	
*kaŋi	>	kaŋ	'eat (vb)/eat s.th. (pl)'
*kakaŋi	>	kakaŋ	'sharp'
*kinikini	>	kinikin	'pinch (vb)/pinch (n)'
*laŋi	>	naŋ	'sky/cloud'
*manu	>	man	'creature'
*masani	>	maran	'smooth'
*panipani	>	panipan	'sea cucumber'
*puŋu	>	puŋ	'fall, rain down/going down'
*pwoŋi	>	pwoŋ	'night'
*raŋi	>	aaŋ(a)	'warm/to heat oneself at a fire'
*tani	>	tan(tan)	'skin disease'
*taŋi	>	taŋ	'cry, weep'
*canu	>	ran	'water/fresh water'
*unu	>	un	'a star'

b. But no loss of final high vowels after non-nasal consonants

*fasu	>	ari	'eyebrow'
*kapi	>	kapi	'bottom'
*kapwu	>	kapu	'dull'
*kariki	>	kauki	'ko crab/ghost crab'
*kuki	>	uki	'fingernail'
*kutu	>	uti	'louse'
*liku	>	niku	'outside'
*masaki	>	maraki	'ache, pain'
*mataku	>	maaku	'fear, afraid'
*peti	>	peti	'to float'

c. And no loss of final non-high vowels after nasals

*kana	>	kana	'food/food; eat s.th. (sg)'
*lama	>	nama	'lake, lagoon'
*laŋo	>	naŋo	'fly (insect)'
*lima	>	nima-	'five'
*marama	>	maama	'moon, light/moonlight'
*maane	>	mmaane	'man, male'
*mena	>	mena	'thing'
*namwo	>	namo	'harbour'
*nima	>	nima	'drink (n)'
*roŋo	>	oŋo	'hear (v)'
*saŋa	>	raŋa	'thigh'
*tina	>	tina	'mother'

d. Long high vowels shorten (after all consonants)

*manifi	>	*manii	>	mani	'thin'
*puunuu	>			benu	'coconut husk'
*teluu	>	*tenii	>	teni-	'three'
*atuu	>	*atii	>	ati	'bonito'
*fatuu	>	*fatii	>	ati	'weave'
*fituu	>	*itii	>	iti	'seven'

What has given rise to the loss of final high vowels after nasals but not after other consonants? I suggest that two distinct phonetic developments led to significant devoicing of final high vowels after nasals, and that a further phonetic effect resulted in the loss of these voiceless high vowels due to their weak perceptual cues.[14]

Ohala (1983: 201) suggests that high vowels create significant back pressure in comparison with non-high vowels: 'Although the magnitude of the oral back

---

[14] Of all Micronesian languages, only Gilbertese and two Trukic languages, Woleaian and Pulo Anna, regularly attest pMC historical word-final short vowels before pause. In all other Micronesian languages, pMC short vowels have been lost word-finally. My account differs from that of Marck (1977). He suggests that Gilbertese may have once had a more general rule of final-vowel devoicing, and that the restriction of this to final high vowels could have been due to Polynesian influence from Tuvalu. I follow Jackson (1983), however, who suggests final devoicing of *i already in Proto-Micronesian.

pressure is not very great, it does reduce the transglottal pressure drop and could, in conjunction with other factors . . . contribute to vowel devoicing.' In the Gilbertese case, one contributing factor is the occurrence of these vowels before pause, where in many languages the vocal cords become slightly abducted: for instance, in related Trukic languages Woleaian and Pulo Anna, reflexes of all proto-Micronesian word-final short vowels (in words of more than one syllable) are voiceless (Jackson 1983: 218).[15]

A final and quite interesting potential contributing factor is the muting properties of the preceding nasal consonant. As observed by Ohala (1983: 205-6), the aerodynamics of the vocal tract suggest that nasalization will block (or substantially reduce) the audible flow of air produced by turbulence downstream. His reasoning is as follows:

> . . . if air pressure is to be released through one of the vocal tract's valves, then all other valves that would vent that air must be closed. If another valve is open, then a noisy audible flow of air through the intended valve will be lessened or eliminated. From this, we would predict that the devoicing . . . of vowels and glides . . . should be blocked by nasalization—the open velopharyngeal port acting to reduce the oral pressure that contributed to these effects.

In the case of Gilbertese, I am suggesting that final high vowels were devoiced due to back pressure and ambient utterance-final devoicing, and that velic opening simultaneous with this devoicing significantly reduced the oral air pressure to a point where the final devoiced vowels were no longer audible, at which point these words were reanalysed as being nasal-final.[16]

In sum, intrinsic properties of high vowels, the potential pre-pause position of word-final vowels, and the aerodynamics of the vocal tract all appear to have contributed to devoicing and loss of historical word-final short vowels preceded by nasals in Gilbertese.

[15] Another phonetic factor which may have played a role is the well-studied acoustic similarity of nasalization and aspiration, sometimes referred to as rhinoglottophilia (Matisoff 1975; Ohala 1975; Ohala and Amador 1981; Blevins and Garrett 1993). In this particular case, the coarticulatory nasalization of vowels after nasal consonants may have been misperceived as aspiration, contributing to the complete devoicing of high vowels in this context. Note, however, that rhinoglottophilia alone cannot account for the devoicing of high vowels only. If rhinoglottophilia was the sole factor involved, reinterpretation of nasalization as devoicing would be expected to influence all vowels. Furthermore, rhinoglottophilia is incompatible with the muting aerodynamic properties of the preceding nasal discussed below.

[16] An alternative to the phonetic account is one which incorporates phonological constraints directly into sound change. Under this account, high-vowel devoicing occurs everywhere (because of instrinsic aerodynamic properties of these vowels), but high vowels are 'not heard' by speakers only where the resulting string has an optimal syllable coda. In pre-Gilbertese, nasals are the only possible codas word-internally. This, coupled with the cross-linguistic preference for high-sonority codas, could result in the loss of voiceless high vowels after nasals only; cf. e.g. the loss of final voiceless vowels in Kwara'ae after nasals and [l] only (Blevins and Garrett 1996). Under either account, the Gilbertese example is one of rule inversion which synchronically requires a language-specific phonological rule.

The sandhi effects in modern Gilbertese can be traced directly to reanalysis of an earlier stage of the language. In addition to the loss of short final high vowels after nasals, I assume that assimilation of adjacent vowels of the same height occured across word-boundaries. The same process occurs word-internally as a variable rule in modern Gilbertese, where V_1 assimilates to V_2: *natiu ~ natuu* 'my child'; ŋkoe ~ ŋkee '2sg pronoun' (Harrison 1994: 886–7).

(17) The evolution of nasal-mora preservation in Gilbertese

    i. Reanalysis of N{i,u}-final to N-final

        Pre-Gilbertese   Gilbertese

*kaŋi]	>	*kaŋi̥]	>	kaŋ] 'eat (vb)/eat s.th. (pl)'
*manu]	>	*manu̥]	>	man] 'creature'
*kaŋi] [k...]]	>	*kaŋi̥] [k...]]	>	kaŋ] [k...]]
*manu] [t...]]	>	*manu̥] [t...]]	>	man] [t...]]

    ii. Reanalysis of N{i,u}-final to N-final in high-vowel sandhi contexts (on analogy with reanalysed forms in i.)

*kaŋi] [i...]]	>			kaŋ] i [i...]]
*kaŋi] [u...]]	>	kaŋu][u...]]	>	kaŋ] u [u...]]
*manu] [u...]]	>			man] u [u...]]
*manu] [i...]]	>	mani][i...]]	>	man] i [i...]]

    iii. Extensions of nasal-mora preservation (pre-existing /i/-epenthesis)

*kaŋi] [t...]]	>	*kaŋi̥] [t...]]	>	kaŋ] i [t...]]
*manu] [k...]]	>	*manu̥] [k...]]	>	man] i [k...]][17]
*kan] [i...]]	>			kan] i [i...]]
*kan] [u...]]	>			kan] u [u...]]
*kan] [k...]]	>			kan] i [k...]]

    iv. Origins of nasal gemination

        pMC *fanua 'land, island' > *an.wa > an.na 'dry land'
        pMC *aniani 'to bail out' > *an.yani > annan
        In sandhi contexts

*kaŋi] [a...]]	>	*kaŋ.y] [a...]]	>	kaŋ] ŋ [a...]]
*manu] [a...]]	>	*man.w] [a...]]	>	man] n [a...]]

        Generalized to N-final stems

*kan] [a...]]	>			kan] n [a...]]

    v. No reanalysis

*kan]		kan] 'to want'
*kana]		kana] 'food/food; eat s.th. (sg)'

The reanalysis of N{i,u}-final words as N-final (17i) triggered reanalysis of sandhi assimilation (17ii), where the first part of the long vowel is interpreted

---

[17] It is conceivable that, once devoiced, the original quality of the vowel was no longer recoverable. However, it is also possible that the reanalysis of *manu > man in phrase-final position, was simply extended to this context, with the ill-formed coda in forms like /man + k . . . / saved by the general /i/-epenthesis strategy.

as a stray mora, not associated with any underlying morpheme. These structures led Gilbertese speakers to assume final nasal-mora preservation, parallel with the already existing processes of epenthesis (17iii) and nasal gemination (17iv). Nasal gemination was formerly transparently derived from nasal + [− high] vowel sequences. However, the reanalysis of stems in (17i) was extended to these contexts as well, resulting in an opaque source for the geminate nasal. As a result, the alternations in (17iv) as well as those in (17i,ii) were all interpreted as instances of nasal-mora preservation.

I suggest that a similar situation occurred in late seventeenth-century southern British English, when *r*-loss first took place (Lass and Higgs 1984: 98). McCarthy's proposed constraint FINAL-C, which prohibits (lax) vowel-final words, must have already been in evidence when *r*/ø alternations occurred, leading them to be reanalysed as instances of 'repair' for FINAL-C violations. The general schema I am suggesting for this sort of reanalysis is shown in (18).

(18) Rule inversion as Constraint satisfaction
  Stage I: Constraint C in evidence.
  Stage II: Sound change results in surface alternations which can be reinterpreted as instances of constraint-C satisfaction.
  Stage III: Alternation is instantiated (often inverted) as a phonological rule indexed to Constraint C.

Synchronically, rule (6), like rule (15), has no phonetic basis; both are due to the optimal reanalysis of regular sound change in the context of a constraint-based grammar.

4. THE ACQUISITION OF PHONOLOGICAL RULES

Within OT, the claim that all constraints are universal immediately restricts the learning task to two domains: the ranking of constraints, and the morpheme-specific nature of certain constraints. Within the domain of constraint-ranking, the situation might be complex: C_1 might dominate C_2 in one component of the grammar, while C_2 dominates C_1 in a different subcomponent of the lexicon (see Itô and Mester 1995; Inkelas, Orgun, and Zoll, Chapter 13 below). An apriori argument against language-specific phonological rules is that these rules are not easily acquired. I suggest, on the contrary, that the two phonological rules discussed here have two properties which greatly simplify the learning task.

The first property is their exceptionless nature and productivity. Both English *r* sandhi and Gilbertese nasal sandhi are exceptionless processes which apply both to native vocabulary items and to loans. McCarthy (1993: 172) highlights this productivity for /r/-less dialects of American English:

The most striking evidence of this productivity involves the regular and virtually unsuppressible transfer of *r* deletion, *r* insertion, and *r* linking to borrowed words and even to other languages. Loans and nonce forms that end in *r* must lose it finally or before a consonant: *Not/e Dame University, palave/, Oma/, Ishta/, Kareem Abdul-Jabba/*. Likewise, new words ending in a, ə, or ɔ, invariably require intrusive *r* before a vowel: *Françoisr is coming, rumbaring, subpoenaring, guffawring, baahring* (of sheep), *blahrer* 'more blah', *a Pollyannarish attitude, schwar epenthesis, the Beqaar in Lebanon*. And, as Jespersen (1909) notes with examples from Danish and German, *r* deletion and *r* insertion are prominent features of the foreign accent of British (and Bostonian) English speakers: *det brændef gansker op, lukker op, hatter ich, sagter er.*

The same is true for Gilbertese nasal sandhi. The alternations shown in (11) apply to all nasal-final words in the language, including loans like: *peen* 'pen', *Saam* 'Sam', *betin* 'basin', *Buritan* 'Britain', *Tun* 'June', *karatin* 'kerosene', *pumkin* 'pumpkin', *tiotipan* 'saucepan', *tiring* 'shilling', *kiing* 'king'.

The second property is the widespread nature of these sandhi processes. In English, some of the most common words and morphemes (*are, for, -er*, etc.) take part in *r/ø* alternations, while in Gilbertese, nasal-final morphemes include some of the most common lexical items and bound morphemes: *kan* 'want', kam^w '2sgSUBJ', *pon* 'verily', *man* 'creature, animal, insect, etc.', *-n* 'construct suffix'. In both languages, vowel-initial words are common and not limited to any part of speech, so that contexts for sandhi occur in a majority of utterances.

Given the productivity and ubiquity of the two phonological rules presented above, the task of learning is greatly facilitated. Rules can be learned by generalizing over surface alternations. In the case of Gilbertese nasal sandhi, once the constraints on well-formed syllables have been learned, including the moraic status of coda nasals, universal constraints allow the learner to map the surface pattern onto one of mora preservation under MAX_{mora}. The wrinkle in the system is the failure of morpheme-final nasals to geminate when followed by high vowels, with high-vowel lengthening occuring instead. I submit that this irregularity, formulated as rule (15), is easily learned via the transparency and robustness of surface alternations, and is due to its association with MAX_{mora}, whose high ranking is evidenced in the other sandhi alternations.

In sum, though phonological rules encode highly language-specific sound patterns, provided these patterns are exceptionless and in great abundance, they should be easily learned. In this sense, learning a phonological rule is parallel to learning the segment inventory of a given language: ample data of a non-ambiguous nature allows the child to extract significant and distinctive sound patterns.

5. LARDIL NOMINATIVES: A MORPHOLOGICAL WORD-FORMATION RULE

5.1 *Problems with the OT account*

A potentially troubling feature of many OT accounts is the interleaving of purely phonological constraints with seemingly idiosyncratic morphologically governed constraints or even syntactic constraints (Tranel 1994, Perlmutter 1995). Consider the P&S analysis of Lardil nominal alternations (Hale 1967; 1973; Wilkinson 1988) of the sort shown in (19). (Throughout this section 'ng' writes the velar nasal, 'rt, rl, rn' write the post-alveolar/retroflex series, 'rr' writes the alveolar tap/trill, and 'r' writes the post-alveolar glide.)

(19) Some Lardil nominals

Stem	Nominative	Non-fut. Acc.	Gloss
a. /kentapal/	kentapal	kentapal-in	dugong
b. /ngaluk/	ngalu	ngaluk-in	story
c. /yiliyili/	yiliyil	yiliyili-n	oyster sp.
d. /mayarra/	mayarr	mayarra-n	rainbow
e. /wirte/	wirte	wirte-n	inside
f. /mela/	mela	mela-n	sea
g. /mungkumungku/	mungkumu	mungkumungku-n	wooden axe
h. /pulumunitami/	pulumunita	pulumunitami-n	young female dugong
i. /wun/	wunta	wun-in	rain
j. /mar/	mar.rta	mar-in	hand
k. /kang/	kangka	kang-in	speech
l. /yak/	yaka	yak-in	fish

In order to account for the loss of stem-final vowels in the nominative, P&S propose the constraint in (20), which is ranked among purely phonological constraints as shown in (21). *COMPLEX bars complex codas and onsets; CODA-COND admits only nasals homorganic with following stops and the apical sonorants {n,l,r,rn,r,rr} in coda position; ONS requires that all syllables have onsets; FTBIN is the familiar constraint requiring that feet be binary under syllabic or moraic analysis; LX=PR requires that a lexical word be a prosodic word demanding that all lexical words be minimally disyllabic; ALIGN in Lardil requires alignment of right edges of stems and syllables where possible, accounting for the augmentation of stems like (19i-k)—/mar/ 'hand' to *mar.rta* in the nominative, not *mara; -COD is the general constraint prefering open syllables to closed ones, but its low ranking means that FREE-V can freely give rise to -COD violations as in (19a,b).

(20) FREE-V. Word-final vowels must not be parsed (in the nominative).

(21) Lardil constraint ranking (P&S)
$\{$*COMPLEX, CODA-COND, ONS, FTBIN, LX=PR$\} >>$ FILL$^{Nuc} >>$
FREE-V $>>$ ALIGN $>>$ FILL$^{Ons} >>$ PARSE $>>$ -COD

By ranking FREE-V below LX=PR, final vowel deletion is blocked in stems like (19e,f) where FREE-V would create a subminimal word. On the other hand, ranking FREE-V above PARSE is necessary, since the alternative ranking would always render FREE-V vacuous.[18]

Two important questions arise here. First, in what sense is FREE-V a universal constraint, given its morphological association with nominative case? P&S (p. 101) argue as follows:

Although FREE-V takes the bull by the horns, it would not perhaps be put forth as the canonical example of a universal markedness principle. It appears to be a morphologized reflex of the prosodic weakness of final open syllables, which are liable to de-stressing, de-voicing, shortening, truncation, and so on, under purely phonological conditions . . . It also has connection with the commonly encountered constraint to the effect that stems or words must end in a consonant . . . Any theory must allow latitude for incursions of the idiosyncratic into grammar. What is important for our program is that such incursions are best expressible as *constraints*; that they are (slightly) modified versions of the universal conditions on phonological form out of which core grammar is constructed; and that they interact with other constraints in the manner prescribed by the general theory.

If incursions of the idiosyncratic as well as universal markedness principles are all expressed as constraints, there is no formal way of distinguishing the two classes of constraints, and the general claim of OT, that constraints are universal and violable, is greatly weakened.

A second more general question is whether FREE-V, which appears to be an inflectional word-formation rule, as shown in (22), belongs in the phonological component at all.[19]

(22) Lardil nominatives: a morphological word-formation rule (N = noun; + Nom = nominative case)

    i. $[\Sigma] \ldots V]_{NominalStem} \rightarrow [\Sigma] \ldots \emptyset]_{N[+ Nom]}$
        elsewhere: $]_{NominalStem} \rightarrow]_{N[+ Nom]}$
    or
    ii. $\ldots V]_{NominalStem} \rightarrow \ldots \emptyset]_{N[+ Nom]}$
        elsewhere: $]_{NominalStem} \rightarrow]_{N[+ Nom]}$

Is the grammar modular, with independent but interacting phonetic, phonological, morphological, and syntactic components, or is it a massive set of interwoven constraints from different subsystems of grammar? Lapointe and Sells (1996), in response to Tranel (1994) and Perlmutter (1995), have made the quite reasonable suggestion that mixing of constraints across rule compo-

---

[18] Within Correspondence models of OT (M&P), FREE-V would need to be reformulated essentially as a non-correspondence between input and output, as follows: NOM: The final short vowel of a nominal stem (input) corresponds to zero in the nominative word (output). This also looks like a problematic feature of the OT analysis, since it directly contradicts the spirit of Correspondence, but I will not dwell on it here.

[19] Cf. Goldsmith (1993: 35), where Lardil truncation is analysed as an M→W rule.

nent boundaries should be disallowed. In the following discussion I would like to provide further support for this view by demonstrating the extent to which V-deletion in Lardil nominatives is an idiosyncratic case of diachronic rule inversion, differing from the phonological rules discussed earlier in involving morphological, as opposed to simple phonological, reanalysis.

I maintain that (22) is a language-specific morphological rule. Unlike phonological rules, morphological rules are not indexed to constraints; and unlike phonological constraints, morphological rules are not ranked among phonological constraints. Rather, morphological rules supply input forms to the phonological component. In other words, concatenative morphology yields /kentapal + in/$_{\text{Non-fut. Acc}}$ and /yiliyili-in/ as input forms to the phonology, while rule (22) provides /kentapal/$_{\text{Nom}}$ and /yiliyil/$_{\text{Nom}}$ as contrasting input forms within the nominative inflectional paradigm. By placing rules like (22) in the morphological component, OT can maintain a fixed hierarchy of universal phonological constraints.

Notice that the one fact the ranking in (21) is meant to capture is that vowel deletion in the nominative does not occur if it would result in a subminimal word (19e,f) (a LX = PW violation). How can the morphological rule-based account in (22) give rise to the same interactions? There are two approaches, exemplified by (22i) and (22ii). First, one can simply build the minimal word requirement into the morphological rule, as in (22i). While this might seem to constitute duplication of LX = PW in the grammar, the historical development of absolutive/nominative case-marking in the Tangkic languages, sketched below, gives some plausibility to such duplication. The alternative is to view (22ii) as creating an (input, input) pair. A stem like (19f) /mela/ will give rise to the input pair (/mela/$_{\text{NOM}}$, /mel/$_{\text{NOM}}$). Because the morphological rule in (22ii) is a stem-to-word rule (by definition), this input set is subject to H-Eval with respect to all *word*-referring constraints, a limited case of lexicon optimization of the sort suggested by P&S (p. 191). This account makes the strong claim that any subtractive rule of word-formation will obey word-minimality constraints.[20] I will remain neutral on whether (22i) or (22ii) is the correct statement of the morphological rule. Either alternative is successful in eliminating language-specific information from the constraint component of the grammar, and in maintaining modularity within the grammar.

In the following section I suggest how Lardil nominative case-marking arose. Though final-vowel neutralization appears to have played a role, I suggest that it is the reinterpretation of a final vowel as a case-marker which is primarily responsible for the synchronic subtractive rule in (22). This kind of morphological reanalysis does not play a role in the evolution of phonological rules as exemplified by English /r/-insertion and Gilbertese nasal sandhi, nor is

---

[20] As far as I am aware, the same claim is not made in current OT accounts, since a constraint like FREE-V could be ordered anywhere among phonological constraints.

there any sense in which Lardil final V-loss in the nominative can be viewed as satisfying any already active constraint in the language. These distinctions in rule types suggest distinct roles in the grammar, and support the analysis of V/ø alternations in Lardil nominatives as instances of the morphological word-formation process stated in (22).

5.2 *The evolution of absolutive case marking in Tangkic*

The Tangkic languages of Australia are a non-Pama-Nyungan family, with the internal relationships shown in (23), following Evans (1995). Proto-Tangkic splits into Southern Tangkic and Lardil, with the Southern Tangkic languages subgrouped into mainland and island groups. Languages marked ERG have ergative/absolutive case-marking systems for common nouns; those marked NOM have nominative/accusative case-marking patterns for common nouns.

(23) Tangkic languages
    Proto-Tangkic (ERG)
      Southern Tangkic
        Mainland: Yukulta (ERG), Nguburindi (ERG)
        South Wellesley: Kayardild (NOM), Yangkaal (NOM)
      Lardil (NOM)

Absolutive case in the ergative(ERG)/absolutive(ABS) systems corresponds with nominative case in the nominative(NOM)/accusative(ACC) systems. A peculiar feature of the southern Tangkic languages is that, of the two core cases (ERG/ABS or NOM/ACC), both can be marked by suffixation. Elsewhere in Australia, the absolutive case is typically unmarked.

Phonotactics of the Tangkic languages and allomorphy of absolutive and nominative forms in the Southern Tangkic languages suggest that the absolutive case suffix arose out of an extension of phonologically motivated alternations. In other words, Proto-Tangkic can be reconstructed with a zero marker for absolutive case, with the absolutive/nominative case-marker arising out of the morphological reanalysis of purely phonological alternations.

Yukulta and Kayardild (and Yangkaal) have almost identical suffixal allomorphy for absolutive and nominative nominals respectively, as shown in (24, 25).

(24) Yukulta absolutive allomorphy (Keen 1983: 203)

a.	Ø	after a-final stems > 2 syllables	kamarra	'stone, hill (ABS)'
			marntuwarra	'boy(ABS)'
b.	-ya	after disyllabic i-final stems,	karnti-ya	'wife-ABS'
c.	-ra	after disyllabic a-final stems	rtangka-ra	'man-ABS'
d.	-wa	after disyllabic u-final stems	ngawu-wa	'dog-ABS'
e.	-ta	after {l,n}-final stems	takal-ta	'round-ABS'
f.	-rta	after (rl,rn)-final stems	miyarl-rta	'spear-ABS'
g.	-ka	after {ng}-final stems	kalarang-ka	'mosquito-ABS'
h.	-a	after {rr,t,k}-final stems	rtamurr-a	'short-ABS'
			ngit-a	'wood-ABS'
			wik-a	'shade-ABS'

NB: *[rr.t]; explains absence of C-augment in /rr/-final stems.

(25) Kayardild (and Yangkaal) nominative allomorphy (Evans 1995: 124–5)

a.	Ø	after a-final stems > 2 syllables	bardaka	'belly(NOM)'
			kunawuna	'child(NOM)'
b.	-ya	after disyllabic i-final stems, (variable after longer i-final stems)	birdi-ya	'bad-NOM'
			yakuri-ya	'fish-NOM'
c.	-a	after disyllabic a-final stems	mala-a	'sea-NOM'
d.	-wa	after disyllabic u-final stems (variable after longer u-final stems)	maku-wa	'woman-NOM'
			mawurru-wa	'spirit home-NOM'
e.	-da	after {l,n}	nal-da	'head-NOM'
f.	-rda	after {r, rn}	ngarn-rda	'beach-NOM'
			mar-rda	'hand-NOM'
g.	-k	after {ng}-final stems	kang-ka	'language-NOM'
h.	-a	after {rr,d,k}-final stems	ngilirr-a	'cave-NOM'
			yarbud-a	'snake-NOM'
			dulk-a	'country-NOM'

NB Kayardild has no /rl/ ; *rl> r.

The only paradigm differences between the two languages are in disyllabic /a/-final stems, where Yukulta shows [ra] allomorph of the nominative and Kayardild and Yangkaal both have [a]. I assume this is the result of the *r > Ø/ a_a in the South Wellesley languages.

The pattern of alternations in (24, 25) after C-final stems are familiar from the study of Lardil nominals, where, as we saw above (19i–l), sub-minimal words are augmented in the same way: if the stem-final C is a possible coda, it is maintained as a coda in the inflected form, with a following homorganic consonant serving as onset to the word-final [a], and elsewhere, the augment is simply the unmarked vowel [a]. In cases where /-a/ is added to vowel-final bases in Yukulta, ONSET triggers the occurrence of a glide homorganic with the preceding vowel: [y] after /i/, [w] after [u] and [ɹ] after [a].[21]

However, the Southern Tangkic languages differ from Lardil in not allowing C-final words, as shown in (26).

(26)

	C-final stems?	C-final words?
Yukulta	Yes	No
Kayardild/Yangkaal	Yes	No*
Lardil	Yes	Yes

*Except phrase-finally; see below.

I hypothesize that at the earliest stage, proto-Tangkic (pT) had a -ø marker for absolutive case, and that, additionally, the language tolerated C-final words, as Lardil does. Some evidence for the existence of C-final words in pT can be seen in Kayardild, where underlying stem-final laminals contrast in non-nominative forms (/nith-/ 'name' versus /ngij-/ 'wood'), but this contrast is neutralized in the nominative (*nida* versus *ngida*). The neutralization in the nominative suggests that these consonants were once word-final, and that a common constraint restricting word-final consonants to apicals was in force.[22] Additional evidence for this hypothesis comes from comparative evidence outside of Tangkic (Evans 1995: 75): compare Kayardild /nith-/ with Bajamal *nij* 'name'; Kayardild /miij-/ 'louse; lobster' with Ngalakan *mij* 'louse'.

How then can a case-marker arise on the previously unmarked case forms? I propose that the original source for the Tangkic absolutive case-marker was the phonological augment occurring on subminimal words (e.g. dulka̲) and on C-final words (yarbuda̲), which at some point became ill-formed in proto-Southern Tangkic (pST).[23] The augment [-a] which at this point occurred on a great number of absolutive forms was reanalysed as a case-marker. The first three stages of evolution are summarized in (27).

(27) Evolution of absolutive case marker in Tangkic

Proto-Tangkic [pT] * -Ø   Absolutive
                        C-final stems

Stage I.   [pT] Augmentation to satisfy LX=PW constraint (retained in all languages.)
Stage II. [pST] Augmentation to satisfy *C constraint
Stage III. [pST] Augment /-a/ reanalysed as absolutive case-marker where alternations occur (*-ø / -a allomorphy)

---

[21] The occurrence of the retroflex glide /ɹ/ in the a_a context is the epenthesis rule referred to in note 5. However, I have been unable to determine whether this rule also reflects a historical process of -loss. Yukulta has no ɹ-final stems (Keen 1983: 196); if ɹ-final stems can be reconstructed for Proto-Tangkic, then ɹ-insertion in (24c) is analagous to English r-sandhi.

[22] In Lardil, where the stem-final consonants have been maintained, the underlying stem-final contrast between /th/ and /j/ has been neutralized in favour of an analysis where alternations are conditioned by the following suffixal vowel.

[23] Evans (1995: 137) suggests that the innovation of a constraint against C-final words may have arisen through contact with the northern Nyungic languages which share the same constraint.

Subsequent to these changes, the Southern Tangkic languages appear to have extended case-marking, as outlined in (28). First, absolutive case-marking was extended to what appears to be the unmarked prosodic base for affixation in the Tangkic languages, the foot or minimal word (i.e. the unmarked prosodic base for affixation was itself a word), accounting for synchronic affixation in (24,25 b–d). Subsequently case-marking was extended in Kayardild and Yangkaal to longer {i,u}-final stems, presumably because longer /a/-final stems were already analysed as incorporating the nominative /-a/ (despite its occurrence in other inflected forms.)

(28) Subsequent extension of ABS/NOM marking in Southern Tangkic

Stage IV. Absolutive /-a/ suffixation extended to prosodic base = [Σ]. Trisyllabic [a]-final stems interpreted as [[Σ]a]$_{ABS}$ (but no levelling).

Stage V. Nominative /-a/ optionally extended to remaining i/u stems (Kayardild and Yangkaal only).

What then happened in Lardil, where nominative case-marking is absent, and the constraint against C-final words is no longer in evidence? Synchronically, Lardil has rules of word-final vowel lowering which only apply to underlyingly word-final vowels.[24] Assuming these are the phonologized reflexes of regular sound change, I propose the sound changes in (29a–c). Historically, these sound changes would have resulted in the etymologies shown in (29i–iii), where all word-final vowels with the exception of /i/ preceded by a non-lamino-palatal, were neutralized to [a].[25]

(29) Pre-Lardil word-final vowel lowering

  a. *i > a/ C^y_]$_{Wd}$ i. *wurdalji > *wurdalja > wurdal 'meat'
  b. *u > a/ _]$_{Wd}$ ii. *yalulu > *yalula > yalul 'flame'
  c. *i > {e,ɛ,æ}/_]$_{Wd}$ iii. *yiliyili > *yiliyile > yiliyil 'oyster sp.'

It is this phonological neutralization of /i/, /u/, and /a/ word-finally, along with its allowance of C-final words, which appear to have given rise to the very different evolution of case-marking in Lardil. As shown in (30), subsequent to V-lowering (30ii), the final [a] of the stem could be reanalysed as an instance of nominative /-a/, with deletion of preceding stem-final /u/ (30iii).

(30) Loss of non-zero NOM in Lardil
  i.   yalulu-ø (cf. Non-fut. ACC yalulu-n)   thungal (from proto-Tangkic)
  ii. yalula-ø (final V-lowering)   n.a.
  iii. yalulø-a (final [a] reanalysed as NOM /-a/)   n.a.
  iv. yalulø-ø (loss of NOM /-a/; gen. of ø   n.a.
       of /i,a/-final stems; unmarked prosodic
       base = Σ)
  v.   yalulu + V-deletion   n.a.

---

[24] Within OT this constraint against [+ hi] final vowels would need to be formulated as a constraint holding of input forms: cf. /ngawu/ ngawa 'dog NOM' but /mungkumungku/ mungkumu (*mungkuma) 'wooden axe NOM'.

[25] It is unclear to me at what point phonemic /e/ arose, so I omit it from discussion here.

Subsequently, the paradigm was levelled by loss of all nominative /-a/s, in favor of the ø form of the case-marker, still occurring in some /i/-final and all / a/-final stems like (19f) /mela/ 'sea'. The extension of the NOM/ABS suffix in the Southern Tangkic languages to disyllabic bases appears to be the mirror image of the substraction of the same suffix from disyllabic bases in Lardil. If we assume, as in (28) Stage IV, that the unmarked prosodic base for affixation was the prosodic word, then we can begin to explain the synchronic restriction of final V-deletion in the nominative, as expressed directly in (22i).

This step, (30iv), can be further motivated by notions of morphological markedness.[26] The sense in which the absolutive/nominative is the unmarked case form is optimally expressed by absence of a case-marker. But given nominatives like *yalul* paradigmatically opposed to non-future forms like *yalulu-n*, this loss of the nominative suffix was reinterpreted as (phonological) final-V deletion,—the rule which remains to this day. In sum, the synchronic rule of nominative formation through final V-deletion is the result of historical morpheme subtraction and phonological reanalysis. Only in the most indirect sense does it reflect 'the prosodic weakness of final open syllables, which are liable to de-stressing, de-voicing, shortening, truncation, and so on, under purely phonological conditions', as suggested by P&S above.

In fact, a purely phonological constraint of the FREE-V sort does occur in one of the Tangkic languages, but its effects are quite different from the morphological rule in Lardil. As shown in (31), Kayardild has a rule of phrase-final [a] deletion.[27] At the end of every planned pause, unstressed short [a] is not pronounced. As expected, this rule can give rise to ill-formed syllable types including word-final clusters, which are otherwise illicit, ill-formed codas, and even violations of the minimal word constraint (31c). Of course, this is precisely what we expect of a phrase-level rule whose origins are ultimately phonetic. *Contra* P&S, it seems unlikely that a phonologization of a phrase-final phonetic process of final-vowel weakening would ever show the minimal word effects so salient in Lardil.

---

[26] P&S (p. 101) note that similar subtractive V-deletion occurs in Estonian nominatives. However, the Estonian case is much more complicated in that there are multiple allomorphs of the nominative, not all involving truncation (*nimi* 'name-NOM' versus *nime* 'name-GEN'). Tonkawa nominalizations (/nodoxo/ 'to hoe', *nodox* 'hoe') also show subtractive final V-deletion (Hoijer 1933). In Tonkawa the subtractive morpheme appears to be related to the vowel loss which occurs under independent nominal formation with /-an/: /naxdje-/ 'to build a fire' versus *naxdj-an* 'fire'; /x'ene-/ 'to sweep' versus *x'en-an* 'broom'. The historical development of the Lardil rule suggests that morphological (un)markedness might play a role in all 'subtractive' morphophonological rules: subtractive morphology evolves as the deletion of a previous morpheme in the unmarked member of a morphological paradigm.

[27] The same rule occurs in Yaangkal (Evans 1995). Hale (1973) discusses the Yaangkal data briefly, but does not observe that vowel-deletion is limited to phrase-final position.

(31) Kayardild phrase-final [a]-loss (Evans 1995: 63-4)
Word-final short [a] is lost before planned pauses at the end of a breath group.

    a. jirrkur-ung-ka   thaa-th_,   thaa-tha   jirrkur-ung-k_
       north-ALL-NOM return-ACT return-ACT north-ALL-NOM
       'They came back to the north, to the north they came back'
    b. kirrka-miburl-d_   c. kirrk-_
       nose-eye-NOM   nose-NOM
       'face'   'nose'

In sum, if this proposal for the evolution of absolutive/nominative case-marking in Tangkic is on the right track, morphological analysis of final [a] as the nominative and morphological paradigm levelling in pre-Lardil are crucial ingredients of the historical evolution of synchronic V-deletion in the nominative, and argue strongly against FREE-V as a (slightly modified) instance of a universal phonological constraint.

6. CONCLUDING REMARKS

I have attempted to highlight the extent to which fairly well-understood sound changes and instances of morphological reanalysis and levelling can give rise to language-specific phonological and morphological rules. I have suggested that phonological rules are best viewed as alternate strategies to Gen within OT grammars, indexed to the specific constraints for which they are the specialized 'repair' strategy. On the other hand, morphological rules are best viewed as language-specific statements outside of the phonology proper which provide input forms to the phonology. If all language-specific information relevant to regular sound patterns in natural languages can be exiled to constraint-indexed phonological rules or to word-formation rules within the morphology proper, then the debate between derivational and non-derivational grammars is one that cannot be decided on the basis of universal versus language-specific information alone, since both models are able to integrate universal and parochial aspects of sound patterns. While Gilbertese nasal sandhi and Lardil nominative formation are only two examples, it is hoped that this study will inspire other researchers to investigate properties of language-specific rules, and their proper place within grammars directly incorporating phonological markedness and phonetic naturalness.

258 *Empirical Studies*

REFERENCES

Blevins, J., and Garrett, A. (1993). 'The evolution of Ponapeic nasal substitution', *Oceanic Linguistics* **32**: 199–236.

—— —— (1996). 'Compensatory C/V "metathesis"'. Paper presented at the Austronesian Formal Linguistic Association III, University of California, Los Angeles, Apr.

—— and Harrison, S. P. (1995). 'Trimoraic Feet in Gilbertese: A Constraint-Based Analysis'. MS, University of Western Australia.

Cowell, R. (1951). *The Structure of Gilbertese*. Beru, Gilbert Islands: Rongorongo Press.

Chomsky, N., and Halle, M. (1968). *The Sound Pattern of English*. New York: Harper & Row.

Delattre, P. (1951). 'The physiological interpretation of sound spectrograms', *Publications of the Modern Language Association of America* **65**: 864–75.

—— and Freeman, D. C. (1968). 'A dialect study of American r's by x-ray motion picture', *Lingruistics* **44**: 29–68.

Dixon, R. M. W. (1980). *The Languages of Australia*. Cambridge: Cambridge University Press.

—— (1990). 'Compensating phonological changes: an example from the Northern dialects of Dyirbal', *Lingua* **80**: 1–34.

Evans, N. (1995). *A Grammar of Kayardild*. Berlin: Mouton de Gruyter.

Fant, G. (1968). 'Analysis and synthesis of speech processes', in B. Malmberg (ed.), *Manual of Phonetics*. Amsterdam: North-Holland, 171–272.

Goldsmith, J. (1990). *Autosegmental and Metrical Phonology*. Oxford: Blackwell.

—— (1993). 'Harmonic phonology', in J. Goldsmith (ed.), *The Last Phonological Rule*. Chicago: Chicago University Press, 21–60.

Greenberg, S. (1995). 'The ears have it: the auditory basis of speech perception', Proceedings of the 13th International Congress of Phonetic Sciences, iii. 34–41.

Hale, K. (1967). 'Some productive rules in Lardil Mornington Island syntax', Papers in Australian Linguistics, No. 2, 63–73. Canberra: *Pacific Linguistics* A-11.

—— (1973). 'Deep-surface canonical disparities in relation to analysis and change: an Australian example', in T. A. Sebeok (ed.), *Current trends in linguistics*, xi. The Hague: Mouton, 401–58.

Harrison, S. P. (1994). 'Kiribati', in D. T. Tryon (ed.), *Comparative Austronesian Dictionary: An Introduction to Austronesian Studies*, pt. 1, fascicle 2: 879–93.

—— (1995). 'A Grammar of Gilbertese'. MS, University of Western Australia.

Hoijer, H. (1933). *The Tonkawa Language*. Berkeley, Calif.: University of California Press.

Inkelas, S., and Orgun, C. O. (1995). 'Level (non)ordering in recursive morphology: evidence from Turkish'. Paper presented at the Conference on Morphology and Its Relation to Syntax and Phonology, University of California, Davis.

Itô, J., and Mester, A. (1995). 'The core–periphery structure of the lexicon and constraints on reranking', in J. N. Beckman, L. W. Dickey, adn S. Urbanczyk (eds.), *Papers in Optimality Theory* (University of Massachusetts Occasional Papers 18). Amherst: GLSA, 181–209.

Jackson, F. H. (1983). '*The Internal and External Relationships of the Trukic Lan-

guages of Micronesia'. Ph.D. dissertation, University of Hawaii. Distributed by University Microfilms International.

Kahn, D., (1980). *Syllable-Based Generalizations in English Phonology*. New York: Garland Press, 1980.

Keen, S. (1983). 'Yukulta', In R. M. W. Dixon and B. Blake (eds.), *Handbook of Australian Languages, III*. Amsterdam: John Benjamins, 190–304.

Ladefoged, P., and Maddieson, I. (1996). *The Sounds of the World's Languages*. Cambridge, Mass.: Blackwell.

Lapointe, S., and Sells, P. (1996). 'Determining the Optimal Boundary between Syntax and Phonology in Optimality Theory'. MS, University of California, Davis, and Stanford, University.

Lass, R., and Higgs, J. A. W. (1984). 'Phonetics and language history: American /r/ as a candidate for an archaism'. In J. Higgs and R. Thewall (eds.), *Topics in Linguistic Phonetics in Honour of E. T. Uldall*. New University of Ulster.

Lehiste, I. (1970). *Suprasegmentals*. Cambridge, Mass.: MIT Press.

Lindau, M. (1978). 'Vowel features', *Language* **54**: 541–63.

—— (1985). 'The story of /r/', in V. A. Fromkin (ed.), *Phonetic linguistics: Essays in Honor of Peter Ladefoged*. Orlando, Fla.: Academic Press, 157–68.

McCarthy, J. J. (1991). 'Synchronic rule inversion', in L. A. Sutton, C. Johnson, and R. Shields (eds.), *Proceedings of the 17th Annual Meeting of the Berkeley Linguistics Society*. Berkeley, Calif.: Berkeley Linguistics Society, 192–207.

—— (1993). 'A case of surface constraint violation', in C. Paradis and D. LaCharité (eds.), *Constraint-Based Theories in Multilinear Phonology, Canadian Journal of Linguistics* **38**: 169–95.

—— and Prince, A. (1995). 'Faithfulness and reduplicative identity', in N. Beckman, L. W. Dickey, and S. Urbanczyk (eds.), *Papers in Optimality Theory* (University of Massachusetts Occasional Papers 18). Amherst: GLSA, 249–384.

Maddieson, I. (1984). *Patterns of Sounds*. Cambridge: Cambridge University Press.

Marck, J. C. (1977). 'A preliminary manual of Micronesian sound correspondences'. Paper presented at the Symposium on Austronesian Linguistics of the Summer Meeting of the Linguistics Society of America, Honolulu, Hawaii, Aug.

Matisoff, J. A. (1975). 'Rhinoglottophilia: the mysterious connection between nasality and glottality', in C. A. Ferguson, L. M. Hyman, and J. J. Ohala (eds.), *Nasálfest: Papers from a symposium on nasals and nasalization*. Stanford, Calif.: Stanford University Linguistics Dept, 265–87.

Myers, S. (1991). 'Persistent rules', *Linguistic Inquiry* **22**: 315–44.

Ohala, J. J. (1975). 'Phonetic explanations for nasal sound patterns', in C. A. Ferguson, L. M. Hyman, and J. J. Ohala (eds.) *Nasálfest: papers from a symposium on nasals and nasalization*. Stanford, Calif.: Stanford University Linguistics Dept., 289–316.

—— (1983). 'The origin of sound patterns in vocal tract constraints'. in P. F. MacNeilage (ed.), *The Production of Speech*. New York: Springer, 189–216.

—— (1985). 'Around *Flat*', in V. A. Fromkin (ed.), *Phonetic Linguistics: Essays in Honor of Peter Ladefoged*. Orlanda, Fla.: Academic Press, 223–41.

—— and Amador, M. (1981). 'Spontaneous nasalization', *Journal of the Acoustic Society of America* **68**: S54–5 (abstract).

—— and Kawasaki-Fukumori, H. (forthcoming). 'Alternatives to the sonority hierarchy for explaining the shapes of morphemes', in E. H. Jahr and S. Eliasson (eds.), *Memorial volume for Einar Haugen*. Berlin: Mouton de Gruyter.

Paradis, C. (1988*a*). 'On constraints and repair strategies', *Linguistic Review* **6**: 71–97.

—— (1988*b*). 'Towards a theory of constraint violations', *McGill Working Papers in Linguistics* **5**: 1–44.

Perlmutter, D. (1995). 'Explanation of allomorphy and the architecture of grammars'. Paper presented at the Conference on Morphology and Its Relation to Syntax and Phonology, University of California, Davis.

Prince, A. (1990). 'Quantitative consequences of rhythmic organization', in *Parasession on the syllable in phonetics and phonology*, Chicago Linguistic Society: 355–98.

—— and Smolensky, P. (1993). 'Optimality Theory: Constraint Interaction in Generative Grammar'. MS, Rutgers University and University of Colorado, Boulder.

Selkirk, E. O. (1984). *Phonology and Syntax: The Relation between Sound and Structure*. Cambridge, Mass.: MIT Press.

—— and Shen, T. (1990). 'Prosodic domains in Shanghai Chinese', in S. Inkelas and D. Zec (eds.), *The Phonology–Syntax Connection*. Chicago: University of Chicago Press.

Tranel, B. (1994). 'French liaison and elision revisited: a unified account within Optimality Theory'. Paper presented at the Linguistic Symposium on Romance Linguistics 24.

Uldall, E. T. (1958). 'American 'molar' r and 'flapped' r', *Revista do Laboratório de Fonética Experimental da Faculdade de Letras da Universidade de Coimbra* **4**: 103–6.

University of Hawaii, (1990). 'Proto-Micronesian Word-List'. Dep. of Linguistics.

Vennemann, T. (1972). 'Rule inversion'. *Lingua* **29**: 209–42.

Wilkinson, K. (1988). 'Prosodic structure and Lardil phonology', *Linguistic Inquiry* **19**(3): 325–34.

8

Non-derivational Phonology Meets Lexical Phonology

GEERT BOOIJ

1. INTRODUCTION

A proper theory of phonology has to provide at least the three subtheories
listed in (1):

(1) (i)   a theory of the nature of phonological representations
    (ii) a theory of the form of phonological generalizations
    (iii) a theory of the organization of phonology as part of the grammar

Autosegmental phonology, Prosodic Phonology, and the theory of Feature
Geometry are examples of theories that deal with (aspects of) the nature of
phonological representations.

The issue of how to express phonological generalizations has become one of
the foci of recent phonological research. The basic ingredients of the classical
SPE approach, and of Lexical Phonology in its standard form, are rules and
derivations. We now observe a shift to constraint-based approaches such as
Constraints-and-Repairs Phonology (Paradis 1988–9) and Harmonic Phonology
(Goldsmith 1990; 1993), in which both rules and constraints play a role, and
Optimality Theory (OT). In the latter theory, rules have been completely
abolished in favor of a hierarchy of constraints, and there is no derivational,
serial computation of the correct phonetic form of a word (Prince and Smolensky 1993). In another approach, Declarative Phonology, rules have been
replaced with stative, declarative statements that express well-formedness
constraints that apply conjunctively (Coleman 1995).

Lexical Phonology (henceforth LP) in its different varieties is in essence a
theory of the organization of the grammar, that is, of how phonology
interacts with other components of the grammar, in particular morphology
and syntax. In addition, it is a substantial theory of the form, interaction,
and application of rules (Elsewhere Condition, Strict Cyclicity, and Level
Ordering).

The three subtheories mentioned above are not completely independent.
For instance, given a richer theory of prosodic structure and prosodic

domains, our theory about the organization of the grammar can often be simplified (Booij 1994). The enrichment of phonological representations by Autosegmental Phonology has also led to simpler formulations of phonological generalizations. Therefore, it is worthwhile to investigate to what extent the insights and generalizations of LP, which have been formulated in a rules-and-derivations-framework, carry over to, or are in conflict with, constraint-based theories of phonological generalizations. This is the main aim of this chapter. Therefore, I will first discuss the theoretical core of LP in section 2. Subsequently, I will discuss how the different claims of Lexical Phonology bear on constraint-based theories. First, LP makes use of rule ordering, in particular counterbleeding and counterfeeding order, for the expression of phonological generalizations. These devices are not available in non-derivational phonology. Cases of counterbleeding order will be discussed in section 3, those of counterfeeding order in section 4. Second, rule-based generative phonology acknowledges morpholexical rules, i.e. phonological rules of a restricted nature in the sense that they are conditioned by lexical and/or morphological properties. Can the generalizations expressed by such rules also be expressed in non-derivational phonology? This is the topic of section 5. In section 6 I give my main conclusions: There is no evidence for rule-ordering effects (in the sense of serial rule application, with extrinsic rule ordering) in Dutch that cannot be reanalysed in a way compatible with OT, and perhaps preferably so. There is, however, strong evidence for level-ordering effects. OT is compatible with this notion of derivation. Even when restated within Correspondence Theory, the facts discussed continue to argue for some degree of serial computation in phonology.

2. THE CORE OF LEXICAL PHONOLOGY

The core hypotheses of LP (cf. Pesetsky 1989; Kiparsky 1982; Booij 1981) are the following:

(2) (i) There is a systematic difference between lexical and postlexical phonology.
     (ii) Morphology and phonology apply in tandem.

The first hypothesis reflects the classical distinction between word phonology and sentence phonology, and will be discussed in section 3. Clearly, this hypothesis is not exclusive to Lexical Phonology.

The second hypothesis means, to put it simply, that you take a word, and apply the applicable phonological rules right away (= first cycle); you may then apply a morphological rule to that word, which creates a new domain of application for the phonological rules of the language, the second cycle, which in turn can be input for another morphological operation that creates a third cycle, and so on.[1]

The difference between the traditional cyclic application of phonological rules and LP is that, in the first approach, phonology is ordered after morphology, and that it has to be stipulated that phonological rules apply to the most internal morphological domain first, then to the next morphological domain, etc. It incorrectly excludes the possibility of morphology being dependent on derived phonological properties of its bases.

Hypothesis (2ii) predicts that

(3) a. the phonological rules of a language that apply to words apply cyclically, at least in principle;
   b. the morphological rules of a language may refer to both underived and derived phonological properties of their input words.

The cyclic application of phonological rules in turn predicts that

(4) phonological and morphological rules may make use of phonological information that is no longer present in the phonetic forms of words.

The claims in (2–4) are in fact a consequence of an even simpler idea, namely the following minimal assumption:[2]

(5) Apply a rule when possible.

This principle predicts, for instance, that the rule of word stress of a language applies immediately to a given word, before it is subject to (further) morphological operations. Thus, cyclicity of stress assignment follows from principle (5). Since words are formed in the lexical component, the rules of word phonology will apply to those words right away, before they enter the syntax, which gives the effect that word phonology precedes sentence phonology.

Why is cyclic rule application desirable? One important reason is that it accounts for the fact that morphological operations, for instance the choice of a particular affix, may be dependent on derived phonological properties of the base to which that affix attaches, for instance the stress pattern or prosodic structure. Another argument is that, as far as stress assignment is concerned, cyclic application accounts for the fact that in some languages the stress pattern of a complex word is not affected by every affix that it contains: the

---

[1] The formulation 'you take a word, and apply the applicable phonological rules' implies that it is words that form cyclic domains, not morphemes. This is in line with the conclusions of Brame (1974) and Harris (1983), who argue that cyclic domains must be dominated by a lexical category node. It is also in line with the lexeme-based view of morphology as advocated in Aronoff (1976) and Anderson (1992). That is, morphology is not seen primarily as the 'syntax of morphemes', but as a set of language-specific rules for the creation of complex words.

[2] The point that Lexical Phonology is simply a consequence of this minimal assumption is also made by Kaye (1992: 141).

distinction between stress-shifting and stress-neutral affixes can be expressed by attaching the latter after stress assignment.

The question then arises how we block reapplication of the stress rule after the attachment of a stress-neutral affix. In the standard version of LP this is achieved by means of level-ordering: the main stress rule only applies on the first level, whereas stress-neutral affixes are attached on a second level. However, level-ordering has a number of problematic properties (cf. Booij 1994), and we can do without it as far as stress is concerned in the following way. Stress-shifting affixes are specified as cyclic, which means that they erase the stress pattern of their base, thus inducing reapplication of the main stress rule (Halle and Vergnaud 1987). Stress-neutral suffixes, on the other hand, are specified as non-cyclic in the sense that they do not erase the stress pattern of their base. Thus the main stress rule cannot reapply because existing metrical structure must be respected. The only kind of stress that can be assigned to stress-neutral suffixes is secondary stress, a rhythmic kind of stress (Booij 1995: 105–13).

Principle (5) does not predict that all phonological rules of a language apply in the lexicon. Rules that apply within the domain of the syllable, the foot, or the prosodic word can already apply in the lexicon because these prosodic categories are already available during the construction of words (Booij 1988; Inkelas 1989). However, many rules have domains larger than the word, e.g. the phonological phrase. Such rules are by definition postlexical (i.e. syntactic) rules, since their applicability depends on the availability of domains created on the basis of syntactic structure.

Within the lexical level some rules must be construed as postcyclic (that is, word-level) because they must apply after all morphology has been performed. For instance, the rule of Coda Devoicing in Dutch states that obstruents are voiceless in coda position. This rule cannot apply cyclically, because we would then derive wrong phonetic forms, such as [hɛltɪn] for *held-in* 'heroine', derived from *held* /hɛld/ 'hero', instead of the correct [hɛldɪn]: suffixation causes the morpheme-final underlyingly voiced obstruent to appear in onset position, and hence it remains voiced.[3] Its postcyclicity follows from a prohibition on absolute neutralization. In other words, the rule cannot apply cyclically because of Strict Cyclicity, the principle that forbids the cyclic application of rules in a non-derived environment (prosodic structure such as 'Coda' does not count as derived environment, since otherwise Strict Cyclicity would be made vacuous).

---

[3] The distinction between lexical and postlexical rules is a reflection of the classical distinction between 'word phonology' and 'sentence phonology' that can be found in the *Projet de terminologie standardisée* of the Prague Linguistic Circle ('phonologie du mot' versus 'phonologie de la phrase', *Travaux du Cercle Linguistique de Prague* **4**: 309–23), and in van Wijk (1939: 132): 'woordphonologie' versus 'zinsphonologie'.

So we get in LP three levels at which phonological rules can apply (Booij and Rubach 1987):

(6) lexical level: cyclic level
                         word level
    postlexical level

The theoretical discussion within the framework of LP also includes a number of related issues, such as the hypothesis of Strict Cyclicity, and the distinguishing properties of lexical rules versus postlexical rules. I will leave these issues out of the discussion, because they do not bear directly on the issues discussed in this chapter.[4]

3. COUNTERBLEEDING ORDER

Counterbleeding order poses a challenge to non-derivational theories because it requires an extrinsic ordering of rules, whereas the constraints of non-derivational phonology can be ranked, but cannot be ordered since they apply simultaneously. So let us investigate what kind of generalization counterbleeding order is meant to express. Our first case of counterbleeding order concerns the ordering of lexical rules before postlexical rules. The second case involves counterbleeding order within one cycle of the lexical phonology of a language.

3.1 *Lexical versus postlexical phonology*

The issue at hand is that of the number of levels of abstraction in phonology. Certain generalizations only hold at a certain systematic level of abstraction, and may be opaque at the phonetic surface. In OT, this kind of opacity does not necessarily lead to the postulation of levels, because constraints are violable, and therefore they are also able to express generalizations that are violated at the phonetic surface. But the point is that a certain level of abstraction, in particular the lexical level, plays a systematic role. First, I will argue that candidates have to be evaluated in two steps, at the lexical and the postlexical level. Second, certain constraints are only valid for words, which means that there is a different constraint-ranking at the postlexical level.

In this connection, I would like to stress that there is no logical conflict between Optimality Theory and (a restricted form of) serial computation. The intrinsic content of OT concerns the form of phonological generalizations, and this does not necessarily exclude each form of serialism. This is pointed out explicitly in Cohn and McCarthy (1994: 4 ff., 47 ff.); note, moreover, that in

---

[4] See Hargus and Kaisse (1993) and Booij (1994) for a survey and discussion of these issues.

the appendix to McCarthy and Prince (1993) two levels are distinguished for the phonology of Axininca Campa.

The lexical/postlexical distinction is also acknowledged in Goldsmith (1990; 1993) and in Lakoff (1993). For instance, Goldsmith (1993: 32) posited a level between the underlying level and the phonetic level, the W-level. He gave the following characterization of these levels:[5]

(7) M-level, a morphophonemic level, the level at which morphemes are phonologically specified;

W-level, the level at which expressions are structured into well-formed syllables and well-formed words, but with a minimum of redundant phonological information; and

P-level, a level of broad phonetic description that is the interface with the peripheral articulatory and acoustic devices.

The relevant point here is that Goldsmith acknowledges one intermediate stage between the input level and the output level, the word level, which can roughly be equated with the phonemic level of structuralist phonology. In LP this is the level reached when all lexical rules have applied, and before the postlexical rules apply.

An important motivation for the distinction between a lexical level and a postlexical level is that at the lexical level certain generalizations hold that may be made opaque in surface structure due to phonological processes that apply to sequences of words in a sentence. In particular, many languages have segments that show the effects of a syllabic position in which they do not surface (cf. Hargus 1993). A clear example from Dutch is the following. Dutch has a number of vowel-initial clitics, most of which begin with a schwa. These clitics obligatorily form one prosodic word with the preceding word, since they cannot form a proper prosodic word of their own (Booij 1995; 1996): a prosodic word must contain at least one syllable with a full vowel. Moreover, a prosodic word cannot begin with a schwa, which shows that syllables headed by a schwa must have an onset. The latter constraint is only met when a schwa-syllable occurs in non-word-initial position, where it will always have an onset consonant. Therefore, schwa-initial clitics are predictably enclitics (except in sentence-initial position). Consequently, word-final obstruents of the preceding host word fill the onset positions of the syllables headed by the clitic-initial vowels. Yet those obstruents that are voiced underlyingly, are voiceless in such onset positions (σ = syllable):

---

[5] In Goldsmith's view, there are intra-level and cross-level rules. Intra-level rules apply simultaneously at one particular level, and are harmonic, i.e. they only apply if they improve the phonological representation. Cross-level rules express correspondences between two levels, and are not necessarily harmonic; they are not to be seen as directional, and are not extrinsically ordered.

(8) (ik) heb 't 'I have it' /hɛb ət/ (hɛ)$_\sigma$(pət)$_\sigma$
    (hij) had 't 'he had it' /had ət/ (ha)$_\sigma$(tət)$_\sigma$
    (ik) heb 'r 'I have her' /hɛb ər/ (hɛ)$_\sigma$(pər)$_\sigma$

So, we first have to apply the rule of Coda Devoicing at the word level, and then, at the postlexical level, the attachment of vowel-initial clitics to the preceding words leads to resyllabification, i.e. the devoiced obstruent is shifted to onset position. This is a typical example of counterbleeding order. This order need not be stipulated, but follows from the organization of the grammar assumed in LP, and in all other models that assume the lexical/postlexical distinction.

Instead of formulating Coda Devoicing as a rule, we can also express this generalization in the form of a constraint: the feature [+ voice] is not licensed for obstruents in coda position, and hence it will be delinked in that position. In OT terms we might say that this is a Coda Condition that implies that the feature [+ voice] cannot be parsed for obstruents in coda position. Whatever the form of this phonological generalization, the point is that it only holds at a certain level of abstraction of the grammar, before the effects of cliticization on the syllabification of words in syntactic contexts are taken into account.

It is not possible to solve this problem by adhering to one level of application of rules/constraints and by considering the obstruents involved as ambisyllabic when followed by such clitics, as proposed by Coleman (1995) within the Declarative Phonology framework, which does not acknowledge different levels of representation:

(9) Many standard examples of structure-changing operations can be reanalysed as purely structure-building. Analyses employing a resyllabification operation . . . which removes a consonant from coda position and attaches it to the onset node of the following syllable, can be replaced by an analysis in which the coda consonant is shared with the onset of the following syllable (ambisyllabicity). (Coleman 1995: 360)

This solution is not viable for Dutch, because ambisyllabicity blocks Coda Devoicing. This can easily be seen from words with a short vowel. Dutch is subject to the constraint that a rhyme has to contain at least two positions. In a word-internal VCV sequence, the C will therefore be ambisyllabic (Van der Hulst 1984; Booij 1995: 32), as shown here for the word *adder* /adər/ 'snake':

(10)
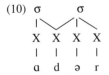

Here, the /d/ will be realized as [d]. Coda Devoicing, formulated in (11), does not apply.

(11) Coda
       |
       ×
       |
    [−son]

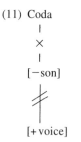

    [+voice]

In terms of licensing we can say that in (10) the feature [+voice] of the /d/ is licensed parasitically (Goldsmith 1990), by also being linked to the onset position. In a rule-based approach, application of the rule of Coda Devoicing will be blocked by the Uniform Applicability Condition (UAC) of Schein and Steriade (1986: 727), as shown in Booij (1995: 32), or by Hayes's Linking Constraint (Hayes 1986), which states that association lines in structural descriptions are interpreted as exhaustive.

The implication of this phenomenon for OT is that the set of candidates must be evaluated in two steps, at the lexical level and at the postlexical level. To make the discussion more concrete, let us assume the following constraints:

(12) Schwa-Onset: a syllable headed by schwa must have an onset.
       Coda Devoicing: [+voice] is not licensed for obstruents in coda position.

(The Schwa-Onset constraint is not exactly the same as the general Onset constraint that requires filling of onsets, because Dutch prosodic words can begin with a full vowel.) In the derived word *hebber* /hɛb+ər/ [hɛbər] 'greedy person', the /b/ will (also) be parsed as an onset, and hence it will remain voiced. On the other hand, the /b/ of *heb* [hɛp] has to devoice, even if it becomes the onset of the following clitic syllable, as in the last example of (8), *heb er* 'have her'. Therefore, evaluation must take place in two steps; otherwise, Coda Devoicing would not get a chance to apply in word+clitic combinations. In other words, as far as Coda Devoicing in Dutch is concerned, lexical morphemes and lexical combinations of morphemes must be evaluated before postlexical morpheme combinations are evaluated. Note that this is a case where the surface opacity of obstruent devoicing is not a matter of another constraint dominating Coda Devoicing: Schwa-Onset does not interact with Coda Devoicing in the sense that Coda Devoicing is violated due to the higher-ranked Schwa-Onset constraint. The minimal pair *hebber*—*heb er* [hɛbər]—[hɛpər] can only be accounted for by evaluation in two steps.

The case of Dutch is by no means an isolated example. There are many cases attested in the literature where a phonological generalization that holds at the lexical level is made opaque by resyllabification at the sentence level. Booij (1984) and Booij and Rubach (1987) mention a number of phonological generalizations concerning French that are made opaque by postlexical resyllabification (*liaison* and *enchaînement*), and Harris (1994: 182–3) mentions similar facts of Spanish: certain rules apply to coda consonants which subsequently become the onsets of the following vowel-initial words. These are all cases of counterbleeding order. For instance, in French connected speech word-final consonants syllabify with the initial vowel of the next word of the same phonological phrase, as in *première amie* 'first girlfriend' (prə)(mjɛ)(ra)(mi). Yet, the second vowel of *première* is [+low] according to the rule of Closed Syllable Adjustment, which says that mid vowels are [+low] in closed syllables. So resyllabification would bleed Closed Syllable Adjustment, if resyllabification applied before Closed Syllable Adjustment. Therefore, the counterbleeding order is required. This order follows from the fact that Closed Syllable Adjustment is a rule that can already apply in the lexicon, whereas resyllabification is a postlexical rule because it applies to sequences of words in phonological phrases. Interestingly, Kenstowicz (1994) came to the same conclusion that constraint evaluation has to take place in two stages, based on analyses of stress patterns in Carib, Shanghai Chinese, and Polish.[6]

An implication of this two-stage derivation/evaluation is that we must allow for resyllabification, albeit of a restricted type: an obstruent which is at one stage in coda position shifts to an onset position in the next stage. That is, the grammar must allow for certain information to be overwritten. In Rubach and Booij (1990) it has been proposed that resyllabification has to be allowed for, but is restricted to coda erasure at the right edges of morphemes.

In his article on the organization of the grammar, Mohanan (1995: 64) makes the following comment on the issue under discussion here:

(13) One can subscribe to the hypothesis that phonological theory needs to separate the module of word-internal structure from the module of structure across words, without necessarily assuming that the former module precedes the latter in a procedural sense. In a non-sequential conception, the modules and the levels of representation that are associated with them, are 'co-present', as structures along a multidimensional space, where information from different 'levels' or dimensions of organization is simultaneously accessible to principles of the grammar.

Although I agree that multidimensional representations are necessary (see Booij and Lieber 1993 for arguments in favor of the co-presence of the morphological and the prosodic structure of words), I do see a problem for this 'parallel' interpretation of the lexical/postlexical distinction which is

[6] It is possible to avoid a two-stage evaluation by making use of empty positions which are linked to other positions. For the case under discussion, this implies that the onset obstruents in word + clitic combinations are co-indexed with an empty coda position in the host word. Onset obstruents would then be devoiced because they are co-indexed with a coda position. Such an approach is only motivated if evidence could be provided for such 'traces' in phonology, and I am not aware of such independent evidence. Moreover, such a solution does not explain why the onset position does not parasitically license the feature [+voice] in that position.

illustrated by the Dutch case under discussion: both modules pertain to the same dimension of structure, namely prosodic structure. Thus, the lexical and the postlexical representation of the prosodic structure of a Dutch word + clitic combination make contradictory predictions with respect to the phonetic realization of morpheme-final underlyingly voiced obstruents. The question is: is an underlying /d/ that occurs in coda position in one dimension, and in onset position in another one, to be realized as a [t] or a [d]? In a derivational, i.e. serial, approach we can say that the lexical level comes first, and that therefore such an underlying /d/ is to be pronounced as a [t]. What the derivational metaphor correctly expresses is that the lexical level takes priority over the postlexical level, and this is what phonological theory has to express as a universal of grammatical organization.

3.1.1 *Correspondence theory*

There seems to be an alternative in OT for capturing the distinction between the lexical and the postlexical level: the generalized theory of Correspondence advocated, for instance, in McCarthy (1995), which allows for constraints on the relation between the output forms of related words. Similar ideas have been put forward by Burzio (1995; 1996) and Flemming & Kenstowicz (1995), who also argue in favor of identity constraints on the output forms of related words. The introduction of output–output constraints means that the paradigmatic relations between words play a role in the computation of the phonetic form of a word. That is, it is a form of paradigmatic phonology.

Suppose now that we assume an identity constraint that requires the phonetic forms of morphemes in different contexts to be identical. Clearly, this must be a violable constraint because otherwise morphemes would never be allowed to have allomorphs. In the case under discussion it is only featural identity that is required; the prosodic structure might be different: the /b/ of *heb* 'have' is a coda, but that of *heb er* 'have her' is an onset. The Feature Identity constraint will induce overapplication of Coda Devoicing: the /b/ in *heb er* is devoiced although it should not be, since it is in onset position.

Note, however, that we still have to differentiate between suffixes and clitics with respect to their effect on the phonetic forms of morphemes: the Feature Identity constraint should not apply to morphemes followed by a suffix. For instance, whereas the morpheme *heb* surfaces as [hɛp] in isolation and before clitics, it surfaces as [hɛb] before vowel-initial suffixes. If we do not have recourse to ordering of rules, we therefore have to assume co-phonologies. That is, a language then has more than one phonological system. Each subsystem is formed by a language-specific ranking of the universal constraints. Each of the co-phonologies applies to a particular domain of the language, for instance, the word domain or the domain of non-native words. In the case under discussion, we have to assume two co-phonologies for Dutch: one in which faithfulness constraints dominate the Feature Identity Constraint (the lexical co-phonology, in which the feature [+voice] of the relevant obstruents is parsed), and one in which the Feature Identity Constraint dominates Faithfulness (postlexical phonology, in which the relevant feature [+voice] is not parsed).

It seems to me that using Correspondence Theory for the elimination of evaluation in two steps, at the lexical and the postlexical level, is not right, because it forces us to assume two co-phonologies with different rankings of the Feature Identity constraint, whereas the facts discussed here directly follow without different rankings if we evaluate in two steps, at the lexical level and subsequently at the postlexical level (see Inkelas, Orgun, and Zoll, Chapter 13 below, for specific discussion of the issue of co-phonologies).

3.1.2 *The systematicity of the lexical level*

The lexical level defended here as an intermediate step in the computation of phonetic forms has a systematic role in the grammar, in that the constraints of word phonology are different from those of sentence phonology. For instance, many constraints that apply to consonant clusters in Dutch words, do not apply to postlexical combinations of consonants in prosodic words that are clitic–host combinations:

(14) tf-   't valt 'it falls'
    kb-   'k ben 'I am'
    ks-   'k zal 'I will'
    tɣ- |'t gaat 'it goes'

Similarly, Dell (1995) pointed out that the phonotactics of French at the word level is much more restricted than that after the application of inflection and syntax, which reflects the traditional distinction between 'phonological syllable' and 'phonetic syllable'.

In sum, the classical distinction between word phonology and sentence phonology, which forms part of the LP model of the grammar, should be maintained whatever the format of one's phonological generalizations.

What the derivational metaphor of evaluation in two steps expresses is that the postlexical phonology may make the effects of the lexical phonology opaque, whereas the inverse, lexical phonology making the postlexical phonology opaque, does not occur. That is, we should not interpret the two phonologies as co-phonologies that apply simultaneously, but as sequentially ordered phonologies. In this way, we also avoid the need to assume a Feature Identity Constraint with two different rankings.

3.2 *Cyclic application of rules*

Cyclic rule application has been a persistent topic in generative phonology since SPE. The cyclic application of rules has been part and parcel of Lexical

Phonology, and follows from the basic claim of Lexical Phonology that phonology and morphology apply in tandem, as outlined above.

What I will not discuss here is how far cyclic application of stress rules (the classic case of rule cyclicity) is necessary in order to derive the correct stress patterns of complex words.[7] I will focus on two other aspects of the cyclicity hypothesis in LP:

(15) (i) morphological rules may refer to derived phonological properties of their inputs;
    (ii) morphological and phonological rules may refer to phonological properties that never come to the surface.

The question, then, is how far these insights concerning the organization of the grammar imply a derivational approach to phonology.

A straightforward example of the dependence of morphology on derived phonological properties of its inputs is the case of German past participles, which are formed by suffixation of *-en* (strong verbs) or *t/d* (weak verbs), and by simultaneous prefixation of *ge-* if the first syllable of the verbal stem carries main stress:

(16) *Verb stem*   *Past participle*
    lauf 'walk'   gelaufen
    filtríer 'filter'   filtriert
    reaktivíer 'reactivate' reaktiviert

Such a generalization can, but need not necessarily, be expressed in the form of a cyclic derivation in which first stress is assigned to the verbal stem, and subsequently past-participle formation takes place. It is also possible to express this generalization as an output constraint which states that the presence of *ge-* is only licensed by a following syllable with main stress, because the information on the stress pattern of the verbal stem will be present at the surface.

Another illustration of the first of these two implications of the LP model is noun pluralization in Dutch. Dutch has two competing suffixes for pluralization, *-s* /s/ and *-en* /ən/. The selection of the correct suffix is determined by the stress pattern of the base word:

(17) *-en* after a stem ending in a stressed syllable
    -s after a stem ending in an unstressed syllable

The following examples illustrate this selection pattern:

(18) (a) dam 'id.'   dámm-en
       kanón 'gun'   kanónn-en
       kanáal 'channel' kanál-en
       lèdikánt 'bed'   lèdikánt-en
       ólifànt 'elephant' ólifànt-en

---

[7] A survey and analysis of the discussions of this topic can be found in Cole (1995).

(b) kánon 'canon'	kánon-s
bézəm 'sweep'	bézəm-s
tóga 'gown'	tóga-s
proféssor 'id.'	proféssor-s

Although there are a number of complications with respect to the pluralization of loanwords and certain types of complex word,[8] this generalization concerning the role of stress is an established insight in Dutch morphology (cf. Booij and van Santen 1995: 64 ff.).

The basic properties of the Dutch stress system are as follows. Main stress falls on the penultimate syllable of a word, unless its last syllable is superheavy (i.e. contains a VVC- or VCC-rhyme); in the latter case main stress falls on the final syllable. However, certain French loan words such as *kanón* 'gun' and *trompét* 'trumpet' have final stress although they do not end in a superheavy syllable, and therefore have to be diacritically marked as [+ F] (mnemonically for [+ French]). We also find words with antepenultimate stress, in which the last syllable has to be marked as extrametrical. So, unless its last syllable is superheavy, marked as [+ F], or extrametrical, a Dutch word ends in a syllabic trochee. Secondary stress is determined by a lexical rule of alternating stress. Furthermore, syllables headed by schwa never bear stress. Thus to a large extent the stress patterns of Dutch words are predictable.

The facts concerning the selection of the correct plural suffix given above form a perfect illustration of LP's claim that phonology and morphology apply in tandem, and that morphology may be dependent on derived phonological properties. On the first cycle, stress is assigned to the nominal stem. On the second cycle, where the plural suffix is attached, the rule can make use of the relevant, predictable information concerning the stress pattern of the nominal stem.

These plural suffixes, like all inflectional suffixes of Dutch, are stress-neutral: they do not influence the stress pattern of their stems. We have to create some provision for this. For instance, if the *-s* of *toga's* 'gowns' counted for stress assignment, the last syllable of this plural form would be superheavy, since its rhyme consists of a long vowel followed by a consonant /s/, and hence carry main stress. This is incorrect, since it is the first syllable of this word that carries main stress. In LP stress neutrality can be expressed by the ordering of rule blocks: the rules of inflectional morphology are ordered after the Main Stress Rule of Dutch. Alternatively, we may not assume ordered rule blocks, but mark stress-neutral suffixes as noncyclic suffixes in the sense of Halle and Vergnaud (1987), which implies that they do not trigger reapplication of the

---

[8] For instance, in some types of complex word with a suffix ending in schwa, the derivational suffix may determine the selection of the plural suffix: diminutive nouns, which end in schwa, always require *-s* as their plural suffix. English loans often have a plural suffix *-s* even when they end in stressed syllable, as in *tram-s*.

Main Stress Rule of Dutch, as outlined in section 2. This latter alternative is to be preferred, because there exist complex words in Dutch in which a stress-neutral suffix precedes a stress-shifting one (Booij 1995), which is an obvious problem for the ordered-blocks analysis.

Is a non-derivational account of these facts possible? To begin with, the prosodic constraint involved in the selection of plural suffixes can be used as an argument for output constraints instead of rules that select the correct allomorph. The effect of the generalizations given in (17) is that a plural noun will always end in a disyllabic trochee. That is, the following (violable) output constraint can be assumed for Dutch:

(19) Words end in a syllabic trochee.

The advantage of such an output constraint is that the functional motivation for the conditions on the choice between -*s* and -*en* is expressed, whereas a generalization such as (17) does not express this: if the inverse conditions applied (-*s* after stressed syllables, -*en* after unstressed syllables), the rules would not be more complicated.

A consequence of this OT-type of approach to allomorphy is that GEN generates two candidate sets for each plural noun, one for the noun ending in -*s* and one for the same noun ending in -*en*. Similar arguments for such an output constraint-based approach to prosodically determined allomorphy are provided by Tranel (1994) for French and by Kager (1995) for Estonian.

Given a constraint-based account of the plural suffix allomorphy of Dutch, the question remains how we account for the fact that the plural affixes do not affect the location of the main stress. In computing the prosodic structure of a plural noun, the plural suffix must be ignored as far as the location of main stress is concerned. Otherwise, a plural form such as *toga's* /to:ɣa:s/ 'gowns' would get final stress, just like *soláas* /so:la:s/ 'solace', because both words end in a superheavy syllable. Stress neutrality can be accounted for in derivational theories by cyclic derivation:

(20) 1st cycle   /to:ɣa:/
      Main Stress Rule   ó:
      2nd cycle
      Suffixation   +s
      Main Stress Rule   [blocked; see below]
      phonetic form   [tó:ɣa:s]

Application of the Main Stress Rule on the second cycle is blocked because the suffix -*s* is marked as a suffix that does not induce stress erasure, and therefore the existing metrical structure is respected.

It is not possible to obtain this cyclicity effect by an alignment constraint (McCarthy and Prince 1994) which requires the right edge of a stem to align with the right edge of a foot. This kind of solution is proposed in Cohn and

McCarthy (1994) for Indonesian. As they point out, this works for cases in which the stem is followed by a suffix of the CV form. Vowel-initial suffixes of Indonesian, on the other hand, do not allow for such an alignment because the suffix-initial vowel forms a syllable with the stem-final consonant, and Cohn and McCarthy (1994) claim that it is precisely in such cases that there is no cyclicity effect. In the Dutch case under discussion here, however, there is preservation of the location of main stress of the stem, although there is no alignment of the right edge of the stem and the right edge of a foot, as the following examples illustrate (the right stem edge is indicated by]):

(21) tóga-s 'gowns'

kanál-en 'channels'

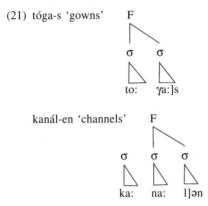

That is, the stress-neutral suffixes must be incorporated into the prosodic structure of the words they belong to after the initial determination of the prosodic structure (including main stress assignment). Subsequently, the prosodic structure will be partially recomputed. This is necessary because the output constraint on plural nouns that they must end in a trochee must evidently be evaluated with respect to the prosodic structure of the whole plural form, including the inflectional suffix. Therefore, the cyclicity effect under discussion here cannot be obtained through alignment.[9]

So it seems that we have to assume two stages here *within* word phonology, which can be characterized in terms of alignment differences: at the first level the right edge of prosodic structure must align with the morphological boundary before the inflectional suffix; at the second level the right edge of the prosodic structure must align with the right word edge. That is, we have to assume two steps in the computation of the proper form of a word.[10]

An alternative for cyclic derivation is the use of anti-allomorphy constraints (Burzio 1995; 1996), also called identity constraints (Flemming and Kenstowicz

---

[9] The same problem holds for the solution suggested by Kenstowicz (1994: 21).
[10] Orgun (1994) reaches the same conclusion that not all cyclicity effects can be accounted for by means of alignment conditions, on the basis of data from Turkish.

1995), or correspondence constraints (McCarthy 1995). The idea is that there is a class of constraints that require the output form of the stem of a complex word to be maximally similar to the output form of the corresponding lexical item. For example, we might assume an identity constraint (Head Identity) that requires the head of the prosodic word of *toga's* 'gowns', the vowel /o:/, to match the head of the prosodic word of *toga*.

Stress neutrality is not a property of all Dutch suffixes, however: non-native suffixes do affect the location of the main stress, and such stem + non-native suffix combinations behave with respect to stress assignment as if they are underived. Therefore, the Head Identity constraint does not apply to the non-native part of the morphological system of Dutch. We are thus forced to assume two co-phonologies for Dutch: a native and a non-native co-phonology, with different constraint rankings. In the native co-phonology, the constraint that final superheavy syllables are the heads of prosodic words (Superheavy) is dominated by the Head Identity constraint that requires identity with respect to prosodic headship. In the non-native co-phonology, the ranking of these two constraints is the inverse. Compare the evaluation of *toga's* with the evaluation of the de-adjectival noun *absurditéit* 'absurdity', derived from the adjective *absúrd* 'id.' with the non-native suffix *-iteit* '-ity':

(22)

	Head Identity	Superheavy
→ tóga-s		*
togá-s	*!	

	Superheavy	Head Identity
absúrd-iteit	*!	
→ absurd-itéit		*

The existence of co-phonologies implies cyclic evaluation of constraints: each suffix in its turn determines which co-phonology governs the evaluation. For instance, the plural form of *absurditeit* 'absurdity' is *absurditeit-en*. For the evaluation of this word we have to use the native co-phonology because the plural suffix induces native phonology. In order to check Head Identity, we have to look at the output form of its stem, *absurd-iteit*. The output form of this word can only be computed by first computing the output of its base *absurd*. Crucially, we cannot directly compare *absurditeiten* with *absurd*, because then we would have to conclude that the Head Identity Constraint is violated (in *àbsurditéiten* the part *absurd* does not bear main stress). That is, the introduction of correspondence constraints involves cyclic evaluation of complex words in languages with co-phonologies, a form of serial computation.

4. COUNTERFEEDING RULE ORDER

Counterfeeding order is a form of extrinsic rule ordering that is clearly at odds with non-derivational phonology. I should add, however, that it is also a form of rule ordering that should be avoided as much as possible in derivational phonology. It is to be avoided since it is essentially stipulative, and does not follow from the organization of the grammar, unlike the application of lexical rules before postlexical ones, or the application of a rule on a cycle before the application of another rule on the next cycle.

Whereas cyclicity is not necessarily in conflict with a constraint-based approach, the extrinsic ordering of rules within a cycle clearly is. So the question is whether we can do away with this kind of extrinsic ordering. The combination of cyclic application and extrinsic ordering of rules that is often found in LP analyses can be illustrated on the basis of the following facts of Dutch discussed in Booij (1995: 80 ff.). Non-native words ending in a syllable with a VC rhyme that does not bear main stress exhibit vowel lengthening: the vowel of the last syllable is lengthened before non-native suffixes, which are all vowel-initial. Consider the following examples:

(23) kán[ɔ]n 'canon'   kan[o:]níek 'canonical'
     mót[ɔ]r 'engine'   mot[ó:]risch 'engine-'
                               mot[o:]ríek 'way of moving'

     sát[ɑ]n 'id.'   sat[á:]nisch 'satanical'
     álfab[ɛ]t 'alphabet'   alfab[é:]tisch 'alphabetical'
     proféss[ɔ]r 'id.'   profess[o:]ráal 'professorial'
                               profess[o:]ráat 'professorate'

     organisát[ɔ]r 'organizer' organisat[ó:]risch 'organizational'
     álcoh[ɔ]l 'id.'   alcoh[ó:]lisch 'alcoholic-A'
                               alcoh[o:]líst 'alcoholic-N'

The crucial condition is that the syllable that is lengthened does not bear main stress in the base word. Given this stress condition on vowel lengthening, the vowels of monosyllabic base words will never be lengthened because they always have main stress. The stress pattern of the base word, however, is not preserved in the complex word: as pointed out above, non-native suffixes erase the stress pattern of the base word when the stress pattern of the derived word is computed. In the complex words, main stress falls on the last stressable syllable (except for words with the suffix *-isch*, where main stress falls on the last syllable before the suffix). We also find near-minimal pairs such as *kànoníek* [ka:no:ni:k] 'canonical' derived from *kánon* 'canon' versus *kànon-níer* [ka:nɔni:r] 'gun man', derived from the word *kanón* 'gun':

(24) *No lengthening*

tón 'id.'	t[ɔ]nnáge 'number of tons'
blók 'block'	bl[ɔ]kkéer 'to block'
kanón 'gun'	kan[ɔ]nníer' gun man'
modél 'id.'	mod[ɛ]lléer 'to model'
librétto 'id.'	libr[ɛ]ttíst 'id.'

The stress of all base words involved is regular, and hence predictable by rule (except for disyllabic words such as *kanón* 'gun': this word forms a minimal pair with the regularly stressed *kánon* 'canon'). So the basic ingredients of rule-based LP for expressing the generalization involved are: cyclic assignment of stress, and extrinsic ordering of vowel lengthening before stress assignment. These rules have to be ordered in counterfeeding order, because otherwise Stress Erasure would feed Vowel Lengthening, with incorrect results (lengthening of the second vowel) for a word like *kanonnier* derived from *kanón*. For instance, the LP derivation of *kanonnier* runs as follows:

(25)

1st cycle	[ka: nɔn]$_N$
Main Stress Rule	ʌ́
2nd cycle	[[ka: nʌ́n]$_N$i:r]$_N$
Vowel Lengthening	blocked
Stress Erasure	ɔ
Main Stress Rule	í:
Secondary Stress	à
output	[kà:nɔní:r]

This derivation presupposes again that non-native suffixes are cyclic suffixes in the sense of Halle and Vergnaud (1987), which means that they erase the stress pattern of their base word, after which the Main Stress Rule is reapplied to the whole string including the suffix. This nicely illustrates the idea that phonological rules may refer to phonological properties that never come to the surface.

Note that the blocking of vowel lengthening cannot be made dependent on the presence of the diacritic feature [+ F] that is necessary to get exceptional main stress on words such as *kanón* and *trompét*. The reason is that there are also words such as *tón* and *librétto* with regular stress, where the stressed vowel also resists lengthening.

If this type of analysis were the only possible account, it would form a strong case in favor of a rule-based approach to phonology, in the spirit of Bromberger and Halle (1989), who claim that it is extrinsic ordering of rules that distinguishes phonology from the other components of the grammar. However, as has been pointed out by e.g. Lakoff (1993) and Coleman (1995), it is possible to reanalyse the Bromberger–Halle data without making use of extrinsic ordering. Generally, the use of extrinsic ordering of rules should be avoided as much as possible in a constrained theory of phonology, since extrinsic ordering adds to the number of stipulations in the grammar of a particular language. It is preferable to have a theory of rule or constraint inter-action that can do without the device of stipulated extrinsic ordering. In this respect extrinsic ordering is different from cyclic rule application, because the latter need not be stipulated, but follows from the principle 'apply a rule when possible'. It is also the goal of LP to reduce the order of application of rules as much as possible to universal principles such as the Elsewhere Condition.

4.1 *Correspondence constraints?*

One possible solution to this descriptive problem within the correspondence theory proposed by Flemming and Kenstowicz (1995) is the following: 'the constraint requiring a stem final vowel to be long is dominated by a constraint that matches the head of the prosodic word of the base with the corresponding vowel in the derived structure'. What this formulation implies is the following: in a word such as *kanonnier* (derived from *kanón*) the vowel of the second syllable may not be lengthened because it may not be different from the vowel of the second syllable of *kanón*, this vowel being the head of the prosodic word of the base (i.e. it bears main stress). On the other hand, the vowel of the second syllable of *kanoniek* can be lengthened because this vowel does not correspond to the head of the prosodic word of the base, which is the first vowel of the base, the /a/. This is a typically paradigmatic solution: although there is no primary stress on the second syllable of *kanonnier* that can block the lengthening, there is such a primary stress on the corresponding base word.

Although I do not want to exclude the possibility that paradigmatic relations may play a role in phonology, it is at present a very unconstrained device. Therefore, it is worthwhile to investigate whether an alternative analysis with-out correspondence constraints is possible. Such an analysis would run as follows. Non-native words in Dutch often appear to have two different forms in derivational morphology, one for non-native suffixation and one for native suffixation. Sometimes, the allomorph that is used in non-native suffixation is not even pronounceable as such, that is, it is not a proper prosodic word, as is the case for the allomorph *filtr* of the word *filter* 'id.'. Also, it is often impossible to derive one allomorph from the other by means of a phonological rule. Consider the following examples (from Booij 1995: 83):

(26) orkest 'orchestra'   orkestr-eer 'to orchestrate'
     gymnasium 'grammar school'   gymnasi-ast 'grammar school pupil'
     trauma 'id.'   traumat-isch 'traumatic'
     functie 'function'   function-eer 'to function'
     horizon 'id.'   horizont-aal 'horizontal'
     orgel 'organ'   organ-ist 'organ player'

The conclusion to draw from these examples is that for such (non-native) words two stem allomorphs have to be listed, one that is subcategorized for non-native suffixation and one that has no subcategorization, the default allomorph. The default allomorph is chosen when the word is used as a simplex word, in prefixation, and in native suffixation.

We might then use the same strategy for cases such as *kánon—kànoníek*, and list two stem allomorphs in the lexicon for the relevant word: /ka:nɔn/ and /ka:no:n/. The only disadvantage of this solution is that we do not derive one allomorph from the other by means of a regular rule of phonology, as was possible in the analysis presented above. Note, however, that the rule of vowel lengthening does not have the character of an automatic phonological rule anyway, since its application is restricted to non-native complex words. It also has exceptions such as *claxonneer* 'to sound one's horn', derived from the English loan *kláxon* 'horn'.

As argued by Aronoff (1994), there is ample evidence from a number of languages for lexical rules that derive one stem allomorph from another one in a systematic way (see also Spencer 1988).[11] In the case under discussion here, this rule would have the following form:

(27) Non-native morphemes ending in . . . VC_1V_iC have an allomorph in
     . . . $VC_1V_iV_iC$ subcategorized for non-native suffixation.
     Condition: the morpheme does not bear the diacritic feature [+ F].

By requiring the absence of [+ F] (= [+ French]), we ensure that only those morphemes in -VC_1VC that do not carry main stress get an allomorph with a long vowel in the final syllable. So *kánon* /ka:nɔn/ 'canon' has an allomorph /ka:no:n/, but *kanón* 'gun', with the exceptional word-final stress triggered by the feature [+ F] does not. Monosyllabic words such as *ton* and polysyllabic words such as *librétto* do not have the phonological form required by the allomorphy rule, and hence do not exhibit vowel lengthening.

There is independent evidence for a stem allomorphy analysis in these cases. Non-native nouns ending in -*on* or -*or* also exhibit this vowel-length alternation optionally in singular–plural pairs:

(28) | *Singular* | *Plural* | *Derived word* |
|---|---|---|
| démon 'demon' | démons/dem[ó:]nen | dem[ó:]nisch 'demoniac' |
| eléktron 'electron' | eléktrons/elektr[ó:]nen | elektr[ó:]nisch 'electronic' |
| mótor 'engine' | mótors/mot[ó:]ren | mot[ó:]risch 'engine-' |
| dóctor 'doctor' | dóctors/doct[ó:]ren | doct[o:]ráal 'doctoral' |

---

[11] Note that Spencer (1988) uses the term 'morpholexical rule' for lexical redundancy rules that relate two or more listed allomorphs, whereas I use the term, like Anderson, as a synonym of 'morphophonological rule', i.e. a phonological rule conditioned by non-phonological (morphological and/or lexical) properties.

The crucial observation is that a difference in plural suffix correlates with a difference in the location of the main stress, although normally plural suffixes do not affect the stress patterns of their base words. These facts follow directly if we assume two allomorphs for these words, as proposed above. The only exceptional aspect of the behavior of these words in *-on* and *-or*, then, is that the allomorph that is normally used only for non-native suffixation may also be used for inflectional suffixation. When the allomorph *demon* is used, the prosodic output constraint on plural nouns requires *-s*, because the predictable stress pattern is *démon*. The allomorph *demoon*, on the other hand, will receive main stress on its final syllable, because this syllable is superheavy, and thus forms a foot of its own. After prosodic integration of the suffix *-en*, the word will end in a trochee, as required.[12]

In sum, what we have seen here is that in some cases the extrinsic ordering of rules can be avoided by making use of rules of stem allomorphy. Thus, these data do not constitute decisive evidence in favor of a rule-based approach to phonology.

4.2 *Non-native allomorphy*

Another relevant case of allomorphy is the following. When a Dutch non-native word has two allomorphs, one of them may be unpronounceable, i.e. it does not form a proper phonological word. The generalization is that, unlike non-native suffixation, native suffixation always requires its inputs to be fully prosodically licensed. Consider the following examples:

(29) filter 'id.'   [− native]: filtr-eer 'to filter', filtr-aat 'filtrate'
                           [+ native]: filter-en 'to filter, inf.', filter-ing 'id.'
     regel 'rule'   [− native]: regl-ement 'rules'
                           [+ native]: regel-en 'to arrange, inf.', regel-ing 'arrangement'
     exempel 'example'   [− native]: exempl-arisch 'exemplary'
                           [+ native]: exempel-en 'examples'
     arbiter 'id.'   [− native]: arbitr-age 'refereeing', arbitr-eer 'to referee'
                           [+ native]: arbiter-en 'to referee', inf.'
     center 'id.'   [− native]: centr-eer 'to center', centr-aal 'central'
                           [+ native]: center-en 'to center', inf.'
     cilinder 'cylinder'   [− native]: cilindr-isch 'cylindrical'
     integer 'honest'   [− native]: integr-eer 'to integrate', integr-iteit 'integrity'
                           [+ native]: integer-e 'honest', inflected form

A [− native] stem allomorph such as *filtr* cannot be completely licensed prosodically: a coda /tr/ of this monosyllabic stem would violate the Sonority

---

[12] The plural suffix *-en* is exceptional here in that it attaches to an allomorph that does not occur as an independent word. For instance, *demoon* does not occur as word. The normal base identity constraint for native suffixation should not apply.

Sequencing Generalization, and hence the /r/ will remain extrasyllabic unless some action is taken. In the case of non-native suffixation, the vowel-initial suffix triggers resyllabification, as in $(fil)_\sigma(tre:r)_\sigma$. Thus, the /r/ is prosodically licensed. When the morpheme *filtr* is to be realized as a word, the default vowel of Dutch, the schwa, is inserted before the /r/, and hence we get the form /fɪltər/. It is this form that feeds native suffixation. So, although a native vowel-initial suffix could have saved the /r/ of *filtr*, this is not the proper solution for words with native suffixes, and the schwa has to be inserted.

In a classical LP approach this array of facts can be accounted for by assuming two morphological levels: a level of non-native suffixation followed by a level of native suffixation. The rule of schwa insertion will then be ordered after the first, and before the second level of suffixation. That is, a form of extrinsic ordering seems to be necessary.

In constraint-based phonology it is possible to analyse these facts by making use of constraints of correspondence.[13] The schwa insertion in a word such as *filter-en* can be seen as a case of overapplication of schwa epenthesis, triggered by an output–output identity constraint that holds for the native phonology of Dutch: the phonetic form of a stem used in native suffixation must be identical to the phonetic form of that stem when realized as a word in isolation. In a rule-based approach without extrinsic ordering, on the other hand, the two allomorphs cannot be derived from a common underlying form.

Again, the use of correspondence constraints does not eliminate serial computation completely. For instance, if we have to evaluate the candidates for the complex word *filtr-eer-ing* 'filtration', the native suffix *-ing* induces evaluation on the basis of the constraint-ranking of the native phonology, in which the relevant identity constraint is undominated. However, in order to evaluate this constraint we cannot directly compare *filtr-eer-ing* to the phonetic form of the morpheme /fɪltr/, [fɪltər]. This would give the wrong conclusion that the relevant identity constraint has been violated. Instead, we have to evaluate *filtr-eer-ing* with respect to the phonetic output of the stem *filtr-eer* which the grammar also computes. The conclusion will then be that there is no violation of the identity constraint. However, in order to compute the proper phonetic output of *filtr-eer*, we have to check the candidates with respect to all constraints, including the (now dominated) identity constraint in the ranking as defined for the non-native phonology: the constraint appears to be violated, but that does not matter in non-native phonology, where faithfulness between input and output is apparently ranked higher than the identity constraint.

In short, if we interpret phonological strata (level ordering) as co-phonologies, complex words must be evaluated cyclically, and hence we have to allow for serial computation.

---

[13] This solution was suggested to me by Bernard Tranel.

5. MORPHOLEXICAL RULES

Generative phonology deals not only with purely phonological generalizations, in the derivational model in the form of automatic phonological rules, but also with morpholexical rules, i.e. phonological generalizations that only hold for a specific lexical or morphological class of words.

An interesting consequence of the LP model is that morpholexical rules need not necessarily precede automatic phonological rules. The effect of an automatic phonological rule on a cycle can be relevant for the application of a morpholexical rule on the next cycle (within a cycle, morpholexical rules apply before phonological rules). The allomorphy of the Dutch diminutive suffix can be used to illustrate this point. The Dutch diminutive suffix has five allomorphs, *-tje, -je, -etje, -kje, -pje*. The allomorphs *-etje* and *-kje* both appear after a stem that ends in a velar nasal; the allomorph *-etje* appears after stems ending in a sonorant consonant, if the last syllable bears (primary or secondary) stress; after an unstressed syllable ending in the velar nasal the allomorph *-kje* appears:

(30) ríng 'id.'   ring-etje
     seríng 'lilac'   sering-etje
     hórizòn 'id.'   horizonn-etje

     wándel-ìng 'walk'   wandel-ing-etje
     óefen-ìng 'exercise' oefen-ing-etje

     stróm-ing 'stream'   strom-in-kje
     léid-ing 'pipe'   leid-in-kje

     kóning 'king'   konin-kje
     páling 'eel'   palin-kje

As pointed out above, the native suffixes of Dutch, including the inflectional suffixes, are stress neutral. This also applies to the deverbal nominalizing suffix *-ing*. The determination of the location of main stress in Dutch depends on the segmental structure of the last (three) syllables (Kager 1989). However, as amply motivated in Booij (1995), the assignment of secondary stress is a completely rhythmical matter in which notions like syllable weight and stress neutrality do not play a role. The rule of Secondary Stress creates an alternation of stressed and unstressed syllables without creating stress clashes. Therefore, in a word like *wandeling* (a deverbal noun derived from the verb *wandel* 'to take a walk') the last syllable receives secondary stress.

In the classical LP model, the form of the diminutive noun *wandelingetje* is derived as follows:

(31) *1st cycle*   [wɑndəl]
     Main Stress   á
     Sec. Stress   not applicable

2nd cycle	[[wɑ́ndəl]ɪŋ]
Sec. Stress	ì
3rd cycle	[[[wɑ́ndəl]ìŋ]tjə]
Stress rules	not applicable
Allomorphy rule	ətjə
Phonetic form	[wɑ́ndəlìŋətjə]

On the third cycle, no stress rule applies. The Main Stress Rule does not apply because the diminutive suffix, like *-ing*, is stress-neutral. The rule of Secondary Stress does not apply because syllables headed by schwa can never bear stress.

In a non-derivational framework, there are two possibilities for analysing these data. The problem that must be solved is that the schwa epenthesis in words such as *wandelingetje* is not triggered by an automatic phonological rule of schwa epenthesis; it only applies to diminutive words. This can easily be seen from the pair *stil-te* /stɪltə/ 'silence' versus *still-etje* /stɪlətjə/ 'chamberpot': although these words have the same adjectival stem, *stil* 'silent', and both contain a /t/-initial suffix, it is only before the diminutive suffix that a schwa is inserted. Therefore, in a constraint-based non-derivational phonology we have to assume a specific co-phonology for diminutives, a set of constraint rankings that is unique to the diminutive suffix. Alternatively, since we certainly want to avoid a proliferation of morpheme-specific co-phonologies, we may list the five allomorphs of the diminutive suffix, and provide each with the relevant phonological subcategorization. The relation between the five allomorphs is then to be expressed by allomorphy rules, i.e. lexical redundancy rules that relate these forms to each other. Thus, the choice for a constraint-based phonology appears to favor a non-phonological analysis of that kind of allomorphy that is not conditioned by 'pure' phonology.

As pointed out above, the allomorph *-etje* requires the preceding syllable to bear (primary or secondary) stress. In a theory of phonology based on output constraints this is no problem: the phonological subcategorization functions as an output constraint that checks the stress pattern of the diminutive. Thus, when GEN generates both *wándelìngetje* and *wándelìngkje*, it is the first form that is selected, whereas for a noun such as *koning* it is *kóninkje* that is selected, not *kóningetje*, because in this latter word the second syllable does not bear stress.

Interestingly, these conclusions concerning allomorphy support the conclusion reached above as to how to account for the phenomenon of vowel lengthening in non-native words: the allomorphs must be listed, and related by means of redundancy rules, instead of being derived from a common underlying form.

We thus see that the category of morpholexical rules does not form a problem for non-derivational theories of phonology if we accept an allomorphy analysis for the alternations involved.

6. Conclusions

The empirically attested types of rule interaction that form part of the motivation of the LP model of phonology show that a non-derivational conception of phonology, in which there is only one set of ranked constraints that apply simultaneously, is problematic.

First, all phonological theories must distinguish generalizations within the word phonology from generalizations concerning sentence phonology. The effects of prosodically conditioned rules of word phonology may be made opaque by resyllabification effects at the sentence level, and therefore evaluation in two steps appears to be necessary.

Second, although we can probably do without extrinsic ordering of individual phonological rules, the most typical case of 'serial' phonology, certain phenomena require there to be more than one stage at which rules can apply or constraints can be evaluated: we need cyclicity.

This implies that the three levels of LP—the cyclic level, the postcyclic (= word) level, and the postlexical level—cannot be given up in constraint-based phonologies. Moreover, we still need a principle such as Strict Cyclicity that tells us which constraints must be evaluated cyclically, and which constraints should only be evaluated at the word level.

The insights concerning the interaction of phonology and morphology that have been expressed in the LP model of the organization of the grammar have to be preserved, whatever one's theory of the form of phonological generalizations. In an OT framework, they can be partially expressed by means of alignment and correspondence constraints, but evaluation in more than one step remains necessary. A restricted form of serialism appears to be necessary, even in primarily parallel models of phonology.

Finally, we have seen that in non-derivational phonology the generalizations expressed by morpholexical rules lead to a proliferation of morpheme-specific rankings of constraints. The only way to avoid this is another analysis of this kind of allomorphy. Instead of deriving the allomorphs from a common underlying form, the classical strategy of generative phonology, each allomorph is lexically represented. As Goldsmith (1995*a*: 9) rightly points out, we should not take the classical (= phonological) approach to allomorphy which Goldsmith summarizes in the formula 'minimize allomorphy' for granted. Thus constraint-based phonology may contribute to a principled choice as to which allomorphy belongs to the domain of phonology, and where morphology, the module that deals with the selection of morphemes, takes over.

Acknowledgements

This chapter is based on a paper given at the Essex workshop on Derivations and Constraints in Phonology organized by Iggy Roca. A preliminary version of it was published in J. Durand and B. Laks (eds.), *Current Trends in Phonology: Models and Methods*, (Paris: CNRS and Salford: Salford University Press), under the title 'Lexical Phonology and the derivational residue' (pp. 69–97). I would like to thank Bill Idsardi, Gjert Kristoffersen, two anonymous referees, and the editor, Iggy Roca, for their helpful comments on the draft of this article.

REFERENCES

Anderson, S. (1992). *A-morphous Morphology*. Cambridge: Cambridge University Press.
Aronoff, M. (1976). *Word Formation in Generative Grammar*. Cambridge, Mass.: MIT Press.
—— (1994). *Morphology by Itself*. Cambridge, Mass.: MIT Press.
Booij, G. (1981). 'Rule ordering, rule application, and the organization of grammars', in W. U. Dressler et al. (eds.), *Phonologica 1980*. Innsbruck: Institut für Sprachwissenschaft.
—— (1984). 'French C/Ø-alternations, extrasyllabicity, and Lexical Phonology', *The Linguistic Review* **3**: 181–207.
—— (1988). 'On the relation between Lexical Phonology and Prosodic Phonology', in P. M. Bertinetto and M. Loporcaro (eds.), *Certamen Phonologicum*. Turin: Rosenberg & Sellier, 63–76.
—— (1994). 'Lexical Phonology, a review', *Lingua e Stile* **29**: 525–55.
—— (1995). *The Phonology of Dutch*. Oxford: Clarendon Press.
—— (1996). 'Cliticization as prosodic integration, the case of Dutch', *The Linguistic Review* **13** 219–42.
—— and Lieber, R. (1993). 'On the simultaneity of morphological and prosodic structure', in S. Hargus and E. Kaisse (eds.), *Studies in Lexical Phonology*. San Diego: Academic Press, 23–42.
—— and Rubach J. (1987). 'Postcyclic versus post-lexical rules in Lexical Phonology', *Linguistic Inquiry* **18**: 1–44.
—— and van Santen, A. (1995). *Morfologie: De woordstructuur van het Nederlands*. Amsterdam: Amsterdam University Press.
Brame, M. (1974). 'The cycle in phonology: stress in Palestinian, Maltese, and Spanish', *Linguistic Inquiry* **5**: 39–60.
Bromberger, S., and Halle M. (1989). 'Why phonology is different', *Linguistic Inquiry* **20**: 51–70.
Burzio, L. (1995). 'The rise of Optimality Theory', *GLOT International* **1**(6): 3–7.
—— (1996). 'Surface constraints vs. underlying representations', in J. Durand and B. Laks (eds.), *Current Trends in Phonology*. Paris: CNRS / Salford: University of Salford Press.
Cohn, A., and McCarthy J., (1994). 'Alignment and Parallellism in Indonesian Phonology'. MS, Cornell University / University of Massachusetts, Amherst.
Cole, J. (1995). 'The cycle in phonology', in Goldsmith (1995*b*: 72–113).
Coleman, J. (1995). 'Declarative Lexical Phonology', in J. Durand and F. Katamba

(eds.), *Frontiers of Phonology: Atoms, Structures, Derivations*. London: Longman, 333–82.

Dell, F. (1995). 'Consonant clusters and phonological syllables in French', *Lingua* **95**: 5–26.

Flemming, E., and Kenstowicz, M. (1995). 'Base-identity and Uniform Exponence: Alternatives to Cyclicity'. MS, Dept. of Linguistics, MIT.

Goldsmith, J. (1990). *Autosegmental and Metrical Phonology*. Oxford: Blackwell.

—— (1993). 'Harmonic Phonology', in Goldsmith (ed.), *The Last Phonological Rule*. Chicago: Chicago University Press, 21–60.

—— (1995*a*). 'Introduction', in Goldsmith (1995b: 1–15).

—— (ed.) (1995*b*). *The Handbook of Phonological Theory*. Oxford: Blackwell.

Halle, M., and Vergnaud, J.-R. (1987). *An Essay on Stress*. Cambridge, Mass.: MIT Press.

Hayes, B. (1986). 'Inalterability in CV phonology', *Language* **62**: 321–53.

Hargus, S. (1993). 'Modelling the phonology–morphology interface', in S. Hargus and E. Kaisse (eds.), *Studies in Lexical Phonology*. San Diego, Calif.: Academic Press, 45–74.

—— and Kaisse E. (1993). 'Introduction', in Hargus and Kaisse (eds.), *Studies in Lexical Phonology*. San Diego, Calif.: Academic Press, 1–19.

Harris, J. (1983). *Syllable Structure and Stress in Spanish*. Cambridge, Mass.: MIT Press.

—— (1994). 'Integrity of prosodic constituents and the domain of syllabification rules in Spanish and Catalan', in K. Hale and S. J. Keyser (eds.), *The View from Building 20: Essays in Linguistics in Honor of Sylvain Bromberger*. Cambridge, Mass: MIT Press, 177–94.

Hulst, H. van der (1984). *Syllable Structure and Stress in Dutch*. Dordrecht: Foris.

Inkelas, S. (1989). 'Prosodic Constituency in the Lexicon'. Dissertation, Stanford University.

Kager, R. (1989). *Metrical Theory of Stress and Destressing in English and Dutch*. Dordrecht: Foris.

—— (1995). 'On Affix Allomorphy and Syllable Counting'. MS, University of Utrecht.

Kaye, J. (1992). 'On the interaction of theories of Lexical Phonology and theories of phonological phenomena', in W. U. Dressler et al., (eds.), *Phonologica 1988*. Cambridge: Cambridge University Press, 141–55.

Kenstowicz, M. (1994). 'Cyclic vs. noncyclic constraint evaluation', *MIT Working Papers in Linguistics* **21**: 11–42.

Kiparsky, P. (1982). 'From Cyclic Phonology to Lexical Phonology', in H. van der Hulst and N. Smith (eds.), *The Structure of Phonological Representations*, Part 1. Dordrecht: Foris, 131–75.

Lakoff, G. (1993). 'Cognitive phonology', in J. Goldsmith (ed.), *The Last Phonological Rule*. Chicago: Chicago University Press, 117–45.

McCarthy, J. (1995). 'Extensions of Faithfulness: Rotuman Revisited'. MS, Dept. of Linguistics, University of Massachusetts at Amherst.

—— and Prince A., (1993). 'Prosodic Morphology, I: Constraint Interaction and Satisfaction'. MS, University of Massachusetts, Amherst, and Rutgers University.

——— ——— (1994). 'Generalized alignment', in G. Booij and J. van Marle (eds.) *Yearbook of Morphology 1993*. Dordrecht: Kluwer, 79–153.

Mohanan, K. P. (1995). 'The organization of the grammar', in J. Goldsmith (ed.), *The Handbook of Phonological Theory*. Oxford: Blackwell, 24–69.

Orgun, C. O. (1994). 'Monotonic Cyclicity'. MS, University of California, Berkeley.

Paradis, C. (1988–9). 'On constraints and repair strategies', *The Linguistic Review* **6**: 71–97.

Pesetsky, D. (1989). 'Russian Morphology and Lexical Theory'. MS, Dept. of Linguistics, MIT.

Prince, A. and Smolensky P., (1993). 'Optimality Theory: Constraint Interaction in Generative Grammar'. MS, Rutgers University/University of Colorado.

Rubach, J., and Booij G. (1990). 'Edge of constituent effects in Polish', *Natural Language and Linguistic Theory* **8**: 427–64.

Schein, B., and Steriade, D. (1986). 'On geminates', *Linguistic Inquiry* **17**: 691–744.

Spencer, A. (1988). 'Arguments for morpholexical rules', *Journal of Linguistics* **24**: 1–29.

Tranel, B. (1994). 'French Liaison and Elision Revisited: A Unified Account Within Optimality Theory'. MS, University of California, Irvine.

Wijk, N. van (1939). *Phonologie: Een hoofdstuk uit de structurele taalwetenschap*. 's Gravenhage: Martinus Nijhoff.

9

Berber Syllabification: Derivations or Constraints?

G. N. CLEMENTS

1. INTRODUCTION

This chapter addresses one of the central questions raised by the recent development of constraint-based approaches to phonology: is it possible to eliminate derivations from phonological analysis? As is well known, classical generative phonology and many of its offspring proposed to characterize the sound patterns of natural languages—understood both as static patterns of phoneme distribution and as regular patterns of alternation—in terms of grammars consisting of ordered (or in some versions, unordered) rewrite rules, applying one after the other to an input form to derive a sequence of lines, the last of which is the surface form. The ordered sequence of lines created in this way constitutes a *derivation*.

If all derivations could be reduced to two lines (the input and output), the notion of derivation as such would be theoretically uninteresting. However, countless studies have shown that information crucial to the application of many rules is present neither in the input nor in the output, but in intermediate lines of the derivation, that is, at stages at which some but not all rules have applied (see Kenstowicz 1994 for recent discussion). This result is theoretically interesting; but if we regard the linguist's description as an analogue of the speaker's internalized knowledge of grammar in some sense, the crucial intermediate lines must be regarded as suspect, since no independent (i.e., system-external) evidence of either a linguistic or psychological nature has come forward to attest to their cognitive reality.[1]

In contrast, some recent constraint-based models of phonology have proposed frameworks in which the role of derivations is reduced or eliminated altogether. Perhaps the most radical such proposal is that of Declarative Phonology, which constructs surface forms according to sets of surface-true constraints describing well-formed surface configurations (see e.g. Scobbie

---

[1] There is some evidence, however, that the output of certain subsets of rules, constituting lexical strata, may have a cognitive status (Mohanan 1982).

1993 and references therein). In this framework there are no derivations whatsoever (even in the theoretically uninteresting sense), as there is no distinction between underlying representations (input) and surface representations (output).

We shall be concerned here with another framework which severely reduces the role of derivation in phonology: the parallel-processing or non-derivational version of Optimality Theory, as presented in Prince and Smolensky (1993), McCarthy and Prince (1993*a*; 1993*b*), and related work. In their foundational presentation of this framework, Prince and Smolensky (1993) stress that the parallel-processing version is not the only possible conception of Optimality Theory, and briefly sketch the outlines of a serial-processing (or derivational) approach to constraint satisfaction. However, neither these writers nor any others, to my knowledge, have devoted significant attention to this approach (see, however, Blevins in Chapter 7 above [Editor]), and indeed McCarthy and Prince (1993*a*) identify parallelism as one of four defining principles of the theory, stating without qualification that 'there is no serial derivation'. It is therefore the parallel-processing version of the theory that I will consider here. (We shall see in the later discussion, however, that McCarthy and Prince do allow a limited role for derivation in their account of stratal organization.)

This study undertakes to examine the success with which Optimality Theory, in the latter sense, can be applied to a complex set of data on Berber syllabification described in two publications by Dell and Elmedlaoui (1985; 1988). In their account, Imdlawn Tashlhiyt Berber (ITB) has a set of rules collectively referred to as Core Syllabification (CS) which apply serially in several passes to construct CV (or 'core') syllables over unsyllabified input strings. Subsequent rules gather as-yet unsyllabified material into codas, and prune excess syllabifications created by the CS rules in pre- and postpausal position. D&E show that this conceptually simple framework correctly describes a wide range of complex phonological data. As their description relies crucially on rule ordering, it offers an interesting challenge to nonderivational models of phonology.

Prince and Smolensky address this challenge directly, assigning ITB a central illustrative role in their presentation of the theory: 'Our first goal will be to establish that the notion of optimality is, as claimed, indispensable to grammar . . . We will argue this point from the results of Dell and Elmedlaoui in their landmark study of syllabification in Imdlawn Tashlhiyt Berber' (1993: 10). As this citation indicates, their main goal in discussing ITB is not to demonstrate the superiority of a nonderivational approach to phonology—indeed, they briefly sketch an analysis of ITB phonology within a derivational version of Optimality Theory—but to show the importance of the notion of *optimality*, as formalized in terms of constraint domination and harmonic ordering. P&S view ITB as a case where treating grammar as optimization rather than rule (or constraint) application can lead to a deeper explanation of the facts.

But, of course, any success at developing a convincing non-derivational analysis of materials that previously seemed to require an ordered-rule treatment lends further plausibility to the non-derivational interpretation of the theory.

While P&S suggest the direction that a full analysis of ITB might take, they do not discuss much of the evidence that presents a potentially severe challenge to the theory (again, in its non-derivational interpretation). This evidence includes the regular surface exceptions to the CS rules found at the edges of the syllabification domain, treated by D&E in terms of 'annexation rules', and the interaction between ITB syllabification and word formation. Moreover, their study discusses only a few forms, several of which are invented. Their demonstration is therefore incomplete, and one may wonder whether a non-derivational analysis along the lines they suggest can be successfully generalized to a more representative fragment of ITB phonology.

The present study takes up this challenge, attempting to extend a non-derivational, optimality-based analysis along the lines initiated by P&S to a larger fragment of ITB phonology, while focusing on aspects that present a potential problem for non-derivational theories of phonology. Its principal goals will be (i) to determine whether such an account is possible at all, and (ii) if so, to see whether it can offer a deeper explanation of ITB phonology than the rule-based account originally offered by D&E. A related though subsidiary goal will be to submit P&S's constraint system to critical evaluation within the overall logic of their general aims and assumptions, in the interest of placing our analysis on the firmest grounds possible.

The following discussion begins with an overview of previous analyses of ITB syllabification, and then proceeds to develop a new account. Section 2 lays out the basic principles of D&E's analysis, whose basic insight is that ITB syllabification favors the creation of high-sonority peaks over low-sonority peaks, to the extent consistent with independent constraints. Section 3 then summarizes P&S's constraint-based analysis, whose fundamental claim is that ITB syllabification favors the creation of low-sonority margins over high-sonority margins. It shows that this analysis relies crucially on certain constraints that express 'antitendencies' (in a sense to be explained below), and that the incorporation of such constraints in the theory leads to a problem of overgeneration (i.e. to the generation of implausible typologies); it is therefore proposed that such constraints should be excluded from the theory. Sections 4–6 propose a new analysis of ITB consistent with this proposal, which addresses the central goals of this chapter as set out above. Section 4 introduces the new analysis, and applies it to representative data of the sort considered by P&S. Section 5 takes up the study of the pre- and postpausal clusters that motivated D&E's 'annexation rules'. Section 6 then examines the interaction of syllabification with principles of word formation, considering one type of imperfective formation as well as the system of templatic morphology. Section 7 summarizes our results, and evaluates the overall success of an Optimality-theoretic approach in eliminating derivations from the grammatical description of ITB.

2. Dell and Elmedlaoui's Rule-Based Account

Dell and Elmedlaoui's studies (1985; 1988) are concerned with the Imdlawn Tashlhiyt dialect of Berber as spoken by the second author. I follow D&E in referring to this variety as ITB. The underlying system of ITB speech sounds is presented below.[2]

(1) ITB consonants:
  a. contoids:

  b. vocoids:

    y   w   a

All segments have syllabic and nonsyllabic variants except /a/, which is always syllabic; in this study, syllabic contoids are underlined, and the syllabic realizations of / y, w / are written [i, u]. Length is indicated by the use of double symbols, as in *tamanns* 'near him'. Emphasis (dorsopharyngealization) is a distinctive morpheme-level feature, symbolized by an exclamation point written before the unit it characterizes, as in *!tlbzt* 'step onto'.

As a broad generalization it may be stated that, with only marginal exceptions, all underlying strings in ITB can be fully syllabified without recourse to epenthesis or deletion. This is because all segments—sonorants, fricatives, and even stops—may be pressed into service as syllable peaks when necessary to ensure full syllabification. In the limit case, even words consisting entirely of voiceless obstruents are fully syllabifiable, as shown by examples such as (tf̱)(tk̲t) 'you suffered a sprain' (D&E 1985: 116), where the separate syllables are enclosed in parentheses.

In spite of its tolerance of typologically unusual syllable peaks, ITB syllabification obeys strict principles. One fundamental principle, which I will term the Onset Principle, is stated by Dell and Elmedlaoui as follows (1985: 113):

---

[2] In the interest of consistency I adopt the transcription symbols of D&E (1988), which follow IPA practice except for the use of y to designate the palatal nonsyllabic vocoid [j], x to designate the voiceless uvular fricative [χ], γ to designate the voiced uvular fricative [ʁ], and ! to indicate emphasis. However, I retain their earlier use of [ʷ] to indicate labialization (rounding). In underlying representations, the segments designated by the symbols in (1), including the vocoids, are unspecified for syllabicity.

(2) Onset Principle: All syllables in ITB must have an onset.

This constraint is strictly obeyed everywhere except in postpausal position, where onsetless syllables are freely tolerated. Syllabification is carried out according to principles that favor syllables with high-sonority peaks over syllables with low-sonority peaks. D&E (1985: 109) note the following empirical generalization, which I term Peak Preference (the apostrophes in this citation indicate that the preceding segment is a syllabic peak):

(3) Peak Preference
When a string . . . PQ . . . could conceivably be syllabified either as . . . P'Q . . . or as . . . PQ' . . . (i.e. when either syllabification would involve only syllable types which, taken individually, are possible in ITB), the only syllabification allowed by ITB is the one that takes as a syllable peak the more sonorous of the two segments.

This principle assumes the following sonority scale:

(4)

Class	Conventional symbol	Examples
low vocoid	a	a
high vocoids	y	y w
liquids	r	r l
nasals	n	m n
voiced fricatives	z	z ʒ ɣ ɣ^w ʕ ɦ
voiceless fricatives	s	f s ʃ x x^w ħ
voiced stops	d	b d g g^w
voiceless stops	t	t k k^w q q^w

The Peak Preference generalization (3) has no formal status in D&E's analysis, but represents a descriptive observation which their formal analysis attempts to capture.

D&E's formal analysis is carried out in terms of a rule-and-constraint model, according to which rules apply in an ordered sequence and are blocked if their output would violate a constraint. The principal mechanism of syllabification is the set of related rules that I will refer to collectively as the Core Syllabification Rule, or CSR, which D&E state as follows (1985: 111):

(5) Core Syllabification
Associate a core syllable with any sequence (Y)Z, where Y can be any segment and Z is a segment of type T, where T is a variable to be replaced by a certain set of feature specifications.

Core syllables are therefore of the form CV, where C and V are single segments and V (consonant or vowel) represents the syllable peak. The CSR as just stated is a rule schema. Individual rules are derived from it by replacing T with feature specifications corresponding to each of the sonority classes in (4). The expansions follow the order set out in (4); for example, the first rule replaces 'T' with the feature set [−consonantal, +low], the second with the feature set [−consonantal, −low], and so forth. The resulting list of rules is applied from top to bottom, gathering up as yet unsyllabified material into CV syllables on each successive pass. Each rule is constrained by the Onset Principle (2), which blocks application if the resulting output would be a (non-initial) onsetless syllable. Rule application continues until all segments have been syllabified. At this point, any leftover segments are gathered into codas by the Coda Rule.

The CSR and Coda Rule apply across word boundaries. Their operation can be illustrated with a few representative examples.[3]

(6)		a. / d w-rgaz /	b. / y-dda w-rgaz /
	CSR(a)	dwr(ga)z	yd(da)wr(ga)z
	CSR(y)	(du)r(ga)z	(i)d(da)wr(ga)z
	CSR(r)	−	(i)d(da)(wr̲)(ga)z
	CSR(z)	−	−
	Coda Rule	(dur)(gaz)	(id)(da)(wr)(gaz)

		c. / ra-t-lwl-t /	d. / kywt /	e. / y-ywy /
	CSR(a)	(ra)tlwlt	−	−
	CSR(y)	(ra)t(lu)lt	(ki)wt	(yi)(wi)
	CSR(t)	(ra)t(lu)(lt̲)	(ki)(wt̲)	−
	Coda Rule	(rat)(lu)(lt̲)	−	−
	annexation rule	(rat)(lult)	(kiwt)	−

In these derivations, each expansion of the CSR is identified by the appropriate conventional symbol given in (4); for example, 'CSR(a)' is shorthand for the expansion of the CSR which creates core syllables with low-vowel peaks, and so forth. In (6a), CSR(a) creates the core syllable (ga), and CSR(y) then creates the core syllable (du). The potentially applicable rules CSR(r) and CSR(z) are blocked by the Onset Principle. As a final step, all remaining unsyllabified consonants are gathered into codas by the Coda Rule. The other examples are derived in a similar way (the 'annexation rule' of examples (6c,d) will be discussed in section 5). D&E cite example (6d) (among others) as motivating left-to-right rule application; this mode of application explains the fact that CSR(y) creates a core syllable over /ky/ and not /yw/, which would lead to the incorrect form *[kyut]. Example (6e) is included to show that in applying each rule from left to right, we must apply the longest expansion of the expression (Y)Z first; if we had applied the shorter expansion first, we would incorrectly derive *[iyuy]. (This principle is, of course, simply the orthodox interpretation of the SPE parenthesis notation.)

The priority of syllables with high-sonority syllable peaks over those with

---

[3] The glosses of these examples are: (a) 'with the man', (b) 'the man has come', (c) 'you will be born', (d) (in /ti-kyw-t/) 'type of cactus', (e) (in /y-ywy t-!yt-t s dar-wn /) 'he brought (the eye to your place)'.

low-sonority peaks, as remarked in the Peak Preference generalization (3), follows in this analysis from the device of sequential rule ordering: the fact that the CSR starts applying at the top of the sonority scale guarantees that /a/ will always be syllabified as a syllable peak, and the fact that it proceeds from top to bottom assures that lower-sonority segments will be syllabified as peaks only after all available higher-sonority segments have been recruited in this function.

3. PRINCE AND SMOLENSKY'S REANALYSIS

Prince and Smolensky propose to show that a non-derivational version of Optimality Theory can provide a superior account of the facts and generalizations noted by D&E. They point out that any theory which makes available a rule like the CSR (5) suffers from formal arbitrariness: even if we grant that this rule is empirically well supported, any formal system rich enough to allow its expression will also allow the expression of countless rules with undesirable properties. Thus, for example, the traditional theory has no principled way of excluding the expression of an implausible rule similar to the CSR except that its successive scans of the input string follow the *reverse* order of sonority, from least to most sonorous.

In contrast, OT incorporates general principles of harmony directly into grammatical theory in the form of universal, violable constraints whose language-specific rankings determine the phonological patterns of each language. In this framework, the fact that a given language shows a preference for widely attested patterns such as high-sonority syllable peaks should be a direct consequence of the choice of primitive elements from which the grammatical description is constructed, rather than the fortuitous result of rule interaction.

P&S develop their analysis of ITB syllabification by a method of successive approximation. Their initial analysis (pp. 11–21) introduces the two constraints ONSET and HNUC. ONSET is stated as follows:

(7) The Onset Constraint (ONS): Syllables must have onsets (except phrase-initially)

Like D&E's Onset Principle (2), which it generalizes, it allows exceptions in initial syllables, a point to which we return in the later discussion. The Nuclear Harmony Constraint (HNUC) states that higher-sonority nuclei are preferred to lower-sonority nuclei, and thus captures much of the import of D&E's Peak Preference generalization (3). HNUC generates a list of all the nuclei (= peaks) in each candidate syllabification, arrayed from most to least sonorous; evaluation proceeds by comparing the sonority of the sets of syllable peaks displayed in the HNUC column and eliminating candidates with less sonorous peaks than those of another candidate. The following tableau represents a number of the more plausible syllabifications of the form [txznt] 'you sg. stored (pf.)' (D&E 1985: 106).

(8)	/t-xzn-t/	ONSET	HNUC
→	a. tx̱.znṯ		n x
	b. tx̱.znṯ		n t!
	c. ṯ.xẕ.nṯ		z! t t
	d. txẕ.nṯ		z! t
	e. txẕ.nṯ	*!	n z
	f. txẕ.nṯ	*!	n x

Here, candidate (a) represents the correct syllabification, even though (e) better satisfies HNUC. This demonstrates that ONSET must be ranked above HNUC in the constraint hierarchy. Of the candidates that satisfy ONSET, candidate (a) has the most harmonic set of syllable peaks, and is therefore selected as the output form.[4]

These two constraints introduce the necessary conceptual tools for the subsequent discussion. The revised analysis (pp. 132–4, 163–9) differs from the preliminary one primarily in replacing the graded constraint HNUC with a *complex* of binary (categorical) constraints governing the affinity of segments to particular syllable positions according to their sonority rank. The set of constraints governing peak position is the following:

(9) Peak Hierarchy: *P/t >> *P/d >> *P/s >> *P/z >> *P/n >> *P/r >> *P/i >> *P/a

Each *P/α is interpreted as the statement 'α must not be parsed as a syllable Peak'. Thus, for example, any syllabic voiceless stop [p], [t], [k], etc. violates *P/t, any syllabic voiced stop violates *P/d, and so forth. The constraints are universally ranked as shown. All else being equal, a syllable peak violating a lower-ranked constraint is more harmonic than one violating a higher-ranked constraint; in this sense, (9) can be said to define a scale of peak harmony.

P&S further propose to recognize a Margin Hierarchy with the same properties as the Peak Hierarchy, except that segments are ranked in the opposite order, expressing the view that to the extent that a given segment forms a good syllable peak it forms a poor margin, and vice-versa.

(10) Margin Hierarchy: *M/a >> *M/i >> *M/r >> *M/n >> *M/z >> *M/s >> *M/d >> *M/t

Each *M/α is read 'α must not be parsed as a syllable Margin (Onset or Coda)'. (10) defines a scale of syllable margin harmony. One significant result of the replacement of the graded constraint HNUC with the binary constraints

---

[4] Evaluation by HNUC is carried out according to a recursive procedure involving the comparison of marks in the HNUC column, as suggested by our use of the exclamation point indicating fatal violations. See P&S (1993: 68–73) for fuller discussion of this procedure.

(9) and (10) is that the individual members of a hierarchy need no longer be ranked adjacent to each other in the grammar, a property exploited by P&S in their treatment of low-vowel sequences.[5]

The fundamental claim of P&S's revised analysis is that all members of the Peak Hierarchy are ranked below all members of the Margin Hierarchy. This means that candidate syllabifications are first evaluated on the basis of their margins and only subsequently on the basis of their peaks. Notice that, to establish this ranking, it is sufficient to show that the lowest-ranked member of the Margin Hierarchy, *M/t, dominates the highest-ranked member of the Peak Hierarchy, *P/t; it will follow by transitivity of rank ordering that all members of the Margin Hierarchy must dominate all members of the Peak Hierarchy.

This is the strategy adopted by P&S. They offer two examples in support of their claim, the first of which is shown in (11):

(11)	/tkt/ (invented)	*M/t	*P/t
→ a.	t̠.k̠t̠	k	t t
b.	t̠k̠t̠	t t!	k

This is a hypothetical form, with P&S's judgement as to the winning candidate indicated by the arrow. Here, candidate (b) incurs two violations of *M/t while candidate (a) only incurs one. The reverse ranking of *M/t and *P/t would give the opposite result. Thus, if (a) is the correct output, we may infer that *M/t dominates *P/t in the constraint ranking.

As it happens, however, the form generated by the CSR is not (a), but (b). We must pause to establish this point here, as the new analysis proposed in the next section will differ from P&S's analysis in selecting (b) as the most harmonic syllabification of this and similar forms, and we must show that this result is not incorrect.

As we have seen, the CSR as stated by D&E—and as restated by P&S (p. 12)—scans inputs from left to right, and takes the longest expansion of the expression (Y)Z first. The first subsequence in the input /tkt/ that matches YZ is therefore / tk . . . / and not / t . . . /. Accordingly, the CSR creates the core syllable (tk̠), and the leftover [t] is subsequently attached by the Coda Rule. Thus the syllabification predicted by the CSR is the one shown in (11b).

---

[5] The low vocoid /a/ is always realized as a vowel in ITB. According to François Dell (pers. comm.), the underlying sequence /aa/ is realized phonetically either as a long vowel [a:] or as the sequence [aya]; for example, underlying /y-nna as/ 'he told him' is realized as [in.na:s] or as [in.na.yas]. The long-vowel realization is obligatory in morpheme-internal sequences. In their account, P&S cite the epenthetic realization only, using it in support of the claim that *M/a is detached from the other members of the Margin Hierarchy (pp. 132–4). As the facts are somewhat more complex than their discussion suggests and have not yet been documented in print, I will not discuss low-vowel realizations further in this chapter. However, we will see independent support for the claim that the Peak and Margin Hierarchies form 'detachable' binary constraint sequences in the later discussion (section 5).

This syllabification is, moreover, in conformity with Dell and Elmedlaoui's intuitions, as shown in the course of their discussion of the imperfective stem (1988: 10–12). In D&E's account, the imperfective is formed from the basic (perfective) stem of the verb by geminating whichever segment of the stem is syllabified as an onset by the CSR. Thus we have examples like the following:

(12) *Basic stem*   *Syllabified*   *Imperfective*
                    basic stem   *stem*
  a. rʃq   (r̩)(ʃq)   rʃʃq
     bxl   (b̩)(xl̩)   bxxl
     kʃm   (k̩)(ʃm̩)   kʃʃm
  b. mrz   (mr̩z)   mmrz
     frn   (fr̩n)   ffrn
     xng   (xn̩g)   xxng

Though /tkt/ is not an existing stem, D&E discuss a parallel (though equally hypothetical) form, /sxf/, which like /tkt/ consists of three segments of equal sonority ranking, and we would expect these two forms to show parallel behavior. D&E state that the imperfective of such a stem, following the regular rule, would be *ssxf*. This judgement implies that [s] must be an onset in the core syllabification of the basic stem *sxf*, which must accordingly be syllabified (sx̩f), and not (s̩)(x̩f) as predicted by the analysis shown in (11). By parallel reasoning, /tkt/, with its identical sonority profile, should be syllabified (tk̩t). Thus the evidence from hypothetical forms like /tkt/, whatever weight we might want to give it, does not support the ranking of the Margin Hierarchy over the Peak Hierarchy.

P&S's second example, /fdt/, fares better than the first, since, though equally hypothetical, its correct syllabification can be confirmed with a parallel existing form. P&S's analysis of this example is shown below:

(13) /fdt/ (invented)	*M/f	*M/d	*M/t	*P/t	*P/d	*P/f
→ a. f.d̩t		d		t		f
b. fd̩t	f!		t		d	
c. fd̩t		d	t!			f

This is the syllabification predicted by the CSR. Furthermore, the parallel form /rʃq/ 'be happy' given by D&E, showing the same descending sonority ramp, is syllabified (r̩)(ʃq), as we just saw in (12). We may therefore conclude that candidate (13a) is indeed the correct syllabification of the hypothetical /fdt/, in spite of its poor showing on the Peak Hierarchy scale. It follows that *M/t dominates *P/t, since the reverse ranking would eliminate (13a) in favor of (13c).[6] It follows by transitivity of constraint ranking that all members of *M/α dominate all members of *P/α.

---

[6] Candidate (c) is, however, the correct realization in prepausal position, due to the operation of Prepausal Annexation, discussed in section 5.2. The present analysis, following P&S, abstracts away from the effects of this rule.

In the new analysis, the Margin Hierarchy typically subsumes the role of the Peak Hierarchy, in its earlier incarnation as Hnuc, in candidate evaluation. This fact is evident from a comparison of the new tableau for / t-xzn-t / shown below with the tableau given earlier in (8).

(14) /t-xzn-t/	ONSET	*M/n	*M/z	*M/s	*M/t	*P/t	*P/s	*P/z	*P/n
→ a. tx.znt			z		t t		x		n
b. tx.znt			z	x!	t	t			n
c. t.xz.nt		n!		x		t t		z	
d. txz.nt		n!		x	t	t		z	
e. txz.nt	*!			x	t t			z	n
f. txz.nt	*!		z		t t		x		n

ONSET still outranks the members of the Margin Hierarchy, eliminating candidates (e) and (f). Candidates (c) and (d) are eliminated by *M/n, and the survivors, (a) and (b), tie on *M/z. Consequently, evaluation passes down to *M/s which eliminates (b), leaving (a) as the winner. (In this example, the ranking of the Margin Hierarchy above the Peak Hierarchy is not crucial.)

The domination of *M/t over *P/t in the constraint ranking, crucially motivated by (13), leads to a striking and quite unexpected consequence: P&S's final analysis of ITB no longer expresses D&E's Peak Preference generalization (3), according to which syllabification proceeds by comparison of syllable peaks, but expresses the view that syllabification primarily involves comparison of *syllable margins*. In this respect, P&S's insight into the basic mechanisms underlying ITB syllabification is fundamentally different from D&E's.

This consequence depends crucially upon the presence of *M/t in the constraint ranking. There is reason to believe, however, that a theory containing *M/t may raise intractable problems. To see this, let us recall that *M/t expresses the constraint that 'members of sonority class *t* [voiceless stops] must not be parsed as a syllable Margin'. Strikingly, this statement does not represent any cross-linguistic tendency or markedness statement, since languages show no tendency to disfavor voiceless stops as syllable margins. Quite to the contrary, voiceless stops are optimal syllable margins across languages; all known languages syllabify voiceless stops as margins in at least some circumstances, and the great majority do in all circumstances. We might say instead that this constraint expresses an *antitendency*—the contrary of a universally observed tendency—which is regularly and consistently violated in all known languages.

Analogous remarks hold of certain other constraints in the Peak and Margin Hierarchies. Thus, *P/a encapsulates the statement that 'members of sonority class *a* [low vocoids] must not be parsed as a syllable Peak'. This statement also expresses an antitendency, since low vocoids constitute the optimal representative of the class of syllable peaks across languages. Similarly, all languages regularly violate the peak constraint *P/i and the margin constraints *M/d, *M/s, . . ., *M/r, not just under pressure from higher-level constraints but in unmarked syllabification contexts. Thus, for example, the great majority of known languages regularly syllabify high vocoids as syllable peaks if they constitute sonority peaks, and fricatives as syllable margins even when they constitute sonority peaks. In contrast to these, most or all of the other Peak and Margin Hierarchy constraints (*P/r, *P/n, *P/z, *P/s, *P/d, *P/t, *M/a, *M/i) express genuine cross-linguistic tendencies; most languages balk at syllabifying fricatives and stops as syllable peaks even in contexts where they constitute sonority peaks, and most resist all pressure to syllabify low vocoids as margins (as indeed does ITB). It seems that P&S's Peak and Margin Hierarchies have grouped together two substantively different types of constraint, and it would be reasonable to ask whether those which express antitendencies really belong in a theory based on the notion of optimality.

That the answer to this question is probably a negative one is shown by the fact that the inclusion of such constraints in the constraint system predicts classes of typologically implausible grammars. To see this, let us examine a hypothetical system including the universally violated constraints *P/a and *M/t and some version of PARSE, interpreted as legislating against extrasyllabic segments. It is easy to see that such a system can express grammars in which all segments (including vocoids) are typically parsed as margins, the only well-formed nucleus being the epenthetic vowel. Such grammars can arise if all members of the Peak Hierarchy *P/α are ranked above PARSE and all members of the Margin Hierarchy *M/α below it. An example is given below:

(15)	/ta/	*P/α	PARSE	*M/α	ONSET	*CODA	FILL
→ a.	tØ̧a̧			a t		*	*
b.	ta	a!		t			
c.	<t><a>		*!*				

In this grammar, the optimal syllabification of /ta/ is one in which [a] functions as coda and the epenthetic vowel as peak. Notice that this grammar can be mimicked in a rule-based theory by allowing syllabification to be carried out in terms of a CVC template which licenses no segments in the V position. An equally arbitrary grammar can be created by reversing the positions of *P/α and *M/α in tableau (16); in this grammar, all segments are typically syllabified as peaks, leading to the optimal syllabification of /ta/ as two syllables, (ţ)(a).

(16)	/ta/	*M/α	PARSE	*P/α	ONSET	*CODA	FILL
→	a. ṭ.a			t a	*		
	b. ta	t!		a			
	c. <t><a>		*!*				

Again, this result is implausible. At the outset of this section we noted that the ability of rule-based theories to express implausible rules amounts to a strong inadequacy; but if constraint-based theories are allowed to express equally implausible grammars, such as the one generating tableaux (15) and (16), they are subject to exactly the same criticism.

Our judgement that (ta) is a more harmonic syllabification than either (tØạ) or (ṭ)(a) derives from two observations: that CV syllables—D&E's 'core syllables'—are the universally preferred syllable type (Jakobson 1962: 526; Clements and Keyser 1983), and that the preferred CV syllables have low-sonority onsets and high-sonority peaks (Clements 1990). This insight is not captured in a constraint system including the full Peak and Margin Hierarchies, if each of them can potentially dominate all other constraints in a constraint system. If Optimality Theory is to succeed in excluding the arbitrariness inherent in traditional rule analysis, it must systematically exclude constraints that can lay the basis for arbitrary constraint interactions such as these. A minimal and quite conservative step toward achieving this result would be to eliminate the class of constraints expressing antitendencies from the universe of entertainable constraints. As long as such constraints are allowed, they can always occur in high-ranked position in a constraint hierarchy where they can outrank constraints expressing genuine tendencies, and predict the existence of implausible grammars; this result subverts the desirable criterion (assumed by e.g. McCarthy and Prince, 1995a) that free re-rankings of universal constraints should generate possible grammars.

It might be objected that one can always exclude typologically implausible constraint interactions by universal constraint rankings. Universal constraint rankings are required in any case to order the members of the universal Peak and Margin Hierarchies, as we have seen. Following this strategy, we could exclude the arbitrary grammars discussed above by placing appropriate conditions on the admissable rankings of *P/α, *M/α, PARSE, and other constraints, as necessary. However, this solution is not particularly satisfying, as we prefer to express the range of possible linguistic systems through the free interaction of theoretical primitives; and it is not clear that it is even feasible, given the large number of constraints that will constitute the full system. A major goal of later sections will be to show that it is possible, in the case of ITB, to replace constraints expressing antitendencies with constraints that do not, with no loss in descriptive adequacy.

To summarize the discussion of this section, we have seen that P&S's analysis accounts for basic features of ITB syllabification in terms of two basic principles, the ONSET constraint and a Margin Hierarchy all of whose members are crucially ranked above the Peak Hierarchy. Their analysis incorporates the view that syllabification proceeds by comparing syllable margins, rather than peaks. However, this analysis relies crucially upon the use of a constraint, *M/t, which leads to potential overgeneration.

The remaining discussion proceeds as follows. Section 4 lays out the elements of a new analysis in which P&S's full Peak and Margin Hierarchies are replaced by reduced hierarchies, eliminating constraints which express antitendencies. To do the work of the excluded members of the Margin Hierarchy, two new constraints are introduced which evaluate candidates in terms of their sonority sequencing properties. Sections 5 and 6 extend this analysis to two areas not discussed by P&S: the treatment of D&E's annexation rules, and the intricate relation between syllabification and certain rules of word formation.

4. A NEW APPROACH TO ITB SYLLABIFICATION

Let us first review the surface-level observations that D&E's rule analysis was designed to capture. These include the Onset Principle (2) as well as the Peak Preference generalization (3), which, given a choice of alternative syllabifications, selects the one with the more sonorous peak.

Certain of P&S's constraints directly capture these generalizations. P&S's ONSET (7) is a restatement of the Onset Principle, of which it is a straightforward generalization. We restate it below, eliminating the condition which restricts it to non-phrase-initial position, for reasons that will become apparent in the later discussion.

(17) ONSET: Syllables must have onsets.

Similarly, the residue of the Peak Hierarchy that remains after we have eliminated *P/a and *P/i, which arrays syllabic consonants from most to least harmonic (*P/t >> *P/d >> *P/s >> *P/z >> *P/n >> *P/r), directly expresses the generalization that high-sonority syllabic consonants are preferred to low-sonority ones. In the following discussion, I will refer to this hierarchy as the reduced Peak Hierarchy to distinguish it from P&S's full hierarchy.

However, these constraints are not sufficient to describe the full range of ITB data, and we must now examine additional constraints that will be required in a more complete analysis. D&E note a further important surface generalization in the following terms (1985: 126):

(18) In no syllables is the coda more sonorous than the peak.

As they note, this generalization is a logical consequence of their analysis: 'there should not exist a syllable like *kmr* with *m* as its syllabic peak, for such a sequence would have been syllabified as *k(mr)* by the pass for the liquids, which precedes the pass during which the nasal *m* becomes available for grouping with the preceding *k*.' Dell and Tangi (1993) term this generalization the Rising Rhyme Principle, and propose it as a formal constraint on syllabi-fication in the Ath-Sidhar Rifian dialect. This principle is, of course, just a special case of the well-known Sonority Sequencing Principle, which as stated by Jespersen 1904 prohibits sonority from increasing as we proceed from the syllable peak to the margins. We will incorporate this principle directly into the constraint system, and state the special case that applies to codas as follows:

(19) *RR: the Coda cannot exceed the Peak in sonority (rhymes do not rise in sonority).

This constraint holds without exception in D&E's data.[7]

Given the sonority scale in (4), *RR correctly favors the syllabification of e.g. / t-xzn-a-s / 'she stored for him (pf.)' (D&E 1985: 106) as (t̩)(xẕ)(nas) and not (txẕ)(nas). This syllabification provisionally demonstrates the ranking of *RR above the members of the reduced Peak Hierarchy, as shown below:[8]

(20)

/t-xzn-a-s/	*RR	*P/t	*P/s	*P/z
→ a. t̩.xẕ.nas		t		z
b. txẕ.nas	*!		x	

There is a further logical consequence of D&E's analysis, which I will call the Sonority Peak Principle (SPP), and will state as follows:

(21) SPP: within the syllabification domain, sonority peaks contain syllable peaks.

A sonority peak is any local maximum of sonority, such as the [r] in [krm] or [rmk]. Constraint (21) requires that any such peak occurring in the syllabifica-tion domain must constitute a syllable peak; thus [r] must be a peak in the examples just cited. (In the special case where the sonority peak extends across two or more segments, as in /kywt/, it requires that at least one of them be a syllable peak.) Note that (21) does not require *syllable* peaks to be *sonority* peaks; thus the syllabic consonants [t̩] and [ẕ] of (t̩)(xẕ)(nas) just above, though not sonority peaks, do not constitute violations. (21) is a special case of

---

[7] In contrast, there are many syllables whose onset is more sonorous than the peak. Such syllables arise just in case the selection of the more sonorous segment as peak would create a violation of the Onset Principle. For example, /t-ywn-t-a-s/ 'you climbed on him' is syllabified (ti)(wn̩)(tas) and not *(ti)(un)(tas), which contains a violation of the Onset Principle (D&E 1985: 110).

[8] This ranking will be confirmed in the later discussion. Notice that candidate (b) also incurs two violations of the *CODA constraint, while (a) only incurs one. However, we cannot explain the choice of candidate (a) by ranking *CODA above *P/t. We will see much evidence that *CODA is a weak and rarely decisive constraint in ITB, ranked below all other constraints discussed in this study, including *P/t. Thus, for example, both (i)(gi)(dr̩) and (i)(gidr) are well-formed syllabifica-tions of /ygydr/ 'eagle' in final position; if *CODA were ranked above *P/r, as would follow necessarily from its ranking above *P/t, it would exclude the second candidate. See also n. 10.

Jespersen's principle that 'in every group of sounds there are just as many syllables as there are clear relative peaks of sonority' (1904: 188). The SPP has exceptions in ITB only in pre- and postpausal clusters, and we will see in the next section that these exceptions actually lie outside the syllabification domain; accordingly, we can regard the SPP as undominated in ITB.[9]

The role of the SPP in ITB is illustrated in the following tableau with my earlier example, /rʃq/ 'be happy'. As usual, only relevant constraints are included. As [r] is a sonority peak in this example, it must be syllabified as a syllable peak. This has been done in candidate (a) but not in candidate (b), which therefore incurs a fatal SPP violation. This example demonstrates the crucial ranking of the SPP above *P/t, and hence above all other members of the reduced Peak Hierarchy.[10]

(22)	/rʃq/	SPP	*P/t	*P/s	*P/r
→ a.	r̩.ʃq̩		q		r
b.	rʃq̩	*!		ʃ	

Taken together, SPP and *RR perform most of the function of the CSR in the new constraint system. These two constraints are mutually unranked, and are undominated in the system.

Let us now establish the ranking of ONSET (17) with respect to SPP and *RR. To do this, we must first consider the formulation of ONSET more closely. Up to now, we have assumed that ONSET applies only to noninitial syllables. Why should this be so?

P&S briefly raise this question and refer the reader to McCarthy and Prince (1993a) for further discussion. In this work (as well as in McCarthy and Prince 1993b), McCarthy and Prince propose a family of *alignment constraints* whose typical function is to align grammatical and prosodic categories with each other. They argue that ONSET, stated with full generality as in (17), can be violated in the initial syllable of a prosodic domain in order to satisfy an alignment constraint, for example, to assure the alignment

---

[9] Many languages present violations of the SPP; e.g. given the sonority scale in (4), this principle is violated by the English monosyllable *stop*, with its two sonority peaks *s* and *o*. The existence of such violations is not, of course, inconsistent with theories which tolerate surface-level constraint violations, such as OT. In the case of English, the SPP is overruled by the constraints *P/t, . . ., *P/z excluding syllabic obstruents.

[10] Anticipating the upcoming discussion of ONSET, which shows that this constraint must apply to initial as well as non-initial syllables, we could alternatively explain the preference for (a) over (b) on the assumption that *CODA, which is violated only in (b), outranks ONSET, which is violated only in the initial syllable of (a). However, that the contrary ranking, ONSET >> *CODA, is correct is confirmed by the fact that sequences ABC in which B is a sonority peak are regularly syllabified (ABC), with a *CODA violation, and not (AB)(C), with an ONSET violation; thus e.g. /krm/ 'be dried out' (D&E 1988: 11) is syllabified (kr̩m) and not *(kr̩)(m̩). Further confirmation for this ranking will come from the discussion of / t-xzn-t / in (26).

of the left edge of a foot or prosodic word with the leftmost segment in a grammatical stem or word.

Let us see how an analysis along these lines can be applied to the ITB data. What we require is a constraint which aligns the left edge of the unit which forms the syllabification domain with the left edge of a grammatical word. What can the syllabification domain in ITB be? We know that it is larger than the prosodic word, since core CV syllables regularly span word boundaries, and there is little convincing evidence that word boundaries play any role in syllabification (though see Elmedlaoui, 1985 for brief discussion possibly motivating such a view). Pending fuller study of the ITB prosodic hierarchy, let us tentatively identify the ITB syllabification domain as the Phonological Phrase (PhPhr). The appropriate alignment constraint can then be stated as follows:[11]

(23) ALIGN (PhPhr,L,Wd,L): The left edge of the phonological phrase must coincide with the left edge of a grammatical word.

Let us refer to this as ALIGN-L, for short. It requires the first segment in the phonological phrase to be identical to the first segment of its first grammatical word. ALIGN-L therefore prohibits syllabifications in which the first segment in the phrase does not belong to the grammatical word (as when its first segment is epenthetic), or is not the first segment in the word (as when the first segment is deleted or unparsed).

With this background, we may return to our example /rʃq/ (22). If ONSET is stated with no restriction as in (17), the first candidate, (r̩)(ʃq), now presents a genuine violation in its first syllable. However, it satisfies higher-ranking ALIGN-L, unlike competitors with an epenthetic onset. The new analysis is given in the following tableau:[12]

(24)	/rʃq/	ALIGN-L SPP	ONSET	*P/t	*P/s	*P/r
→ a.	r̩.ʃq		*	q		r
b.	Ør̩.ʃq	*!		q		r
c.	rʃq	*!			ʃ	

Here, (r̩)(ʃq)—candidate (a)—is the most harmonic of the three candidates. Candidate (b) violates ALIGN-L since its first onset, the epenthetic position-holder indicated by Ø, is not a member of the grammatical word [rʃq]. Candidate (c) also satisfies ONSET but violates the higher-ranking SPP, since

---

[11] A similar constraint governs the right edge of the phonological phrase. I postulate a parallel ALIGN-R constraint to express this fact.

[12] In the interest of clarity, here and below I adopt the convention of using vertical lines only to separate constraints whose ranking has been motivated in the earlier or current discussion. We shall later see that *P/t dominates ONSET in the constraint ranking. Summaries of constraint rankings are given at the end of sections 4 and 5.

its sonority peak, [r], is not a syllable peak. This tableau confirms the ranking of both Align-L and SPP above Onset.[13]

Consider next the relative ranking of *RR and Onset. Below I give a revised tableau for /t-xzn-a-s/, superseding the earlier one in (20).

(25)

/t-xzn-a-s/	Align-L	SPP	*RR	Onset	*P/t	*P/s	*P/z
→ a. t̪.xẓ.nas				*	t		z
b. txẓ.nas			*!			x	

Candidate (a), with its Onset violation, is selected over (b) with its *RR violation, showing that *RR outranks Onset. Note that SPP is irrelevant here, since the sole sonority peak in this form is [a] and it is syllabified as peak. (26) gives a revised tableau for /t-xzn-t/, allowing a comparison with P&S's analyses of this form discussed in the preceding section (cf. (8), (14)).

(26)

/t-xzn-t/	Align-L	SPP	*RR	Onset	*P/t	*P/s	*P/z	*P/n
→ a. tx.znt						x		n
b. tx.znt		*!		*	t			n
c. t̪.xẓ.nt̪	*!			*	tt		z	
d. txẓ.nt̪	*!				t		z	
e. txẓ.nt̪				*!			z	n
f. txẓ.nt̪		*!	*			x		n

In (26) the sonority peak is [n], and this constitutes a syllable peak in candidates (a), (b), (e), and (f) but not in (c) and (d), which are thereby eliminated by the SPP. Candidates (b) and (f) are eliminated by their first-syllable violation of *RR. This leaves only (a), which violates *P/s, and (e), which violates Onset in its second syllable. Since (a) is in fact the correct syllabification, we must assume that Onset is ranked over at least *P/s, as indicated in the tableau.[14]

It is instructive to compare this analysis with P&S's given in (14). In the new analysis the correct syllabification is determined entirely by the structural constraints SPP, *RR, and Onset, which entirely subsume the function of P&S's Margin Hierarchy. Indeed, we have so far seen no use for the reduced Peak and Margin Hierarchies, whose role—though a significant one—will become apparent only later in the discussion.

---

[13] We could also explain the choice of candidate (a) over candidate (b) on the assumption that Align-L and Onset are unranked with respect to each other, since independent constraints, such as Fill[ONS], could explain the dispreference for (b). We will leave this question open at this point, but will see independent justification for the ranking Align-L >> Onset in the later discussion (see (32)).

[14] Tableau (26) also confirms that the SPP cannot be replaced by *Coda, ranked above Onset. Under this assumption, candidate (d), which does not violate *Coda, would be selected over candidate (a), which does.

To complete the basic analysis, we must consider the additional candidate syllabifications of /t-xzn-a-s/ and /t-xzn-t/ shown below:

(27) a. /t-xzn-a-s/: (txznas)
     b. /t-xzn-t/:   (txznt)

Given the constraints proposed so far, the syllabification (txznas) is actually better than either of the candidate syllabifications of /t-xzn-a-s/ given in (25) due to the fact that it presents no ONSET or *RR violation; indeed, it is flawless in terms of the constraints considered so far, if we exclude the low-ranked *CODA from consideration. Similarly, (txznt) beats candidate (a) as the most highly valued syllabification of /t-xzn-t/ in (26) as it does not violate *P/s. Of course, neither of these syllabifications is acceptable in ITB; why should this be so?

The problem clearly lies in their initial clusters. It is widely observed that, all else being equal, complex syllable constituents are more restricted in their distribution than simplex ones, and are often totally disallowed; for this and similar reasons they are often considered to be phonologically marked (see e.g. Clements 1990; Blevins 1995). P&S incorporate this observation into the universal constraint set in the form of the constraint *COMPLEX, interpreted to mean 'no more than one C or V may associate to any syllable position node'. They add that this constraint is intended only as a cover term for further interacting factors that determine syllable structure. It will be sufficient, however, for the purposes of the following discussion, though for the sake of clarity I will factor it into separate onset and coda constraints, referred to as *COMPLEX^{Ons} and *COMPLEX^{Cd}:

(28) *COMPLEX^{Ons}: no more than one C may associate to the Onset node.
     *COMPLEX^{Cd}: no more than one C may associate to the Coda node.

It will become apparent that these constraints, like ALIGN-L, SPP, and *RR, are undominated in the ITB constraint system.

*COMPLEX^{Ons} must outrank ONSET and *P/t if we are to explain the fact that the syllabification (t)(xz)(nas) given in (25a) is better than (txznas), in spite of its ONSET, *P/t, and *P/z violations. This is shown in the following tableau:

(29) /t-xzn-a-s/	SPP	*RR	*COMPLEX^{Ons}	ONSET	*P/t	*P/s	*P/z
→ a. t.xz.nas				*	t		z
b. txznas		*!					

*COMPLEX^{Ons} can explain another pattern in ITB syllabification, the preference for apparent left-to-right syllabification in sequences of vocoids. This pattern is discussed by D&E in regard to examples like /ty-kyw-t/ 'type of cactus', whose second syllable is syllabified (kiwt) rather than (kyut) (see derivation (6d) above). This choice can be understood as resulting from the *COMPLEX^{Ons} violation in (kyut) rather than from a principle of directional rule application.

The evidence for left-to-right syllabification elsewhere in ITB is slender, given the relatively small number of supporting examples beyond the special case just mentioned, as well as a fair number of counterexamples. Potential evidence comes from forms with sonority plateaux, sequences of equal sonority rank. A representative selection of cases is shown below.

(30) Syllabification of sonority plateaux
    a. Examples supporting left-to-right syllabification

		I	II	
i.	/rks-x/	r̥.ksx̥	*rk̥.sx̥	'I hid'
ii.	/bayn-n/	ba.yṇn	*bay.ṇn	'they (m.) appear'
iii.	/y-swfw-yyt/	i.su.fuyyt	*i.suf.wiyt	'let him illuminate'
iv.	/ldy-yyy/	l̥.diy.yi	*l̥d.yi.yi	'pull me!'

    b. Examples supporting right-to-left syllabification

i.	/wgm-n/	u.gṃn	ug.mṇ	'they (m.) drew (water)'
ii.	/y t-!bdry-n/	*i.tb̥d.rin	it.b̥d.rin	'for the cockroaches'
iii.	/tt-bddal/	?	ttb̥d.dal	'exchange'
iv.	/y-ftk baba-s/	?	if.tk̥.ba.bas	'his father suffered a sprain'

Forms predicted by left-to-right syllabification are shown in column I, and forms predicted by right-to-left syllabification are shown in column II; asterisks show D&E's explicitly stated ungrammaticality judgements.[15] The constraint system developed up to this point does not choose between the alternative syllabifications given in each column (all score equally in terms of $*P/\alpha$, Onset, *Coda, etc.), and so predicts, in the absence of other relevant constraints, that both should be possible. This prediction is correct in one case, (30bi), where D&E observe that both syllabifications are correct, but not generally.

As these and many other examples show, there does not seem to be any clear-cut preference for left-to-right syllabification of sonority plateaux. Elmedlaoui (1985) gives many further exceptions to the left-to-right directionality principle, and proposes several subgeneralizations overriding this principle. D&E themselves do not place great weight on the directionality principle: 'we believe that [it] is not concerned with left-to-right ordering *per se*, but rather with favoring applications of CS that maximize the sonority differences between the terms Y and Z' (D&E 1985: 127, n. 22), that is, between the onset and the peak. However, there are counterexamples to this alternative interpretation as well, such as (30bii), and it is possible that not one but several subsidiary principles are at work, perhaps along lines suggested by Elmedlaoui. Finally, some of the indeterminacy in the data may reflect the difficulty of the judgements required in determining where the syllable peak actually

---

[15] The starred first example, (29ai), may not be pertinent to the discussion, since phrase-final syllabic obstruents are excluded for independent reasons; see the discussion of Prepausal Annexation below (in general, D&E's judgements on the syllabification of citation forms reflect the operation of this rule).

occurs on two adjacent segments of equal sonority rank (D&E 1985: 115). In the face of these observations, I will not introduce any direct analogue of D&E's directionality principle in the present analysis, but will join them in leaving a residue of unresolved cases such as those in (30) for further study.[16]

In addition to *COMPLEX^Ons, our analysis requires *COMPLEX^Cd. To see this, consider the syllabifications of /t-ywn-t-a-s/ 'you climbed on him' shown in the following tableau:

(31) /t-ywn-t-a-s/	ALIGN-L	SPP	*RR	*COMPLEX^Ons	COMPLEX^Cd	ONSET	*P/n
→ a. ti.wn̩.tas							n
b. ti.un.tas					*!		
c. tyun.tas			*!				
d. tiwn.tas					*!		

Candidates (b) and (c) are excluded by their ONSET and *COMPLEX^Ons violations, while candidate (d) is excluded by its *COMPLEX^Cd violation. Candidate (a) violates only *P/n, which must therefore be ranked below ONSET, a fact which follows from the previously established ranking of *P/t under ONSET.

We have now assembled the basic elements of our analysis. We have added three new constraints, ALIGN-L, SPP, and *RR, which capture most of the import of D&E's Peak Preference principle (3), and have retained P&S's *COMPLEX to exclude syllables with clusters. The constraints given so far must be arrayed in the following rank order:

(32) 1. ALIGN-L (23), SPP (21), *RR (19), *COMPLEX (28)
     2. ONSET (17), *P/t,d
     3. *P/s, . . ., r

The individual members of *P/α are of course universally ranked, such that *P/t >> *P/d, etc.

5. PHRASE-EDGE CLUSTERS IN ITB

We will now see how our analysis can be extended to account for the phrase-edge clusters that motivated D&E's 'annexation rules'. These rules challenge the non-derivational version of Optimality Theory since they crucially apply to intermediate forms generated by the CSR and map them into distinct surface forms. Our task will be to determine whether a plausible nonderivational account of phrase-edge clusters can be found. We take up Postpausal Annexation (section 5.1) and Prepausal Annexation (section 5.2) in that order.

---

[16] Another set of counterexamples to the left-to-right directionality principle involves a number of words containing high vocoids which appear to behave as if they had the same sonority rank as consonants (Elmedlaoui 1985; D&E 1985: 114–15). Professor Elmedlaoui informs me that in at least some cases, these consonantal glides can be shown to derive historically from obstruents.

5.1 *Postpausal annexation*

D&E (1988: 5) state the rule of Postpausal Annexation as follows:

(33) Postpausal Annexation
'We assume the existence of a late rule which applies to every postpausal noncontinuant obstruent which is a nucleus . . . and incorporates it into the onset of the next syllable'.

This rule is crucially ordered after the CSR, which feeds it. Thus postpausal /txz/ is first syllabified as (t)(xz̲) by the CSR and then consolidated into a single syllable (txz̲) by Postpausal Annexation. A few examples showing the operation of this rule are given below. Column I shows the underlying form, column II the intermediate forms created by the CSR, and column III the surface forms created by Postpausal Annexation.

(34)

I	II	III	
/t-xzn-a-s/	t̲.xz̲.nas	txz̲.nas	'she stored for him'
/tzmt/	t̲.zm̲t	tzm̲t	'it (f.) is stifling'
/gnw/	g̲.nu	gnu	'sew'
/gzy/	g̲.zi	gzi	'vaccinate'
/tt-bddal/	tt.bd̲.dal	ttbd̲.dal	'exchange' (impf.)
/tlwrtnt/	t̲.lur.tn̲t	tlur.tn̲t	'she gave them (f.) back'

There are two major properties of Postpausal Annexation that must be accounted for in any analysis. The first is the fact that only *stops* are targeted for annexation. The special status of stops in this rule is surely not arbitrary, but must be related to the fact that stops are at the low end of the sonority scale, and thus make the poorest possible syllable peaks. This fact is directly expressed by the reduced Peak Hierarchy, which ranks *P/t,d universally above all other members of the *P/α constraint family. If this is the correct account, our analysis should derive the special status of stops in Postpausal Annexation from the presence of the independent constraints *P/t,d in the universal constraint hierarchy.

A second important property of the rule is that it applies only *postpausally*, i.e. at the left edge of the phonological phrase, and never phrase-internally. Again, this fact is surely not arbitrary: it is widely reported in the phonological literature that the left and right edges of the syllabification domain frequently allow longer clusters than are tolerated in internal syllables (see e.g. Borowsky 1986; Clements 1990). To explain this fact, it has been proposed that the external members of domain-edge clusters may not be incorporated into the onset as such, but remain *extrasyllabic* (Clements and Keyser 1983), and are thus exempted from the general constraints on syllable structure, which in the case of ITB prohibit tautosyllabic consonant clusters. In several proposals to this effect, extrasyllabic segments are not regarded as totally stray elements but are linked to prosodic structure at a higher level of the prosodic hierarchy (see e.g. Milliken 1988; Rubach and Booij 1990; Rialland 1994), where they are preserved from deletion by Stray Erasure (Steriade 1982). Such analyses make the empirical prediction that extrasyllabic segments, though exempted from all rules and constraints applying at the level of the syllable, should systematically undergo all phonological rules and constraints applying at the prosodic level at which they are attached.[17]

If we adopt this analysis, we may treat the initial member of postpausal CC clusters as extrasyllabic. However, we must find a way of accounting for the fact that only *stops* can be extrasyllabic. Following the logic of the analysis in the preceding section, our strategy must be to seek a constraint X that excludes extrasyllabic segments (expressing the fact that such segments are dispreferred across languages), and which is ordered between the constraints *P/t,d ruling out syllabic stops and the lower-ranking constraints ruling out other syllabic consonants: thus, *P/t,d >> X >> *P/s, . . . , r. It will follow from this ranking that, while syllabic fricatives and sonorants are generally preferred to extrasyllabic ones (X >> *P/s, . . . , r), extrasyllabic stops are preferred to syllabic (i.e. nuclear) ones (*P/t,d >> X), all else being equal.

Let us take X to be another member of the family of alignment constraints, one which in this case requires the left edge of the syllabification domain (which we take to be the phonological phrase) to align with the left edge of a syllable. This constraint can be stated as follows:

(35) ALIGN (PhPhr, L, σ, L): the left edge of a phonological phrase must coincide with the left edge of a syllable

(35) legislates against the occurrence of extrasyllabic segments at the left edge of the syllabification domain. We shall see shortly that a similar constraint governs the right edge of the domain as well (as these two constraints will prove to be crucially non-adjacent in the overall constraint ranking, they cannot be collapsed into one, or replaced by a single constraint against extrasyllabic segments such as PARSE[seg]). Extrasyllabic segments will therefore always violate these constraints wherever they occur; but under what circumstances can they actually appear?

To answer this question, let us examine figure (36), illustrating several imaginable prosodifications of the sequence /txz/ as it occurs in postpausal [txz.nas] 'she stored for him'.[18]

---

[17] This account of extrasyllabicity is at variance with the view that each unit in the prosodic hierarchy is strictly dominated only by units of the next level up (the Strict Layer Hypothesis). However, this principle has well-known violations (see e.g. McCarthy and Prince, 1993*b*: section 2 and n. 40).

[18] This figure presupposes that the only units of the ITB prosodic hierarchy are the syllable and the phonological phrase. A fuller study of ITB phonology may well show the need for intermediate prosodic levels. For example, rules of emphasis assimilation (D&E 1985: 118) and obstruent

(36)

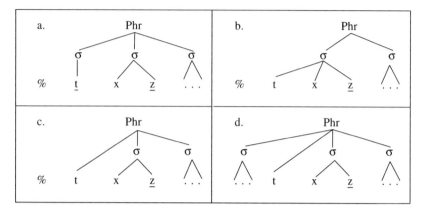

(36a) shows a configuration in which syllabic (nuclear) *t* occurs in phrase-initial position, indicated by the conventional symbol %. This configuration satisfies Alignment constraint (35) but violates *P/t. (36b) shows the adjunction of *t* to the syllable onset, a configuration which satisfies (35) and *P/t, but which violates *COMPLEX^{Ons}. Figure (36c) shows extrasyllabic *t*, a configuration satisfying *P/t and *COMPLEX^{Ons} but violating Alignment (35). Finally, figure (36d) illustrates a prosodification in which extrasyllabic *t* occurs phrase-internally. We will assume that this configuration is ruled out in ITB by a further alignment constraint, requiring all pairs of syllables to be strictly adjacent in the syllabification domain (McCarthy and Prince 1993*b*). This constraint is stated below:

(37) ALIGN(σ, L, σ, R): the left edge of each syllable must coincide with the right edge of another syllable

Under this analysis, what is wrong with (36d) is the fact that the first two syllables are separated by the extrasyllabic *t*. For convenience of reference, I will refer to constraint (37) as Syllable Adjacency (SA).

The winning candidate among the first three of these configurations will depend on the relative ranking of *COMPLEX^{Ons}, *P/t, and ALIGN(PhPhr, L, σ, L). In ITB, these three constraints are ranked in the order just stated. Conse-

voicing assimilation (El Medlaoui 1995: §II.5) apply in domains roughly coextensive with the word. Exactly how the domains of these (and other rules) are to be formally characterized awaits further study. If it turns out that an additional prosodic unit intervenes between the phonological phrase and the syllable, the analysis illustrated in (36) will have to be revised accordingly. In particular, following our present assumptions, extrasyllabic consonants such as the one shown in (36c) will link to the intermediate unit, rather than directly to the phrase. Such a revision would appear to have no consequences for the analysis proposed here, however, since the alignment constraints (35) and (41) will operate in the same way no matter what suprasyllabic unit the extrasyllabic consonant attaches to.

quently, only (36c), presenting a violation of the lowest-ranked of the three, is well-formed. Tableau (38) illustrates this analysis for the example /t-lwr-tn-t/ 'she gave them (f.) back'; as usual, only relevant constraints are shown:[19]

(38) /t-lwr-tn-t/	SA	*COMPLEX^{Ons}	*P/t	ALIGN(PhPhr, L)	ONSET	*P/n
postpausally:						
→ a. %<t>.lur.tṇt				*		*
b. %tlur.tṇt		*!				*
c. %t.lur.tṇt			*!		*	*
internally:						
a. . . . <t>.lur.tṇt	*!					*
b. . . . tlur.tṇt		*!				*
→ c. . . . t.lur.tṇt			*			*

In postpausal position (top of the tableau), candidate (a) is the most harmonic, since though it violates ALIGN(PhPhr, L, σ, L) it does not violate higher-ranking *COMPLEX^{Ons} or *P/t. Internally, however, this candidate is ruled out by Syllable Adjacency (SA), and so the candidate violating the lower-ranking constraint *P/t is selected instead. Note in particular that the first candidate in (38), as illustrated in (36c), does not violate ALIGN-L (23), since its leftmost element, *t*, though extrasyllabic, is nevertheless the leftmost element of the phrase.

To summarize the discussion so far: we have seen that the challenge posed for the nonderivational version of OT by phrase-initial clusters can be successfully met in an analysis incorporating relatively uncontroversial assumptions and constraints. This analysis has been able, moreover, to derive certain arbitrary features of Postpausal Annexation—its limitation to stops and its restriction to the edge of the syllabification domain—from other well-motivated constraints.

5.2 Prepausal annexation

Let us now turn to the analysis of phrase-final clusters. These clusters are created in D&E's analysis by a rule of Prepausal Annexation:

(39) Another rule operates on every prepausal open syllable with an obstruent as a nucleus and turns it into a complex coda of the preceding syllable. (D&E 1988: 5) The application of [this rule] is obligatory when the last segment is an obstruent, and it is optional when that segment is a sonorant. (D&E 1985: 120)

Thus obstruents can never be peaks in final position in the phrase, while sonorants show a pattern of free variation in this position. This rule, like

---

[19] The ordering of ALIGN(PhPhr,L) over ONSET is required by forms like /ndr/ 'moan' (D&E 1988: 13), whose correct syllabification is (ṇ)(dṛ), with an ONSET violation, and not <n>(dṛ), with an ALIGN violation.

Postpausal Annexation, is strictly derivational, as it is crucially fed by the CSR. Some examples follow. As in (34), column I represents underlying forms, column II the intermediate forms derived by the CSR, and column III the surface forms derived by Annexation.

(40)

I	II	III		
a. final obstruents:				
/y-nna ns/	in.na.ns̲	in.nans		'he said: spend the night!'
/y-!sbwkd/	!is.bu.kd̲	!is.bukd		'he poked (his father's) eye out'
/y-rks/	ir.ks̲	irks		'(his father) hid'
/y-stγ/	is.tγ̲	istγ		'he cracked (the door)'
b. final sonorants:				
/ygydr/	i.gi.dr̲	(*same or*)	i.gidr	'eagle'
/y-wrm/	yu.rm̲	(*same or*)	yurm	'he tasted'
/rgl/	r.gl̲	(*same or*)	rgl	'lock!'
/dwm-n/	du.mn̲	(*same or*)	dumn	'they (m.) last'

To account for this pattern, which is analogous to that of Postpausal Annexation, we will postulate a constraint similar to Alignment constraint (35), requiring strict alignment of the right edge of the phonological phrase with the right edge of a syllable:

(41) ALIGN (PhPhr, R, σ, R): the right edge of a phonological phrase must coincide with the right edge of a syllable.

This constraint must be ranked below *P/t, *P/d, *P/s, and *P/z to express the total exclusion of syllabic obstruents in absolute phrase-final position. We illustrate with a representative tableau (42) for /y-nna ns/ 'he said: spend the night!'.

(42) /y-nna ns/	SA	*COMPLEX^{Cd}	*P/s	ALIGN(PhPhr, R)
prepausally:				
→ a. in.nan<s> %				*
b. in.nans %		*!		
c. in.na.ns̲ %			s!	
internally:				
a. in.nan<s> . . .	*!			*
b. in.nans . . .		*!		
→ c. in.na.ns̲ . . .			s	

My account here assumes the same treatment of extrasyllabic consonants as that given earlier, and is parallel to the analysis I gave of the Postpausal Annexation facts.

Consider next the case of phrase-final syllabic sonorants, which are only optionally 'annexed' in prepausal context. There is a simple way of accounting for this optionality that does not require any new theoretical mechanisms. Let us suppose that two adjacent constraints are *freely* ranked if each way of ranking them leads to an equally correct choice of candidates. The notion of free ranking can be interpreted in terms of the following algorithm:

When two constraints C_1 and C_2 are freely ranked, two tableaux are constructed for each input, in one of which $C_1 \gg C_2$ and in the other of which $C_2 \gg C_1$. The winning candidates in each tableau are retained as alternative output forms.

This approach can be generalized to the case where one constraint is freely ranked with *several* adjacent constraints by allowing each C in the above statement to stand for a set of constraints. Suppose that C_1 is a single constraint X and C_2 is a set of three adjacent constraints $\{P, Q, R\}$, where $P \gg Q \gg R$ in the constraint ranking. If C_1 is freely ranked with C_2, then two tableaux are constructed for each input, one having the ranking $X \gg P \gg Q \gg R$ and the other the ranking $P \gg Q \gg R \gg X$. Naturally, transitivity holds over all rankings so that, for example, all constraints that dominate R in the second of these tableaux also dominate X.[20]

Let us suppose, then, that in the ITB constraint system, the pair of adjacent constraints $\{*P/n, *P/r\}$ is freely ranked with ALIGN(PhPhr, R, σ, R). This assumption yields the analysis of prepausal /ygydr/ 'eagle' shown in the pair of tableaux in (43). (As usual, only relevant constraints are displayed.)

(43) a.

/ygydr/	*COMPLEX[Cd]	*P/r	ALIGN(PhPhr, R)
→ a. i.gid\<r\> %			*
b. i.gidr %	*!		
c. i.gi.dr̥ %		r!	

b.

/ygydr/	*COMPLEX[Cd]	ALIGN(PhPhr, R)	*P/r
a. i.gid\<r\> %		*!	
b. i.gidr %	*!		
→ c. i.gi.dr̥ %			r

Candidate (a) is the winner in (43a) and candidate (c) is the winner in (43b). Both are therefore retained as variant output forms.

The analysis so far provides a correct account of forms with final two-

---

[20] This approach (see also Itô and Mester in Chapter 14 below) is distinct from the notion of 'equal ranking' proposed by Kager (n.d.), which is formulated as follows: When two constraints C_1 and C_2 are ranked equally, the evaluation procedure branches at that point. In one branch, constraint C_1 is ranked above the constraint C_2, while in the other branch the ranking is reversed. The winning candidates in each branch are retained as the output forms. One crucial difference between the two lies in the fact that while the notion of *free* ranking can be easily generalized to sets of constraints in the way just shown, the notion of *equal* ranking cannot, at least without further elaboration. This is because any constraint (in a system excluding free ranking) has just one rank in the full constraint ranking. It follows from this that a constraint cannot hold the same rank as two other constraints each of which hold different ranks.

member clusters, and we must now consider forms with final three-member clusters. These include examples like /y-rks/ 'he hid' (40a), realized as [irks] phrase-finally. The problem with this and similar forms is that $*\text{COMPLEX}^{\text{Cd}}$ (28) excludes all syllabifications with a CC coda, including both (irks) and (irk)<s>.

A solution to this problem is suggested by a closer examination of the data. The following list shows all final three-member clusters in D&E's data. It can be seen that these clusters fall into two general types, (a) those beginning with a tautomorphemic geminate, and (b) those whose second member is a (non-nasal) stop.

(44) *Cluster*   *Example*

	Cluster	Example	
a.	yyt	i.su.fuyyt	/y-swfw-yyt/
	yyt	i.ʒa.rayyt	/i-ʒara-yyt/
	yyl	yuyyl	/y-wyyl/
	llm	illm	/y-llm/
	nnk	!as.munnk	/!azmw-nn-k/
	nns	ta.manns	/tama-nn-s/
b.	rks	irks	/y-rks/
	stɣ	istɣ	/y-stɣ/
	ʃkd	iʃkd	/yʃkd/
	xkm	uglxkm	/wgl-x-km/
	ftk	iftk	/y-ftk/

Cluster type (a) reflects the existence of an exceptionless constraint in ITB which prohibits syllabifying the second element of a tautomorphemic geminate as peak (D&E 1985: 120–5). This constraint rules out syllabifications such as (i)(su)(fu)(yit) for the first example, which would otherwise be maximally harmonic. Note, however, that the correct syllabification of this example, (i)(su)(fuyyt), shows an apparent violation of $*\text{COMPLEX}^{\text{Cd}}$, but is none the less preferred to the syllabification (i)(su)(fuy)(yt) with its violation of *P/t. We cannot explain this preference on the assumption that *P/t outranks $*\text{COMPLEX}^{\text{Cd}}$ due to examples like /ra-t-kty/ 'she will remember' (D&E 1985: 113), which is syllabified (ra)(tk)(ti) (with a *P/t violation) and not (ratk)(ti) (with a *CODA violation), showing that syllabic stops are preferred to complex codas in internal syllables.

To deal with this problem, I propose that ITB phonology licenses two extrasyllabic positions at the end of the phonological phrase. The first, linked to the PhPhr node, is subject to the condition that it must be filled by either the second element of a geminate or a stop. The other, linked to the Utterance node, is unconditioned. I will term these positions 'appendices' for convenience, though no constituent status is attributed to them. These positions and their licensing conditions are shown in (45).

(45)

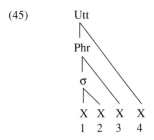

condition: 3 = 2 or 3 = [-continuant, -sonorant]

Phrase-appendices (position 3 in the diagram) are of course subject to the SPP (21), which forbids sonority peaks that are not syllable peaks within the syllabification domain. Let us consider our earlier example, *irks*. Since the phrase-appendix [k] is not a sonority peak, it is not required to be a syllable peak, and so does not violate the SPP. On the other hand, the utterance-appendix [s] is not subject to the SPP, since it lies outside the syllabification domain, and so even though it is a sonority peak, it also does not violate the SPP. A tableau for *irks* is given below:

(46)

/y-rks/	SA	SPP	*COMPLEX^{Cd}	*P/s	ALIGN(PhPhr, R)
prepausally:					
→ a. ir<k><s> %					*
b. irks %			*!		
c. ir.k$\underline{s}$ %				s!	
internally:					
a. ir<k><s> ..	*!				*
b. irks ..			*!		
→ c. ir.k$\underline{s}$ ..				s	

Similar analyses can be given of the other examples in (44).

Consider, in contrast, a form such as (ma)(ra)(tgt) 'what will happen of you?' from underlying /ma ra-t-g-t/ (D&E 1985: 113) whose final syllable does not undergo Prepausal Annexation. In D&E's account, this is because a crucial condition for the application of this rule is not met: the syllabic *g* is not final in its syllable. The present account offers a different explanation: if [g] were incorporated as a phrase appendix it would constitute a sonority peak that is not a syllable peak within the syllabification domain (the phrase), and would therefore incur a violation of high-ranking SPP.

The correctness of this solution to the problem of three-member clusters will ultimately depend on an examination of more data than are provided in D&E (1985; 1988). However, several further observations support this approach. First, schema (45), by providing two appendix positions, correctly predicts that initial and final clusters can have no more than three members (onset or coda plus two appendices). There is no room in the prosodic structure for further segments, since any additional ones would have to be stray segments. I assume that such segments violate the undominated constraint *STRAY, stated below:

(47) *STRAY: Root nodes are linked to prosodic structure.

*STRAY is of course the Optimality-Theoretical counterpart of Stray Erasure (Steriade 1982).

Second, this structure also allows us to explain an apparent anomaly in our analysis up to this point. This concerns the prepausal form [i.gid<r>] (43), whose final consonant, *r*, appears to violate the SPP. Under the present account, this form is anomalous only if *r* is analyzed as a phrase appendix. If we suppose instead that *r* is an utterance appendix, it lies outside the domain of the SPP and no longer incurs a violation.

A third source of support can be drawn from a subtle difference in predictions between D&E's analysis and the one proposed here. This difference involves the forms (u)(gṃn) ~ (ug)(mṇ) 'they (m.) drew (water)' from underlying /wgm-n/, discussed earlier in connection with (30). D&E state that both forms are correct in prepausal position. Given the possibility of the second syllabification, the optional application of D&E's Prepausal Annexation rule predicts a possible third variant, (ugmn). This variant, however, is not reported. We have already seen that the present analysis correctly predicts both of the observed variants, and we can now see that it excludes the monosyllabic form (ugmn) due to the fact that its second consonant *m* violates both of the conditions on the phrase-appendix: it is not an oral stop and it violates the SPP.[21]

A fourth consideration in favor of this analysis is the fact that it generalizes straightforwardly to *initial* three-member clusters as well. Such clusters can be created by the imperfective prefix /tt-/, as illustrated by examples such as [ttfu.wat] 'spend', from intermediate /tt-fwwat/ (D&E 1985: 121–2). The expected syllabification [tt̩.fu.wat] is blocked by the constraint, mentioned earlier, which prohibits taking the second element of a tautomorphemic geminate as a peak. However, the initial syllable appears to violate *COMPLEX^{Ons}. We may account for such examples on the assumption that the mirror image of schema (45) defines extrasyllabic positions in phrase-initial position too. In this analysis, the first *t* is an utterance appendix, and the second *t* a phrase

---

[21] A similar example is /rks-x/ 'I hid' (D&E 1985: 114–15). In the non-final form /ss-rks-x-t/ 'I hid him', D&E indicate a hesitation between the syllabification (ssṛ)(kṣxt), conforming to left-to-right rule application, and the syllabification (ssṛk)(sx̩t), conforming to right-to-left application. If both of these syllabifications are in fact correct, we would expect /rks-x/ 'I hid' to have the parallel phrase-internal syllabifications (ṛ)(kṣx) and (ṛk)(sx̩). In prepausal position, the latter parsing should feed the obligatory application of Prepausal Annexation, predicting the final form *(ṛksx); however, the reported prepausal form is (ṛ)(kṣx). As before, the present analysis excludes the prepausal form *(ṛksx) on the basis of its ill-formed phrase appendix [s], which violates both conditions on this position.

appendix; note that the latter, being a segment of the lowest-sonority class, will never violate the SPP.

The ranking of the major constraints used in the above analysis is summarized in (48).

(48) a. Undominated constraints (mutually unranked)
  *STRAY (47)
  Syllable Adjacency (37)
  ALIGN(PhPhr, L, Wd, L) (23)
  SPP (21)
  *RR (19)
  *COMPLEX^{Ons}, *COMPLEX^{Cd} (28)
  b. Dominated constraints (in rank order)
  *P/t,d
  ALIGN(PhPhr, L, σ, L) (35)
  ONSET (17)
  *P/s, z

```
              /              \
*P/n, r                       ALIGN(PhPhr, R, σ, R) (41)
ALIGN(PhPhr, R, σ, R) (41)    *P/n, r
              \              /
                   *CODA
```

To summarize the results of this section, I have shown that patterns of initial and final clusters in ITB can be given a plausible analysis within a non-derivational version of Optimality Theory. Of the two approaches to ITB, the latter provides a better explanation of the interactions among the syllabification principles. In the derivational analysis, it was necessary to mention the class of stops in three different rules, all of which have the effect of restricting the contexts in which they can function as syllable peaks: the CSR stipulates that stops are the last segments to be recruited as syllable peaks, Postpausal Annexation stipulates that stops are the sole targets for phrase-initial annexation, and Prepausal Annexation stipulates that stops (and fricatives) are the sole targets for the obligatory case of phrase-final annexation. As these rules are formally independent of each other, the derivational analysis is unable to explain the 'conspiracy' according to which all ITB rules restricting the occurrence of syllable peaks apply in preference to segments lying at the *bottom* of the sonority scale. The constraint-based analysis developed here, in contrast, captures this generalization directly through its rank-ordering of the Peak Hierarchy constraints with respect to the constraints with which they interact. The fact that stops are highly restricted in their ability to function as syllable peaks is explained uniformly by the fact that *P/t,d lie near the top of the constraint ranking.

6. Syllabification and Word Formation

I shall finally consider how the principles of syllabification developed so far interact with the principles of word formation. I consider first a rule of imperfective formation (section 6.1) and then take up the problem raised by the system of templatic morphology (section 6.2).

6.1 *Imperfective formation*

D&E state the principle governing one type of imperfective formation, to which I have referred briefly in the earlier discussion, as follows:

> Certain verbs of ITB form their imperfective stem by geminating one of the consonants of their root . . . The segment which is geminated in the imperfective stem is that segment which is syllabified as an onset by [the CSR] in the basic stem. (D&E 1988: 10–11; see also D&E 1991)

This statement presents a potential challenge to a non-derivational theory of phonology, since it is crucially defined on the output of the CSR, before the annexation rules have applied. To show that this ordering is crucial, I repeat a selection of illustrative forms from (12), showing first the basic stem, then the output of the CSR, then the output of the annexation rules, and finally the imperfective stem:

(49)	*Basic stem*	*CSR*	*Annexation*	*Imperfective stem*
a.	rʃq	(r)(ʃq)	(rʃq)	rʃʃq
	bxl	(b)(xl)	(bxl)	bxxl
	kʃm	(k)(ʃm)	(kʃm)	kʃʃm
b.	mrz	(mrz)	n/a	mmrz
	frn	(frn)	n/a	ffrn
	xng	(xng)	n/a	xxng

The problem form for a nonderivational analysis is the first one, /rʃq/ 'be happy'. Here Prepausal Annexation turns the onset created by the CSR (as shown in column 2) into a coda (as shown in column 3). D&E's statement allows us to predict gemination correctly only if we can refer to the immediate output of the CSR, before the annexation rules apply to it.

There is a quick but ultimately unsatisfactory solution to this problem. Recall that in the analysis of the preceding section, the external members of phrase-edge CC clusters are extrasyllabic. Thus, our predicted syllabification of the first example is not (rʃq) but (rʃ)<q>, in which the final consonant is extrasyllabic, and the syllabifications of the next two examples are similarly <b>(xl) and <k>(ʃm). In all these forms, the consonant that must be geminated in the imperfective can be characterized as the first *syllable margin* (onset or coda). As this information is present in the surface forms, it follows that imperfective formation does not require reference to an intermediate stage of derivation and does not offer crucial evidence against a non-derivational model of phonology.

What is unsatisfactory about this account is that it assumes that the output of the phonology, which constitutes surface phonological representation, can constitute the input to morphological derivation. Such a situation is rare at best; in the normal case, morphological derivation must apply either to underlying representation or to the output of an early subset of the phonological rules (the lexical rules). In particular, we do not expect to find word-formation rules that make crucial reference to high-level prosodic categories such as the phonological phrase (PhPhr), which in standard rule-based models are only introduced at the postlexical level; but we saw in the preceding section that organization into phonological phrases is crucial to the selection of surface syllabifications such as (rʃ)<q>, which, in the alternative account just offered, form the input to imperfective formation.

Let us consider an alternative account of imperfective formation that makes use of the notion of *stratal organization*. This notion has a place in the version of OT proposed by McCarthy and Prince (1993*a*), who distinguish between a prefix level, a suffix level and a word level in the phonology and morphology of Axininca Campa. They summarize their view of Axininca Campa stratal organization in the following terms:

Each level constitutes a separate mini-phonology, just as in ordinary rule-based Lexical Phonology (e.g., Kiparsky 1982, Mohanan 1982, Borowsky 1986) or in the level-based rule + constraint system of Goldsmith (1990, 1991). The constraint hierarchies at each level will overlap only in part, and will in fact specify somewhat different constraint rankings. Each level selects the candidate form that best satisfies its parochial constraint hierarchy; the winning candidate is fully interpreted by filling in empty moras or incomplete root-nodes and by erasing unparsed material. This interpreted representation then becomes the input, the underlying representation, for the next level in the derivation. (pp. 24–5)

As the last word in this quotation explicitly shows, the notion of stratal organization introduces derivations into the model, where it characterizes the relation between adjacent levels. In this conception, the organization of the phonology is non-derivational *within* strata and derivational *across* strata; McCarthy and Prince's affirmation that 'there is no serial derivation' must be understood in this sense.

Let us attempt to view ITB phonology and morphology in terms of a multistratal model minimally including one lexical stratum and one postlexical stratum. On this view, imperfective formation can be treated as a 'normal' word-formation rule in the sense that it belongs to the lexical stratum and not the postlexical stratum. Let us further assume, as seems reasonable, that no PhPhr and Utterance nodes are present in lexical representations. If these nodes are not present, there will be no licensing nodes for extrasyllabic consonants (phrase and utterance appendices). As a result, extrasyllabic consonants will violate the undominated constraint *STRAY (47), requiring all segments to be linked to prosodic structure at some level. Assuming that this constraint is undominated, consonants violating any member of the *P/α family will be preferred to those violating *STRAY.

To illustrate this analysis, a selection of candidate syllabifications of /rʃq/ present in the output of the lexical phonology is given in (50):

(50) /rʃq/	*STRAY	*COMPLEX^{Cd}	ONSET	*P/t
→ a. r̩.ʃq			*	q
b. rʃ<q>	*!		*	
c. r̩ʃq		*!	*	

In candidate (b) the extrasyllabic consonant enclosed in brackets is a stray segment, as just explained, and is therefore eliminated by its *STRAY violation. Candidate (c) presents a complex coda and so violates *COMPLEX^{Cd}. Candidate (a), then, is the most harmonic.

I conclude that the facts involving the type of imperfective formation discussed in this section probably require a distinction between two strata, a lexical and a postlexical one. By recognizing this distinction, we introduce a derivational level intermediate between underlying and surface representation corresponding to the level of *lexical representation* in Lexical Phonology. This is a derivational level for which cognitive status has sometimes been claimed (Mohanan 1982).[22]

6.2 *Templatic morphology*

We turn finally to the larger class of morphological derivatives involving templatic morphology. As we shall see, these forms provide a further challenge to a strictly non-derivational and hence monostratal interpretation of Optimality Theory. In their 1992 study, D&E analyse these derivatives in terms of prosodic templates, following the model proposed by McCarthy (1979) for Classical Arabic. The templates required for ITB in this analysis consist of sequences of skeletal units C, V, the latter of which are always preassociated with a vowel. D&E propose templates such as the following:

---

[22] The distinction between a lexical and a postlexical stratum has a number of further ramifications for the analysis presented here, of which I will mention just one. In the bistratal analysis of /rʃq/, the output of the lexical stratum is (r̩)(ʃq) and that of the postlexical stratum is (rʃ)<q>, as seen earlier. In McCarthy and Prince's stratal model as cited above, it is the *interpreted* representation, with syllable structure intact, that becomes the input for the next level in the derivation. This means that (r̩)(ʃq), with two syllables, is the input to the postlexical stratum and (rʃ)<q>, with one syllable, the output. The postlexical 'mini-phonology' must thus have the ability to destroy the second syllable, mimicking the effect of D&E's annexation rule in this respect.

(51)　　　　u　　a　　　　　TIRRUGZA template
　　　　　　　|　　|
　　(C) C C V C C V
　　　　　\ /
　　　　　α

　　u　　i　　　　　　　UKRIS template
　　|　　|
　　V C C V C

Parenthesized slots indicate positions that are optionally filled, and two slots linked to a shared α represent positions that must be linked to a single consonant of the melody tier (which is accordingly realized as a geminate). D&E elaborate a set of ranked, violable constraints predicting the well-formed patterns of association between base forms and templates. They observe that among the phonemes of the base, only *consonants*—a term they use to refer to both nonsyllabic vocoids and contoids—are transferred to the derived word. As in Arabic, consonants are mapped onto templatic C-slots, but unlike in Arabic, vowels—vocoids with syllabic function—are not mapped onto V-slots due to the presence of the prelinked vowels which pre-empt them.[23]

D&E do not explicitly relate their morphological analysis to their earlier analysis of the syllable, and the question naturally arises where the principles of templatic word formation apply in the course of syllabification. A close reading of their study shows that the point of interface must correspond to that point in the derivation at which CSR(a) and CSR(i) have applied, but the later rules CSR(r, . . ., t) have not; this is the point at which all instances of /a/ and appropriate instances of /y, w/ (those that do not introduce ONSET violations) have been assigned to V slots in CV core syllables, but before any syllabic consonants have been created.

This result is problematical not only for a strictly non-derivational version of OT but also for the bistratal model of ITB proposed in the preceding section, whose level of lexical representation corresponds to the output of *all* members of the CSR, not just CSR(a, i). Let us therefore examine the evidence for this conclusion more closely. It is easy to verify that CSR(a, i) must have already applied at the point where the templatic derivatives are formed, since the base-to-template mapping rules must crucially distinguish the vowels [i, u] from the consonants [y, w]. Consider, for example, the following TIRRUGZA deriva-tives, as transcribed by D&E:

---

[23] In their work in prosodic morphology (e.g. 1995*b*), McCarthy and Prince have suggested that prosodic templates should be expressed in terms of syllables and other higher-level prosodic units, rather than in terms of skeletal (CV or X) units. As far as I can determine, a reanalysis of ITB in prosodic terms, whatever its merits, would not substantially affect the present discussion.

(52)   *Base*   *Derivative*
   a. 'man'   a-rgaz   t-i-rrugza
   b. 'dummy'   a-!nttayfu   t-i-!nttuyfa
   c. 'sharif'   ʃʃrif   t-i-ʃʃurfa
   d. 'to dream'   wurga   t-i-wwurga
   e. 'heir'   a-m-kkusu   t-i-mmukksa

(52a) establishes the basic pattern. The derived form *t-i-rrugza* can be predicted by mapping the base consonants *r*, *g*, *z* onto the obligatory C-positions
of the TIRRUGZA template in (51) (geminating the first, as required), and
discarding the vowels of the base form in favor of the prespecified melody [u
. . . a]. The remaining examples follow suit. In these derivations, it is crucial
that the segment which we transcribe as underlying /y/ counts as the consonant
[y] in (52b) where it maps onto a templatic C-slot, and as the vowel [i] in (52c)
where it does not. For the same reasons, the manifestation of underlying / w /
must count as a consonant in (52d) and as a vowel in (52e) (recall that the [u]
of TIRRUGZA derivatives is the prespecified template vowel). Thus the
mapping principles illustrated here presuppose the operation of at least
CSR(a) and CSR(i), the latter of which creates the distinction between [i, u]
and [y, w].

We can also verify that the remaining CS rules, CSR(r, . . ., t), *cannot* have
applied at the point at which the templatic morphology is defined. Consider,
for example, the base /krs/ 'tie in a bundle', whose UKRIS derivation is
schematized in (53a) below. Here, the base form is shown below the dashed
line and the prosodic template above. Notice that the base form has a CCC
skeleton, guaranteeing correct C-to-C associations to the template.

(53) a. (UKRIS template)   b. (UKRIS template)

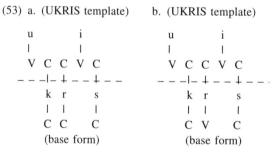

If CSR(r) had applied to the base form prior to template mapping, as shown in
(53b), it would have assigned /r/ a syllable peak (V), creating an illegitimate
V-to-C association. D&E's representation of /krs/ as shown in (53a) is fully
typical of the representations they give elsewhere in their article; in no input
(or output) form is any consonant linked to a V-position, even in the many
cases where the application of the CSR would have created such a linkage. The
justification for this treatment is clear. On an analysis in which *only* CSR(a,i)
have applied at the point where template mapping is defined, the principle

which maps melody units onto template positions is simple to state: all and only segments occupying C-slots in the base (extensionally equivalent to D&E's 'consonants') are assigned to C-slots in the derived template. If instead *all* CSR rules had applied prior to template mapping, creating representations like that in (53b), template mapping would have to apply to a formally arbitrary class of segments (nonsyllabic sounds and contoids), statable only in terms of a disjunction.

We conclude, then, that D&E's mapping principles apply to forms that occur in the immediate output of CSR(a,i). It is natural to ask why these principles apply at this point rather than at some other randomly chosen point in the derivation, such as between CSR(n) and CSR(z). Is this result fortuitous, or does it follow from some principle of grammatical organization? Though they do not explicitly raise this question, D&E present no evidence that this particular step in the derivation corresponds to a well-marked level in the phonology, such as the output of a lexical rule stratum—though the very fact that a large class of word-formation principles converges on this point might be taken as circumstantial evidence for such a view.

Let us suppose that the lexical phonology and morphology of ITB contains not one but two lexical strata, the first of which derives the templatic derivatives and the second of which derives the imperfective forms. One possible interpretation along these lines, among others, would be the following. The Stratum 1 phonology derives the distinction between the vowels [i, u] and the nonsyllabic vocoids [y, w] but creates no syllabic consonants, and of course no prosodic structure at the level of the phonological phrase or above. The output of the Stratum 1 phonology forms the input to the Stratum 1 morphology, represented by the templatic derivatives. Let us assume that the output of the Stratum 1 morphology is resubmitted to the Stratum 1 phonology, so that its output is correctly syllabified. The output of the Stratum 1 phonology and morphology, in this sense, constitutes a first derivational level (L1). This level forms the input to Stratum 2, in which the full set of syllabic consonants appears, but higher-level prosodic structure is still absent. The output of the Stratum 2 phonology forms the input to the Stratum 2 morphology, perhaps constituted in ITB by the special class of imperfective derivatives discussed above, whose output is resubmitted to the Stratum 2 phonology as before. The output of the Stratum 2 phonology and morphology, taken together, constitutes derivational level 2 (the level of lexical representation). This level forms the input to the Stratum 3 (postlexical) phonology, in which the phonological phrase (PhPhr) and other higher-level prosodic structure appear for the first time. The output of this stratum forms the level of surface phonological representation (L3).

This account, when properly developed, requires that each level have its appropriate mini-phonology (cf. Chapter 13 below for discussion of mini-phonologies [Editor]). For example, to guarantee that no consonants are syllabic at L1, that all consonants are potentially syllabic at L2, and that certain domain-edge consonants are desyllabified at L3 requires the appropriate reranking of the members of *P/α with respect to the constraints with which they interact at each level. Due to the tentative nature of the present analysis (required by the incomplete nature of the data at my disposal) and to space limitations, I will not attempt to carry out a formal analysis of the different rankings here. Nor will I speculate as to what formal mechanism may be responsible for suppressing higher-level prosodic nodes like PhPhr in the lexical strata, as several possibilities suggest themselves, none being clearly superior to the others.

To summarize, the interaction of phonology and morphology discussed in this section appears to require stratal organization in the grammar. The primary weakness of the stratal account, if it has one, is that all the evidence supporting a distinction among different strata has been drawn from word formation; there is no purely phonological evidence that syllabification should be carried out in three derivational steps. Nor do I know of any convincing explanation for why imperfective formation should be assigned to a later lexical stratum than the templatic word formation rules. These qualifications notwithstanding, the currently available evidence strongly suggests the need for multistratal organization in ITB, and hence a well-defined role for derivation.

7. Summary and Conclusions

As I stated at the outset, this chapter has two main goals. It proposed first to see whether the non-derivational version of Optimality Theory proposed by P&S can be successfully extended to a larger range of ITB data than these writers considered, including data involving pause-conditioned 'annexation' rules and phonology–morphology interactions. We have seen that their basic syllable model can be extended to the annexation data with certain modifications, none of which required abandonment of the basic premises of the theory. However, our discussion of the phonology–morphology interface showed that it may be necessary to recognize several phonological and morphological strata, distinguished by different constraint rankings ('mini-phonologies'), and crucially ordered in the sense that the output of earlier strata forms the input to later strata. This result requires that the full theory must allow derivations *across* strata, perhaps along lines envisaged by McCarthy and Prince (1993*a*).

A second goal was to see whether a non-derivational account can offer deeper insights into ITB phonology than a rule-based account along the lines proposed by D&E. Here we were able to draw upon the resources of the strictly non-derivational version of OT to provide a unified account of what appeared to be a 'rule conspiracy' in D&E's account: the fact that rules conspire to severely restrict the contexts in which syllabic stops can appear. Standard rule frameworks can bring such 'conspiracies' to light but cannot explain them directly in terms of the formal structure of the analysis. The optimality-based analysis succeeds in explaining the existence of this conspiracy by extracting the generalization that underlies it—stops are low in sonority and hence make poor syllable peaks—as a principle of universal grammar, *P/t,d, universally ranked above all other members of the Peak Hierarchy. In this sense, the Optimality Theory account provides a more satisfactory account of the organization of ITB grammar.

A related but subsidiary goal was to examine P&S's constraint system from a critical perspective. I have argued on purely empirical grounds that the inclusion of certain members of P&S's full Peak and Margin Hierarchies leads to a problem of typological overgeneration. We traced this result to the fact that the constraints in question, *P/a, i and *M/t, . . ., r, expressed *antitendencies*, contraries of widely attested tendencies and markedness principles. In response to this problem, it was proposed that all constraints of this type should be eliminated from the universal constraint system. We have seen that an analysis eliminating the problematical constraints could successfully account for the data considered by P&S and extend to new data as well.

This result has further consequences for the issue of theory comparison. Perhaps the most significant criticism of rule-based theories has been that their basic theoretical construct, the notion 'rule of grammar', allows the expression of countless implausible rules and hence implausible grammars. They are therefore incapable of characterizing the class of possible human languages as far as their phonological components are concerned. In the face of such difficulties, some linguists have appealed to the view that cross-linguistic tendencies and regularities are a product of forces which are largely external to the language faculty itself. If we consider grammatical theory to be a theory of the language faculty, it would follow that phonology (as a part of the theory of grammar) need not concern itself with such tendencies. An unfortunate result of this position is that it tacitly passes the burden of explaining many of the most basic features of phonological systems to some unidentified area(s) of study lying outside phonological theory proper.

Optimality Theory offers a potential solution to this problem, to the extent that the members of the universal constraint set are selected on solid empirical grounds (see Myers, Chapter 4 above for extensive discussion). The most widely accepted members of the proposed constraint set include such constraints as ONSET and *CODA which together express the widely attested cross-linguistic preference for CV syllables. The fact that these constraints allow insightful accounts into the organization of many phonological systems is related to the fact that they represent widely observed linguistic tendencies. In contrast, an alternative theory making use of contrary constraints expressing antitendencies (*ONSET and CODA) could mimic the effect of arbitrary rules and rule orderings (in which e.g. the Coda rule is crucially ordered before the Onset rule), and would consequently predict many implausible grammars. *Only if such constraints are systematically eliminated* can OT place itself in a position to solve the problem of arbitrariness inherent in rule-based theory.

The present study is a preliminary one, and many important questions remain to be addressed. For example, the question of how ITB phonology and morphology interact has been barely touched upon; I have offered a few tentative suggestions in this regard, but further analysis of ITB phonology and morphology, drawing in part on published work not discussed here (D&E 1989; 1991), may very well lead to a different view from the one sketched here. Second, I have not examined the syllabification of geminates, for which D&E (1985) already offer a constraint-based analysis, nor have I said anything about the rich system of morphosyntactically conditioned alternations (D&E 1989; 1991), phonologically conditioned segmental alternations (D&E, forthcoming), stress and intonation, lexical and morphological exceptions, dialect variation, and so forth. Finally, I have found a few potential exceptions to the analysis presented here, and I follow a venerable tradition in relegating them to a footnote.[24] It is hoped that this study will stimulate further research into these questions.

ACKNOWLEDGEMENTS

I have benefited from the opportunity to present earlier versions of this material at the Essex Workshop on Derivations and Constraints in Phonology, September 1995, and at my phonology seminar at the University of Paris in 1994–5; I would like to thank the participants at these gatherings, and in particular J.-E. Boltanski, for their interest and comments. Special thanks are due to Mohamed Elmedlaoui for sharing many of his intuitions with me and amplifying my understanding of several aspects of ITB phonology, and to François Dell, Alan Prince, and Iggy Roca for offering very useful comments

---

[24] Besides the exceptions discussed in connection with the directionality problem (see (30)), the constraint system proposed here does not exclude the hypothetical syllabification of prepausal /t-ftk-t/ 'you suffered a sprain' as (tft)(kt), or of /rks-x/ 'I hid' as (rk)(sx), both of which are excluded in D&E's analysis by left-to-right application of the CSR, or (if this fails) by Prepausal Annexation. From /y-ftk/ 'suffered a sprain', the constraints proposed here predict the possible non-final output (i)(ftk) as well as the observed (if)(tk) (D&E 1985: 120) (note that the latter form violates the left-to-right directionality principle). D&E do not specifically state whether these predicted variants are ill-formed; if they are, other constraints will be needed to exclude them under the present analysis. In addition, Elmedlaoui (1985) presents many forms which are exceptions both to the present analysis and to that of D&E (1985; 1988). I should add, however, that the present analysis successfully handles at least one form that was an exception for D&E, in addition to those in the right-hand column in (29b): their analysis predicts that /ra-t-kʃm/ 'she will enter' should be syllabifiable as (ra)(tkʃm) in prepausal position through the optional application of Prepausal Annexation (D&E 1985: 120), while my analysis correctly excludes this form by virtue of its violation of the *RR.

and suggestions on an earlier draft of this chapter. Of course, I take full responsibility for any remaining errors of fact or interpretation.

References

Blevins, J. (1995). 'The syllable in phonological theory', in J. Goldsmith (ed.), *A Handbook of Phonological Theory*. Oxford: Blackwell, 206–44.

Borowsky, T. (1986). 'Topics in the Lexical Phonology of English'. Ph.D. Dissertation, University of Massachusetts, Amherst.

Clements, G. N. (1990). 'The role of the sonority cycle in core syllabification', in J. Kingston and M. Beckman (eds.), *Papers in Laboratory Phonology I: Between the Grammar and Physics of Speech*. Cambridge: Cambridge University Press, 283–333.

—— and Keyser, S. J. (1983). *CV Phonology: A Generative Theory of the Syllable*, Cambridge, Mass.: MIT Press.

Dell, F., and Elmedlaoui, M. (1985). 'Syllabic consonants and syllabification in Imdlawn Tashlhiyt Berber', *Journal of African Languages and Linguistics* 7: 105–30.

—— —— (1988). 'Syllabic consonants in Berber: some new evidence', *Journal of African Languages and Linguistics* 10: 1–17.

—— —— (1989). 'Clitic ordering, morphology, and phonology in the verbal complex of Imdlawn Tashlhiyt Berber' (part 1). *Langues Orientales Anciennes: Philologie et Linguistique* 2, 165–94.

—— —— (1991). 'Clitic ordering, morphology, and phonology in the verbal complex of Imdlawn Tashlhiyt Berber' (part 2), *Langues Orientales Anciennes: Philologie et Linguistique* 3: 77–104.

—— —— (1992). 'Quantitative transfer in the nonconcatenative morphology of Imdlawn Tashlhiyt Berber', *Journal of Afroasiatic Languages* 3: 89–125.

—— —— (forthcoming). 'Consonant releases in Imdlawn Tashlhiyt Berber', *Linguistics*.

—— and Tangi, O. (1993). 'On the vocalization of /r/ in Ath-Sidhar Rifian Berber', *Linguistica Communicatio* 5(1–2): 5–53.

Elmedlaoui, M. (1985). 'Le Parler berbère chleuh d'Imdlawn (Maroc): segments et syllabation'. Doctoral thesis, University of Paris VIII.

El Medlaoui, M. (1995). *Aspects des représentations phonologiques dans certaines langues chamito-sémitiques*. Rabat: Université Mohamed V.

Goldsmith, J. (1990). *Autosegmental and Metrical Phonology*. Oxford: Blackwell.

—— (1991). 'Phonology as an intelligent system', in D. J. Napoli and J. A. Kegl (eds.), *Bridges between Psychology and Linguistics*. Hillsdale, NY: Lawrence Erlbaum, 247–67.

Jakobson, R. (1962). *Selected Writings, I: Phonological Studies*, expanded ed. The Hague: Mouton.

Jespersen, O. (1904). *Lehrbuch der Phonetik*. Leipzig: B. G. Teubner.

Kager, R. (n.d.) 'Generalized alignment and morphological parsing'. MS, University of Utrecht.

Kenstowicz, M. (1994). *Phonology in Generative Grammar*. Oxford: Blackwell.

Kiparsky, P. (1982). 'Lexical morphology and phonology', in I.-S. Yang (ed.), *Linguistics in the Morning Calm*. Hanshin, Seoul: Linguistic Society of Korea, 3–91.

McCarthy, J. (1979). 'Formal Properties of Semitic Phonology and Morphology'. Ph.D. dissertation, MIT.

—— and Prince, A. (1993*a*). 'Prosodic morphology', pt. 1. MS, University of Massachusetts, Amherst, and Rutgers University.

—— —— (1993*b*). 'Generalized alignment', in G. Booij and J. van Marle (eds.), *Yearbook of Morphology 1993*. Dordrecht: Kluwer, 79–153.

—— —— (1995*a*). 'Faithfulness and reduplicative identity'. MS, University of Massachusetts, Amherst, and Rutgers University.

—— —— (1995*b*). 'Prosodic morphology', in J. Goldsmith (ed.), *A Handbook of Phonological Theory*. Oxford: Blackwell, 318–66.

Milliken, S. (1988). 'Protosyllables: A Theory of Underlying Syllable Structure in Nonlinear Phonology'. Ph.D. Dissertation, Cornell University.

Mohanan, K. P. (1982). 'Lexical Morphology and Phonology'. Ph.D. dissertation, MIT.

Prince, A., and Smolensky, P. (1993). 'Optimality Theory: constraint interaction in generative grammar'. Technical Report 2 of the Rutgers Center for Cognitive Science. Piscataway, NJ: Rutgers University.

Rialland, A. (1994). 'The phonology and phonetics of extrasyllabicity in French', in P. A. Keating (ed.), *Phonological Structure and Phonetic Form: Papers in Laboratory Phonology, III*. Cambridge: Cambridge University Press, 136–59.

Rubach, J. and Booij, G. E. (1990). 'Edge of constituent effects in Polish', *Natural Language and Linguistic Theory* **8**(3): 427–64.

Scobbie, J. M. (1993). 'Constraint violation and conflict from the perspective of declarative phonology', *Canadian Journal of Linguistics/Revue canadienne de linguistique* **38**(2): 155–67.

Sievers, E. (1881). *Grundzüge der Phonetik*. Leipzig: Breitkopf & Hartel.

Steriade, D. (1982). 'Greek Prosodies and the Nature of Syllabification'. Ph.D. dissertation, MIT.

10

r, Hypercorrection, and the Elsewhere Condition

MORRIS HALLE and WILLIAM J. IDSARDI

1. INTRODUCTION

Our purpose in this article is to contribute to the current debate regarding the differing theoretical assumptions between Optimality Theory (OT) and the more traditional theory of derivations employing ordered rules. Such a discussion of fundamental issues is greatly facilitated if there is a body of data at hand that satisfies two desiderata: (1) the data are of a degree of complexity that makes it necessary to invoke more than just the most elementary resources of the competing theories, and (2) the phenomena are well-enough understood so that obviously inadequate solutions can be rejected without extensive investigation of the most basic facts. One body of data that satisfies these desiderata is the well-known shibboleth of the Eastern Massachusetts *r*. We are fortunate, moreover, in that these data have been reviewed in two recent papers by John McCarthy (1991; 1993), a native speaker of the dialect, who happens also to be one of the leading phonologists of our generation. In addition, much of the same data have been discussed in chapter V of Harris (1994), where parallel developments in other dialects of modern English are also considered.

2. THE DISTRIBUTION OF *r* IN EASTERN MASSACHUSETTS ENGLISH

It is well known that speakers of the Eastern Massachusetts dialect 'drop their *r*s'. This aspect of New England speech has been taken note of even by popular culture, as evidenced by the T-shirts sported by tourists proclaiming 'I pahked my cah in Hahvahd Yahd'. In addition to dropping *r*s, speakers of the dialect also insert *r*s after non-high vowels. As a result, words that in many other English dialects are phonetically distinct, such as *spa* and *spar* or *tuna* and *tuner*, are pronounced alike in (almost) all contexts in the Eastern Massachusetts dialect. This is illustrated by the examples in (1).

(1) a. the spa[r] is broken   the spar is broken.
     b. the spa seems broken   the spaɾ seems broken
     c. algebra[r] is difficult   Homer is difficult
     d. algebr[ə] bores me   Hom[ə] bores me
     e. the study of algebr[ə]   the study of Hom[ə]

As McCarthy explains in detail, the general loss of surface contrast does not also result in a loss of contrast in underlying representations. For example, such nearly identical stems as *Volta* and *alter* must have distinct underlying representations, because the stems behave differently under level I affixation; for instance in the forms in (2):

(2) Volt[ej]ic   alt[ər]ation
     algebr[ej]ic   Hom[er]ic

By admitting that these stems contrast in their underlying representation, we also admit that the phonology of the Eastern Massachusetts dialect includes machinery for both the insertion of *r* in some contexts (e.g. (1c)) and the deletion of *r* in other contexts (e.g. (1d)).

The level I affixation facts just reviewed are not the only evidence supporting the above conclusions. McCarthy (1991) reviews a number of additional facts, some of considerable complexity, all of which lead to the same conclusion: the dialect must distinguish in underlying representations syllables that end with a non-high vowel from syllables that end in non-high vowel + *r*, and as a consequence the dialect must include machinery for r-insertion as well as *r*-deletion. However *r*-insertion does not take place either before level I suffixes, as illustrated in (2), or in morpheme-internal position, as illustrated in (3).

(3) Aida *A[r]ida   Thais *Tha[r]is

An important topic discussed in detail in McCarthy (1991), but not in McCarthy (1993), is the treatment of stem-final liquids. Liquid-final stems that have a nucleus ending in a [+high] glide [j,w] are subject to schwa epenthesis when the stem is word-final or is followed by a level II suffix. This is illustrated with *l*-final stems in (4a). As shown in (4b), no epenthesis takes place stem-medially or before a level I suffix.[1]

(4) a. feel   [fijəl]
        feeling   [fijəlɪ̃ŋ]
        file   [fajəl]
        foal   [fowəl]
        fail   [fejəl]

---

[1] The majority of the examples in (4) and below appear in McCarthy (1991); in a few cases we have supplemented these with examples obtained from native speakers of the dialect among our acquaintances. We follow McCarthy's transcriptions of the long/tense vowels as involving an off-glide. This is crucial for the OT account because of the work done by the Final-C constraint, but this choice is not important to the rule-based account.

b. Healey   [hijlij]
   Gaelic   [gejlɪk]
   polar   [powlə]

It is to be noted that schwa epenthesis before *l* takes place even when the following morpheme begins with a vowel. Thus, the stem *feel* is disyllabic not only before pause, but also in *feel ill* and *feel sick*, and in *feeling*.[2] The liquid *r* exhibits exactly the same behavior as *l*. The behavior is, however, masked by the fact that *r* is deleted in syllable coda, i.e. before pause or consonant.

(5) a. fear   [fijə]
       fearing   [fijərɪŋ]
       fearless   [fijəlɪs]
       fear Ann   [fijər æn]
       fear Dan   [fijə dæn]
    b. see Ann   [sij æn]
       see Dan   [sij dæn]
    c. Byron   [bajrən]
       viral   [vajrəl]

As shown in (5a), like before *l*, schwa is epenthesized before stem-final *r* at the end of the word, before consonant and before level II suffixes. The examples in (5b) show that schwa is not inserted stem-medially or before level I suffixes. It is important to note that schwa epenthesis takes place in *r*-final stems, regardless of whether or not the *r* is deleted.[3] Although underlying stem-final *r*s trigger schwa epenthesis regardless of whether or not they are subject to deletion, inserted *r*s do not trigger schwa epenthesis. There is therefore no schwa epenthesis in the examples in (1) or in those in (6).

(6) draw[r]-ing
    draw[r] Ann
    rumba[r]-ing
    rumba[r] acts

The reason for this is that, as observed by McCarthy, *r* is inserted after [−high] nuclei. Since schwa epenthesis occurs after [+high] nuclei, it is to

---

[2] According to McCarthy (1991: 198), the bisyllabic pronunciation of *feeling* is found only in 'more monitored speech'. We have chosen to focus on this speech style because our informal observations suggest that it is the normal pronunciation with many speakers. Moreover, from an expository point of view it is somewhat simpler than McCarthy's more casual style.

[3] A comparison of *desire* [dəzajə]—*desirous* [dəzajrəs] with *idea* [ajdijə]—*ideal* [ajdijəl] shows that we must distinguish *r*-final stems from schwa-final stems, for if *r*-final stems (such as *desire*) were represented as ending in a schwa, we should have no account for the appearance of *r* before level I suffixes. Moreover, we should also lack an account for the facts of McCarthy's more casual speech, and we would have to limit schwa epenthesis to *l*. This argument is independent of the argument offered with respect to the data in (2) above.

be expected that there would be no schwa insertion before inserted *r*.[4] Finally, McCarthy draws attention to the fact that the underlying *r* in syllable onset is phonetically distinct from *r* elsewhere:

> Preliminary phonetic investigation shows that the principal difference between, say, 'sawr eels' [sɔr ijlz] and 'saw reels' [sɔ rijlz], is that the r in 'sawr eels' is considerably more vocalic, with more energy at all frequencies. (1993: 179)[5]

This difference between *r*s parallels the more familiar allophonic variation exhibited by *l*, the other liquid of English.[6] McCarthy assumes that this phonetic difference is reflected formally by the distinction between an *r* that is assigned to the syllable onset exclusively and an *r* that is ambisyllabic.[7] The main facts about the Eastern Massachusetts dialect that have been noted in the discussion to this point are summarized in (7).

(7)   i. Although phonetically indistinguishable, the stem final rhymes of such words as *algebra* and *Homer* must be distinguished in their underlying representations. The difference in the rhymes is required to account for the different behavior of the stem under suffixation.

ii. Stems that in their underlying representation end with a diphthongal nucleus in a [+high] segment followed by a liquid, epenthesize schwa before the liquid if the liquid is rhyme-final or followed by a level II suffix.

iii. Stems that in their underlying representation end with a [−high] vowel, insert *r* in the syllable coda when followed by a vowel.

iv. Coda *r* is deleted.

v. The liquids [r,l] in syllable onset differ phonetically from liquids in syllable coda.

3. OPTIMALITY ACCOUNTS

3.1 *Traditional Optimality Theory*

As noted, McCarthy's 1993 paper considers only *r*-insertion and *r*-deletion and does not offer an OT account of schwa epenthesis. His analysis of these data is

[4] It is, however, not the case that *r* is inserted after [−high] nuclei everywhere (cf. e.g. (3); see also n. 13 below).

[5] Some spectrographic data on the contrast are given in Olive *et al.* 1993.

[6] The Eastern Massachusetts dialect shares this distinction with the RP dialect. Thus, Jones (1950: 90–1) states that in RP '[t]wo chief varieties are distinguished, a fairly 'clear' l with resonance approximating to i, and a 'dark' l with resonance approximating u . . . The fairly clear l's are used when a vowel or j follows . . . Definitely dark varieties of l are used finally and before consonants . . . ' The difference between the two *l*s in feature terms is evidently that of [±back], and a rule to this effect will have to be included in the phonology of these dialects since the contrasts are peculiar to these dialects of English; in fact, many languages have a neutral *l* that is neither 'light' nor 'dark'.

[7] In the rule-based alternative presented in Section 24 below, we treat McCarthy's ambisyllabic *r*s as coda *r*s.

based on the two constraints in (8), which we reproduce from McCarthy (1993):

(8) a. The constraint CODA-COND . . . prohibits [r] in post-nuclear position of a syllable, or, equivalently, requires that [r] be in the onset. CODA-COND is responsible for the loss of etymologic /r/ preconsonantally and utterance-finally. (McCarthy 1993: 172)

b. FINAL-C governs the shape of the final syllable in a prosodic (i.e. phonological) word . . . a Prosodic Word (PrWd) cannot end in a (short) vowel, though it can end in a consonant or glide. (McCarthy 1993: 176)

The effect of these constraints is illustrated in the tableau in (9), which summarizes the information in McCarthy's 1993 tableaux (17) and (18). In (9), syllable boundaries are represented by dots; 'R' indicates that the *r* is inserted, rather than underlying, and the sequences 'r.r' and 'R.R' in (9iv) are used to represent ambisyllabic *r*.

(9)

	Candidates	Coda-Cond	Final-C
☞ i.	Wan.da. left. Ho.me. left.	✓	*
ii.	Wan.daR. left. Ho.mer. left	*!	✓
iii.	Wan.da. a.rrived Ho.me. a.rrived.	✓	*!
☞ iv.	Wan.daR. Ra.rrived. Ho.mer. ra.rrived.	✓	✓

McCarthy's remarks about these candidates are quoted in (10).[8]

(10) The candidates [in (9i)] obey the dominant constraint CODA-COND, whereas the candidates [in (9ii)] violate it. Thus [the candidates in (9i)] are selected as the actual output forms; the fact that they violate the lower-ranked constraint FINAL-C is irrelevant according to the principles of OT. The candidates [in (9iii) and (9iv)] all obey the dominant constraint CODA-COND. This tie is resolved in the usual way, by passing the candidates on to the rest of the constraint hierarchy, in this case FINAL-C . . . [which] then rejects [(9iii)]. (McCarthy 1993: 186)

McCarthy observes that in order for the examples (9iv) to obey the CODA-COND it is necessary to assume the *r* is ambisyllabic. McCarthy also notes some possible consequences for this view; we reproduce these comments in (11).

---

[8] McCarthy (1993: 189) states that Fill-V and Parse-V are ranked above Final-C, but ranked on a par with respect to Coda-Cond.

(11) There are at least two principled ways to incorporate this refinement into the enforcement of CODA-COND. First, if enforcement is subject to the Linking Convention . . . any *r* which is linked to both coda and onset position is immune to this constraint. Second, if CODA-COND is reformulated as a positive condition licensing *r* only in onsets . . . the fact that ambisyllabic *r* is also in a coda will not affect it. Either of these alternatives is fully satisfactory on all counts. (McCarthy 1993: 180)

Likewise, Final-C is satisfied with an ambisyllabic *r*; it does not require that the last consonant be wholly within the PrWd. McCarthy and Prince (1993*b*) compare Final-C, which is satisfied by 'sloppy' alignment, with the constraint Align-Left [i.e. Align(Stem, L, PrWd, L)], which requires 'crisp' alignment at the beginning of stems in English. McCarthy and Prince (1993*b*) point out that Align-Left must dominate Final-C so as to ensure crisp alignment and thus prevent ambisyllabic *r* from appearing in strings such as *Wanda retrieved*, for if the *r* in this string were ambisyllabic it would satisfy Final-C. Their argument is quoted in (12).

(12) a. Some care is required to complete the argument at the level of formal detail. One approach runs as follows. For purposes of Align-Left we need a string that 'is a' PrWd, whose first element is also the first element of the Stem. But in (103b) [see (12b), which illustrates the rejected candidate form of *saw Ted*; McCarthy and Prince assume that flapped *t* occurs when *t* is ambisyllabic] the string *Ted* fails to stand in the 'is a' relationship to the node PrWd, in the sense that if all the (graph-theoretic) edges emerging from its terminals are traced upward, they do not converge on the one PrWd node. Therefore there is no string that 'is a' PrWd in this upward sense (although tracing downward from PrWd would yield the string *Ted* as its contents), and the constraint cannot be met. The sketch of formal Alignment at the end of section 2 is based on the superannuated notion that linguistic structure correspond to acyclic graphs—trees in particular; given dual motherhood of nodes, we must sharpen our sense of 'is a'. (McCarthy and Prince 1993*b*: 147–8)

b. PrWd   PrWd
  / | \/ | \
  s   ɔ t   ə d

Reduced to its essentials, the idea here is that constraints such as Align or Coda Cond or Final-C are specified with a vantage point. When the vantage point is that of the segment, Align constraints must be understood 'crisply'. When the vantage point is that of a higher prosodic category, Align constraints can be understood as 'sloppy'. We can restate the constraints CODA-COND and FINAL-C as in (13) so as to make it clearer that the constraints will be satisfied here by ambisyllabic elements.[9]

---

[9] The upward/downward idea of McCarthy and Prince (1993*b*) shows that McCarthy's speculation regarding the Linking Condition of Hayes (1986), quoted above, was not correct. The Coda condition could be formulated in a sloppy manner (which would disallow even geminate *r*, compare the restriction in Hebrew against gutturals either as geminates or wholly within Codas—McCarthy, 1994), and Final-C could be formulated in a crisp manner.

(13) a. CODA-COND: No *r* should be wholly within a syllable Coda.

b. FINAL-C: Every word must end with (part of) a consonant.

The introduction of a vantage point obviously increases the number of constraints, since many Align constraints can now come in both 'crisp' and 'sloppy' varieties. And because the set of all constraints is taken to be part of Universal Grammar, each available constraint must be present in every grammar, though the constraint may be ranked very low. Thus, for instance, in addition to the sloppy constraint Final-C, there must also be a crisp constraint which we will call Final-C!. We will examine the effects of this crisp version below. At the time of the composition of McCarthy (1993), all insertion and deletion of elements in OT accounts was handled indirectly, by violations of the Fill and Parse constraints respectively. In the case of insertion an abstract place holder (graphically represented by an unfilled square) was inserted into strings in the Gen set, and if a candidate containing such a place holder was selected as optimal by the constraint hierarchy the place holder was ultimately filled by the default phoneme, i.e., by the least marked vowel if the place holder occupied the position of a syllable head, and by the least marked consonant elsewhere. In view of this, epenthesis must invariably insert a default phoneme. As McCarthy notes, (14), this poses a serious problem for his account of *r*-insertion.

(14) The problem with this approach is that r is demonstrably not the default consonant in English . . . This means that the output form 'Wandar arrived' must differ segmentally (melodically), rather than just prosodically, from the corresponding input form /Wanda arrived/. Thus, this form goes beyond the standard Optimality-Theoretic view of the candidate set as consisting of all possible melody-conserving prosodic rearrangements of the input. Melody is not conserved in 'Wandar arrived', so it is necessary first of all to broaden the candidate set to include this form. (McCarthy 1993: 189)

To broaden the candidate set, McCarthy proposes to have recourse to a special rule of *r*-insertion, (15).

(15) By a 'rule' here I mean a *phonologically arbitrary stipulation* one that is outside the system of Optimality. [emphasis added] This rule is interpreted as defining a candidate set {Wanda, Wandar}, and this candidate set is submitted to the constraint hierarchy. That is, this rule enlarges the candidate set to include non-melody-conserving candidates like 'Wandar arrived' (and *'Wandar left'), which are then evaluated by the constraints in the familiar way. (McCarthy 1993: 190)

This move, however, is unsatisfactory both on conceptual and on empirical grounds. Conceptually, reliance on an arbitrary stipulation that is outside the system of Optimality is equivalent to giving up on the enterprise. Data that cannot be dealt with by OT without recourse to rules are fatal counterexamples to the OT research programme (see, however, Blevins, Chapter 7 above [Editor]).[10]

From an empirical point of view the proposed extension encounters a number of serious problems overlooked by McCarthy. For instance, McCarthy's general *r*-insertion rule (Ø → r) will extend the Gen sets not only for inputs such as *Wanda* but also for the other cases illustrated in (16) (LaCharité and Paradis 1993: 139 also note these problems with McCarthy's rule of *r*-insertion).

(16) /wanda/ → {wanda, wandar} 'Wanda'
  /sij/ → {sij, sijr} 'see'
  /sijr/ → {sijr, sijrr} 'sear'

Of course, McCarthy could write a more specific rule of *r*-insertion (such as (29) below) that would be restricted to applying only after [−high] vowels. But the use of standard generative rules is sufficient to solve the problem, without OT constraints, candidates, and evaluation.

Consider, in particular, the candidates for the word *seeing* in (17). The brackets mark PrWd constituents. Following Selkirk (1995) the level I/II distinction is encoded here by either attaching the affix within the lowest PrWd (level I) or Chomsky-adjoining it to the PrWd, creating recursive PrWd structure. Recall that the discussion above showed that it is necessary to recognize both crisp and sloppy versions of some constraints. In view of this, we can no longer rule out such dual versions of other similar constraints. In particular, since, as we have seen above, Final-C is a sloppy constraint, the constraint set must also include its crisp analogue Final-C!, which we have ranked here as low as possible. Notice, however, that this constraint hierarchy selects the incorrect candidate from the set (17).

(17)

/si:+ɪŋ/	Coda-Cond	Final-C	Onset	NoComplexCoda	Final-C!
☞ [[sij.]rɪŋ]	√	√	√	√	√
[[sij.]jɪŋ]	√	√	√	√	*!
[[sijr.]rɪŋ]	√	√	√	*!	*
[[sij.]ɪŋ]	√	√	*!	√	√
[[sijr.]ɪŋ]	*!	√	*	*	√

---

[10] In an earlier part of the paper, McCarthy specifically rejects an analysis of this kind, i.e. one in which phonemes are inserted only to be deleted by a later rule (overriding constraint). As an alternative to his ambisyllabification analysis, McCarthy considers an analysis in which 'all vowel-final words will receive intrusive r at Word level, but intrusive r will be deleted phrasally when it cannot be resyllabified as an onset' (1993: 181). He rejects this analysis out of hand: 'This analysis

We must therefore conclude that the account in McCarthy (1993) failed to provide a satisfactory analysis of the data in terms of the then current version of OT.

3.2 *A Correspondence Theory approach*

The problems just noted—(1) the need for a rule to extend the Gen set, instead of relying on the insertion of the unmarked phoneme, and (2) the incorrect choice of [sij.rɪŋ] as the surface manifestation of *seeing*—can be dealt with rather differently in McCarthy and Prince's 1995 Correspondence Theory (COT). COT drops the inert prosodic position analysis of epenthesis in Prince and Smolensky (1993), and simply allows Input and Output to diverge. A relation between elements of I(nput) and O(utput), is established and the relative deviation of this relation from the conceptual ideal of identity is measured by I/O constraints, such as MaxIO. The guiding idea behind Correspondence Theory is that the phenomenon of reduplication provides the model for all of phonology, with the correspondence between Base and Reduplicant serving as the model for the I/O relation. The question that must asked at this point is how this new approach will ensure that *r* appears in the output instead of some other 'default consonant', say *t*. One obvious answer is to admit 'positional defaults'. This answer was in effect already available in Prince and Smolensky (1993), because that theory distinguished Fill violations in the syllable peak from those in syllable margins. Since phonological theory distinguishes Onsets from Codas, nothing prevents us from saying that *r* is the default consonant in Codas, and that *t* is the default Onset. What is interesting about the cases under discussion is that the inserted *r* is ambisyllabic, and thus counts as both Onset and Coda. The constraint rankings in (18) will select the correct candidate from the set in (16).

(18) Coda-Cond >> MaxIO(C), Align-Left >> Final-C >> Dep(C) >> *Coda/*t*
    >> *Coda/*r*, *Ons/*r*

MaxIO in (18) is the COT analogue of Parse (in its role as maintainer of underlying segments, not in its role as enforcer of the Strict Layer Hypothesis of Selkirk, 1995). Dep is the COT counterpart of Fill. The constraints *Coda/*t* and *Coda/*r* in (18) belong to a family of constraints, modelled on Prince and Smolensky (1993) syllable structure constraints (see, however, Clements, Chapter 9 above [Editor]). Their role here is to give a ranking of undesirable segments in Codas. Since MaxIO(C) outranks this entire family, the family's effect is limited to inserted elements. Moreover, since Final-C outranks Dep(C), we will

may be a descriptive success, but it is an explanatory failure. The derivations are dubious, because many r's are inserted at Word level only to be deleted phrasally in what Pullum 1976 calls the "Duke of York gambit"' (p. 182). The rejected analysis, however, is in all relevant respects indistinguishable from McCarthy's account. Specifically, McCarthy's proposed 'phonological rule' inserts *r*s that are then excluded from the output by the OT constraints that apply subsequently. For some additional discussion, see below.

be effectively limited to inserting ambisyllabic consonants. According to Prince and Smolensky 1993 the Onset hierarchy is universal and has the form in (19).

(19) *Ons/*a* >> . . . >> *Ons/*y* >> . . . .. >> *Ons/*r* >> . . . .. >> *Ons/*t*

The ranking in (19) accords with the idea that *t* is the least objectionable epenthetic onset. But then, in order to ensure that it is *r* that is inserted in the cases under discussion, we must make certain of two things. First, we must make sure that *r* is the least objectionable coda; i.e. *Coda/*r* must be dominated by all other *Coda/X constraints. Second, *Coda/*t* must dominate *Ons/*r* so that it is better to have an Onset containing (part of) *r* than a Coda containing (part of) *t*. Moreover, in order for these constraints to do their work properly, they must be interpreted as 'sloppy'. That is, the *Coda/X constraints do not care if the segment in question is also linked to an Onset position, i.e. they do not care if the consonant is ambisyllabic. By contrast, Coda-Cond does care about sloppiness. In fact, Coda-Cond is just the strict version of *Coda/*r*. However, it is suspicious to require the two such closely related constraints in (20).

(20) Coda-Cond: No *r* wholly within a Coda
       *Coda/r: No (part of) *r* within a Coda

And it is even more suspicious that the two almost identical constraints must be ranked so far apart, as in (18).[11] An additional problem is posed by the facts of schwa epenthesis before coda liquids, which interact crucially with *r*-deletion. These facts, which were covered in McCarthy (1991) but omitted in McCarthy's (1993) OT analysis, are extremely important in evaluating the adequacy of the OT analysis. In rule-based terminology these two processes apply in counterbleeding order, with schwa epenthesis preceding *r*-deletion. It is clear that the constraints implementing schwa epenthesis must be ranked fairly high, because the output violates Final-C, whereas simple failure to maintain *r* in the output would not, as shown in (21).

(21)

fear / _ C	Coda-Cond	Final C	MaxIO(C)
a. [fijr]	*!	✓	✓
☞ b. [fij]	✓	✓	*
c. [fijər]	*!	✓	✓
d. [fijə]	✓	*!	*

[11] This is especially troubling in connection with theories of constraint learning such as Tesar and Smolensky (1993), because every positive example for moving Coda-Cond up in the rankings will also be motivation to move *Coda/*r* up in the ranking. Because of this learning problem, we predict this ranking of constraints to be unstable; thus any consonant other than *r* would be a better choice as the default Coda.

Both (21b) *[fij] and (21d) [fijə] violate MaxIO, because both fail to preserve *r* in the output. Moreover, [fijə] (21d) is worse than *[fij] (21b) in two additional ways. First, in epenthesizing schwa, [fijə] (21d) also violates Dep(V), which states that every vowel in the output should have an input correspondent (similar to the role formerly played by Fill). Second, [fijə] violates Final-C, which *[fij] (21b) does not by virtue of its final [j].

We begin the discussion of these problems by examining schwa epenthesis before *l*, for there is no *l*-deletion (in this dialect) to complicate matters there. The constraint in (22) will do the appropriate work with *l*.

(22) *j{rl}. Do not end a syllable with j + liquid.

Now we must rank MaxIO(C) above Dep(V), so that adding vowels is better than eliminating consonants. Consider the candidates for *feel* in (23).

(23)

feel	*j{rl}.	Coda-Cond	Final-C	MaxIO(C)	Dep(V)
a. [fijl]	*!	√	√	√	√
b. [fij]	√	√	√	*!	√
☞ c. [fijəl]	√	√	√	√	*
d. [fijlə]	√	√	*!	√	*

The constraint ranking in (23) does the correct work: (23c) [fijəl] is chosen over (23d) [fijlə] by virtue of Final-C, which requires that words end with consonants. This ranking, however, will not do the correct work with *r* as shown in (24).

(24)

fear	*j{rl}.	Coda-Cond	Final-C	MaxIO(C)	Dep(V)
a. [fijr]	*!	*	√	√	√
☞ b. [fij]	√	√	√	*	√
c. [fijər]	√	*!	√	√	*
d. [fijə]	√	√	*!	*	*
e. [fijrə]	√	√	*!	*	*

Here the ranked constraints choose [fij] (24b) as the best candidate. It is obvious that a more specific constraint must be at work, which identifies the sequence /j + liquid/ in the input and forces epenthesis directly. But even if we can rule out [fij] (24b) by forcing epenthesis, we must get the epenthetic vowel in the right place. For [fijəl] in (23c) we could appeal to Final-C or to

Align(Stem, R, PrWd, R) to force epenthesis inside the stem (and thus violate Stem Contiguity). But with (24d) [fijə] there is no surface *r* to appeal to, so Final C, Align-Right, and Contiguity are all useless in this regard. In fact, Stem Contiguity would pick [fijrə] (24e) as the best candidate, for it maintains Stem Contiguity while preserving all the underlying elements of the stem, thereby satisfying MaxIO. Since we see no principled way to solve this problem, let us just formulate a brute-force I/O constraint, as in (25).

(25) /j{rl}/ ⇒ [jə] For input /j + liquid/, have at least [jə] in the output.

Constraint (25) yields the correct results in this case, as shown in (26).

(26)

fear	/j{rl}/ ⇒ [jə]	Coda-Cond
a. [fijr]	*!	*
b. [fij]	*!	√
c. [fijər]	√	*!
☞ d. [fijə]	√	√
e. [fijrə]	*!	√

However, constraint (25) as formulated has too much power, for it will also force epenthesis where it is not needed. Where *l* or *r* can be ambisyllabic (or wholly in the following onset), as in *velum* and *Byron*, the constraint incorrectly selects [vijələm] and [bajərən], rather than the correct schwa-less forms [vijləm] and [bajrən]. But it seems that whatever constraint one proposes to prevent the insertion of schwa in such cases—for example a constraint mandating [r,l] in the Onset of the syllable following coda [j,w]—the constraint must be ranked above (25) and will therefore choose *[fij.rə] (26e) as the winning candidate for *fear*. In sum, our attempts to formulate an OT account of the facts of the Eastern New England *r* and related matters have not produced encouraging results. While these failures do not exclude the possibility that an adequate OT solution may yet be discovered, the burden of proof is clearly on proponents of OT. We turn now to an alternative account based on rules and principles.

4. AN ACCOUNT BASED ON RULES AND PRINCIPLES

4.1 r-*deletion*.

It will be recalled that r-deletion occurs before consonants and at the end of clauses, i.e. in syllable coda. This is expressed more formally in rule (27).

(27)

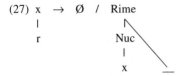

4.2. Schwa epenthesis

As illustrated in (4) and (5) above in the dialect under discussion here, McCarthy's 'monitored speech', schwa is epenthesized before a rhyme-final liquid when preceded by a diphthong ending in a [+high] vowel or glide. Rule (28) provides a formal account of this.

(28)

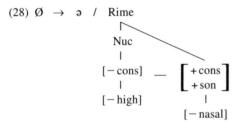

It was noted above that schwa is inserted also word-internally before level II suffixes beginning with a vowel. If we assume that (28) is a level II (noncyclic) rule and that it is ordered before any rules of resyllabification, rule (28) will insert schwas correctly.[12]

4.3 *r*-insertion

We quoted McCarthy's observation (1993: 178) that the 'intrusive' *r* in '*Wanda*[*r*] *arrived*' and the 'linking' *r* in '*Homer arrived*' are phonetically identical but that they differ from the onset *r* in '*Wanda returned*'. If we assume that there is no resyllabification across word boundaries, this difference in quality of the *r* is then totally context-determined: one kind of *r* appears in coda, another *r* appears in onset. Whatever the phonetic difference—and its nature remains to be elucidated by phonetic research—there is one *r* in the onset and another in the coda. Since the inserted 'intrusive' *r* is phonetically identical with the 'linking' *r* in the coda of *Homer* we formulate

---

[12] McCarthy (1991: 198) cites forms such as *goal of* and *feel it* and the participles *feeling* and *fearing* as having no inserted schwa in his more casual speech. In order to account for these forms it would be necessary to assume that resyllabification is ordered before schwa insertion, (29). McCarthy gives no information about the pronunciation of phrases like *feel ill* and *feel sick* in his dialect. If there is insertion only in *feel sick*, but not in 'feel ill' nothing further needs to be added. If—as in the speech of several of our informal consultants—there is insertion in both phrases, it will be necessary to posit that a clitic (such as *of* or *it*) is incorporated into the word on its left.

the rule of *r*-insertion (29) so that it inserts *r* into syllable coda. However, unlike schwa epenthesis, *r*-insertion requires the presence of a following vowel, which may be in the same word (*draw*[*r*]*ing*) or may be in the next word (*Wanda*[*r*] *arrived*). The *r*-insertion rule must therefore also be part of the phrase-level rule block, i.e. Level III. Moreover, as noted by McCarthy, 'intrusive *r* is found only at the end of lexical words. The lexical word with intrusive *r* may itself be contained inside a larger word by virtue of a Level II suffix (*drawring*, *withdrawral*) but the consistent generalization is that intrusive r is limited to lexical-word final position' (1993: 176). This morphological restriction can be captured instead by restricting the operation of (29) to derived environments, and by restricting (29) to Level II and subsequent (noncyclic) levels of the phonology. (See Kiparsky, 1993 for the separation of the derived environment condition from the lexical/cyclic conditions.)

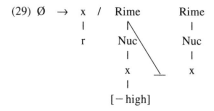

(29) Ø → x / Rime ... Rime
with r, Nuc, Nuc, x, x, [−high]

We recall that the context in which *r*-deletion (27) occurs is the syllable coda. *r*-insertion also occurs in syllable coda, but only if additional conditions are satisfied. An immediate consequence of this fact is that if *r*-deletion is ordered after *r*-insertion, all effects of *r*-insertion will be eliminated in the output. This, therefore, is not a viable ordering of the rules. Unfortunately, the reverse order—i.e. *r*-deletion preceding *r*-insertion—results in derivations where the effects of *r*-deletion are repaired by *r*-insertion. This type of rule interaction has been termed by Pullum 'the Duke of York gambit' and objections to it have been raised on the grounds that the gambit subverts the essential difference between rules, which reflect idiosyncratic facts of a language, and repairs, which are consequences of general structural principles obeyed by the language.

There is, however, yet a third solution. Rules precisely of this kind were studied by Kiparsky (1973) in a paper that is in our opinion among the most important contributions to phonology. Kiparsky proposed that, when rules of the kind just described arise in a language, they are subject to a special convention on their application. The special importance of Kiparsky's proposals derives from the fact that his conventions on rule application must—obviously—not be part of the phonology of any language, but are part of UG, part of the principles that determine what may or may not arise in a particular language. Specifically, Kiparsky's principle tells us that if, by some quirk of circumstance, a language develops two rules that are formally similar in precisely the same way as *r*-insertion and *r*-deletion, then *r*-insertion must be ordered before *r*-deletion and, moreover, that the two rules are disjunctively ordered so that strings of the form of the output of the *r*-insertion rule may not be subject to *r*-deletion. We have reproduced Kiparsky's formulation in (30).

(30) Two adjacent rules of the form

A → B / P ___ Q

C → D / R ___ S

are disjunctively ordered if and only if:

(a) the set of strings that fits PAQ is a subset of the set of strings that fit RCS;

(b) the structural changes of the two rules are either identical or incompatible.

Kiparsky explains that 'incompatible' changes have opposite effects, such as, assigning the feature [+F] and [−F], or, as in the case under discussion here, inserting a segment and deleting it. When rules satisfying these conditions are found in a language, they are ordered so that the more complex one—(29) in our case—precedes the less complex one—here (27). The rules, moreover, must apply disjunctively, i.e. both rules may never apply to the same string. This has usually been interpreted to mean that if a string is subject to rule (29) it is not also subject to rule (27). In the examples *draw[r]ing* and *Wanda[r] arrived* this gives the correct result: since the *r*s here are inserted by rule (29), they are not subject to deletion by rule (27). It has been pointed out to us by Francois Dell (p.c.) that prior application of (29) is not a necessary condition for blocking the application of (27). For instance, *r*-insertion does not apply to the examples in (31), yet they are not subject to *r*-deletion.

(31) a. Lear is . . .

b. the rear is . . .

c. fire away [fajərəwej]

d. layering empowering

e. fear Ann [fijər æn]

To account for these examples we need to generalize the condition on disjunctivity as given in (30).[13] Any two rules meeting the Elsewhere Condition prerequisites are subject to the following constraint: the less complex rule may not apply to a string that has the form of the output of the more

---

[13] McCarthy devotes considerable attention to *r*-insertion after function words (prepositions, pronominal clitics, auxiliary verbs). He shows that *r*-insertion does not occur if the function word is part of the same constituent as the following word; e.g. no insertion occurs in *I'm gonna eat* or in *Didja eat.* By contrast, when the function word is not part of the same constituent as the next word, *r*-insertion occurs; e.g. *I said I was gonna[r] and I did* or *we oughta[r] if we're asked* (McCarthy 1993: 176). This is explained if we assume that in *I'm gonna eat* and *Didja eat?* the cliticized function word is morphologically (and phonologically) part of the following word. The space separating the words in the conventional orthography is thus misleading. Since *r*-insertion (31) takes place after [−high] vowels only if they come at the end of a constituent that is a lexical category or phrase, cliticization of the function word to the following word prevents *r*-insertion. In cases such as *We oughta[r] if we're asked*, the function word cannot cliticize across the clause boundary, and consequently cliticizes to the preceding word. Then, because the function word is at the end of a constituent, *r*-insertion (31) will apply.

complex rule. That is, the less complex rule is blocked if the current representation is compatible with the structural change of the more complex rule. Since application of the more complex rule will obviously generate such strings, the proposed generalization subsumes under it all previously noted cases.

One might ask at this point why there are dialects with rules with 'incompatible' structural changes of the kind illustrated above, i.e. dialects where one rule inserts an element into the string which then is deleted by another rule. These are typical instances where the undesirable 'Duke of York gambit' might arise, were it not for the fact that such rules are subject to the Elsewhere Condition. We believe that some light on the reason for the existence of such pairs of rules is shed by the phenomenon of hypercorrection.

Hypercorrection typically arises when a phonetic contrast is lost by a group of speakers who are in contact with speakers in whose speech the contrast is maintained. Once the speakers of the innovative dialect become aware of the fact that they are pronouncing certain words differently from many of the individuals with whom they are in contact, it is not uncommon for the former to take corrective steps to eliminate the differentiating trait. The corrective rule, however, often fails to restore the status quo ante and produces instead hypercorrection.

It is well known that the deletion of coda *r* is relatively widespread among English dialects and historically prior to *r*-insertion. These facts fit well with the suggestion that *r*-insertion is a corrective rule of the type sketched above. Speakers notice that coda *r*s are missing in their utterances and attempt to correct this by *r*-insertion in some intervocalic contexts. Once the *r*-insertion rule is added, however, the Elsewhere Condition orders it with respect to *r*-deletion, whose domain of application is somewhat more limited in dialects with *r*-insertion than it is in dialects without this rule. (For a discussion of such dialects, see Sledd 1966; Harris 1994: ch. V). This naturally leads to another question: why is the rule of *r*-insertion as complicated as it is? That is, why isn't the rule formulated to simply insert *r* everywhere? The answer is again found in the operation of the Elsewhere Condition. If the rule of *r*-insertion is more general than the rule of *r*-deletion, then by the Elsewhere Condition that general *r*-insertion rule must follow the *r*-deletion rule, and be disjunctive with it. Because *r*-deletion deletes all coda *r*s the hypothetical general *r*-insertion rule would then be blocked from creating any coda *r*s. Thus, the Elsewhere Condition has an intimate relation with hypercorrection by rule addition: the added rule must be more specific than the original rule.

A reviewer has also asked whether the reinterpretation of the Elsewhere Condition does not amount to a trans-derivational constraint. The reinterpretation of the Elsewhere Condition is not a trans-derivational constraint because no access to previous or subsequent representations in the derivation (or in other derivations) is necessary. Rather, the application of a rule to the current representation is blocked in one particular circumstance—if the form is compatible with the structural description or change of a more specific rule. Thus, what is required is a limited access to the formal encodings of other rules, not to other representations or derivations. Of course, what this suggests is that phonological rules are organized in the grammar partially by their formal properties. In other words, the Elsewhere Condition is really a universal principle of phonological grammar organization. A system of phonological rules is not mentally encoded simply as a blind list; rather, rules with similar function and properly nested environments are bound together in the grammar. Thus, the reinterpreted Elsewhere Condition provides intrinsic ordering and structure to phonological rules and derivations.

In sum, the three ordered rules (28), (29), and (27), supplemented by the revised version of Kiparsky's Elsewhere principle, not only capture the facts of the Eastern Massachusetts dialect but also allow us also to gain some insight into the evolution of these dialectal phenomena, as well as into the reasons for the rather special interaction among the three rules. By contrast, as discussed in section 2, an OT account of these data encounters a number of non-trivial difficulties, and it remains to be shown that it is possible to construct an OT account for these data that not only grinds out the facts but also explains the reason for their existence.[14]

ACKNOWLEDGEMENTS

We would very much like to thank François Dell, Iggy Roca, and all of the participants at the Essex Workshop on Derivations and Constraints in Phonology. We would also like to thank the reviewers (especially John Harris) for their insightful and provocative comments. Though we would like to discuss the various possible questions and alternatives that they raise, time and space considerations preclude doing so here. Morris Halle gratefully acknowledges the support of the Humanities Research Board of the British Academy for travel expenses to attend the workshop. William Idsardi gratefully acknowledges the support of the University of Delaware Research Foundation.

REFERENCES

Burzio, L. (1995). 'The rise of Optimality Theory', *GLOT International*, **1**(6).
Chomsky, N., and Halle, M. (1968). *The Sound Pattern of English*. New York: Harper & Row.
Halle, M. (1996), 'Comments on Luigi Burzio's "The rise of Optimality Theory"', GLOT International, **1**(9/10): 27–8.

[14] For some recent discussion of explanatory adequacy in phonology, see Halle (1996).

Harris, J. (1994). *English Sound Structure*. Oxford: Blackwell.
Hayes, B. (1986). 'Inalterability in CV phonology', *Language* 62: 321–51.
Jones, D. (1950). *The Pronunciation of English*. Cambridge: Cambridge University Press.
Kiparsky, P. (1973). '"Elsewhere" in phonology', in S. Anderson and P. Kiparsky (eds.), *A Festschrift for Morris Halle*. New York: Holt, Rinehart & Winston, 93–106.
—— (1993). 'Blocking in nonderived environments', in S. Hargus and E. Kaisse (eds.), *Studies in Lexical Phonology*. New York: Academic Press, 277–314.
LaCharité, D., and Paradis, C. (1993). 'Introduction: The emergence of constraints in Generative Phonology and a comparison of three current constraint-based models', *Canadian Journal of Linguistics* 38: 127–53.
McCarthy, J. (1991). 'Synchronic rule inversion', *Proceedings of the Annual Meeting of the Berkeley Linguistics Society*, 17: 192–207.
—— (1993). 'A case of surface constraint violation', *Canadian Journal of Linguistics* 38: 169–95.
——— (1994). 'The phonetics and phonology of Semitic pharyngeals', in P. Keating, (ed.), *Phonological Structure and Phonetic Form: Papers in Laboratory Phonology iii*. Cambridge: Cambridge University Press, 191–233.
—— and Prince, A. (1986). 'Prosodic Morphology'. MS, University of Massachusetts and Brandeis University.
—— —— (1993a). 'Prosodic Morphology I: Constraint Interaction'. MS, University of Massachusetts and Rutgers University.
—— —— (1993b). 'Generalized alignment', in G. Booij and J. van Marle (eds.), *Yearbook of Morphology 1993*. Dordrecht: Kluwer. 79–153.
—— —— (1995). 'Faithfulness and Reduplicative Identity'. MS, University of Massachusetts and Rutgers University.
Olive, J., Greenwood, A., and Coleman, J. (1993). *Acoustics of American English Speech*. New York: Springer.
Prince, A., and Smolensky, P. (1993). 'Optimality Theory: Constraint Interaction in Generative Grammar'. MS, Rutgers University and University of Colorado.
Pullum, G. (1976). 'The Duke of York gambit', *Journal of Linguistics* 12: 83–102.
Schein, B., and Steriade, D. (1986). 'On geminates', *Linguistic Inquiry* 17: 691–744.
Selkirk, E. (1995). 'The prosodic structure of function words', in J. N. Beckman, L. W. Dickey, and S. Urbanczyk (ed.), *Papers in Optimality Theory* (University of Massachusetts Occasional Papers in Linguistics 18). Amherst, GLSA, 439–70.
Sledd, J. (1966). 'Breaking, umlaut and the Southern drawl', *Language* 42: 18–47.
Smolensky, P. (1995). 'On the explanatory adequacy of Optimality Theory'. Talk presented at the conference on Current Trends in Phonology, Abbaye de Royaumont, France, June 1995.
Tesar, B., and Smolensky, P. (1993). 'The Learnability of Optimality Theory: An Algorithm and Some Basic Complexity Results'. MS, Johns Hopkins University.
Wells, J. (1982). *Accents of English*. (3 vols). Cambridge: Cambridge University Press.

11

Underlying Representations in Optimality Theory

MICHAEL HAMMOND

1. INTRODUCTION

There are alternations in English like *column* [káləm]–*columnar* [kəlʌ́mnər] and *damn* [dǽm]–*damnation* [dæ̀mnéʃən], yet there are no similar alternations involving non-coronal obstruents, e.g. [brʌ́k]-[brʌ́kpər] or [brʌ́k]-[brʌ̀kpéʃən]. In this chapter I substantiate this generalization and argue that it cannot be treated in a derivational theory and can only be treated in a constraint-based theory where morphemes are themselves constraints.

2. SOME FACTS FROM ENGLISH

As a first approximation, word-final syllables of English can be closed by at most a single consonant if the vowel is tense or diphthongal, and at most two consonants if the vowel is lax.

(1) | *Tense/diphthong* | | *Lax* | |
|---|---|---|---|
| teak | [tik] | think | [θɪŋk] |
| hoop | [hup] | stump | [stʌmp] |
| nape | [nep] | help | [hɛlp] |
| soak | [sok] | ramp | [ræmp] |
| roof | [ruf] | lymph | [lɪmf] |
| strike | [strajk] | milk | [mɪlk] |

If the vowel is lax and there are two consonants, those consonants must obey the sonority hierarchy.[1] Legal sequences of consonants after a lax vowel are given in (2) below.[2]

---

[1] It would probably be better to simply say that the vowels of English divide into the two classes indicated. Several vowels do not exhibit the behaviour one would expect based on other diagnostics for tense/lax; e.g. the vowels [ɔ] and [a] can occur word-finally in stress position like other tense vowels, e.g. *paw* and *spa*, but can precede two consonants like lax vowels, e.g. *pork* and *park*. On the other hand, the vowel [ʊ] cannot occur word-finally in stressed position but can appear only before a single word-final consonant, e.g. *good*.

[2] The liquids diverge in sonority, with [r] being more sonorous than [l]. This is shown in examples like *Carl* [karl].

(2) nasal + obstruent   ramp   [ræmp]
    liquid + obstruent   help   [hɛlp]
    liquid + nasal   helm   [hɛlm]

If we characterize tense vowels as occupying two (moraic) positions, and assume coda consonants are moraic, then word-final English rhymes can be characterized as maximally trimoraic.

However, final syllables can be augmented with an unbounded number of coronal obstruents.[3] These coronals can be inflectional (3a), derivational (3b), or part of the same morpheme (3c), and can violate the sonority hierarchy in that they can follow other obstruents.

(3) a. inflectional   hopes   [hops]   thinks   [θɪŋks]
                           liked   [lajkt]   helped   [hɛlpt]
    b. derivational   ninth   [najnθ]   twelfth   [twɛlfθ]
    c. tautomorphemic   round   [rawnd]   text   [tɛkst]
                           lounge [lawndʒ]   ax   [æks]

A form like *texts* [tɛksts] shows at least three appended coronal consonants, and there appears to be no upper bound.

A number of puzzles face any formalization of this generalization in terms of syllable structure. For example, it is not at all clear how to express the fact that the sonority hierarchy seems to not apply to the adjoined coronals. For our purposes, it is sufficient to note that any number of coronal obstruents can be adjoined to any licit word-final sequence of consonants. The schema in (4) below expresses the fact that final syllables may contain up to three moras and be adjoined by an unbounded number of coronal obstruents. (Unexpressed is the fact that the sonority hierarchy applies only to the moraic material.)

(4) Word-final syllables

$$\mu\mu\mu + \begin{bmatrix} COR \\ -\text{son} \end{bmatrix}_0$$

Evidence in support of this generalization comes from various underlying sequences that do not meet it and are resolved in various ways.[4] However, a striking fact about all of these cases is that the offending word-final consonant is always either a coronal or a sonorant.

First, there are words that end in a superficial syllabic liquid. A number of these can be argued to have underlying representations with a nonsyllabic liquid. One class of cases involves forms with stressed antepenults, and heavy penults.

[3] These facts are discussed by Halle and Vergnaud (1978). An anonymous reviewer maintains that these facts were discussed in earlier work by Fudge, but I have been unable to track this reference down.
[4] The cases that follow are drawn from discussions by Chomsky and Halle (1968), Selkirk (1982), and Borowsky (1986).

(5) cylinder   [síləndɽ]
    collinder   [kál/əndɽ]
    carpenter   [kárpəntɽ]

SPE (Chomsky and Halle 1968) argues that such forms actually contain only two vowels in underlying representation, e.g. /silindr/. If one makes this assumption, one can account for how stress can surface on the antepenult, to the left of a superficially heavy penult (as is typical of English monomorphemic nouns).

A similar argument can be made from cases, as in (6), where an underlying final syllabic [ɽ] or [ḷ] corresponds to a nonsyllabic liquid when in a derived prevocalic context.[5]

(6)

hinder	[híndɽ]	hindrance	[híndrəns]
carpenter	[kárpəntɽ]	carpentry	[kárpəntri]
cylinder	[síləndɽ]	cylindrical	[səlíndrəkḷ]
remember	[rəmémbɽ]	remembrance	[rəmémbrəns]
disaster	[dəzǽstɽ]	disastrous	[dəzǽstrəs]
burgle	[bɽ́gḷ]	burglary	[bɽ́gləri]
twinkle	[twíŋkḷ]	twinkling$_N$	[twíŋklɪŋ]

Another case that can be argued to be an unsyllabifiable sequence resolved on the surface involves words with a final <y> [i] and aberrant stress much like in (5). Some of these are exactly like the forms in (5), and some exhibit different regularities.

(7) a.   galaxy   [gǽləksi]
        industry   [índəstri]
        modesty   [mádəsti]
   b.   Abernathy [ǽbɽnæ̀θi]
        melancholy [mélənkàli]
        necromancy [nékrəmæ̀nsi]

The forms in (7a) behave just like those in (5), and are treated by supposing that the final [i] is actually a glide (not syllabic) in underlying representation. Forms like *Ábernàthy* in (7b) exhibit an unusual stress pattern that can also be treated this way. A primary can occur to the left of a secondary typically only if the secondary stress is word-final, e.g. *Álcatràz, ánecdòte*. This generalization can be extended to forms like *Ábernàthy* if we make the assumption that the final [i] is underlyingly a glide.[6]

---

[5] Chomsky and Halle also cite forms like *schism, schismatic* here. I will return to these below.

[6] Iggy Roca reminds me that this is all contingent on how one represents a glide. If glides are simply vowels in non-nuclear positions, then this account falls apart. (There is, of course, no problem if glides are featurally distinct from vowels, as in SPE.) I propose a three-way moraic distinction in underlying/input representations. Glides, like [j], are nonmoraic; short/lax vowels, like [ɪ], are monomoraic; long/tense vowels, like [i], are bimoraic (cf. Hayes 1989).

There are other cases, however, where a final consonant is not salvaged by syllabifying it. Examples include the following.

(8) hymn   [hím]   hymnal   [hímnəl]
    damn   [dǽm]   damnation   [dǽmnéʃən]
    column   [káləm]   columnar   [kəlÁmnər]

Here an [n] is deleted when it cannot be adjoined to the preceding syllable.

In all the cases so far, particular consonants undergo specific changes (deletion or syllabification); there are also cases where the same consonant can be salvaged in different ways. There are two classes of cases involving [g] followed by a nasal.

(9) a. paradigm   [pǽrədàjm]   paradigmatic   [pæ̀rədɪgmǽtɪk]
       phlegm   [flɛ́m]   phlegmatic   [flɛ̀gmǽtɪk]
       syntagm   [síntæ̀m]   syntagmatic   [sìntæ̀gmǽtɪk]
    b. sign   [sájn]   signature   [sígnətʃr̩]
       malign   [m̩əlájn]   malignant   [məlígnənt]

These differ from the cases above in two regards. First, it is the nonfinal consonant that is deleted here. Second, the cases in (9a) involve a final sonorant that is non-coronal.

A somewhat different case was mentioned in note 5 above, exemplified by forms like *schism* or *Maoism*. Like the cases in (9a) these involve [m], but they differ in that they are not preceded by /g/ and are resolved by syllabifying the /m/, rather than by deleting the preceding consonant.

To summarize to this point, we have seen that, while word-final English syllables are in general limited to three moras and governed by the sonority hierarchy, these syllables can be augmented in two ways. First, these syllables can be followed by an unbounded number of coronal obstruents that can surface directly, e.g. *texts*, etc. In addition, there are other forms ending in various sonorant consonants where these consonants also cannot be accommodated by the three-mora limit and the sonority hierarchy, e.g. *cylinder*, *galaxy*, *damn*, *sign*, and *schism*. These latter examples undergo various changes to produce a well-formed output. Grouping both cases together, the relevant consonants are coronal and/or sonorant. This rather surprising generalization is stated as follows.

(10) Coronal/Sonorant Generalization (CSG)
     Consonants that cannot be included in the three-mora span governed by the sonority hierarchy on the right edge of an English word must be coronal and/or sonorant.

I will argue that Optimality Theory (OT) as it stands cannot accommodate this generalization, and must be altered in a dramatic fashion to do so. In addition, I show that, while a constraint-based theory can be revised to treat (10), a derivational theory has a far more difficult time of it.

3. ANALYSIS: FIRST PASS

The input–output pairings motivated above can all be treated readily in terms of OT. Following Prince and Smolensky (1993), the consonants that can become syllable peaks are treated by ranking the constraints *PEAK/X below PARSE/X. The constraint schema *PEAK/X prevents a consonant from being a syllable peak. The PARSE/X constraint prevents a consonant from being deleted. Deletion is treated by ranking PARSE/X below *PEAK/X.[7]

Thus a form like *carpenter*, where the offending consonant is syllabic on the surface, has at least the following candidate outputs.

(11)

/karpVntr/	*PEAK/n	PARSE	*PEAK/r
☞ [kárpəntr̩]			*
[kárpənt]		*!	

A form like *hymn* gets a different resolution because *PEAK/n is ranked differently.

(12)

/hɪm/	*PEAK/n	PARSE	*PEAK/r
☞ [hɪm]		*	
[hɪmn̩]	*!		

What about /m/? Recall that sometimes /m/ becomes syllabic, as in *schism*, and sometimes a neighbouring consonant deletes, as in *paradigm*. This can be treated by supposing that, while it is in general better to syllabify /m/ than to delete it (PARSE/m >> *PEAK/m), it is better to delete /g/ than to syllabify /m/ (*PEAK/m >> PARSE/g).

(13)

/skɪzm/	PARSE/m	*PEAK/m	PARSE/g
☞ /skɪzm̩/		*	
/skɪz/	*!		

---

[7] This is also readily treated in terms of Correspondence Theory (McCarthy and Prince, 1995) by violating MAX$_{IO}$.

(14)

/flɛgm/	Parse/m	*Peak/m	Parse/g
☞ /flɛm/			*
/flɛg/	*!		
/flɛgm̩/		*!	

An important observation about the data above that does *not* emerge from these constraints and this ranking is the Coronal/Sonorant Generalization, or CSG, in (10): in all these cases, where a consonant occurs on the right edge of a word in English and is not syllabifiable, the relevant consonant is coronal and/or sonorant. The critical cases are repeated below.

(15) y galaxy
     r cylinder
     l burgle
     n damn
     m phlegm/schism

Before considering the import of this observation, let us consider another class of segments that occurs underlyingly yet is unsyllabifiable on the surface.

4. Some More Facts

There are sequences of nasal followed by a voiced non-coronal stop (16a,b).

(16) a. iamb   [ájæ̀m]   iambic   [àjǽmbɪk]
        bomb   [bám]   bombard   [bàmbárd]
        crumb   [krʌ́m]   crumble   [krʌ́mbl̩]
     b. long   [lɔ́ŋ]   longer   [lɔ́ŋgɾ]
        strong [strɔ́ŋ]   stronger [strɔ́ŋgɾ]
     but:
     c. hand   [hǽnd]   handy   [hǽndi]
        fiend   [fínd]   fiendish [fíndɪʃ]
        avenge [əvɛ́nd͡ʒ]   avenger   [əvɛ́nd͡ʒɾ]
        strange [strénd͡ʒ]   stranger [strénd͡ʒɾ]

This last group is not governed by the CSG, as these sequences are in principle directly syllabifiable since they do not violate the sonority hierarchy or exceed the moraic limits of the final syllable. Hence the nonparsing of the [b] or [g] in (16a,b) must have some other source.

Confirmation of this distinction comes from a comparison of the vowels that can precede nasal + stop sequences. When the nasal + stop sequence is coronal, then we get both tense and lax vowels, as expected. However, when the sequence is terminated by a voiced labial or dorsal, then the preceding vowel must be one of the vowels that otherwise allow two following consonants on the surface.

(17) iamb   [ájæ̀m]   cf. bank   [bǽŋk]
     bomb   [bám]   cf bark   [bárk]
     crumb   [krʌ́m]   cf. bunk   [bʌ́ŋk]
     long   [lɔ́ŋ]   cf. honk   [hɔ́ŋk]

If we were to treat the nonparsing of /b/ and /g/ in (16a,b) on a par with the nonparsing of consonants from the previous section, we would miss several related facts. First, the cases in (16a,b) would violate the CSG. Second, the cases in (16a,b) do not violate the sonority hierarchy. Third, they never exceed the trimoraic maximum. These cases can be treated straightforwardly, however, if we assume that beyond the requirements already discussed, there is a minimum sonority distance restriction on codas. While a nasal followed by a voiceless stop satisfies both the sonority hierarchy and minimal sonority distance, a nasal followed by a voiced stop does not satisfy minimal sonority distance.

Support for an approach built on minimum sonority distance comes from the observation that onset sequences are subject to a similar sonority distance restriction involving voicing. While stop + liquid clusters involving voiced and voiceless clusters are well-formed in English, fricative + liquid clusters are not. Fricative + liquid clusters involving voiced fricatives are clearly marginal.

(18) a. $\begin{bmatrix} \text{voiceless} \\ \text{fricative} \end{bmatrix}$ + liquid   flip, frill, throw, slip, shrink, etc.

    b. $\begin{bmatrix} \text{voiced} \\ \text{fricative} \end{bmatrix}$ + liquid   Vladimir, zloty

We therefore assume a constraint on sonority distance in codas that rules out nasals followed by voiced stops.[8]

(19) Sonority distance in codas
    The sequence nasal + [voiced stop] is too similar in sonority for codas.

If the relevant constraint is placed above PARSE/g and PARSE/b, then the right results are achieved.

Notice that, as formulated, (19) would also seem to exclude sequences involving voiced coronal stops in codas. Since such sequences do surface, e.g. (16c), we assume that (19), like the sonority hierarchy generally, does not apply to adjoined coronal consonants.[9]

---

[8] There should surely be a fleshed out theory of sonority distance, but doing so would take us far afield. See Hammond (in prep.)

[9] As with the restriction of the sonority hierarchy to the three-mora span, I have no theoretical motivation for this observation.

To summarize thus far, English words must end in one of the following three ways. First, words may end in syllabifiable maximally trimoraic sequences which may be followed by some string of (syllabifiable) coronal obstruents. Second, words may end in syllabifiable maximally trimoraic sequences followed by unsyllabifiable coronals and/or sonorants (which are either subject to nonparsing or surface as syllabic). Third, words may end in sequences of V + N + [voiced stop], where if the voiced stop isn't coronal, it is subject to nonparsing.

We have seen that it is a straightforward matter to treat the resolution of these three situations. What is difficult is to account for why only these three cases arise. The problem is perhaps best seen with a schematic example. Imagine an English root /brʌkp/. In isolation, the final /p/ would be subject to nonparsing: [brʌk]. However, under suffixation, the /p/ would surface before a vowel-initial suffix: /brʌkp/+ic would surface as: [brʌkpɪk]. No such alternation exists in English, and no-one has ever offered an explanation for this fact.

5. DERIVATIONAL ACCOUNT 1: MORPHEME STRUCTURE CONDITIONS

The simplest account of the CSG would be a morpheme structure condition (Chomsky and Halle 1968; Stanley 1967) that simply excluded morphemes like /brʌkp/ from underlying representations.[10] The problem with this account is that it is insufficiently general. I will cite evidence below that shows that it is not morphemes of this shape that are excluded, but any *combination* of morphemes of this shape.

English has a number of affixes which are composed of a single consonant (20). Strikingly, all such affixes are coronals.

(20)

Plural	books	[bʊks]	bugs	[bʌgz]	bushes	[bʊʃɨz]
Genitive	Luke's	[luks]	Bob's	[babz]	Mitch's	[mɪtʃɨz]
Past	looked	[lʊkt]	begged	[bɛgd]	fitted	[fɪtɨd]
Participle	shown	[ʃon]			written	[rɪtən̩]
Ordinalizer	fifth	[fɪfθ]				
Nominalizer	width	[wɪtθ]				
Nominalizer	galaxy	[gæləksi]				

---

[10] As one anonymous reviewer notes, one might contemplate allowing morpheme structure conditions in OT. The current argument would also apply to such a hybrid theory.

This limitation on the identity of monosyllabic affixes follows if the CSG governs not just single morphemes but all combinations of morphemes. Any coronal or sonorant consonant can be an affix, because whatever stem such an affix will combine with will always result in a form satisfying this generalized CSG. A morpheme structure condition by its very nature could not generalize to sequences of morphemes.[11] The only possibility under such an account would be to posit a separate morpheme structure condition which simply excludes non-coronal or non-sonorant single consonant affixes. Hence, we reject a morpheme structure account of the CSG.[12]

6. DERIVATIONAL ACCOUNT 2: LEVELS

Another possible account of the CSG in a derivational framework would be to suppose that there is an earlier pass of syllabification which eliminated any sequence violating the CSG. This account will be rejected as well.

The way it works is as follows. Inputs are drawn from the morphology or lexicon and undergo a first pass of syllabification that leaves any segment violating the CSG unsyllabified at the right edge. Such segments are then deleted. There is then a second pass of syllabification that goes much as suggested in the OT analysis above. Such an account builds on level-ordering much as in classical lexical phonology (Kiparsky 1982).

(21) Input   /brʌkp/   /hɪkmn/
     Level 1   \brʌk\   \hɪmn\
     Level 2   [brʌk]   [hɪm]

This account is quite problematic. First, there is no evidence for this first pass of syllabification. It is completely ad hoc to capture the CSG. If we look a little closer, however, we can see that in fact this account simply doesn't work. Consider the derivations of hypothetical /brʌkp/ versus /brʌkp+ɪk/ compared with *hymn–hymnal*.

(22) Input   /brʌkp/   /brʌkp+ɪk/   /hɪmn/   /hɪmn+əl/
     Level 1   \brʌk\   \brʌkp+ɪk\   \hɪmn\   \hɪmn+əl\
     Level 2   [brʌk]   [brʌkp+ɪk]   [hɪm]   [hɪmn+əl]

[11] One possibility suggested by an anonymous reviewer would be to allow cyclic morpheme structure conditions on a derivational analysis. A serious problem for such an approach is that derivational theories of phonology that manipulate cyclicity as a theoretical descriptor have typically not treated the inflectional phonology of English as being cyclic (see e.g. Halle and Mohanan 1985.) Hence some sort of cyclic application of morpheme structure conditions would fail to treat the inflectional affixes above.

[12] Notice that this account predicts the possibility of sonorant non-coronal affixes. The only candidate for such an affix in English is the objective *-m* in words like *whom, him, them*.

Positing two levels simply doesn't eliminate the possibility of alternations of the first kind. The CSG does not emerge from a two-level account.

7. OT Account 1: Lexicon Optimization

Let us now consider an OT treatment of the CSG. The simplest account would be to try to treat the absence of underlying representations like /brʌkp/ as a consequence of some sort of lexicon optimization (Prince and Smolensky 1993). Lexicon optimization refers to the process whereby the simplest input for a fixed output is chosen. Imagine some output X is known and several possible inputs are compatible with it. Lexicon optimization says that, all else being equal, the input that results in the fewest constraint violations is chosen.[13]

It would seem fairly obvious how to apply this to the /brʌkp/ problem. Given some output [brʌk] and a set of possible input forms including /brʌkp/ and /brʌk/, lexicon optimization would surely insist that /brʌk/ be selected as input. This is because the mapping from /brʌkp/ to [brʌk] would necessitate a violation of Parse, while the mapping from /brʌk/ would not.

There are two problems with this view. First, while the lexicon optimization approach can correctly exclude /brʌkp/ as the underlying representation for a non-alternating form [brʌk], it fails to account for why there could simply be no alternation like [brʌk]–[brʌkpɪk]. That is, lexicon optimization would select /brʌk/ as the input for [brʌk], only in the absence of alternation evidence supporting /brʌkp/ as the input.[14] A second problem with the lexicon optimization view is that it would fail to generalize to the treatment of single-consonant affixes. Since lexicon optimization governs the representation of lexical items, there is no way for it to govern the shape of an affix that would only violate the generalization when considered in combination with other morphemes. I thus dismiss the lexicon optimization approach here.[15]

8. OT Account 2: M-parse

Another possible account of these facts in terms of OT would invoke the M-parse constraint (Prince and Smolensky, 1993). This constraint assigns a violation when a morpheme is not pronounced. This allows for a morpheme

---

[13] Iggy Roca points out to me that lexicon optimization may be circular. If so, this would argue compellingly against any treatment of the CSG in terms of lexicon optimization (cf. however Pulleyblank and Turkel, Chapter 5 above, for a promising development).

[14] See Inkelas (1994).

[15] Note that I am not dismissing lexicon optimization (or something like it) as a reasonable mechanism for other parts of the grammar.

to be unpronounced when an appropriate constraint outranks M-PARSE. For example, haplology can be treated by allowing a constraint excluding adjacent identical material to outrank M-PARSE.

The problem with this approach simply is that M-PARSE does not work. Imagine a consonantal affix /p/. An analysis in terms of M-PARSE would allow such an affix to surface in contexts not violating the CSG and not in other contexts where the CSG would be unviolated, yet such an affix with such a distribution does not occur in English. Hence, an analysis built on M-PARSE is rejected as well.

9. OT ACCOUNT 3: MORPHEME CONSTRAINTS

To capture the CSG, we need constraints that can govern the input and that can limit what can constitute a morpheme in the language. To deal with this, I draw on the theory of morpheme constraints (Hammond 1995; Russell 1995).[16] The basic logic of my proposal is that there are constraints on phonological form that outrank constraints on the form of morphemes. Such constraints thus block form–meaning pairings that would violate them.

Let us assume that the pairing of form and meaning is achieved through constraints. This assumption entails two things. First, there will be constraints like CAT = kæt. Second, if such constraints are to play any role in candidate evaluation, then it must be the case that the input is phonologically unspecified. That is, the input for a form like [kæt] is simply CAT, a semantic or morphosyntactic representation devoid of phonology.

The constraint proposed then entails tableaux like (23).

(23)

CAT	CAT = kæt
☞ kæt	
kæn	*!
bark	*!

This proposal raises a number of important questions, which are addressed in the following section. For now, let us see how it solves the problem of the CSG.

To capture the CSG, we must assume first that there is a constraint or set of constraints that correspond to the CSG, and second, that that constraint or constraint set is top-ranked, so that it outranks any morpheme constraint. Such

---

[16] The terminology here is due to Elzinga (1995). In earlier work I have referred to these by the less perspicuous name of 'parochial constraints'.

a constraint (set) must disallow any labial or dorsal obstruent after another obstruent at the right edge of a form. There are a variety of ways to enforce this restriction, but choosing among them involves issues of segmental representation that are irrelevant here. For explicitness, I will adopt the following: segments specified for a place of articulation are excluded at the right edge if the preceding segment is an obstruent. (This assumes that coronals are unspecified for place.)

(24) CSG
    * [−son] PLACE]

This constraint, or some equivalent, is top-ranked.[17]

Consider now how such an arrangement results in the array of facts we have seen for English. Imagine a surface form [brʌk]. The language learner has several hypotheses for the morphemic identity of such a string: /brʌk/ or /brʌkp/. The former commits the learner to a surface form [brʌk], while the latter entails an unparsed final segment [brʌk(p)]. These differing hypotheses result in the following tableau.

(25)

?	CSG
☞ brʌk	
brʌk(p)	*!

Given two candidate analyses, the CSG throws out the violating one.[18]

What we need to consider is a case where the learner has some reason to believe that surface [brʌk] really has a final consonant. This 'reasoning' can be characterized as a hypothesis about what the morpheme is that underlies the surface form [brʌk]. If the learner hypothesizes that [brʌk] is really /brʌkp/, then the learner is positing a constraint ? = brʌkp. However, by the assumption that the CSG is top-ranked and that morpheme constraints are not, we end up with tableau (26), which is in relevant respects no different from (25).

(26)

?	CSG	? = brʌkp
☞ brʌk		*
brʌk(p)	*!	

---

[17] Notice again that (24) does *not* recapitulate generalizations regarding syllable structure. Inputs that pass (24) are not all directly syllabifiable.
[18] The same work would be done by lexicon optimization so far.

Hence, top-ranked CSG results in the absence of morphemes that violate the CSG even when the learner might have evidence (such as alternations) to suppose that there might be a morpheme that violates the CSG.[19]

Consider now the case of single-consonant affixes. Imagine the learner is confronted with some form [brʌkəp]. The learner thinks that maybe [əp] is a consonantal morpheme /p/. The alternative is to believe that the possibly epenthetic vowel is actually underlying. This hypothesis results in the second candidate in the following tableau.

(27)

? + ?	CSG	? = p
brʌk□p	*!	
☞ brʌkəp		*

Here again, the CSG forces the learner to reject the hypothesis that there is a suffix that violates it.

The morpheme constraint proposal thus treats the CSG phenomenon in a simple and direct fashion. Unlike the proposals considered above, it handles the single-consonant suffix problem without complication.

10. REMAINING QUESTIONS

The morpheme constraint proposal raises a number of questions which I treat in this section.

The first thing to note is that the morpheme constraint proposal is not really very radical. In many ways it is quite similar to previous proposals in non OT frameworks. First, readers familiar with lexical phonology will note that morpheme constraints are similar to the 'identity rules' proposed by Kiparsky (1982) in his attempt to derive the Strict Cycle Condition from the Elsewhere Condition. There are clear differences between this proposal and that one, however. First, that proposal was explicitly derivational and the current one is not. Second, that proposal is word-based and the current one is not. Thus, on Kiparsky's view, the output of every morphological level is an identity rule.

---

[19] An anonymous reviewer notes that another possible response to a conflict between the CSG and some hypothesized morpheme is that the relevant morpheme constraint may enter the constraint hierarchy *above* the CSG. This would result in a morpheme that violates the CSG. This apparently does not happen in English, so there must be some pressure against such a ranking. It may very well happen in the acquisition process with subsequent reranking by adulthood so that the CSG is again top-ranked. I have no evidence bearing on this question, however, and will not speculate further.

On the current proposal, only lexical entries and morphology are morpheme constraints.

In fact, the identity rule proposal is completely incapable of describing the current facts. The critical observation that the identity rule proposal is built on is, for example, that monomorphemic forms like *nightingale* [nájtŋgèl] do not undergo rules like Trisyllabic Shortening, while morphologically derived forms like *tonic* [tánək] do. (Cf. *tone* [tón].) Kiparsky's insight was that if the lexical entry for *nightingale* were augmented or replaced with a rule 'nightingale → nightingale', that rule would be in a specific–general relationship with Trisyllabic Shortening and thus block it. Critically, there was no such identity rule for *tonic* which thus allows it to undergo Trisyllabic Shortening. The central insight thus distinguishes morphologically simple and morphologically complex forms, while the CSG phenomenon applies to *both* morphologically simple and morphologically complex forms.

Another proposal rather like the current one is found in Declarative Phonology (e.g. Bird 1990; Coleman 1991; Scobbie 1991). The proposals are actually quite similar, though couched in frameworks that have one very sharp distinction. In OT, constraints are violable; in declarative phonology, they are not. This difference has a number of extremely important consequences, but evaluation of this issue is not the goal of this chapter.

Yet a third proposal that has interesting similarities with the current one is the very long tradition of processual morphology.[20] In this family of theories, morphology *per se* is expressed as rules, as opposed to elements. One critical difference between the proposal here and processual morphology is whether roots are constraints or, equivalently, whether roots are processes. This is a critical part of the proposal above, since the CSG holds not just of affixed elements but of bare roots as well. Roots are not processual in processual morphology.

Finally, let us briefly consider another proposal made within OT recently that bears certain similarities to the current proposal: Direct OT (Golston 1996). Under the Direct OT view, morphemes are represented as arrays of constraint violations. This view thus shares a rejection of the traditional lexicon with the current view. However, the two positions are really very distinct otherwise. Under Direct OT, lexical entries are quite distinct from constraints, though they are of course defined in terms of them.

In sum, while the proposal here draws on and shares the insights of much earlier work, it is a distinct empirical proposal to be evaluated on its own merits.

The current proposal raises several theoretical issues in the context of OT. First, the morpheme constraint proposal might seem to expand the constraint

---

[20] For treatments in the generative era, see e.g. Matthews (1972), Anderson (1992), and Steele (1995).

set to ridiculous extremes. While the earliest work on OT maintains that the constraint set is universal and finite, the current proposal would seem to commit us to an unbounded and obviously non-universal constraint set. This objection is actually a red herring. First, while classical OT maintained a universal constraint set, it still allowed for an unbounded and language-specific lexicon. Thus the task for the language learner still involved determining the content of the language-specific lexicon. Under the current proposal, the information from the lexicon has simply been recast as constraints. The *other* constraints, those that are not morpheme constraints, may still be characterized as universal and finite. Thus there is no massive expansion in information to be learned under the current proposal.

A second objection to the universality question is that it is hardly plausible to continue to think that the constraint set is universal. For example, even under classical OT, there are constraints like (in Tagalog) 'align -*um*- on the left edge of the word'. To the extent that putatively universal constraints can refer to individual lexical items, the infinity of the lexicon is *already* part of the constraint set. Hence, there is no argument against the current proposal from the universality of the constraint set.

11. CONCLUSION

I have argued that English is subject to a generalization such that forms may not end in sequences composed of an obstruent followed by a labial or dorsal obstruent. This fact cannot emerge naturally from any reasonable derivational account or in orthodox OT.

We have already dismissed various derivational alternatives, but, in fact, we would not expect this generalization to be treatable in derivational terms. One obvious reason is that sequences that potentially violate the CSG are not resolved derivationally. That is, while one might argue that /hɪmn/ being pronounced [hɪm] is because of a derivation that deletes the [n], the same kind of reasoning cannot apply to the absence of /brʌkp/. There is simply no surface form for the latter; hence there can be no derivation *per se*.

A second problem for any derivational account is that the key insight that makes the CSG a problem is that morphologically simple and morphologically complex forms *conspire* to avoid certain sequences. (I say this is a conspiracy because the consonantal affixes in isolation are not a violation of the CSG; it is only when they combine with certain stems that they violate it.) Similar conspiracies in stress and syllabification were precisely the motivation for a nonderivational theory to begin with (Prince and Smolensky 1993). Derivational phonology is computationally restrictive in that each rule only has access to the output of the preceding rule. It is precisely this attractive restrictiveness that dooms a derivational treatment of the CSG.

If, however, we adopt a constraint-based theory like OT, and morphemes are recast as constraints, and those constraints can be outranked by specific phonological constraints, then the generalization is readily treated. This analysis thus constitutes a general argument for the nonderivational OT framework and a specific argument for morpheme constraints.

ACKNOWLEDGEMENTS

Thanks to Diana Archangeli, Colleen Fitzgerald, Dirk Elzinga, Amy Fountain, Diane Ohala, Iggy Roca, and several anonymous reviewers for useful comments and discussion. All errors are my own.

REFERENCES

Anderson, S. R. (1992). *Amorphous Morphology*. Cambridge: Cambridge University Press.
Bird, S. (1990). 'Constraint-Based Phonology'. Dissertation, University of Edinburgh.
Borowsky, T. (1986). 'Topics in the Lexical Phonology of English'. Dissertation, University of Masachusetts.
Chomsky, N., and Halle, M. (1968). *The Sound Pattern of English*. New York: Harper & Row.
Coleman, J. (1991). 'Phonological Representations'. Dissertation, University of York.
Elzinga, D. (1995). 'Fula Consonant Mutation and Morpheme Constraints'. MS, University of Arizona.
Golston, C. (1996) 'Direct OT: representation as pure markedness', *Language* **72**: 713–748.
Halle, M., and Mohanan, K. P. (1985). 'Segmental phonology of Modern English', *Linguistic Inquiry* **16**: 57–116.
—— and Vergnaud, J.-R. (1978). 'Metrical Structures in Phonology'. MS, MIT.
Hammond, M. (1995). 'There is no lexicon!'. MS, University of Arizona, ROA-43.
Hammond, M. (in prep.) *English Prosody*.
Hayes, B. (1989). 'Compensatory lengthening in moraic phonology', *Linguistic Inquiry* **20**: 253–306.
Inkelas, S. (1994). 'The consequences of optimization for underspecification', *NELS* **24**: 287–302.
Kiparsky, P. (1982). 'Lexical morphology and phonology', in I.-S. Yang (ed.), *Linguistics in the Morning Calm*. Seoul: Hanshin, 3–91.
Matthews, P. H. (1972). *Inflectional Morphology*. Cambridge: Cambridge University Press.
McCarthy, J., and Prince, A. (1995) 'Faithfulness and Reduplicative identity', in J. N. Beckman, L. W. Dickey, and S. Urbanczyk (eds.), *Papers in Optimality Theory* (University of Massachusetts Occasional Papers 18). Amherst: GLSA, 249–384.

Prince, A. and Smolensky, P. (1993). 'Optimality Theory'. MS, Rutgers University and University of Colorado.

Russell, K. (1995). 'Morphemes and Candidates in Optimal Theory'. MS, University of Manitoba. ROA-44.

Selkirk, E. (1982). 'The syllable', in H. van der Hulst and N. Smith, (eds.), *The Structure of Phonological Representations*, pt. II. Cinnaminson: Foris.

Scobbie, J. (1991). 'Attributive Value Phonology'. Dissertation, University of Edinburgh.

Stanley, R. (1967). 'Redundancy rules in phonology', *Language* **43**: 393–436.

Steele, S. (1995). 'Towards a theory of morphological information', *Language* **71**: 260–309.

12

Phonological Derivations and Historical Changes in Hebrew Spirantization

WILLIAM J. IDSARDI

1. INTRODUCTION

Chomsky (1995: 224) cites Hebrew spirantization as an example of a phonological phenomenon whose conditioning factors are rendered opaque (even absent) by the operation of later processes in the phonological derivation in standard rule-based generative phonology. Because Optimality Theory (OT, Prince and Smolensky 1993) is built on surface output conditions (and in later versions input–output and output–output correspondence constraints), any such cases of intermediate representations are non-trivial questions to be addressed.

Idsardi (forthcoming) examines some aspects of the synchronic grammar of Tiberian Hebrew which interact with spirantization, and concludes that no non-derivational version of OT can handle all of the facts of Tiberian Hebrew spirantization. The present chapter extends these findings by examining the historical development of Hebrew, concentrating on changes that interact with spirantization. Idsardi (forthcoming) considers several possible OT grammars of Tiberian Hebrew, using various versions of Optimality Theory. The present paper considers only the account in McCarthy (forthcoming), and the generative account offered in Idsardi (forthcoming).

2. TIBERIAN HEBREW SPIRANTIZATION

2.1 *Basic facts*

Non-emphatic stops alternate with fricatives in Tiberian Hebrew (TH), the language of the Bible as annotated by the Masoretes. Alternations such as (1) (adapted from McCarthy 1979) are typical.

(1) a. [t ~ θ, k ~ x]   ka:θáv 'write 3MS PERF' (Josh. 8: 32)
               jixtó:v 'write 3MS IMPF' (Isa. 44: 5)
       b. [g ~ ɣ, d ~ ð]   ga:ðlú: 'be great 3P PERF' (Jer. 5: 27)
               jiɣdá: lu: 'be great 3MP IMPF' (Ruth 1: 13)

Modern Hebrew (MH) retains only the [p ~ f], [b ~ v], and [k ~ x] alterna-tions, having lost the alternations [t ~ θ], [g ~ ɣ], and [d ~ ð]. This is dis-cussed in more detail below. The basic generalization in TH is that fricatives appear postvocalically and stops appear elsewhere (postconsonantally and at the beginning of words following pause), but this has several complications, which are discussed briefly below, and in more detail in Idsardi (forthcoming).

TH had the consonant system in (2), following Prince (1975: 8–9). Stop–spirant pairs in the obstruent series are paired vertically.

(2) *Obstruents*   *Sonorants*
    a. p b t d ṭ s z ṣ (ś) ʃ k g q   m n l r j w ḥ ʕ h ʔ
    b. f v θ ð   x ɣ

The consonants in (2a) are both phonemic and phonetic; the consonants in (2b) are only phonetic.

Although spirants usually appear following a surface vowel, there are a number of complications to this generalization. The range of environments in which spirants appear in TH is given in (3)[1] (see Idsardi forthcoming for further examples and discussion).

(3) Spirants occur:
    a. after vowels present at both UR and SR (as in (1), above)
    b. after vowels present at UR but not at SR (deleted vowels):
       /katab + u/ → [ka:θvú:] 'write 3P PERF' (Ezra 4: 6)
       compare /katab/ → [ka:θáv] 'write 3MS PERF' (Josh. 8: 32)
    c. after vowels present at SR but not at UR (epenthetic vowels):
       /malk/ → [mélex] 'king' (Gen. 14: 1)
    d. between words in the same phrase:
       [wayyaʕălú: ve:θ-ʔé:l] 'and go up 3MP IMPF Bethel' (Judg. 20: 18)
    e. after a vowel when an intervening syllable-final laryngeal is deleted
       [ma:ṣá:(ʔ)θi:] 'find 1S PERF' (1 Kgs. 21: 20)
    f. across the glides /j,w/:
       [ḥa:jθá:] 'live 3FS PERF' (Gen. 12: 13)
    g. with degeminated consonants:
       /rabb/ → [rav] 'great, much MS' (Gen. 24: 25)
       compare /rabb-im/ → [rabbí:m] 'many MP' (Num. 20: 11)
    h. to both onsets and codas [ka:θáv] 'write 3MS PERF' (Josh. 8: 32)

It is particularly important to notice that the occurrence of spirants is not predictable from the surface syllabic position of the consonant. Spirants occur both as codas and as onsets. The conditioning factor is rather the adjacency to a preceding nucleus (Schein and Steriade 1986), not to the syllabic affiliation of the segment in question.

However, even with the occurrence of spirants in all the positions catalogued

---

[1] Underlining is used to draw attention to the place of interest in the form, not to indicate spirantized variants.

in (3), spirant members of stop–spirant pairs are banned from other environments, catalogued in (4).

(4) Spirant realizations of stop–spirant pairs do not occur:
    a. postpausally
    b. after consonants (except (3b) and (3f) cases)
    c. with surface geminates (cf. (3g)):
       underlying /rabb-im/ → [rabbí:m] 'many MP' (Num. 20: 11)
       derived /ja-n-kateb/ → [jikka:θé:v] 'write 3MS IMPF Nifʕal' (Esther 8: 5)
    d. across gutturals (cf. (3f))
       [jaẖbó:t] 'strike 3MS IMPF' (Isa. 27: 12)
    e. when 'metathesized' into postconsonantal position:
       [ləhištabbéaẖ] 'praise INF Hitpaʕel' (Ps. 106: 47)
       cf. [wəhiθba:ré:x] 'and bless 3MS PERF Hitpaʕel' (Deut. 29: 18)
    f. after a deleted vowel following a prefix (cf. (3b)):
       /ja-katob/ → [jixtó:v] 'write 3MS IMPF' (Isa. 44: 5)
       /na-katab/ → [nixtáv] 'write 3MS PERF Nifʕal' (Esther 8: 8)
       compare /katab-u/ → [ka:θvú:] 'write 3P PERF' (Ezra 4: 6) where the deleted
         vowel is later in the stem
       and /b#katob/ → [bixθó:v] 'when writing' (Ps. 83: 6) where the deleted vowel
         follows a proclitic
    g. following a word ending in a glide (cf. (3d,f)):
       [wajṣáw da:wí:ð] 'and order 3MS JUSS David' (1 Chr. 22: 17)

There are also other spirants which do not alternate with stops (e.g. [s ʃ]). These fricatives can occur in all the relevant phonetic environments listed above.

The crucial test cases for any theory of spirantization is the difference in behaviors between (3b) and (4f), for together they show that spirantization does not uniformly occur following all deleted vowels. Because these cases are so crucial, it will be necessary to briefly review the morphology of the verb stem in Hebrew.

The perfect, imperfective and intensive perfect (Piʕel) forms for the verb root /ktb/ 'write' are shown in (5). Sound triliteral verb stems can show four different surface shapes: CVCVC, CVCCVC, CVCC, and CCVC. Vowel length is phonologically predictable, and there are different agreement markers for the Perfect and Imperfect aspects.

(5)

	Perfect		*Imperfect*		*Piʕel Perfect*	
1S	ka:θáv-ti:	CVCVC	ʔe-xtó:v	CCVC	kittáv-ti	CVCCVC
2MS	ka:θáv-ta:	"	ti-xtó:v	"	kittáv-ta:	"
2FS	ka:θáv-t	"	ti-xtəv-í:	"	kittáv-t	"
3MS	ka:θáv	"	ji-xtó:v	"	kittév	"
3FS	kaθv-á:	CVCC	ti-xtó:v	"	kittəv-á:	"
1P	ka:θáv-nu:	CVCVC	ni-xtó:v	"	kittáv-nu:	"
2MP	kəθav-tém	"	ti-xtəv-ú:	"	kittav-tém	"
2FP	kəθav-tén	"	ti-xtó:v-na:	"	kittav-tén	"
3MP	ka:θv-ú:	CVCC	ji-xtəv-ú:	"	kittəv-ú:	"
3FP	ka:θv-ú:	"	ti-xtó:v-na:	"	kittəv-ú:	"

McCarthy (1979) represents a watershed in the analysis of stem-shape patterning in Semitic morphology. Previous accounts, such as Prince (1975), had built stem shapes from an underlying CVCVC form through morpho-phonological rules of deletion and insertion. McCarthy suggested instead that the stem shape was supplied morphologically for the particular binyan and aspectual class, with the root consonants then associating to the template. In the case of the CVCC stems, however, McCarthy (1979) also derived this stem shape from /CVCVC/ with a phonological rule of vowel deletion. More recently, McCarthy and Prince (1990), McCarthy (1993), and Dobrin (1993) have argued for a return to the idea that *all* verb stem shapes are based on a CVCVC stem. They argue that the stem shapes CCVC, CVCC, and CVCCVC must be derived through morphophonological processes because these shapes do not define valid prosodic constituents and are therefore incoherent from the standpoint of Prosodic Morphology. For example, the first C in the CCVC case is syllabified not with the stem but with the preceding prefix. Therefore the prosody of a stem exhibiting this shape is a mora plus a syllable, [µ σ], which is not a valid prosodic constituent. The shape CVCCVC is also incoherent, they argue, because it is not a valid foot type, being too large to be either a trochee or an iamb. McCarthy and Prince derive the CVCCVC shape by infixing a prosodic position (a mora) after the first syllable of the CVCVC stem. The CCVC case is handled in Arabic by a phonological rule of vowel deletion (McCarthy 1993: 202). Rappaport (1985) likewise argues that the Hebrew imperfective CCVC shape arises from a phonological process of vowel deletion. In order to generate the correct surface forms (including spirantization) in the Hebrew case, however, prefixed stems must undergo two levels of calculation, both cyclic and noncyclic; see Rappaport (1985) for details. The existence of the cyclic level is crucial in capturing the difference in spirantization of consonants following deleted vowels; compare [jix_to:v] 'write 3MS IMPF' with [ka:θ_vu:] 'write 3MS PERF.' No spirantization occurs with the /t/ following the deleted vowel in the imperfective, but the spirant [v] does occur following the deleted vowel in the perfective. Any analysis of spirantization must capture this distinction. In Rappaport's derivational analysis (carried over into this chapter) this is accounted for by deleting the vowel in the imperfective in the cyclic stratum, while deleting the vowel in the perfective noncyclically; see the next section for details.

2.2 *A rule-based analysis*

Idsardi (forthcoming) accounts for the behavior of spirantization in Tiberian Hebrew with the rules in (6) and (7). Of course there are other morphological and phonological rules in Tiberian Hebrew, see especially Prince (1975), Dresher (1983), Rappaport (1985), and Malone (1993) for examples and analyses. The summary of rules in (6) and (7) is limited to those rules that interact relatively directly with spirantization. The morphological component is responsible for constructing the underlying representations for the phonological component. In the case of Tiberian Hebrew, the rules relevant for spirantization are the limited infixation of /t/ in the Hitpaʕel (commonly analysed as metathesis), and the construction of stem forms by infixation (medial gemination) and vowel deletion (the CCVC stem shape characteristic of the imperfect tenses). Assuming that syllable structure is encoded in the basic template form (and thus available in the morphology) the rules are then as in (6).

(6) a. Medial gemination $\emptyset \to x$ / $[_{Piʕel, etc.} [CV\_\_ _\sigma]$
    b. Hitpaʕel formation   i. $\emptyset \to x$ / $[_{Hitpaʕel} x \_\_$
                                   | / \
                             [− son]   [− son] Coronal
                         ii. $\emptyset \to /t/$ / $[_{Hitpaʕel} \_\_$

If the Hitpaʕel infixation, (6bi), applies, then all Guttural features spread rightward from the stem-initial consonant. The consequence of this is that the infix will agree in voicing and [RTR] (emphasis) with the stem-initial segment. As noted by Gesenius (1910: 149), some stems beginning with /n/, /k/ or /r/ exceptionally form their Hitpaʕel forms through infixation. The infixation is also general in other Semitic languages. The analysis of the Hitpaʕel formation as infixation solves a problem with voicing assimilation in Modern Hebrew, see below.

The phonological rules are given in their application order in (7). Each rule is specified for whether it applies cyclically, noncyclically, or in both strata. Explication and justification for the formulations of the rules can be found in Idsardi (forthcoming).

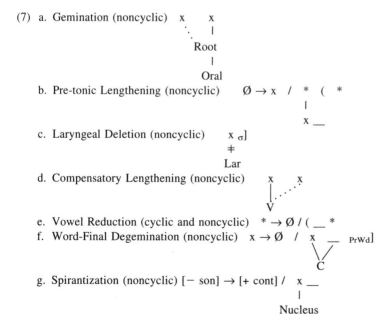

(7) a. Gemination (noncyclic)   x   x
                                 ˙. |
                                      Root
                                        |
                                      Oral
    b. Pre-tonic Lengthening (noncyclic) $\emptyset \to x$ / * (*
                                                              |
                                                              x __
    c. Laryngeal Deletion (noncyclic)   x _σ]
                                        ╪
                                       Lar
    d. Compensatory Lengthening (noncyclic)   x   x
                                              |.··˙·
                                              V
    e. Vowel Reduction (cyclic and noncyclic)   * → $\emptyset$ / (__ *
    f. Word-Final Degemination (noncyclic)   x → $\emptyset$ / x __ _PrWd]
                                                 \ /
                                                  C
    g. Spirantization (noncyclic) [− son] → [+ cont] / x __
                                                       |
                                                    Nucleus

h. Schwa Deletion (cyclic and noncyclic)   ə → Ø / V$_\sigma$][C __ $_\sigma$]
                                                                    |
                                                                   Oral

i. Closed syllable i (cyclic and noncyclic)   V → /i/ / __ C $_\sigma$]
                                              / \ |
                                          [− high] [− round]   Oral

j. n Deletion (cyclic)   x   C
                            ǂ |
                            n   Oral

Idsardi (forthcoming) argues that, because the stop/spirant distinction was not contrastive in TH, the 'stops' in (2) were underlyingly without any value for the [cont] feature. Spirantization (7g) provides these items with [+ cont], and a general rule supplies the [− cont] default otherwise, with these rules disjunctively ordered by Kiparsky's (1973) Elsewhere Condition (cf. Chomsky's 1951 MR34).

As discussed above, the appearance of the shortened stem shapes CCVC and CVCC is governed by the operation of the rules of Vowel Reduction and Schwa Deletion on the base stem shape CVCVC. Derivations of forms exhibiting this operation are shown in (8). Verb forms containing prefixes (Nifʕal, Imperfectives, etc.) are subject to the cyclic block of rules; forms without prefixes do not undergo a cyclic calculation. Imperatives and infinitive absolute forms, which appear not to have a prefix, are analyzed here as having a Ø- (zero) prefix, and are therefore subject to the cyclic rules.

(8) *Morphology*

	[[ja-katob $_{cyc}$]-u $_{non}$]	[katab-u $_{non}$]	[b#[Ø-katob$_{cyc}$] $_{non}$]
Cyclic	jakatob	n/a	katob
Reduction	x (x		(x
	(ja)(ka)(to)b		(ka)(to)b
Deletion	x (x		
	(jak)(to)b		
	x (x		
Closed σ i	(jik)(to)b		
Noncyclic	x (x x	x (x x	(x
	(jik)(to)(bu)	(ka)(ta)(bu)	(bə)(ka)(to)b
Lengthening		x)(x x	
		(ka:)(ta)(bu)	
Reduction	x (x	x)(x	
	(jik)(tə)(bu)	(ka:)(tə)(bu)	
Spirantization	x (x	x)(x	(x
	(jix)(tə)(vu)	(ka:)(θə)(vu)	(bə)(xa)(θo)v
Deletion		x)(x	(x
		(ka:θ)(vu)	(bəx)(θo)v
Closed σ i			(x
			(bix)(θo)v
Other rules:	[jixtəvú:]	[kà:θvú:]	[bixθó:v]

As discussed in Idsardi (forthcoming), the proclitic of infinitive construct form /l#katob/ → [lixtov] is lexically specified as [+ cyclic]. Therefore, the derivation of this form is parallel to the imperfective forms in the relevant respects.

2.3 *An Optimality Theoretic analysis*

The most important change from generative models of phonology to Optimality Theory is the total elimination of phonological rules. Instead of rules, surface well-formedness constraints rank output candidates in terms of how well they meet surface-orientated conditions. Thus, in principle all constraints are violable, and the grammar of a language is an ordering of the universal constraints from most to least important. The general form of the theory is 'generate and test', as in (9).

(9) Gen(input) = {candidates}
     Eval({ candidates }, { constraints }) = output

We will not construct a substantial partial OT grammar for Hebrew here, but will assume that constraints can be formulated and ranked to generate the surface patterns for processes other than spirantization. The surface orientation of OT constraints allows us to be somewhat agnostic about how the rest of the constraints are formulated and ranked, since the constraints should be in terms of surface properties, or input–output relations.

McCarthy (forthcoming) offers a novel approach to the problem of accounting for phonological opacity within a non-derivational version of OT. Because of the importance of the concept of opacity in the rest of the discussion, I give the definition of opacity in Kiparsky (1976: 178–9) in (10).

(10) [A] process P of the form
          A → B / C __ D
       [is] opaque to the extent that there are phonetic forms in the language having either (i) or (ii):
       (i)   A in the environment C __ D . . .
       (iia) B derived by the process P in the environment 'other than C __ D'
       (iib) B not derived by the process P (i.e. underlying or derived by another process) in the environment C __ D

Hebrew spirantization is a typical example of an opaque rule, because later rules, such as vowel deletion, obscure the application environment in the surface form. The ordering of spirantization before deletion is an opacity of type (10iia), because at the surface a spirant appears postconsonantally.

McCarthy proposes that OT constraints be parameterized for certain aspects of their evaluation. His formulation of the Tiberian Hebrew spirantization constraint is given in (11).

(11) No-V-Stop Tiberian Hebrew Version (with opacity . . .)

*	Condition	Level
α	V	Indifferent
β	[− son, − cont]	Surface
Linear Order	α > β	Indifferent
Adjacency	Strict	Indifferent

McCarthy explains that 'in correspondence terms, the meaning of this constraint is this: the constraint is violated if a surface stop β or its underlying correspondent is immediately preceded by a vowel'. By parameterizing the constraint in this way, spirantization is predicted following surface vowels (epenthetic or underlying) and if a consonant was preceded by a vowel in the underlying representation.

As discussed in Idsardi (forthcoming), the claim that all underlying V–Stop sequences show surface spirantization of the stop is false. In particular, imperfective verb forms do not show spirantization of the second root consonant even though it is underlyingly preceded by a vowel (as argued in e.g. McCarthy 1993, discussed above), for example TH [jixbað], MH [jixbad] 'he will be heavy'. Therefore McCarthy's account does not correctly differentiate between the two behaviors following deleted vowels illustrated by the contrast between (3b) and (4f), a distinction which persists in MH. However, I shall not be primarily concerned with this problem in the following discussion. Instead, I seek to test the claim that the absence of opacity is less marked, and that languages will change diachronically so as to become less marked, and therefore less opaque.

3. Modern Hebrew Phonology

3.1 *Basic facts*

Hebrew has undergone many changes since the Biblical period. Some of these changes are of interest with regard to the proper analysis of spirantization. Here I will consider only the standard Israeli Hebrew dialect, as described for example in Rosén (1962; 1977), Bolozky (1978; 1980), Berman (1978), and Baltsan (1992). I will not consider Sephardic or Ashkenazic dialects, where they differ from the descriptions below. The history of the development of Hebrew is complex, and is full of uncertainties. The widespread use of unpointed scripts throughout the history further complicates the always difficult problem of interpreting orthographic conventions. With all these caveats, a summary of the changes from TH to MH given in Bolozky (1978: 11–13) is given in (12).

(12) a. *Mergers and phonemic restructuring*

[O]f the original set of six spirant alternants . . . only the two labials /b/ and /p/ and the voiceless velar /k/ have spirant counterparts — [v], [f], and [x], respectively.

The voiceless pharyngeal fricative /ħ/[=ḥ] is typically pronounced exactly like its velar counterpart [x].

[T]he glide /w/ is generally pronounced exactly like the labial spirant [v].

[T]he so-called 'emphatic' consonants /ṣ/, /ṭ/, and /q/ no longer occur in any native Hebrew speech . . . [and] are today pronounced as the dental affricate [ts], the dental stop [t], and the velar stop [k], respectively.

b. *Degemination*

Another loss in the consonantal system is the nonrealization of consonantal gemination.

c. *Guttural deletion*

[T]he voiced pharyngeal fricative /ʕ/ *'ayin* has coalesced with the glottal stop /ʔ/ *aleph* and is most generally deleted, just as are original glottal stops.

With the addition of the phoneme /f/ through borrowings such as [fibrek] 'fabricate', [falafal] 'falafal' (Zilkha 1989), and [fintez] 'he fantasized', [festival] 'festival' (Ravid 1995: 82), Modern Hebrew has the underlying consonant system shown in (13).

(13) *Obstruents*   *Sonorants*
    p b t d s z t͡s ʃ k g   m n l r j ʕ h ʔ
    f v   x

See below for the lack of spirantization with /k/ < TH /q/, and justification for the inclusion of /ʕ ʔ/ in the underlying inventory.

It is particularly fascinating that so much of the relevant data regarding spirantization remains much the same in Modern Hebrew. For example, the contrast between infinitive constructs in /l#/ and /b#/ which motivated Prince's (1975) cyclic analysis continues, as observed by Berman (1978: 288). Some examples from MH are given in (14).

(14) a. [lispor]   'to count'   [bisfor]   'on counting'
     b. [liʃpox]   'to pour'   [biʃfox]   'on pouring'
     c. [limkor]   'to sell'   [bimxor]   'on selling'

As Idsardi (forthcoming) shows, this data cannot be handled in any nonderivational version of OT. The continuation of this pattern of data for thousands of years indicates that this is a robust fact of the language, and must be handled in any theory of phonology. However, in this chapter I will concentrate on some of the things that have changed in the grammar of Hebrew that interact with spirantization, and evaluate whether they have decreased opacity in the grammar or not.

3.2 *Implications for the analyses*

In the following sections I will examine the diachronic implications for the two analyses of Tiberian Hebrew. What must be changed in the grammars of the two analyses from TH to MH?

The two theories predict rather different things. The rule-based theory predicts rule change (in parameters for target/environment/level/conditions; see Archangeli and Pulleyblank 1995), rule loss, and rule addition, especially to the end of the grammar, as explained by Halle and Kiparsky:

(15) the new rules are ordinarily added at the end of the grammar . . . (Halle 1962: 68)

the vast majority of sound changes are rules added to the end of the existing sequence of phonological rules . . . (Kiparsky 1970: 309)

Rule addition at the end of the grammar is the most important type of change for the purposes of the present chapter. Rules added at the end of the grammar do whatever they do. They may be in feeding, bleeding, counterfeeding, or counterbleeding relationships with rules earlier in the grammar. This theory predicts it should be possible, even normal, for languages to show an increase in the opacity of the grammar through rule addition. Of course, if the system becomes so opaque that it cannot be readily learned, it will then be restructured.

The OT perspective is diametrically opposed, as is shown by the quotes from McCarthy (forthcoming).

(16) Kiparsky's concern is with understanding how minimization of opacity drives diachronic change. (p. 1)

Accepting Kiparsky's . . . dictum that phonological opacity is marked, I will stipulate that the default form of a phonological constraint—the form in which it is represented in UG—has all of its level specifications set to 'surface'. A constraint of this type is a *true output target* . . . It is not opaque, since the conditions of obedience or violation can be read off of surface structure in a completely transparent way. (p. 6)

It is clear that, in contrast to the rule approach which has no direct measure of opacity, there is explicit representation of opacity in the OT constraint parameters, and the default state for these parameters is for true surface (transparent) evaluation. Therefore, with OT we would not expect increases in grammar opacity to be favored occurrences in language change.

The rest of this section will examine the changes in the historical development of Hebrew relating to spirantization, focusing on what changes in the grammars would account for these changes, and whether or not these changes increased the opacity of the grammar.

3.2.1 *Phonemic restructuring*

The most notable change in Hebrew spirantization has already been mentioned—the restriction of the set of spirantizable stops. The problem this presents is succinctly explained by Bolozky (1978: 33):

(17) Spirantization no longer applies to all six members of the three pairs of non-back stops, but is confined to the alternations of *p, b,* and *k* with the fricative *f, v,* and *x*, respectively. Note that these three sets of stop–spirant alternations cannot be associated with any accepted 'natural' phonological class of segments.

It is possible to exclude the coronals by restricting spirantization to Peripheral stops (Rice 1994; this restriction is attested in Samaritan Hebrew; see Murtonen 1990), but this still leaves MH */g/ → [ɣ] to be explained.[2]

I believe that an illuminating answer arises from examining the set of outputs of the spirantization process in Modern Hebrew, [f v x]. In Biblical Hebrew these sounds were only phonetic variants of the spirantizing stops, but this is not the case in Modern Hebrew. Owing to historical mergers (TH /w/ > MH /v/ and TH /ḥ/ > MH /x/) MH acquired new phonemes /v x/. Due to borrowings MH has also acquired the phoneme /f/. It has not, however, acquired a phoneme /ɣ/, although [ɣ] is a phonetic variant of /k/ and /x/ through voicing assimilation (see below). Therefore, if we restrict the operation of spirantization to produce only phonemes as outputs, we can uniquely identify the set of stops undergoing the rule. But this is simply the Structure Preservation condition of Lexical Phonology (Kiparsky 1982). Of course, the addition of new phonemes has also meant that there are now instances of spirants in positions where they could have been created by the spirantization rule (e.g. following surface vowels, [patax] 'he opened' <TH /pataḥ/, introducing opacity of type (10iib) into the language.

Elan Dresher (pers. comm.) has suggested a slight variation on this story (see also Faber 1986; Katz 1993). Since for many centuries Hebrew was primarily a liturgical language, spirantization might have been restricted to producing phonemes in the first language of the speakers. Interestingly, the major European first languages of relevant interest (German, Russian, Polish) all have phonemic /f v x/ and lack phonemic /ɣ/. Thus, we might have two slightly different stories regarding the development of the structure-preserving restriction. The first says that under the influence of languages with /f v x/ Hebrew innovates /f v x/. Then spirantization changes to be structure-preserving. The second story would allow the speakers' first-language phoneme set including /f v x/ to restrict the operation of spirantization directly, without first 'importing' the phonemes into Hebrew. This is a very subtle and clever distinction, and may shed light on other inter-language phenomena, but cannot be resolved for the present case.

[2] Asterisks (*) are only used to mark ungrammatical forms, not to indicate historical sources.

Work in Lexical Phonology (Kaisse 1990; Rice 1990; Hyman 1993; Iverson 1993) has demonstrated that noncyclic rules can be structure-preserving, and Kiparsky (1993) shows that rules must be individually marked as to whether they are subject to the Derived Environment Condition. Thus the fact that a rule obeys Structure Preservation is not an infallible indication that the rule is cyclic. So let us leave the spirantization rule in the noncyclic stratum, but mark the rule as Structure-Preserving, and thereby preclude /g/ from being spirantized to [ɣ]. It seems premature at this point to speculate whether the structure-preserving restriction then directly prevented /t d/ → [θ ð] (or forced /t d/ → /s z/? see Faber 1986) or whether spirantization was separately restricted to Peripheral segments.

Employing output conditions like Structure Preservation would seem to play directly to OT's strengths. But it is extremely important to realize that it is only the output of the spirantization process itself that has been made structure-preserving. In particular it is incorrect to view Structure Preservation as a constraint on surface outputs in MH. This can be very clearly seen by examining the interaction of spirantization with regressive Voicing Assimilation (Bolozky 1978: 16). Bolozky notes two idiosyncrasies of the rule in careful speech: /v/ does not induce voicing on a preceding segment (a phenomenon shared with Russian) and /x/ does not become [ɣ]. Bolozsky notes that in fast speech these restrictions can be lifted. As regards /x/ ↛ [ɣ], we can account for the careful speech restriction by saying that Voicing Assimilation is subject to Structure Preservation in careful speech, but that the Structure Preservation restriction on voicing assimilation is lifted in fast speech. Bolozky gives the examples in (18) (see also Kisseberth 1977: 51–2).

(18) | *Careful speech* | *Fast speech* | | *TH root* |
|---|---|---|---|
| [exzir] | [eɣzir] | 'returned tr.' | /ħzr/ |
| [jixboʃ] | [jiɣboʃ] | 'he will conquer' | /kbʃ/ |

Thus in fast speech it is possible for /k/ → /x/ → [ɣ]. Notice that the output does not meet Structure Preservation, for there is no phoneme */ɣ/. But, the spirantization process by itself is structure-preserving. Now consider a minimally different case, that of /g/ between a vowel and a voiceless obstruent, as in (19).

(19) /ja-gasos/ → [jiksos] *[jixsos] 'he will agonize/be about to die'
      /ja-gaxon/ → [jikxon] *[jixon] 'he will lean'

It is impossible to chain together spirantization and Voicing Assimilation so as to produce */g/ → /ɣ/ → [x], even though the output segment would be structure preserving because /x/ is a phoneme. Thus it is *not* the overall Input–Output relation that is relevant for Structure Preservation, but only the operation of the spirantization process. Since /g/ → [ɣ] is not structure-preserving, the process of spirantization is blocked, and therefore when Voicing

Assimilation applies /g/ → [k]. Note also that the existence of forms such as [jiksos] is an opacity of type (10i).

In contrast, an examination of the surface forms in terms of Structure Preservation in OT makes the wrong predictions, as shown in (20).

(20) /ja-gasos/	*Voicing Assimilation*	*Structure-Preserving*	*Spirantization*
a. jiksos	✓	✓	*!
b. jixsos	✓	✓	✓
c. jiɣsos	*!	*	✓
d. jigsos	*!	✓	*

Since the output [x] is an element of the phonemic inventory, the candidates (20a) and (20b) tie for the purposes of Structure Preservation. Therefore *[jixsos] should be the preferred candidate because it also satisfies the spirantization constraint, an unwanted Emergence of the Unmarked effect. Thus, it is clear that an explanation in terms of Structure Preservation as an OT output constraint fails. The proper results fall out directly if Structure Preservation is applied as a constraint on the application of individual rules. The correct results do not follow if Structure Preservation is calculated over entire derivations.

Thus, OT cannot use a general constraint for Structure Preservation, but must break Structure Preservation into several separate constraints. One of these could be an Ident constraint freezing the relevant partial segment structure which identifies /g/, as in (21).

(21)

$$\text{Ident} \left(\begin{array}{c} \text{Root} \\ /\ |\ \backslash \\ [-\text{cont}]\ \text{Place}\ \text{Laryngeal} \\ |\qquad\ \backslash \\ \text{Dors}\ \ [+\text{voice}] \end{array} \right)$$

But this is not the end of the matter. We must properly rank the constraints so as to allow /g/ → [k] but not /g/ → [ɣ] or /g/ → [x]. That is, [−cont] is more frozen than [+voice]. The relevant ranking would obviously have to be Voicing Assimilation (VA) >> (21) >> (11). However, if (21) is evaluated as a binary constraint, this still yields the wrong results, through the same unwanted Emergence of the Unmarked effect, as shown in (22).

(22) /ja-gasos/	VA	(21)	(11)
a. jiksos	✓	{[− voice]}	*
b. jixsos	✓	{[− voice], [+ cont]}	✓
c. jifsos	✓	{[− voice], [+ cont], [Lab]}	✓
d. jiɣsos	*!	{[+ cont]}	✓
e. jigsos	*!	✓	*

If (21) is evaluated as a binary constraint, then (22a–c) all meet the voicing assimilation requirement and tie on (21) as well (all of them violating it).

Evaluation would then fall to the relative performance on the spirantization constraint, which (22b,c) meet and (22a) fails. Since (22b) is more faithful to the input in terms of retaining the Dorsal articulation (Max-Dorsal), (22b) would be the winning candidate. Since (22a) is the correct output, (21) must be evaluated as a gradient constraint, or be exploded into some kind of contextual Ident constraints, such as Ident ([−cont]) for /g/, perhaps through a parameterized constraint like (23).

(23) *   *Condition*   *Level*
      α   g   Indifferent
      β   [+ cont]   Surface
      Relation   β ∈ α   Indifferent

This constraint means that no instance of a [+ cont] feature should be contained in a surface segment [g], or in a surface segment whose input correspondent is /g/. Constraint (23) is effectively a kind of anti-correspondence constraint barring /g/ from surfacing as any kind of continuant [γ x z s . . .] (see Archangeli and Suzuki, Chapter 6 above, for similar discussion [Editor]). The problem here with both (21) and (23) is that they both simply stipulate that underlying /g/ cannot change its value for [− cont]. That is, they are simply brute force formal ways of excluding /g/ from spirantization. In contrast, the rule-based Structure Preservation account explains the behavior of /g/ in terms of an independently necessary phonological structure—the phoneme inventory. But because the relevant evaluation of the adherence to Structure Preservation is the output of the spirantization rule (an intermediate level), it is impossible to use Structure Preservation evaluated over surface forms, as OT would require, and therefore constraints specific to /g/ must instead be formulated.

One minor clarification regarding voicing assimilation should be made at this point. As Bolozky (1978: 22) shows, the Hitpaʕel 'metathesis' interacts with voicing assimilation so that application to /z/-initial stems yields [-zd-] rather than [-st-], as the surface output, as in (24).

(24) /hit-zaken/   [hizdaken]   'grow old'
     /hit-zarez/   [hizdarez]   'hurried'
     /hit-zakef/   [hizdakef]   'stood up'

As Bolozky points out, one possible conclusion from such data is that voicing assimilation precedes metathesis. Bolozky rejects this interpretation on the general grounds that morphologically conditioned rules do not follow low-level phonetic rules. This conclusion is correct, and can be reinforced. Given the morphological restriction of the metathesis to the Hitpaʕel, and the existence of cognate infixes in related languages, the correct analysis is morphological infixation, as in (6b) above. As discussed above, the Guttural features spread from the stem-initial consonant onto the infixed position, resulting in both voice and emphasis assimilation in TH. Since emphasis has been lost in MH, only the voicing assimilation is apparent.

Modern Hebrew now has what many observers have described as apparent surface exceptions to spirantization with surface [k]s that (generally) correspond to TH /q/, which, being emphatic, was systematically exempt from spirantization. Bolozky (1978: 34) summarizes the situation:

(25) Historical /q/ has merged with /k/, and yet has remained totally unaffected by
Spirantization, as shown by such forms as: [kara] '(he) read' ~ [jikra] 'will read';
[kana] 'bought' ~ [jikne] 'will buy'; [dakar] 'stabbed'; [zarak] 'threw'; and so on.
This also makes Spirantization opaque for many cases of phonetic [k] now
occuring to which the rule does not apply.

As Bolozky points out, the existence of non-spirantizing [k] < TH /q/ increases the opacity of the grammar, as it introduces new instances of (10i).

There are two possible answers to this problem: preserve the historical distinction in the synchronic grammar, or differentiate between the two /k/s with some other feature. In the rule-based analysis, if we assume that MH retains underlying /q/, then there must be a rule that absolutely neutralizes /q/ to [k]. Clearly, this is a rule added subsequent to TH, and therefore we expect it to be added to the end of the grammar, and therefore for the rule to follow spirantization. This is exactly the behavior that is observed, and therefore this case would also confirm the rule-ordering theory of diachronic change. This is a plausible explanation for the change, but I have argued above that phonemic restructuring does take place, so what phonemic restructuring would be predicted in this case?

In MH the voiceless velars display a three-way contrast in behavior: one is always a spirant [x] (< TH /ḥ/); one is always a stop [k] (< TH /q/); and one undergoes the stop/spirant alternation [k ~ x] (< TH /k/). This can be explained simply if we adopt a three-way distinction in the underlying representation of [cont], giving three distinct underlying segments: /x/ with [+cont], /k/ with [−cont], and /K/ without any specification for [cont]. As in TH, spirantization in MH is restricted to 'filling in' unspecified values for [cont], but it is further restricted by Structure Preservation to do so only if the output is an existing underlying segment.

Of course, the appearance of new phonemes /f/ and /v/ entails that they will be non-alternating and always [+cont]. But this analysis also makes the prediction that the 'exceptional' behavior of MH /k/ < TH /q/ should be able to lexically diffuse, and MH should gain non-alternating /p/ and /b/. This does seem to be happening, so that '[t]here are some borrowed verbs with initial *b* that is not spirantized in postvocalic position' (Bolozky 1980: 6), for example:

(26) [bilef]   'he lied, bluffed'
     [mebalef]   'he is lying, bluffing'
     [jebalef]   'he will lie, bluff'

The same can be observed to a more limited extent with /p/, for example [pitpet] 'he talked a lot' [lepatpet] 'to talk a lot', (Bolozky 1978: 35). Ravid (1995: 82) gives further examples: [ibdu] 'lost Pl', [mikroskop] 'microscope', and [zlob] 'big, ungainly person'. These are obviously also additions to the language which are opaque under the definition in (10i). Notice that this results in cases which cannot be treated as lexical exceptions to spirantization at the level of the morpheme (the co-phonology approach; see also Inkelas et al. 1994; and Chapter 13 below), because within a single morpheme one segment can spirantize normally while another is 'exceptional', such as TH /pqḥ/ 'open eyes' MH [pakax] 'he opened eyes', [jifkax] 'he will open eyes'.

The opacities resulting from the neutralizations and phonemic restructuring observed in Modern Hebrew have another important effect—they render the memorization of URs ambiguous in some cases when the learner is provided with insufficient evidence from a paradigm. In Modern Hebrew there are two sources for [x], MH /x K/ (= TH /ḥ k/) and two sources for [k], /k K/ (= TH /q k/). Thus, a learner when encountering a form with, for example, an initial [k] can propose either /k/ or /K/ in that position in the memorized form. Likewise, upon hearing [x] following a vowel the learner can propose either /x/ or /K/. These choices (quite possibly made with inadequate information) will then determine whether the newly memorized item will alternate or not in the learner's grammar; and mistakes (and uncertainties) of just this sort do occur, as documented in Bolozky (1980) and Ravid (1995) posing serious problems for Lexicon Optimization in OT.

Now let us consider how we might handle TH /q/ in MH using OT. First let us assume that we retain TH /q/ as MH /q/. Then we must obviously bar surface [q], perhaps through a general constraint against gutturals. Specifically, we would like to ban the surface manifestation of retracted tongue root, *[RTR]. But this is not sufficient, as we must also prevent /q/ from surfacing as [+cont] [x], while allowing /k/ to be [+cont] on the surface. The constraint will be substantially similar to (23), as shown in (27).

(27)

*	Condition	Level
α	q	Indifferent
β	[+ cont]	Surface
Relation	β ∈ α	Indifferent

However, (23) and (27) cannot be combined into a single constraint without also blocking spirantization of /k/, for the set of features shared by /q/ and /g/ also characterizes /k/.

The representational reanalysis into an underlying three-way distinction between /k/, /x/, and /K/ is more successful. Then all that is needed in OT is a highly ranked Ident([cont]) constraint, forcing input–output correspondent pairs to agree for the feature [cont]. However, the problem of /g/ remains. It would be possible, of course, to specify /g/ as [−cont] underlyingly and thereby ban it from spirantization. However, this analysis would then produce a strangely skewed underlying inventory, because there would be a [−cont] /g/ without a minimally contrasting [+cont] */γ/ or an unspecified */G/. But by hypothesis underlying segments can be unspecified for [cont], and then it is odd that we must choose the more formally marked /g/ over the less marked /G/ as the sole voiced velar segment. Thus, as might be expected, OT forces us to take a less historical, more surface-orientated analysis of the behavior of TH /q/ in MH. The rule-based analysis can use this same analysis, or a historically orientated one.

The historical development of TH /q/, then does not particularly favor one theory or the other. However, the non-spirantization of /g/ along with the existence of a surface phone [γ] (from /x K/ through voicing assimilation) is difficult to handle in OT, but falls out directly in the rule-based Structure Preservation account. All of these changes also increase the opacity of the grammar by Kiparsky's definitions, which is not the development favored by OT.

3.2.2 Degemination

As discussed above, surface geminates were immune from spirantization in TH, and the MH counterparts are still realized as stops, but they are no longer surface geminates, as Bolozky (1978: 34) explains:

(28) Gemination, which historically blocked Spirantization—as in *dibber* 'spoke', *sipper* 'told', *makkar* 'acquaintance', *tabbax* '(a) cook', *tappil* 'parasite'—is no longer manifested, but Spirantization is still invariably blocked where it used to exist—a circumstance which again renders the rule opaque . . .

As expected in the rule-based diachronic model, the addition of a general rule degeminating consonants, as in (29), is added to the end of the grammar, and thus follows the spirantization rule.

(29) x → Ø / __ x
　　　　　　　\ /
　　　　　　 Root

This is exactly the analysis proposed in Chomsky (1951), with Spirantization (MR34) ordered prior to Degemination (MR44). Thus in rule-based terms there is a counterfeeding relation between spirantization and degemination, and this has increased the opacity of the grammar under clause (10i).

How will we handle this in OT? Obviously, we need a surface constraint against geminates. But, again, this is insufficient for the whole story. We must somehow prevent underlying geminates from surfacing as continuants. Again, following the general plan of (11) and (23), we can propose (30).

(30) *	Condition	Level
	x　x	
α	\ /	Indifferent
	[− son]	
β	[+ cont]	Surface
Relation	β linked to α	Indifferent

That is, underlying geminates retain [−cont] although they lose their bi-positional status through an analysis similar to the account of the failure of spirantization to affect /g/. The appropriate constraint ranking would be *Geminate >> (30) >> (11). Though underlying geminates must degeminate, it is still better for them to retain [−cont], as shown in (31).

(31)
	/dibber/	*Geminate	(30)	Spir
	[dibber]	*!	√	*
☞	[diber]	√	√	*
	[diver]	√	*!	√
	[divver]	*!	*	√

Notice that conceptually the OT account is already at a disadvantage. The rule-based account had to make one new statement: the degemination rule. This was added at the predicted place at the end of the grammar, and all other effects immediately followed. The OT account, on the other hand, must not only rerank the *Geminate constraint towards the top of the grammar but also change the settings in (30) away from their default values of 'surface', which were sufficient to characterize the constraint as it operated in TH. That is, the most favored development under the OT account would be to simply rerank *Geminate, and retain the unmarked values of 'surface' evaluation on (30). This predicts the non-opaque pattern whereby historical geminates would spirantize. But, in fact, MH is opaque in this respect. Thus, this development is natural and expected under the rule-based theory, and unnatural and unexpected in the OT account.

There are two additional, empirical problems for the OT account. The first problem with (30) is that derived geminates also block spirantization. One process deriving geminates is /n/ deletion, (7j), illustrated in MH in (32):[3]

(32)
nava 'he derived from'	jiba	'he will derive from'
nafal 'he fell'	jipol	'he will fall'
nafax 'he breathed his last'	jipax	'he will breathe his last'
nifkad 'he has been missing'	jipaked	'he will be missing'
	(/ja-n-paked/ → jappaked → [jipaked])	

The /n/ deletion can most clearly be seen in the future of the Nifʕal binyan. The [+cyclic] proclitic preposition /min#/ and the definite marker /ha#/ also

---

[3] As Bolozky points out, the loss of /n/ and compensatory gemination is restricted to certain (base) verbs. Thus while /nbʕ/ 'derived from' has future [jiva], /nbħ/ 'bark' has future [jinbax]. The (derived) nifʕal binyan verb forms regularly show loss of /n/ and no spirantization in the future, though at the surface the stop immediately follows the future prefix vowel: *jipaem* 'he will be moved', *jipaer* 'it will be opened up', *jipade* 'he will be redeemed', *jipaga* 'he will be hurt', *jipaked* 'he will be missing', *jipaxed* 'he will be frightened', *jipara* 'he will be paid up', *jipared* 'he will separate', *jiparek* 'it will be unloaded', *jiparem* 'it was ripped', *jipares* 'it will be spread out', *jiparet* 'it will be changed', *jiparec* 'it will be broken into', *jipasek* 'it will be stopped', *jipasel* 'he will be disqualified', *jikashel* 'he will fail', *jibael* 'he will have sexual intercourse', *jibadek* 'he will be examined', and numerous others.

caused gemination of the following consonant in TH, and MH has (as expected) the corresponding surface stops rather than fricatives. Since these geminate segments are derived rather than underlying, (30) is of no help in accounting for the non-spirantization. Rather, we would have to formulate a post-*n* constraint as in (33).

(33) *	Condition	Level
α	*n*	Indifferent
β	[−son, +cont]	Surface
Linear Order	α > β	Indifferent
Adjacency	Strict	Indifferent

However, (33) results in a constraint ranking paradox, as follows. For Niffal forms like /ja-n-paked/ → [jipaked], (33) must be ranked higher than (11), because (11) is violated at the surface in such forms. But for forms like /ganaB-u/ → [ganvu] 'they stole', (11) must be ranked above (33) because (33) is violated at the surface in such forms. We can get around this problem for these two cases by setting the Adjacency evaluation parameter in (33) to 'Underlying', and ranking (33) >> (11). However, this will not suffice when we examine the imperfective verb cases. In rule-based terms, the cyclic application of vowel deletion feeds gemination in such forms: /ja-napol/ → janəpol → jinpol → jippol → [jipol]. These forms are especially interesting because /n/ is not next to the /p/ at either the underlying or the surface level. In fact, /n/ is completely absent at the surface, so any effective modification of (33) must evaluate some aspect of underlying structure. Our only choice is then to modify the adjacency parameter to be 'consonant to consonant' (cf. McCarthy forthcoming: 15). But this then reinstates the problem for [ganvu].

The second empirical problem for the OT account is that TH did have a more restricted degemination rule which applied at the end of words, (7f), and fed spirantization, (3g). Some of these alternating forms survive in MH, such as /CVC$_i$C$_i$/ nouns, as in (34), from Bolozky (1978: 38).

(34) kaf	'spoon'	kapot	'spoons'
tof	'drum'	tupim	'drums'
rav	'large'	rabim	'large pl.'
dov	'bear'	dubim	'bears'

These examples fall out from the rule-based analysis with no further stipulations. Since the general degemination rule is added to the end of the grammar, it does not directly affect the specific degemination rule earlier in the grammar. Furthermore, the ordering of these two rules is consistent with the Elsewhere Condition, with the more specific rule applying before the more general rule (see also Halle and Idsardi, Chapter 10 above, for discussion of rule addition and the Elsewhere Condition). The specific rule was already ordered before spirantization. In adding the general rule to the grammar, the Elsewhere

Condition requires that the new rule be ordered after the specific rule. In this particular case the new rule meets this condition by being ordered after spirantization. Therefore spirantization is sandwiched between two degemination rules, and these surface forms are correctly generated.

In contrast, this data is a problem for the OT analysis. The TH situation is not hard to handle. The TH version of (30) is evaluated at the surface, and the anti-geminate constraint is restricted to word-edges. But in MH the parameter settings have changed in (30) to partially 'Indifferent', and (30) must be ranked above (11). But this will also prevent spirantization of word-final degeminated stops, contrary to fact. Although alternations such as (34) are being lost in MH (Bolozky 1980), they are being levelled in only one direction, toward a spirant realization in all cases, indicating loss of the underlying geminates on a word-by-word basis. We do not observe the sudden levelling of (34) into stops, as would be predicted by (30). Therefore, we must rank another constraint in the grammar above (30), one possibility is (35), which (assuming the three-way underlying contrasts) will have to ranked below Ident([cont]) .

(35) * V [−son, −cont] $_{PrWd}$]

Evidence for ranking (35) below Ident([cont]) comes from words ending in /k/ < TH /q/.

Once again, the major development from TH to MH can be simply stated as an additional rule or a reranked constraint. What is different between the two cases is that placing the rule at the end of the generative grammar accounts for the rest of the facts without further stipulations, whereas in the OT account several additional constraints must be reranked or reparameterized in order to generate the correct forms. This is because the change to MH has increased the opacity of the grammar, with degemination creating new instance of (10i) type opacity.

3.2.3 *Guttural loss*

We have discussed already the change from TH /ḥ/ to MH /x/. The other TH gutturals, /ʔ h ʕ/, all show some effacements in MH, some of which is also observable in TH. Syllable-final /ʔ/ is deleted in TH, with a following stop being spirantized, (7e). In the very rare cases where /ʔ/ is maintained syllable-finally, it blocks spirantization, for example [wajʔpóːð] 'and surround 3ms impf.' (Lev. 8: 7).

The other gutturals, /h ʕ/, act variably in TH, either inducing post-guttural epenthesis or staying in syllable-final position. When in syllable-final position, they block spirantization of a following stop. Thus we have TH data such as in (36).

(36) a. /ʕbd/ 'work'   [ʕa:vaθ] 'work 3ms perf.' Ezek. 29: 18
                            [yaʕăvo:θ] 'work 3ms impf.' Gen. 25: 23
                            [neʕba:θ] 'work 3ms perf. Nifʕal' Eccles. 5: 8
                            [maʕba:θe:hem] 'work pl.' Job 34: 25
   b. /ʕbr/ 'pass over'   [ʕa:var] 'pass over 3ms perf.' Gen. 15: 17
                            [jaʕăvo:r] 'pass over 3ms impf.' Amos 8: 5
                            [maʕba:ra:] 'passage' Isa. 10: 29
   c. /ʕkr/ 'trouble'   [ʕa:xar] 'trouble 3ms perf.' 1 Sam. 14: 29
                            [jaʕka:rxa:] 'trouble 3m s impf. ms' Josh. 7: 25
                            [neʕka:r] 'trouble 3ms perf. Nifʕal' Isa. 10: 29
   d. /hpk/ 'change'   [ha:fax] 'overturn 3ms perf.' Lev. 13: 3
                            [ʔehpo:x] 'overturn 1s impf.' Zeph. 3: 9
                            [nehpax] 'overturn 3ms perf Nifʕal' Exod. 7: 15
                            [mahpe:xa:] 'overthrow' Isa. 1: 7
                            [mahpexeθ] 'stocks' Jer. 20: 2
                            [tahpu:xo:θ] 'perversities' Deut. 32: 20

In MH [ʕ] has disappeared; /ʕ/ can show up as [ʔ] in prevocalic position, and is deleted elsewhere. The same distribution applies to /h/, which can surface as [h] prevocalically, and is deleted elsewhere. This yields data in MH such as in (37), where the deleted segments /ʕ h/ are shown in parentheses.

(37) a. /ʕbd/ 'work'   [ma(ʕ)bada] 'laboratory' (Klein 1987)
                            [ma(ʕ)bad] 'deed, action' (Alcalay 1974)
   b. /ʕbr/ 'pass over'   [ma(ʕ)bara] 'immigrant's transit camp' (Zilkha 1989)
                            [ma(ʕ)boret] 'ferryboat' (Zilkha 1989)
   c. /ʕkr/ 'trouble'   [ne(ʕ)kar] 'to be spoiled' (Zilkha 1989)
   d. /hpk/ 'change'   [ta(h)puxan] 'perverse' (Klein 1987)
                            [ta(h)puxot] 'instability' (Zilkha 1989)
                            [ma(h)pax] 'reverse, change' (Klein 1987)
                            (also the name of one of the accent signs)
   e. /hbl/ 'vapor'   [ma(h)bil] 'steaming' (Klein 1987)
                            [ma(h)bel] 'steam generator' (Alcalay 1974)

This change also increases the opacity of the language, as these are additional instances of (10i).

The absolute neutralization of /ʕ/ to [ʔ] or [Ø] (the same distribution as /ʔ/) has led some to propose that TH /ʕ ʔ/ are merged into MH /ʔ/. Unfortunately, this account does not yield the correct spirantization facts, as loss of /ʔ/ still results in spirantization, [joxal] 'will eat' (Bolozky 1978: 18), whereas loss of /ʕ/ does not (36a-c). This also shows that we cannot handle /ʕ/ deletion as a feeding relationship between the rules /ʕ/ → /ʔ/ and /ʔ/-deletion. But since /ʕ/ → /ʔ/ is a new rule (not existing in TH), the prediction is that it will be added to the end of the grammar. This correctly accounts for the facts, and is also the analysis in Chomsky (1951), where Spirantization (MR34) precedes /ʕ/ → /ʔ/

(MR42). Likewise, the general loss of /h ʕ/ is an innovation, and this rule, (38), should be added to the end of the grammar.

(38) [−cons] → Ø / ___ σ]
     |
     Guttural

This prediction is exactly borne out, with the general guttural deletion in syllable-final position following spirantization, but with the continuation of the TH /ʔ/-deletion preceding spirantization, as it did in TH. Notice that this is the same effect observed with the two degemination rules. The more specific, historical rules are retained before spirantization while the general rules are added to the end of the grammar, following spirantization, and this ordering is in accordance with the Elsewhere Condition.

For the OT account, we will have to raise the ranking of the constraint barring /h ʕ/ from syllable-final position in the MH grammar because [h ʕ] are not observed in this position. But if this is the only reranking that we do, we will incorrectly predict that the now postvocalic stops will spirantize, contrary to fact. Thus, we also have to add a constraint preventing spirantization following underlying /h ʕ/, as in (39).

(39) *

	Condition	Level
α	h / ʕ	Indifferent
β	[−son, +cont]	Surface
Linear Order	α > β	Indifferent
Adjacency	C-to-C	Indifferent

The problems with this account are similar to those encountered with (33). C-to-C adjacency is required to explain forms like /na-ʕakar/ → [nekar], but it will then incorrectly block spirantization in post-guttural epenthesis cases, such as segolate nouns, for example /zaʕp/ → [záʔaf] 'rage, anger', but (39) incorrectly predicts *[zaʔap]. Put in surface-orientated terms, spirantization is only blocked by underlying /ʕ h/ when these segments themselves delete. (Even this statement is not completely accurate phonetically, as it is possible to elide /h ʕ/ quite generally.) But no formulation of that generalization is possible within the parameterized OT constraint theory. Finally, one additional problem with (38) is finding the feature combination which will pick out /h ʕ/ to the exclusion of /ʔ/. Notice that defining this segment class was unnecessary in the rule-based theory because /ʔ/-deletion applies first, allowing the added rule, (38), to be more general and delete all gutturals.

4. SUMMARY AND CONCLUSIONS

The examination of the role of spirantization in the grammar of Modern Hebrew shows that Modern Hebrew in fact has richer and more opaque relationships among phonological processes than did Tiberian Hebrew. The innovations in Modern Hebrew do not give rise to decreased opacity as expected in OT (cf. also Koutsoudas et al. 1974 in this respect). Rather, the changes can be succinctly described only in a rule-based framework, where they are clustered at the end of the grammar. In contrast, the OT account of each of the developments examined here entails making extra changes in constraint parameters or rankings.

For example, the loss of geminates in MH and its attendant effects on spirantization should be simply statable in phonological theory. The rule-based theory adds a general degemination rule, (29), to the end of the grammar. Being at the end of the grammar, it is surface-true. The correct effects follow without making any other changes to the grammar. It is simple to bar geminates from phonetic forms in OT: simply put a constraint against surface geminates at the top of the grammar. Being undominated, it will be surface-true. But, unfortunately, if this is the only change we make, we will not generate the correct forms of MH. Instead, we must formulate and rank new constraints such as (30), (33), and (35) to generate the actual patterns of MH. Furthermore, there is nothing in the historical record to suggest that the hypothetical OT grammar obtained by simply making *Geminate undominated was an intermediate stage. In fact, it is clear that it could not have been an intermediate stage, as it would have completely neutralized the geminate/non-geminate distinction, which then could not have been reinstated. Therefore, it is evident for the cases we have considered here that the rule-based theory does a much better job of accounting for the diachronic changes.

In OT as developed in McCarthy (forthcoming), opacity is a fundamental concept, and OT grammars highly value transparent (surface-true) solutions. Since OT is specifically designed to disfavor opacity, the increase in opacity observed in the transition from Tiberian Hebrew to Modern Hebrew is unexpected and problematic for OT. In contrast, rule systems are not so easily characterized in terms of opacity, and in the present case the original hypothesis of Halle (1962) that new rules are added to the end of the grammar succinctly accounts for the interactions between various diachronic neutralizations and spirantization. Thus OT is not only wrong in the narrow technical sense that it cannot adequately handle cases like MH [jipol], but also wrongheaded as it is not yielding interesting questions or answers regarding the general principles of grammar and grammatical change.

ACKNOWLEDGEMENTS

I would especially like to thank Peter Avery, Noam Chomsky, Elan Dresher, Morris Halle, Rolf Noyer, Tom Purnell, Tova Rapaport, Keren Rice, and the reviewers for discussions of the material presented here. I would also like to thank the participants of the Montreal–Ottawa–Toronto Phonology meeting in Ottawa, February 1995, Iggy Roca and the participants of the Essex Workshop on Derivations and Constraints in Phonology, September 1995, and Gene Buckley, Sean Crist, and the participants at the University of Pennsylvania Linguistics Colloquium in Philadelphia, February 1996, for exciting discussions of these issues. This research was partially supported by a grant from the University of Delaware Research Foundation.

REFERENCES

Alcalay, R. (1974). *The Complete Hebrew–English Dictionary*. Bridgeport, Conn.: Prayer Book Press/Hartmore House.

Archangeli, D., and Pulleyblank, D. (1995). *Grounded Phonology*. Cambridge, Mass.: MIT Press.

Baltsan, H. (1992). *Webster's New World Hebrew Dictionary*. New York: Prentice-Hall.

Bolozky, S. (1978). 'Some aspects of Modern Hebrew phonology', in R. Berman (ed.), *Modern Hebrew Structure*. Tel Aviv: University Publishing Projects, 11–67.

—— (1980). 'Paradigm coherence: evidence from Modern Hebrew', *Afroasiatic Linguistics* **7** (4): 1–24.

Chomsky, N. (1951). 'Morphophonemics of Modern Hebrew'. Master's Thesis, University of Pennsylvania, Philadelphia. Published 1979, New York: Garland.

—— (1995). *The Minimalist Program*. Cambridge, Mass.: MIT Press.

Dobrin, L. M. (1993). 'Underdeterminacy in prosodic morphology', *Papers from the 29th Regional Meeting of the Chicago Linguistics Society*. Chicago Linguistics Society, 137–153.

Dresher, B. E. (1983). 'Postlexical phonology in Tiberian Hebrew', *Proceedings of the Second West Coast Conference on Formal Linguistics*. Stanford University, 67–78.

Faber, A. (1986). 'On the origin and development of Hebrew spirantization', *Mediterranean Language Review* **2**: 117–38.

Gesenius, W. (1910). *Gesenius' Hebrew Grammar*, ed. and enlarged by E. Kantzsch. 2nd English edn. by A. E. Cowley. Oxford: Oxford University Press.

Halle, M. (1962). 'Phonology in a generative grammar', *Word* **18**: 54–72.

Hyman, L. (1993). 'Structure preservation and postlexical tonology in Dagbani', in S. Hargus and E. Kaisse (eds.), *Studies in Lexical Phonology*. New York: Academic Press, 235–54.

Idsardi, W. (forthcoming). 'Tiberian Hebrew spirantization and phonological derivations', *Linguistic Inquiry*.

Inkelas, S., Orgun, O., and Zoll, C. (1994). 'Subregularaties as cogrammars: The theoretical status of nonproductive patterns and exceptions in grammar'. MS, University of California, Berkeley.

Iverson, G. (1993). '(Post)lexical rule application', in S. Hargus and E. Kaisse (eds.), *Studies in Lexical Phonology*. New York: Academic Press, 255–76.

Kaisse, E. (1990). 'Toward a typology of post-lexical rules', in S. Inkelas and D. Zec (eds.), *The Phonology–Syntax Connection*. Stanford, Calif.: CSLI, 127–44.

Katz, D. (1993). 'The phonology of Ashkenazic', in L. Glinert (ed.), *Hebrew in Ashkenaz: A Language in Exile*. Oxford: Oxford University Press, 46–87.

Kiparsky, P. (1970). 'Historical linguistics', in J. Lyons (ed.), *New Horizons in Linguistics*. New York: Penguin, 302–15.

—— (1973). '"Elsewhere" in phonology', in S. Anderson and P. Kiparsky (eds.), *A Festschrift for Morris Halle*. New York: Harper & Row, 93–106.

—— (1976). 'Abstractness, opacity and global rules', in A. Koutsoudas (ed.), *The Application and Ordering of Grammatical Rules*. The Hague: Mouton, 160–86.

—— (1982). 'Lexical phonology and morphology', in I.-S. Yang (ed.), *Linguistics in the Morning Calm*. Seoul: Hanshin, 3–91.

—— (1993). 'Blocking in nonderived environments', in S. Hargus and E. Kaisse (eds.), *Studies in Lexical Phonology*. New York: Academic Press, 277–314.

Kisseberth, C. (1977). 'The interaction of phonological rules and the polarity of language', in A. Koutsoudas (ed.), *The Application and Ordering of Grammatical Rules*. The Hague: Mouton, 41–54.

Klein, E (1987). *A Comprehensive Etymological Dictionary of the Hebrew Languages for Readers of English*. New York: Macmillan.

Koutsoudas, A., Sanders G., and Noll, C. (1974). 'On the application of phonological rules', *Language* **50**: 1–28.

McCarthy, J. (1979). 'Formal Problems in Semitic Phonology and Morphology'. Doctoral dissertation, MIT.

—— (1993). 'Template form in prosodic morphology', *Proceedings of the Formal Linguistics Society of Mid-America III*. Bloomington: Indiana University Linguistics Club, 187–217.

—— (forthcoming). 'Remarks on phonological opacity in Optimality Theory', to appear in J. Lecarme, J. Lowenstamm, and U. Shlonsky (eds.), *Proceedings of the Second Colloquium on Afro-Asiatic Linguistics*.

—— and Prince, A. 1990. 'Prosodic morphology and templatic morphology', in M. Eid and J. McCarthy (eds.), *Perspectives on Arabic Linguistics III*. Philadelphia: Benjamins, 1–54.

Malone, J. (1993). *Tiberian Hebrew Phonology*. Winona Lake, Ind.: Eisenbrauns.

Murtonen, A. (1990). *Hebrew in its West Semitic Setting: A Comparative Survey of non-Masoretic Hebrew Dialects and Traditions*, pt. 2: *Phonetics and Phonology*. New York: E. J. Brill.

Prince, A. (1975). 'The Phonology and Morphology of Tiberian Hebrew'. Dissertation, MIT.

—— and Smolensky, P. (1993). 'Optimality Theory: Constraint Interaction in Generative Grammar'. Technical report, Center for Cognitive Science, Rutgers University, and Dept. of Computer Science, University of Colorado, Boulder.

Rappaport, M. (1985). 'Issues in the Phonology of Tiberian Hebrew'. Dissertation, MIT.

Ravid, D. (1995). *Language Change in Child and Adult Hebrew: A Psycholinguistic Perspective*. Oxford: Oxford University Press.

Rice, K. (1990). 'Predicting rule domains in the phrasal phonology', in S. Inkelas and D. Zec (eds.), *The Phonology–Syntax Connection*. Stanford, Calif.: CSLI, 289–312.

—— (1994). 'Peripheral in consonants', *Canadian Journal of Linguistics* **39**: 191–216.

Rosén, H. (1977). *Contemporary Hebrew*. The Hague: Mouton.

—— (1962). *A Textbook of Israeli Hebrew*. Chicago: University of Chicago Press.

Schein, B. and Steriade, D. (1986). 'On geminates', *Linguistic Inquiry* **17**: 691–744.

Zilkha, A. (1989). *Modern Hebrew–English Dictionary*. New Haven, Conn.: Yale University Press.

13

The Implications of Lexical Exceptions for the Nature of Grammar

SHARON INKELAS, C. ORHAN ORGUN, and
CHERYL ZOLL

1. Introduction

This chapter explores the consequences of lexical exceptions for the nature of grammar, drawing a comparison between two types of phonological theory: rule theory (or derivational theory), which uses rules to capture alternations and constraints to capture static patterns, and Optimality Theory (Prince and Smolensky 1993), which uses constraints to handle alternations as well as static patterns. We conclude that in order to deal with lexical exceptions, rule theory is forced to use morpheme-specific co-phonologies (subgrammars), a practice which engenders such serious problems that it must be rejected outright. By contrast, Optimality Theory is capable of avoiding morpheme-specific co-phonologies. The fact that OT has violable constraints allows it to employ a principled prespecification approach to lexical exceptions. As we demonstrate, prespecification has a number of advantages over the co-phonology approach and none of its fatal problems. The chapter concludes with a discussion of the positive implications of OT for a principled underlying representation, and with some speculation on the grammatical status of static patterns.

2. Case Studies

We begin by setting out two case studies which will inform the discussion. (Clearly it would be desirable to consider more examples, but space limitations force us to refer the reader to other, related works; see especially Inkelas, 1994; forthcoming, and Inkelas and Orgun, 1995; forthcoming for a richer panoply of data). Both examples are from Turkish, and form part of a larger ongoing study by two of the authors on the lexical phonology of Turkish.

2.1 *Labial attraction*

Our first example of lexical exceptionality involves a static pattern which induces no alternations but has none the less been claimed to have grammatical status in Turkish.

As originally described by Lees (1966) and developed in subsequent work by Itô et al. (1993; 1995: 818), Ní Chiosáin and Padgett (1993), and Itô and Mester (1995), Labial Attraction is an alleged root-structure constraint to the effect that if a labial consonant occurs between the vowel /a/ and a following high back vowel, that high vowel must be round, i.e. /u/. (In fact, a consonant may occur immediately adjacent to the labial, on either side, but we omit this immaterial detail for notational ease.)

(1) A root obeys Labial Attraction if the following statement is true:
'∀ /aB[+ bk, + hi]/, [+ bk, + hi] = /u/'
(where 'B' represents any labial consonant)
A root disobeys Labial Attraction if the same statement is false.

Some roots overtly conforming to Labial Attraction are listed in (2):[1]

(2) karpuz   'watermelon'
    sabun   'soap'
    habur   (the place name 'Habur')
    javru   'cub'

As Clements and Sezer (1982) note, Lees's Labial Attraction constraint admits numerous exceptions, some of which are listed below:[2]

(3) kapɯ   'door'
    kalamɯʃ   (the place name 'Kalamış')
    tavɯr   'attitude'

Labial Attraction induces no alternations, holding strictly within roots and never across morpheme boundaries, as shown by the suffixed forms in (4a).

---

[1] Turkish data are presented in phonemic transcription using IPA symbols (and following the common practice of representing the low back unrounded vowel, [ɑ], as [a]). Syllable boundaries (marked with a dot) are indicated only when directly relevant to the discussion. Upper-case letters stand for archiphonemes, unspecified for alternating features (in the case of low vowels ('E'), [back]; in the case of high vowels ('I'), [back] and [round]; in the case of plosives (e.g. 'B'), [voice]). Data represent the speech of the alphabetically second author, a native speaker of (Standard) Istanbul Turkish.

[2] Itô et al. (1993; 1995) have claimed that Labial Attraction is true of the native vocabulary of Turkish. In fact, however, a number of the roots (including some which Itô et al. (1993) list) are loans (e.g. *karpuz* 'watermelon', from Greek, *armut*, 'pear', from Persian, *sabun* 'soap', from Arabic, *ʃampuan* 'shampoo', from French and so on), while a number of native roots (e.g. *kapɯ* 'door') are exceptions to the constraint. It may be that the constraint held at one time in the history of the language; *kapɯ* used to be pronounced *kapu* (and still is, by some older speakers), and there are a few forms with frozen suffixes whose vowels conform to Labial Attraction (e.g. *yamuk* 'crooked', with a frozen adjective suffix *-uk*), suggesting that the constraint may even have induced alternations at one time.

The forms in (4b) serve as a control to show that the same suffixes can, elsewhere, appear with round vowels; these result from vowel harmony, which assimilates them to a preceding round vowel.

(4) a. i. kitap   'book'
        kitab-ɯ   'book-accusative'   *kitabu
     ii. tambura-m   'stringed instrument-1sg.poss'
        tambura-m-dɯ   'stringed instrument-1sg.poss-past'   *tamburamdu
    b. i. sabun   'soap'
        sabun-u   'soap-accusative'
        sabun-du   'soap-past'

2.2 *Coda devoicing*

Our second example is a pattern which *does* induce alternations. Coda Devoicing is a well-known alternation in Turkish whereby plosives surface as voiced in onset position but as voiceless in coda position (Lees 1961; Lewis 1967; Underhill 1976; Kaisse 1986; Rice 1990; Inkelas and Orgun 1995). An example involving /t ~ d/ is given below:

(5) a. ka.nat   'wing'
    b. ka.nat.-lar   'wing-plural'
    c. ka.na.d-ɯ   'wing-accusative'

The generalization is described as coda devoicing (Kaisse 1986; Rice 1990) rather than, for example, onset voicing, because of the large number of roots ending in consistently voiceless plosives:

(6) a. dev.let   'state'
    b. dev.let.-ler   'state-plural'
    c. dev.le.t-i   'state-accusative'

Coda Devoicing admits a small number of lexical exceptions, roots which end in plosives that surface as voiced even in coda position (Kaisse 1986; Hayes 1990; Inkelas and Orgun 1995):[3]

(7) a. e.tyd   'study'
        e.tyd.-ler   'study-plural'
    b. ka.ta.log   'catalog'
        ka.ta.log.-dan 'catalog-ablative'

---

[3] As noted in Lewis (1967), monosyllabic roots follow a different pattern in which it is alternating plosives that are the exception. For an account of this, see Inkelas and Orgun (1995).

3. LEXICAL EXCEPTIONS IN RULE THEORY

We turn now to the manner in which rule theory handles exceptions of the two types we have just exemplified. Recall that by 'rule theory' we mean any theory that uses rules to account for alternations and (inviolable) constraints to account for static patterns. Rule theories include the Theory of Constraints and Repair Strategies (Paradis 1988) and standard generative phonology (see e.g. McCarthy 1986 and Yip 1988).

Two options have historically been utilized by rule theory to deal with lexical exceptions: morpheme-specific co-phonologies and prespecification. Both date back to Chomsky and Halle (1968) and have been in use ever since. The morpheme-specific co-phonology method designates a morpheme in underlying representation as an exception to an existing rule (negative rule exception features) or as exceptionally triggering a rule that does not ordinarily apply (minor rules). (There are a few other types of underlying designation as well; for a full overview of the rule features used by Chomsky and Halle, 1968, and subsequent authors, see Zonneveld, 1978.)[4] Prespecification, by contrast, is the strategy of specifying a lexical item with its exceptional structure, under the assumption that the underlying structure will block the purely structure-filling insertion rules to which the form is an exception (see e.g. Ringen 1975).

For static patterns that are handled by constraints, such as Labial Attraction, only the morpheme-specific co-phonology option is available in rule theory to handle exceptions. Because output constraints perform no operation, there is no sense in which complicating the underlying phonological structure of a morpheme can affect the applicability of a constraint to its surface structure.

For alternations that admit exceptions, both prespecification and co-phonology options have been taken in the rule theory literature.[5] We will show here, however, that, of the two, only the co-phonology option has been and can be satisfactorily implemented from a formal standpoint in rule theory. The prespecification method enjoys a long history, great intuitive appeal, and staunch defenders (including authors of this chapter). However, it has a subtle but devastating formal flaw when implemented in rule theory: the apparently

---

[4] For a sampling of works using the rule feature approach see Lees (1961), Lightner (1965), McCawley (1968), Postal (1968), Harris (1969), Saciuk (1969), Kisseberth (1970), Lakoff (1970), Schane (1973), Zonneveld (1978), Ringen (1978), Kiparsky (1982), and Halle and Vergnaud (1987). The rule feature approach is defended as superior to prespecification by Kiparsky (1973*a*; 1973*b*).

[5] A sampling of past uses of prespecification to handle exceptions in rule theory includes Ringen (1975); van der Hulst (1985; 1988); Mester (1986); Myers (1987); Vago (1988); Pulleyblank (1988); Archangeli and Pulleyblank (1989); Buckley (1992; 1994*a*; 1994*b*); Paradis and Prunet (1993); Ringen and Vago (forthcoming). For a defence of prespecification over morpheme-specific co-phonologies (specifically, rule exception features), see e.g. Harris (1977*a*; 1977*b*), Inkelas and Cho (1993), Inkelas (1994) and Inkelas and Orgun (1995). Prespecification is employed to handle related phenomena by Inkelas and Cho (1993) (for geminate inalterability) and Kiparsky (1993) (for nonderived environment blocking).

intrinsic inability of rule theory to formalize adequately the critical difference between a purely structure-filling insertion rule and a structure-changing insertion rule. The former will be halted by prespecification and admit exceptions, while the latter will ride roughshod over prespecified structure and be exceptionless. Without this distinction, it is impossible to predict the behavior of an insertion rule when confronted with prespecified structure.[6]

Two basic strands of attempts to denote rules as purely structure-filling can be isolated in the literature. The simplest and most ambitious is the proposal of Poser (1982), Mascaró (1987), and Cho (1990) (see also Kiparsky, 1985; 1993) that all insertion rules are structure-filling, and that all structure-changing insertion rules (including spread) can be decomposed into deletion rules and structure-filling insertion rules.[7] If no insertion rules are structure-changing, then in principle there is no formal difficulty with the prespecification method. Though elegant (albeit stipulative), this approach is overly restrictive, lacking, for example, the ability to account for chain shifts in which the original featural make-up of a segment is a crucial predictor of its outcome when subjected to the structure-changing shift operation (see Clements 1991; McCarthy 1993*b*; 1994; Orgun 1995; Cho 1995; Kirchner 1996). If, as in the vowel height chain shift discussed by Clements (1991), in which Bantu vowels shift from low to mid and from mid to high, the height specification of a vowel were deleted and then replaced, all vowels would incorrectly become underspecified and would therefore neutralize. Furthermore, the decomposition of apparently structure-changing rules suffers from a conspiracy problem: in cases where the deletion component operates solely in order to enable the insertion component to apply, the two components must have exactly the same conditioning environment, missing the generalization that they are really part of the same alternation.

The alternative approach is that of Pulleyblank (1986) and many others, who propose that what defines a purely structure-filling rule is the designation of its target as unspecified for a given feature or features.

(8) Purely structure-filling rule (see Pulleyblank, 1986 for an autosegmental version)
   $[\emptyset F] \rightarrow [+ F] / X \underline{\quad} Y$

However, the ability to refer to 'zeroes' creates more problems than it solves, incorrectly permitting the influence of underspecification to extend beyond the

---

[6] See Kiparsky (1993) for a review of attempts to block structure-filling rules from incorrectly neutralizing exceptional (and other) underlying structure. Kiparsky concludes that no past principles, including the Alternation Condition, the Revised Alternation Condition, and the Strict Cycle Condition, are sufficient, and that it is instead necessary to make individual rules purely structure-filling to get the desired results.

[7] Kiparsky (1985) allows structure-changing rules to exist, as the marked case, by stipulating in the rule itself that pre-existing structure must be deleted. However, his formalism does not allow for the existence of rules which will apply either in the presence or in the absence of pre-existing structure.

intended use of permitting insertion of the underspecified structure. For example, direct reference to underspecification makes it possible to formulate a constraint forbidding two adjacent underspecified segments, or a rule which inserts one feature (F) only in segments unspecified for another (G). Apart, perhaps, for the characterization of purely structure-filling insertion rules, there is no evidence that rules or constraints can directly refer to the underspecification of a segment; some of the undesirable consequences of allowing rules to do so have been explored by Stanley (1967).[8]

In summary, prespecification is clearly intractable as a means of accounting for lexical exceptions to the inviolable constraints of rule theory; we have also concluded that it is formally flawed as an account of exceptions to rules. We are left with morpheme-specific co-phonologies as the encoders of lexical exceptions to constraints and static patterns.

4. THE CASE AGAINST MORPHEME-SPECIFIC CO-PHONOLOGIES

Having concluded that morpheme-specific co-phonologies are necessary to the description of lexical exceptions in rule theory, we now proceed to develop an argument *against* morpheme-specific cophonologies. (Ultimately, we will conclude that rule theory has no acceptable method of dealing with lexical exceptions.) The argument in this section is essentially theory-neutral, applying equally to rule theory and to constraint-based theories.

It is clear that co-phonologies are required to handle cases of competing sets of alternations triggered in disjoint sets of morphological constructions; such co-phonologies, referred to as the 'levels' or 'strata' of Lexical Phonology (Kiparsky 1982; Mohanan 1982), have been in use for a long time and are widely accepted.[9] However, *morpheme*-specific cophonologies are an entirely different analytic device engendering a number of serious problems, which we will now proceed to detail.

---

[8] A related implementation of direct reference to underspecification is offered by Archangeli and Pulleyblank (1994: 293 ff.), who propose FREE TARGET as one of their rule parameters. This specification is intrinsically relevant only to insertion rules, and ensures that the target is not linked to the type of structure being inserted by the rule. Unfortunately, Archangeli and Pulleyblank are not explicit about the formal description of rule environments, making it difficult to evaluate the ramifications of direct reference to underspecification there. In any case, any restrictions on reference to underspecification present in Archangeli and Pulleyblank's approach are there by stipulation; their fundamental insight, that rules are parameterized, has no inherent bearing on the nature of structure-filling rule application.

[9] For more recent theoretical developments related to this use of co-phonologies, see e.g. Buckley (1995) and Inkelas and Orgun (1995; forthcoming).

4.1 *Exceptions to static patterns (the Distributional Method)*

We begin by examinating the implications of using morpheme-specific co-phonologies to handle lexical exceptions to static patterns such as Labial Attraction. In the interest of clarity, we will give a name to this methodology:

(9) DISTRIBUTIONAL METHOD for establishing co-phonologies: Given a phonological property P, assume that its presence is enforced by grammar. If not all morphemes in the language possess property P, then establish two co-phonologies: one which requires the presence of P and another which requires its absence. Assign each morpheme to one of these two co-phonologies.

In the case of Labial Attraction, the property P is obedience to Labial Attraction. The Distributional Method causes two co-phonologies to be defined for Turkish, one which enforces Labial Attraction and another which does not.

(10) *Co-phonology A: enforces Labial Attraction.* morphemes which are consistent with the requirements of Labial Attraction, e.g. (in Turkish) *sabun* 'soap' or *kitap* 'book'.

Co-phonology B: does not enforce Labial Attraction. Members: only morphemes which directly violate Labial Attraction, e.g. (in Turkish) *kapɯ* 'door'.

The problems we raise in the following subsections arise from the consequences of following the Distributional Method in a systematic way.

4.1.1 *Uninteresting co-phonologies*

A first objection to the Distributional Method is that many, if not most, of the cophonologies it causes to be defined hold absolutely no interest at all to the linguist. For example, consider the property of lacking a syllable coda (reified as a constraint in rule theory by Itô, 1986 and in OT by Prince and Smolensky, 1993). All languages have morphemes without codas, and most languages have morphemes with codas. Thus in most languages two classes exist: one in which codas are absent and one in which codas are present. The Distributional Method automatically defines a separate co-phonology for each class, one which prohibits and one which requires codas.[10] We term the relevant constraint 'NoCoda', following Prince and Smolensky (1993); but recall that we are assuming the rule theory framework in which constraints are inviolable.

(11) *Co-phonology C (enforces 'NoCoda'): No syllable may have a coda.*
Members of Co-phonology C: all roots consistent with 'NoCoda' (in Turkish, e.g. *su* 'water', *iki* 'two', *adana* (the place name 'Adana')).

Co-phonology D (does not enforce 'NoCoda'): At least one syllable must have a coda.
Members of D: all roots in violation of 'NoCoda' (in Turkish, e.g. *ham* 'unripe', *karpuz* 'watermelon', *istanbul* (the place name 'İstanbul'))

---

[10] It is crucial for the system to be deterministic that Co-phonology D require a coda. If it simply tolerated but did not require codas, then the co-phonology membership of a word with only open syllables would be indeterminate between co-phonologies C and D.

Proceeding apace, the Distributional Method will define separate co-phonologies for vowel-initial and consonant-initial roots in Turkish. We use the term 'Onset' for this constraint (though it should not be confused with the Onset constraint of Prince and Smolensky, 1993):

(12)   *Co-phonology E (enforces ' Onset'): All roots begin with a consonant.*
        Members of E: all roots that obey Onset (in Turkish, e.g. *bebek* 'baby', *masa* 'table', *su* 'water')

        Co-phonology F (does not enforce' Onset'): All roots begin with a vowel.
        Members of F: all roots that disobey Onset (in Turkish, e.g. *anne* 'mother', *aaf* 'tree', *ek* 'affix')

But co-phonologies C, D, E, and F are of no particular interest. No insight is gained by establishing separate grammars for *su* and *ham*, respectively, or for *bebek* and *anne*, respectively, in Turkish.

    In essence, for any detectable pattern which is formulable as a constraint and which admits surface exceptions, it is always the case that the morphemes of the language *can* be divided into two classes on the basis of that constraint. Our point is that if the Distributional Method is assumed, they *must* be. The Distributional Method simply does on a systematic basis what linguists have done on an elective basis, presumably when the constraint in question is of interest to them (as Labial Attraction was to Itô, *et al.*, 1993, and Ní Chiosáin and Padgett, 1993). However, the Distributional Method does not have the discretion that individual linguists do, and so it blindly and automatically defines co-phonologies whether they are interesting or not. Needless to say, it is necessary to suspend intuitions and discretion when evaluating the formal power of a theory; a method must be applied systematically in order to see what it will achieve. In the case of the Distributional Method, it achieves cophonologies that are of no interest.

4.1.2 *Too many co-phonologies*

A second, related problem for the Distributional Method is that, applied consistently, it results in the postulation of one co-phonology per (phonologically distinct) morpheme. Consider, by way of illustration, the interaction of the co-phonologies responsible for the distribution of Labial Attraction (Co-phonologies A and B) (10) and those responsible for the occurrence of coda consonants (Co-phonologies C and D) (11). Because Labial Attraction and coda presence are logically independent, their respective memberships intersect, as shown in (13), yielding four distinct co-phonologies. (In the chart, 'yes' means that the form is consistent with the relevant constraint; 'no' means that it is not.)

(13)

Cophonology	Labial Attraction	NoCoda	Example member word	
A,C	yes	no	karpuz	'watermelon'
A,D	no	no	tavɯr	'attitude'
B,C	yes	yes	tapu	'title'
B,D	no	yes	kapɯ	'door'

But of course Labial Attraction and coda presence are not the only two phonological properties found in Turkish morphemes. As soon as it detects another independent phonological property, e.g. onset presence (regulated by Co-phonologies E and F) (12), the Distributional Method will define four new phonologies:

(14)

Co-phonology	Labial Attraction	NoCoda	Onset	Example member word	
A,C,E	yes	yes	yes	tapu	'title'
A,C,F	yes	yes	no	osamu[11]	(the foreign name 'Osamu')
A,D,E	yes	no	yes	habur	(the place-name 'Habur')
A,D,F	yes	no	no	armut	'pear'
B,C,E	no	yes	yes	kapɯ	'door'
B,C,F	no	yes	no	a:bɯru:	'dignity'
B,D,E	no	no	yes	kalamɯʃ	(the place-name 'Kalamış')
B,D,F	no	no	no	apɯʃ	'astride'

It is obvious that this kind of breakdown can continue virtually indefinitely. As long as two morphemes exhibit any differences at all that are characterizable by a well-formed constraint, the Distributional Method forces the grammar to capture the distinct pattern of each morpheme with a distinct co-phonology. This is too many co-phonologies.

4.1.3 *Possible solutions*

There are two possible solutions we know of to the problem of morpheme-specific co-phonology proliferation caused by the Distributional Method. One is extrinsically to limit the number of morpheme-specific co-phonologies a language can define, e.g. by placing a requirement of statistical significance on patterns that can be encoded by constraints (and hence sponsor morpheme-specific co-phonologies). The underlying assumption would be that only these patterns come to the attention of the language learner and are encoded in grammar.

While this approach would reduce the *number* of co-phonologies, it still would have no effect on the problem of counterintuitive, unwanted morpheme-

---

[11] The native-speaker author imported this proper name into Turkish (which is easy to do) for purposes of filling out this table.

specific co-phonologies that the Distributional Method defines. The reason is that the Distributional Method still lacks any judgement as to which morpheme-specific co-phonologies it makes sense to include in the grammar of a language, and which are due to the vagaries of history and better left unencoded. To illustrate, we turn to an example of a statistically significant but linguistically irrelevant static pattern that occurs in Slave (Athapaskan).

As Rice (1988; 1989) has shown, French loans are the dominant source of initial /l/ in Slave words. French nouns have been borrowed in their definite form, and thus have an initial [l] corresponding to the definite article *le* of French. A few of the very large number of nouns of this type are illustrated in (15):

(15) *Slave*   *English*   *French*

    líʃabú   hat   le chapeau
    líbahdú   barge   le bateau
    lígarí, lígar cards   les cartes
    lamé   mass   la messe
    líselí, lísel salt   le sel
    lífilí   thread   le fil

In her comprehensive (1989) grammar of Slave, Rice cites exactly seven [l]-initial forms which do *not* come from French, a sampling of which is given in (16).

(16) lamǫ   'ring'
    leʤai   'window'
    la   'work'
    láidi   'where is it?'

The crucial point is that if a noun is [l]-initial, the probability is very high that the nucleus of the first syllable will be [i]. This pattern is, of course, due entirely to historical factors: [i] is the reflex in Slave of the vowel of the definite article in French, found in most [l]-initial nouns (as in the representative list in (15)). If, however, it proves statistically significant, as it presumably will, the linguist committed to encoding all statistically significant patterns in grammar will have to encode this one as well. The grammar of Slave will have to contain a co-phonology defined by the requirement that [l]-initial words have [i] in the first syllable.

To any linguist finding this to be an undesirable situation, statistical significance will not be the savior of the Distributional Method. The problem with the statistical method is that statistical significance suggests that a certain pattern is not due to chance. It does follow from this that there might be a cause for the pattern, but it does not follow that the cause must be in the synchronic grammar.

A second logical option for improving the Distributional Method would be to limit the variety, rather than the number, of co-phonologies possible in a given language. One interesting approach along these lines has been suggested by Itô and Mester (1993; 1995) in a discussion of the phonotactics of native and loanwords in the vocabulary of Japanese.

Itô and Mester observe that the etymologically native (Yamato) vocabulary items in Japanese all obey the following three constraints:

(17) *Constraints obeyed by all Yamato lexical items*
  *P: Single [p] is prohibited
  *NT: Post-nasal obstruents must be voiced
  *DD: Voiced geminate obstruents are prohibited

Some loanwords also obey these constraints and can for all purposes be classified as Yamato. Others, however, violate one or more of the constraints in (17). Based on the observed patterns of constraint violation, Itô and Mester define two additional co-phonologies for these loans. A loan is classified as 'Foreign' iff it violates the *DD constraint; a form violating only *NT or *P (or both), but not *DD, is classified as 'Assimilated Foreign':

(18) *Co-phonology*   *Definition*   *Examples*

'Foreign'	*DD necessarily violated	*beddo* 'bed'
'Assimilated Foreign'	*DD necessarily obeyed; at least one of *NT, *P necessarily violated	*peepaa* 'paper', *hantai* 'opposite'

The Foreign and Assimilated Foreign co-phonologies of Japanese are excellent examples of co-phonologies that the Distributional Method would define. They are not supported by alternations; rather, they are defined by properties with a static, partial distribution. They are thus the type of morpheme-specific cophonologies whose potential for proliferation is a concern.

Itô and Mester observe that the differences between Yamato, Foreign, and Assimilated Foreign, are not random, but rather show a range of degrees of assimilation to the constraints characterizing the etymologically native words. On the basis of this observation, Itô and Mester (1993; 1995) propose a general organizational system of the lexicon in which one co-phonology (in the case of Japanese, Yamato) is designated as the 'core'; all other, 'peripheral' cophonologies are allowed to differ from the core only by virtue of imposing fewer of the core constraints. A prediction that the model makes, according to Itô and Mester, is that loanwords will never be subject to a stricter set of constraints than that imposed on native items.

If general, this proposal would certainly limit the number of constraints available to define morpheme-specific cophonologies to those true of the entire 'core' vocabulary. However, it does not seem to be cross-linguistically viable. For one thing, when a language with fairly loose phonotactics borrows from languages with stronger phonotactics, it will indeed be the case that loanwords obey tighter constraints than native items. Turkish, for example, has certain vowels in its inventory which are not found in English or French, languages from which it has borrowed many items. As a result, English loans can be described as obeying a constraint against the presence of the vowel /ø/, which is not imposed on native words; similarly, French loans are all consistent with a constraint against the presence of /ɯ/, which does not hold in native words.

Another possible cause for scepticism is the learnability of the system. In the absence of knowledge as to which lexical items are etymologically native, how is the learner to know which items to use in defining the 'core' co-phonology? In Turkish, for example, some native items are monosyllabic and others are disyllabic. How does the learner know not to posit 'be monosyllabic' or 'be disyllabic' as constraints defining the native core?

4.1.4 *Summary*

The decision to capture a static pattern which admits exceptions comes at the price of accepting the Distributional Method, which has thus far resisted all attempts to constrain it to the point where it would come even close to modelling the instincts of linguists. It seems that if we are to capture roots obeying Labial Attraction in a separate co-phonology, the hobgoblin of consistency also requires us to define all of the undesirable co-phonologies discussed in this section. Following Clements and Sezer's (1982) suggestion to abandon Labial Attraction, with which we would probably concur, does not solve the more general problem, either; the point is that if the Distributional Method is used at all, it must be used systematically, and the cost of doing so is unacceptable.

4.2 *Morpheme-specific co-phonologies and exceptions to alternations*

In the preceding section we confined ourselves to the discussion of static patterns, reaching the conclusion that morpheme-specific co-phonologies are entirely unsuitable as a means of capturing any lexical exceptions which those patterns admit.

Let us now consider the situation of lexical exceptions to alternations. Do problems with morpheme-specific cophonologies disappear once we turn away from static patterns? We will answer this question by returning to the case study of Coda Devoicing, an exception-admitting alternation in Turkish. If morpheme-specific co-phonologies are used to handle the lexical exceptions to Coda Devoicing, we will require morphemes to be segregated into the following two co-phonologies:

(19) Co-phonology G: Coda Devoicing rule applies
       Co-phonology H: Coda Devoicing does not apply

4.2.1 *Locating area of exceptionality*

The essential problem for the morpheme-specific co-phonology approach to lexical exceptions to alternations is that it is descriptively inadequate, lacking the ability to locate the area of exceptionality with a morpheme. Consider, with respect to the Coda Devoicing alternation, the following Turkish data:

(20) *Nominative*   *Accusative*   *Gloss*

    edʒ.dat   edʒ.da:d-ɯ   'ancestors'
    is.tib.dat   is.tib.da:d-ɯ   'despotism'

Each of these nominative forms contains two plosives, one which is voiced in coda position and one which is voiceless. Each simultaneously obeys and violates the Coda Devoicing rule. How, if exceptionality is an overall feature of the morpheme, are we to indicate in underlying form which coda plosive in these roots is the villain?[12]

A similar problem arises with another alternation in Turkish, the rule of intervocalic velar deletion (see e.g. Lees 1961; Lewis 1967; Underhill 1976; Zimmer and Abbott 1978; Sezer 1981). Examples illustrating velar deletion are shown below:

(21) bebek   'baby'   bebe-i   'baby-accusative'
     t͡ʃit͡ʃek   'flower'   t͡ʃit͡ʃe-e   'flower-dative'
     gel-edʒek   'come-future'   gel-edʒe-im   'come-future-1sg'
     ol-adʒak   'happen-future'   ol-adʒa-a   'happen-future-dative'

All the morphemes in (21), as well as the complex words they form, obey the Velar Deletion rule. However, there are a number of morphemes which do not (as indicated by the double-underlined strings):

(22) gaga   'beak'
     abluka   'blockade'

Based on these facts, we could simply say that the morphemes in (21) belong to Co-phonology I, in which Velar Deletion applies, while those in (22) belong to Co-phonology J, which does not contain the rule.

(23) Co-phonology I: Intervocalic velars are deleted (Velar Deletion applies)
     Co-phonology J: Intervocalic velars are not deleted (VD does not apply)

The problem we are interested in arises in the data in (24). Here, the very same root both resists Velar Deletion, suggesting that it belongs to Co-phonology I, *and* undergoes it (when suffixed with a vowel-initial suffix), suggesting that it belongs to Co-phonology J.

---

[12] Lest it be thought that the morpheme-internal voiced codas in (20) are somehow licensed by the following onset, which happens also to be voiced, forms like *kutb-u* 'pole(-acc)', *makbul* 'accepted', and many others show that plosive voicing is independent of the voicing of a following consonant.

(24) sokak　'street'　soka-ɯ　'street-accusative'
　　 mekik　'shuttle'　meki-i　'shuttle-accusative'

These forms illustrate the same problem we saw above: the very same root contains two structures providing contradictory evidence about the morpheme's co-phonology membership. There is exceptionality within the morpheme somewhere, but not everywhere, and the co-phonology approach is too insensitive to make the necessary discrimination.

The Turkish cases might be solved, with some loss of insight, by complicating the relevant rules to apply only to morpheme-final consonants.[13] However, the same approach cannot be extended to a similar example from Spanish discussed in various works by Harris (1969; 1977*a*; 1977*b*; 1985), in which some but not all mid vowels diphthongize under stress, as shown in (25).[14]

(25) a.　Diphthongizing　c[o]ntò　'he told'　n[e]gò　'he denied'
　　　　 /e,o/:

　　　　　　　　　　　c[wé]nto　'I tell'　n[jé]ga　'he denies'
　　　　　　　　　　　[o]rfandád　'orphanhood'
　　　　　　　　　　　[wé]rfano　'orphan'

　 b.　Non-diphthongizing　m[o]ntó　'he mounted'　p[e]gó　'he hit'
　　　　 /e,o/:

　　　　　　　　　　　m[ó]nto　'I mount'　p[é]go　'I hit'

Pursuing the morpheme-specific cophonology approach to lexical exceptionality, Spanish must have two cophonologies, one (K) in which Diphthongization applies, and another (L) in which it does not.

(26) *Cophonology K: Diphthongization applies.* Members: the roots in (25a).
　　 Cophonology L: Diphthongization does not apply. Members: the roots in (25b).

However, as Harris shows, this approach falters in the face of data like that in (27), where the very same root contains *two* mid vowels, one which diphthongizes under stress and the other which does not (Harris 1985: 42).

(27) r[é]pr[o]bo (N.)　/e/ does not diphthongize under stress
　　 r[e]pr[wé]bo (V.)　/o/ *does* diphthongize under stress

---

[13] In fact, even this move would not be sufficient, as shown by forms such as /birik-edʒek-i/ → [birikedʒei] 'accumulate-fut-3poss', in which only one of the two morpheme-final velars deletes. The rule would have to refer to morpheme boundaries preceding a certain class of morphemes. A reviewer suggests the possibility of dividing schizophrenic roots like these into multiple domains for co-phonology application, e.g. [edʒ][da:d-ɯ] or [sok][ak-ɯ]. However, the domains that would be required to get Coda Devoicing and Velar Deletion to apply correctly to these 'mixed' roots do not correspond to independently motivated phonological constituents. Without any independent check, this approach generates even greater co-phonology proliferation than we have already seen, and must be rejected.

[14] Data are taken from Harris (1985), except for *huérfano*, which comes from Saporta (1959: 52).

It is impossible to characterize the morpheme atomically as belonging either to Co-phonology K or to Co-phonology L.

One option that has been taken in the past is the use of diacritic features in the feature matrix of individual segments; these features are visible to phonological rules and can either trigger or block them, as the case may be (see e.g. Chomsky and Halle 1968; Zonneveld 1978). But since such features amount to co-phonologies, we essentially end up with a system in which each segment is potentially in its own co-phonology. If it is possible to interpret this situation at all, one wonders how rules which are conditioned by material outside the segment are to apply. In any case, once one concedes that information about exceptionality must be prespecified at the segmental level, it makes more sense to consider the prespecification alternative, in which it is actual phonological structure, not diacritic features, that is prespecified. This is the approach that OT makes possible, as we show in the next section.

5. Lexical Exceptions in Optimality Theory

It is now time to look at lexical exceptions from a different perspective, that of OT, in which constraints are used to handle both static patterns and alternations. The crucial difference, for our purposes, between OT and rule theory is that in OT, constraints are violable. As we will demonstrate, this makes it possible for OT to use the prespecification method for handling lexical exceptions. As a consequence, morpheme-specific co-phonologies, and all the problems that they entail, can be entirely avoided.

That said, morpheme-specific co-phonologies *have* been imported into OT as a means of capturing lexical exceptionality; see e.g. Kisseberth (1993), Kirchner (1993), Pater (1994), and Cohn and McCarthy (1994). However, not only do the same problems arise that we discussed in the previous section; in addition, the morpheme-specific co-phonology approach stands in contradiction to the fundamental assumption in OT that constraints are violable. In the case of lexical exceptions, co-phonologies are defined on the basis of a set of morphemes all of which—or none of which—violate a given constraint. By defining away the possibility for constraints to be violated, the morpheme-specific co-phonology approach prevents the analyst from benefiting from constraint violability and from noticing emergent generalizations of the type, called 'emergence of the unmarked', discussed by McCarthy and Prince (1994).

In OT all that is needed in order for a lexical item to resist the effects of a constraint is for the faithfulness constraints which protect the underlying structure of that lexical item to be ranked higher than the constraint in question. This approach has been used by Inkelas (1994; forthcoming) for exceptions to vowel harmony, coda devoicing, and stress in Turkish, and by Roca (1996) for Spanish plural formation.

In the case of Labial Attraction, lexical exceptions to the constraint (which, recall, requires a high vowel to be /u/ if the preceding vowel is /a/ and a labial consonant intervenes) are simply prespecified lexically with an unrounded vowel, /ɯ/. In the case of the morpheme /kapɯ/ 'door', the faithfulness constraint (PARSE, for Prince and Smolensky, 1993; MAX, for McCarthy and Prince, 1994; MATCH, for Orgun, 1995) banning deletion of input material outranks Labial Attraction, preventing the /ɯ/ from surfacing as /u/.

(28) How prespecification works to characterize exceptions to Labial Attraction

	kapɯ	FAITH	LABIAL ATTRACTION
☞ a.	[kapɯ]		*
b.	[kapu]	*!	

Similarly, prespecification can easily handle exceptions to Coda Devoicing, our example of an alternation admitting lexical exceptions. Plosives which alternate with respect to voicing (e.g. the final consonant of /kanaD/ 'wing') are underspecified for [voice] (29a), while those which always surface as voiced (e.g. in /etyd/ 'study') are prespecified as [+ voice] (29b); those which always surface as voiceless (e.g. in /devlet/ 'state') are prespecified as [−voice] (29c). As proposed by Hayes (1990) and Inkelas and Orgun (1995), Coda Devoicing is a purely structure-filling alternation, meaning, in OT, that the requirement that coda plosives be voiceless is dominated by a constraint prohibiting the deletion of input [voice] specifications.

(29) How prespecification works to characterize Coda Devoicing and its exceptions

a.	/kanaD/	FAITH	CODA DEVOICING
☞ i.	[kanat]	*	
ii.	[kanad]	*	*!

b.	/etyd/	FAITH	CODA DEVOICING
i.	[etyt]	*!	
☞ ii.	[etyd]		*

c.	/devlet/	FAITH	CODA DEVOICING
☞ i.	[devlet]		
ii.	[devled]	*!	*

Prespecification has a number of advantages over the co-phonology approach, the most obvious being that it does not contribute to co-phonology proliferation. When prespecification is the method of capturing lexical exceptions, only one (co-)phonology is needed.

Another advantage of prespecification is that it deals handily with 'mixed' morphemes, those in which one segment is exceptional and another, well-behaved. Recall, for example, the mixed morphemes confronting the Coda Devoicing rule in Turkish, which posed an embarrassing problem for the morpheme-specific co-phonology approach. All that needs to be said in the prespecification approach is that the exceptional, voiced plosives are prespecified for [+ voice], while the obedient, alternating ones are underlyingly unspecified, supplied with the appropriate value for [voice] by the structure-filling grammar.

(30) /ed͡ʒda:D/   /istibda:D/   /pɯrelyd/
      | | |
     vd   vd   vd

As long as the grammar is designed such that the faithfulness constraint protecting underlying [voice] specifications outranks the constraint requiring coda plosives to be voiceless, the exact nature of the lexical exceptionality of these morphemes we have discussed is trivially easy to describe.[15]

Similarly, as Harris (1985) shows, prespecification is the solution to the dilemma of mixed morphemes in Spanish. Recall that there are morphemes in which one mid vowel in a morpheme undergoes Diphthongization in the appropriate stress context, but another does not. Harris (1985) proposes a simple prespecification treatment, assigning diphthongizing vowels an unlinked timing unit which gets filled only under stress:

(31) Short vowel   True diphthong   Alternating vowel
       X   X   X   X   X
       | | | |
       i   i   e   i

As long as Diphthongization is purely structure-filling, meaning that the constraint requiring stressed mid vowels to be diphthongs is ranked below the constraint requiring prelinked vowels to be preserved, there is no need to create two cophonologies in Spanish, one which forces diphthongization and the other which does not. All morphemes can belong to the same co-phonology, at least as far as Diphthongization is concerned.

To conclude, we have demonstrated that the only alternative to prespecification, namely morpheme-specific co-phonologies, is an untenable approach to

---

[15] What to prespecify in the case of exceptions to Velar Deletion is not quite as obvious; Inkelas and Orgun (1995) offer reasons to think that it is syllable structure which is prespecified, and that the Velar Deletion alternation affects only velars which are not syllabified in the input.

lexical exceptionality; moreover, we have shown that prespecification is capable of describing the kinds of intricacy that one actually finds in exceptionality. In sum, prespecification is the most constrained while simultaneously the only descriptively adequate way of handling lexical exceptionality to static patterns and alternations. It is made possible in OT precisely because of the ability of constraints in OT to be violated; lexical resistance (exceptionality) results when faithfulness constraints preserve underlying structure from the ravages of lower-ranked constraints.

Put another way, OT is intrinsically suited to the prespecification approach to exceptions because it is intrinsically suited to capturing the notion of a structure-filling alternation. This notion is what rule theory has been unable to formalize adequately, for good reason: as Kiparsky (1982) notes, the same rule can apply in a structure-filling manner in one instance but in a structure-changing manner in another. Structure-fillingness is best understood as a property of a given input–output mapping, rather than a property of a rule, divorced from the particular forms it is applying to.

6. THE PRINCIPLED NATURE OF PRESPECIFICATION

Past proposals to use prespecification to handle lexical exceptionality have often come under criticism for being unprincipled (see e.g. Mester and Itô 1989; Steriade 1995). The principal concern seems to be that if underlying representation can be adjusted to fit the observed data, then no predictions can be made about which forms actually occur in a language. It has even been suggested that the problem is enhanced in OT, whose practitioners typically opt to impose no constraints at all on underlying representation.[16]

However, we would like to argue, with Inkelas (1994), that the situation is exactly the opposite. It is precisely the 'richness of the input' aspect of OT (McCarthy 1995) which makes the prespecification account so successful. In OT, it does not technically matter what underlying representation is given to a morpheme so long as whatever underlying representation is chosen leads to the correct surface form. In fact, it is possible in some cases for any of a variety of possible underlying representations to work in any given case. How, then, is underlying representation determined? The solution that has been offered within OT by Prince and Smolensky (1993) is Lexicon Optimization. According to Prince and Smolensky (1993) (see also Itô *et al.*, 1993; 1995; and Inkelas, 1994), that underlying representation is chosen which leads to the violation of the fewest highly ranked constraints in the generation of surface

---

[16] See, however, Prince and Smolensky (1993), who entertain the possibility of using *SPEC as a constraint whose only effect is on underlying representation. Also, Archangeli and Suzuki in Chapter 6 above [Editor].

form (see Pulleyblank and Turkel, Chapter 5 above, for akin discussion). Each morpheme has exactly one best underlying representation. As a result, there is no reason to worry about indeterminacy in underlying representation.

As illustration, a sample Lexicon Optimization tableau with one constraint (adapted from Itô *et al.*'s (1995: 593) discussion of postnasal obstruent voicing in Japanese) is shown below.[17] All inputs given will yield the same output, according to the grammar postulated by Itô *et al.* That input is selected to be stored in underlying representation which violates the fewest high-ranking constraints in grammar. In this simple *tableau des tableaux* (to use the term of Itô *et al.*, 1993; 1995), only FAITH is shown; the optimal input is (d), the most faithful to the output form *tombo*. Even though the shared voicing structure would be assigned by the grammar and is thus redundant, Lexicon Optimiza-

(32)

		Input	Output	FAITH	Comments
	a.	/toMPo/	tombo	**!	MP specified for voice in output only
	b.	/tomPo/ | vd	tombo	*!	P specified for voice in output only
	c.	/toMbo/ | vd	tombo	*!	M specified for voice in output only
☞	d.	/tombo/ V vd	tombo		voice faithful between input and output

tion causes it to be stored lexically anyway.

Not surprisingly, FAITH constraints will always favor a fully specified form in the absence of higher-ranked constraints forcing underspecification. Thus for structures which exceptionally fail to show the expected alternations and instead maintain a constant surface form, Lexicon Optimization will naturally cause them to be stored underlyingly in their surface form—that is, to be prespecified.

Given a theory of Lexicon Optimization and a single grammar, underlying specification is constrained, in fact determined, by the surface forms of morphemes. If *SPEC (Prince and Smolensky 1993) is one of the constraints in the grammar, then the best underlying form is the one that adheres the most closely to *SPEC, all other things being equal (i.e. given that it can generate the correct surface forms). However, underlying form is still principled even if

[17] See Inkelas (1994) for discussion of Lexicon Optimization in cases of alternations.

constraints such as *SPEC are not part of the grammar at all. Even if, as
explicitly advocated in Inkelas (1994), no constraints at all are dedicated to
shaping underlying form, Lexicon Optimization still ensures that underlying
representation is deterministic (some problems are, however, pointed out in
Chapter 1 above, pp. 37–8 [Editor]). It provides a principled way of deciding
underlying form while allowing exceptionality to be handled using prespecification, precisely the combination of goals that derivational theories have
been unable to achieve.

7. The Grammatical Status of Partial Static Patterns

Having now argued that prespecification is the best, if not the only, treatment of
lexical exceptions to alternations and static patterns, we now would like to offer, in
closing, some speculation about the validity of encoding partial static patterns in
grammar in the first place. The observation that inspires us to question whether
constraints like Labial Attraction should be part of the grammar of Turkish is the
following: because of Lexicon Optimization, the lexicon of Turkish will look the
same *whether or not* Labial Attraction is actually part of the grammar. To see this,
consider the following Lexicon Optimization tableau for the root whose surface
form is *sabun* 'soap', which conforms to Labial Attraction. There are two workable options for its underlying representation. One (34a) is for its surface [u] to be
underlyingly unspecified for roundness; the other (34b) is for surface [u] to be
underlyingly fully specified as /u/. In each case the same surface sequence will
result. (A third possibility, where /u/ is underlyingly specified as ɯ, is unworkable,
since there is no way it could generate the desired output, and so it does not even
make it into the Lexicon Optimization tableau.)

(33)

	Input	Output	No insertion	Labial Attraction	Vowel harmony
a.	/sabIn/	[sabun]	*!		*
☞ b.	/sabun/	[sabun]			*

Because both forms obey Labial Attraction and violate Vowel Harmony
equally, the only difference between them is that one gratuitously violates
the faithfulness constraint against feature insertion while the other does not.
No matter how the constraints are ranked, it is clear that input (33b) will
always win. But what this means is that Labial Attraction is not doing anything
in the grammar. If the constraint were absent, forms exhibiting Labial Attraction would still be prespecified; they would be considered exceptions to Vowel
Harmony, rather than as constituting a minor subregularity. In fact there is no

grammatical evidence that can determine whether or not Labial Attraction should be a part of the grammar.[18]

Evidence of an extragrammatical sort has sometimes been offered instead; the literature includes a number of psycholinguistic experiments designed to test whether apparent regularities which admit exceptions are actually part of the competence of native speakers. Zimmer (1969), for example, tested the status of Labial Attraction by asking native speakers to judge the Turkishness of nonsense words containing /aBɯ/ and /aBu/ sequences, respectively. Although Zimmer's interpretation of his data has been questioned by Itô et al. (1993), Zimmer, who found no statistically significant preference for /aBu/ sequences over /aBɯ/ ones, concluded that his experiment offered no support for considering Labial Attraction to be part of the grammar of Turkish. By contrast, Zimmer did find a statistically significant preference for /aCu/ sequences over /aCɯ/ ones (where the intervening C could be any consonant), a perplexing result. Our speculation about Zimmer's findings is that, whether Labial Attraction is part of the grammar of Turkish or not, the only use a speaker could make of it is by making analogies to words exhibiting the pattern. Since the grammar never forcibly imposes Labial Attraction on words not already conforming to it, any effects Labial Attraction might have on a speaker's performance would be on an unpredictable, analogical basis. The same is true of the /aCu/ pattern, which is a possible generalization one could make over some roots in Turkish, but not one that any linguist has chosen to make, as it conditions no alternations. For whatever reason, it appears that some speakers in Zimmer's experiment chose to draw an analogy between nonsense words that they heard and Turkish words containing /aCu/ sequences, but not Turkish words containing /aBu/ sequences. However, this behavior should not, we contend, be used as evidence that the relevant static patterns are encoded in the grammar of Turkish.

Though it may seem like an esoteric, trivial issue, given the lack of empirical evidence either way, the decision whether or not to encode a static pattern in grammar may have important implications, the most obvious being that if certain constraints hold only in static form, the form of phonological theory will vary according to whether or not those constraints are deemed worthy of inclusion in grammars. In light of the theoretical claims that have been made over the years on the basis of static patterns, this is a legitimate concern.

---

[18] The assumption that all constraints are universal makes this issue moot except in the case of a constraint (such as, arguably, Labial Attraction) that only one language provides evidence for. However, the universality assumption has been challenged by e.g. McCarthy (1993*a*) and Blevins (Ch. 7 above).

8. Conclusion

We have argued that prespecification is the only workable treatment of lexical exceptions to alternations and static patterns; we have chronicled the many ways in which its competitor, the use of morpheme-specific co-phonologies, is fatally flawed. This conclusion has important implications for the choice between Optimality Theory, in which all alternations and static patterns are captured by (potentially) violable constraints, and rule theory, in which alternations are handled using rules, and static patterns are handled by (inviolable) constraints. Only OT is suited to the formalization of purely structure-filling alternations, giving it an advantage over rule theory in the use of prespecification to handle lexical exceptions. And only OT, with its violable constraints, can handle lexical exceptions to static regularities at all.

The weight to put on this evidence in support of OT over rule theory ultimately comes down to the importance placed on exceptions. Lexical exceptions have played roles of various strengths in the history of generative phonology, starring in the early days of generative phonology and autoseg-mental phonology but waning in recent years as emphasis has shifted to the systematic exceptionality that arises through constraint-ranking in Optimality Theory. In this chapter, however, we have shown that lexical exceptionality can be united with systematic exceptionality: both follow from constraint violability. In the case of lexical exceptions, faithfulness to the input is the higher-ranking constraint.

Our conclusion will also, we hope, ease fears about the uncontrolled nature of underlying representation in OT. It is indeed possible to use underlying representation to account for the behavior of morphemes; Lexicon Optimization not only allows this, but in fact mandates it. The 'richness of the input' in OT is the only approach to underlying representation which allows a descriptively adequate and theoretically constrained analysis of lexical exceptions, permitting them to continue to shed light on the structure of grammar.

Acknowledgements

A version of this paper was presented at the TREND II workshop at Stanford University and at the University of Washington. We are grateful to both audiences for helpful suggestions, and to Carole Paradis, Iggy Roca, Richard Wiese, and Draga Zec and four reviewers of this volume for comments on earlier versions of the manuscript.

REFERENCES

Archangeli, D., and Pulleyblank, D. (1989). 'Yoruba vowel harmony', *Linguistic Inquiry* **20**: 173–218.

—— —— (1994). *Grounded Phonology*. Cambridge, Mass.: MIT Press.

Buckley, E. L. (1992). 'Kashaya laryngeal increments, contour segments, and the moraic tier', *Linguistic Inquiry* **12**: 487–96.

—— (1994*a*). 'Default feature prespecification: the two [i]'s of Kashaya', in M. Gonzàles (ed.), *Proceedings of the Northeast Linguistics Society 24*. Amherst, Mass.: GLSA, 17–30.

—— (1994*b*). *Theoretical Aspects of Kashaya Phonology and Morphology*. Stanford: CSLI.

—— (1995). 'Constraint domains in Kashaya', in J. Camacho, L. Choueiri, and M. Watanabe (eds.), *Proceedings of the Fourteenth West Coast Conference on Formal Linguistics*. Stanford: CSLI, 47–62.

Cho, Y. Y. (1990). 'Parameters of Consonantal Assimilation'. Dissertation, Stanford University.

—— (1995). 'Rule ordering and constraint interaction in OT'. Paper presented at the 21st meeting of the Berkeley Linguistics Society.

Chomsky, N., and Halle, M. (1968). *The Sound Pattern of English*. New York: Harper & Row.

Clements, G. N. (1991). 'Vowel height assimilation in Bantu languages', in K. Hubbard (ed.), *Proceedings of the Special Session on African Language Structures*. Berkeley, Calif.: Berkeley Linguistics Society, 25–64.

—— and Sezer, S. (1982). 'Vowel and consonant disharmony in Turkish', in H. van der Hulst and N. Smith (eds.), *The Structure of Phonological Representations*, pt. II. Dordrecht: Foris, 213–55.

Cohn, A., and McCarthy, J. (1994). 'Alignment and Parallelism in Indonesian phonology'. ROA-25.

Halle, M., and Vergnaud, J.-R. (1987). *An Essay on Stress*. Cambridge, Mass.: MIT Press.

Harris, J. (1969). *Spanish Phonology*. Cambridge, Mass.: MIT Press.

—— (1977*a*). 'Remarks on diphthongization and Spanish stress', *Lingua* **41**: 261–305.

—— (1977*b*). 'Spanish vowel alternations, diacritic features and the structure of the lexicon'. *Proceedings of the North East Linguistics Society* **7**: 99–113.

—— (1985). 'Spanish diphthongization and stress', *Phonology Yearbook* **2**: 31–45.

Hayes, B. (1990). 'Precompiled lexical phonology', in S. Inkelas and D. Zec (eds.), *The Phonology–Syntax Connection*. Chicago: University of Chicago Press, 85–108.

Holden, K. (1976). 'Assimilation rates of borrowings and phonological productivity', *Language* **52**: 131–47.

Inkelas, S. (1994). 'The consequences of optimization for underspecification', in J. Beckman (ed.), *Proceedings of the Northeastern Linguistics Society* **25**: 287–302.

—— (forthcoming). 'Exceptional stress-attracting suffixes in Turkish: representations vs. the grammar', in H. van der Hulst, R. Kager, and W. Zonneveld (eds.), *Prosodic Morphology*. Cambridge: Cambridge University Press.

—— and Orgun, C. O. (forthcoming). 'Level (non)ordering in recursive morphology:

evidence from Turkish', in S. Lapointe (ed.), *Proceedings of the Davis Workshop on Morphology and Its Relations to Syntax and Phonology*. Stanford, Calif.: CSLI.

—— —— (1995). 'Level ordering and economy in the lexical phonology of Turkish', *Language* **71**: 763–93.

—— and Cho, Y. Y. (1993). 'Inalterability as prespecification', *Language* **69**: 529–74.

Itô, J. (1986). 'Syllable Theory in Prosodic Phonology', Dissertation, University of Massachusetts, Amherst.

—— and Mester, A. (1993). 'Japanese Phonology: Constraint Domains and Structure Preservation'. Linguistics Research Center Publication LRC-93–06, University of California, Santa Cruz.

—— —— (1995). 'Japanese phonology', in J. Goldsmith (ed.), *The Handbook of Phonological Theory*. Cambridge, Mass.: Blackwell, 817–38.

—— —— and Padgett, J. (1993). 'Licensing and Redundancy: Underspecification in Optimality Theory'. University of California, Santa Cruz, LRC-93–07.

—— —— —— (1995). 'Licensing and underspecification in Optimality Theory', *Linguistic Inquiry* **26**: 571–613.

Kaisse, E. (1986). 'Locating Turkish devoicing', in M. Dalrymple et al. (eds.), *Proceedings of the Fifth West Coast Conference on Formal Linguistics*. Stanford, Calif.: Stanford Linguistics Association, 119–28.

Kiparsky, P. (1973*a*). 'Phonological representations: how abstract is phonology?' in O. Fujimura (ed.), *Three Dimensions in Linguistic Theory*. Tokyo: TEC, 5–56.

—— (1973*b*). 'Phonological representations: abstractness, opacity and global rules', in O. Fujimura (ed.), *Three Dimensions in Linguistic Theory*. Tokyo: TEC, 56–86.

—— (1982). 'Lexical morphology and phonology', in I.-S. Yang (ed.), *Linguistics in the Morning Calm*. Seoul: Hanshin, 3–91.

—— (1985). 'Some consequences of Lexical Phonology', *Phonology Yearbook* **2**: 85–138.

—— (1993). 'Blocking in non-derived environments', in S. Hargus and E. Kaisse (eds.), *Phonetics and Phonology* **4**: *Studies in Lexical Phonology*. San Diego, Calif.: Academic Press, 277–313.

Kirchner, R. (1993). 'Turkish Vowel Disharmony in Optimality Theory'. ROA-4.

—— (1996). 'Synchronic chain shifts in Optimality Theory', *Linguistic Inquiry* **27**: 341–50.

Kisseberth, C. (1970). 'The treatment of exceptions', *Papers in Linguistics* **2**: 44–58.

—— (1993). 'Optimal domains: a theory of Bantu tone. A case study from Isixhosa', Rutgers Optimality Workshop 1.

Lakoff, G. (1970). *Irregularity in Syntax*. New York: Holt, Rinehart & Wilson.

Lees, R. (1961). *The Phonology of Modern Standard Turkish*. Bloomington: Indiania University Publications.

—— (1966). 'On the interpretation of a Turkish vowel alternation', *Anthropological Linguistics* **8**: 32–9.

Lewis, G. (1967). *Turkish Grammar*. Oxford: Oxford University Press.

Lightner, T. M. (1965). 'On the description of vowel and consonant harmony', *Word* **21**: 244–50.

Mascaró, J. (1987). 'A Reduction and Spreading Theory of Voicing and Other Sound Effects'. MS, Universitat Autònoma de Barcelona.

McCarthy, J. (1986). 'OCP effects: gemination and antigemination', *Linguistic Inquiry* **17**: 207–63.

—— (1993*a*). 'A case of surface constraint violation'. *Canadian Journal of Linguistics* **38**: 169–96.

—— (1993*b*). 'The parallel advantage'. Rutgers Optimality Workshop 1.

—— (1994). 'On coronal "transparency"', Trilateral Phonology Weekend II, Stanford University.

—— (1995). 'Extensions of Faithfulness: Rotuman Revisited'. ROA-110.

—— and Prince, A. (1994). 'An overview of Prosodic Morphology', pt. 1: 'Templatic form in reduplication'. Utrecht University Workshop on Prosodic Morphology.

McCawley, J. D. (1968). *The Phonological Component of a Grammar of Japanese*. The Hague: Mouton.

Mester, A. (1986). 'Studies in Tier Structure'. Dissertation, University of Massachusetts, Amherst.

—— and Itô, J. (1989). 'Feature predictability and underspecification: palatal prosody in Japanese mimetics', *Language* **65**: 258–93.

Mohanan, K. P. (1982). 'Lexical Phonology'. Dissertation, Massachusetts Institute of Technology.

Myers, S. (1987). 'Vowel shortening in English', *Natural Language and Linguistic Theory* **5**: 485–518.

Ní Chiosáin, M. and Padgett, J. (1993). 'On the Nature of Consonant–Vowel Interaction'. Linguistics Research Center publication LRC-93–09, University of California, Santa Cruz.

Orgun, C. O. (1995). 'Correspondence and identity constraints in two-level Optimality Theory', in J. Camacho (ed.), *Proceedings of the Fourteenth West Coast Conference on Formal Linguistics*. Stanford, Calif.: Stanford Linguistics Association.

Paradis, C. (1988). 'On constraints and repair strategies'. *The Linguistic Review* **6**: 71–97.

—— and Prunet, J.-F. (1993). 'On the validity of morpheme structure constraints', in C. Paradis and D. LaCharité (eds.), *Constraint-Based theories in Multilinear Phonology*, *Canadian Journal of Linguistics* **38**: 236–56.

Pater, J. (1994). 'Against the underlying specification of an "exceptional" English stress pattern', *Proceedings of the Conference on Contrast*, University of Toronto.

Poser, W. J. (1982). 'Phonological representation and action at-a-distance', in H. van der Hulst and N. Smith (eds.), *The structure of phonological representations*, pt. II. Dordrecht: Foris, 121–58.

Postal, P. (1968). *Aspects of Phonological Theory*. New York: Harper & Row.

Prince, A., and Smolensky, P. (1993). 'Optimality Theory: Constraint Interaction in Generative Grammar'. MS, Rutgers University and the University of Colorado, Boulder.

Pulleyblank, D. (1986). *Tone in Lexical Phonology*. Dordrecht: Reidel.

—— (1988). 'Feature hierarchy and Tiv vowels', *Phonology* **5**: 299–326.

Rice, K. (1988). 'Continuant voicing in Slave (Northern Athapaskan): the cyclic application of default rules', in M. Hammond and M. Noonan (eds.), *Theoretical Morphology*. San Diego, Calif.: Academic Press, 371–88.

—— (1989). *A Grammar of Slave*. Berlin: Mouton de Gruyter.

—— (1990). 'Predicting rule domains in the phrasal phonology', in S. Inkelas and D.

Zec (eds.), *The Phonology–Syntax Connection*. Chicago: University of Chicago Press and CSLI Publications, 289–312.

Ringen, C. O. (1975). 'Vowel Harmony: Theoretical Implications'. Doctoral dissertation, Indiana University. Published in 1988 in the Outstanding Dissertations Series by Garland, New York.

—— (1978). 'Another view of the theoretical implications of Hungarian vowel harmony'. *Linguistic Inquiry* 9: 105–15.

—— and Vago, R. M. (forthcoming). 'A constraint based analysis of Hungarian vowel harmony', in I. Kenesei (ed.), *Approaches to Hungarian* 5.

Roca, I. (1996). 'The phonology–morphology interface in Spanish plural formation', in U. Kleinhenz (ed.), *Interfaces in Phonology*. Berlin: Akademie Verlags, 210–30.

Saciuk, B. (1969). 'The stratal division of the lexicon', *Papers in Linguistics* 1: 464–532.

Sezer, E. (1981). 'The k/Ø alternation in Turkish', in G. N. Clements (ed.), *Harvard Studies in Phonology*. Bloomington: Indiana University Linguistics Club, 354–82.

Stanley, R. (1967). 'Redundancy rules in phonology', *Language* 43: 393–436.

Steriade, D. (1995). 'Underspecification and markedness', in J. Goldsmith (ed.), *A Handbook of Phonological Theory*. Cambridge, Mass.: Blackwell, 114–74.

Underhill, R. (1976). *Turkish Grammar*. Cambridge, Mass.: MIT Press.

Vago, R. (1988). 'Height harmony in Pasiego', *Phonology* 5: 343–62.

van der Hulst, H. (1985). 'Hungarian vowel harmony', in H. van der Hulst and N. Smith (eds.), *Advances in Nonlinear Phonology*. Dordrecht: Foris, 267–304.

—— (1988). 'The geometry of vocalic features', in H. van der Hulst and N. Smith (eds.), *Features, Segmental Structure and Harmony Processes*, pt. II. Dordrecht: Foris, 77–125.

Yip, M. (1988). 'The Obligatory Contour Principle and phonological rules: a loss of identity', *Linguistic Inquiry* 19: 65–100.

Zimmer, K. (1969). 'Psychological correlates of some morpheme structure conditions', *Language* 45: 309–21.

—— and Abbott, B. (1978). 'The k/Ø alternation in Turkish: some experimental evidence for its productivity', *Journal of Psycholinguistic Research* 7: 35–46.

Zonneveld, W. (1978). *A Formal Theory of Exceptions in Generative Phonology*. Lisse: Peter de Ridder.

14

Correspondence and Compositionality: The Ga-gyō Variation in Japanese Phonology

JUNKO ITÔ and ARMIN MESTER

1. Voiced Velar Nasalization in Japanese Phonology

1.1. *Introductory remarks*

This chapter is a contribution to the study of surface-to-surface, or output–output, correspondence constraints in Optimality Theory (see McCarthy and Prince, 1995 for an authoritative statement of the original proposal, as well as numerous other works cited there). The particular question to be investigated concerns the tension between two widely shared theoretical assumptions about the computation of phonological form, which, taken together, seem to lead to a contradiction. First, there is the central tenet of OT summarized in (1): phonological constraints are constraints on outputs.

(1) Output-orientation
Phonological constraints apply to outputs alone or govern input–output relations; they apply simultaneously in the course of the selection of the most harmonic candidate (Prince and Smolensky, 1993).

In most current conceptions (see Prince and Smolensky, 1993 for some discussion of alternatives) (1) has (2) as a corollary.

(2) Nonsequentiality and Noncyclicity
There is no sequential phonological derivation in the sense of traditional generative phonology. There is no set of rules and operations applying in a certain order; there are also no cyclic derivations, in the sense that phonological operations first apply only within the smallest morphological domains available and work upwards through a series of more and more inclusive morphological domains.

At the same time, a large body of work in phonological theory and analysis since Chomsky and Halle 1968 (SPE) lends strong support to the view that the computation of the phonological structure of complex inputs must proceed in some sense 'from the inside out': the phonological structure associated with certain subdomains of the whole form plays a privileged role ('cyclic' effects). In order to have a relatively theory-neutral way of referring to the phenomena in question, we borrow some terminology from formal semantics and state that the computation of complex phonological structures fulfills some form of compositionality (3).[1]

(3) Compositionality

Phonological form is computed compositionally: the phonological form of a morphologically complex input is a function of the phonological form of its parts, and of their mode of combination.

As a concrete illustration that prefigures one of the central topics of the chapter, let us take a compound consisting of two stems, *stem₁ ⌢ stem₂*. Compositionality (3) means that its phonological output form should obey the statement in (4):

(4) ϕ (stem₁ ⌢ stem₂) = ϕ (stem₁) + ϕ (stem₂)

The phonological output form (ϕ (x)) of an input that consists of the morphological concatenation (⌢) of two stems, stem₁ and stem₂, is identical with the phonological combination (+) of the phonological output forms of the two stems.

Even though there is nothing inherently derivational about Compositionality,[2] which simply expresses a relation between the phonological output form of a whole and the phonological output forms of its parts (see Orgun, 1995 for discussion), it is fair to say that a strong link between compositionality effects and derivationalism has been forged in the work of Chomsky and Halle (1968) and the succeeding generation of generative phonologists, where such effects have been consistently ascribed to cyclic rule application, with very few dissenting voices (most importantly Liberman and Prince, 1977 and Selkirk, 1980). In the cyclic-derivationalist view, the reason why properties of ϕ *(stem₂)*, for example, are mirrored in ϕ *(stem₁ ⌢ stem₂)* lies in the cyclic application of the relevant rules to larger and larger parts of the input form: first separately to the individual stems, as if they stood in isolation, and only subsequently to the whole form. This tradition of cyclic analysis culminated in the theory of Lexical Phonology (Pesetsky, 1979; Kiparsky, 1982; Mohanan, 1986), with some differences in comparison to the original SPE proposal that should not obscure the invariance of the basic approach.

Seen from the perspective of cyclicity-based approaches to compositionality

---

[1] (3) is vague in a number of respects, just as informal versions of the semantic principle of compositionality on which it is modeled (see von Stechow, 1991: 95, where the origin of a principle of this kind in Gottlob Frege's work is discussed). For an application of the idea of compositionality in Montague Phonology, see Bach and Wheeler (1981).

[2] But is there something inherently compositional about derivations, which are restricted to the *addition* of morphological or phonological structure? As René Kager (pers. comm.) points out, the very notion of 'addition' amounts to a stipulation in itself, and if so, the derivational theory's 'explanation' of compositionality is only circular.

effects in phonology, then, Compositionality (3) stands in conflict with Non-sequentiality and Noncyclicity (2), and casts doubt on the programme of Optimality Theory.[3] We will argue that no such conclusion is in fact warranted—rather, compositionality effects are the results of constraints on outputs alone.

Within the theoretical context of OT, it is natural to view Compositionality (3) not as a phonological constraint or principle in itself but rather as a family of related constraints (a subgroup of the Faithfulness family of constraints) which are of the surface–surface (output–output) variety and hold between parts of a form and the form as a whole (for earlier versions of this proposal, see e.g. Benua, 1995; Kenstowicz, 1995; McCarthy, 1995; Orgun, 1995; Itô *et al.*, 1996). Like all optimality-theoretic constraints, these constraints are ranked with respect to others, and are crucially violable. The basic idea is indicated in (5), in a schematic form: Compositionality effects are the results of correspondence constraints that link, for example, the bound occurrence of a stem within a compound word (ϕ_2) to its occurrence as an independent word ($\phi_{2'}$).

(5)

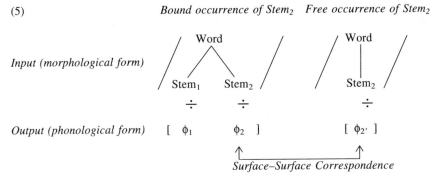

This chapter approaches the issue through a detailed analysis of one particular phonological system, taking up a classical problem in the phonology of Japanese. A salient characteristic of the conservative dialect of Tokyo Japanese[4] is the nasalization of voiced velar plosives (*ga-gyō bionka*, henceforth 'Voiced Velar Nasalization', abbreviated as VVN).[5] At first glance, VVN is

---

[3] Setting aside sequential variants of OT, see Prince and Smolensky (1993: chs. 2 and 5) for discussion and Black (1993) for a worked-out alternative model.

[4] Specifically, the variety of the language spoken by older residents of the (mostly affluent) Yamanote area of the metropolitan region. As a prestige dialect, it forms the basis for the modern standard language (*hyōjungo*), enjoying a semi-official status in government and broadcasting, which is reflected in standard pronunciation dictionaries (see Vance, 1987: 1, 110 for further details).

[5] Partially having to do with sociological factors relating to the existence of nonalternating dialects, and to the fact that many younger speakers of the Tokyo dialect no longer consistently observe the $g \sim \eta$ alternation, language mavens and other cultural commentators refer to the phenomenon as 'the *ga-gyō* problem' (i.e. the problem related to the *g*-column of the kana syllabary).

nothing but a classical case of allophony, consisting in the replacement of word-internal *g* by its allophonic variant ŋ. As a result, the two voiced velar segments *g* and ŋ stand in (largely, see below) complementary distribution, as illustrated in (6), with *g* occurring initially, ŋ medially.[6]

(6)   PrWd

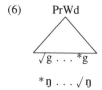

The theoretical interest of this alternation, as we will show, lies in the combination of factors that block word-internal replacement of *g* by ŋ in a variety of contexts, leading to a superficially more complicated picture than what (6) suggests. Depending on the context, VVN may be blocked, optional, or obligatory. Some of the factors that lead to the different behavior of VVN can be traced to stratal distinctions (e.g. native versus loan), morphological structuring, and derived versus underived environments. This would seem to be exactly the type of correlation that the derivational mechanisms, in particular those of Lexical Phonology, are designed to handle. The apparent derivational complexity of the phenomenon therefore presents a challenge for OT. We will show in this chapter that Correspondence Theory (in particular, Surface–Surface correspondence) offers a streamlined OT analysis of this complex set of factors. Perhaps more surprisingly, once the facts are considered in their totality, it turns out that the correspondence-theoretic analysis is actually superior to a Lexical Phonology account: the latter turns out to be not at all straightforward, requiring rather arbitrary assumptions which must be imposed from the outside.

The chapter is organized as follows. After presenting the basic facts of the VVN alternation and its treatment in OT below, section 2 turns to the main point, the interaction of VVN with morphological structure, and presents an analysis that makes crucial use of compositional correspondence constraints requiring identity between pairs of surface structures. Section 3 argues that a correspondence-theoretic account within OT is superior to a derivational and rule-based alternative based on a traditional model of phonology. Section 4 concludes the paper by taking up some additional issues related to VVN in Japanese.

[6] Cf. Trubetskoi (1949: 293): 'En japonais il existe entre *g* et ŋ un rapport de variante combinatoire, *g* n'apparaissant qu'à l'initiale de mot et ŋ qu'entre voyelles: ici également l'opposition *g* : ŋ ne peut différencier une pair de mots, mais cette opposition sert à délimiter le mot, *g* indicant toujours le début d'un mot.' Note that Japanese syllable structure, in particular the Coda Condition against consonantal Place (see Itô, 1986; 1989 and subsequent work), rules out any possibility of PrWd-final *g* or ŋ.

1.2. *Facts and basic analysis*

In traditional allophonic rule terms, VVN can be formulated as in (7): underlying *g* appears as *g* in initial position, but is changed into ŋ in all other environments.

(7) Voiced Velar Nasalization (VVN)

$$/g/ \quad \begin{matrix} \nearrow & [g] \text{ / } _{\text{PrWd}} \text{ [[} \_\_ \\ \searrow & [\eta] \text{ / elsewhere} \end{matrix}$$

Examples of PrWd-initial *g* are given in (8a), followed by examples with PrWd-medial ŋ in (8b). As indicated, choosing the other variant leads to illformedness in both environments (the alternating segments are indicated by bold type).

(8) a. Initial g

[g . . . .]	*[ŋ . . . .]	
geta	*ŋeta	'clogs'
giri	*ŋiri	'duty'
guchi	*ŋuchi	'complaint'
go	*ŋo	'(game of) Go'
garasu	*ŋarasu	'glass'

b. Internal ŋ

*[. . . g . . .]	[. . . ŋ . . .]	
*kagi	kaŋi	'key'
*kago	kaŋo	'basket'
*kaŋgae	kaŋŋae	'thought'
*sasageru	sasaŋeru	'give'
*uguisu	uŋuisu	'(Japanese) bush warbler'
*tokage	tokaŋe	'lizard'
*igirisu	iŋirisu	'England'

Differentiated in terms of morphological context, the nasal variant appears obligatorily in morpheme-internal position (9a–c), stem-finally before vowels (9d–e), and suffix/clitic-initially (9f–h).

(9) MCat   + Suffix/Clitic

a.	kuŋur	+ u	'pass through-present'	} morpheme-internal
b.	kaŋo	+ ni	'basket+locative'	
c.	tokaŋe	+ wa	'lizard+topic'	
d.	oyoŋ	+ oo	'swim-hortative'	} stem-final
e.	toŋ	+ anai	'sharpen-neg-present'	
f.	kayoobi	+ ŋa	'Tuesday-nominative'	} suffix/clitic-initial
g.	mikka	+ ŋurai	'approximately three days'	
h.	gorira+no	+ ŋotoshi	'like a gorilla'	

The complementary distribution induced by VVN manifests itself in morpheme alternations in the case of bound roots, as in (10), which show the expected position-dependent variants. For example, /gai/ 'outside' is realized as [gai] when it is the first member of a compound (*gai-jiN* lit. 'outside-person', i.e. 'foreigner'), but as [ŋai] in second position (*koku-ŋai* lit. 'country-outside', i.e. 'abroad').

(10) Bound roots

PrWd[g . . . .]			PrWd[. . . . . ŋ . .]		
gai	+ jiN	'foreigner'	koku	+ ŋai	'abroad'
go	+ zeN	'morning'	shoo	+ ŋo	'noon'
gam	+ peki	'quay, jetty, wharf'	kai	+ ŋaN	'sea shore'
gi	+ kai	'parliament'	shiŋ	+ ŋi	'deliberation'
guu	+ zeN	'accidental occurrence'	soo	+ ŋuu	'meet accidentally'
gen	+ zai	'currently'	sai	+ ŋeN	'reappearance'

The compounds in (10) are made up of Sino-Japanese roots which only appear as bound morphemes.[7] The fact that they do not have a corresponding free form (i.e. *gai, *go, *gaN, *gi, *guu, *geN, etc., as independent words) will figure centrally in the later analysis.

In their treatment of the basic allophonic relation between g and ŋ, which we adopt here in its essentials, McCarthy and Prince (1995: 353–5) take nasalization as resulting from the interaction of three constraints, ranked as in (11): the context-sensitive constraint prohibiting ŋ in initial position[8] outranks the context-free segment markedness constraint *g banning voiced dorsal obstruents everywhere, which in turn outranks a relevant faithfulness constraint.[9]

---

[7] The closest equivalent in English are so-called 'Greek compounds', such as *cosmo-politan, micro-cosm, helico-pter, ptero-dactyl.*

[8] Found frequently cross-linguistically: McCarthy and Prince (1995) point to English and Southern Paiute; see also section 4.1 below.

[9] Vance (1987: 111) points out (citing work by Donegan and Stampe) 'that a velar voiced stop is more difficult than one articulated further forward, because the air chamber between the glottis and the obstruction is smaller and therefore fills up more quickly'. McCarthy and Prince (1995) adopt this view and propose a constraint against voiced velar stops, noting that this constraint 'phonologizes the familiar articulatory effect of Boyle's Law: It is difficult to maintain voicing when the supraglottal cavity is small; indeed, some nasal airflow is a typical accommodation to this articulatory challenge. The difficulty of maintaining voicing is obviously greatest when the supraglottal cavity is smallest.' Empirical data bearing on this issue appear in Hayes (1996), which presents cross-linguistic inventory statistics which support the position that the velar place of articulation is indeed the least favoured for obstruent stop articulations among the major places of articulation (see also section 4.1 below). Vance himself rejects a direct appeal to aerodynamics as an explanation of g-nasalization in Tokyo Japanese, arguing that such nasalization is not otherwise attested as a natural process resolving the velar voicing problem, and pointing to the existence of intervocalic voicing as a natural process attested in many languages. We anticipate that within a theory with violable constraints, Vance's objections are not insurmountable—e.g. intervocalic voicing of voiceless stops might be due to a dominant and overriding constraint favouring uninterrupted voicing domains—and simply adopt a phonologization of the aerodynamic account for our analysis. In a similar way, the constraint against word-initial ŋ should properly be seen in the context of the status of foot/syllable-initial ŋ and other cases of segment distributions skewed against initial position (such as retroflexes favoring postvocalic position; see Steriade, 1995 and work cited there). These and other legitimate questions are worth pursuing, but are tangential to our enterprise here.

(11) *[ŋ   *_{PrWd}[nas(dorsal) ('ŋ is prohibited PrWd-initially')
|
*g   *obs(dorsal)/[+voice] ('Voiced dorsal obstruents are prohibited')
|
IdentLS(nas)   Lexical–Surface correspondents are identically specified for [nasal]

In a broader perspective, (11) is simply a particular instantiation of the basic scheme (12) for the analysis of allophonic relations in OT: some constraint with syntagmatic effects is ranked over a conflicting context-free markedness constraint, which in turn dominates a relevant faithfulness constraint.[10]

(12)   constraint with syntagmatic effects
|
context-free markedness constraint
|
faithfulness constraint

In order to see how the analysis in (11) works, consider the composite tableaux for *kaɲi* and *geta* in (13) and (14).[11] In these multi-input displays, we first focus on the a-inputs /kagi/ and /geta/, respectively, with oral voiced velar segments. As the tableaux show, the candidate with internal ŋ is judged as optimal in (13) (we assume that a higher-ranked IdentLS(Place) rules out candidates like *kabi* or *kani*). On the other hand, the g-initial candidate wins the competition in (14) because of the overriding influence of the constraint *[ŋ.

(13) kaɲi 'key'

Input a. /kagi/ (...[−nas]...)	*[ŋ	*g	IdentLS(nas)	
b. /kaɲi/ (...[+nas]...)				
c. /kaGi/ (...[0nas]...)				
				a.
kagi (...[−nas]...)		*!		b. *
				c. *
				a. *
+ kaɲi (...[+nas]...)				b.
				c. *

---

[10] See Itô and Mester (1995*b*: 195–205) for general remarks, illustrated by other allophonic relations in Japanese; see also Merchant (1996) for the *ich*-Laut/*ach*-Laut allophony in German. Jaye Padgett (pers. comm.) points out that the syntagmatic constraint at the top of this hierarchy need not necessarily be stated in terms of a specific environment, but could have a much more general content (such as a spreading imperative), whose effects would in certain contexts counteract those of the markedness constraint.

[11] The analysis in (13) and below assumes binary feature specifications, as in the standard version of Correspondence Theory (McCarthy and Prince, 1995), i.e. *g* is [+dorsal, +voiced,

(14) geta 'clogs'

Input a. /geta/ ([−nas]. . .)	*[ŋ]	*g	IdentLS(nas)
b. /ŋeta/ ([+nas]. . .)			
c. /Geta/ ([0nas]. . .)			
+ geta ([−nas]. . .)		*	a. b. * c. *
ŋeta ([+nas]. . .)	*!		a. * b. c. *

As observed by McCarthy and Prince 1995, since the segment structure constraints—both the context-free *g and the context-sensitive *[ŋ]—outrank the relevant faithfulness constraint IdentLS(nas), the nasality specification of voiced velars in inputs is irrelevant for the output distribution of the two segments. The full tableaux in (13) and (14) above demonstrate that identical results are obtained with input g (the a-rows), with input ŋ (the b-rows), and with underspecified candidates (the c-rows). The low ranking of IdentLS(nas) means that the faithfulness constraint simply cannot play a role in the determination of the winner. Provided everything else is equal, some version of lexicon optimization (see Itô *et al.*, 1995: 593 for a formal analysis of this notion, building on Prince and Smolensky, 1993 and Stampe, 1972) selects the /ŋ/-input in (13) and the /g/-input in (14). This would mean nonuniformity in underlying structure, a familiar situation in OT.

We note in passing an interesting aspect of the interaction of surface ŋ with voiced obstruents. The relevant situation arises in connection with Rendaku, a junctural process which voices the initial segment of the second member of a compound (see Itô and Mester, 1986). For example, in (15a) the *t* in *tama* 'ball' turns into *d* in *teppoo-dama*, literally, 'gun ball'. Lyman's Law regularly blocks voicing if the second compound member already contains a voiced obstruent. The internal *b* in *taba* blocks the voicing of the initial *t*, resulting in *satsu-taba,* not *satsu-daba* (15b). Against this background, consider the forms

−nasal], and ŋ is [+dorsal, +voiced, +nasal]. In the present context, this is strictly a matter of convenience. The analysis to follow can also be executed with privative [voice] and [nasal] features, which would require a slightly different conception of feature identity constraints (see Walker, 1996 and works cited there). Dan Karvonen (pers. comm.) points out that insofar as the analysis expresses segment markedness relations by means of constraints such as *g and *ŋ, the ranking *g >> *ŋ must hold. We will return to some issues involving markedness in the appendix (section 4).

in (15c) with internal ŋ. It turns out that ŋ blocks compound voicing as well (*hasami-toŋi*, **hasami-doŋi*), i.e. surface ŋ here patterns with the voiced obstruents (15b) and not with the nasals (15a).[12]

(15) a. Rendaku (sequential voicing in compounds)

tama	'ball'	teppoo + **d**ama	'bullet'
tana	'shelf'	garasu + **d**ana	'glass shelf'

b. Blocking of Rendaku voicing in stems containing voiced obstruents (Lyman's Law)

taba	'bundle'	satsu + $\left\{ {}_{*\mathbf{d}}^{\mathbf{t}} \right\}$ aba	'wad of bills'
ta**d**e	'knotweed'	haru + $\left\{ {}_{*\mathbf{d}}^{\mathbf{t}} \right\}$ade	'redshank'

c. Blocking of Rendaku voicing in stems containing ŋ

toŋi	'sharpen'	hasami + $\left\{ {}_{*\mathbf{d}}^{\mathbf{t}} \right\}$ oŋi	'knife grinder'
toŋe	'thorn'	bara + $\left\{ {}_{*\mathbf{d}}^{\mathbf{t}} \right\}$ oŋe	'rose thorn'

In our earlier work (Itô and Mester 1989; 1990), this was taken as evidence that the underlying segment must be *g* even in dialects with VVN. In the present theory, even though 'freedom-of-the-input' reasoning makes the explanation less direct (see (13) and (14) above), it remains true that Lyman's Law, an OCP-effect on obstruent voicing, treats all ŋ's that stand in the *g~*ŋ relation as part of the voiced obstruent system. Although not without interest in itself, a full analysis of Lyman's Law and similar OCP-interactions goes beyond the limits of the present chapter (see Itô and Mester, 1996 for a proposal).

With the basic allophonic analysis of Voiced Velar Nasalization (10) in place, we are now in a position to turn to the morphologically complex cases, where VVN presents the analyst with an intriguing junctural puzzle.

2. SURFACE–SURFACE CORRESPONDENCE AND COMPOSITIONALITY

Obligatory and optional phonological processes are typically associated with different types of morphological juncture (internal versus external sandhi, lexical versus postlexical level, etc.; see e.g. Kiparsky, 1985). The surprising fact about VVN is the systematic occurrence of both optional and obligatory instantiations of the process in one and the same morphological environment. This raises a serious problem for the traditional strategy in phonology of tying

---

[12] Not every ŋ is included in the Lyman's Law triggers. Any ŋ outside of the *g~*ŋ relation, such as a 'genuine nasal' in coda position, is Lyman's Law-neutral: teŋka 'empire', onna +deŋka 'petticoat government', keŋka 'quarrel', oyako+geŋka 'quarrel between parent and child', etc. Both *teŋka* and *keŋka* are Sino-Japanese compounds that exceptionally undergo Rendaku, which is otherwise restricted to Yamato (native) items. Prototypical Yamato items with coda-ŋ always have a following *g* (because of the independent NC-restriction of Itô *et al.*, 1995; see also Hayes, 1996) and are therefore not useful for the isolation of the Lyman's Law-behaviour of coda-ŋ by itself.

such contrasting modes of application (here, obligatory versus optional) to different types of boundary/level. This section will show that this fact, far from being some small additional complication, is the key to the grammar of VVN, since it reveals the central role of surface–surface correspondence constraints and of free ranking (lack of ranking specification for certain pairs of constraints in individual grammars) within the overall analysis.

2.1. A junctural puzzle

Japanese compounds behave accentually as single prosodic words, in the cross-linguistically established sense of permitting at most a single accent (see e.g. Poser, 1990; Kubozono, 1995; 1996; Kubozono and Mester, 1995).[13] The central observation is that even when both stems contain a lexical accent, the compound never appears with two accents. As a general rule, the initial member loses its lexical accent (e.g. *kúuki* 'air' + *mákura* 'pillow' → *kuukimákura*, or *bíjin* + *konkúuru* → *bijinkonkúuru* 'beauty contest'). For present purposes, we assume that this outcome is brought about by a high-ranking Lex≈Pr constraint (or rather, by MCat–PCat alignment constraints; see Prince and Smolensky, 1993; McCarthy and Prince, 1995) requiring that for every MWd, there exists a PrWd which is simultaneously Left- and Right-aligned with it (see Hewitt and Crowhurst, 1995 on such conjoined constraints). Given a compound word consisting morphologically of two stems, then, its (optimally related) phonological structure will be a single PrWd, as in (16).

(16)

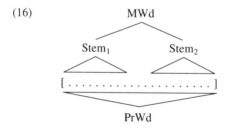

The structure in (16), taken together with the analysis of VVN as developed up to this point, makes a clear prediction: *g* should be found only in Stem₁-initial (qua PrWd-initial) position: *geta* + *bako* 'clog cabinet', etc.; in all other

---

[13] We follow the 'prosodic word' terminology of Kubozono and Mester (1995). Within Japanese accentology, a specialized terminology has developed since McCawley (1968), reflecting a more differentiated conception of the prosodic domains involved, and the relevant prosodic unit has also been called 'accentual phrase' and 'minor phrase' (see e.g. Pierrehumbert and Beckman, 1988; Selkirk and Tateishi, 1988). Nothing hinges on our particular choice of terminology, and the analysis can be easily restated in other terms. This also means that we do not exclude the possibility that further internal prosodic structure exists below the PrWd level that takes each stem to be some independent prosodic unit.

positions, ŋ should be found to the exclusion of g: *kaŋe* + *ŋuchi* lit. 'shadow mouth', i.e. 'malicious gossip', etc.

The facts, however, are somewhat different. While it is true that Stem₁-initial position permits g and only g, it is not true that Stem₂-initial position allows ŋ and only ŋ. Rather, as illustrated in (17), instead of consistent nasalization, we find variation between ŋ and g. Thus the word for 'garden clogs', for example, can appear either as *niwa+geta* or as *niwa* + *ŋeta* (although the two variants are accentually identical).

(17) Compounding with g-initial Stem₂: optional VVN

geta	'clogs'	niwa	+ $\left\{ {g \atop ŋ} \right\}$eta	'garden clogs'
goro	'grounder'	pitchaa	+ $\left\{ {g \atop ŋ} \right\}$oro	'a grounder to the pitcher'
gara	'pattern'	shima	+ $\left\{ {g \atop ŋ} \right\}$ara	'striped pattern'
gei	'craft, art'	shirooto	+ $\left\{ {g \atop ŋ} \right\}$ei	'amateur's skill'
go	'Go game'	oki	+ $\left\{ {g \atop ŋ} \right\}$o	'Go played with a handicap'

As is well known, compounds (provided their second element is a native stem) are the canonical site for Rendaku voicing, which requires the initial segment of Stem₂ to be voiced (e.g., *sushi* versus *maki-zushi* 'rolled sushi', and *tana* 'shelf' versus *hon-dana* 'book-shelf'; see Itô and Mester, 1986 and also (15) above). This leads to a further complication of the picture. In the same Stem₂-initial position where (17) shows optional VVN, we find obligatory VVN, without any variation, when the voiced velar is due to Rendaku voicing (instead of being underlyingly voiced). Illustrative examples appear in (18): whenever a voiced velar in Stem₂-initial position corresponds, via Rendaku, to k in the independent form of the stem, it obligatorily appears as ŋ.

(18) Compounds involving Rendaku: obligatory VVN

kuni	'country'	yuki	+ $\left\{ {ŋ \atop *g} \right\}$uni	'snow country'
kami	'paper'	ori	+ $\left\{ {ŋ \atop *g} \right\}$ami	'origami paper'
kaeru	'frog'	gama	+ $\left\{ {ŋ \atop *g} \right\}$aeru	'toad frog'
keŋka	'fight'	oyako	+ $\left\{ {ŋ \atop *g} \right\}$eŋka	'parent-child fights'
kaki	'writing'	yoko	+ $\left\{ {ŋ \atop *g} \right\}$aki	'horizontal writing'
kusuri	'medicine'	nuri	+ $\left\{ {ŋ \atop *g} \right\}$usuri	'medical ointment/cream'
kirai	'dislike'	onna	+ $\left\{ {ŋ \atop *g} \right\}$irai	'woman-hater, misogynist'

As schematically shown in (19), on the next page, the underlying voiced velar g shows variation, with optional VVN, whereas Rendaku-induced g shows obligatory VVN and no variation.

McCawley (1968: 86–7), who was the first to draw theoretical attention to

(19) a. Underlying /g/ (cf. (17))   b. Rendaku-induced /g/ (cf. (18))

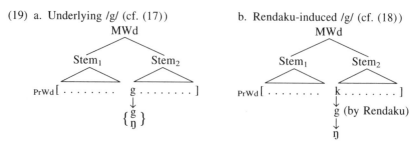

these facts, points out that this difference in behavior between underlying *g*'s (19a) and Rendaku-induced *g*'s (19b) in compounding is puzzling, since no plausible junctural explanation suggests itself. Positing different junctures (or levels) for the two cases would be nothing but a diacritic for optional versus obligatory VVN, and would mean missing the overall generalization: that the two cases are exactly alike in every other respect, for example, accentually. Similar considerations show that it would also not do to assume that there is some 'optional' internal prosodic word formation for the second stem in (19a): crucially, variable VVN here does not correlate with variable accent patterns.[14]

2.2 *Optional nasalization as a free ranking effect*

We begin our analysis with the case of optional VVN: when Stem$_2$ is *g*-initial in isolation, the compound juncture gives rise to variation, as depicted in (20). This raises two interrelated questions: (i) Why is PrWd-internal *g* possible here? and (ii) why do we find variation between *ŋ* and *g*, instead of a uniform outcome?

(20) a.   MWd   b. in isolation: MWd

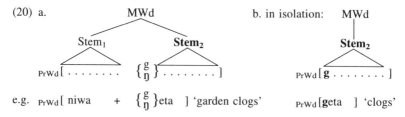

e.g. ₚᵣwd[niwa   +   {$_\text{ŋ}^\text{g}$}eta] 'garden clogs'   ₚᵣwd[geta] 'clogs'

The simplest and most attractive answer to the first question is already contained in (20): in a sense to be made precise, *g* is possible in compound-internal position (*niwa* + *geta*) because Stem$_2$ also occurs in isolation (*geta*),

---

[14] From a different (and mainly historical) perspective, Martin (1987) notes that the behavior of *k* and *g* under compounding in Tokyo Japanese is noteworthy in view of the probable historical origin of VVN, namely, a pattern of intervocalic weakening effects. Such a consonant gradation pattern has been reconstructed for the proto-language, and is still found in the Tohoku dialect of northern Japan (Muraki, 1970; Kanai, 1982); (a) /hata/ → ha**d**a 'flag'; (b) /kaki/ → ka**g**i 'persimmon'; (c) /hada/ → ha**ⁿd**a 'skin'; (d) /kagi/ → ka**ŋ**i 'key'. Intervocalic voiceless stops (a, b) undergo voicing, and intervocalic voiced stops (c, d) are nasalized in a non-neutralizing way: /d/ is

where it shows *g* (and only *g*) as its first segment. This appeal to a correspond-ing independent form finds both a natural place and a precise formalization in the context of recent work on Surface–Surface correspondence (Benua, 1995; McCarthy, 1995; Itô *et al.*, 1996; Kenstowicz, 1995). The idea, then, is to focus on the fact that the related simplex (non-compounded) form of Stem$_2$ (e.g. *geta* 'clog') shows surface PrWd-initial *g*. A version of the relevant Surface–Surface correspondence constraint IdentSS is given in (21). It is responsible for the PrWd-internal *g* in the compound *niwageta* by requiring segmental correspondence to the related surface form *geta*.

(21) IdentSS(Stem$_{bound}$, Stem$_{free}$)
  The bound form of a stem is segmentally identical with its corresponding free form:
  $\{(\text{Stem}_{bound} = \text{Stem}_{free}) \wedge [\phi\,(\text{Stem}_{free}) = p]\} \supset (\phi\,(\text{Stem}_{bound}) = p)$

A pair consisting of a bound and a free occurrence of a stem incurs one violation of IdentSS for each pair of nonidentical correspondent segments (i.e. the unit of measurement here is the segment and not the feature, a point that will turn out to be important in section 2.3 below).

 Taking up our remarks at the beginning of this chapter (see section 1), IdentSS is nothing but one element from a set of low-level surface–surface identity constraints through which the overall imperative of compositional computation of complex forms is implemented in an optimality-theoretic grammar, distributed over the constraint system. The instantiation for com-pounds is given in (22) (here repeated from section 1).

(22) $\phi\,(\text{stem}_1 \frown \text{stem}_2) = \phi\,(\text{stem}_1) + \phi\,(\text{stem}_2)$
  The phonological output form ($\phi\,(x)$) of an input that consists of the morphological concatenation ($\frown$) of two stems, stem$_1$ and stem$_2$, is identical to the phonological combination (+) of the phonological output forms of the two stems.

 There is, strictly speaking, no 'principle of compositionality' in the sense of some unshakable truth. In OT the compositionality imperative is, rather, distributed over the constraint hierarchy in the familiar way, namely, in the form of individually ranked and individually violable constraints. This is a more flexible and arguably superior conception of compositionality than a mono-lithic all-or-nothing principle. Note, again, the fallacy of projecting some kind of quintessentially derivational nature onto the facts of compositionality. The essen-tial insight behind the derivational metaphor is the asymmetry of compositional

prenasalized to [^{n}d], and /g/ appears fully nasalized as [ŋ]. But the derived voiced stops in [hada] (a) and [kagi] (b) do not undergo further nasalization. Against this background, the interaction of VVN with Rendaku is surprising: *g* weakens only optionally to ŋ (19a), whereas *k* obligatorily shifts all the way to ŋ (19b). Gradation systems typically exhibit a chain-shift pattern, where shifts occur in staggered stages, i.e. in a contrast-preserving ('counterfeeding') way (see Pullum, 1983 for relevant discussion, and see also Kirchner, 1996 for an OT analysis of such phenomena).

relations; i.e. the isolation form of the parts crucially enters into the form of the whole, not vice versa. But this primacy of the parts is hardly surprising, and it is not absolute—as Prince and Smolensky (1993: ch. 3) have shown, 'bottom-up' effects are found alongside 'top-down' effects in the phonologies of natural languages—a situation naturally captured by ranked and violable constraints.

Our next task is to find a place for the new constraint IdentSS (21) within the basic analysis discussed in section 1 (here repeated in (23)).

(23) *[ŋ   >>   *g   >>   IdentLS

As it turns out, this provides us with a very simple way of solving the second of the problems raised above: why is ŋ possible at all at the beginning of Stem$_2$, given that g is required by (21)? The answer must be that the compositional correspondence constraint IdentSS (21) does not reign supreme, but rather occupies a dominated position in the ranking. More precisely, as shown in (24), it occupies the same rank as the segmental markedness constraint *g, i.e. two constraints are unranked with respect to each other. We refer to this kind of scenario as *free ranking*.[15]

(24) *[ŋ   >>   { *g / IdentSS }   >>   IdentLS

Postponing further discussion for a moment, we interpret the lack of ranking here as follows: A violation of *either* constraint can count as dominating a violation of the other; the choice is left open by the grammar. Free ranking derives two winners in a two-competition (two-tableau) scenario, as in (25a, b), with one competition per ranking. In (25) and subsequent tableaux, 'Surf' denotes the independent surface form of Stem$_2$, and italicization expresses the Surface–Surface correspondence relation.

(25) a. **[IdentSS >> *g]** -ranking

Lex: /niwa-geta/ Surf: [*geta*]	*[ŋ	**IdentSS**	***g**	IdentLS
☞ [niwa *geta*]			*	
[niwa *ŋeta*]		*!		*

    b. **[*g >> IdentSS]** -ranking

Lex: /niwa-geta/ Surf: [*geta*]	*[ŋ	***g**	**IdentSS**	IdentLS
[niwa *geta*]		*!		
☞ [niwa *ŋeta*]			*	*

With the [IdentSS >> *g]-ranking (25a), the *g*-candidate *niwageta* is the winner, because being identical to the related surface form *geta* is more important than avoiding the voiced velar *g*. On the other hand, the [*g >> IdentSS]-ranking (25b), with a stronger aversion to voiced velars, awards the palm to the ŋ-candidate *niwaŋeta*. In both (25a) and (25b), the *[ŋ constraint is fulfilled by all candidates (there is no PrWd-initial ŋ), and IdentLS plays no crucial role since the competition is already decided by the higher-ranking markedness constraint *g and the compositional correspondence constraint IdentSS. Even if the input for the tableaux above was taken to be *niwa-ŋeta*, the winners would still be the same.

In the free ranking approach in (25a, b), strict domination holds within each competition, even though it is not observed in the grammar (i.e. in the overall constraint ranking). As an alternative where strict domination does not even hold for individual competitions, there is the *tied ranking* interpretation: two (or more) constraints are true equals, in the sense that a violation of neither constraint ever counts as dominating a violation of the other. This type of ranking has been invoked in ranking paradox situations where any specific dominance relation between two constraints derives incorrect results for some inputs (for an example, see Ní Chiosáin, 1995). Closer to the purpose at hand, tied ranking opens up the possibility for a single competition to yield two optimal candidates, and has been used in Müller (1995) and Smolensky (1996) to account for optionality phenomena in syntax.

Tied ranking means that violations of the two constraints IdentSS and *g count as equivalent: It is just as bad to violate IdentSS as it is to violate *g. In (26), on the next page, this is indicated by assigning the two relevant constraints to the same column in the tableau, without a separating vertical line. It stands to reason that tied ranking only produces two winners in a single competition when the candidates in question perform equally well with respect to all other constraints, including the lower-ranked ones. This condition is frequently not fulfilled, as shown in (26a, b), where the (otherwise inert) low-ranked constraint IdentLS breaks the tie in favor of the input-faithful candidate. In this tied ranking scenario, the *input* specification of the voiced velar segment becomes all of a sudden crucial (different from the free-ranking analysis presented earlier)—now the source for optionality lies in the indeterminacy of the input, and not in the constraints or their ranking.

Another relevant input candidate is (26c) where the voiced velar is unspecified for [nasal] (indicated by capitalization). The relevant competing candi-

[15] Building on an idea first put forth in Prince and Smolensky (1993: 51), this approach to optionality and variation has proved fruitful in sociolinguistics (see e.g. a number of the papers presented at NWAV XXIII) and has been taken up in work by e.g. Kiparsky (1993*b*), Kager (1994), Liberman (1994), Reynolds (1994), Sells *et al.* (1994), Anttila (1995), and Hayes and MacEachern (1996).

(26) a.

Lex: /niwa-geta/ Surf: [geta]	*[ŋ]	IdentSS	*g	IdentLS
☞ [niwa *geta*]			*	
[niwa *ŋeta*]		*		*!

b.

Lex: /niwa-ŋeta/ Surf: [geta]	*[ŋ]	IdentSS	*g	IdentLS
[niwa *geta*]			*	*!
☞ [niwa *ŋeta*]		*		

c.

Lex: /niwa-Geta/ Surf: [geta]	*[ŋ]	IdentSS	*g	IdentLS
☞ [niwa *geta*]			*	*
☞ [niwa *ŋeta*]		*		*

dates (assuming a high-ranking constraint requiring surface specification as either [+nasal] or [−nasal] are treated equally by Ident LS(nas) and emerge as co-winners in a single competition.[16]

Indeterminacy in input specification (see section 1 above), hitherto considered analytically awkward, would here be put to full advantage: surface indeterminacy (i.e. optionality) directly results from lexical indeterminacy. This is an intriguing outcome which, while deserving further attention, will be left for future exploration. The remainder of the chapter adopts the more conservative free ranking interpretation (24–25), which adheres to the strict domination doctrine of Prince and Smolensky (1993).

2.3 *Rendaku voicing and obligatory nasalization*

Besides accounting for the optionality of VVN at compound junctures, the analysis in (24) has the additional benefit of explaining the surprising asym-

---

[16] As in Müller (1995) and Smolensky (1996); see also Hammond (1994) for an analysis deriving stress variability in Walmatjari from the fact that the constraint system is not fine-grained enough to determine a single winner in all situations.

metry noted above in (19) between underlying voiced velars in Stem$_2$-initial position, and cases whose voicing is Rendaku-induced (variation in the former cases, no variation in the latter). The minimal-pair contrasts in (27) (due to Kamei, 1956 and Kindaichi, 1967) are reported to be very clear for speakers of a consistent VVN-dialect.

(27)

Underlying [+ voi]: optional VVN			*Rendaku-induced [+ voi]: obligatory VVN*		
boN + $\{ {}^{g}_{\eta} \}$oro	'mediocre grounder'		boN + ŋoro	'Bon period'	
	goro	'grounder'		koro	'time'
oo + $\{ {}^{g}_{\eta} \}$ama	'big toad'		oo + ŋama	'big kettle'	
	gama	'toad'		kama	'kettle'
ita + $\{ {}^{g}_{\eta} \}$arasu	'plate glass'		ita + ŋarasu	'pain crow'	
	garasu	'glass'		karasu	'crow'
kita + $\{ {}^{g}_{\eta} \}$iši	'kita technician'		kita + ŋiši	'north shore'	
	gishi	'technician'		kishi	'shore'
ki + $\{ {}^{g}_{\eta} \}$umi	'yellow berry'		ki + ŋumi	'yellow group'	
	gumi	'berry'		kumi	'class'

It turns out that our analysis already contains the basic ingredients for the solution, once the familiar Rendaku voicing requirement is incorporated into the constraint system. The requirement is stated informally in (28) as a sequential voicing constraint SeqVoi, which can be taken as a constraint-based counterpart[17] to the (language-specific) voicing morpheme figuring in earlier analyses (see Itô and Mester, 1986; and see Anderson, 1992 for recent discussion of alternatives to the traditional concept of a morpheme within a rule-based framework).

(28) Sequential Voicing (SeqVoi):
   'In [$_{wd}$ X$_1$ X$_2$], X$_2$ begins with a [+voi] segment.'
   (informal statement)

SeqVoi (28) is not dominated by any of the other constraints here under investigation (even though dominated in the overall analysis by the OCP,

---

[17] This formulation is chosen here mainly in order to sidestep some distracting technical complications of the analysis. The status of SeqVoi (28) in our analysis is akin to that of Free-V in Prince and Smolensky's (1993) analysis of Lardil since it is presumably a language-particular constraint—even though one could always declare it universal, in the uninteresting Pickwickian sense of being ranked at the bottom of the hierarchy in most, if not all, languages except Japanese (and, perhaps, the Northern Athapascan language Slave; see Rice 1988). A formal OT analysis of sequential voicing is developed in Itô & Mester (1996), in the context of an investigation of its interaction with the OCP.

which is responsible for Lyman's Law effects; see (15) above and Itô and Mester, 1986). The constraint diagram (29) shows that SeqVoi (28) ranks crucially above the Ident constraints and the markedness constraint *g.

(29)   *[ŋ   SeqVoi

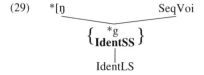

$$\left\{ \begin{array}{c} *g \\ \textbf{IdentSS} \end{array} \right\}$$

IdentLS

Tableaux for the illustrative input /yuki + kuni/ 'snow country', where the selection of the winning candidate crucially involves Rendaku, are given in (30) for the two different-ranking scenarios, [IdentSS >> *g] (30a) and [*g >> IdentSS] (30b).

The central result is that in this case ranking variation does not translate into variation in the output. With either ranking, the same candidate is selected, namely, the ŋ-candidate *yuki+ŋuni*. This is so because the compositional correspondence constraint IdentSS is violated both by the g-candidate (*yuki+guni*, with Rendaku-voicing) and the ŋ-candidate (*yuki+ŋuni*, with Rendaku-voicing and nasalization), since neither is identical (in its second part) to the isolation form *kuni*. Therefore, IdentSS is unable to distinguish between the two, whatever its ranking. The only candidate to fulfill IdentSS (and IdentLS) is the k-candidate (*yuki+kuni*), which loses the competition early in violating high-ranking SeqVoi. This means that the markedness constraint *g is all-powerful, selecting the ŋ-candidate (*yuki+ŋuni*) in both competitions.

(30) /yuki+kuni/ 'snow country'
    a. [**IdentSS** >> *g] -ranking

Lex: /yuki-kuni/ Surf: [*kuni*]	*[ŋ	SeqVoi	**IdentSS**	*g	IdentLS (nas)
[yuki *guni*]			*	*!	
☞ [yuki *ŋuni*]			*		*
[yuki *kuni*]		*!			

    b. [*g >> **IdentSS**] -ranking

Lex: /yuki-kuni/ Surf: [*kuni*]	*[ŋ	SeqVoi	*g	*IdentSS	IdentLS (nas)
[yuki *guni*]			*!	*	
☞ [yuki *ŋuni*]				*	*
[yuki *kuni*]		*!			

Obligatoriness of ŋ in Rendaku contexts thus follows without special plead-ing, and the fact that *k* goes all the way to ŋ is not a surprise, given surface–surface correspondence. Since they do not correspond to any isolation surface form, Rendaku-induced *g*'s are not under the protection of IdentSS.

It is essential in this context that IdentSS (see (21) above) operates at the level of the segment and is not specific to an individual feature like [nasal] (cf. the Input–Output constraint IdentLS(nas)). Two occurrences of a stem fulfill IdentSS (i.e. are segmentally identical) if all pairs of correspondent segments are identical. Segment identity itself is determined in a categorical ('yes/no') way and not in a gradient way, in terms of individual features shared. The latter could be implemented (i) by a single gradiently violable segment identity constraint, or (ii) by a family of feature-specific identity constraints). Either scenario yields wrong results: In (i), the ŋ-candidate would show two viola-tions (*[+nas] and *[+voi]) and therefore lose to the *g*-candidate in (30a), which only has one violation: *[+voi]. In (ii), the ŋ-candidate would violate both IdentSS[nas] and IdentSS[voi], whereas the *g*-candidate would violate only the latter. This shows the importance of a non-gradient notion of segment identity, besides all gradient measures of similarity.[18] Taking note of the fact that this is a necessity for the present analysis, we speculate that the difference between the two Ident constraints is a reflection of a more fundamental difference between 'input–output' (LS) faithfulness and 'output–output' (SS) identity, an issue beyond the scope of the present investigation.[19]

2.4 *Obligatory nasalization of bound elements*

Besides Rendaku-voiced velars discussed in the preceding subsection, there are also underlying voiced velars which do not show optionality at compound junctures. Again, there are well-known minimal pairs (Kamei, 1956; Kindai-chi, 1967) illustrating the contrast between optional and obligatory VVN, as shown in (31). For example, we have a contrast between 'poison moth' and 'poison fang', where 'poison moth' can be pronounced *doku-ga* or *doku-ŋa*, but 'poison fang' is obligatorily *doku-ŋa*.

---

[18] See Cohn and McCarthy (1994: 54) for a related case. Note also that IdentSS in Japanese is still limited to segmental identity—the prosodic form of free and bound occurrences can differ (e.g. accentually).

[19] Care must be taken in characterizing constraints like IdentSS (21) in terms of 'gradience' and 'multiple violation'. Even though it does not matter *how much* an individual segment diverges from its correspondent, it does matter *how many* segments are different from their correspondents. IdentSS measures identity in terms of whole segments, but, as René Kager (pers. comm.) reminds us, can incur multiple violations, depending on the number of nonidentical pairs of segments: *pata/bata* and *pata/mata* show one violation, *pata/bati* and *pata/mati* two, etc.

(31)

Stem₂ occurs as a free form: optional VVN		Stem₂ does not occur as a free form: obligatory VVN	
doku + { g ŋ }a	'poison moth'	doku + ŋa	'poison fang'
ga	'moth'	*ga	'fang' (→ kiba)
seN + { g ŋ }o	'thousand-five'	seN + ŋo	'post-war'
go	'five'	*go	'after' (→ ato)
ko + { g ŋ }aN	'solitary wild goose'	ko + ŋaN	'lake shore'
gaN	'wild goose'	*gaN	'shore (→ kishi)'
ai + { g ŋ }o	'matched go-players'	ai + ŋo	'tender care'
go	'Go'	*go	'care' (→ mamoru)

As (31) shows, this is not a haphazard collection of optional and obligatory nasalized forms. A correlation is found between optionality and the status of the second compound element as an independent lexical item (i.e. occurring in isolation), as indicated in the right-hand column in (31). For example, *ga* in the meaning of 'moth' can occur as a free (non-compounded) form, but not when it refers to 'fang', in which case it only occurs as a bound element. When referring to a fang in isolation, the alternative lexical item *kiba* (shown in parentheses to the right of the ungrammatical form) is used.[20]

Why, then, is nasalization optional when Stem₂ can stand alone as an independent word, and obligatory when it cannot? It is of course possible to appeal to a distinction in morphological category, e.g. between bound stems and free stems, and rely on a junctural solution for these cases (as in Itô and Mester, 1989; 1990). But from the present vantage point, such proposals merely serve to encode the crucial factor: the existence or nonexistence of a free form. The strength of the present analysis is that no such appeal to morphological category distinction is necessary or warranted, since the analysis developed so far already covers these new cases, without any change or extension: Just as in the case of Redaku-induced voicing discussed in the preceding subsection, variation is absent in this case because the IdentSS constraint is irrelevant for candidate selection in these cases, wherever it is

---

[20] The same Kanji character (GA) is used for both the (Sino-Japanese) bound form +*ga*+ (*ondoku* 'sound reading') and the isolation (Yamato) form *kiba* (*kundoku* 'meaning reading'). This kind of contrast is perhaps most equivalent in English to Greek/Latinate versus Germanic morphemes, such as *penta-* and *five*, where only the Germanic form *five* can be used as an independent lexical item. As Iggy Roca (pers. comm.) has reminded us, the notion of an independently existing form is not as straightforward as it might at first seem. What seems to be involved, beyond mere existence, is the establishment of a true connection between dependent and independent occurrence. Thus some Sino-Japanese stems have independent uses, which are arguably not connected in a derivational way to their bound occurrences inside established compounds. See n. 21 for related discussion.

ranked. In this case, however, the relevant candidates all tie with respect to IdentSS not because they all violate it (as in the Rendaku case), but because they all fulfill it: when the second member is a bound form, there is no surface correspondent, and hence IdentSS is vacuously satisfied, and either ranking leads to the ŋ-candidate, as shown in (32).[21]

[21.] An alternative approach to optionality that comes to mind in this context could exploit differences in the *accessibility* of independent correspondents in cases like (32). The vacillation between g and ŋ is traced back not to some ranking variation, but rather to the character of the candidate set itself that enters the selection process (namely, as either equipped with an SS-relation or without such a relation.) More specifically for the case at hand, the ranking is fixed as [*[ŋ >> IdentSS >> *g >> IdentLS], and the optionality effect is captured by whether or not the surface form of the compound member in isolation is available to the computation. In (a), the surface form [geta] is available, and hence IdentSS is instrumental in selecting the g-candidate. On the other hand, in (b), no independent surface form is available, making IdentSS powerless.

a.

Lex: /niwa-geta/ Surf: [geta]	*[ŋ	Ident-SS	*g	Ident-LS
☞ [niwa geta]			*	
[niwa ŋeta]		*		*!

b.

Lex: /niwa-geta/ Surf: —	*[ŋ	Ident-SS	*g	Ident-LS
[niwa geta]		vac.	*!	
☞ [niwa ŋeta]		vac.		*

There may be some empirical evidence that favors this kind of interpretation. Although all the relevant compounds exhibit optionality, speakers note that some compounds usually have ŋ, others tend to have g, and still others are truly optional (cf. NHK, 1985). When the compound itself is more widely used than the individual item, ŋ is preferred, whereas if the individual item is more common than the compound, g is preferred. When both the compound and the individual item are just as common (or rare), then no preference is given. Which words belong to which type differs widely with respect to individual speakers—not surprisingly, since usage of a certain word or compound surely differs among individual speakers. Although more serious empirical and statistical work would have to be done on the topic, the noted tendencies might be attributed to the accessibility of the independent correspondent. When the speaker perceives the particular compound to be compositional, then the compositional correspondence constraint IdentSS is relevant (leading to the g-candidate), but not otherwise (leading to the ŋ-candidate).

(32) /doku-ga/$_{Lex}$ 'poison fang' ☞ [doku ŋa]

a.

Lex: /doku-ga/ Surf: —	*[ŋ	**IdentSS**	*g	IdentLS
[doku ga]			*!	
☞ [doku ŋa]				*

b.

Lex: /doku-ga/ Surf: —	*[ŋ	*g	*IdentSS	IdentLS
[doku ga]		*!		
☞ [doku ŋa]				*

2.5 *Summary*

To recapitulate the analytical results of this section, we have achieved a single unified analysis (33) for what at first appears to be a diverse patterning of VVN in compounds summarized in (34) and (35).

(33) *[ŋ   » $\left\{{}^{*}\text{g} \atop \textbf{IdentSS}\right\}$ »   IdentLS

(34) VVN Variation
Stem$_2$ occurs in isolation.

doku + $\left\{{\textbf{g} \atop \textbf{ŋ}}\right\}$ama 'poison toad'   gama 'toad' (section 2.2)

(35) No VVN Variation
a. Stem$_2$ occurs in isolation, but undergoes Rendaku in compounds.
doku + ŋuchi 'abusive language'   kuchi 'mouth' (section 2.3)
b. Stem$_2$ does not occur in isolation.
doku + ŋa 'poison fang'   *ga 'fang' (kiba) (section 2.4)

   Classical OT ranking logic tells us that the ranking of two constraints makes a difference only when the two competing candidates each pass, and fail, one of the constraints, as in (36), here leading to variation due to the free ranking of these two constraints, IdentSS and *g.

(36)

L: /doku-gama/ S: [gama]	**IdentSS**	*g
☞ [doku *gama*]		*!
[doku *ŋama*]	*	

L: /doku-gama/ S: [gama]	*g	**IdentSS**
[doku *gama*]	*!	
☞ [doku *ŋama*]		*

On the other hand, if the candidates either both violate (37a) or both satisfy (37b) one of the constraints, then the constraint in question (here, IdentSS) has no deciding power. When a constraint is in this way irrelevant, it stands to reason that its ranking with respect to the other constraint will also be irrelevant—hence different rankings have no effect and lead to the same winner.

(37) a. IdentSS violated

L: /doku-kuchi/ S: [*kuchi*]	**IdentSS**	***g***
[doku *guchi*]	*	*!
☞ [doku *ŋuchi*]	*	

L: /doku-kuchi/ S: [*kuchi*]	***g***	**IdentSS**
[doku *guchi*]	*!	*
☞ [doku *ŋuchi*]		*

b. IdentSS satisfied

L: /doku-ga/ S: —	**IdentSS**	***g***
[doku *ga*]		*!
☞ [doku *ŋa*]		

L: /doku-ga/ S: —	***g***	**IdentSS**
[doku *ga*]	*!	
☞ [doku *ŋa*]		

The upshot of the analysis is that the complex of optionality/obligatoriness factors that has defied a junctural solution turns out to have at its core a fairly simple OT constraint-ranking analysis. In order to complete the argument, we now turn to a possible lexical phonological account along lines previously pursued in our earlier work (Itô and Mester, 1989; 1990), and show why the OT analysis is superior.

3. A DERIVATIONAL ALTERNATIVE

VVN exhibits many of the characteristics and correlations that Lexical Phonology (LP), supported by appropriate assumptions about featural underspecification, is designed to handle: the distinction between obligatory and optional VVN is reminiscent of properties typically associated with lexical vs. post-lexical rule application; alternation in derived contexts (*gai+jiN* 'foreigner' vs. *koku+ŋai* 'abroad') is accompanied by a corresponding lack of contrast in underived contexts (*kaŋi*, **kagi* 'key'), a correlation that is the hallmark of the strict cycle; and finally, different phonological behavior in morphologically complex cases is expected to follow from cyclicity, as it is built into the architecture of standard LP (Kiparsky, 1982; 1985).

An account along such lines recalls the central strategy of classical generative phonology (Chomsky and Halle, 1968), faithfully preserved in LP: to seek the explanations for complex phonological patterns in the inner workings of a multi-staged derivational phonology, with cyclic vs. non-cyclic rule application, Structure Preservation, lexical levels, underspecified representations gradually filled up by batteries of default rules, etc. As Itô and Mester (1989; 1990) have shown, an analysis of VVN using the resources of Lexical Phonology indeed looks initially very promising, viewed in the abstract from an eagle's perch. However, in order to be able to make any valid comparison between the OT analysis developed here and such a derivational alternative, we must at least sketch a concrete LP analysis which actually captures all the generalizations of VVN.

3.1. *Cyclic default rules and specificational blocking*

Within a derivational analysis, Voiced Velar Nasalization is conceived of as a rule, here formulated as in (38).

(38) VVN: [+voiced, +dorsal] → [+nas] / ... __   (where ... is non-null)

The first analytical step is to invoke an obligatory/optional distinction between a lexical and a postlexical application of (38). Lexical applications are responsible for the obligatory appearance of ŋ in word-internal contexts (e.g. *kaŋi* 'key', *tookyoo+ŋa* 'Tokyo-NOM'). Postlexically, (38) should apply optionally at compound junctures, leading to variation (e.g. *niwa-geta* ~ *niwa-ŋeta* 'garden clogs').

A moment's reflection reveals, however, that distinguishing the two levels in this way is not sufficient to account for the junctural puzzle noted in section 2.1: when the compound juncture is occupied by a velar whose voicing is Rendaku-induced, then ŋ is obligatory (e.g. *yuki-ŋuni* 'snow country', *kuni* 'country'). Differentiating compound types (between those that undergo obligatory VVN or optional VVN) in terms of further level distinctions is not an acceptable solution, since, as discussed in detail in section 2, there is no other correlating difference, either morphological or prosodic, between compounds like 'snow country' (*yuki-ŋuni* with Rendaku and obligatory ŋ), and 'garden clogs' (*niwa-geta~niwa-ŋeta* with optional ŋ) except for the fact that Rendaku happens to be able to leave an audible mark on the former but not on the latter.

What is necessary to get the derivational analysis off the ground is to start with the assumption that lexical VVN also applies obligatorily to compounds (to account for the cases involving Rendaku) but that it is blocked—by some mechanism to be discussed below—from applying in those cases where the *g* must be protected against obligatory nasalization, so as to remain a candidate for later optional postlexical VVN. A partial derivation of the relevant forms is given in (39). The bolded lexical outputs show *yuki-ŋuni* with ŋ and *niwa-geta* with *g*; only the latter is available for the optional postlexical application of VVN, leading to variation in its postlexical output, *niwa-geta* and *niwa-ŋeta*. Variation is not found for *yuki-ŋuni*, since its ŋ is derived by the obligatory lexical application of VVN.

(39) Lexical:

Compound cycle	yuki-kuni	niwa-geta
Rendaku:	. . . g . . .	–
VVN (obligatory):	. . . ŋ . . .	'*blocked*'
Lexical output:	**yuki-ŋuni**	**niwa-geta**
Postlexical		
VVN (optional):	–	. . . $\left\{ {g \atop ŋ} \right\}$ . . .
Postlexical output:	**yuki-ŋuni**	**niwa-$\left\{ {g \atop ŋ} \right\}$eta**

The remaining challenge is to explain why lexical VVN is blocked in *niwa-geta*. In the earlier cycle [*geta*], *g* is initial and the structural description of VVN is not met. In the compound cycle, however, *g* has become word-internal through compounding; in other words, *g* stands in a derived environment— why is it not subject to obligatory VVN? It is clear that neither Cyclicity nor the Strict Cycle Condition of standard Lexical Phonology (Kiparsky, 1982; 1985) provides a solution; the answer has to be sought elsewhere. As demonstrated in Itô and Mester (1989; 1990), the blocking effect can be achieved by shifting the explanatory burden away from the Strict Cycle Condition and towards a very different assumption: that lexical rules are strictly feature-filling (i.e. they cannot change feature specifications), coupled with cyclic default rules. More precisely, the analysis incorporates the following assumptions (40).[22]

(40) a. Underspecification of the feature [nasal] for velar segments.
   b. Lexical (cyclic) VVN is feature-filling, assigning [+nasal] to non-initial *g*'s.
   c. Postlexical VVN is feature-changing.
   d. A cyclic default rule fills in [−nasal] (or, if [nasal] is treated as privative, another appropriate feature, such as [oral] or [raised velum]) on initial *g*'s.

This basic scheme is illustrated in (41), where voiced velars underspecified for nasality are indicated by capital G. Lexical VVN supplies the specification [+nasal] in *kaGo* → *kaŋo* 'basket', and the cyclic default rule fills in [−nasal] in *Gomi* → *gomi* 'rubbish'.

(41)

	/kaGo/ 'basket'	/Gomi/ 'waste, rubbish'
VVN (feature-filling)	kaŋo	–
Cyclic [−nas] default:	–	gomi

[22] In making these assumptions, the LP analysis of VVN developed in Itô and Mester (1989; 1990) is in many ways reminiscent of the revised model of Lexical Phonology that was later independently proposed in Kiparsky (1993a).

For *niwa-geta* in (42), the cyclic default rule applies on the earlier [*geta*]-cycle, thereby preventing VVN on the compound cycle [*niwageta*]. The optional postlexical version of the rule—which is assumed to be feature-changing, different from the lexical version—is not blocked by the prior application of the default rule, and derives the optional surface ŋ-variant correctly.

(42) Lexical

Stem cycle	/niwa/	/Geta/
VVN+cyclic default:	niwa	geta
Compound (word) cycle:	niwageta	
VVN (feature-filling, obligatory):	*'blocked'*	

Postlexical

VVN (feature-changing, optional):   niwa$\{\begin{smallmatrix} g \\ ŋ \end{smallmatrix}\}$eta

Given (40), lexical VVN only applies to voiced velar archisegments (i.e. segments underspecified for the feature nasal). At a given stage of the derivation, such archisegments will be available only if there is no earlier cycle in which VVN or the cyclic default rule could have taken place. In other words, the analysis encodes morphological structure as feature structure. For example, the suffix /-Ga/ (43) 'Nominative' does not constitute a cyclic domain, and as a result its voiced velar will for the first time be subject to VVN on the cycle of the full suffixed form *geta-Ga* 'sandals-NOM', where it undergoes VVN. If the suffix constituted a cycle on its own, the default rule would have inserted [−nasal] on this domain, thereby wrongly preventing lexical, hence obligatory, nasalization.

(43)

	/Geta/	/-Ga/
Stem cycle	Geta	
VVN + default	geta	
Word cycle	geta Ga	
VVN + default	ŋ	
Output:	geta ŋa	'clogs+NOM'

In order to account for the VVN-behavior of stems that do not happen to occur as independent forms, it is necessary to assume that they (mostly of Sino-Japanese origin) fail to constitute cyclic domains. This entails that such stems become available for lexical rule application only on the cycle where they are conjoined with another lexical element (typically another stem). Given the lack of an earlier cycle, archisegmental G is preserved undisturbed up to this point, setting the form up for lexical (hence obligatory) VVN. This account is illustrated by the stem /-Gai-/ 'outside' (*koku*+ŋ*ai* 'abroad', cf. *gai* +*jiN* 'foreigner') in (44).

(44)

	/-koku-/	/-Gai-/
Stem cycle	–	–
Word cycle	koku + Gai	
VVN+default:	koku + ŋai	

Compounds with Rendaku-derived *g*'s unquestionably have an internal cycle—but they lack a *relevant* internal cycle, i.e. a cycle on which the default rule could have filled in [−nasal] (on a voiced velar). As illustrated in (45), the underlying form /kuni/ is an internal cycle, but the voiced velar does not yet exist on that cycle. Consequently, lexical VVN applies correctly to derive *yuki-ŋuni* 'snow country', with obligatory ŋ.

(45) Stem cycle   /yuki/   /kuni/
      Output   yuki   kuni

      Compound cycle   yuki kuni
      Rendaku   G
      VVN   ŋ
      Output   yuki ŋuni

We have, then, succeeded in constructing a viable account of both optional and obligatory VVN within a derivational model, crucially relying on the assumptions in (40).

3.2. *Assessment and comparison*

Before turning to the comparison with the OT analysis, we should first critically look back at the derivational analysis that has been arrived at within the conceptual framework of Lexical Phonology and Featural Underspecification Theory. The analysis has at least two problematic aspects of a general nature that are worth mentioning, the first with respect to Underspecification Theory, the second with respect to a central tenet of standard Lexical Phonology.

First, in relying on specificational blocking by the insertion of a [−nasal] feature in the phonological derivation, the feature is in effect being treated as a diacritic to prevent the segment from undergoing nasalization. This reveals itself in the form of ternary distinctions that arise at certain points in the derivation: there are voiced velars with no nasal specification, voiced velars with [+nasal], and voiced velars with [−nasal], illustrated by examples like *suŋi+geta-Ga* 'cedar+clog-NOM', which, at the beginning of the highest cycle, has the form / . . . *[+nas]* . . . *[−nas]* . . . *[∅nas]* . . . /. There is no difference at all between the two non-nasal voiced velars, except in one respect: one of them is supposed to undergo lexical VVN, the other one is not supposed to undergo it.[23] This raises the disturbing possibility that the seemingly principled underspecification account has hardly moved beyond diacriticity: lacking independent

---

[23] Note that the issue raised here is more basic than the narrow technical concern about a ternary distinction [+/−/∅] arising in connection with a binary conception of [nasal]. As shown in Itô and Mester (1989), the issue is rather a diacritic use of feature structure, which carries over to a privative conception of [nasal], in which *suŋi+geta-Ga* might take the form / . . . *[nasal]* . . . *[oral]* . . . *[∅]* . . . / (∅ stands for 'neither nasal nor oral'), or to an equivalent feature-geometric implementation with further node structure, such as a [soft palate] node.

motivation, underspecification of [nasal] only serves to encode relevant aspects of morphological structure in terms of abstract contrasts (which are themselves brought about by judiciously ordered default rules). Underspecification thus performs only a mechanical role in the derivational algorithm.

The second troubling aspect is the central analytic assumption that the rule of VVN applies as a cyclic lexical rule. The problem here is that the rule is (semi-)allophonic, and clearly not structure-preserving (there is no underlying ŋ in Japanese). Since Structure Preservation is one of the properties generally ascribed to cyclic lexical rules, having to posit a non-structure-preserving lexical VVN rule is at least worrisome. On the other hand, it has been shown in other cases (e.g. by Borowsky, 1986 for several Level 2 rules in English) that Structure Preservation needs to be weakened. Simply abolishing it would be a short-sighted move, since the structure-preserving character of the vast majority of morphophonemic alternations remains a fact calling for an explanation (see Myers, 1991 for pertinent discussion).

The two general concerns mentioned so far may not be serious impediments to the derivational analysis at hand, but they should be taken into account in an overall assessment of the principles and goals of Lexical Phonology.

As a starting-point of our comparison between the OT analysis in section 2 and the derivational alternative in section 3.1, we will look at what exactly is involved in accounting for the main set of empirical generalizations of VVN, summarized in section 2.4 and repeated below in (46) and (47).

(46) Optional VVN if Stem$_2$ occurs in isolation

doku + $\{ {g \atop ŋ} \}$ama 'poison toad'   gama 'toad'

(47) Obligatory VVN if:
a. Stem$_2$ does not occur in isolation.
    doku + ŋa 'poison fang'   *ga 'fang' ($\rightarrow$ kiba)

b. Stem$_2$ occurs in isolation, but undergoes Rendaku in compounds.
    doku + ŋuchi 'abusive language'   kuchi 'mouth'

In the OT analysis, the optionality in (46) follows from the free ranking of the two constraints IdentSS and *g, while in the LP analysis the postlexical application of VVN is optional. The LP analysis might seem to have a competitive edge here, since it is sometimes surmised that postlexical optionality follows directly from the theory and does not have to be stipulated. However, the validity of such a claim is questionable, since many well-established postlexical processes (e.g. flapping, downstep) are in fact obligatory.[24] This means,

---

[24] There is also some question whether lexical application automatically implies obligatoriness. Obligatory application is certainly the unmarked state of affairs for lexical rules, but, e.g. Kiparsky's (1986) re-analysis of the interaction between stress and umlaut in Chamorro crucially relies on optional lexical rules.

in a derivational theory, which conceives of optionality as a property of *rules*, that each individual rule needs to be annotated as 'optional' or 'obligatory', in order to declare its mode of application. Adding a label 'x' does not amount to a serious formal account (let alone explanation) of x-behavior (here, optionality), and is not connected to anything else in the grammar. Sometimes this is all we can do at the present stage of our knowledge—but sometimes we can do better. Free ranking, even without considering its further advantages for this case (see below), constitutes an analytically superior move, since it at least attempts to explicate optionality behavior by something else (instead of simply offering a label), thus potentially establishing connections to other phenomena.

The obligatory appearance of ŋ in (47) follows in the OT analysis again from the freely ranked constraints IdentSS and *g. As discussed in detail in section 2.4, whichever ranking is chosen, IdentSS does not play a deciding role, because it is either vacuously satisfied (47a) or violated (47b) in the relevant candidates.

In the LP analysis, the obligatoriness of (47) is accounted for by the appropriate selection of cyclic domains and cyclic default rules. For (47a), an independent cycle on Stem$_2$ must be avoided, since such a cycle would induce default insertion of [−nasal], thus preventing the factually required VVN on the higher cycle. The absence of a cycle here is usually ascribed to the generalization that bound stems do not constitute cyclic domains (Brame, 1974; Kiparsky, 1982; Inkelas, 1989). Two points are worth noting in this connection.

First, there is no intrinsic reason in the cyclic theory itself that would prevent a cycle on stems that do not occur as independent words (as opposed to stems that occur as free forms); so this particular restriction, instead of being a consequence of a derivational theory, amounts to a separate stipulation.

The second point arises in considering what it means to be a bound stem: an item that does not occur as a prosodic word by itself in surface structure. So, when we say that bound stems do not constitute a cycle, we are in effect denying a cycle to items that do not happen to constitute surface prosodic words by themselves. That is, only stems with a surface prosodic word status at the *end* of the derivation constitute cyclic domains *earlier* in the derivation. This is quite close to the IdentSS correspondence constraint in the OT analysis, but the two are by no means theoretical equivalents. While surface correspondence requirements are a natural outgrowth of an output-oriented theory like OT, and amply supported in other areas, such as reduplication (see McCarthy and Prince, 1995), they must be added on from the outside in a derivational approach. In a theory predicated on the assumption that lexical phonological rules apply cyclically, following an inside-out path through the morphological structure of the word, the prosodic surface status of some deeply embedded substring of a whole form should be irrelevant for the way the substring is treated at an early point of the derivation. To the extent, therefore, that correspondence to other related output forms *is* a real force in phonology, the derivational theory is at a disadvantage since such information has to be transmitted back upstream, into the derivation—for the case at hand, by means of restrictions on cyclic domains that make covert reference to output structure.

It is of course possible to *encode* the crucial distinctions by means of appropriately chosen nodes and labels[25]—the decisive point is that the correspondence theoretic OT analysis gets by without such encodings and is in this sense a *minimal* theory of compositionality effects.

For the Rendaku-derived *g*-cases (47b), it is crucial that the cyclic default rule inserting [−nas] affects only voiced velars and no other segments. In particular, it must not affect the voiceless velar *k*: every *k* from an earlier cycle, after undergoing Rendaku voicing, changes to *ŋ*, so the cyclic default rule must not have applied to it. But why should the cyclic default rule apply only to *g*, and not to *k* (or, for that matter, to any other segments)? After all, in order to have explanatory merit, a cyclic application of default rules must have the status of a general convention. Principles like the Redundancy Rule Ordering Constraint (RROC) of Radical Underspecification Theory (Archangeli, 1984) are of no help (among other things, the insertion of the marked value of a feature by a phonological rule does not trigger the RROC-insertion of the unmarked value of the feature, let alone on one and only one kind of segment, to the exclusion of all others). It seems unavoidable to conclude that the cyclic default rule is a liability of the LP analysis, since it must be a language-specific rule ordered in the cycle after VVN.

To sum up, the main characteristics of the LP analysis are: (i) optional and obligatory application of VVN; (ii) selection of cyclic domains; and (iii) blocking by cyclic default rules. Although these properties initially seem to follow from the theory itself, closer consideration reveals that this is not so: each involves a language-specific stipulation and/or special pleading. For each case, we need an assumption designed to account for a particular type of example. After optionality is declared for some cases, the obligatoriness of the two other cases each rests on additional unrelated (and somewhat questionable) assumptions.

In contrast, the crucial analytical move of the OT analysis consists in the free ranking of two constraints, one of them being the compositional correspondence constraint IdentSS. It is legitimate to ask what, if anything, is different about the free ranking stipulation in comparison with the stipulation of optionality for one rule. Free ranking in itself is indeed not of overwhelming

[25] In HPSG-oriented theories, such as Orgun's (1994) sign-based approach or Matsui's (1996) JPSG phonology model, this point would carry over in a declarative-nonderivational context, as long as the central element of the derivational approach is preserved: the encoding of the distinction by means of additional nodes and category labels.

interest; rather, it is noteworthy that, given the content of the constraints involved, the free ranking analysis captures further facts beyond the optionality behavior itself. Instead of understanding optionality as the application mode of a given process, the OT account reduces it to a local property of the constraint system and links optionality to other properties and phenomena in a deductive way, providing a unified account of optional and obligatory VVN. The strength of the OT analysis, in other words, is that it is woven from a single cloth, tying various facts together in a more intrinsic way.

4. Appendix: Other Issues

This appendix provides some background for the analysis of VVN developed in the chapter. Section 4.1 investigates the empirical underpinnings of the central segmental markedness considerations. In 4.2 we turn to some additional factors affecting the relation between *g* and *ŋ*, tying up some loose ends and completing the analysis developed in the preceding sections.

4.1. *Markedness relations*

If Universal Grammar contains some constraint against dorsal nasals (*ŋ), any *ŋ* in the output is a violation of *ŋ. Any analysis, therefore, that views VVN as a way of complying with the constraint against voiced dorsal obstruents (*g) must hold that the ranking is *g >> *ŋ: If the ranking was the opposite, or if the two constraints were unranked, *ŋ* would not be consistently preferred over *g* (in word-internal position, and abstracting away from correspondence effects). This raises the question of whether any direct markedness relation between the two segments can be substantiated. McCarthy and Prince (1995: 353) point out that 'UG does not provide a fixed hierarchy of the form *ŋ >> *g or of the form *g >> *ŋ, since neither segment is obviously more marked than the other'.

We are somewhat unclear about the criteria that are often invoked in making the leap from segment distributions in inventories to markedness relations in Universal Grammar. In our attempt to understand the basis of such relationships, we have made some simple calculations based on the data reported in UPSID (Maddieson 1984: 35, 60), arranged in (48) so that each cell contains the number of occurrences of the relevant type of segment.

(48) Frequency of Plain Consonants in UPSID data (Maddieson 1984: 35, 60)

Manners	Labials	Coronals	Dorsals	(Average)
[−voi] Plosives	263	309	283	285
[+voi] Plosives]	199	195	175	190
Nasals	299	316	167	261
(Average)	254	273	208	245

In (49), each cell of (48) is divided by the associated *row* average in order to calculate *index(x,y)*, the 'index of representation' of Place *x* within Manner *y*. In (50), each cell in (48) is divided by the associated *column* average, obtaining *index(y,x)*, the index of representation of Manner *y* within Place *x*. *Index(x,y)* > 1 means that Place *x* is overrepresented within Manner *y*; *index(x,y)* < 1 means underrepresentation.

(49) Representation of places within manners: *index (place, manner)*

Manners	Labials	Coronals	Dorsals	(Average)
[−voi] Plosives	0.92	1.08	0.99	(1.00)
[+voi] Plosives]	1.05	1.03	0.92	(1.00)
Nasals	1.15	1.21	0.64	(1.00)
(Average)	1.03	1.12	0.85	(1.00)

(50) Representation of manners within places: *index (manner, place)*

Manners	Labials	Coronals	Dorsals	(Average)
[−voi] Plosives	1.04	1.13	1.36	1.16
[+voi] Plosives]	0.78	0.71	0.84	0.77
Nasals	1.18	1.16	0.80	1.06
(Average)	(1.00)	(1.00)	(1.00)	(1.00)

Since the relevant reference points (averages) are different (i.e. manner average vs. place average), the two indices are usually different for a given place/manner combination. For example, *index(labial, voiced plosive)* in (49) is 199/190 = 1.05, i.e. labials are very slightly overrepresented among voiced plosives. On the other hand, *index(voiced plosive, labial)* in (50) is 199/254 = 0.78, i.e. voiced plosives are significantly underrepresented among labials.[26] The comparisons emerging from (49) and (50) are summarized in (51) and (52), respectively, with notable underrepresentation (index < 0.9) indicated by boldface.

(51)

Manner class	Place comparisons based on (49)
a. Voiceless	Coronal > Dorsal > Labial
b. Voiced	Labial > Coronal > Dorsal
c. Nasal	Coronal > Labial > **Dorsal**

[26] This indicates that the question whether some segment or class of segments is 'marked' or 'unmarked', without an explicit reference group, is hard to assess.

(52)

Place class	Manner comparisons based on (50)				
a. Labial	Nasal	>	Voiceless	>	**Voiced**
b. Coronal	Nasal	>	Voiceless	>	**Voiced**
c. Dorsal	Voiceless	>	**Voiced**	>	**Nasal**
d. average	Voiceless	>	Nasal	>	**Voiced**

The summary generally confirms markedness (or 'underrepresentation', in the more neutral terminology chosen here) statements made in the literature. In the voiceless class, *p* (0.92) is slightly underrepresented (51a), as is *g* (0.92) in the voiced class (51b). The only major departure from the standard index of 1 is found in the nasal class (51c) with the dorsal ŋ (0.64), which is responsible for bringing down the average dorsal index (0.85) in (51d). If the average of the different manners is to be taken as an indicator of general markedness, then Dorsal is more marked than Labial overall, suggesting a refinement of the usual dichotomy, which contrasts (unmarked) Coronal with (marked) Noncoronal. For manner comparisons within a given place class (52), we find notable underrepresentation (index < 0.9, indicated by boldtype) for the voiced plosives within all place classes (*b*: 0.78, *d*: 0.81, *g*: 0.84), and for the nasals within the dorsal class (ŋ: 0.80).

Returning to our point of interest, the relation between *g* and ŋ, it is important to bear in mind that an index of representation has two arguments; in other words, it is defined only strictly internal to a given reference group. Noting that the relevant reference group for *g* and ŋ is a Place class, namely Dorsal in (50) and (52c), we find that ŋ (0.80) has an index only slightly lower than that of *g* (0.84). In other words, the two can be considered equally underrepresented within the dorsal class. The manner classes in (49) and (51) provide no basis on which *g* and ŋ could be legitimately compared: it is true that *g* is underrepresented with respect to *d* and *b* (reference group: voiced plosives), and ŋ with respect to *n* and *m* (reference group: nasals)—but no direct comparison between the two dorsals in question emerges from this, confirming McCarthy and Prince's (1995) assessment that neither can be said to be universally more marked than the other. Rather, there are constraints against voiced dorsal obstruents and dorsal nasals, which can be ranked with respect to each other in individual grammars.

4.2. *Suppression of nasalization and faithfulness promotion*

Throughout this chapter, our analysis of VVN has been concerned with a conservative version of the Tokyo dialect, i.e. with a pattern of speech showing consistent observance of the VVN alternation. Within Modern Japanese, this dialect coexists with a large number of varieties which do not exhibit the *g~ŋ* alternation and admit ŋ only as the allophone of a nasal consonant before dorsals (as in *keŋka* 'quarrel'); in a number of other dialects, the prestige position of Tokyo speech has led to a partial adoption of the *g~ŋ* alternation, resulting in more or less sporadic cases of VVN accompanied by high variability, hypercorrections, and similar sociolinguistic symptoms. Abstracting away from this kind of social and geographical variation by focusing on a consistent VVN-dialect, our analysis has proceeded under the assumption that the occurrence of PrWd-internal *g* is always due to compositional correspondence (viz. to a related *g*-initial stem, see section 2). In order to round off the picture, we will briefly deal with another source of internal *g*, a parochial promotion of faithfulness (crucially, above the conflicting markedness constraint *g).

The richest source of word-internal *g* consists in unassimilated loanwords (53), an important subpart of the contemporary Japanese lexicon (Shibatani, 1990; Itô and Mester, 1995*a*; 1995*b*).

(53) [. . . **g** . . .]   *[. . . ŋ . . .]
    a. egoisuto   *eŋoisuto   'egoist'
    b. puroguramu   *puroŋuramu   'program'
    c. suroogaN   'slogan'
    d. koNgo   'Congo'
    e. porutogaru   'Portugal'

Such internal *g*'s conform to the foreign (mostly English) source word. They tend to be replaced by ŋ as the form becomes assimilated and partially nativized, as illustrated by the long-established loanwords like *iŋirisu* 'England' (54a). There are also forms where the foreign source already contains ŋ, as in (54b).[27]

(54) a. *igirisu   iŋirisu   'England'
      *orugaN   oruŋaN   'organ' (musical instrument)
    b. *kiŋgu   kiŋŋu   'king' [kɪŋ]
      *zooriŋgeN   zooriŋŋeN   'Solingen' [zoːlɪŋən]

In the approach to the phonological lexicon developed in Itô and Mester (1995*b*), non-nasalized *g* in loanwords, as in (53), is a case of lexicon-internal variation reducible to lexicon-internal ranking variation (specifically, of correspondence-sensitive constraints). For the case at hand, the crucial point is

---

[27] Some forms occupy a transitional status in terms of nativization (*doguma ~ doŋuma* 'dogma'), and pronunciation dictionaries show some degree of divergence (e.g. whereas the NHK pronunciation dictionary (NHK, 1985) lists the loanword corresponding to 'organ' *as orugaN*, it appears as *oruŋaN* in Kindaichi (1958)). Conceivably, prosodic position might also play some role here, with foot-initial position (as in (54b)) (vs. foot-medial position, as in (54a)) serving as some kind of secondary licenser for *g* (assuming left-aligned footing, as suggested in Itô and Mester, 1992).

that IdentLS(nas) occupies a higher rank, resulting in the lexicalized ranking IdentLS(nas) »*g (58).

(55) a. Ranking in the grammar   b. Lexically marked ranking

       *[ŋ   *[ŋ

        | |

       *g IdentLS(nas)

        | |

   IdentLS(nas)   *g

Taking up our earlier treatment (Itô and Mester, 1995*b*), we suggest that the relation of the lexicalized ranking [Ident-LS(nas) >> *g] (55b) to the general ranking [*g >> Ident-LS(nas)] (55a) posited in the grammar can be conceived of in terms of a generalized notion of 'taking precedence'. The familiar notion of precedence (lexicographic precedence, in Strict-Domination-OT, following Prince and Smolensky, 1991; 1993) is an instance of a first-level precedence, as in (56a).[28] The next logical step is to consider the possibility of 2nd level precedence statements, as in (56b), which express relations between 1st level precedences, i.e. constraint rankings.

(56) a. First-level precedence (>>)
      relation between constraints—constraint ranking $C_n >> C_m$

    b. Second-level precedence (>> >>)
      relation between constraint rankings (i.e. between first level precedences)
      $[C_n >> C_m] >> >> [C_m >> C_n]$

Note now that the relation of a lexicalized ranking like [Ident-LS(nas) » *g] to the ranking [*g » Ident-LS(nas)] posited in the grammar is of a particular kind: the two rankings conflict,[29] the first (lexically marked) relates to the second (lexicon-wide) ranking as the specific to the general, and the first (specific) ranking is visibly active in the lexicon of Japanese (as evidenced by the existence of outputs like *egoisuto* instead of *eŋoisuto*). In other words, their relation falls under Prince and Smolensky's 1993 Pāṇinian theorem on constraint ranking (appropriately generalized to accommodate precedence relations of any level), and (57) must hold.

(57) [IdentLS(nas) >> *g]$_{lex}$ >> >> [*g >> IdentLS(nas)]

A tableau illustrating the lexicalized ranking appears in (58).

---

[28] This raises the question of whether constraints themselves can be formally understood as zero-level preference relations holding between linguistic structures. This is conceivable for many among the currently used constraints: thus the constraint Onset declares that a consonant-initial syllable is preferable to (>) a vowel-initial syllable, and the constraint NoCoda declares a consonant-final syllable to be inferior to a vowel-final syllable. Syllable well-formedness constraints as 0th level preference relations on structures: Onset: $_\sigma[C >{}_\sigma[V;$ NoCoda: $V]_\sigma > C]_\sigma$. It remains to be seen, however, whether all constraints can be profitably expressed in such a comparativist format, and what the consequences would be for the formal theory of candidate competition and selection.

[29] In a second-level sense of 'conflict': the two rankings result in grammars selecting a different output for at least one input.

(58)

/egoisuto/ 'egoist' [IdentLS(nas) >> *g]lex	*[ŋ	IdentLS(nas)	*g
☞ egoisuto			*
eŋoisuto		*!	

For the forms in (54) with normal VVN, it can simply be assumed that they are subject to the general ranking [*g >> IdentLS(nas)], as shown in (59) for the form *iŋirisu.*[30]

(59)

/igirisu/ 'England'	*[ŋ	*g	IdentsLS(nas)
igirisu		*!	
☞ iŋirisu			*

Apart from unassimilated loanwords, word-internal *g* occurs in VVN-dialects in certain areas of the native lexicon under the pressure of construction-specific Ident-constraints, namely, Ident-BR and Ident-κ.[31] One relevant context, mimetic (sound-symbolic) reduplication, has recently been given a correspondence-theoretic analysis by McCarthy and Prince (1995). Within the Japanese lexicon, mimetics form a separate stratum with special phonological and morphological characteristics (McCawley, 1968; Hamano, 1986; Mester and Itô, 1989; Itô and Mester, 1995a; 1995b). Mimetic stems are subject to regular VVN: as shown in (60), stem-internally *ŋ* occurs to the exclusion of *g*.

(60) moŋu + moŋu   'mumbling'   *mogu + mogu
      iŋa + iŋa   'irritating voice' *iga + iga

Mimetics are thus subject to the same analysis as all core elements of the lexicon, as illustrated in (61)[32]—sound-symbolism apparently provides no special license for word-internal *g*.

[30] However, it is not entirely clear whether this is the correct way of dealing with the cases in (54b), where the *ŋ* in the Japanese form is probably not merely a case of the emergent native *ŋ*-pattern, but a Japanese *ŋ* corresponding to an *ŋ* in the source word. If it is appropriate to incorporate such considerations within the purview of formal grammar (see Silverman, 1992 and Yip, 1993 for different proposals in this context), this might call for a further extension of Correspondence Theory—the crucial correspondence relation would here reach out to a related output in a different language. In the most general sense, of course, the two items—loanword and source word—stand in some kind of relation. What remains to be seen is whether it is theoretically fruitful to extend the linguistic (grammatical) notion of correspondence to cover such relations between languages.

[31] See Itô et al. (1996) for some discussion of the close connection between (i) the lexicalized promotion of a faithfulness constraint and (ii) the proliferation of separately rankable construction-specific faithfulness constraints.

[32] Identical results are obtained from the alternative inputs /moŋu/ or /moGu/ (with underspecification of [nasal]); see (13) in Section 1.

(61)

/mogu/	*[ŋ]	*g	IdentsLS(nas)
mogu		*!	
☞ moŋu			*

There is one context, however, where VVN is suppressed: when mimetic stems are reduplicated, *g* at the beginning of the second part is never nasalized, but it remains *g*, just as its correspondent at the beginning of the first part (62).

(62) gara + gara   'rattle'   *gara + ŋara, *ŋara + ŋara
       geʲi + geʲi   'centipede'   etc.
       goto + goto   'sound of large moving objects'
       gii + gii   'scraping'
       guu + guu   'snoring'
       goo + goo   'strong windy sound'
       gatsu + gatsu   'starvingly'
       goro + goro   'rolling'
       gee + gee   'retching'

For this kind of underapplication of an allophonic alternation in reduplication, we adopt McCarthy & Prince's analysis, reproduced below in (63).[33]

(63)

/gara–RED/	Ident-BR (nas)	*[ŋ]	*g	IdentLS (nas)
a. ŋara-ŋara		*!		*
b. gara-ŋara	*!		*	
c. ☞ gara-gara			**	

---

[33] There is a possible alternative analysis of internal *g* in mimetic reduplication which links the phenomenon directly to a genuine prosodic property of the forms in question. As pointed out by Haruo Kubozono (pers. comm.), the accentual characteristics of mimetic forms reveal in many cases that they consist of two separate prosodic words. If so, the reduplication-specific property enforced by base-reduplicant identity is a prosodic one (*two prosodic words*—perhaps word-onset must correspond to word-onset?), whereas all segmental effects are secondary. In this analysis, 'internal *g*' is not internal in the relevant sense, so there is no underapplication here of an allophonic process. In addition, the lack of underapplication in other reduplicated forms noted below in the text (see (64)) is fully expected (as normal compounds, they constitute single prosodic words). A genuine (but isolated) example of non-prosodic overapplication pointed out to us by Michinao Matsui (pers. comm.) is found in connection with the morphophonemic alternation whereby single /h/ in Japanese corresponds to geminate /pp/: The ('lexically reduplicated') form *haha* 'mother', when combined with the gemination-inducing prefix *baka-* 'foolish', yields *bakappapa* 'foolish mother' and not **bakappaha* or *??bakahhaha* (this can also be conceived of as underapplication, taking /p/ to be underlying; see Matsui, 1996: 125, n. 10).

Internal non-nasalized *g* is specific to mimetics—it does not hold in general for reduplication. Thus in intensifying and pluralizing reduplication (64) we find the normal replacement of *g* by ŋ. This is true both for bound reduplicative compounds like *ge+ŋe* 'lowest' and for free reduplicative compounds like *kuni+ŋuni* 'various countries' (with Rendaku-induced *g* further replaced by ŋ; see section 2 above).

(64) ge + ŋe   'lowest'   *ge + ge
     ga + ŋa (taru) 'rugged'   *ga + ga
     kuni + ŋuni   'various countries'
     kane + ŋane   'for a long time'

A final case of non-nasalized internal *g* occurs in the recitation of the kana syllabary, where each column is treated as a single phonological word with antepenultimate accent: *a-i-ú-e-o*, *ka-ki-kú-ke-ko*, etc. In the case of the *g*-column (*ga-gyō*), we find (65a), with nonnasalized PrWd-internal *g*, instead of (65b).

(65) a. ga gi gú ge go   b. *ga ŋi ŋú ŋe ŋo

One way of analysing this case would be to assimilate it to that of the loanwords seen earlier, i.e. to claim that the recitation of the kana-syllabary is likewise governed by the lexicalized ranking [Ident-LS(nas) » *g]. However, it is not clear whether this gets to the core of the phenomenon, which is arguably not the preservation of *g* per se, but rather the establishment of uniformity throughout the 'paradigm' (here, the *g*-column) (see e.g. Raffelsie-fen, 1995: 39 for this approach to paradigm uniformity effects). Making this idea more concrete, we will assume that the invariance of the onset element throughout all members of a kana-column (**ka-ki-ku-ke-ko**, **ma-mi-mu-me-mo**, etc.)[34] is expressed in the grammar by means of a surface–surface (output–output) correspondence relation κ (mnemonic for 'kana'), akin to base–reduplicant correspondence in the case of mimetic reduplication (see (60) and (61) above). κ links the correspondent onset elements into what we can refer to as a κ-chain. One possible formulation of the identity constraint on members of such chains is given in (66).[35]

---

[34] This extends to the case of the onsetless vowel kana *Øa-Øi-Øu-Øe-Øo* as identity of zero onsets, in ways familiar from the analysis of poetic rhyme and alliteration (cf. *Øin* and *Øout* alongside *part and parcel, spic and span*, etc.), see Jakobson (1963) and Kiparsky (1973) for discussion.

[35] An alternative would be to formulate chain identity more simply as in: 'The members of a κ-chain must be identical.' In this case, for a set of chain members M, the domain of evaluation is the Cartesian Product $M \times M$, and each pair (m_i, m_j) with $m_i \neq m_j$ counting as a violation. This is perhaps a more elegant way of stating the constraint (which avoids the conceptually clumsy reference to the first chain element), with potentially different empirical results (note that (67b) has 6 violations in this mode of reckoning, thereby losing to (67a) with 4 violations). On the other hand, it is conceivable that reference to the first member is an irreducible fact, for substantive reasons (see Beckman, 1995 and Padgett, 1995 for discussion of such prominence-related factors).

(66) Ident-κ: The members of a κ-chain must be identical to its head (i.e. its initial member).

Notating κ by means of co-superscription of correspondent elements, tableau (67) shows how kana column uniformity is enforced by adding the constraint Ident-κ at the top of the constraint hierarchy.

(67)

/ga-gi-gu-ge-go/	*Ident-κ	*[ŋ]	*g	IdentLS (nas)
a. g^{κ}a-ŋ$^{\kappa}$i-ŋ$^{\kappa}$u-ŋ$^{\kappa}$e-ŋ$^{\kappa}$o	*!***		*	****
b. g^{κ}a-g$^{\kappa}$i-ŋ$^{\kappa}$u-ŋ$^{\kappa}$e-ŋ$^{\kappa}$o	*!**		**	***
c. ŋ$^{\kappa}$a-ŋ$^{\kappa}$i-ŋ$^{\kappa}$u-ŋ$^{\kappa}$e-ŋ$^{\kappa}$o		*!		*****
d. ☞ g^{κ}a-g$^{\kappa}$i-g$^{\kappa}$u-g$^{\kappa}$e-g$^{\kappa}$o			*****	

Within the total analysis, Ident-κ turns out to be a dominated constraint, as shown by the fact that kana column uniformity is violated, for example, in the *s*-column (*sa-gyoo*): *sa-ʃi-su-se-so*. Building on the analysis in Itô and Mester (1995*a*; 1995*b*), this is correctly captured by the constraint ranking in (68), where the constraint IdentLS(ant), different from IdentLS(nas), ranks above Ident-κ and above the antagonistic markedness constraint *ʃ. On the other hand, both Ident-constraints are dominated by the sequential constraint *si*.

(68) *si >> IdentLS(ant) >> Ident-κ >> *ʃ

An illustrative tableau is given in (69).

(69)

/sa-si-su-se-so/	*si	IdentLS (ant)	Ident-κ	*ʃ
a. s^{κ}a-ʃ$^{\kappa}$i-ʃ$^{\kappa}$u-s$^{\kappa}$e-s$^{\kappa}$o		**!	**	**
b. ☞ s^{κ}a-ʃ$^{\kappa}$i-s$^{\kappa}$u-s$^{\kappa}$e-s$^{\kappa}$o		*	*	*
c. ʃ$^{\kappa}$a-ʃ$^{\kappa}$i-ʃ$^{\kappa}$u-ʃ$^{\kappa}$e-ʃ$^{\kappa}$o		**!***		*****
d. s^{κ}a-s$^{\kappa}$i-s$^{\kappa}$u-s$^{\kappa}$e-s$^{\kappa}$o	*!			

ACKNOWLEDGMENTS

The names of the authors appear in alphabetical order. Even though the research reported here has undergone several major overhauls since its first presentation at the 1989 Features and Underspecification Conference held at MIT, Alan Prince and Moira Yip, who gave us substantive written comments and helpful suggestions on the 1989 version, might still recognize the outlines of the original paper. Thanks are due to audiences at MIT, UC Irvine, Osaka University, UCLA, UC Santa Cruz, Kobe University, and Stanford University for their comments and questions, in particular to Bruce Hayes, Motoko Katayama, Pat Keating, Paul Kiparsky, Haruo Kubozono, Yuki Kuroda, John McCarthy, Orhan Orgun, Philip Spaelti, Donca Steriade, and Rachel Walker. For a careful and critical reading of the current version of the paper, we are indebted to René Kager, Dan Karvonen, and Jaye Padgett, whose extensive written comments led to numerous improvements in both content and style. Finally, we would like to thank Iggy Roca for giving us the opportunity to contribute to this volume. This work was partially supported by faculty senate grants from the University of California at Santa Cruz and by the National Science Foundation under grant SBR-9510868.

REFERENCES

Anderson, S. R. (1992). *A-Morphous Morphology*. Cambridge: Cambridge University Press.
Anttila, A. (1995). 'Deriving Variation from Grammar: A Study of Finnish Genitives'. MS, Stanford University, California.
Archangeli, D. (1984). 'Underspecification in Yawelmani Phonology and Morphology'. Dissertation, Massachusetts Institute of Technology.
Bach, E., and Wheeler, D. (1981). 'Montague Phonology: A First Approximation'. Amherst: University of Massachusetts. Occasional Papers in Linguistics [UMOP] 7: 27–45.
Beckman, J. N. (1995). 'Shona height harmony: markedness and positional identity', in J. Beckman, S. Urbanczyk, and L. Walsh (eds.), UMOP 18: *Papers in Optimality Theory*. Amherst, Mass.: GLSA, 53–75.
Benua, L. (1995). 'Identity effects in morphological truncation', in J. Beckman, S. Urbanczyk, and L. Walsh (eds.), UMOP 18: *Papers in Optimality Theory*. Amherst, Mass.: GLSA, 77–136.
Black, H. A. (1993). 'Constraint-Ranked Derivation: A Serial Approach to Optimization'. Dissertation, University of California, Santa Cruz.
Borowsky, T. (1986). 'Topics in the Lexical Phonology of English'. Doctoral dissertation, University of Massachusetts, Amherst.
Brame, M. (1974). 'The cycle in phonology: stress in Palestinian, Maltese, and Spanish', *Linguistic Inquiry* 5: 39–60.
Chomsky, N. and Halle, M. (1968). *The Sound Pattern of English*. New York: Harper & Row.
Cohn, A. and McCarthy, J. J. (1994). 'Alignment and parallelism in Indonesian phonology'. MS, Cornell University, Ithaca, NY, and University of Massachusetts, Amherst. ROA-25. To appear in *Linguistic Inquiry*.

Hamano, S. (1986). 'The Sound-Symbolic System of Japanese'. Dissertation, University of Florida.

Hammond, M. (1994). 'An OT Account of Variability in Walmatjari Stress'. MS, University of Arizona, Tucson. ROA-20.

Hayes, B. (1996). 'Voicing in NC clusters', handout of talk given at University of California, Santa Cruz.

—— and MacEachern, M. (1996). 'Folk Verse Form in English', MS, University of California, Los Angeles. ROA-121.

Hewitt, M. S., and Crowhurst, M. J. (1995). 'Conjunctive Constraints and Templates in Optimality Theory'. MS, University of North Carolina, Chapel Hill.

Inkelas, S. (1989). 'Prosodic Constituency in the Lexicon'. Dissertation, Stanford University.

Itô, J. (1986). 'Syllable Theory in Prosodic Phonology'. Dissertation, University of Massachusetts, Amherst.

—— (1989). 'A prosodic theory of epenthesis', *Natural Language and Linguistic Theory* 7: 217–59.

—— Kitagawa, Y., and Mester, A. (1996). 'Prosodic faithfulness and correspondence', *Journal of East Asian Linguistics* 5: 217–94.

—— and Mester, A. (1986). 'The phonology of voicing in Japanese: theoretical consequences for morphological accessibility', *Linguistic Inquiry* 17: 49–73.

—— —— (1989). 'Gagyoo: Featural and Prosodic Characteristics'. MS, University of California, Santa Cruz.

—— —— (1990). 'Proper containment and phonological domains', handout distributed at KATL, Osaka University, Dec. 1990.

—— —— (1992). 'Weak layering and word binarity'. Linguistics Research Center Report No. 92–09. University of California, Santa Cruz.

—— —— (1995a). 'Japanese phonology', in J. Goldsmith (ed.), *Handbook of Phonological Theory*. Oxford: Blackwell, 817–38.

—— —— (1995b). 'The core–periphery structure of the lexicon and constraints on reranking', in J. Beckman, L. W. Dickey, and S. Urbanczyk (eds.), *Papers in Optimality Theory* University of Massachusetts Occasional Papers in Linguistics 18: Amherst: GLSA, 181–210.

—— —— (1996). 'Rendaku I: Constraint Conjuction and the OCP'. Handout of talk presented at the Kobe Phonology Forum, Japan, and at the Western Conference on Linguistics, University of California, Santa Cruz. ROA-144.

—— —— and Padgett, J, (1995). 'Licensing and underspecification in Optimality Theory', *Linguistic Inquiry* 26: 571–614.

Jakobson, R. (1963). 'On the so-called vowel alliteration in Germanic verse', *Zeitschrift für Phonetik, Sprachwissenschaft, und Kommunikationsforschung* 16.

Kager, R. (1994). 'Generalized Alignment and Morphological Parsing.' MS, Research Institute of Language and Speech, Utrecht University. ROA-36.

Kamei, T. (1956). 'Ga-gyō no Kana' (The Kana of the ga-column), *Kokugo to Kokubungaku* 39 (9): 1–14.

Kanai, Y. (1982). 'A case against the morphophonemic–allophonic principle', *Linguistic Inquiry* 13: 320–3.

Kenstowicz, M. (1995). 'Cyclic vs. non-cyclic constraint evaluation', *Phonology* **12**: 397–436.

Kindaichi, H. (ed.) (1958). *Meikai Nihongo Akusento Jiten* [Japanese Accent Dictionary]. Tokyo: Sanseido.

—— (1967). *Nihongo On'in no Kenkyū[MB1]* [Studies in Japanese Phonology]. Tokyo: Tokyōdō.

Kiparsky, P. (1973). 'The role of linguistics in a theory of poetry', *Daedalus* **102**: 231–45.

—— (1982). 'Lexical Morphology and Phonology', in I. S. Yang (ed.) *Linguistics in the Morning Calm*. Seoul: Hanshin, 3–91.

—— (1985). 'Some consequences of Lexical Phonology', *Phonology Yearbook* **2**: 82–138.

—— (1986). 'Systematic Optionality in the Lexical Phonology of Chamorro'. MS, Stanford University, California.

—— (1993a). 'Blocking in nonderived environments', in S. Hargus and E. Kaisse (eds.), *Phonetics and Phonology IV: Studies in Lexical Phonology*. San Diego, Calif.: Academic Press, 277–313.

—— (1993b) 'Variable rules', handout distributed at Rutgers Optimality Workshop 1, Oct. 1993.

Kirchner, R. (1996). 'Synchronic chain shifts in Optimality Theory', *Linguistic Inquiry* **27**: 341–50.

Kubozono, H. (1995). 'Constraint interaction in Japanese phonology: evidence from compound accent', in R. Walker, O. Lorentz, and H. Kubozono (eds.) *Phonology at Santa Cruz, IV*. Linguistics Research Center, University of California, Santa Cruz, 21–38.

—— (1996). 'Lexical markedness and variation: a nonderivational account of Japanese compound accent', West Coast Conference on Formal Linguistics 15.

—— and Mester, A. (1995). 'Foot and accent: New Evidence from Japanese compound accentuation', handout distributed at LSA Meeting, New Orleans, Jan. 1995.

Liberman, M. (1994). 'Optionality and Optimality'. Fragment of a draft, University of Pennsylvania.

—— and Prince, A. (1977). 'On stress and linguistic rhythm', *Linguistic Inquiry* **8**: 249–336.

McCarthy, J. J. (1995). 'Extensions of Faithfulness: Rotuman Revisited'. MS, University of Massachusetts, Amherst.

—— and Prince, A. S. (1995). 'Faithfulness and reduplicative identity', in J. N. Beckman, L. W. Dickey, and S. Urbanczyk (eds.), *Papers in Optimality Theory* (University of Massachusetts Occasional Papers 18). Amherst: GLSA. 249–384.

McCawley, J. D. (1968). *The Phonological Component of a Grammar of Japanese*. The Hague: Mouton.

Maddieson, I. (1984). *Patterns of Sounds*. Cambridge: Cambridge University Press.

Martin, S. E. (1987). *The Japanese Language through Time*. New Haven, Conn.: Yale University Press.

Matsui, M. (1996). 'An introduction to JPSG phonology', in T. Gunji (ed.) *Studies on the Universality of Constraint-Based Phrase Structure Grammars*. Osaka University, 111–42.

Merchant, J. (1996). 'Alignment and fricative assimilation in German', *Linguistic Inquiry* **27**: 709–19.

Mester, A., and Itô, J. (1989). 'Feature predictability and underspecification: palatal prosody in Japanese mimetics', *Language* **65**: 258–93.

Mohanan, K. P. (1986). *The Theory of Lexical Phonology*. Dordrecht:, Reidel.

Müller, G. (1995). 'Partial Wh-Movement and Optimality Theory'. MS, Seminar für Sprachwissenschaft, University of Tübingen.

Muraki, M. (1970). 'A sound change in a Tohoku dialect', *Papers in Linguistics* **3**: 341–7.

Myers, S. (1991). 'Structure preservation and the Strong Domain Hypothesis', *Linguistic Inquiry* **22**: 379–85.

Ní Chiosáin, M. (1995). 'Prosodic Well-formedness and Sonority Constraints: Epenthesis in Irish'. MS, University College Dublin. ROA-89.

NHK (JAPAN BROADCASTING CORPORATION) (1985). *Nihongo Hatsuon Akusento Jiten* [Japanese Pronunciation Accent Dictionary]. Tokyo: Nihon Hōsō Kyōkai.

Orgun, C. O. (1994). 'Monotonic Cyclicity and Optimality Theory', in M. Gonzàles (ed.), Proceedings of the 24st Annual Meeting of the North-East Linguistic Society. University of Massachusetts, Amherst: GLSA, 461–74.

—— (1995). 'Correspondence and identity constraints in two-level Optimality Theory', West Coast Conference on Formal Linguistics 14.

Padgett, J. (1995). 'Feature classes', in J. N. Beckman, L. W. Dickey, and S. Urbanczyk (eds.), *Papers in Optimality Theory* (University of Massachusetts Occasional Papers 18). Amherst: GLSA, 385–420.

Pesetsky, D. (1979). 'Russian Morphology and Lexical Theory'. MS, Cambridge, Mass.

Pierrehumbert, J., and Beckman, M. (1988). *Japanese Tone Structure*. Cambridge, Mass.: MIT Press.

Poser, W. J. (1990). 'Evidence for foot structure in Japanese', *Language* **66**: 78–105.

Prince, A., and Smolensky, P. (1991). 'Notes on Connectionism and Harmony Theory in Linguistics'. Technical Report CU-CS-533-91. Dept. of Computer Science, University of Colorado, Boulder.

—— —— (1993). 'Optimality Theory: Constraint Interaction in Generative Grammar'. MS, Rutgers University, New Brunswick, and University of Colorado, Boulder.

Pullum, G. K. (1983). 'Morphophonemic rules, allophonic rules, and counterfeeding', *Linguistic Inquiry* **14**: 179–84.

Raffelsiefen, R. (1995). 'Conditions for stability: the case of schwa in German', Theorie des Lexikons 69. University of Düsseldorf.

Reynolds, W. T. (1994). 'Variation and Phonological Theory'. Dissertation, University of Pennsylvania, Philadelphia.

Rice, K. (1988). 'Continuant voicing in Slave (Northern Athapaskan): the cyclic application of default rules', in M. Hammond and M. Noonan (eds.), *Theoretical Morphology*. San Diego, Calif.: Academic Press.

Selkirk, E. O. (1980). 'The role of prosodic categories in English word stress', *Linguistic Inquiry* **11** (3): 563–605.

—— and Tateishi K, (1988). 'Constraints on minor phrase formation in Japanese', in

Papers from the 24th Annual Regional Meeting of the Chicago Linguistic Society. Chicago: CLS, 316–36.

Sells, P., Rickford, R., and Warsow, T. (1994). 'An Optimality-Theoretic Approach to Variation in Negative Inversion in AAVE'. MS, Stanford University. ROA-53.

Shibatani, M. (1990). *The Languages of Japan.* Cambridge: Cambridge University Press.

Silverman, D. (1992). 'Multiple scansions in loanword phonology: evidence from Cantonese', *Phonology* 9(2): 289–328.

Smolensky, P. (1996). 'On the comprehension/production dilemma in child language', *Linguistic Inquiry* 27: 720–31.

Stampe, D. (1972). 'How I Spent My Summer Vacation (A Dissertation on Natural Phonology)'. Dissertation, University of Chicago.

Steriade, D. (1995). 'Underspecification and markedness', in J. Goldsmith (ed.) *Handbook of Phonological Theory.* Oxford: Blackwell, 114–74.

Trubetskoi, N. S. (1949). *Principes de phonologie,* trans. J. Cantineau. Paris: Klincksieck.

Vance, T. (1987). *An Introduction to Japanese Phonology.* New York: SUNY Press.

von Stechow, A. (1991). 'Syntax und Semantik', in A. von Stechow and D. Wunderlich (eds.), *Semantik: Ein internationales Handbuch der zeitgenössischen Forschung.* Berlin: de Gruyter, 90–148.

Walker, R. (1996). 'Neutral Segments and Locality', MS., University of California, Santa Cruz.

Yip, M. (1993). 'Cantonese loanword phonology and Optimality Theory', *Journal of East Asian Linguistics* 2: 261–92.

15

Rhythmic Vowel Deletion in Optimality Theory

RENÉ KAGER

1. INTRODUCTION

A challenge to any theory of phonology is to reconcile two radically different kinds of interaction: *conspiracy* and *opacity*. A conspiracy is a situation in which independent processes interact in such a way that they create a uniform pattern in surface forms. In contrast, opacity is an interaction by which one process obscures the context of application of another process—resulting in a loss of transparency in the surface form.

One of the principal reasons for which rule-based theory has recently come under attack is that it offers no satisfactory explanation for conspiracies. Rule-based theory fails in this respect, since it states generalizations in the form of structural descriptions, which are checked against representations at various steps during a serial derivation. All that is relevant for rule application is that some representation matches the context of a rule at the point in the derivation at which that rule applies. In this view the level of the output is no more privileged than any intermediary level. In contrast, Optimality Theory (Prince and Smolensky, 1993; McCarthy and Prince, 1993b) defines grammatical well-formedness as the result of an interaction of conflicting constraints on surface forms, thus abandoning the concept of ordered rules. Focusing on the output allows a more principled explanation of conspiracies. In OT, a convergence to surface patterns is the expected situation, since the output is the single level at which generalizations can be stated.

As compared to its success in capturing conspiracies, OT has up till now at least not been equally successful in capturing opacities. In rule-based theory, opacity is just the expected situation, since generalizations may hold at inter-mediary levels, but then be lost in the output, where other rules may have obscured them.[1] Opacity poses a challenge for OT, a theory that, in its

---

[1] Doug Pulleyblank kindly reminds me of proposals in derivational theory that minimize opacity in rule interactions (e.g. Kiparsky, 1971). This is a valid observation, but it leaves unaffected the crucial point: derivational theory, being a theory employing ordered rules, is *in principle* capable of expressing rule opacity, and to that extent it also predicts it. This point has been emphasized by Kisseberth (1970; 1973), Kenstowicz and Kisseberth (1979), and others.

standard interpretation at least, is deprived of any intermediate levels that do not correspond to morphological strata (but cf. Chapters 16, 17, and 18 below [Editor]).

This chapter is devoted to one specific type of opacity, the case of rhythmic vowel deletion. This is a cross-linguistically common process that deletes vowels in alternating syllables. The standard rule-based analysis attributes the rhythmicity of vowel deletion to its context—weak syllables of iterative disyllabic feet. Opacity is an inherent result of this analysis, for the following reason. Deletion of vowels is followed by a resyllabification of surrounding consonants. Consequently the context of deletion may be irrecoverable from the output. A rule-based scenario typically includes the following ordered rules (i–iv): (i) syllabification; (ii) iterative foot construction; (iii) deletion of vowels in weak syllables of feet; and (iv) resyllabification. The derivations in (1) illustrate these rules by forms from two languages that will figure prominently in this chapter, Macushi Carib (iambic, 1a) and South-eastern Tepehuan (trochaic, 1b).

(1)	UR	a.	/wanamari/	b.	/maa-matuʃidʒaʔ/
	Syllabification		wa.na.ma.ri		maa.ma.tu.ʃi.dʒaʔ
	Foot construction		(wa.nàː). (ma.ríː)		(máa.ma). (tù.ʃi). (dʒàʔ)
	Vowel deletion		(w .nàː). (m .ríː)		(máa.m). (tù.ʃ). (dʒàʔ)
	Resyllabification		(wnàː). (mríː)		(máam). (tùʃ). (dʒàʔ)
	PR		[(wnàː). (mríː)]		[(máam). tuʃ.dʒaʔ]

In languages in which the context of deletion correlates with rhythmic stress in surface forms, such as Macushi Carib, deletion is transparent with respect to its metrical context. But in the case of South-eastern Tepehuan, where no surface rhythmic pattern is present, deletion cannot be conditioned by surface feet. Here vowel deletion apparently destroys its own context, by deleting the vowel that is the head of the weak syllable in the foot. 'Metrical opacity' presents a challenge to surface-oriented Optimality Theory. This chapter tackles this challenge by arguing that vowel deletion in South-eastern Tepehuan is not due to iterative feet, but rather to the minimization of the number of unstressed syllables that remain unparsed by a single word-initial foot. This analysis is fully surface-based, thereby removing the opacity problem.

This dual treatment of (what appears to be) a unitary phenomenon may seem to amount to a loss of generalization: there are now two types of grammar that achieve the same kind of surface result—alternating phonetic loss of underlying vowels. However, this loss of generalization is apparent only, since there are independent arguments for a distinction between these types of language. Actually, there is no unitary phenomenon of rhythmic vowel deletion, but instead there are two varieties: *gradient* and *categorical*.

Gradient rhythmic vowel deletion is phonologically incomplete, occurring in free variation with vowel reduction. It preserves the syllabicity of the 'deleted' vowel, which may be signalled by phonetic cues (open transitions at the deletion site, etc.). It preserves the foot-based context in the output, in the form of secondary stresses. Since its context is fully recoverable from the output, gradient reduction/deletion involves no opacity. The language that exemplifies this is Macushi Carib, discussed in Section 2.

Categorial rhythmic vowel deletion is phonologically complete, and has no vowel reduction counterpart. It destroys the syllabicity of the deleted vowel, which is clear from the fact that syllable-governed phonology refers exclusively to the output syllabification. Moreover, there is no secondary stress pattern that coincides with the alternating deletion pattern. (As a matter of fact, South-eastern Tepehuan has no secondary stress at all.) OT predicts that categorial deletion cannot be conditioned by iterative feet, since that would involve opacity. In Section 3 I will first argue against an iterative-foot-based analysis on independent grounds. I will then propose an OT analysis which is based on the idea that vowel deletion in South-eastern Tepehuan serves a cross-linguistically well-known output target: exhaustivity of metrical parsing. It minimizes the number of syllables outside the single initial foot (e.g. [(máam)] in the output of 1b). The apparent 'rhythmicity' of the deletion pattern follows from constraint interaction: input consonants must be preserved, while output consonants must be properly syllabified ('no complex margins'). From this it follows that the optimal strategy to reduce violations of exhaustive metrical parsing, while preserving the input consonantism, is the deletion of alternating vowels.

My conclusion will be that OT (but not rule-based theory) predicts the clustering of properties of rhythmic vowel deletion found in Macushi and South-eastern Tepehuan on a broader typological basis. It is a virtue of OT, rather than a liability, that it makes a distinction between two phenomena that are only apparently identical.

2. Macushi Carib

2.1. *Rhythmic vowel deletion preserves syllabicity*

The rhythmic pattern of Macushi, a member of the Carib family spoken in Guyana and Brazil, was first described by Hawkins (1950). His paper focuses on the rhythmic vowel deletion rule, without discussing an alternating stress pattern as its conditioning factor. Hawkins reports that vowels in odd-numbered syllables, counting from left to right, are deleted. The last vowel in each stress contour is always retained. Abbott (1991) relates deletion to an alternating stress pattern: 'A short unstressed vowel is reduced to open transition [transcribed as [ᵊ],RK] before stops, and may be completely lost before voiced consonants.' Complementing the rhythmic deletion pattern, Abbott (1991: 145) reports a short-long rhythmic pattern in sequences of open syllables within the phrase, with even-numbered syllables long: 'The final CV in a phonological phrase (i.e., a phrase bounded by pause) is always long and stressed, but within the phrase, even across grammatical word boundaries, the pattern is that the even numbered V or CV syllable, counting from the left, is long.' Abbott defines 'long' as 'having stress and vowel length'. This pattern is illustrated for different lengths of syllable in (2), where foot boundaries are indicated that will be motivated below:[2]

(2) 2σ /pata/   (pᵊtáː)   'place' (A: 147)
        /pe-pɨn/   (pᵊpɨ́n)   'no, never' (H: 89)
    3σ /piripi/   (prìː).(píː)   'spindle' (H: 89)
        /upata/   (ᵊpàː).(táː)   'my place' (A: 146)
    4σ /erepamɨ/   (ᵊrèː).(pmɨ́ː)   'I arrive' (A: 146)
        /pirɔtɔ-rɨ/   (pᵊrɔ́ː).(trɨ́)   'gunshot' (H: 89)
    5σ /u-manari-rɨ/   (màː).(nrìː).(rɨ́ː)   'my cassava grater' (H: 89)
        /y-akina-tɔʔ-ton/ (yᵊkìː).(nᵊtɔ̀ʔ).(tɔ́n) 'something to comb him
                                                  with' (H: 88)
    6σ /u-wanamari-rɨ/ (wàː).(nmàː).(rrɨ́ː)   'my mirror' (H: 87)
    7σ /arimarakayamɨ/ (rìː).(mràː).(kyàː).(mɨ́ː) 'dogs' (A: 146)

Rhythmic vowel deletion may actually produce vowel–zero alternations in stems, due to prefixation, which affects the odd–even count:[3]

(3) a. /wanamari/   (wnàː).(mríː)   'mirror' (H: 87)
    b. /u-wanamari-rɨ/ (wàː).(nmàː).(rrɨ́ː)   'my mirror' (H: 87)

In sum, we find that foot parsing is iambic by two converging criteria: rhythmic vowel reduction (or deletion) and rhythmic vowel lengthening. Both indicate the strength of even-numbered syllables, and the weakness of odd-numbered syllables. Moreover, the quantity-sensitivity of iambic feet is apparent from both processes. First, vowels in heavy syllables (Cvv, CvC) are immune to deletion. Second, heavy syllables disrupt the parity count of both lengthening and reduction (underlying length of vowels has been indicated by gemination):

(4) a. /seepɔrɔ/   (sèe).(prɔ́ː)   'along here' (A: 147)
    b. /peʔmara/   (pèʔ).(mráː)   'free' (A: 147)
    c. /eerepamɨ/   (èe).(rᵊpàː).(mɨ́ː)   'I arrive' (A: 146)

---

[2] Forms below which are taken from Hawkins (1950) are marked by 'H', while those from Abbott are marked by 'A'. In the former I have added length on vowels where this should fall according to Abbott's description. Lengthening data reported in Carson (1982) deviate slightly from those in Abbott (1991). Carson describes vowel-lengthening as a compensatory process: 'when a short vowel is suppressed, the vowel that immediately precedes a stop consonant in its vicinity is lengthened.' Her description differs in various other aspects from Hawkins (1950) and Abbott (1991), in particular in positing lexical tone rather than stress. Because of these rather large differences I suspect that Carson's description was based on a different dialect from those studied by Hawkins and Abbott. For this reason I have not used any of Carson's examples.

[3] In fact, without alternations we would not know the underlying values of most vowels.

d.	/waimu̱yami̱/	(wài).(myàː).(míː)	'rats' (A: 147)
e.	/ʃiʔ-mi̱ri-kɔ̱-pe/	(ʃìʔ).(mrìː).(kᵊpéː)	'little now' (H: 88)
f.	/aʔta̱ en-kɔ̱ne-kaʔpi̱/	(àʔ)(tèn)(knèː)(kàʔ)(píː)	'the hammock that he made' (H: 88)
g.	/u̱-y-en-kuʔ-ti̱-saʔ-ya/	(yèː).(kùʔ).(tᵊsàʔ).(yáː)	'if anyone deceives me' (H: 88)

The contexts of application of reduction and lengthening are stated maximally general by iambic feet, which present the contexts of both processes simultaneously.

Both lengthening and vowel reduction are cross-linguistically common processes in iambic languages, increasing the durational differences which are inherent to the iamb: *a quantitatively unbalanced rhythm unit* (Hayes, 1995) of a light plus a heavy syllable. From a typological perspective some analysis is preferrable that expresses this connection between foot type and reduction. But then vowel reduction must crucially preserve the weak syllable in the iamb as a degenerate syllable, containing a nucleus that is void of vocalic features (indicated below by •):

(5) [Cv.Cv] → [C• .Cvv]

If the vowel were categorially deleted, the disyllabic iambic target would be lost. This is, to some extent, a theory-internal argument. However, there is additional evidence that vowel deletion is an extreme type of reduction, i.e. of a gradient rather than a categorial nature. First, according to Abbott (1991) it is an optional process: reduction need not go all the way to deletion. Since reduced vowel and 'zero' seem to be mutually interchangeable realizations, it would be difficult to draw the line between both. The gradient nature of vowel deletion shows its phonetic, rather than phonological, character. Second, deletion is literally incomplete in certain contexts: before stops, an open transition is retained at the site of the 'deleted' vowel. I interpret this to be the phonetic realization of the empty nucleus:

(6)	a.	/y-eʔma̱-tan-ti̱ʔ/	(yèʔ).(mᵊtàn).(tíʔ)	'you (pl.) go pay it' (H: 88)
	b.	/y-akina̱-tɔʔ-ton/	(yᵊkìː).(nᵊtɔ̀ʔ).(tɔ́n)	'something to comb him with'

Without a phonetic counterpart of syllabicity, the closed versus open transition contrast between [. . . nt . . .] (cf. 6a) and [. . . nᵊt . . .] (cf. 6b) is not explainable.[4]

Third, if deletion were complete, it would violate otherwise unviolable

---

[4] Hawkins (1950: 88) argues open transition to be 'nonsyllabic and nonvocalic (1) because the space between the consonants has no clear vowel quality; (2) because no contrastive vowel qualities are there present; (3) because the transition does not take as much time as the vowels do; and (4) because no vowel phoneme with which this can be phonetically or structurally identified occurs elswehere in the language'. He adds that 'the contrast between open and closed transition, however, remains as an unexplained contrastive residue in the phonemic analysis'.

phonotactic laws of consonant clusters. For example, the word onsets /wn/ and /yk/ that arise across the deletion site in (3a) and (6b) are not otherwise attested initially in roots. It then turns out that resyllabification cannot apply by the principles that govern initial syllabification.

Fourth, there is corroborating evidence from lengthening that 'deleted' vowels still function as empty nuclei in the phonology. We saw earlier that iambic lengthening affects open syllables, but not closed syllables. If vowel deletion were complete, it would trigger resyllabification of an onset as the coda of the preceding syllable, thereby closing it. Then lengthening would be incorrectly blocked (since closed syllables generally fail to lengthen). For example, we would expect *[wnam.riː] rather than [wnaːmriː] (cf. 3a).

An allophonic process of obstruent voicing provides yet another argument for an empty nucleus. Abbott (1991: 140) reports that 'Voicing occurs following a long syllable (CVV, CVC or VC) in which there is a long vowel or a final n or ʔ (this does not include all cases of rhythmically long vowels)'. From various examples which she provides it is clear that both 'underlying' and 'derived' syllable weight may trigger obstruent voicing (7a–d). But Abbott never transcribes a voiced obstruent in a position following a site of reduction or deletion (7e–f). (Abbott's transcriptions abstract away from deletion; I have indicated reduction vowels by underlining.)

(7) a. /seeporɔ/   [see.bɔ.rɔː]   'along here' (A: 147)
    b. /mɔʔta/   [mɔʔ.da]   'move' (A: 140)
    c. /uyapɔnse/   [u.yaː.bɔŋ.ze]   'my bench' (A: 140)
    d. /yepɔtɔrɨ/   [ye.pɔː.dɔ.rɨː]   'lord' (A: 140)
    e. /sɨrɨrɨpe/   [sɨ.rɨː.rɨ.peː]   'today' (A: 144)
    f. /eraʔmata/   [e.raʔ.ma.taː]   'go get it' (A: 147)

If deletion were to affect syllabification, it would produce outputs such as *[(srɨːr).(beː)], in which bold-face /b/ would be in the position for voicing, following a heavy syllable.

There is yet a third syllable-sensitive process which provides evidence for the lack of resyllabification. Nasals in coda position cannot license place of articulation, and they are homorganic with the following consonant, or realized as [ŋ] at the end of a word and before /r/ (8a). Now observe that a nasal that precedes a deletion site always retains its place features (8b–c):[5]

(8) a. /anraʔ/   [aŋraʔ]   'heron' (A: 142)
    b. /peʔmara/   [peʔmara]   'free' (A: 147)
    c. /aimutuŋ/   [aimutuŋ]   'white' (A: 142)

If deletion would trigger resyllabification, the expected outputs would be *[peʔŋ.ra] and *[ain.tuŋ]. Crucially, all three syllable-sensitive processes

---

[5] Form (8b) is actually presented by Abbott with its underlined vowel deleted, while form (8a) is presented in a broader transcription that abstracts away from vowel deletion.

point to the same syllabification of consonant clusters that are adjacent to 'deletion' sites. This prediction is not made by a derivational analysis with true vowel deletion, given the fact that (in principle at least) a syllable-sensitive rule may be extrinsically ordered before or after vowel deletion.[6]

In sum, there are four arguments that RVD preserves a nucleus in the output—and hence is phonologically incomplete. First, its target (the canonical iamb LH) is disyllabic. Second, it is optional, while vocalic traces (open transitions) may remain at the deletion site. Third, it does not respect otherwise general phonotactics (since it creates ill-formed consonant clusters). Fourth, three syllable-sensitive processes (vowel-lengthening, obstruent-voicing, and nasal assimilation) show that deletion fails to trigger resyllabification.

2.2. *Rule-ordering theory versus Optimality Theory*

Consider first a rule-based analysis of this pattern:

(9) a. Foot construction: assign iambs from left to right (treating CvC as heavy).
    b. End Rule (Right): label the rightmost foot as strong.
    c. Iambic lengthening: lengthen the vowel of a syllable in strong position.
    d. Iambic reduction: reduce the vowel of a syllable in a weak position.

This analysis is illustrated by sample derivations below:

(10)	UR	/piripi/	/y-akina-tɔʔ-tɔn/	/ʃiʔ-miri-kɨ-pe/
	Iambs	(pi.ri).(pi)	(ya.ki).(na.tɔʔ).(tɔn)	(ʃiʔ).(mi.ri).(kɨ.pe)
	ER(R)	(pi.ri).(pí)	(ya.ki).(na.tɔʔ).(tɔ́n)	(ʃiʔ).(mi.ri).(kɨ.pé)
	Lengthen	(pi.riː).(píː)	(ya.kiː).(na.tɔ́ʔ).(tɔ́n)	(ʃiʔ).(mi.riː).(kɨ.péː)
	Reduce	(priː).(píː)	(yᵊ.kiː).(nᵊtɔʔ).(tɔ́n)	(ʃiʔ).(mriː).(kᵊ.péː)
	PR	[(prìː).(píː)]	[(yᵊkìː).(nᵊtɔ̀ʔ).(tɔ́n)]	[(ʃiʔ).(mrìː).(kᵊ.péː)]

Now consider an OT analysis of the Macushi footing pattern. The preservation of input vowels—in the form of empty nuclei—is due to the 'faithfulness' constraint MAX (McCarthy and Prince, 1995). This requires input segments to have some *correspondent* in the output. (Correspondence is a relationship between elements in two segment strings, in this case input and output; see McCarthy and Prince, 1995.)

(11) MAX
    Every segment in the input has a correspondent in the output.

MAX does not require a correspondent of an input segment to retain the feature content of that input segment—it only asserts that 'something' be

---

[6] Doug Pulleyblank remarks that resyllabification is not necessarily triggered by vowel deletion in a rule-based approach. However, resyllabification is considered to be an 'automatic rule' by most derivational analysts.

identifiable in the output as a realization of the input vowel, e.g. an open transition.[7]

Next I assume a 'cover constraint' FT-FORM, merely as a shorthand notation for four undominated constraints that together define the iamb as a foot of the shape (LH) or (H). This includes the constraint responsible for vowel lengthening (PK-PROM: 'The element x is a better peak than y if the intrinsic prominence of x is greater than that of y', Prince and Smolensky, 1993):

(12) FT-FORM (cover constraint)

a.	FTBIN	Feet are binary under moraic or syllabic analysis.
b.	WSP	Heavy syllables are prominent within the foot.
c.	RHTYPE=IAMB	Feet are right-headed.
d.	PK-PROM	Peak (x) ≻ Peak (y) if $|x| > |y|$.

Vowel reduction (or the loss of vocalic features) in weak syllables is due to undominated REDUCE.

(13) REDUCE
Weak syllables dominate no vocalic features.

To obtain an iterative foot parsing, PARSE-σ (14) must dominate ALL-FT-R (15).

(14) PARSE-σ
All syllables must be parsed by feet.

(15) ALL-FT-R
All feet must stand at the right edge of PrWd.

This constraint interaction (McCarthy and Prince, 1993*a*) produces exhaustive footing that is oriented towards the right edge of the word. Let us see how this works. First, PARSE-σ must be undominated because of exhaustivity. It must crucially dominate ALL-FT-R, since every foot that is not strictly at the right word edge incurs a violation of ALL-FT-R. But even in its dominated position, ALL-FT-R has two effects. It minimizes the number of feet per word. Since feet are maximally disyllabic, the effect is an alternating rhythm. Its second effect is to limit monosyllabic feet to the right periphery—this will become clear immediately below in tableau (18). Notice that the *left-to-right* specification of footing in the rule-based analysis translates into a *right-edge* orientation in the OT analysis.

---

[7] Bill Idsardi objects that null vowels constitute a representational extension of the theory, since 'if null vowels are not phonetically present, then the analysis of Carib sneaks a derivation in through the back door. The OT calculation is not calculating surface phonetic forms, but "end-of-phonology" forms, subject to further phonetic interpretation.' I disagree. Under any theory, a line should be drawn between phonology and the domain of phonetic interpretation. A well-argued assumption (Keating, 1988; Cohn, 1990) is that this coincides with the distinction between categorial ('symbolic') and gradient ('temporal and spatial') rules. Since durational reduction of unstressed vowels is a gradient process in Macushi Carib (as it is in many other languages), it must belong to phonetic interpretation.

The fact that vowels are reducible at all is due to an interaction of REDUCE and IDENT. The latter is the faithfulness constraint that militates against loss of input features in the output (McCarthy and Prince, 1995).

(16) IDENT
    If a segment is specified as [αF] in the input, then it must be specified as [αF] in the output.

Clearly REDUCE must dominate IDENT. The last crucial ranking, that of ALL-FT-R above IDENT, will be motivated by the tableaux (18–19).

In sum, the alternating reduction pattern is due to the following hierarchy:

(17) MAX, REDUCE, FT-FORM, PARSE-σ >> ALL-FT-R >> IDENT

This hierarchy is illustrated in tableaux (18–19). In (18) we see a trisyllabic form:

(18) Input: /piripi/	MAX	REDUCE	FT-FORM	PARSE-σ	ALL-FT-R	IDENT
a. ☞ (p• .riː).(piː)					*	*
b. (piː).(r• .piː)					**!	*
c. (piː).(riː).(piː)					*, *!*	
d. p• .(r• .piː)				*!		**
e. (p• .ri).(piː)			PK-PROM!		*	*
f. (pi.riː).(piː)		*!			*	
g. (pr• .piː)	*!					*

'Rightward directionality' of foot parsing is due to ALL-FT-R, which excludes (18b–c) in favor of (18a). Note that violations of ALL-FT-R are counted by measuring the distance in numbers of syllables between every right foot edge and the right word edge. Of the three candidates (18a–c) that violate none of the undominated constraints, (18c) is the only one that has no reduced vowels, hence no violations of IDENT. However, it is excluded by ALL-FT-R, of which it has three violations, while the optimal candidate (18a) has only one. This establishes the ranking ALL-FT-R >> IDENT.

Next consider tableau (19) to see how a consonant cluster affects the foot parsing:

(19) Input: /ʃiʔ-miri-kɨ-pe/	MAX	REDUCE	FT-FORM	PARSE-σ	ALL-FT-R	IDENT
a. ☞ (ʃiʔ).(m• .riː).(k•.peː)					** ****	**
b. (ʃiʔ).(m• .riː).(kɨː).(peː)					*, **, ****!	*
c. (ʃiʔ).(miː).(riː).(kɨː).(peː)					*, **, ***, *!***	
d. (ʃ• ʔ.miː).(r• .kɨː).(peː)			WSP!		*, ***	**
e. (ʃiʔ).(mi.riː).(kɨ.peː)		*!*			** ****	
f. (ʃiʔ).(mriː).(kpeː)	*!*				*, **	

The activity of WSP now becomes visible: the three-foot candidate (19d) is rejected by it even though this has fewer violations of ALL-FT-R than the optimal candidate (19a).

Let us now summarize the argument. A foot-based analysis of RVD in Optimality Theory requires that feet governing RVD can be inferred from the output on the basis of phonetic cues or phonotactic diagnostics. Arguments given earlier substantiate this: there are phonetic cues (open transitions) for syllabicity at deletion sites, while foot structure is diagnosed by the presence of both secondary stress and vowel length (phonotactically the lengthening pattern shows that no resyllabification takes place, since it is not inhibited by consonant clusters resulting from deletion). More generally, the prediction is that if RVD is foot-based, then it must be gradient. Conversely, if RVD is categorial, then it cannot be foot-based. The latter prediction will be shown correct for South-eastern Tepehuan in section 3. Before that, I have to point out a refinement in the analysis of Macushi Carib.

2.3. *Excursus: phonotactic restrictions on deletion*

Hawkins (1950: 88–9) mentions certain phonotactic conditions under which RVD fails to apply. He reports that 'a vowel in the basic form is retained if it precedes or follows any cluster of . . . two consonants in which the first consonant is a member of Group I'.

(20) a. /pakra-yamɨn?/   pakraymɨn?   (*pᵊkraymɨn?)   'bush hogs'
     b. /ptakay-pe/   ptakaype   (*ptᵊkaype)   'traira-fish now . . . '
     c. /kratu-pe/   kratᵊpe   (*krᵊtupe)   'alligator now . . . '

Group I is the class of obstruents /p, t, k, s, ʃ, r/. Since ternary onsets are disallowed, the obstruent-plus-consonant cluster in the quote from Hawkins defines the (phonotactically well-formed) complex onset in Macushi. It may therefore seem plausible to attribute the blocking of vowel deletion in (20) to syllable phonotactics (e.g. 'no ternary onsets'). But we have seen in previous examples that vowel reduction/deletion is *not* phonotactically structure-preserving. (That is, consonant clusters may arise across a deletion site that are not elsewhere attested in morphemes.) Instead we attribute the ill-formedness of vowel deletion in (20) to an undominated constraint *CC:[8]

(21) *CC
     A complex onset must not be adjacent to an empty nucleus.

---

[8] A similar situation is disallowed in Dutch, possibly by the same constraint—schwa may not be the head of a syllable that has a complex onset, see Kager (1990), van Oostendorp (1995). However, there is no evidence for a ban on post-schwa complex onsets in Dutch.

This symmetrical constraint rules out pre-cluster reduction (20a), as well as post-cluster reduction (20b–c).

The problem for a rule-based analysis is that the metrical parsing is influenced by phonotactic patterns that arise only *after* vowel reduction. This is illustrated by the forms (22ab). The predicted metrical parsing, resulting from the rightward assignment of iambs, is shown in (22a). The metrical parsing that is required for the attested form, and which is motivated by the reduction of the second vowel, is shown in (22b):

(22) a. (kra.tu).(pe)   *[krᵊtuːpeː]
    b. (kra).(tu.pe)   [kraːtᵊpeː]

The problem is not so much how to block (22a): this may be due to *CC, interpreted as an output filter on vowel reduction/deletion. Instead, the problem is how to derive the foot parsing (22b) that makes correct predictions about reduction/deletion. An ordering paradox is evident: vowel reduction depends on metrical parsing, while metrical parsing must in turn depend on reduction.[9] Hence foot parsing must have global look-ahead in order to apply properly. This raises a problem for a rule-based analysis, since globality is excluded by most proponents of rule theory.

The look-ahead of metrical parsing to whatever phonotactic effects it might have in the output is just the kind of situation that one would expect under OT. The 'shift' in position of feet follows from REDUCE, which selects the metrical parsing (kraː).(tu.péː) in (23a) over the parsing (kra.tuː).(péː) in (23c), with a non-reduced initial syllable.

(23) Input: /kratu-pe/	*CC	MAX	REDUCE	FT-FORM	PARSE-σ	ALL-FT-R
a. ☞ (kraː).(tᵊ.peː)						**
b. (kraː).(tuː).(peː)						*, **!
c. (kra.tuː).(peː)			*!			*
d. (kᵊ.tuː).(peː)		r!				*
e. (krᵊ.tuː).(peː)	*!*					*

The tableau of /ptakay-pe/ minimally differs from the preceding tableau (23). Here WSP rejects the two-foot output (24b), which is due to the heaviness of the second syllable, which in its turn is due to the consonant cluster preceding the final vowel.

---

[9] Incidentally, note that these data present evidence for the assumption that reduced vowels are featurally empty due to a phonological constraint. If vowel reduction were completely phonetic, its influence of metrical parsing could not be explained.

(24) Input: /ptakay-pe/	*CC	Max	Reduce	Ft- Form	Parse- σ	All-Ft-R
a. ☞ (ptaː).(kay).(peː)						*, **
b. (ptaː).(k• y.peː)				WSP!		**
c. (pta.kay).(peː)			*!			*
d. (p• .kay).(peː)		t!				*
e. (pt• .kay).(peː)	*!					*

This concludes the analysis of Macushi Carib. I now turn to South-eastern Tepehuan.

3. South-eastern Tepehuan

3.1. *Patterns of vowel deletion*

South-eastern Tepehuan (Willett, 1982; Willett, 1991) is an Uto-Aztecan language spoken south-east of Durango in Mexico. It has a number of vowel alternations, among them apocope, rhythmic syncope, and shortening. These three alternations occur in a domain identified as the *stem* by Willett (1982). The stem includes the root, plus a reduplicant prefix, plus a number of stem-formation suffixes.

Before we can look into the vowel alternations, we must discuss the place of the accent in the stem. Accent falls on the initial stem syllable when it is heavy (i.e. either long-voweled, diphthongal, or closed) (25a–c). It falls on the second stem syllable if this is heavy while the first syllable is light, see (25d–f). Note that no stem begins with a sequence of two light syllables—this output gap is due to rhythmic syncope. The accent pattern can be captured by a single iambic foot (H) or (LH) at the left edge:

(25) a. (vóo).hi   'bear'   d. (ta.káa).ruiʔ   'chicken'
     b. (vát).vi.rak   'went to bathe'   e. (sa.pók)   'story'
     c. (táat).piʃ   'fleas'   f. (ta.pɨɨʃ)   'flea'

Both aspects of my analysis (non-iterativity and iambic foot-shape) will be motivated below.

The first vowel alternation, shown in (26), is due to a *shortening* of long vowels in unstressed syllables. (The reduplicant is marked off the root by –):

(26) a.i /kooʔ/   (kóoʔ)   'snake'
     a.ii /koo-kooʔ/   (kóo).koʔ   *(kóo).(kòoʔ)   'snakes'
     b.i /kaam/   (káam)   'cheek'
     b.ii /kaa-kaam/   (káa).kam   *(káa).(kàam)   'cheeks'

c.i	/topaa/	(to.páa)		'pestle'
c.ii	/to-topaa/	(tót).pa	*(tót).(pàa)	'pestles'
d.i	/tapɨɨʃ/	(ta.pɨ́ɨʃ)		'flea'
d.ii	/ta-tapɨɨʃ/	(tát).pɨʃ	*(tát).(pɨ̀ɨʃ)	'fleas'

Shortening of non-accented vowels demonstrates that surface forms are single-footed.

The second vowel alternation is due to *apocope*, which, like syncope, minimizes the number of unfooted syllables in the stem. Short vowels are deleted word-finally, except when a sequence of consonants (as in 27d) or when /h/ (as in 27e) precedes. Prefixes are outside the stem, as I have indicated by #, while suffixes are integrated.[10]

(27)	a.i	/hiɲ# novi/	hiɲ# (óv)		'my hand'
	a.ii	/hiɲ# noo-novi/	hiɲ# (ɲóo).nov		'my hands'
	a.iii	/novi-ʔn/	(no.víʔɲ)		'his hand'
	b.i	/tu# huana/	tu# (huán)		'he is working'
	b.ii	/tu# huana-t/	tu# (huá).nat		'he was working'
	c.	/nakasɨʈi/	(nák).sɨʈ		'scorpion'
	d.	/hupna/	(húp).na *(húpn) *CC]σ		'pull out'
	e.	/voohi/	(voo).hi *(vóoh) *h]σ		'bear'

The condition that a vowel–consonant sequence must precede for deletion to take place reflects inviolable phonotactics: no process may produce branching codas, or /h/ codas.

Interestingly, neither apocope nor shortening affects final long vowels which can be syllabified in the strong position of an iamb, e.g.

(28)	a.i	/gaa/	(gáa)			'cornfield'
	a.ii	/ga-gaa/	(ga.gáa)	*(ga.gá)	*(gá?ŋ)[11]	'cornfield'
	b.	/ʔaʈii/	(ʔa.ʈíi)	*(ʔa.ʈí)	*(ʔáʈ)	'child'

We thus find that the output goal of apocope/syncope is *not* to minimize the number of syllables as such, but to minimize the number of syllables that stand *outside the foot*. Since apocope would not yield an improvement with respect to this output goal in the examples of (28), it does not apply.

The third vowel alternation is due to *syncope*: vowels in even-numbered open syllables are dropped. Examples (29g–j) illustrate that syncope may delete long vowels and diphthongs following an initial Cvv syllable. All examples (except 29a) show that syncope freely applies across a reduplicant-stem boundary, so that the domain must be the stem. Notice that regular prefixes are outside this domain (29i–j).

---

[10] In (27a.i–ii) a 1sg. object prefix /hiɲ-/ occurs, in (27b) an extent prefix /tu-/; (27a.iii) contains a 3sg. possessive suffix, and (27b.ii) a past imperfective suffix.

[11] The de-obstruentization of voiced obstruents in coda position will be discussed below.

(29) a. /tɨroviɲ/   (tɨr).viɲ   'rope'
   b. /tɨɨ-tɨroviɲ/   (tɨ́ɨt).ro.piɲ   'ropes'
   c. /to-topaa/   (tót).pa   'pestles'
   d. /taa-tapɨɨʃ/   (táat).pɨʃ   'fleas'
   e. /taa-takaaruiʔ/   (táat).ka.ruiʔ   'chickens'
   f. /tu# maa-matuʃidʒaʔ/   tu# (máam).tuʃ.dʒaʔ   'will teach'
   g. /gaa-gaagaʔ/   (gáaʔŋ).gaʔ   'he will look around for it'
   h. /sui-suimaɽ/   (súis).maɽ   'deer (pl.)'
   i. /hiɲ# ɲuu-ɲuutʃiʃ/   hiɲ# (ɲúuɲ).tʃiʃ   'my brothers-in-law'
   j. /hiʃ# mai-maikak/   hiʃ# (máim).kak   'sweet (pl.)'

The examples in (30) illustrate the lack of syncope after a *light* first syllable. In (30a–d) this is shown for the context #CvCvv and in (30e–f) for the context #CvCv(v)C.

(30) a. /takaaruiʔ/   (ta.káa).ruiʔ   'chicken'
   b. /vo-voohi/   (va.póo).hi   'bears'
   c. /va-vaiɲum/   (va.pái).ɲum   'metals'
   d. /vi-viadikaiʔ/   (vi.piáʔɲ).kaiʔ   'lizards'
   e. /ka-karvaʃ/   (ka.kár).vaʃ   'goats'
   f. /ha-haannuɽ/   (ha.háan).nuɽ   'clothes'

In contexts where both are possible, *apocope* is preferred over *syncope*:

(31) a. /hiɲ# noo-novi/   hiɲ#(ɲóo).nov   *hiɲ#(ɲóon).vi   'my hands'
   b. /ʃi# ʔomiɲi/   ʃi#(ʔo.míɲ)   *ʃi#(ʔóm).ɲi   'break it!'
   c. /naa-nakasɨɽi/   (náan).ka.sɨɽ   *(náan).kas.ɽi   'scorpions'

So far we have been looking into the context of syncope—let us now look into its *effect*: does it result in full (or partial) vowel deletion? Four independent phonotactic diagnostics indicate that syncope amounts to the complete deletion of the nucleus, i.e. of *syllabicity*.

First, syncope strictly respects the canonical syllable (Cv, Cvv, CvC, CvvC), which has an obligatory non-branching onset and an optional non-branching coda, with either a long or short vowel as its nucleus. Syncope is blocked wherever it would create a complex coda or a complex onset.

(32) /ka-karvaʃ/   (ka.kár).vaʃ   *(kákr).vaʃ   *(kák).rvaʃ   'goats'

Second, the language has a *mutation* process (restricted to reduplicated forms) by which intervocalic /v/ changes into [p]. This consonant mutation is conditioned by the output syllabification (i.e. it applies 'after' syncope), as shown by the forms (33c–d):

(33) a. /va-vaavasi/   (va.páa).vaʃ   'pheasants'
   b. /tɨɨ-tɨroviɲ/   (tɨ́ɨt).ro.piɲ   'ropes'
   c. /to-tovaa/   (tót).va   *(tót).pa   'turkeys'
   d. /noo-noviɲ/   (nóon).viɲ   *(nóon).piɲ   'his hands'

Third, a process of *coda de-obstruentization* changes voiced obstruents in codas into pre-glottalized nasals—while agreeing in place of articulation with the following consonant. Again, it is output syllabification that matters here.

(34) a. /gaa-gaaga?/   (gáa**ʔŋ**).ga?   'he will look around for it'
      b. /gio-giotir/   (gió**ʔn**).tir   'plains'
      c. /vi-viadikai?/   (vi.piá**ʔŋ**).kai?   'lizards'

Fourth, output syllabification is relevant to another coda weakening process of /h/-*assimilation,* by which /h/ assimilates completely to a following consonant.

(35) /hiɲ# hii-hiikuʈ/   hiɲ#(híik).kuʈ   'my uncles'

Observe that syncope is not blocked by a constraint barring /h/ from syllable coda, as we saw earlier for apocope. The difference is that here /h/ can be 'saved' by complete assimilation to the following consonant.

In sum, no syllable-sensitive phonology of South-eastern Tepehuan refers to the 'initial' syllabification.[12] Instead all such phonology refers to the 'resyllabified' output of apocope and syncope, in a phonologically transparent way. Below I will return this important observation.

3.2. *A rule-based analysis*

The rule-based analysis expresses syncope as the deletion of vowels in weak syllables of iterative feet. The core of such an analysis has been given by Rice (1992) in the form of the five ordered rules in (36a-d, 36f). To complete the analysis I have added four rules Apocope (36e), De-obstruentization (36g), Conflation (36h), and Shortening (36i).

(36) a. *Syllabify*:   Assign syllable structure.
      b. *Metrify*:   Build left-headed quantity-sensitive feet from left to right.
      c. *Destressing*:   Remove the rightmost of two adjacent heads, unless the rightmost head dominates a syllable which is heavier than the leftmost. In that case, delete the left one.
      d. *End Rule Left*:   Promote the leftmost foot to main stress.
      e. *Apocope*:   Delete final short vowels (and resyllabify).
      f. *Syncope*:   Delete vowels in non-head syllables (and resyllabify).
      g. *De-obstruentization*: Nasalise voiced obstruents in coda position.
      h. *Stress Conflation*:   Remove feet that do not support the main stress.
      i. *Shortening*:   Shorten vowels in metrically weak syllables.

---

[12] There is a rule of palatalization that 'precedes' vowel deletions, but this does not refer to syllable structure, just to adjacency of root nodes.

This analysis is illustrated in (37) by derivations of stems beginning with #HL or #LL:

(37) UR	a. /maa-matuʃidʒaʔ/	b. /naa-nakasɨɾi/	c. /to-topaa/
Syllabify	maa.ma.tu.ʃi.d͡ʒa	naa.na.ka.sɨ.ɾi	to.to.paa
Metrify	(maa.ma).(tu.ʃi).(d͡ʒaʔ)	(naa.na).(ka.sɨ).(ɾi)	(to.to).(paa)
Destress	–	–	–
End Rule L	(máa.ma).(tu.ʃi).(d͡ʒaʔ)	(náa.na).(ka.sɨ).(ɾi)	(tó.to).(paa)
Apocope	–	(náa.na).(ka.sɨɾ)	–
Syncope	(máam).(tuʃ).(d͡ʒaʔ)	(náan).(ka.sɨɾ)	(tót).(paa)
Deobstruent	–	–	–
Conflation	(máam).tuʃ.d͡ʒaʔ	(náan).ka.sɨɾ	(tót).paa
Shortening	–	–	(tót).pa
PR	[(máam).tuʃ.d͡ʒaʔ]	[(náan).ka.sɨɾ]	[(tót).pa]

Although the analysis derives these forms correctly, it runs into conceptual problems.

First, the complete lack of surface secondary stress must be accounted for by a rule of 'stress conflation' (Halle and Vergnaud, 1987), eliminating feet that do not support the main stress. This obscures the iterative metrical pattern on which syncope is based, rendering it opaque. From the viewpoint of the language learner, the abstractness of this analysis, as well as the extrinsic rule ordering on which it is based, are problematic.

Second, out of the four trochees that the analysis sets up to define the context of syncope—(LL), (HL), (H), and (L)—three never surface (only H does). Two of these abstract trochees, degenerate L and unbalanced HL, are cross-linguistically marginal at best (Hayes, 1995). This contributes to the abstractness of the analysis. Even worse, the surface stress contours at the stem's left edge, #H and #LH, are easily interpreted as *iambic*, given the fact that foot constituency is inaudible. The trochaic analysis assigns a 'misaligned' parsing #L(H) to the latter sequence, thereby adding to its abstractness (a mismatch between foot type and surface stress patterns).

Third, iterative unbalanced trochees by themselves do not suffice to predict the syncope and accent pattern. One problematic case comprises inputs beginning with a sequence #HH—recall that syncope may delete a long vowel or diphthong in the second syllable if the initial syllable is heavy (29g–j). Here the monosyllabic foot on the second syllable must be deleted prior to syncope, since syncope only affects unstressed syllables (38c). But now compare such cases to inputs that begin with a sequence #LH. These surface with accent on their second syllable, which must—somehow—be protected against destressing and subsequent syncope (38a–b). Rice (1992) proposes a quantity-sensitive destressing rule (36c): if both syllables are of equal weight (#HH, cf. 38c), it deletes the right-hand foot, but if the left-hand syllable is lighter (#LH, cf. 38a–b), the left-hand foot is deleted:

(38) UR	a. /ka-karvaʃ/	b. /vi-viadikaiʔ/	c. /gaa-gaagaʔ/
Metrify	(ka).(kar).(vaʃ)	(vi).(via.di).(kaiʔ)	(gaa).(gaa).(gaʔ)
Destressing	ka.(kar).(vaʃ)	vi.(via.di).(kaiʔ)	(gaa).gaa.(gaʔ)
End Rule L	ka.(kár).(vaʃ)	vi.(viá.di).(kaiʔ)	(gáa).gaa.(gaʔ)
Syncope	–	vi.(viád).(kaiʔ)	(gáag).(gaʔ)
Deobstruent	–	vi.(viáʔŋ).(kaiʔ)	(gáaʔŋ).(gaʔ)
Conflation	ka.(kár).vaʃ	vi.(viáʔŋ).kaiʔ	(gáaʔŋ).gaʔ
PR	[ka.(kár).vaʃ]	[vi.(viáʔŋ).kaiʔ]	[(gáaʔŋ).gaʔ]

The quantity-sensitive destressing rule that compares the relative weight of the first two syllables is a powerful device. Even worse, it misses the generalization that destressing and syncope conspire toward outputs that begin with iambs: (H) or (LH). Finally, notice that initial light syllables in words beginning with #LH fail to undergo syncope, even though destressing places them in a metrically weak position. Rice does not address this problem, but clearly this situation reflects an *output constraint* on syncope: it must not create syllables with branching onsets or codas. Output constraints on serial rules defeat the strictest version of rule-based theory.

In sum, the rule-based analysis identifies iterative feet as the context of syncope. This metrical structure arises only momentarily as an intermediary step in the derivation but it is lost in the output—due to syncope, resyllabification, and conflation. *Opacity* of syncope is the result—a situation that is highly compatible with the serial point of view, but a potential embarrassment to OT. Yet rule-based analysis, in order to be able to set up syncope as the result of an opaque metrical structure, was forced to accept various types of flaws: an odd foot typology, output constraints on syncope, quantity-sensitive destressing, etc. Moreover, a rule-based analysis fails to express various *conspiracies* in the phonology of South-eastern Tepehuan: the accented syllable is heavy, no rule leads to an output violating the canonical syllable, etc. Let us now consider an OT analysis of these data.

3.3. *An OT analysis*

The rule-based analysis given above cannot be translated into an OT analysis, since the metrical context (iterative feet) does not occur in the output in the form of a secondary stress pattern. In the rule-based analysis, this metrical context is destroyed by syncope plus resyllabification, while conflation wipes out any traces of secondary stress feet.

3.3.1. *Basic ideas*

The intuition behind an OT analysis is that syncope and apocope serve 'exhaustivity' of metrical parsing. They serve this goal by minimizing the number of syllables that are not parsed by the initial foot—a (H) or (LH) iamb. This effect is shown schematically in the Cv-skeletal forms in (39). The outputs in the middle column are 'better' than those in the rightmost column because they contain a smaller number of unparsed syllables. In the rightmost column, non-application of apocope (39a), syncope (39b), or of neither (39c), would result in outputs that contain a larger number of unparsed syllables:[13]

(39)	Inputs	Optimal outputs	Less-than-optimal outputs
a.i	/CvCvCv/	(Cv.CvC)	*(Cv.Cv).Cv
a.ii	/CvvCv/	(CvvC)	*(Cvv).Cv
b.i	/CvvCvCvC/	(CvvC).CvC	*(Cvv).Cv.CvC
b.ii	/CvvCvCvCvCvC/	(CvvC).CvC.CvC	*(Cvv).Cv.Cv.Cv.CvC
c.i	/CvCvCvCv/	(CvC).CvC	*(Cv.Cv).Cv.Cv
c.ii	/CvvCvCvCvCv/	(CvvC).Cv.CvC	*(Cvv).Cv.Cv.Cv.Cv

The optimal forms in (39) cannot be compressed any further by deletion of additional vowels *without violating rigid syllable phonotactics*: syllables must have non-branching margins. Forms in the rightmost column in (40), even though they are preferrable over those in the middle column for exhaustivity, are ruled out by syllable shape constraints:

(40)	Inputs	Optimal outputs	Less-than-optimal outputs
a.i	/CvvCvCvC/	(CvvC).CvC	*(CvvCCC)
a.ii	/CvCvCvCv/	(CvC).CvC	*(Cv.CvCC)

We already begin to see the outlines of an explanation for the alternating character of vowel deletion. Syncope of vowels in adjacent syllables necessarily leads to consonant clusters that cannot be parsed by canonical syllables. And we also see a connection now between syncope and apocope: both improve metrical parsing. The explanation for why apocope applies 'more generally' than syncope is that final vowels happen to be 'easier' targets for deletion: no consonants follow that might phonotactically interfere. (There is some independent pressure for apocope in the phonology as well, as we will see later.)

If the 'target' of vowel deletion is exhaustive parsing of syllables into feet, then we predict that no deletion will take place when nothing can be gained by it—that is, when deletion would yield no progress in terms of syllable parsing. This is exactly what we find. In (41) apocope/syncope fails to reduce the number of syllables that are left unparsed by the foot. Everything else being equal, it is always better to be 'faithful' to input segments:[14]

[13] These skeletal structures correspond to actual examples that have been presented above, as follows: (39a.i) to (31b) /ʃi# ʔomiɲi/; (39a.ii) to (27c.i) /tu# huana/; (39b.i) to (27a.ii) /hiɲ# noonovi/; (39b.ii) to (29f) /tu# maa-matuʃidʒaʔ/; (39c.i) to (27c) /nakasiɾi/; and (39c.ii) to (31c) /naanakasiɾi/.

[14] Actual examples corresponding to (41a–b) are (28b) /ʔaɾii/ and (30c) /va-vaiɲum/. I have not found any examples whose input shape is /CvCvvCv/. These are predicted to undergo apocope into (Cv.CvvC).

(41)   *Inputs*   *Optimal outputs*   *Less-than-optimal outputs*
   a.   /CvCvv/   (Cv.Cvv)   *(CvC)
   b.   /CvCvvCvC/   (Cv.Cvv).CvC   *(CvC).CvC

A second output target of syncope is related to quantity-sensitivity: *the stressed syllable must be heavy* (i.e. CvC, Cvv, or CvvC) in the output (compare Macushi Carib, discussed earlier). This means that syncope affects all inputs beginning with #CvCv, to prevent a (LL) foot.

(42)   *Inputs*   *Optimal outputs*   *Less-than-optimal outputs*
   a.   /CvCvCvCv/   (CvC).CvC   *(Cv.Cv).CvC, *(CCv.CvC)
   b.   /CvCvCvC/   (CvC).CvC   *(Cv.Cv).CvC, *(CCv.CvC)

It is correctly predicted that the second vowel in such sequences is deleted. Phonotactics ('no branching onsets') rule out the deletion of the first vowel, which would produce an ill-formed output *(CCv.CvC). Unlike the rule-based analysis, no abstract intermediate trochee (LL) is needed to obtain this result.

Could a rule-based analysis be based on the same idea, setting up a single foot at the left edge, then apocopate, and finally syncopate?[15] Perhaps, but it is immediately clear that it would be very difficult to deal with 'rhythmic deletion' in examples such as (39b.ii). Without iterative foot structure, what sets syllables to be syncopated apart from those that are immune? A solution would be to write the 'double-sided CV context' into the syncope rule V → Ø / CV ___ CV, and to apply this rule from left to right through the domain, resyllabifying its output after each application. Even then, a major problem arises with respect to quantity: since both short and long vowels are deletable, why syncopate CvvCvvCvC, but not CvCvvCvC? Although perhaps such an analysis may be feasible, it would totally obscure the relationship between syncope and foot structure.

3.3.2. *The constraints and their ranking*

The idea of an OT analysis is that exhaustivity of metrical parsing, and heaviness of the accented syllable, are both given priority over realizing underlying vowels in the output. However, the forces that lead to vowel deletion are counterbalanced by phonotactics: syllables must not have branching onsets.[16]

To implement all this, we start by fixing the metrical constraints that account for the shape and position of the accent foot. South-eastern Tepehuan, like Macushi Carib, has an iambic foot inventory (H) and (LH). Accordingly, I adopt Ft-Form as a cover constraint:

---

[15] The idea of such a rule-based analysis was suggested to me by Doug Pulleyblank.

[16] As we will see in section 3.3.4 on reduplicated forms, we must also recognize morphological forces opposing deletion.

(43) Ft-Form (cover constraint)

a.	FtBin	Feet are binary under moraic or syllabic analysis.
b.	WSP	Heavy syllables are prominent within the foot.
c.	RhType=Iamb	Feet are right-headed.
d.	Pk-Prom	Peak (x) ≻ Peak (y) if |x| > |y|.

South-eastern Tepehuan truly differs from Macushi Carib in having maximally one foot per word, rather than iterative feet. This difference is due to a reranking, as compared to Macushi Carib, of foot alignment and Parse-σ (McCarthy and Prince, 1993*a*). Since All-Ft-L takes precedence over Parse-σ, every foot is adjacent to the left PrWd edge:

(44) All-Ft-L
    Align (Ft, L, PrWd, L)

(45) All-Ft-L, Ft-Form » Parse-σ

The interaction All-Ft-L and Parse-σ, which produces non-iterative footing, is illustrated in tableaux (46) and (47):[17]

(46)	/ka-karvaʃ/	All-Ft-L	Ft-Form	Parse-σ
a.	☞ (ka.kár).vaʃ			*
b.	(ka.kár).(vàʃ)	**!		

(47)	/vatvirak/	All-Ft-L	Ft-Form	Parse-σ
a.	☞ (vát).vi.rak			**
b.	(vát).(vi.ràk)	*!		

Next, the set of syllable shapes that are well-formed in South-eastern Tepehuan is {Cv, Cvv, CvC, CvvC}, i.e. an obligatory non-branching onset (48a–b), and an optional non-branching coda (48b). Moreover, the fact that CvC syllables cannot occur in weak positions of iambs (LH) shows that such syllables must be heavy (48c).

(48) σ-Form (cover constraint)

a.	Onset	Syllables must have onsets.
b.	*Complex	Syllables must not have complex margins.
c.	Weight-by-Position	Codas must be moraic.

Next consider that all three vowel alternations involve deletion or shortening. More generally, South-eastern Tepehuan allows neither epenthesis nor lengthening, of any segment type. For example, Stress-to-Weight cannot be

---

[17] The violation of WSP due to the CvC syllable outside the accent foot in candidates (46a) and (47a) will be discussed below. The preservation of input vowel quality in unstressed vowels is due to the ranking Ident >> Reduce, which I have not indicated here.

satisfied by lengthening the second vowel in stems beginning with #CvCv. That is, we never find inputs such as /tɨroviɲ/ realized as *(tɨróː).viɲ, rather than (tɨr).viɲ. The avoidance of vowel epenthesis and lengthening motivates undominated DEP (McCarthy and Prince, 1995):

(49) DEP
   Every segment in the output has a correspondent in the input.

DEP is another 'faithfulness constraint'—one that sees to it that the input and output are maximally identical. It penalizes any output segment that cannot be traced back to a segment of lexical representation—ruling out epenthesis. It is the logical counterpart of MAX, which requires that input segments have correspondents in the output.

Unlike vowels, consonants remain generally unaffected—they may participate in alternations of place, but they are never deleted nor inserted under pressure of metrical constraints. For example, the stem /karvaʃ/ might surface as a single (LH) iamb without any violation of PARSE-σ, if only one of its medial consonants were deleted: *(ka.váʃ), or *(ka.ráʃ). This apparently never occurs—all outputs must preserve the consonants of their inputs. Therefore MAX-C must be undominated as well:[18]

(50) MAX-C
   Every consonant in the input has a correspondent in the output.

DEP and MAX-C limit the options of South-eastern Tepehuan to accommodate its word shapes to metrical constraints to the *deletion of vowels* (e.g. syncope, apocope) or parts of vowels (e.g. shortening). This means that vowel–zero alternations must be due to a constraint interaction in which MAX-V is crucially dominated by metrical constraints.

(51) MAX-V
   Every vocalic element in the input has a correspondent in the output.

What constraints must dominate MAX-V such that apocope and syncope arise? Clearly PARSE-σ is among these constraints, since it forces vowel deletion. By transitivity, all constraints dominating PARSE-σ must dominate MAX-V as well:

(52) ALL-FT-L, FT-FORM, σ-FORM, DEP, MAX-C >> PARSE-σ >> MAX-V

The 'rhythmicity' of the syncope pattern follows from this ranking—there is no need to set up an intermediate representation of iterative trochees, as in the rule-based analysis.

A major 'rhythmic' property of syncope follows directly from (52): the fact that adjacent syllables do not both syncopate. If they did, the outcome would collide with syllable shape constraints, since this would stack up consonants

---

[18] I assume that consonants are distinguished from vowels segmentally, by [± consonantal].

that cannot be parsed as onsets or codas due to *COMPLEX. There is no remedy in simplifying such clusters by deletion of consonants: this escape route is effectively shut off by MAX-C. Another fact of syncope (that the rule-based analysis attributed to trochaic feet) now follows as well: vowels in initial syllables are immune from syncope, since vowel deletion in #CvCv would produce an output #CCv, again in violation of *COMPLEX. Furthermore, syncope may never affect a closed syllable, since that always results in violations of *COMPLEX. Again, this is attributed to abstract intermediate deletion feet in the rule-based analysis. Finally, it is correctly predicted that syncope/apocope are blocked in vowels preceded by more than one consonant—the maximum that can be accommodated as a coda in the preceding syllable. Actually, the rule-based analysis does not make this prediction at all.

3.3.3. Non-reduplicated stems

I will first illustrate, and develop, the analysis for non-reduplicated stems. Reduplicated stems will be treated in section 3.3.4, since they involve interaction with morphology-based constraints. Due to relative shortness of unreduplicated stems, it turns out that the activity of the constraint PARSE-σ cannot be motivated on the basis of such stems, since other constraints obscure its effects. However, PARSE-σ (and its ranking above MAX-V) will be motivated later on the basis of reduplicated stems.[19]

Tableau (53) shows the effect of undominated constraints: ALL-FT-L, FT-FORM, σ-FORM, DEP and MAX-C. The optimal output (53a) cannot be improved with respect to PARSE-σ without violating any of these.

(53) /tɨroviɲx/	ALL-FT-L	FT-FORM	σ-FORM	DEP	MAX-C	PARSE-σ	MAX-V
a. ☞ (tɨr).viɲ						*	o
b. (tɨ.víɲ)					r!		o
c. (tɨróo.víɲ)				o!		*	
d. (tro.víɲ)			*!				ɨ
e. (tɨrvɲ)			*!				o, i
f. (tɨ.ró).viɲ		PK-PROM!				*	
g. (tɨr.víɲ)		WSP!					o
h. (tɨr).(vìɲ)	*!						o

---

[19] As a service to the interested reader, I refer ahead to the tableaux of [(ɲúuɲ).tʃiʃ] in (67), [(táat).pɨ̀ʃ] in (79), [(tɨ́ɨt).ro.piɲ] in (80), and [(máam).tuʃ.dʒaʔ] in (81).

Next, (54) shows the role of the faithfulness constraint MAX-V, which blocks vowel deletion by rejecting candidate (54b). Both the optimal candidate and its competitor (54b) have one unparsed syllable, and both contain a well-formed foot. That is, vowel deletion does not apply when nothing is gained by it in terms of foot shape or metrical parsing.

(54) /takaarui?/	ALL-FT-L	FT-FORM	σ-FORM	DEP	MAX-C	PARSE-σ	MAX-V
a. ☞ (ta.káa).rui?						*	
b. (ták).rui?						*	a!a
c. (ta.káar?)			*!				ui
d. (tak.rúi?)		WSP!					aa
e. (ta.káa).(rùi?)	*!*						

Notice that no violations of WSP have been indicated for the candiates (54a–b), even though both have an unstressed heavy syllable; there is no inconsistency here, as I will argue in section 3.3.5 on vowel-shortening.

When we consider a vowel-final input such as /nakasɨṭi/, we find that PARSE-σ and MAX-V make the incorrect prediction that its output should be *(na.kás).ṭi, rather than the actual attested form (nák).sɨṭ. Both outputs have identical numbers of unparsed syllables, but the former is slightly more faithful to its input vocalism (since it preserves all but one vowel, rather than all but two). The ill-formedness of the output *(na.kás).ṭi must therefore be due to another factor: it ends in a vowel, and hence violates a cross-linguistically common requirement that the stem must end in a consonant. This is stated as STEM CLOSURE (Prince, 1990: 381):

(55) STEM CLOSURE
   All stems end in C.

STEM CLOSURE is the functional analogue of apocope in a rule-based analysis. Tableau (56) shows that it ranks above MAX-V, since the output candidate (56a) that is selected by STEM CLOSURE is less faithful to its input vocalism than its competitor (56b). Notice that the indicated ranking PARSE-σ » STEM CLOSURE cannot be motivated by this tableau. (However, we will find indirect evidence for this ranking directly below.)

(56) /nakasɨṭi/	ALL-FT-L	FT-FORM	σ-FORM	DEP, MAX-C	PARSE-σ	STEM CLOSURE	MAX-V
a. ☞ (nàk).sɨṭ					*		a, i
b. (na.kás).ṭi					*	*!	i
c. (nák).sɨ.ṭi					**!	*	a
d. (nak.sɨ́ṭ)		WSP!					a, i
e. (na.ká).sɨ.ṭi		PK-PROM			**	*	
f. (nák).(sɨ̀ṭ)	*!						a, i

Tableau (57) again shows that apocope is favored over syncope, for a vowel-final stem that is slightly shorter.

(57) /ʃi# ʔomiɲi/	ALL-FT-L	FT-FORM	σ-FORM	DEP, MAX-C	PARSE-σ	STEM CLOSURE	MAX-V
a. ☞ ʃi# (ʔo.míɲ)							i
b. ʃi# (ʔóm).ɲi					*!	*	i
c. ʃi# (ʔo.míi).ɲi				i!		*	*
d. ʃi# (ʔo.mí).ɲi		PK-PROM!				*	*

Next we must reconsider disyllabic stems ending in a long vowel, whose input shape is CvCvv, e.g. /topaa/ 'pestle'. Due to the ranking STEM CLOSURE >> MAX-V the analysis (incorrectly) predicts that such stems lose their final vowel. Only consider two output forms [(to.páa)] and *[(tóp)] to see this. These candidates are evaluated equally by all higher-ranking constraints, as both have a well-formed, left-aligned foot, and no unparsed syllables. Therefore STEM CLOSURE selects *[(tóp)], the candidate that ends in a consonant, over the more faithful candidate [(to.páa)].

The blocking of apocope in such words must be due to an independent factor, which I identify as a 'minimality' effect. Specifically, apocope fails since the resulting output [(tóp)] would violate the constraint that a Prosodic Word is minimally disyllabic. This constraint is stated as DISYLL below, minimally adapting a constraint of the same name in McCarthy and Prince (1993*a*):

(58) DISYLL
    The PrWd is minimally disyllabic.

Note that we cannot identify the disyllabicity requirement as a foot, since the minimal foot equals a single heavy syllable. There is cross-linguistic support for a disyllabicity constraint from quantity-sensitive languages which have bimoraic feet (e.g. Japanese, Itô 1990; Axininca Campa, McCarthy, and Prince 1993*a*; Guugu Yimidhirr and Kager 1995*a*).

In South-eastern Tepehuan DISYLL must be ranked above STEM CLOSURE, as the following tableau shows:

(59) /topaa/	ALL-FT-L	FT-FORM	DEP, MAX-C	PARSE-σ	DISYLL	STEM CLOSURE	MAX-V
a. ☞ (to.páa)						*	
b. (tóp)					*!		aa
c. (to.pá)		PK-PROM!				*	a

Note that DISYLL is ranked below PARSE-σ, since /CvvCv/ input stems surface without their final vowel, e.g. /tu# huana/ [tu# (huán)] (27b.i). This interaction is shown in (60):

(60) /huana/	ALL-FT-L	FT-FORM	DEP, MAX-C	PARSE-σ	DISYLL	STEM CLOSURE	MAX-V
a. ☞ (huán)					*		a
b. (huá).na				*!		*	
c. (huá.na)		RHTYPE=I!				*	

Since DISYLL dominates STEM CLOSURE, but is in its turn dominated by PARSE-σ, we find a ranking PARSE-σ >> DISYLL >> STEM CLOSURE. By transitivity, we now find evidence to rank PARSE-σ with respect to STEM CLOSURE, a ranking that was so far unestablished.

We have seen that apocope is blocked by the disyllabic minimality requirement. We may then ask whether disyllabicity is enforced by epenthesis as well, for example in monosyllabic stems. The answer is negative. South-eastern Tepehuan has monosyllabic stems, but none undergoes vowel epenthesis. This motivates the ranking DEP >> DISYLL. Tableau (61) illustrates this ranking for the monosyllabic stem /ban/ 'coyote', where the epenthetic vowel appears as a capital:

(61) /ban/	ALL-FT-L	FT-FORM	DEP, MAX-C	PARSE-σ	DISYLL	STEM CLOSURE	MAX-V
a. ☞ (bán)					*		
b. (ba.nÁA)			AA!			*	

Since DISYLL is dominated by PARSE-σ, which is itself dominated by FT-FORM and DEP, we predict that FT-FORM and DEP both dominate DISYLL. This prediction is correct. Stems of the shape /CvCv/ undergo apocope, falling below the disyllabic minimum, for example /novi/ [(nóv)] 'my hand' (cf. 27a.i). In tableau (62) a faithful candidate (62b), which preserves the final input vowel, is ruled out by FT-FORM. This 'bad' double-light iamb cannot be improved upon by final lengthening as in (62c), due to DEP:

(62) /novi/	ALL-FT-L	FT-FORM	DEP, MAX-C	PARSE-σ	DISYLL	STEM CLOSURE	MAX-V
a. ☞ (nóv)					*		i
b. (no.ví)		PK-PROM!				*	
c. (no.víI)			I!			*	

This concludes the basic analysis of apocope and syncope. An analysis of the third vowel alternation, shortening, will be given in section 3.3.5.

3.3.4. *Reduplicated stems*

South-eastern Tepehuan uses reduplication for a number of morphological categories, of which plurality in nouns is the most important. Two types of reduplicant prefix occur: Cv- (short) and Cvv- (long). The choice between both cannot be predicted from the stem's quantitative (or segmental) make-up, although certain interesting tendencies can be observed.[20] The idiosyncratic nature of the type of reduplicant (short versus long) is shown in the pairs (63a–c) below, for stems that have the skeletal structure CvC, CvvC, and CvvCvC:

(63) a.i   /Cv—huk/   (hu.húk)   'pines'
      a.ii /Cvv—ban/   (báa).ban   'coyotes'
      b.i   /Cv—gaat/   (ga.gáat)   'bows'
      b.ii /Cvv—kaam/   (káa).kam   'cheeks'
      c.i   /Cv—haaraʃ/   (ha.háa).raʃ   'crabs'
      c.ii /Cvv—ɲuutʃiʃ/   (ɲuuɲ).t͡ʃiʃ   'brothers-in-law'

I assume that stems select length of the reduplicant by lexical specification. Moreover, this length requirement must be respected in the output. To see what is at stake we must look into vowel-shortening.

The current constraint ranking falsely predicts that a long reduplicant shortens to Cv in order to form a maximal foot (Cv.CvX) together with the stem-initial syllable. In (64a), this false prediction is due to PARSE-σ, while in (64b), it is due to MAX-V:

(64) | | *Input* | *Predicted output* | *Actual output* |
      |---|---|---|---|
      | a.i | /RED—ban/ | *(ba.bán) | (báa).ban |
      | a.ii | /RED—novi/ | *(no.nóv) | (nóo).nov |
      | a.iii | /RED—tɨroviɲ/ | *(tɨ.tɨ́r).viɲ | (tɨ́ɨt).ro.piɲ |
      | a.iv | /RED—nakasiʈi/ | *(na.nák).siʈ | (náan).ka.siʈ |
      | b.i | /RED—ɲuutʃiʃ/ | *(ɲu. ɲúu).tʃiʃ | (ɲúuɲ).t͡ʃiʃ |
      | b.ii | /RED—matuʃidʒaʔ/ | *(ma.mát).ʃi.d͡ʒaʔ | (máam).tuʃ.d͡ʒaʔ |

Non-shortening of long reduplicants cannot be attributed to MAX-V, since this is ranked below PARSE-σ. Moreover, MAX-V fails to explain the actual output form [(ɲúuɲ).t͡ʃiʃ] in (64b.i), since this is less faithful to input vocalism than its competitor [(ɲu. ɲúu).tʃiʃ].

Rather, the generalization is that the (stem-specific) requirement on the length of the reduplicant vowel must always be respected in the output. To capture this, I assume that the reduplicant's nucleus can be required to be

---

[20] e.g. polysyllabic stems that begin with a closed syllable always select a short reduplicant, so that the reduplicated stem starts with a (LH) foot. Although this suggests control by the constraint system, I have not been able to fully predict it by ranked constraints.

bimoraic (Shaw, 1992). South-eastern Tepehuan places this constraint under control of specific stems:

(65) RED = NUC$_{\mu\mu}$

    The reduplicant must be a syllable with a bimoraic nucleus (for specific stems).

This is equivalent to postulating two allomorphs of the plural prefix, whose distribution is lexically determined—a cross-linguistically common situation. There is no need to postulate two co-phonologies here (on co-phonologies, see the contributions by Inkelas, Orgun, and Zoll (Chapter 13); and Booij (Chapter 8)).

RED = NUC$_{\mu\mu}$ must rank above PARSE-σ, as tableau (66) shows:

(66) /RED-ban/	ALL-FT-L	FT-FORM	RED=NUC$_{\mu\mu}$	PARSE-σ	DISYLL	STEM CLOSURE	MAX-V
a. ☞ (báa).ban				*			
b. (ba.bán)			*!				
c. (bán).ban			*!	*			
d. (báa).(bàn)	*!						

Tableau (67) shows that, as predicted by transitivity, RED = NUC$_{\mu\mu}$ ranks above MAX-V. This is the first of a series of tableaux presenting firm evidence for PARSE-σ. The optimal output (67a) is less faithful to its input vocalism than candidate (67b), but is selected on the grounds of its smaller number of unparsed syllables.

(67) /RED-ɲuutʃiʃ/	ALL-FT-L	FT-FORM	RED=NUC$_{\mu\mu}$	PARSE-σ	DISYLL	STEM CLOSURE	MAX-V
a. ☞ (ɲúuɲ).tʃiʃ				*			uu
b. (ɲúu).ɲu.tʃiʃ				**!			u
c. (ɲu.ɲúu).tʃiʃ			*!	*			
d. (ɲúu).(ɲu.tʃiʃ)	*!						u

Note that syncope may obscure the identity of the reduplicant and the *base*. An example is the vowel [uu] in the reduplicant of (ɲúu-ɲ).tʃiʃ, which has no correspondent in the output, but depends on the vowel [uu] in the input. In terms of constraint-ranking, the prosodic constraints of foot shape and foot position, syllable-shape, and PARSE-σ, must dominate constraints on reduplicant–base correspondence.[21]

---

[21] This may appear as a case of a reduplicant that is more faithful to the input than the base is. McCarthy and Prince (1995) suggest that languages universally rank reduplicant–base faithfulness above reduplicant–input faithfulness. Actually, the South-eastern Tepehuan data do not unambiguously counterexemplify this, since all we know is that R-B identity must be dominated by prosodic constraints.

(68) *Ft-shape, Ft-position,* σ-*shape* >> Parse-σ >> *R-B Identity*

I will not pursue the issue of the correspondence relationship between reduplicant and input here.

3.3.5. *Vowel-shortening and WSP*

Next let us turn to unstressed vowel-*shortening*. This is exemplified for open
syllables in (69a), and for closed syllables in (69b).

(69)	a.i	/taa-takaarui?/	(táat).ka.rui?	*(táat).kaa.rui?	'chickens'
	a.ii	/to-topaa/	(tót).pa	*(tót).paa	'pestles'
	b.i	/kaa-kaam/	(káa).kam	*(káa).kaam	'cheeks'
	b.ii	/taa-tapɨɨʃ/	(táat).pɨʃ	*(táat).pɨɨʃ	'fleas'

Actually, the tools for shortening in unstressed open syllables are already in
our hands, in the form of the ranking WSP >> Max-V. This predicts that
unstressed vowels shorten 'in order to' avoid a violation of WSP (Cvv being
heavy, and Cv light). But we must sharpen this initial analysis quite a bit. So
far we have tacitly assumed that heavy syllables outside the accent foot do *not*
constitute violations of WSP. If they did, WSP would incorrectly block every
vowel deletion that results in a closed syllable outside the accent foot. See
(56a) versus (56b–c), which I repeat below for convenience:

(70) (nák).sɨɽ > (na.kás).ɽi, (nák).sɨ.ɽi

This indicates that WSP must be ranked below both Parse-σ and Stem Closure. But that sets up a ranking paradox: WSP must also be undominated to
keep closed syllables from weak positions of iambs. I will break this paradox
by elaborating on a distinction between two logically possible interpretations
of quantity-sensitivity, both of which are found in the metrical literature. On
the one hand, any heavy syllable (CvC, Cvv, CvvC) must be banned from weak
positions of feet (this interpretation of quantity-sensitivity is due to Hayes,
1980, and occurs in much later work on foot typology, e.g. Hayes, 1995). I will
refer to it as WSP-Ft:

(71) WSP-Ft
      Bimoraic syllables must not occur in weak positions of feet.

As stated above, this constraint does not distinguish degrees of syllable weight,
e.g. Cvv and CvC from CvvC. Violations of it are counted absolutely, rather
than gradiently.

On the other hand, a more general interpretation of quantity-sensitivity has
been proposed in Prince (1983) and Prince and Smolensky (1993). Their
Weight-to-Stress Principle rules out any heavy syllable that does not occupy
a strong position in a foot:

(72) WSP
Heavy syllables are prominent in foot structure and on the grid.

WSP is violated by both unstressed footed and unfooted heavy syllables. As I will argue below, this constraint measures violations in a gradual fashion, so that a violation that is due to an unstressed CvC syllable is less severe than a violation that is due to an unstressed CvvC syllable. This will then predict vowel shortening.

This dual interpretation of the Weight-to-Stress Principle allows us to rank WSP (72) below PARSE-σ, while we can maintain WSP-FT (71) as a part of the undominated cover constraint FT-FORM, thus guaranteeing quantitatively well-formed iambs. That is, the effects of both constraints are empirically distinguishable in South-eastern Tepehuan since WSP-FT (the specific constraint) dominates WSP (the general constraint), while two other constraints (PARSE-σ, STEM CLOSURE) are ranked in between.

The new (now complete) ranking is given below:

(73) ALL-FT-L, FT-FORM (*including* WSP-FT), σ-FORM, DEP, MAX-C, RED = NUC$_{\mu\mu}$ >> PARSE-σ >> DISYLL >> STEM CLOSURE >> WSP >> MAX-V

An illustration of this analysis is provided by tableau (74). All three candidates (74a–c) have no violations of undominated constraints, and violate PARSE-σ to the same degree. The shortening of the long stem vowel is due to WSP, which rules out candidates (74b) and (74c), each of which has one additional heavy syllable as compared to the optimal candidate (74a). Candidate (74e), which would be an improvement over (74a) in terms of PARSE-σ and MAX-V, is excluded by WSP-FT.

(74) /RED-takaaruiʔ/	ALL-FT-L	FT-FORM	RED = NUC$_{\mu\mu}$	PARSE-σ	STEM CLOSURE	WSP	MAX-V
a. ☞ (táat).ka.ruiʔ				**		*	a, a
b. (táat).kaa.ruiʔ				**		**!	a
c. (táa).tak.ruiʔ				**		**!	aa
d. (ta.tàk).ruiʔ			*!	*		*	aa
e. (taat.káa).ruiʔ		WSP-FT!		*		**	a
f. (táa).(ta.kàa).ruiʔ	*!, ***						

In (74) I have indicated violations of WSP on a binary ('all-or-none') basis, since we have not yet seen the crucial evidence for a gradual interpretation.

The analysis of reduplicated CvCvv stems involves a final vowel-shortening that is due to WSP. Again we find that WSP must dominate MAX-V:

(75) /Red-topaa/	All-Ft-L	Ft-Form	Red=Nuc$_{\mu\mu}$	Parse-σ	Stem Closure	WSP	Max-V
a. ☞ (tót).pa				*	*		o, a
b. (tót).paa				*	*	*!	o
c. (tot.páa)		wsp-ft!			*	*	o
d. (tót).(pàa)	*!				*		o

Observe that Red = Nuc$_{\mu\mu}$ is not violated, since /topaa/ is not a stem that triggers it. There is yet another plausible candidate to be considered, [(to.tóp)]. The fate of this ill-formed output form will be discussed in section 3.3.6.

In the following tableau, we find additional evidence that WSP is dominated by Stem Closure:

(76) /Red-novi/	All-Ft-L	Ft-Form	Red=Nuc$_{\mu\mu}$	Parse-σ	Stem Closure	WSP	Max-V
a. ☞ (nóo).nov				*		*	i
b. (nóon).vi				*	*!		o
c. (nóo).no.vi				**!	*		
d. (no.nóv)			*!				i
e. (nóo).(nòv)	*!						i

So far we have been looking into vowel-shortening in unstressed open syllables—this could still be captured by the binary weight distinction between Cv and Cvv/CvC. But gradual evaluation by WSP is relevant for shortening in unstressed closed syllables, e.g. /Red-kaam/ [(káa).kam], (63b.ii). Such forms tell us that CvC must be *lighter* than CvvC. If not, vowel-shortening would not yield any gains in terms of WSP.[22]

We thus find that WSP (66) uses a gradual interpretation of syllable weight, one based on 'intrinsic prominence'. Interestingly this precisely matches the heaviness scale which Prince and Smolenky (1993: 40) give for 'prominence-driven' stress systems:

(77) CvvC > Cvv, CvC > Cv

Prince and Smolensky (1993) and Hayes (1995) argue that weight scales typically occur in languages whose stress assignment is not strictly foot-based (cf. PkProm in Prince and Smolensky's analysis of Kelkar's Hindi). South-eastern Tepehuan confirms this picture: *gradual* syllable weight is relevant

---

[22] Of course we cannot assume that CvC is light; CvC must be heavier than Cv as judged from various types of evidence, in particular accentability and stem minimality: stems are minimally CvC or Cvv, never Cv.

outside the foot (WSP), and a *binary* moraic weight distinction (Cv versus bimoraic syllables) *within* the foot (WSP-F$_T$). The shortening of CvvC into CvC which we find outside the foot follows from the gradual evaluation by WSP: unstressed CvC incurs one violation, and unstressed CvvC two.[23]

This is illustrated in tableau (78). The optimal candidate (78a) violates WSP to a smaller degree than candidate (78b), even though the latter is more faithful to the input. This motivates the ranking WSP >> MAX-V.

(78) /RED-kaam/	ALL-FT-L	FT-FORM	RED=NUC$_{\mu\mu}$	PARSE-σ	STEM CLOSURE	WSP	MAX-V
a. ☞ (káa).kam				*		*	a
b. (káa).kaam				*		**!	
c. (kaa.káam)			*!				
d. (kaa.káam)		WSP-FT!				*	
e. (káa).(kàam)	*!						

Tableau (79) proves the same point (compare 79a and 79b), and also presents additional evidence for a ranking PARSE-σ >> MAX-V (compare 79a and 79c).

(79) /RED-tapɨʃ/	ALL-FT-L	FT-FORM	RED=NUC$_{\mu\mu}$	PARSE-σ	STEM CLOSURE	WSP	MAX-V
a. ☞ (táat).pɨʃ				*		*	a, ɨ
b. (táat).pɨɨʃ				*		**!	a
c. (táa).ta.pɨʃ				**!		*	ɨ
d. (tát).pɨʃ			*!	*		*	a, ɨ
e. (táa).(tà.pɨɨʃ)	*!						

As expected, there is independent evidence for the role of WSP from syncope. In some cases the choice of which vowel will be deleted depends on whether the output contains an open or a closed syllable. In such cases the output is selected that has the fewest violations of WSP. In tableau (80), two candidates (80a) and (80b) occur which equally violate PARSE-σ, but the optimal output (80a) has one fewer violation of WSP (it has one unstressed heavy syllable only).

---

[23] WSP is never enforced by vowel-lengthening in stressed syllables. As was explained in section 3.3.2, lengthening is absolutely disallowed because of undominated DEP.

(80) /RED-tɨroviɲ/	ALL-FT-L	FT-FORM	RED=NUC$_{\mu\mu}$	PARSE-σ	STEM CLOSURE	WSP	MAX-V
a. ☞ (tɨ́t).ro.piɲ				**		*	ɨ
b. (tɨ́).tɨr.viɲ				**		*, *!	o
c. (tɨ́).tɨ.ro.piɲ				***!		*	
d. (tɨ.tɨ́r).viɲ			*!	*		*	o
e. (tɨ́ɨt).(ro.pɨ̀ɲ)	*!						ɨ

Observe again that PARSE-σ must dominate MAX-V, so as to exclude candidate (80c).

The next tableau shows rhythmic vowel deletion in the longest form seen so far. The optimal candidate is the one that has the minimal number of unparsed syllables that is possible without violating undominated constraints. The 'rhythmicity' of the deletion pattern is captured by an interaction of output constraints, and requires no iterative feet.

(81) /RED-matuʃidʒaʔ/	ALL-FT-L	FT-FORM	RED=NUC$_{\mu\mu}$	PARSE-σ	STEM CLOSURE	WSP	MAX-V
a. ☞ (máam).tuʃ.dʒaʔ				**		*, *	a, i
b. (máa).mat.ʃi.dʒaʔ				***!		*, *	u
c. (máa).ma.tu.ʃi.dʒaʔ				***!*		*	
d. (ma.mát).ʃi.dʒaʔ			*!	**		*	u
e. (maam.tuʃ).dʒaʔ		WSP-FT!		*		**, *	a, i
f. (máa).(ma.tùʃ).(dʒàʔ)	*!, ***						i

Note that this tableau represents all key aspects of the analysis: the domination of input faithfulness (MAX-V) by exhaustive metrical parsing (PARSE-σ), and the domination of the latter by a complex of constraints that enforce a single left-aligned iamb.

3.3.6. *Vowel deletion and output-to-output correspondence*

Finally I return to the question of what excludes the candidate [(to.tóp)] in tableau (75), with a complete deletion of the final vowel. Given the constraint ranking established so far, this candidate is incorrectly predicted to be optimal, since it has no violations of the constraints that are violated by the attested output [(tót).pa] in (75a), PARSE-σ and STEM CLOSURE. What makes [(to.tóp)] less optimal than [(tót).pa]? I suggest that the presence of the final [a] in the reduplicated form correlates with its status as a stressed vowel in the non-reduplicated form [(to.páa)]. This *output-to-output* correspondence relationship between the head of the basic form and a vowel in the output has been stated as the correspondence constraint HEADMAX (McCarthy, 1995; Alderete, 1995):

(82) HEADMAX (B/O)
Every segment in the base prosodic head has a correspondent in the output.

The notion of 'base' is used here in a more general sense than is usually assumed in the analysis of reduplication. Following Benua (1995), Alderete (1995), and Kager (1995*b*), I assume that the 'base' of an affixed form is the word (an output form itself) to which it is morphologically related by means of affixation. Here the independently existing form [(to.páa)] is the base of the prefixed form [(tót).pa], in which the prefix happens to be a reduplicant. As I will show below, HEADMAX is not crucially dominated by any other constraint in South-eastern Tepehuan.

Tableau (83) illustrates its effect in the reduplicated stem [(tót).pa]:

(83) /RED-topaa/ B: (to.páa)	ALL-FT-L	HEAD-MAX	RED=NUC$_{\mu\mu}$	PARSE-σ	DISYLL	STEM CLOSURE	WSP	MAX-V
a. ☞ (tót).pa				*		*		o, a
b. (to.tóp)	*!							aa

Finally, we must ask whether HEADMAX has any harmful consequences for the analysis of reduplicated forms that were discussed earlier. Upon closer inspection, this happens not to be the case. The vowel that is stressed in the base always recurs in the reduplicated stem, in its 'proper' position in the stem (84a), in the reduplicant prefix (84b), or even in both positions (84c).

(84)

	Input	*Base*	*Reduplicated stem*	
a.i	/topaa/	(to.páa)	(tó-t).pa	'pestle(s)'
a.ii	/novi-ɲ/	(no.ví)	(nóo-n).viɲ	'his hand(s)'
a.iii	/tapɨ̈ʃ/	(tap.ɨ̈ʃ)	(táa-t).pɨʃ	'flea(s)'
b.i	/ɲuutʃiʃ/	(ɲúu).tʃiʃ	(ɲúu-ɲ).tʃiʃ	'brother(s)-in-law'
b.ii	/tɨroviɲ/	(tɨ́r.viɲ)	(tɨ̈-t).ro.piɲ	'rope(s)'
c.i	/karvaʃ/	(kár).vaʃ	(ka-kár).vaʃ	'goat(s)'
c.ii	/novi/	(nóv)	(nóo)-nov	'hand(s)'

This concludes the analysis of rhythmic vowel deletion in South-eastern Tepehuan.

3.4. *Metrical opacity in South-eastern Tepehuan: conclusions*

In sum, rhythmic vowel deletion in South-eastern Tepehuan is 'categorial' in the sense that no traces of deleted vowels appear in the output. Consonants across the deletion site are phonologically adjacent, as we inferred from various syllable-sensitive phonotactic patterns. Moreover, rhythmicity of the vowel deletion pattern finds no surface correlate in the form of secondary stress. The opacity of the metrical context of deletion makes it analysable as foot-based only within a rule-based model. But as I have shown, the derivational foot-based analysis is suspect for independent reasons. It must set up feet (quantity-sensitive trochees) that never surface and whose single role is to 'explain' the syncope pattern, producing circularity. Moreover, the rule-based analysis offers no real explanation of the fact that all syllable-sensitive rules in South-eastern Tepehuan refer to surface ('post-syncope') syllabification rather than to pre-syncope syllables. In contrast, an OT analysis has no intermediate stage of abstract iterative 'syncope' feet. Instead, it rationalizes syncope as a means of minimizing the number of syllables unparsed by the initial foot. The foot is an iamb, i.e. a surface-true foot. It also explains why phonotactic constraints refer to surface syllabification. In sum, derivational theory seems to be too rich in its descriptive possibilites, since it places no inherent limitations on the abstract intermediate representations that condition vowel–zero alternations in surface forms. OT is descriptively more conservative, and also adequately captures the distinction between 'gradient' and 'categorial' types of RVD.

4. Conclusions: a Typological Perspective

I have shown that OT makes the prediction of two types of rhythmic vowel deletion, gradient and categorial. Gradient deletion is actually extreme reduction which preserves syllabicity. This may be foot-based, applying to rhythmically weak syllables in surface feet. In contrast, categorial rhythmic deletion (rhythmic syncope) involves full deletion, with loss of syllabicity, and 'resyllabification'. It is not conditioned by iterative feet, but by other factors. For example, in South-eastern Tepehuan 'rhythmicity' of RVD follows from the ranking ALL-FT-L, FT-FORM, σ-FORM, MAX-C >> PARSE-σ >> MAX-V. This ranking says that the position and shape of feet, and exhaustivity of metrical parsing, have higher priority than faithfulness to input vocalism. That is, the phonology may delete input vowels in order to get closer to the ideal of a single initial foot, with no unparsed syllables. However, this goal cannot be attained at the cost of syllable well-formedness, nor can input consonants be deleted (since σ-FORM, MAX-C >> PARSE-σ). Consequently the optimal vowel deletion strategy is 'rhythmic'—deleting alternating vowels.

These typological predictions require careful checking against more languages. Languages that I know from the literature seem to fall into one or the other class by the majority of criteria. Into the first class (of 'gradient deletion') fall a number of iambic languages that are discussed in Hayes (1995). For example, Unami and Munsee (both Algonquian languages) have vowel reduction up to the point of deletion, which seems to be remarkably free of phonotactic restrictions, while secondary stress is preserved. More examples may be found in the historical phonology of Romance languages. Late Latin (Jacobs, 1989) had a process of post-tonic vowel reduction/deletion which was not phonotactically conditioned, since it led to consonant clusters that were otherwise ruled out in the language. It was only in Gallo-Romance, a later stage at which alternations between reduced vowel and zero had been lost altogether, that the 'illegal' clusters were repaired to match canonical syllables (e.g. Latin *dormitorium* > Late Latin [dɔrm.torju] > Gallo-Romance [dɔr.tojr]). Into the second class ('categorial deletion') fall syncope patterns found in various Arabic dialects (Levantine and Palestinian Arabic syncope and metrical structure are analyzed using Correspondence Theory in Kager, 1995*b*), as do several Uto-Aztecan languages (genetically related to South-eastern Tepehuan) such as Cupeño (Hill and Hill, 1968), Hopi (Jeanne, 1982), and Luiseño (Munro and Benson 1973). Here syncope tends to be conditioned phonotactically (since it is 'repaired' by epenthesis), while the secondary stress pattern (if any) does not signal the site of deletion.[24]

Finally, I wish to point out a general point of this chapter which may bear on the debate between (rule-based) derivational phonology and (constraint-based) OT. This is that one cannot, and should not, directly transfer the conceptual categories of rule-based theory into OT. As I have shown, 'surface opacity with respect to metrical structure' is not a *categorical* problem for a constraint-based theory which views the surface form as the primary level at which generalizations interact. Rather, for independent reasons that have nothing to do with the theoretical viewpoint, the derivational notion 'metrical opacity' should be broken down into two separate cases.[25] Each of these requires a different type of analysis, and each analysis can be stated strikingly well in optimality theoretic-terms.

ACKNOWLEDGEMENTS

Many thanks to the participants in the Essex Workshop on Derivations and Constraints in Phonology for discussing this paper after its presentation. Special thanks to Bill Idsardi, Doug Pulleyblank, and Iggy Roca, for useful comments on an earlier version. None of them is to blame for any errors occurring in it. Research for this paper was sponsored by the Royal Netherlands Academy of Sciences (KNAW).

---

[24] Bill Idsardi (Chapter 12 above) argues that an opaque interaction of spirantization and syllabification in Tiberian Hebrew is problematic to OT.
[25] Another type of metrical opacity, involving 'output-to-output' correspondence', is discussed in Kager (1995*b*).

REFERENCES

Abbott, M. (1991). 'Macushi', in D. C. Derbyshire and G. K. Pullum (eds.), *Handbook of Amazonian Languages, III*. Berlin: Mouton de Gruyter, 23–160.

Alderete, J. (1995). 'Faithfulness to Prosodic Heads'. MS, University of Massachusetts.

Benua, L. (1995). 'Identity effects in mophological truncation', in J. N. Beckman, L. W. Dickey, and S. Urbanczyk (eds.), *Papers in Optimality Theory* (University of Massachusetts Occasional Papers 18). Amherst: GLSA.

Carson, N. M. (1982). 'Phonology and Morphosyntax of Macuxi (Carib)'. Dissertation, University of Kansas.

Cohn, A. C. (1990). 'Phonetic and Phonological Rules of Nasalization'. Dissertation, University of California, Los Angeles.

Halle, M. and Vergnaud, J.-R. (1987). *An Essay on Stress*. Cambridge, Mass. MIT Press.

Hawkins, W. N. (1950). 'Patterns of Vowel Loss in Macushi (Carib)', *International Journal of American Linguistics* 16: 87–90.

Hayes, B. (1980). 'A Metrical Theory of Stress Rules'. Dissertation, MIT. (Distributed by IULC, Bloomington, Ind.)

—— (1995). *Metrical Stress Theory: Principles and Case Studies*. Chicago: University of Chicago Press.

Hill, J. H., and Hill, K. C. (1968). 'Stress in the Cupan (Uto-Aztecan) languages', *International Journal of American Linguistics* 34: 233–41.

Itô, J. (1990). 'Prosodic minimality in Japanese', *Chicago Linguistic Society* 26: 213–39.

Jacobs, H. (1989). 'Nonlinear Studies in the Historical Phonology of French'. Dissertation, University of Nijmegen.

Jeanne, L. M. (1982). 'Some phonological rules of Hopi', *International Journal of American Linguistics* 48: 245–70.

Kager, R. (1989). *A Metrical Theory of Stress and Destressing in English and Dutch*. Dordrecht: Foris.

—— (1990). 'Dutch schwa in moraic phonology'. *Chicago Linguistic Society* 26: 241–55.

—— (1995a). 'Stem Disyllabicity in Guugu Yimidhirr'. MS, Utrecht University.

—— (1995b). 'Surface Opacity of Metrical Structure in Optimality Theory', MS, Utrecht University.

Keating, P. (1988). 'Underspecification in phonetics', *Phonology* 5: 275–97.

Kenstowicz, M., and Kisseberth, C. (1979). *Generative Phonology: Description and Theory*. San Diego, Calif.: Academic Press.

Kiparsky, P. (1971). 'Historical linguistics', in W. Dingwall (ed.), *A Survey of Linguistic Science*. College Park: Linguistics Program, University of Maryland, 576–649.

Kisseberth, C. (1970). 'On the functional unity of phonological rules', *Linguistic Inquiry* 1: 291–306.

—— (1973). 'Is rule ordering necessary in phonology?', in B. Kachru (ed.), *Issues in Linguistics: Papers in Honor of Henry and Renée Kahane*. Urbana: University of Illinois Press, 418–41.

McCarthy, J. (1995). 'Extensions of Faithfulness'. MS, University of Massachusetts.

—— and Prince, A. (1993*a*). 'Generalized alignment', *Morphology Yearbook*, 79–153.

—— —— (1993*b*). 'Prosodic Morphology I: Constraint Interaction and Satisfaction'. MS, University of Massachusetts, Amherst, and Rutgers University.

—— —— (1995). 'Faithfulness, Parallelism and Forms of Identity'. MS, University of Massachusetts, Amherst, and Rutgers University.

Munro, P., and Benson, P. J. (1973). 'Reduplication and rule ordering in Luiseño', *International Journal of American Linguistics* **39**: 15–21.

Prince, A. (1983). 'Relating to the grid', *Linguistic Inquiry* **14**: 19–100.

—— (1990). 'Quantitative consequences of rhythmic organization', *Chicago Linguistic Society* **26**: 355–98.

—— and Smolensky, P. (1993). 'Optimality Theory: Constraint Interaction in Generative Grammar'. MS, Rutgers University and University of Colorado at Boulder.

Rice, C. (1992). 'Binarity and Ternarity in Metrical Theory: Parametric Extensions'. Dissertation, University of Texas, Austin.

Shaw, P. (1992). 'Templatic evidence for the syllable nucleus', *North Eastern Linguistic Society* **23**.

van Oostendorp, M. (1995). 'Vowel Quality and Syllable Projection'. Dissertation, University of Tilburg.

Willett, E. (1982). 'Reduplication and accent in Southeastern Tepehuan'. *International Journal of American Linguistics* **48**: 164–84.

Willett, T. L. (1991), *A Reference Grammar of South-eastern Tepehuan*. Arlington: University of Texas.

16

Attic Greek Accentuation and Intermediate Derivational Representations

ROLF NOYER

Questions relating to levels of representation in phonology have reemerged dramatically in recent years along with the development of alternatives to classical generative theory such as Optimality Theory (OT: Prince and Smolensky, 1993; McCarthy and Prince, 1993a; 1993b; 1995) and Harmonic Phonology (Goldsmith, 1992). In Harmonic Phonology, for example, the grammar defines the class of well-formed expressions by appeal to phonotactic conditions which hold of three privileged levels (M, W, and P) and certain relations which must hold across these levels. In certain prominent versions of OT, similarly, the phonological surface alone is the 'locus of explanatory action', and generalizations holding of any other level of description, such as that of the underlying forms, are deemed epiphenomenal.

What these theories, along with pre-generative, structuralist phonology, all share is an insistence that Universal Grammar permits only PRIVILEGED levels of description, and typically only a small number of these. For example, Cohn and McCarthy (1994) and Buckley (1995) argue that intermediate levels are neither necessary nor desirable in the computation of stress placement in Indonesian and Manam: one level of description—the surface—suffices. On the other hand, Kenstowicz (1996) admits the possibility of intermediate levels for Carib and Polish stress, and McCarthy and Prince (1993a) acknowledge at least two levels of well-formedness in Axininca Campa. Indeed, the apparatus of harmonic evaluation used in OT is not incompatible, in principle, with chained or cyclic calls to the EVAL function. But any OT analysis incorporating intermediate levels, if it is to be of any interest, should acknowledge that intermediate levels have a privileged status in UG, that is to say, additional properties must necessarily attach to such levels: they are not, as in classical generative phonology, mere arbitrary stopping-points along a path to a well-formed output. For if not, a serial OT of this sort is in fact a new theory of rules: harmonic evaluation from arbitary level n to arbitrary level n + 1 is an elaborate (although not necessarily incorrect) restatement of an explicitly stated procedure for rewriting representations at n to those at n + 1.

In classical generative theory, on the other hand, a multiplicity of intermediate levels is admitted (the output of successive rule applications), of which no non-underlying level is necessarily cross-linguistically privileged. Whether a discrete, symbolic surface level is even empirically identifiable is a matter of some subtlety, and depends on assumptions about where phonology ends and gradient phonetics begins. For Chomsky (1964), for example, the output of phonology is not necessarily categorial, although it is expressible in terms of a 'universal phonetic alphabet' whose features have a fixed universal significance. There is no manifest categorial surface level accessible to direct observation: both the UR and the surface, such as it may be, are mental states, both are hypothetical, and both bear a relation to physical phenomena which is indirect and still quite obscure at our present state of knowledge. What are casually known as 'surface forms' in classical generative phonology are consequently often simply those descriptions of articulatory intention containing the level of detail beyond which the analyst has nothing further of interest to say. It is to be emphasized that OT departs radically from this view by insisting that not only is there a unique surface level, but in fact all real statements of grammar refer to this level.

I present evidence here that the placement of accent in surface forms in classical (Attic) Greek is explicable in a satisfying way only if reference is made to a pre-surface representation, an abstract syllabification. The syllabification prior to the well-known Attic syllable contraction rule is neither present in underlying forms nor, as far as we can determine, directly recoverable in surface forms, but is a property only of a pre-surface derivational stage. The abstract representation needed for accent placement is a non-surface-true ORGANIZATION of the underlying form into syllables, where that organization must be calculated by the grammar and then erased at the surface. I show that attempts to generate the same facts without recourse to an abstract syllabification are ad hoc, and covertly reintroduce the intermediate stage of interest.

Arguments for the view that surface syllabification does not determine accent placement were known even to the ancients (Vendryes, 1904: 60, citing Choeroboscus, An. de Bekk. 2. 708, 13), are present in standard handbooks (Kühner, 1844; Smyth, 1956), and are recapitulated in generative accounts such as Sommerstein (1973). These will be reviewed here in current perspective, along with additional evidence: a morphophonological rule of accent placement, which converts circumflex intonation to acute in the non-neuter direct cases of substantives (Steriade, 1988), must also apply at a pre-surface level. I then turn to the more important question of whether the pre-surface syllabification occurs at some level privileged by UG, for example, the word level or the cycle-final level in the sense of Lexical Phonology (Kiparsky, 1982; 1985), or the W-Level of Harmonic Phonology (Goldsmith, 1992). The evidence here is much less robust, but my more tentative conclusion, although unfashionable, is a negative one: the pre-surface syllabifications implicated here are simply arbitrary stopping-points in a series of computations ('rules' in a 'derivation' broadly construed).

The chapter is organized as follows. Sections 1–5 review the facts of Greek morphology and accentuation, along with the syllabic trochee analysis of Steriade (1988), as modified here in terms of the theory of Idsardi (1992). Sections 6–8 show that surface syllable contraction, in some cases fed by S-deletion and deletion of underlying hiatus, renders opaque the syllabification needed both for accentuation and for the morphological rule providing acute intonation in the direct cases of non-neuter substantives. Sections 9–11 provide evidence that contraction and Stray Erasure operate cyclically in substantives, implying that contraction cannot be a mere postlexical effect. Sections 12–13 then introduce the moraic trochee proposal of Sauzet (1983; 1989) and Golston (1989), as recast in terms of OT. Finally, section 14 provides further evidence from accent retraction in verbs, showing that the Sauzet–Golston alternative also does not escape the need for an abstract syllabification.

1. MORPHOLOGICAL PRELIMINARIES

Like the other archaic Indo-European languages, classical Greek lexical categories (N, A, V) are tripartitioned into a BASE consisting of a root followed optionally by a stem-extension, a (sometimes null) THEME, and a inflectional affix or DESINENCE (Benveniste, 1984). If the theme is overt, the base is termed 'thematic' (2); otherwise the base is non-thematic (3).[1] As we will see, the base–theme juncture is a phonologicaly important one, and I will separate the base from the theme by the sign [=]. Derivational prefixes will be denoted with a following [+] while all other boundaries will be denoted [−].[2]

(1)   base = theme − desinence

---

[1] From the perspective of the historical morphology of Indo-European, the first declension stems in /a(a) ~ ęę/ are not normally considered thematic; but from a purely synchronic perspective they class with the thematic stems in Attic Greek.

[2] Nouns and adjectives are cited in the nominative and in the singular unless otherwise specified. The problem of the representation of the tense/lax distinction in the mid vowels will not be taken up here directly. Rather, I will simply use the symbol /α/ to denote the second mora of a long non-high vowel, either an underlying long vowel or a lengthened grade. For /eα/ and /oα/ the result is a long low (or lax) vowel, as opposed to false geminate /ee/ and /oo/ arising from contraction (Lejeune, 1972: 230). This notation mirrors Steriade's (1982) proposal that long lax non-high vowels are VV while long tense non-high vowels are VC on the CV tier. Hence: /eα VV/ → [ęę] = η; /ee VC/ → [ee] = ει; /oα VV/ → [ǫǫ] = ω; /oo VC/ → [oo] = ου; /aα/ = /aa/ → [aa] = ᾱ; /uu/ → [uu > üü] = υυ. It should also be noted that certain of my assumptions about underlying forms are not uncontroversial. For example, I assume that the accusative plural desinence is /es/ in the thematic declensions as well as the athematic ones. However, this choice is not relevant to the main argument of the chapter.

(2) Thematic bases
    a. p^hug = eα−∅   'flight'
    b. ^{h}eαmer = a−is   'day (dat pl)'
    c. oik = o−i   'house (pl)'
    d. naut = eα−s   'sailor'
    e. megar = o−n   'hall (acc sg)'
    f. luu = o−mai   'I am loosing'
    g. t^haumadz = e−te   'you (pl) are amazed'
    h. leips = o−esi   'they are leaving'

(3) Non-thematic bases
    a. poim−en = os   'shepherd (gen sg)'
    b. soαm−at = a   'bodies'
    c. soαkrat−eαs = ∅   'Socrates'
    d. gen−e[s] = i   'race (dat sg)'
    e. di−doα = mi   'I give'
    f. ti−t^he = te   'you (pl) place'
    g. deik−nu = mai   'I am shown'

2. ACCENTUATION: PRETHEORETIC GENERALIZATIONS

The orthographic practices and commentaries of the Alexandrian grammarians make it clear that there were at least two distinctive accents, a circumflex (written ˆ), written only on long (bimoraic) vowels, and an acute (written ´), written on long or short vowels (Vendryes, 1904). An additional accent, the grave, is generally taken to be a contextual variant of the acute. Barring special cases of enclisis, there is normally only one accent per word. According to Steriade (1988), who recapitulates what might be called the traditional view, the circumflex is a falling or HL contour beginning on the first mora of a vowel written circumflex, while the acute is a high on the second mora of a long vowel, or on the only mora if the vowel short. This will be the view adopted here (for extensive discussion, see Devine and Stevens, 1994).[3] Assuming this to be correct, the question of accent placement reduces to an account of the position occupied by an H-tone in a word. In the following transcriptions the location of the H will be denoted by an acute accent.

(4) a. ^{h}ámaks=a   ἄμαξα   'wagon'   acute, short vowel
       |
       H

    b. soάm−at = a   σώματα   'bodies'   acute, long vowel
       |
       H

    c. sóαm=a[t]   σῶμα   'body'   circumflex, long vowel
       | |
       HL

---

[3] The main alternative to this view construes the acute as H spread over the entire rime: hence bimoraic acutes are treated as an H attached to both moras, while a circumflex has H attached only to the second mora (Bally, 1945: 13; Sauzet, 1989).

Traditionally, Greek nouns and adjectives are classified into two types: bary-tones and oxytones.[4] Barytone or recessive bases show accent placement as far to the left as possible given the following 'rule of limitation': if the final is long, the accent cannot fall further to the left than the third-to-last mora (5); if the final is short, the accent cannot fall further to the left than the fourth-to-last mora (6) (Jakobson, 1962).

(5) Barytones with long final
    a. ^{h}amáks=aa−s   'wagon (gen)'
    b. soαm−át=oαn   'bodies (gen pl)'
    c. ant^{h}roάp=o−o   'person (gen)'
    d. deα+meά−teαr   'Demeter'

(6) Barytones with short final
    a. ^{h}ámaks=a   'wagon'
    b. soάm−at=a   'bodies'
    c. ánt^{h}roαp=o−s   'person'
    d. deά+meα−ter   'Demeter (voc)'

As shown by Steriade (1988), a final syllable closed by a cluster such as /ks/ counts as long, hence: /polu+píidak=s/ 'abundant in fountains' has penultimate accent and not antepenultimate accent as in (6c). In addition there are certain other specific conditions; for example the nominative plural desinence /i/ does not count for weight (project a mora), hence /ánt^{h}roαp=o-i̯/ 'person (nom pl)' with antepenultimate accent.

For oxytones, H is not solely placed by the recessive rule but rather reflects morphological constituency, and appears in what is known traditionally as the 'pre-desinential' position (Kiparsky, 1973; Kurylowicz, 1958). A close inspection of the facts reveals certain inadequacies of this formulation, however.

For athematic nouns, the best generalization is that accent recedes leftward subject to the rule of limitation, provided it does not fall further to the left than the syllable containing the last mora of the base.

(7) Athematic oxytones
    a. poi−mén=os   'shepherd (gen)'
    b. agóαn=i   'contest (dat)'
    c. agoάn=oαn   'contests (gen pl)'

In (7a, b) accent recedes to the leftmost mora of the syllable containing the last mora of the base. In (7c), however, the rule of limitation prohibits accent from receding to the first mora of the syllable /goα/; hence accent can recede only to

---

[4] Properly this distinction applies only to non-derived forms. Derived forms are subject to additional complications, (Vendryes, 1904: 188 ff.). For example, certain affixes such as adverbial /ákis/ have surface penultimate stress owing to the underlying accentuation of the affix: this was one of Steriade's (1988) arguments that stress should be assigned to the rightmost accented syllable in Greek. There also exists a small class of fixed penult accent forms such as /olíg=o-s/ 'few' and /megál=o-s/ 'great'.

the second mora of this syllable. The rule of limitation combined with the principles of accent placement for oxytones combine to give the 'penultimate rule': a long penult, if accented, has the acute if the final syllable is long (7c), but circumflex if the final syllable is short (7c).

For thematic bases, 'pre-desinential' means that H will appear on the theme (vowel):

(8) Thematic oxytones
    a. pʰug=éα−s   'flight (gen)'
    b. potam=ó−s   'river'
    c. kʰruusé=o−s [kʰruu.sóos]   'golden'
    d. neα=ó−s [→ neî.αos → ne.ǫós] 'temple'

For thematic bases ending in a consonant (8a, b) or a long vowel (8d, the so-called 'Attic declension'), the H appears on the leftmost mora of the theme. But for thematic bases ending in a short vowel, such as (8c), the surface position of the H-tone reflects an underlying pre-thematic rather than pre-desinential position. In this respect these nouns pattern like athematic nouns, and it appears that Greek speakers must have reinterpreted these nouns as behaving accentually as if athematic.[5]

These matters are complicated by the partial morphologization of the HL/LH intonational constrast (Kurylowicz, 1932; 1935). In oxytone non-neuter nouns and adjectives, the nominative and accusative cases show acute (LH) intonation if the final is accented; in the oblique cases and in neuters, circumflex (HL) intonation is the norm.

(9) Direct versus. Oblique cases

	nom sg	gen sg	dat pl	acc pl	
	LH	HL	HL	LH	
a.	aret=eά	aret=éα−s	aret=á−is	aret=a−és	'virtue'
b.	kriit=eά−s	kriit=ó−o	kriit=á−is	kriit=a−és	'judge'
c.	potam=ó−s	potam=ó−o	potam−ó−αi̦	potam=o−és	'river'

(10) Neuters versus Non-neuters

	Neuter HL	Non-neuter LH	
a.	púur	psaár	'fire'; 'starling'
b.	pʰóαs	pʰoάs	'light'; 'person'
c.	kéαr	tʰeάr	'heart'; 'wild beast'

---

[5] Several additional complications attach to these thematic bases ending in short vowels. All historically barytone (recessive) simplex bases of this type were reanalysed as oxytone in Attic whenever there was also contraction; hence recessive, uncontracted /kʰruúse–os/ 'golden' becomes Attic oxytone contracted /kʰruusé-os → kʰruusóos/ (Chantraine, 1961: 46). As pointed out to me by Patrick Sauzet, the reanalysis of these forms as belonging in some sense to the athematic class is supported by certain heteroclites such as /eu+no-os → eúnoos/ 'well-disposed'. (Note that this form is barytone, but this is because it is derived, not simplex: for details, see section 9.) Such nouns should have a thematic nominative plural /eu+no-oi → eúnoi/, but appear textually with desinence /es/, properly the athematic nominative plural: /eu+no-es → eúnoos/ Lysias 8.19.

Steriade (1988) proposed that circumflex intonation is underlying, and acute intonation is derived by a morphophonological rule which for convenience I will refer to as 'Steriade's Rule':

(11) Steriade's Rule

$$\begin{array}{ccc} [\text{V V}\ _\sigma]\ \# & & [\text{V V}\ _\sigma]\ \# \\ | & \rightarrow & | \\ x & & x \end{array}$$ Domain: [+dir] cases of [−neut] substantives

Steriade's Rule shifts the headship of a final long syllable to its right mora in the direct cases of non-neuter substantives. If the final syllable comes to receive H-tone, H will attach to the head mora. The existence of headship contrasts of this type is abundantly evidenced in Lithuanian (see Halle and Vergnaud, 1987 for discussion). Regardless of technical implementation, it suffices for now to note that some account must be provided by the grammar for the generalization which Steriade's Rule captures.

3. Existing Theoretical Proposals

There exists at present a difference of opinion regarding how properly to construe the facts just reviewed. Since syllable weight and position *vis-à-vis* the end of the word figure in the H-tone placement rule, it is natural to assume that H is placed with respect to some metrical parse, but the relation between the place occupied by the H and metrical structure is open to debate. On one view (Steriade, 1988), the H attaches to the metrically prominent syllable (the head of the rightmost foot). The alternative view, championed recently by Sauzet (1983; 1989) and Golston (1989), holds that the H attaches to the mora preceding the metrically prominent syllable, at least for recessive nouns. A completely satisfactory account of oxytones, however, is not provided by Sauzet–Golston. I will pose the following arguments in terms of the analysis presented by Steriade (1988), showing the necessity of an intermediate level of representation. Then I will revisit the same problems through the lens of the Sauzet–Golston approach, showing that it provides only scant advantage for the problems at hand.

4. Steriade (1988): Syllabic Trochees

On the Steriade view, quantity-insensitive trochees are constructed from right-to-left for barytone bases (12); a final light syllable is extrametrical (13).

(12) a. ^hamáksaas   σ(σH)   'wagon (gen)'
     b. soomátoon   'bodies (gen)'

(13) a. ʰámaksa   (σσ)L   'wagon'
    b. soάmata   'bodies'

Such a system of quantity-insensitive trochees can be derived by the following metrical parameters in the theory of Halle and Idsardi (1995):

(14) Line 0:
    i.   Project nucleus heads on line 0
    ii.   Edge Marking: RLR if final syllable has non-branching rhyme (plus certain other conditions)
    iii.   Edge Marking: LLL
    iv.   Iterative Constituent Construction: Insert (Right to Left, binary
    v.   Head: Left
    Line 1:
    i.   Edge Marking: RRR
    ii.   Head: R
    iii.   Conflate

The outputs of some sample derivations are provided below:

(15) x   x   x
      x)   x)   x)
      (x x) x   (x   x) x   (x (x x)
      ʰámaksa   ántʰrǫǫpos   ʰamáksaas
      | | |
      H   H   H
      'wagon'   'person'   'wagon (gen)'

Intonationally, syllables are left-headed (circumflex), unless adjusted to right-headed either by Steriade's Rule (11) or by the 'Mora Rule' (16). The Mora Rule applies to antepenultimate syllables or penults if the final is long (Steriade, 1988: 14), a condition which will arise whenever the syllable's head is associated with the head of a binary foot (17a,b), but not otherwise (17c).

(16) Mora Rule
    [V V σ]   [V V σ]
     | → |
    (x x)   (x x

(17) a. sóαmata → soάmata   'bodies'
       (x x) x   (x x) x
    b. níikeα → niíkeα   'victory'
       (x x   (x x
    c. sóαma   'body'
       (x)   x

5. OXYTONES

It is natural to assume on this account that the oxytones are lexically listed either with prespecified foot structure or with a diacritic which will trigger a rule, sensitive to morphological constituency, which will insert metrical brackets (Idsardi, 1992; Halle and Idsardi, 1995; Halle, 1996). I will adopt the latter idea. The behaviour of oxytones is explained simply by assuming that they are subject to the following rule:

(18) Oxytonesis
$\emptyset \rightarrow (/ \_\_ x_{c}]$
where C = 'base' for athematic nouns or thematics ending in a short vowel, otherwise C = 'theme'

This rule inserts a left parenthesis onto line 0 of the metrical grid before the last grid mark contained in the the constituent ending with the Theme (19a) or Base (19b,c).

(19) a. p^{h}ug=eα−s 'flight (gen)' thematic
      x (x
  b. poi−men=os 'shepherd (gen)' athematic
      x (x x
  c. k^{h}ruuse =o−s 'golden' thematic
      x (x x   with base ending in short V

Assuming that Oxytonesis is ordered after line 0 projection but before Iterative Constituent Construction, we derive the correct grids for these forms.

6. VOWEL CONTRACTION AND ACCENT

Attic Greek, as opposed to that of earlier authors such as Homer or Herodotus, is characterized by a fairly regular rule of syllable contraction which merges the rimes of two syllables where the second is onsetless.

(20) Contraction (cf. Steriade, 1982: 156)
R   R   R
| | → | \
V   V   V V
|
[−high]

(21) k^{h}ruu.se.=o−s → k^{h}ruu.seos 'golden'
as.te=a → as.tea 'town (pl)'

As pointed out by de Haas (1988), Contraction is motivated by a condition of Avoid Hiatus: if the left rime ends in a high vocoid, that vowel can serve as an onset to the following syllable and Contraction does not apply:

(22) mu−os → mu.wos → mu.os   'mouse (gen)'
     oui−es → o.wi.yes → oi.es   'sheep (pl)'
     graau−os → graa.wos → graa.os   'old woman (gen)'

It is noteworthy that insofar as this explanation is correct, it depends on pre-surface conditions of well-formedness. Attic Greek also exhibited deletion of some instances of intervocalic glide /w y/ in surface forms. Accordingly, surface forms such as /graa.os, oi.es/ do not avoid hiatus at all: hiatus avoidance obtains only in a pre-surface form before deletion of /w y/. Cumbersome though this data may be for surface-oriented approaches, this will not be our central focus here. Rather, I want to focus on the effect of Contraction on the surface placement of accent.

If metrical structure rules refer to the pre-contraction syllabification, very little else need be said. Consider the standard example:

(23) pʰile=e−te   'you (pl) love'
     pʰi(le.e).te   Syllabification, Stress
     pʰi.lée.te   Contraction

If metrical structure is built with reference to the post-contraction syllabification, then with a σσL sequence the wrong result obtains: /*(pʰí.lee).te/, cf. /án.tʰroα.pos/ 'person' without contraction.

In order for this account to follow through, some means must exist to ensure that a syllable break will arise between the base and the theme constituent. Following the insight of Kiparsky (1973), I propose that the theme is a noncyclic affix, while the desinence is a cyclic one (cf. also the analysis of Latvian in Halle, 1992). Assuming that the syllabification rule adjoining a preceding nucleus to a rime is a cyclic rule, then a theme vowel cannot be adjoined into a preceding base's rime without violating the Strict Cycle Condition:

(24) pʰi.le   base syllabification
     pʰi.le ⟨e⟩   noncyclic theme
     pʰi.le .e.te   cyclic desinence

This provides the correct syllabification for accent placement, but this syllabification is later deformed by Contraction.

It is important to recognize that mora-counting is unhelpful, a point emphasized by Sauzet (1983) and Dell and Vergnaud (1984: 31). The number of moras remains constant under contraction of two short vowels (25a), although it changes when a short rime contracts with a long vowel (25b):

(25) a. pʰi.le.e.te → pʰi.lee.te   'you (pl) love'
            μ.μ   →   μμ
     b. ʰer.mé.eαn → ʰerméęn   'Hermes (acc)'
            μ.μμ   →   μμ

It is not necessarily the number of moras which changes from pre-surface to surface syllabification; rather it is the *grouping* of these into syllables, where grouping is a purely organizational matter, not one relating to content.

7. CONTRACTION AND STERIADE'S RULE

Consider now the place of Steriade's Rule in the above derivations. Recall that Steriade's Rule requires that, in the direct cases of non-neuter substantives, a final long syllable has acute rather than circumflex intonation, e.g. /aret–eá–n/ 'excellence (acc)'. Forms arising from contraction are systematic exceptions to this generalization:

(26) a. ^{h}ermé = eαn → ^{h}erméαn   'Hermes (acc)'
　　 b. ^{h}udro − k^{h}ó = os → ^{h}udrok^{h}óos   'Aquarius'
　　 c. galé = eαn → galéαn   'weasel (acc)'
　　 d. k^{h}ruusé = os → k^{h}ruusóos   'golden'

Steriade's Rule cannot be recast as a surface-true constraint since these forms fail to undergo the rule. Rather, Steriade's Rule *qua* well-formedness condition holds of a pre-surface level of representation. In all the cases above, Steriade's Rule will shift the headship of the final syllable to the right mora at the pre-surface syllabification. But this will be irrelevant, since subsequent application of Contraction causes the final rime to be deleted, making its headedness irrelevant at the surface (head moras are denoted here by underlining):

(27) a. ^{h}er.(me.eαn)   syllabification, metrical rules
　　 ^{h}er.(me.eαn)   Steriade's Rule
　　 ^{h}er.(meαn)   Contraction
　　 ^{h}er.méẹn   Coalescence, Tone Assignment
　　 'Hermes (acc)'

8. C-DELETION AND S-DELETION

In addition to the syllable-break imposed by the base–theme juncture, the intervocalic loss of historical *i̯ *u̯ *s gave rise to special accentual circumstances. Certain stems must be treated synchronically as containing an empty C or similar diacritic enforcing hiatus in pre-surface and/or surface syllabification:

(28) (peri-(kleC-es) = a   pre-surface syllabification and metrification
　　 (peri(kléC.e) = a   S-deletion
　　 (peri(kléC.ea   Contraction
　　 pe.ri.klé.aa   Coalescence
　　 'Pericles (acc)'

In a recessive base like /peri–kleC-es–/ 'Pericles', we must assume an empty C enforcing hiatus at the pre-surface syllabification, since otherwise accent should recede to the /i/: /*pe(rí.kle–es) = a/, cf. again /(án.tʰroα).pos/ 'person'. The base-final /s/ is deleted by a cyclic rule of s-deletion, followed by Contraction and concomitant deformation of pre-surface syllabification.

Such forms are to be contrasted with oxytone bases ending in /s/, which are also subject to s-deletion, but have final accent in all forms:

(29) (a.leα.(tʰ−és=)a   pre-surface syllabification and metrification
     (a.leα.(tʰ−é)=a   S-deletion
     (a.leα.(tʰéa   Contraction
     a.leę.tʰę̇ę   Coalescence
     'true (acc)'

Since /aleαtʰ-es–/ is oxytone, it follows that /perikleC–es–/ must be recessive since it has a different pattern of accent. This in turn demands that the pre-surface syllabification contain a hiatus as depicted in (28).

9. Morphologically Complex Forms and Contraction

In this section I turn to the crucial question of whether the syllabification needed for accentuation defines a privileged level, for example, the output of the Lexical Phonology in the sense of Kiparsky (1982; 1985). Suppose, for example, that contraction is merely a postlexical effect. If so, the syllabification needed for the calculation of accent placement can be the word-level syllabification, where the word level is independently defined by morphosyntactic constituency. A derivational phonology with a multiplicity of non-privileged intermediate levels will in that case be unnecessary: at most what will be needed for Greek is a three-level model with static relations of correspondence between the levels (Goldsmith, 1992; McCarthy and Prince, 1995).

To this end it will be instructive to consider morphologically complex forms. It has long been noted that the accent of certain derived nouns cannot be assigned on the basis of the pre-contraction syllabification (Lejeune 1972: 32). Specifically we find cases such as:

(30) [peri+[plo=o-o]] → períploo   'sailing around (gen)'
     [eu+[no=o–αi]]   → eúnǫǫi   'well-disposed (dat)'

In the first generative treatment of these cases, Sommerstein (1973) noted that in certain derived nouns, the accent rule must apply *after* Contraction rather than before. If Contraction applies after all metrification, the wrong results obtain:

(31) (pe.ri+(pló = .oo   pre-surface syllabification and metrification
     *(pe.ri+(plóo   Contraction

Instead of antepenultimate accent, any analysis which has metrification always preceding Contraction will incorrectly predict final surface accent as in 31, rather than the correct surface penultimate accent, as in 30. Yet if Contraction is purely postlexical, and the word-level grammar always produces an uncontracted output, we cannot explain such forms.

The solution proposed by Sommerstein involves cyclic application. Contraction does indeed follow syllabification and metrification, but *on the cycle*. Contraction applies to [plo=.oo], but then metrification has another round on the cycle introduced by the prefix [peri–].[6]

(32) Desinence cycle
    (plo=.o–o   Syllabification and metrification
    (plóo   Contraction
    Prefix cycle
    (pe.(rí+ploo   Syllabification and metrification

As a result, Contraction does indeed precede metrification, but only in derived forms, as required.

Bubeník (1983: 155) takes issue with this approach, pointing out that in prefixed verbs there is no contraction: a form like /peri–ora = e–te/ surfaces with penultimate accent: /perioráate/ 'you (pl) look around'. This fact, however, shows only that Contraction occurs only on the desinence cycle of substantives and not on the desinence cycle of verbs, where Contraction is limited to the word level:

(33) Desinence cycle
    (o.(ra=e).te   Syllabification and metrification
    Prefix cycle
    (pe.(ri+o(ra = e).te   Syllabification and metrification
    Word level
    (pe.(ri+o(ráa).te   Contraction, Coalescence

Further evidence for cyclic effects in substantives is seen in derived forms of bases ending in deletable /s/.

(34) *Simplex base*   *Derived base*
    gen−es=oɑn   tri+eɑr−es=oɑn   UR
    genóǫn   trięęrǫǫn   surface
    'races (gen pl)'   'triremes (gen pl)'

---

[6] These forms apparently evidence a mismatch of morphosemantic and phonological structure. Phonologically, the desinence must be more embedded than the prefix: [peri[plo-oo]], while morphosemantically the desinence takes scope over the root /plo/ 'sail (o-grade)' as modified by the prefix /peri–/. Unlike in Sanskrit or Russian (Halle and Vergnaud, 1987: 82, 84 ff.), Greek prefixes must be considered cyclic constituents external to the constituent headed by the desinence. A full discussion of these matters is however beyond the scope of the present chapter.

In simplex bases, accent remains on the mora implicated by the pre-surface syllabification.

(35) Desinence cycle
    ge.(n–és.oαn   Syllabification and metrification
    ge.(nóαn   S-deletion, Contraction
    Word level
    ge.(nǫ́ǫn   Coalescence

In derived forms however, accent recedes according to the surface syllabification.

(36) Desinence cycle
    eα(r–es.oαn   Syllabification and metrification
    eα(róαn   S-deletion, Contraction
    Prefix cycle
    tri + (eάroαn   Syllabification and metrification

Traditionally, forms such as /tri + ę́ę́r-ǫǫn/ 'triremes (gen pl)' were taken to arise from 'analogy', but there appears to be no evidence that such analogies took place except in morphologically complex forms (cf. Kühner 1844: §59 Anm. 4).[7]

Further support comes from derived s-stem adjectives. While simplex /aleαtʰ-(es–/ 'true' has penultimate stress in the genitive plural and corresponding long-final adverb (37), derived /pʰil + aleαtʰ–es–/ 'in a truth-loving way, frankly' has antepenultimate stress positioned according to post-Contraction syllabification (38):

(37) aleα(tʰ–es-oαs → aleαtʰǫ́ǫs   'truly'

(38) pʰil + aleαtʰ–es=oαs → pʰilalęę́tʰǫǫs   'in a truth-loving way, frankly'

This contrast is obtained again by assuming that the prefix provides a second pass at metrification, at which point Contraction has already applied:

(39) Desinence cycle
    (a.leα.(tʰ–és.=oαs   Syllabification and metrification
    (a.leα.(tʰoαs   S-deletion, Contraction
    Prefix cycle
    (pʰil + a.(leάtʰoαs   Syllabification and metrification

On the prefix cycle, cyclic stress erasure applies, deleting the metrification of the desinence cycle (including the prespecified oxytone stress of the stem). In the surface form of the prefixed adjective, stress is placed in accordance with the post-Contraction syllabification.

---

[7] Crucial evidence would come from the genitive plural of the one barytone simplex s-stem adjective /pleαr-es–/ 'full.' I have been unable to find a textual example of this form: it is not present in any major author as far as I am aware.

The evidence in support of these cyclic effects is not tremendously robust. Depending on one's point of view, the paucity of evidence might be taken as grounds for dismissing such cases as being not synchronically derived at all. On the other hand, it is equally legitimate to draw the opposite conclusion: since positive evidence for cyclic effects is so limited in these cases, they must reflect a deep property of UG, namely cyclic rule application. The important point for now is that, if indeed syllabification shows cyclic effects, it must be ordered before contraction on the cycle, with the result that the output of each successive cycle is a contracted form. The syllabification needed for accentuation is therefore neither the surface form nor some privileged representation produced at the end of a cycle of word formation. Rather, this syllabification is merely an arbitrary intermediate derivational stage.

10. STRAY ERASURE

As mentioned in section 2, Steriade (1988) pointed out that final surface clusters such as /ks/ suffice to create a heavy syllable for the purposes of metrification. In an interesting further argument, Steriade draws attention to the position of accent in bases ending in sonorant–obstruent clusters such as /nt/:

(40) a. k^harient = Ø → k^haríen, NOT *k^hárien   'graceful (neuter)'
         cf. k^hariént-os 'id. (gen)'
     b. p^hoɑnei–ent=Ø → p^hǫǫnéien, NOT *p^hǫǫ́neien 'voiced (neuter)'
         cf. p^hǫǫnéi-ent-os 'id. (gen)'

A base such as /k^harient–/ 'graceful' will delete its final /t/ in suface form, provided /t/ has no following vowel whose syllable it can form an onset to; but in such case, Steriade argues, the underlying cluster /nt/ also suffices to create a final heavy syllable. This explains why such bases have penultimate surface accent: /k^haríen⟨t⟩/ is attested while /k^hárien/—the accentuation expected from the surface string—is not.

These facts are not sufficient to establish the necessity of examining pre-surface forms for accent placement: assuming that output constraints have access to underlying forms in some fashion (McCarthy and Prince, 1995) it is a simple matter for underlying (but not surface) clusters to be mentioned by a constraint.

However, Steriade did not discuss the behaviour of derived forms with respect to accent placement. Evidence here is again quite sparse, but we can point to some suggestive facts.

Adverbs can be derived non-productively from neuter adjectives, and in such cases they exhibit recessive accent:

(41) a. aleαt^{h}és   'true (neuter adj)'
        → áleαt^{h}es   'truly (adverb)'
    b. *e–ú   'good (neuter adj)'
        → éu   'well'

The adverb derived from the /nt/-stem /k^{h}aríen/ 'graceful' has accent on the antepenult:

(42) k^{h}aríen   'graceful, pleasing (neuter adj)'
    → k^{h}árien   'with pleasure'

Assuming that adverb formation (conversion) introduces a new cycle with a new pass at metrification, it then follows that underlying /t/ can no longer count for weight, or, more likely can no longer force the preceding /n/ to count for weight. Whether this is properly understood as cyclic 'Stray Erasure' in the sense of Itô (1986) is unclear, but the fact remains that the /t/ no longer counts in the derived form, but does in the non-derived form, again a cyclic effect:

(43) Desinence cycle
    k^{h}a.(ri.ent)–Ø   Syllabification and metrification
    k^{h}a.(rí.en)   Stray Erasure
    Adverb conversion cycle
    (k^{h}ári)en   Syllabification and metrification

In addition to /k^{h}árien/ there is also a small set of derived forms in which underlying clusters do not count for weight:

(44) a. dámar⟨t⟩ → dús + damar   'wife → ill-wedded (adj)'
        cf. dámart–os 'wife (gen)'
    b. gála⟨kt⟩ → oinó + gala, melí + gala   'milk → wine-milk, honey-milk'
        cf. gálakt–os 'milk (gen)'

Significantly, in no case in the textual record does an underlying cluster influence the placement of accent in a derived form.[8] This can be explained readily if Stray Erasure or its formal equivalent operates cyclically.

11. Summary

The preceding sections have introduced evidence suggesting that Contraction, S-deletion, and some analogue of Stray Erasure operated cyclically in the grammar of Attic Greek. The significance of this finding is that the syllabifica-

---

[8] Kühner (1844: 103) gives /mon+ ódon⟨t⟩-Ø/ 'one-toothed (neut)' which on the present proposal is predicted to be /món+ odon⟨t⟩-Ø/. However, it is extremely unlikely that Kühner was citing from textual attestation rather than from conjecture: I have been completely unable to find this form in any author.

tion needed for accent placement is not in fact cycle-final; rather, it must be calculated on a given cycle of word formation prior to other rules. For this reason, syllabification and metrification cannot be equated with conditions holding at some 'privileged' level of representation; rather, they must be seen as the outcome of processes which establish an arbitrary stopping point along a path to a well-formed output.

12. The Sauzet–Golston Alternative

In this section I revisit the above problems in light of the alternative conception of Greek metrical structure introduced in Sauzet (1983; 1989) and elaborated in Golston (1989). For these authors, H-tone is placed on the mora preceding the metrical prominence in recessive nouns; consequently the foot boundaries implicated on Steriade's analysis are shifted rightward. Moraic trochees (Hayes, 1989; 1995) are constructed from right to left.[9] In contrast to Steriade's syllabic trochee analysis, all syllables closed by consonants count as heavy, with the proviso that a single final consonant does not count for weight. An advantage of this view is that the rules needed for e.g. the Homeric scansion are the same as those needed for stress placement, a desirable confluence.

(45) a. á.ne.mo⟨s⟩   L(LL)   'wind'
     b. sǫǫ́mata   H(LL)   'bodies'
     c. ʰá.mak.sa   L(HL)   'wagon'
     d. dęę́.męę.te⟨r⟩   H(HL)   'Demeter (voc.)'
     e. a.né.moo   (LL)(H)   'wind (gen)'
     f. sǫǫmátǫǫ⟨n⟩   (HL)(H)   'bodies (gen pl)'
     g. ʰa.mák.saa⟨s⟩   L(H)(H)   'wagon (gen)'
     h. dęęmęę́tęę⟨r⟩   (H)(H)(H)   'Demeter'

Sample forms are provided below; note that H links to the mora immediately to the left of the metrically prominent one, to which L links:

(46)   x   x   x
        x(x x)   x   (x x)   (x x) (x)
        ʰámaksa   ántʰrǫǫpos   ʰamáksaas
         | | | | | |
        H L   H   L   H L
        'wagon'   'person'   'wagon (gen)'

---

[9] Sauzet's original proposal (1983; 1989) was framed in terms of a different sort of constituent, the uneven trochee. In Golston's revised analysis (1989), which I follow here, Greek is brought into line with the foot typology of Hayes (1989; 1995).

One advantage attaching to the moraic trochee account is that Steriade's Mora Rule seems no longer to be necessary. Antepenults can have only acute intonation because the H in question will attach to the last mora preceding the metrically prominent penult (45b). Penults preceding long finals will also exhibit acute intonation, since here the metrically prominent syllable is the final long (45e,h).

Nevertheless, the Mora Rule or its equivalent must still be invoked to account for shifts in the accent placement of oxytones:

(47) a. agǫ́ǫn=a   'contest (acc sg)' circumflex penult, with light final
     b. agǫǫ́n=ǫǫn   'context (gen pl)' acute penult, with heavy final

In oxytones, the placement of H cannot be a direct reflex of metrical footing, since this must be invariant to retain the symmetry with the Homeric scansion. Rather, placement of H in oxytones must be at least partly a matter of non-metrical tonal rules. This point is made even more evident by the existence of final oxytone acutes such as /potam=ó-s/ 'river' where there is no mora at all following the H-tone mora, and so the H cannot possibly be attaching to the mora 'before the metrical prominence' in such cases. But if the placement of H in oxytones is not determined by footing, but rather by tonal rules, it remains unexplained why oxytones too are subject to the rule of limitation, which is a reflection of footing.

One way to retain the advantages of the moraic trochee analysis while still incorporating the effects of the Mora rule would be to invoke ranked and violable conditions of well-formedness on Alignment (McCarthy and Prince, 1993*b*) of tonal and prosodic domains (Cole and Kisseberth, 1994). Specifically, a satisfactory generalization appears to be that in athematic oxytones the right edge of the syllable containing the H-tone, call it H-σ, must be aligned (as close as possible) with the right edge of the base (call this constraint OXYTONE). The place of H within the H-σ is, however, as close as possible to that required in a barytone noun: as far left as possible, yet not beyond the domain required by the rule of limitation. This effect can be achieved by a constraint which aligns the left edge of the head Foot (as defined by an optimal metrical parse) with the right edge of the H-tone domain (call this constraint BARYTONE). Tableaux (48, 49) exhibit the choice of the forms in (47) relative to near competitors (the H-σ is underlined).

(48)

	OXYTONE Align {H-σ, Right, Base, Right}	BARYTONE Align {Head Foot, Left, H-Tone, Right}
H] | agǫǫn]a agǫ́na x(x x)	n	μμ !
H] | agǫǫn]a ágǫǫna x(x x)	gǫ!ǫn	
☞ H] L | agǫ ǫn]a agǫ́ǫna x(x x)	n	μ

In /agǫ́ǫn=a/ 'contest (acc)', the penult appears with circumflex intonation because low-ranked BARYTONE forces H leftward towards the locus it would occupy in a normal barytone stem. Since /agǫǫn–/ is an oxytone base, however, higher-ranked OXYTONE prevents H from escaping from that syllable whose right edge is most closely aligned with the right edge of the base (the morphological condition on oxytone accent placement).

(49)

	OXYTONE Align {H-σ, Right, Base, Right}	BARYTONE Align {Head Foot, Left, H-Tone, Right}
H] | agǫǫn]ǫǫn agǫ́ǫnǫǫn x (x) (x)	n	μ !
H] | agǫǫn]ǫ ǫn agǫǫnǫ́ǫn x (x) (x)	ǫǫ!n	
☞ H] | agǫǫn]ǫǫn agǫǫ́nǫǫn x (x) (x)	n	

For final–long /agǫǫ́n–ǫǫn/, BARYTONE no longer pushes H leftward within the syllable chosen for it by OXYTONE: a final long penult makes the second mora of the penult the 'best' locus of H, since it is here that a regular barytone stem would have accent anyway.

Thus the moraic trochee analysis does not escape the Mora Rule, but rather leads directly to a theory in which the Mora Rule is recast as a violable constraint whose effects appear only indirectly in oxytones. The success of this manoeuvre seems to cast a favourable light on the OT approach to at least these facts.

13. CONTRACTION AND SURFACE-LEVEL CONSTRAINTS

While a relatively satisfying account of accent placement in simplex forms can be given in the moraic trochee analysis once we invoke OT, the problems discussed earlier in connection with contraction remain. As on Steriade's (1988) syllabic trochee analysis, it is not the number of moras that determines accent placement but rather a grouping of these:

(50) a.   H
          |
        μ μμ μ
        | | | | syllabic trochees   moraic trochees
        ánt^{h}rǫǫpos   (σσ)L   L(HL)
        4th from last mora   'person'

     b.   H
           |
         μ μ μ μ
         | | | | syllabic trochees   moraic trochees
         anémoo   σ(σH)   (LL) (H)
         3rd from last mora   'wind (gen)'

Contraction again serves to deform the groupings of moras needed for correct accent placement, whether by the recessive rule of limitation or by the morphophonological generalization I called Steriade's Rule. For example, turning again to /p^{h}ile = ete → p^{h}iléete/ 'you (pl) love', what is required of a surface-level analysis is that H associate with the metrically prominent mora in surface form provided that mora *was not* metrically prominent in pre-surface form:

(51) p^{h}ile = (e.te) → p^{h}i.(lee.te)   'you (pl) love'
       | |
       H   H

But what are we to make of this last proviso? Certainly it is inadmissible if no pre-surface metrical prominences are admitted in descriptions available to the grammar. Let us assume furthermore that UG does not permit several metrical structures at once to be assigned to surface forms; rather, the surface metrification should remain that appropriate to the Homeric scansion, as suggested by Sauzet (1989). The only alternative, then, is to invoke a condition which accesses morphological structure in some way. A preliminary formulation would be: associate the H-tone with the metrically prominent mora (rather than the mora preceding the metrical prominence), provided the metrically prominent syllable contains the base–theme juncture.

This condition, however implemented, will work for cases such as /p^{h}ile=ete/ where the contracted syllable is the surface penult (52), but not for similar cases where the contracted syllable is the final (53). (The symbol H = will denote a surface heavy syllable containing a [=] juncture):

(52) p^{h}ile=e–te → p^{h}i(lé=e.te   'you (pl) love'
    L L = L L → L (H =) L

(53) a. e-p^{h}ile=o–n → (ep^{h}í) (lo=on   'I was loving'
      L L L = L   (LL) (H =
    b. tiima=e → (tií) (ma=a   'honour! (sg imperative)'
      H L = L → (H) (H =

If the surface-level conditions on H-tone placement require that H associate with the mora preceding the metrical prominence, except where the metrically prominent syllable contains a [=] juncture, then the wrong predictions arise for (53). These should surface as /*ep^{h}ilóon/, /tiimáa/ since their metrically prominent final heavies contain [=], just as does the penult in /p^{h}iléete/. The correct generalization, then, is that the H-tone associates with the surface metrical prominence only if the metrically prominent syllable contains the [=] juncture *and* is the penult. And yet even this refinement is not correct, since a contraction of final L + H will yield a final accented H:

(54) deαlo=eis → (dęę)(ló=is)   'you (sg) manifest'
    H   L H → H H =

In /deαlo=eis → (dęę)(lóis)/ 'you (sg) manifest', contraction draws together the underlying penult L and final H as a surface-final H containing the juncture [=]. Such cases can be distinguished from unaccented contracted final heavies such as /ep^{h}íloon/ (53a) in that the final heavies contain, as it were, an unparsed mora: /(dęę)(ló⟨e⟩is)/. It does not really matter whether such conditions are to be understood in terms of input–output correspondence (McCarthy and Prince, 1995) or simply via the ability of output constraints to access all the underlying form in any output (Prince and Smolensky, 1993): what is crucial here is not the correspondence between the underlying form and the output but rather a non-underlying, non-surface *organization* of the underlying form.

To summarize, it appears that a surface condition on H placement making reference to the [=] juncture will have to run as follows:

(55) H is associated with the mora preceding the metrical prominence unless the syllable containing the metrical prominence contains the base–theme juncture [=] and
   (1) is a penult with a final light or
   (2) is a final heavy containing an 'unparsed' mora (or the equivalent)

Highly specific conditions of this kind are uninteresting and in no way explanatorily adequate. It remains to be seen, however, whether the effect of the conditions in (55) might be obtained by constraint interaction. But the extraordinary simplicity of the alternative, computation of accent based on a pre-surface syllabification, suggests that attempts in this direction will prove misguided.

14. Accent Retraction in Prefixed Forms

An additional advantage cited by Sauzet (1989: 96–7) for the moraic trochee analysis is that it permits a relatively straightforward explanation for a special rule of limitation imposed in prefixed forms. It has long been observed that, in prefixed words, accent never recedes to a position more than one syllable before the prefix–base juncture [+] (Smyth, 1956: 144; Kurylowicz 1958: 138):

(56) a. perí + t^{h}es, *péri + t^{h}es   'put around! (imperative 2 sg)'
     b. lukó + p^{h}ron, *lúko + p^{h}ron   'Wolf-heart (name)'

When the base is a light syllable, the regular rule of limitation should permit the accent to recede to the antepenult, but in prefixed forms accent systematically appears only on the penult. This behavior can be explained automatically if it is assumed that metrical structure built on the base remains intact upon prefixation: Greek prefixes, although behaving as cyclic for the purpose of contraction, do not introduce Stress Erasure along with a new cycle of metrification. In other words, prefixes respect previously built structure (Halle, 1990; Halle and Kenstowicz, 1991).

(57) Desinence cycle
     (t^{h}es)   Metrification
     Prefix cycle
     (peri)(t^{h}es)   Metrification
     Word level
     perít^{h}es   Tone association

As usual, H-tone attaches to the mora preceding the metrical prominence (here the syllable /t^{h}es/), correctly giving penultimate H-tone. We will suppose that tonal association occurs at the word level, after the last cycle of word formation.

   Sauzet does not extend this idea to retraction in contracted substantives like /perí + ploo/ 'sailing around (gen)', discussed above at (30–2), but specifically denies that they are synchronically analyzable (1989: 95, n. 25) and suggests instead that sound change has given rise to a new declensional pattern. But only a little additional needs to be said to accommodate this data in the moraic trochee account. Assuming, as before, that Contraction is cyclic on the desinence cycle of substantives and is ordered after cyclic metrification, we predict the following:

(58) Desinence cycle

plo=(oo)	Metrification
ploo	Contraction, metrical structure erased
Prefix cycle	
(peri)(ploo)	Metrification
Word level	
períploo	Tone association
'sailing around (gen)'	

The point of interest here is that Contraction on the desinence cycle deletes the final rime in /plo=(oo)/, where this rime projects metrical structure. In a manner similar to the Domino Condition in Winnebago (Hale and White Eagle, 1980; Halle and Vergnaud, 1987), Contraction entails the erasure of metrical structure associated with the deleted rime. This provides a second, post-Contraction opportunity for metrification on the cycle which prosodifies the prefix. Since metrical structure has been erased by Contraction on the desinence cycle, refooting occurs on the prefix cycle. While it would appear prima facie that prefixation does not respect desinence-cycle metrification in contracted substantives like /perí-ploo/, it is in fact Contraction, and not cyclic Stress Erasure, that triggers remetrification of the base. This allows us to retain Sauzet's insight that metrical structure remains intact upon prefixation, while retaining Sommerstein's proposal that retraction in substantives is crucially related to cyclic application.

Having established these facts, we may now turn to cases in which the prefix is the so-called verbal 'augment': a vowel which I will denote /μ/ which may in surface form lengthen a following vowel or surface as /e/ if preceding a consonant (Smyth, 1956: 145–6).

(59) a. μ+ ag=o–n → ęęgon   'I was leading'
     b. μ+ paid–eu=o–n → epaideuon   'I was educating'

Now it is well known that accent cannot recede past the augment, or past prefixal reduplication (Smyth 1956: 144), even when permitted to do so by the regular rule of limitation:

(60) a. apo+ μ + e=n → apę́ęn, *ápęęn   'was absent'
        out + augment + be = 3sg
     b. eis+ μ + elt^h=o–n → eisę́ęlt^{h}on, *eísęęlt^{h}on   'they were entering'
        in + augment + go = theme–3pl

We can explain these facts straightforwardly, given the analysis developed so far. By hypothesis, contraction is cyclic only for substantives. The augment and the prefix are separate metrical domains, since each introduces a cycle on which previous metrical structure is respected. At the word level, H-tone associates to the augment (the mora preceding the word-level metrical prominence). Word-level contraction then deforms this syllable structure, giving the surface syllabification. Tone stability ensures that the accent remains unmoved:

(61) Desinence cycle
    (el)t^h = o–n   Syllabification and metrification
    Augment cycle
    (μ.) + (el).t^h = o–n   Syllabification and metrification
    Prefix cycle
    (ei).(s + μ.) + (el).t^h = o–n   Syllabification and metrification
    Word level
    (ei).(s + μ́.) + (el).t^h = o–n   Tone association
    (ei).(sę́ęl)t^{h}on   Contraction, Coalescence

The placement of H-tone in the surface form is on the mora preceding the metrical prominence, where that metrical prominence reflects again a pre-surface footing. Note the important difference between substantival /perí + ploo/ and verbal /eis + ę́ęlt^{h}on/. In the former case, desinence-level Contraction entails refooting and a repositioning of the H-tone. In the latter case this is not so, and contraction occurs only at the word level, so the position of H reflects a pre-surface organization of syllables.

15. SUMMARY

The preceding two sections have introduced evidence that the moraic trochee analysis of Greek proposed by Sauzet (1983; 1989) and Golston (1989), while providing certain advantages over the syllabic trochee analysis, must still contend with the fact that accent placement depends on a syllabification which is deformed by surface-level syllable contraction. Our main contention is then clear: some non-surface-true organization of the underlying information into syllables is required for a perspicuous explanation of the placement of accent. Surface-level constraints which achieve the same effects by appeal to morphological junctures are ad hoc, and serve merely to covertly (re)construct a previous derivational stage.

    Morphologically complex forms show a certain degree of cyclic effects, although here evidence is less robust. Contraction, and S-deletion feeding Contraction, along with some analogue to Stray Erasure, appear to operate cyclically, at least in substantives. Pre-surface syllabification and metrification must precede these rules on the cycle in that event, showing that the pre-surface syllabification needed for accent placement cannot be equated with cycle-final representations, and hence not with any privileged level such as the 'lexical' or W-level. Moreover, for substantives Contraction on the desinence cycle may lead to refooting and concomitant repositioning of H tone; for verbs, however, refooting triggered by Contraction at the word level does not. Clearly, intricate data such as these will provide the appropriate testing ground for the adequacy of non-derivational phonological theories in future work.

ACKNOWLEDGEMENTS

I have benefited especially from many discussions with Morris Halle. I would also like to thank Patrick Sauzet, Don Ringe, Bill Idsardi, Gene Buckley, Paul Kiparsky, and Chris Golston for ideas and comments (although none of these persons should be held responsible for my conclusions).

REFERENCES

Benveniste, E. (1984). *Origines de la formation des noms en indo-européen*. Paris: Adrien Maisonneuve.

Bubeník, V. (1983). *The Phonological Interpretation of Ancient Greek: A Pandialectal Analysis*. Toronto: University of Toronto Press.

Buckley, E. (1995). 'Alignment and Constraint Domains in Manam Stress'. MS, University of Pennsylvania. 17.

Chantraine, P. (1961). *Morphologie historique du grec*. Paris: Klincksieck.

Chomsky, N. (1964). *Current Issues in Linguistic Theory*. The Hague: Mouton.

―――― and Halle, M. (1968). *The Sound Pattern of English*. New York: Harper & Row.

Cohn, A., and McCarthy, J. (1994). 'Alignment and Parallelism in Indonesian Phonology'. MS, Cornell University and the University of Massachusetts, Amherst. 25.

Cole, J., and Kisseberth, C. W. (1994). 'An Optimal Domains Theory of Harmony'. Cognitive Science Technical Report UIUC-BI-CS-94–02 (Language Series). Champaign–Urbana: Beckman Institute, University of Illinois. 22.

de Haas, W. (1988). *A Formal Theory of Vowel Coalescence: A Case Study of Ancient Greek*. Foris: Dordrecht.

Dell, F., and Vergnaud, J.-R. (1984). 'Les développements récents en phonologie: quelques idées centrales', in F. Dell, D. Hirst, and J.-R. Vergnaud (eds.), *Forme sonore du langage*. Paris: Hermann, 1–42.

Devine, A. M., and Stevens, L. D. (1994). *The Prosody of Greek Speech*. New York: Oxford University Press.

Goldsmith, J. (1992). 'Harmonic phonology', in Goldsmith (ed.), *The Last Phonological Rule*. Chicago: University of Chicago Press, 21–60.

Golston, C. (1989). 'Floating H (and *L) tones in Ancient Greek', *Proceedings of the Arizona Phonology Conference* 3. Coyote Papers, University of Arizona.

Hale, K., and White Eagle, J. (1980). 'A preliminary metrical account for Winnebago accent', *International Journal of American Linguistics* **46**: 117–32.

Halle, M. (1962). 'Phonology in generative grammar', *Word* **18**: 54–72.

—— (1990). 'Respecting metrical structure', *Natural Language and Linguistic Theory* **8**: 149–76.

—— (1992). 'The Latvian declension', in G. Booij and J. van Marle (eds.), *Yearbook of Morphology 1991*. Dordrecht: Kluwer, 33–47.

—— (1996). 'On Stress and Accent in Indo-European'. MS, MIT.

—— and Idsardi, W. J. (1995). 'General properties of stress and metrical structure', in J. Goldsmith (ed.), *Handbook of Phonological theory*. Oxford: Blackwell, 403–43.

—— and Kenstowicz, M. (1991). 'The Free Element Condition and cyclic and noncyclic stress', *Linguistic Inquiry* **22**: 457–501.

—— and Vergnaud, J.-R. (1987). *An Essay on Stress*. Cambridge, Mass.: MIT Press.

Hayes, B. (1989). 'A revised parametric metrical theory', *Proceedings of the Northeastern Linguistics Society* **17**: 274–89.

—— (1995). *Metrical Stress Theory: Principles and Case Studies*. Chicago: Universtiy of Chicago Press.

Idsardi, W. J. (1992). 'The Computation of Prosody', Dissertation, MIT.

Itô, J. (1986). 'Syllable Theory in Prosodic Phonology'. Dissertation, University of Massachusetts, Amherst.

Jakobson, R. (1962) [1937]. 'On Ancient Greek prosody', in *Selected Writings*, I: 262–71. The Hague: Mouton.

Kenstowicz, M. (1996). 'Cyclic vs. noncyclic constraint evaluation', *Phonology* **12**: 397–436.

Kiparsky, P. (1973). 'The inflectional accent in Indo-European', *Language* **49**(4): 794–849.

—— (1982). 'Lexical phonology and morphology', in I. S. Yang (ed.), *Linguistics in the Morning Calm*. Seoul: Hanshin, 3–91.

—— (1985). 'Some consequences of lexical phonology', *Phonology* **2**: 83–138.

Kühner, R. (1844). *Grammar of the Greek language*, Trans. B. B. Edwards and S. H. Taylor. Andover, Mass.: Allen, Morrill & Wardwell.

Kurylowicz, J. (1932). 'On the development of Greek intonation', *Language* **8**(3): 200–10.

—— (1935). 'L'indépendance historique des intonations baltiques et grecques', *Bulletin de la Sociéte de Linguistique de Paris* **35**: 24–34.

—— (1958). *L'Accentuation des langues indo-européennes*. Cracow: Polska Akademia Nauk.

Lejeune, M. (1972). *Phonétique historique du mycénien et du grec ancien*. Paris: Klincksieck.

McCarthy, J., and Prince, A. (1993*a*). 'Prosodic Morphology, I: Constraint Interaction and Satisfaction'. Technical Report 3, Rutgers University Center for Cognitive Science.

—— —— (1993*b*). 'Generalized Alignment', in G. Booij and J. van Marle (eds.), *Yearbook of Morphology 1993*. Dordrect: Kluwer, 79–153.

—— —— (1995). 'Faithfulness and reduplicative identity', in J. N. Beckman, L. W. Dickey, and S. Urbanczyk (eds.), *Papers in Optimality Theory*. (University of

Massachusetts Occasional Papers in Linguistics 18). Amherst, Mass.: GLSA, 249–384.

Prince, A. and Smolensky, P. (1993). 'Optimality Theory: Constraint Interaction in Generative Grammar'. Technical Report 2, Rutgers University Center for Cognitive Science.

Sauzet, P. (1983). 'Essai de traitement métrique de l'accent grec (ancien)'. MS, École Normale Supérieure, Paris.

———— (1989). 'L'accent du grec ancien et les relations entre structure métrique et représentation autosegmentale', *Langages* **24**: 81–111.

Smyth, H. W. (1956) [1920]. *Greek Grammar.* Cambridge, Mass.: Harvard University Press.

Sommerstein, A. (1973). *The Sound Pattern of Ancient Greek.* Oxford: Blackwell.

Steriade, D. (1982). Greek Prosodies and the Nature of Syllabification. Dissertation, MIT.

———— (1988). 'Greek accent: a case for preserving structure', *Linguistic Inquiry* **19**: 271–314.

Vendryes, J. (1904). *Traité d'accentuation grecque.* Paris: Klincksieck.

17

Non-transparent Constraint Effects in Gere: From Cycles to Derivations

CAROLE PARADIS

1. INTRODUCTION

This chapter addresses the case of a constraint in Gere which holds across the board—that is, an undominated (unviolated) constraint in Optimality Theory's (OT) terms—but whose effects are none the less non-transparent on the surface in some cases, although easily recoverable in a derivational framework. I will show that the often non-transparent effects of this constraint evidence the need for a cyclic application of constraints, and support more generally a derivational approach as advocated in Paradis (1995, 1996). More precisely, I aim at showing that phonological rules / constraints may refer to phonological properties that never come to the surface, which is in essence one of the claims of the cyclicity hypothesis in Lexical Phonology (see e.g. Booij, Chapter 8 above). We will see that evidence in favor of such a hypothesis questions the adequacy of non-derivational constraint-based theories. The argumentation will be partially based on a comparison between the Theory of Constraints and Repair Strategies (TCRS; see e.g. Paradis, 1988a; 1988b; 1993), a derivational framework, and OT (Prince and Smolensky, 1993; McCarthy and Prince, 1993), a non-derivational one.

The chapter is organized as follows. In section 2 I present the relevant facts of Gere. The effects of four interacting constraints will be described. It will be shown how the effects of these constraints, which include the non-transparent ones, can be handled straightforwardly in a derivational constraint-based theory such as TCRS. In section 3 we will see why non-transparent constraint effects such as those found in Gere are problematic for a non-derivational approach like OT. These effects force a cyclic application of constraints, which, we will see, is problematic for OT in many respects. The usual OT alternatives to constraint cyclicity such as levels of constraint application, the Identity constraints, and Alignment will be considered and rejected in section 4. Section 5 is devoted to showing that even constraint cyclicity, if it were compatible with OT's view, might not be sufficient, and emphasizes the need for a derivational constraint-based approach as a whole. A conclusion is offered in section 6.

2. RELEVANT FACTS IN GERE

2.1. *General phonological information*

Gere is a Kru language spoken in the Ivory Coast. It has nine oral vowels (*i, u, e, o, ı, ɷ, ɛ, ɔ, a*), each with a phonemic nasal counterpart. Gere also allows phonemic and non-phonemic diphthongs, which will prove important for the analysis proposed in this article. The consonant system of Gere is presented in (1).

(1)		*Labial*		*Dental*		*Palatal*		*Velar*		*Complex*
Stops		p	b	t	d	c	ɟ	k	g	kp gb g^w
Implosives			ɓ		ɗ (l)					
Nasals			m		n		ɲ			ŋ^w (ŋ) ŋm
Fricatives	f		v	s	z					
Glides			w						j	
Liquids					l (r, n)					

Gere's maximal syllable is (C)(C)(G)V, where the glide, if present, forms a diphthong with the following vowel.[1] Vowel sequences or long vowels are automatically heterosyllabic. The shape of non-compound words is either monosyllabic (C)(C)(G)V or bisyllabic (C)(G)V(C)V.[2] Diphthongs and branching onsets are systematically limited to the first syllable of words. Gere has also four lexical tones: High (H), Mid-High (MH), Middle (M), and Low (L), which can combine, and yield tautosyllabic sequences (see Paradis 1983*a*; 1983*b* for more details on the language).

2.2. *Four phonological constraints in Gere: the TCRS view*

The constraint we will focus on, the Sonority Constraint, is presented in (2a), and also discussed in Paradis (1990). It requires that the second member of a diphthong be more sonorous than the first one, i.e. Gere allows rising diphthongs only or, in negative constraint-based terms, prohibits non-rising ones. The Sonority Constraint holds without exception, although its effect is often obscured by the effects of two other constraints in Gere, the Height

---

[1] Labialized segments such as ŋ^w and g^w are represented by C here, along with the other complex or non-complex segments. In other words, labialized consonants and consonant glide sequences are distinct, since the glide in the latter case is not part of the onset but of the nucleus, i.e. it forms a diphthong.

[2] When the onset of the second syllable is filled, the onset of the first syllable does not branch.

Constraint and the Tone Constraint, presented in (2b) and (2c) respectively. The Height Constraint, also discussed in Paradis and Prunet (1990), prohibits sequences of non-high vowels, while the Tone Constraint disallows tautosyllabic falling-tone sequences ending with a non-low tone.

(2) Central constraints in Gere
a) Sonority Constraint	Non-rising diphthongs?	Gere: no (e.g. *ew, *ow)
b) Height Constraint	Sequences of non-high vowels?[3]	Gere: no (e.g. *ɔe, *ɛɔ)
c) Tone Constraint	Tautosyllabic falling-tone sequences?	Gere: no* (e.g. *H/MH-M)

*unless the last tone is low[4]

The fourth relevant constraint is a very common constraint across African languages: it prohibits the glide *w* or labialized consonants from being followed by a round vowel (i.e. *u, o,* and *ω*). This restriction on sequences of round segments can be interpreted, as shown in (3), as an effect of the Obligatory Contour Principle (OCP), activated tautosyllabically on the [round] tier in Gere. Note that *ɔ* in Gere does not behave as a round vowel, since sequences such as *wɔ, ŋ*^{w}*ɔ*, etc. are permitted and commonplace. It is thus assumed that the vowel is labial but not round, at least not underlyingly.[5] The exact representation of the vowel, however, is irrelevant here; for our purpose, it suffices to know that it is not targeted by the constraint below.

(3) OCP Constraint on Labial: *[round] [round] (*wu, *wo, *wω, *k^{w}o, *g^{w}ω, etc.)

Constraints will be handled by the derivational constraint-based framework of TCRS, where violations are fixed up by repair strategies. The application of

---

[3] Paradis and Prunet (1990) suggest that the constraint is in fact the following: *Height Constraint*: * [α high] [α high]. This constraint, which can be interpreted as an effect of the Obligatory Contour Principle on [high], prohibits adjacent [−high] values but also adjacent [+high] ones. It is claimed that, since vowels are underspecified for their [+high] value underlyingly, and that [+high] is inserted only after the constraint has been deactivated, the Height Constraint has no apparent effect on the latter sequences. The exact formulation of the constraint is, however, orthogonal to the analysis presented here; we will therefore not be concerned with it any longer.

[4] It is not uncommon for languages to have restrictions on combinations of phonological elements (consonants, vowels, tones) within a syllabic constituent. (2c) is a constraint of that sort, which limits falling tone sequences within a nucleus to the deepest level of fall. This constraint, whose formulation is actually simplified here (hence its language-specific aspect), is likely to result from several parameter settings—like those suggested below—as is the case of vowel and consonant inventories in general, which might be in some languages asymmetrical too (see Paradis, 1988c; Paradis and Prunet, 1988 on combinations of parameter settings as an explanation for the so-called language-specific constraints) (answers in brackets relate to Gere): Tautosyllabic tone sequences? (yes); All types? (no); Rising? (yes); All types? (yes); Falling? (yes); All types? (no); Any first tone? (yes); Any last tone? (no); Last tone is low? (yes—deepest fall); Last tone other than low? (no).

[5] It might be that the vowel [ɔ] is /ɑ/ underlyingly, i.e. an unrounded low back vowel, or that Gere speakers have a mental organization of rounded vowels which is not in total accordance with the phonetics, not an uncommon behavior (see Kenstowicz, 1994: 1–11 on phonetic illusions and the differences as well as the occasional discrepancies between phonetics and phonology).

repair strategies is governed by universal principles such as the Minimality and the Preservation principles, presented in section 5. Constraints themselves are principles, like the OCP, or (negative) parameter settings, like those in (2). In sections 2 and 3 I will be mainly concerned with the derivational aspect of the framework, rather than with the way repair strategies apply. This latter issue will be briefly addressed in section 5 (see also Paradis and LaCharité, 1993; 1995; 1997 for detailed descriptions and discussions). In TCRS, morphological operations are monitored by phonological constraints at all stages. None the less, a constraint can be deactivated at some level, either lexical or postlexical, provided its domain of activation is specified as a set of continuous strata.[6] While active at a given level or levels, a constraint's application is cyclic. That is, each violation by a morphological operation is detected immediately and repaired at once, before another morphological operation can apply. Repairs are limited to two strategies: insert or delete z, where z stands for any phonological material (features, nodes, links, timing slots, etc.).

2.3. *Transparent versus non-transparent constraint effects*

There are three 3sg. suffix pronouns in Gere, ε, $\mathfrak{o}$, ω—selected according to nominal class—and a 3pl. suffix, ι. As shown in (4), suffixed pronouns in non-causative declarative verbal forms systematically create a diphthong with the preceding stem-final vowel (see directly below for justification).

(4) High stem vowel (non-causative forms)
    a) /nmū-ɔ-'/ → [nmwɔ́] '(I) bite it'
    b) /dī-ɛ-'/ → [d͡ʒɛ́] '(I) eat it'
    (the dash over a vowel indicates a M tone, and the vertical bar a MH one)

The MH tone at the end of the clitic object pronoun is what Paradis (1983*a*; 1983*b*) has called the Intransitive suffix. It systematically appears after a single-vowel pronoun object (i.e. a clitic), or after plain intransitive verbs. The diphthong results from the attachment of the pronoun vowel—which has no timing slot of its own—to the timing slot of the stem vowel, as illustrated in (5a). This yields a weak diphthong in the sense of Kaye and Lowenstamm (1980), i.e. a sequence of two nuclear segments attached to a single timing unit (x) or, in moraic theory, to a single mora (see also Harris 1994: 278).

---

[6] See the Stratum Domain Hypothesis of Pulleyblank (1986: 6), a modified version of Mohanan's (1986: 21).

(5) a. diphthongization   b. representation of a weak diphthong

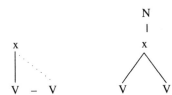

The on-glide on the left of the diphthongs in (4) constitutes the weak member of the diphthongs: recall that Gere allows (sonority) rising diphthongs only. The fact that, when the stem and suffix vowel are identical, as in (6), what is heard is crucially a short monophthong—not a long vowel or a rising diphthong—suggests that the pronoun vowel is slot-less, and that the representation in (5b) accounts well for the facts in Gere.[7]

(6) Identical vowel sequences
  a. /kmɔ̃-ω-'/ → [kmɔ̃'] *[kmwɔ̃'] *[kmɔ̃ɔ̃'] '(I) catch it'
  b. /dī-l-'/ → *[dī'] *[djī'] *[dīi'] '(I) eat them'[8]

Now if we observe in (7) suffixation in verbal stems which end in a non-high vowel, we see that the stem vowel is raised. It is assumed that the mid vowels in Gere are underlyingly [− high] (see Paradis and Prunet, 1990 for arguments). Raising—which will become more evident with the causative forms in (8) and the non-causative forms in (13)—is triggered by the Sonority Constraint in (2a).[9]

(7) Non-high stem vowel (non-causative forms)
  a. /zrɔ̀-ɛ-'/ → [zrwɛ̄'] '(I) beg it'
  b. /plē-ɔ-'/ → [pljɔ̄'] '(I) sell it'

The first two causative forms in (8) constitute minimal pairs with those in (7).

(8) Causative forms with a non-high suffix vowel
  a. /zrɔ̀-CAUS-ɛ-'/ → [zrɔ̃ɛ̄']^10 '(I) make it beg'
  b. /plē-CAUS-ɔ-'/ → [plīɔ̄] '(I) make it sell'
  c. /zrɔ̀-CAUS gbē/ → [zrɔ̄ɔ̄ gbē] '(I) make the dog beg'
  (a grave accent on a vowel represents a L tone)

The stem vowel in (8) is not realized as an on-glide as in (7) because it does not constitute the weak member of a diphthong, i.e. a complex nuclear structure. The vowel sequences in (8) are clearly disyllabic. As already mentioned

---

[7] The realization of the two vowels as one monophthong could not be attributed to a general OCP effect—an attractive alternative at first sight—since sequences such as *ji* and long vowels such as *uu* and *ii* (e.g. *jí* 'to fill', *dūū* 'chest', *klîî* 'crumpled') are common in Gere (see Paradis and Prunet, 1990).   [8] A non-ATR high vowel always harmonizes with an ATR high one.
[9] The fact that the pronoun vowel anchors despite the resulting violation of the Sonority Constraint will be discussed in section 5.
[10] A L-tone is raised when followed by the MH intransitive tone.

in 2.1, sequences of vowels—as opposed to on-glide + vowel sequences—and long vowels are always heterosyllabic in Gere (see Paradis, 1983*a*; 1983*b*, and Paradis and Prunet, 1990 for arguments). This is due to the fact that the causative suffix consists of a bare timing slot, which allows the slotless pronoun vowel to anchor, and thus to form a new syllable, as in (8a) and (8b). Therefore, diphthongization does not occur. When there is no pronoun suffix vowel, the stem vowel simply lengthens, as seen in (8c). Anchoring of the suffix vowel and lengthening of the stem vowel in causative formation are shown in (9a) and (9b), respectively.

(9) a. Anchoring of the suffix vowel   b. Lengthening of the stem vowel

One could object, however, that vowel-raising in (8) is due not to the Sonority Constraint, as in (7), but to the Height Constraint in (2b), which prohibits sequences with two distinct non-high vowels. This is evident from the fact that if the pronoun vowel is already high, as in (10), the stem vowel is not raised (for more examples and detailed derivations, see Paradis 1983*a*: 125 ff.).[11]

(10) Causative forms with a high suffix vowel
     a. /zrɔ-CAUS-ɩ-'/ → [zrɔ́ɩ] *[zrɔ̄ɩ]   '(I) make them beg'
     b. /zrɔ ᴄAUS-ɯ-'/ → [zrɔ́ɯ] *[zrɔ̄ɯ]   '(I) make it beg'

Failure of the vowel to raise in causative formation is due to the fact that the causative, which is suffixed before the pronoun vowel, provides an x-slot to which the pronoun vowel can anchor. As in (8), provision of an x-slot prevents the vowel from having to go through an ill-formed diphthong stage. The derivation of (10a) is provided in (11), where it can be seen that the causative slot associates with the suffix vowel before the latter anchors in the stem slot (11b).[12]

---

[11] The derivations proposed here are slightly different from those in Paradis (1983*a*; 1983*b*), who assumed that single-vowel pronouns were anchored. As a consequence, arbitrary x-slot deletion rules had to be invoked to account for the formation of diphthongs.

[12] Note that whether the stem vowel anchors or not in the Causative suffix before the suffix vowel is associated with it has no bearing on the analysis here. In any case, delinking of the stem vowel once the suffix vowel is associated with the causative slot would be permissible, since it does not result in vowel loss, given that the stem vowel is already anchored.

(11) a. Causative suffixation   b. Anchoring of the suffix vowel

The causative forms in (12), where vowel raising also fails to apply, are derived in the same way.

(12) a. /wɔ́-CAUS-ι-'/ → [wɔ́ι̯] *[wóι̯]   '(I) make them shout'
     b. /wɔ́-CAUS-ɷ-'/ → [wɔ́ɷ̯] *[wóɷ̯]   '(I) make it shout'
    (an acute accent on a vowel represents a H-tone)

Now compare the examples in (12) with those in (13) where, interestingly, the stem vowel is raised in spite of the fact that the pronoun vowel is high and the vowel sequence disyllabic, as in (10) and (12). These examples, which are crucial to the point I want to make here regarding non-transparent constraint effects, are commonplace in Gere (see Paradis, 1983a: 141 ff.).

(13) a) /wɔ́-ι-'/ → [gɷ́ι̯] *[wɔ́ι̯] [gɔ́ι̯]   '(I) shout them'
     b) /wɔ́-ɷ-'/ → [gɷ́ɷ̯] *[wɔ́ɷ̯] *[gɔ́ɷ̯]   '(I) shout it'

Paradis (1983a; 1983b) shows that raising of the stem vowel is well accounted for if it is assumed that the surface disyllabic vowel sequences in (13) go through a (deeper-level monosyllabic) diphthong stage, as in (14), on p. 536. As already shown, a floating pronoun vowel, lacking a slot of its own, links to that of the stem vowel, thus forming a diphthong (14a). In the case at hand, the result is a violation of the Sonority Constraint, which prohibits non-rising diphthongs.[13] To satisfy the Sonority Constraint, the stem vowel raises (14b); however in so doing, it violates the OCP on [round] (see (3)), since high back vowels—in Gere as in most languages—are automatically [+round].[14] Repairing that violation is accomplished by delinking the feature [+round] from the onset consonant, yielding an unrounded *w*, represented here by *g* (14c).[15] When the Intransitive suffix MH is suffixed, it violates yet another constraint, the Tone Constraint in (2c) against tautosyllabic falling

---

[13] Like OCP, constraints in TCRS can trigger repairs (see Kaisse, 1987; Yip, 1988 for numerous examples of OCP yielding repairs) in addition to acting as blockers. As stated in Paradis (1988a; 1988b; 1993), repairs are caused by constraint violations, whose internal sources are: underlying illformedness; morphological operations; and constraint conflicts, the source of the violation here (the reader is referred to Paradis, 1993 for a discussion).

[14] No matter whether or not we assume that ɔ is specified underlyingly for [−round], it is reasonable to believe that rounding is accomplished by a redundancy rule of the type Ø → [+round]/[+back] [−low].

[15] A slight difference can be heard between the velar stop *g* and the unrounded glide *w*. However, since it is not central to our argument, I will ignore this distinction here.

tone sequences (14d).[16] To remedy the Tone Constraint violation, the Intransitive suffix MH is dissociated from the stem vowel slot, and linked to an epenthetic slot that yields, perforce, a distinct syllable (14e). This newly formed syllable is subsequently filled by the closest available vowel, here the second member of the diphthong. This analysis straightforwardly handles the fact that the stem vowel is raised in (13), despite the fact that the surfacing form is disyllabic, i.e. diphthongless, and the pronoun vowel [+ high].

(14) a. Suffixation of the   b. Stem vowel-raising   c. OCP on [round]
        pronoun and formation of   (repair): dissociation   (see (3)): [round]
        an ill-formed diphthong   of [−high] and default   delinking (repair)
        (Sonority Constraint)   insertion of [+ high][17]

   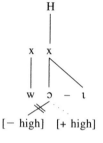   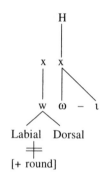

        d. Suffixation of the   e. Repair: insertion of a timing
        Intrasitive and   slot and dissociation of MH
        violation of the Tone   and the pronoun vowel from
        Constraint   the stem vowel's timing slot

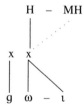   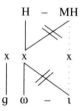

[16] Falling tone sequences such as H-MH/M or MH-M are permitted only if each tone is attached to a syllable of its own. Yet this is not the case of the underlying forms in (12), where the suffix vowel is slotless, and thus forms a diphthong with the stem vowel.

[17] Remember from (7) that the first vowel of a diphthong in Gere is realized as an on-glide. So even if raising does not entirely satisfy the Sonority Constraint here—since it yields a sequence of equal sonority—it is an essential prerequisite to vowel glidation, which finally lowers the sonority of the first vowel below that of the second vowel. Indeed, for a vowel to be turned into a glide, it has to be high. The on-glide is not heard in the form analysed in (14) because the diphthong is undone after a new syllable is inserted (14e) for tonal reasons. However, this point will not be further discussed, since it is rather orthogonal to the point this chapter aims at making.

The same thing happens to the MH tone stems in (15). An ill-formed diphthong is formed before the intransitive tone is suffixed, which yields vowel-raising in the first cycle, as in (14b). In the second cycle, the MH intransitive tone is suffixed—except that, here, its suffixation results in a sequence of two identical MH tones, and a violation of the OCP. To satisfy the OCP, the intransitive MH tone is replaced with a default M tone, thus yielding, at an intermediate stage, an impermissible tautosyllabic falling tone sequence (MH-M), similar to that in (14d). As in (14e), an epenthetic slot is inserted to preserve the Tone Constraint, with which the second member of the tone sequence and of the diphthong associate.

(15) a. /ɓɔ́-ι-'/ → [ɓω̄ι̂] *[ɓɔ̄ι̂] '(I) stop them'
     b. /ɓɔ́-ω-'/ → [ɓω̄ω̄] *[ɓɔ̄ω̄] '(I) stop it'
     c. /vlέ-ι-'/ → [vlíῑ] *[vlέῑ] '(I) cut them'
     d. /vlέ-ω-'/ → [vlī ω̄] *[vlέω̄] '(I) cut it'

What is of particular interest about the data in (13) and (15) is that there is no surface motivation for vowel-raising. Without positing an intermediate stage where the vowel sequences are diphthongized, the examples in (13) and (15) would be unexplainable. On the one hand, the vowel's not being diphthongized on the surface eliminates the Sonority Constraint as a potential cause at that level. On the other hand, the second vowel of the sequence being high precludes a potential effect of the Height Constraint. Indeed, the examples in (13) and (15) stand in marked contrast to the pattern observed in (10) and (12). In the latter, a non-high stem vowel does not raise when an autonomous high pronoun vowel (i.e. one with its own timing slot) is suffixed. One might conclude that vowel-raising in Gere is unsystematic, i.e. that the numerous forms of the kind exemplified in (13) and (15) are simply exceptions to the rule. However, this conclusion would be most unsatisfactory, since raising and non-raising are clearly conditioned in a very predictable way by tonal patterns and by the floating versus anchored status of the pronoun vowels, on the surface as well as during intermediate stages.

3. DERIVATIONAL VERSUS NON-DERIVATIONAL CONSTRAINT-BASED APPROACHES

Non-transparent constraint effects such as those of the Sonority Constraint in (13) and (15) are unproblematic in a derivational constraint-based approach like TCRS. The cyclic application of constraints—here the Sonority Constraint—handles the intermediate stage at which a diphthong is formed in those examples, as well as accounting for the heterosyllabicity of the vowel sequences on the surface, without additional tools. Now the question is: how can a filter-based theory such as OT, where constraints are typically uninvolved in the generation of forms (candidates), account in a principled way for vowel-raising in (13) and (15)? As shown in (16), Eval (/Con) in OT is the set of universal phonological filters which evaluate the whole candidate set generated by Gen, i.e. the place where phonological processes apply or, if one prefers, where inputs undergo modifications.

(16) The organization of phonology in OT

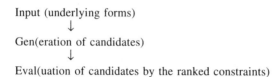

Input (underlying forms)
↓
Gen(eration of candidates)
↓
Eval(uation of candidates by the ranked constraints)

Eval, being a set of filters, has by definition no control over the phonological processes applying in Gen since it deals only with outputs of Gen.

3.1. *One-step assessment of Eval*

Let us first consider the possibility of having a one-step assessment, that is a constraint evaluation of the postlexical outputs. To select the good candidate in (13a), which is *gɔ́ɪ* (/wɔ́-ɪ-'/), the whole candidate set would have to be assessed globally, as in (17), by the filters of Eval. These are ranked on the left in the following tableaux for reasons of space. Note that Parse means 'no deletion' and Fill 'no insertion'; the tie bar under the vowels indicates a diphthong.

(17) One-step assessment → wrong candidate

input: /wɔ́ - ɪ - '/	wɔ̰ɪ	wɔ̰ɪ	gɔ́ɪ	gɔ̰ɪ	wɔ́ / wɪ́	wɔ̰ɪ	gɔ̰ɪ	gɔ̰ɪ	⇒ wɔ́ɪ	gɔ́ɪ
Tone Constraint							*!			
Parse (non-features)	*!	*!	*!	*!	**!	*!		*!		
Sonority Constraint	*		*			*				
OCP on round		*								
Fill (slot)						*			*	*
Parse (features)		*	*	**			**	**		**!

As we can see, the candidate selected in tableau (17) is *wɔ́ɪ*, i.e. the wrong candidate. Let us examine why. The candidate *gɔ̰ɪ* is rejected in (17) because it violates the Tone Constraint, one of the highest-ranked constraints—notice that the four top constraints are not crucially ordered with respect to each other, which is standardly expressed by the dotted line between the constraints. The other candidates, except the two last ones, are also discarded because they all violate the Parse non-feature constraint—another highly ranked constraint[18]—since in all cases the MH intransitive tone was unparsed (/deleted). In the case of wɔ́ / wɩ́, there is also a vowel missing. The struggle is thus between the two remaining candidates, wɔ́ɩ and gɔ́ɩ. They both infringe upon Fill, since they both undergo the epenthesis of a slot, but gɔ́ɩ violates an additional constraint, Parse features. These features are [+round] in the glide and [−high] in the vowel. Paradis and Prunet (1990) clearly show that the underspecified value of [high] in Gere vowels is [+high], not [−high]; otherwise, the Height Constraint could not operate as formulated in (2c).[19] This extra violation is fatal to gɔ́ɩ, no matter how we order the two constraints, i.e. with Fill ranked above Parse features, as in (17), or with Parse features ranked above Fill, as in (18).

(18) /wɔ́ - ɩ - ´/	gɔ́ɩ	wɔ́ɩ	wòɩ	gɔ̀ɩ	gòɩ	wɔ́ / wɩ́	wɔ́ɩ	gòɩ	⇒ wɔ́ɩ	gɔ́ɩ
Tone Constraint	*!									
Parse (non-features)		*!	*!	*!	*!	**!	*!	*!		
Sonority Constraint		*		*			*			
OCP on round		*								
Parse (features)	**		*	*	**			**		**!
Fill (slot)							*		*	*

This yields in both cases wɔ́ɩ as the winning candidate, which is, as already mentioned, the wrong candidate.

3.2. Two-step assessment of Eval

3.2.1. Assessment on a cyclic basis

Now let us examine whether a cyclic application of Eval would solve the problem, i.e. would be able to account for the non-transparent effects of the Sonority Constraint. For this, let us assume that Eval applies right after the pronoun vowel is suffixed, i.e. before the intransitive tone is inserted. The selection of gòɩ in (14c) would work as in (19).

---

[18] 'Parse non-features' is a simplified version of Parse tones, root nodes, and x-slots.

[19] Whether inputs are underspecified or not in OT has no bearing on the argument here, however, since the unparsed feature [−high] is underlying in one way or the other. If underspecification were to be disallowed, only the formulation of the Height Constraint would have to be slightly modified (see n. 3).

540 *Empirical Studies*

(19) First cycle assessment

/wɔ́ - ɪ/	gɔ̰́ɪ	wɔ̰́ɪ	wɔ̰̃ɪ	gɔ̰̃ɪ	wɔ́ / wɪ́	wɔ́ɪ	⇒ gɔ̰́ɪ
Fill (slot)	*!					*!	
Parse (non-features)					*!		
Sonority Constraint		*!		*!			
OCP on round			*!				
Parse (features)	**		*	*			**

The constraint ranking in (19)—where Fill is now the highest-ranked constraint—allows one to select the correct candidate, gɔ̰́ɪ, on the first cycle. This candidate is the one which violates only the lowest-ranked constraint in the constraint hierarchy, Parse features, while the other candidates all violate another constraint, ranked higher in the hierarchy.

(20) Second cycle assessment

/gɔ̰́ɪ - ´/	/gɔ̰́ɪ/	gɔ̰́ɪ	⇒ gɔ̰́ɪ´
Tone Constraint	*!		
Parse (non-features)		*!	
Fill (slot)			*

The selected candidate, gɔ̰́ɪ´, is the correct one, i.e. that with a H-MH heterosyllabic tone sequence. Thus a two-step application of Eval in terms of cycles seems to be able to account for the facts in Gere. This solution is not cost-free, however. First, a cyclic application of Eval renders OT more derivational (serial). Proponents of OT agree that a cyclic application of constraints would be a way of incorporating traditional derivational notions of phonology into OT. As stated by McCarthy (pers. comm.), this would be 'antithetical' to OT's programme. Second, the cyclic solution entails that Eval would have to apply to a non-surface-true form since gɔ̰́ɪ never surfaces as is, i.e. without the intransitive tone. It would be surprising, to say the least, for a filter-based framework to even consider outputs which are not surface-true. It follows from the fact that constraints can be outranked in OT that only a small number of constraints in Eval, i.e. the undominated ones, are expected to be surface-true. However, the candidates selected by Eval must all obligatorily be surface-true, given the non-serialism commitment of OT.

The cyclic option might have to face another (less apparent) problem. Notice that, no matter how Parse is split up in (19), Fill is ranked above all the Parse constraints. However, to derive the final output with the correct tone sequence on the second cycle in (20), this ordering has to be reversed. From the cyclic solution's perspective, this constitutes a ranking paradox akin to the ordering paradoxes that used to afflict standard theory. Recall that even in more traditional lexical approaches, rules are ordered in a given way within a reasonably broad lexical domain (i.e. a whole level at least), and no rule reordering is allowed to take place within that domain.

Of course, the reordering problem for the cyclic option disappears if a broader range of Parse constraints is posited. However, is such a solution really available or even desirable in the case at hand? One could argue that the Parse constraint involved in (20) is different from that in (19), since in (20) it targets tones, while in (19) the Parse constraints apply to root nodes and features. In other words, it could be argued that Parse segments (Parse non-features in (19)) and Parse tones (Parse non-features in (20)) are two different constraints, in which case their different ordering with respect to Fill would not be so surprising. Admittedly, Parse segments might be distinguished from Parse features, with the first one ranked higher since features are assembled into segments. But this is not the case with lexical tones and segments: tones are not part of segments, nor segments part of tones: both are independent and autonomous entities, equally basic and persistent. Dividing a constraint into several constraints inevitably increases the generative power of a grammar, since it multiplies the number of constraint ranking possibilities. Constraint-splitting, when it is unavoidable, must thus be done in a principled way. In the case at hand, it is therefore important to know whether the difference of ranking between Parse segments and Parse tones can be justified on independent grounds or if it is just a convenient descriptive device. After all, Parse means 'preservation of the phonological information contained in or morphologically attached to the input'. Why should segments be more prone to preservation than lexical tones? At least, in the absence of a cogent answer to this question, constraint-splitting—here and elsewhere—should be supported on typological grounds. In other words, one could ask here whether it is a general tendency across languages or in some given languages to give precedence to segment preservation over tone preservation, or if this would have to be an idiosyncrasy of Gere. At this stage, the options in the cyclic solution's perspective appear to be: (1) divide Parse into Parse segments and Parse tones, an alternative which would avoid the ranking paradox under discussion, but which remains to be independently justified in spite of the established use of constraint splitting in OT, or (2) rerank the constraints involved in (19) and (20) cyclically. No doubt this latter option would increase dramatically the derivational power of OT to an extent never reached even by standard Lexical Phonology, in addition to diminishing significantly the predictive power of the framework.

3.2.2. *Assessment on a level-ordered basis*

A partial solution would be to equate the cycles in (19) and (20) with distinct lexical/postlexical levels, since it is admitted by the proponents of OT that Eval can be sensitive to lexical levels: '[e]ach level constitutes a separate mini-phonology, just as in ordinary rule-based Lexical Phonology . . . Each level selects the candidate form that best satisfies its parochial constraint hierarchy' (McCarthy and Prince, 1993: 24).

However, this solution entails problems too. The first problem is empirical: there is no indication that lexical levels exist independently in Gere. As far as I know, these levels would have to be maintained for the sole purpose of the analysis here. Nor is there any indication that one of the suffixes could be concatenated at the lexical level and the other at the postlexical one. As mentioned in 2.3, the intransitive tone is suffixed at the end of intransitive verbs as well as transitive verbs with a clitic object pronoun. It is never found at the end of other objects, which indicates that clitic object pronouns and the Intransitive suffix are closely related, and hence are very likely to be both concatenated at the same level, which seriously challenges the level-ordered option.

However, let us assume the level-ordered option, just for the sake of argument. Eval would still have to apply to a non-surface-true form. As previously stated, the selected candidate on the first cycle, gǒ̰ṵ, never surfaces as is. This is why equating the cycles postulated in (19) and (20) with lexical/postlexical levels would represent only a partial solution for OT in the sense that it would indeed limit the amount of derivationality within OT but would not solve the non-transparency problem, i.e. the fact that the output of the first-step assessment is a non-surface-true form. The level-ordered option also raises a more fundamental question: what are the principled reasons to authorize Eval to apply at the end of levels but not cycles? Why the former morphological domain but not the latter? As far as I know, there is no formal reason ever invoked for doing so but the obvious fact that a cyclic application of Eval would render the framework even more derivational (serial) than it currently is with the level-ordered option. The current tolerance threshold to 'derivations' (serialism) in OT thus seems arbitrary, i.e. a subjective limit to derivation quantity. None the less, it must be clear that either option, cyclic or level-ordered, constitutes a two-step evaluation which is a 'derivational residue'.

4. ALTERNATIVES TO CYCLES AND LEVELS IN OT

It has been argued hitherto that resorting to multi-step constraint application in OT—although partly successful in describing the Gere facts—is not free of practical and conceptual problems, given OT's commitment to non-serialism.

Several attempts have been made in the last few years to get rid of serialism in OT, be it in the form of cycles or of levels. In the main, two devices have been resorted to—Alignment (e.g. McCarthy and Prince, 1994) and Identity constraints (e.g. Kenstowicz, 1995)—which I will consider in turn. It will be shown that both devices fail to handle the opaque effects of the undominated Sonority Constraint.

4.1. *Alignment*

Generalized Alignment is a family of constraints which deal with the correspondences between prosodic and morphological constituents. These constraints are often resorted to in OT to account for (apparent) cyclic effects (see the references in McCarthy and Prince, 1994: 2). Thus one could argue that problematic vowel-raising in (13) is due to the fact that the stem is not aligned with the morphological constituent because of the affixes appended. However, this solution could not be maintained here, since there is alignment in none of the examples under consideration, causative or non-causative. In other words, there is a systematic morphological break between the stem vowel and the pronoun vowel in all cases. More precisely, there is no more or less alignment in the examples in (13) than in those in (7)—if the comparison is to be made with non-causative forms—or those in (12)—if the comparison is to be made with causative forms. Since, on the one hand, vowel-raising applies in the examples in (7), which are monosyllabic, as it does in the examples (13), which are bisyllabic, and, on the other hand, vowel-raising fails to apply in the examples in (12), which are bisyllabic exactly like those in (13), the syllabic differences between all these forms cannot be adequately captured by OT. Syllabic differences are crucial for the derivational TCRS analysis provided in 2.3 but irrelevant to OT, since Eval—being confined to outputs—cannot make the connection between the number of syllables and vowel raising at the intermediate stages.

4.2. *Head Identity*

One might consider replacing cycles or levels with co-phonologies where Head Identity would be ranked differently in each co-phonology. Head Identity, like all Identity constraints, is an anti-allomorphy constraint or, put differently, a correspondence constraint which compares an output with another output, and requires that the head of a non-derived output be identical to that of a morphologically derived one. Thus one could argue that the causative forms pertain to a co-phonology where Head Identity is highly ranked (thus complied with), whereas the non-causative forms, be they monosyllabic as in (7) or bisyllabic as in (13), pertain to another co-phonology where Head Identity is ranked lower. This is exemplified in (21).

(21) a. Co-phonology with Head Identity unviolated: the causative forms in (12)
derived surface form: [wɔ́ɪ̯]   underived surface head: wɔ́

b. Co-phonology with Head Identity violated: the non-causative forms in (13)
derived surface form: [gɔ́ɪ̯]   underived surface head: wɔ́

This account would face several problems, though. First, Head Identity is not respected in the causative forms where the pronoun vowel is not high (cf. (8), where /zrɔ́ - CAUS - ɛ - ʹ/ → [zrœ̄ɛ́]). Second, vowel-raising fails to apply in non-causative bisyllabics where the pronoun vowel is high. As shown in (22), the behavior of non-causative bisyllabics and causatives is identical from this respect.

(22) a. Causatives

With a high pronoun vowel: no vowel-raising

/wɔ́ - CAUS - ɪ - ʹ/   →   [wɔ́ɪ̯] *[wǒɪ̯]   '(I) make them shout'
/wɔ́ - CAUS - ω - ʹ/   →   [wɔ́ὼ] *[wǒὼ]   '(I) make it shout'

With a non-high pronoun vowel: vowel-raising

/wɔ́ - CAUS - ɔ - ʹ/   →   [wɔ̌ɔ́] *[wɔ́ɔ̀]   '(I) make it shout'
/wɔ́ - CAUS - ɛ - ʹ/   →   [wœ̀ɛ́] *[wɔ́ɛ̀]   '(I) make it shout'

b. Non-causative bisyllabics

With a high pronoun vowel: no vowel-raising

/dèe - ɪ - ʹ/   →   [dēɪ́] *[dɪ̄ɪ́]   '(I) begin them'
/dèe - ω - ʹ/   →   [dēὼ] *[dɪ̄ὼ]   '(I) begin it'

With a non-high pronoun vowel: vowel-raising

/dèe - ɔ - ʹ/   →   [dɪ̄ɔ́] *[dēɔ̀]   '(I) begin it'
/dèe - ɛ - ʹ/   →   [dɪ̄ɛ́] *[dēɛ̀]   '(I) begin it'

The link between the causatives and the non-causative bisyllabics would be missed by the co-phonology solution, whereas it is straightforwardly handled by the TCRS derivational analysis proposed in 2.3. Non-causative bisyllabics do not undergo vowel-raising when the pronoun vowel is high, because they, like causatives, do not go through a diphthong stage, i.e. the stem and pronoun vowels can each anchor in an independent slot. When the pronoun vowel is not high, raising occurs because of the height constraint, not the sonority constraint. For the co-phonology solution, however, the facts in (8) and (22) would represent insurmountable problems.[20]

5. CYCLES/LEVELS VERSUS A GLOBAL DERIVATIONAL APPROACH

It thus appears that recourse to the first device examined to account for the Gere facts, i.e. cyclicity, is—although problematic in many respects for OT— hardly avoidable. Now the question is: is such recourse even sufficient? In

---

[20] Not to mention—from a more general perspective—that Head Identity, which is intended to avoid derivations, is not totally deprived of 'derivational residue'. As shown by Booij (Chapter 8 above), Head Identity entails that 'when a language has co-phonologies, complex words must be evaluated cyclically'.

other words, does allowing Eval to assess candidates on a cycle or even a level basis suffice, or do we need an approach which is more globally derivational? The facts reported by Goldsmith (1995) suggest that an openly derivational constraint-based theory might be more adequate than one which declares itself to be non-derivational and allows serialism only through a constraint evaluation per level. Cycles or levels can account for multi-step assessment within morphologically complex forms, but is unable to handle multi-step assessment within morphologically underived ones. Yet such cases exist. Goldsmith (1995) addresses the case of a tonal constraint in Mituku, a Bantu language, which does not hold at the surface. He cogently showed that its violation is not an example of a constraint simply failing to hold, i.e. an outranked constraint in OT's terms. As demonstrated by Goldsmith, the constraint does hold, exceptionlessly—it just does not hold on the surface: it holds at a slightly more abstract level. What is of particular interest about this case in Mituku is that the constraint in question applies intramorphemically, and has to be ordered with respect to another constraint which also applies intramorphemically. Thus recourse to cycles or lexical / postlexical levels as well as to typical OT alternatives such as Identity constraints and Alignment would be useless in this case, since no morphological break whatever is involved.

Even if the level-ordered option with constraint splitting and reranking—the solution most compatible with the OT framework—did not meet the problems pointed out above, it is not obvious that a plainly derivational constraint-based theory like TCRS is not better fitted to handle the facts in Gere, i.e. more explanatory. For the sake of the exposition, let us reconsider the constraint-splitting issue. As already mentioned in section 3.2.1, extrinsic constraint-rerankings on a cycle or level basis could be avoided if a principled reason for splitting Parse into Parse segments and Parse tones could be advanced. Therefore no constraint-reranking would be necessitated. In a more general perspective, the question behind this problem—which is as valid for TCRS as for OT—is why is a floating tone more entitled or prone to receive its own timing unit (see (14e)), which violates Fill, than a floating segment (see (14b)), which abides by Fill? Why is the nature of the tone not merely changed, i.e. why is the MH intransitive tone not replaced with a L tone, for instance, which would yield a permitted falling tone sequence—similarly to what happens to the vowels involved in an ill-formed diphthong—instead of being anchored in an epenthetic slot? As seen, a mid vowel is raised when it constitutes the first element of a diphthong. While OT would most likely resort to constraint-splitting to handle the differences of behaviour between tones and segments— a powerful and essentially descriptive device as long as it is not independently justified—the reason for such differences of behaviour might lie in the fact that segments are decomposable entities, i.e. they are made of nodes and features which can be modified, while tones are generally assumed not to be. In this perspective, changing a tone is perceived as the equivalent of losing it, whereas changing a segment is viewed as a more or less minor modification within the segment, as long as its root node is not deleted.[21]

Assuming that this explanation is valid, however, it is not clear how it can be dealt with or even implemented in OT. Splitting Parse into Parse tone and Parse segment, in order to rank them differently, leaves the explanation provided above completely aside, since constraint-splitting as it currently functions in OT is, as already mentioned, essentially descriptive—for instance, it does not explain why tone preservation is more important than segment preservation—despite the efforts of some authors to restrain or prohibit some constraint rankings within families of constraints such as Parse (see Itô and Mester, 1995; Smolensky, 1995). In contrast, the non-insertion/insertion of a timing slot in (19) and (20) is predicted by TCRS without any extra tool, i.e. from the general principles of the framework. To this effect, I will first present a brief overview of its most basic mechanisms.

As already mentioned, constraints in TCRS are preserved by repair strategies which apply minimally, according to the Minimality Principle in (23).

(23) Minimality Principle: Repairs
    (a) apply at the lowest phonological level to which the violated constraint refers
    and (b) involve as few strategies (steps) as possible.

The lowest phonological level is determined by the Phonological Level Hierarchy in (24). Note that this scale simply reflects the phonological organization required independently of TCRS, where the metrical level is the most important or 'organizational' level, and the terminal feature level the least.

(24) Phonological Level Hierarchy: Metrical level > syllabic level > skeletal level >
    root node > non-terminal feature > terminal feature.

Repairs are also governed by the Preservation Principle in (25).

(25) Preservation Principle: Underlying phonological information is maximally
    preserved.

Now let us reconsider (14a), where the pronoun vowel is unlicensed underlyingly. There are three ways of solving the problem: by inserting a timing unit and attaching it to the pronoun vowel; by anchoring the pronoun vowel in the stem vowel's timing slot; or by deleting the pronoun vowel. The first solution could be the one selected if Gere did not allow diphthongs. However, since it does, the second appears as the most minimal one in the view of the Minimality Principle. According to the Phonological Level Hierarchy in (24), a

[21] Tone modification is commonplace across languages—indeed, tone deletion applies to the MH tone in (15), which is replaced with a default M tone for dissimilation purpose. It also frequently occurs for harmony purposes across languages or because of language-specific constraints on tone sequences. However, I maintain that tone modification is a last-resort device, in contrast to segment modification.

change at the feature level is less dramatic than one at the skeletal (timing slot or mora) level. As for the third solution (deletion of the pronoun vowel), it is rejected by the Minimality Principle since it would needlessly violate the Preservation Principle—more or less the equivalent of general Parse in OT—at a higher level, i.e. the segment level, than the second solution, which violates the Preservation Principle only at the feature level (with [−high] delinking).

In contrast, the rescue of the unlicensed MH intransitive tone in (14d) faces fewer options. Since tones are indivisible entities, only two repairs can be considered: deletion of the MH tone, or insertion of a timing slot to anchor the floating tone. Both solutions are equally minimal, but since the latter is more 'preservative' in the view of the Preservation Principle, it is the one which is selected. One could object, though, that the behaviour of the MH tone in (14) differs from that of the MH tone in (15), where the first option (deletion of the tone) is selected. The answer to this objection lies in the fact that the MH tone of the intransitive does not violate the same constraint in the two cases: in (14) it violates the Tone Constraint (2c), while in (15) it infringes upon the OCP. While the former constraint can be satisfied with the addition of a new syllable—the Tone Constraint refers to syllabicity (see (2c)), the latter cannot; the lowest level it refers to, according to the Minimality Principle, is the tone level. In other words, deletion of the tone in (15) is the only option. This is predicted by TCRS on the basis of universal principles. In OT, however, it would have to be treated as an idiosyncrasy of Gere in terms of language-specific constraint-splitting and ranking.

6. Conclusion

I have endeavoured to show that the non-transparent effects of the unviolated Sonority Constraint in Gere provide evidence of the need for a cyclic application of constraints. OT's usual alternatives to cyclicity, Identity constraints and Alignment, have proved inadequate to handle the Gere facts. We have also seen that the level-ordered option, although the most attractive alternative at first sight in OT's view, can hardly be invoked, since the Intransitive suffix and the clitic object pronouns are most likely appended at the same level.

However, a cyclic application of constraints is not the panacea, since it is not easily compatible with OT's thesis. First, conceptually, it seriously under-mines the declared aserialism of OT. If we accept that constraints may refer to a serial device such as the morphological cycle, can we establish a non-arbitrary limit to serialism? Unless this question is directly and seriously addressed, OT risks being stripped of its essential claims. Second, constraint evaluation on a cyclic basis, no more than one on a level basis, cannot deal with the fact that the (intermediate) output in (19) is not surface-true. This is a serious problem for OT since Eval, by definition, can only select candidates which are surface-true; indeed, the constraints of Eval are not supposed to be able to make reference to phonological information that never comes to the surface. Finally, a constraint evaluation on a cyclic basis as well as on a level one entails, in the case examined, drawbacks such as (so far) unprincipled constraint-splitting or extrinsic constraint-reranking, both of which are easily replaceable by more explanatory devices in a derivational constraint-based framework such as TCRS.

The chapter's specific goal has been to demonstrate the need for constraint cyclicity, a tool that is antithetical to a non-derivational constraint-based theory. Its broader goal has been to show the superiority of a derivational constraint-based approach over a non-derivational one. I have not sought to improve on non-derivational theories in general, or OT in particular—the task is left to advocates of a non-derivational view. From a more general perspective, it is important to remember that, although theory-internal criticism is both necessary and fruitful, phonological theory benefits most when particular theories are criticized from outside as well. What is offered here, then, is an external alternative to a non-derivational constraint-based view.

ACKNOWLEDEGMENTS

I am very grateful to Darlene LaCharité for her numerous and detailed comments on several versions of this chapter. I have also greatly benefited from the illuminating comments of Iggy Roca, the editor of this volume, and Geert Booij, and from discussions with John Goldsmith at the Chicago Society Linguistic Meeting in April 1995 and at the Royaumont Conference in June 1995. Finally, I am indebted to two reviewers, (one of them Doug Pulleyblank), and to Eliane Lebel, my research assistant. I remain solely responsible for the views expressed here, as well as for any remaining errors or omissions. I acknowledge SSHRC grant 410–94–1296 and FCAR grant 95–ER-2305.

REFERENCES

Goldsmith, J. (1995). 'Tone in Mituku: How a floating tone nailed down an intermediate level'. Paper presented at the international congress of Abbaye de Royaumont: Current Trends in Phonology, Royaumont, June. Published in J. Durand and B. Laks, (eds.), (1996), *Current Trends in Phonology: Models and Methods*. Salford: Salford University Press, 267–80.
Harris, J. (1994). *English Sound Structure*. Oxford: Blackwell.
Itô, J., and Mester, A. R. (1995). 'The core–periphery structure of the lexicon and constraints on reranking', *UMass Occasional Papers in Linguistics*, 181–210.

Kaisse, E. (1987). 'Modern Greek continuant dissimilation and the OCP'. Paper presented at the Western Conference on Linguistics, Seattle, Oct. MS. University of Washington.

Kaye, J. and Lowenstamm, J. (1980). Phonological courses. University of Quebec, Montreal.

Kenstowicz, M. (1994). *Phonology in Generative Grammar*. Cambridge, Mass.: Blackwell.

—— (1995). 'Cyclic vs. non-cyclic constraints evaluation', *Phonology* **12**: 397–436.

McCarthy, J. and Prince, A. (1993). 'Prosodic Morphology I: Constraint Interaction and Satisfaction'. MS, University of Massachusetts, Amherst, and Rutgers University.

—— —— (1994). 'Generalized alignment', in G. Booij and J. van Marle (eds.), *Morphology Yearbook 1993*. Dordrecht: Kluwer, 79–103.

Mohanan, K. P. (1986). *The Theory of Lexical Phonology*. Dordrecht: Reidel.

Paradis, C. (1983a). *Description phonologique du guéré*. Abidjan: Presses de l'Université d'Abidjan.

—— (1983b). 'La règle d'élision syllabique et les séquences vocaliques en guéré', in J. Kaye, H. Koopman, D. Sportiche, and A. Dugas (eds.), *Current Approaches to African Linguistics*, ii. Dordrecht: Foris, 181–193.

—— (1988a). 'Towards a theory of constraint violations'. *McGill Working Papers in Linguistics* **5**: 1–43.

—— (1988b). 'On constraints and repair strategies', *The Linguistic Review* **6**: 71–97.

—— (1988c). 'Les paramètres négatifs ou les contraintes particulières dans la grammaire universelle'. Paper presented at the annual congress of the Canadian Linguistics Association, Windsor (Ont.), Canada.

—— (1990). 'Focus in Gere configurational constraints', in J. Hutchison and V. Manfredi (eds.), *Current Approaches to African Linguistics*. Dordrecht: Foris, 53–63.

—— (1993). 'Ill-formedness in the dictionary: a source of constraint violation', in Paradis and LaCharité (1993).

—— (1995). 'Derivational constraints in phonology: evidence from loanwords and implications', in A. Dainora, R. Hemphill, B. Luka, B. Need, and S. Pargman (eds.), *Proceedings of the 31st Chicago Linguistic Society Meeting*. Chicago: Chicago Linguistic Society, 360–74.

—— (1996). 'The inadequacy of faithfulness and filters in loanword adaptation', in J. Durand and B. Laks (eds.), *Current Trends in Phonology*. Salford: Salford University Press, 509–534.

—— and LaCharité, D. (eds.) (1993). *Constraint Based Theories in Multilinear Phonology*. Canadian Journal of Linguistics 38(2): 127–303.

—— —— (1995). 'Saving and cost in French loanword adaptation in Fula: predictions of the TCRS-loanword model', *McGill Working Papers in Linguistics* **11**: 46–84.

—— —— (1997). 'Preservation and minimality in loanword adaptation', *Journal of Linguistics* **33**(1).

—— and Prunet, J.-F. (1988). 'Locality in a theory of constraint violations'. Paper presented at Glow, Budapest, Hungaria, March.

—— —— (1990). 'On explaining some OCP violations'. *Linguistic Inquiry* **21**(3): 456–66.

Prince, A., and Smolensky, P. (1993). 'Optimality Theory: Constraint Interaction in Generative Grammar'. MS, Rutgers University and University of Colorado at Boulder.

Pulleyblank, D. (1986). *Tone in Lexical Phonology*. Dordrecht: Kluwer.

Smolensky, P. (1995). 'On the internal structure of CON in UG', *GLOW Newsletter* **34**: 70.

Yip, M. (1988). 'The obligatory contour principle and phonological rules: a loss of identity', *Linguistic Inquiry* **19**: 65–100.

18

Extrasyllabic Consonants in Polish: Derivational Optimality Theory

JERZY RUBACH

1. INTRODUCTION

This chapter examines the treatment of extrasyllabic consonants in two frameworks: Derivational Theory (DT) and Optimality Theory (OT). The choice of Polish as the source of data has been made for several reasons. First, Polish has a rich system of extrasyllabic consonants. Second, their distribution is complex in the sense that they are not limited to some special position in the word. Third, they interact with assimilation rules, in particular with Final Devoicing, Regressive Assimilation and Progressive Devoicing. Each of these facts puts Polish in the position of an interesting language, since, as I explain below, languages have typically rather restricted systems and simple strategies for dealing with extrasyllabic consonants.

Extrasyllabic consonants are a by-product of syllabification. Universal and language-specific rules and constraints determine what constitutes a well-formed syllable in a given language. Most prominent here is the universal constraint due to Jespersen (1904) that was called by Selkirk (1980) the Sonority Sequencing Generalization. Building on the Sonority Hierarchy (Whitney, 1874; Sievers, 1881), this constraint defines onsets and codas in terms of decreasing sonority, with the most sonorous segments closest to the syllable nucleus and the less sonorous segments further away from the nucleus.

(1) Sonority Sequencing Generalization (SSG)
Stop–Fricative–Nasal–Liquid–Nucleus–Liquid–Nasal–Fricative–Stop

SSG leads to the syllabification of the English word *ulcer* as *ul.cer*, because [ls-] would not be well-formed.[1] A constraint specific to English prohibits stop-nasal onsets, even though such onsets are well-formed from the point of view of SSG. Consequently, *acknowledge* has a syllable boundary between [k] and [n]. In *know*, [k] cannot go into the coda, because there is no syllable to the

---

[1] English maximizes onsets, but in doing so it must observe universal and language-specific constraints; hence the syllabification *ul.cer* rather than *u.lcer*.

left of [k]. Therefore [k] remains unsyllabified (that is, [k] is extrasyllabic) and deletes (Stray Erasure). Deletion is one way of dealing with extrasyllabic consonants. However, more interesting are the cases in which consonants surface phonetically in spite of the fact that they are extrasyllabic. This is possible if a language has a rule of adjunction. Such rules, by definition, override all universal and language-specific constraints and, by brute force, include offending segments into prosodic structure. A case in point is the treatment of final consonants in words such as *fact* and *depth* and, most spectacularly, in *sixths*. Assuming that SSG does not tolerate sonority plateaus, the clusters constitute ill-formed codas: [-kt], [-pθ], [-ksθs]. Consequently, the offending consonants [t], [θ], and [sθs], respectively, are extrasyllabic. However, in surface representation, these consonants must be somehow included into prosodic structure, because only then can they escape Stray Erasure and thus be pronounced (Steriade, 1982; Itô, 1986). The desired effect is achieved by postulating a rule of adjunction which prosodifies extrasyllabic consonants by putting them into a syllable appendix (Fudge, 1969; Fujimura and Lovins, 1978; Halle and Vergnaud, 1980). The consonants that are subject to adjunction in English have a certain property in common: they are all anterior coronal obstruents. We are looking here at a typical situation: an adjunction rule is restricted to a certain class of segments. However, adjunction rules are not always restricted in such ways. For example, in Slovak extrasyllabic segments are drawn from more than one class of segments and they need not have a similar place of articulation.[2]

The following words from Slovak are all monosyllabic:

(2)   rmut 'sadness', rdest 'water-pepper', lkat' 'sob', mzda 'salary'

The initial consonants violate SSG and hence cannot be syllabified. Yet they are pronounced. The problem is solved by postulating an adjunction rule. As observed by Rubach (1993), this rule, while covering all kinds of segments, is clearly defined in terms of position. It affects only and exclusively word-initial segments.

Polish extrasyllabic segments form a richer system than those of English and Slovak. All kinds of consonants can be extrasyllabic (3a), but their distribution is not limited to the word-initial position; for example, [r] occurs in a variety of different configurations (3b).

(3)   a. rdest 'water-pepper', lśnić 'shine', mdły 'nauseous'
       b. rtęć 'mercury', Piotrków (place name), Piotr 'Peter'[3]

---

[2] Levin (1985) shows that it is difficult to proscribe adjunction to specific consonant classes cross-linguistically.

[3] Extrasyllabic consonants need not occur at morpheme edges, as shown by e.g. *Piotrków* (place-name), *krnąbrn+y* 'unruly', *Siedlc+e* (place-name); see also the words in (9) below.

The curiosity raised by distributional facts is further enhanced by the role that extrasyllabic consonants play in voice assimilation. These matters will be the focus of our discussion.

In section 2 I review the facts and state generalizations in terms of Derivational Theory. The same generalizations are then reconsidered in section 3, which proposes an analysis in terms of Optimality Theory. Section 4 summarizes the most important conclusions.

2. DERIVATIONAL THEORY (DT)

The basic facts of Polish voice assimilation are straightforward. Obstruents are devoiced word-finally (4). Elsewhere, they are subject to assimilation, an obstruent-to-obstruent process, which can be either regressive (5) or progressive (6) (NB. y = [ɨ]).

(4) Final Devoicing
klub + y [b] 'club' (nom.pl.)—klub [p] (nom.sg.), majonez + y [z] 'mayonnaise'—majonez [s] (nom.sg.), staw + y [v] 'pond' (nom.pl.)—staw [f] (nom.sg.)

Regressive Voice Assimilation applies both inside words and across word boundaries.

(5) a. Devoicing
grzyb + y [b] 'mushrooms'—grzyb + k + i [p + c] (diminutive)
hard + y [d] 'arrogant'—hard + sz + y [t + š][4]
rajd + y [d] 'trips'—rajd studencki [t st] 'student trip'
obraz + y [z] 'pictures'—obraz pokoju [s p] 'a picture of a room'
   b. Voicing
pros + i + ć [ç] 'ask'—proś + b + a [ʑ + b] 'request'
licz + y + ć [tˢ] (spelled *cz*)—licz + b + a [dᶻ + b] 'number'
las + y [s] 'forests'—las dębowy [z d] 'oak forest'
tort + y [t] 'cakes'—tort brzoskwiniowy [d b] 'apricot cake'

Progressive assimilation is subject to several restrictions. First, it targets fricatives only. Second, it is a word-level rule, that is, it does not apply across word boundaries. Third, the structural change is limited to devoicing.[5]

---

[4] I adopt the convention of enclosing underlying representations in double slashes, intermediate representations in single slashes, and surface representations in square brackets. The following transcription symbols require explanation: [tˢ dᶻ]: alveolar affricates; [š ž]: postalveolar fricatives; [tˢ dᶻ]: postalveolar affricates; [ç ʑ]: prepalatal fricatives; [tᶜ dᶻ ɲ]: prepalatal affricates and nasal; [c ɟ]: postpalatal stops.
[5] Crucially, Progressive Devoicing is a word-level process while Regressive Voice Assimilation is postlexical. This means that in the domain of words the [− voice] [+ voice] disagreement is resolved in favour of Progressive Devoicing; see Booij and Rubach (1987) and Rubach (1996).

(6) Progressive Devoicing

modlitewn + y [tev] 'prayer' (Adj.)—modlitw + a [tf]: *tev → tv → tf*
sakiew + ek [cev] 'bag' (diminutive gen.pl.)—sakw + a [kf] 'bag' (nom.sg.):
kev → kv → kf, and others (see Rubach, 1996)

The behavior of extrasyllabic consonants *vis-à-vis* voice assimilation is illustrated in (7), (8), and (9), which correspond to (4), (5), and (6).

(7) Final Devoicing

kandelabr + y [br] 'lamp' (nom.pl.)—kandelabr [pr] (nom.sg.), katedr + a [dr]
'cathedral'—katedr [tr] (gen.pl.), namydl + i + ć [dl] 'to soap'—namydl [tl]
(imper.), mog + ł + a [gw] 'she could'—móg + ł [kw] 'he could', ojczyzn + a
[zn] 'your country'—ojczyzn [sn] (gen.pl.), przyjaźn + ie [ʐɲ] 'friendship'
(nom.pl.)—przyjaźń [çɲ] (nom.sg.)

Evidently, extrasyllabic consonants are unable to block Final Devoicing. The rule operates as if these consonants were not there. This generalization extends to both Regressive Voice Assimilation and Progressive Devoicing.

(8) Regressive Voice Assimilation
  a. Devoicing
    mędrek [drek] 'crafty person'—mędrk + a [trk] (gen.sg.)
    Siedlec [dletˢ] (place name, gen.pl.)—Siedlc + e [tltˢ] (nom.sg.)
    źdźbł + o [bw] 'stalk'—ździebł + k + o [pwk] (diminutive)
    modl + i + ć się [dl] 'pray'—módl się [tl ç] (imper.)
    przyjaźn + ie [ʐɲ] 'friendships'—przyjaźń polsko-angielska [çɲ p] 'Polish–
    English friendship'
  b. Voicing
    plot + ą [t] 'they weave'—plót + ł + by [dwb] 'he would weave'
    wiatr + y [tr] 'wind'—wiatr zachodni [dr z] 'western wind'
    czasopism + o [sm] 'journal'—czasopism zawodowych [zm z] 'professional
    journal' (gen.pl.)
    taśm + a [çm] 'ribbon'—taśm biurowych [ʐm b] 'office ribbons' (gen.pl.)
    pieśn + i [çɲ] 'song' (nom.pl.)—pieśń bojowa [ʐɲ b] 'war song'

Progressive Devoicing is also insensitive to the presence of extrasyllabic consonants:

(9) Progressive Devoicing

krew + n + y [krev] 'relative'—krw + i [krf] 'blood' (gen.sg.): *krev → krv →
krf*,[6] plw + a + ć [plf] 'spit' (figurative)—s + pluw + a + ć [pluv] 'spit' as well
as non-alternating trwa + ć [trf] 'last', trwog + a [trf] 'fright', and others

---

[6] The hypothesis that the underlying segment is //f// rather than //v// and we have voicing, *f → v*, in *krew+n+y* 'relative' is not an option. This is shown by a minimal contrast between *krew+n+y* [v] and *tref+n+y* [f] 'illegal'. Furthermore, an attempt to derive /v/ from //w// would also be on the wrong track, see Rubach (1996).

The behavior of extrasyllabic consonants towards voice assimilation has been the subject of much debate in recent literature.[7] This debate—introduced originally in a paper by Rubach and Booij (1990b)—has been continued by Bethin (1992), Gussmann (1992), Lombardi (1991) and Rubach (1996). A unifying characteristic of these articles is that they are all set in terms of Derivational Theory, and thus precede Optimality Theory.[8]

Two central questions are raised by extrasyllabic consonants. First, how can we account for transparency effects[9] with regard to voice assimilation? Second, what is the prosodic status of extrasyllabic consonants? That is, where in the prosodic structure do they belong? Notice that they must be somehow included into prosodic structure because they are pronounced. Given that they cannot be syllabified by regular syllabification rules, we are looking at a process of adjunction.

A fruitful line of reasoning with regard to transparency effects is prompted by Final Devoicing. The dilemma is how to make this rule applicable not only to *klub* [klup] 'club' but also to *kandelabr* [kandelapr] 'lamp' and *mechanizm* [mexaɲism] 'mechanism'. A common denominator for these cases is provided by syllabification. In a derivational account, there is a stage at which //b// and //z// are word-final in all the three cases. This stage is found after the regular syllabification rules have applied and the syllables have been gathered into phonological words (PW).[10]

(10)

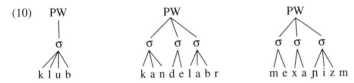

The final consonants *r* and *m* are not syllabified, because they violate SSG which governs regular syllabification. Consequently, *b* and *z* are final, albeit in terms of phonological rather than morphological words. If we make a rather

---

[7] Only sonorants can be extrasyllabic in Polish. This follows from the fact that Polish suspends SSG in the class of obstruents. That is, stops and fricatives occur regularly in either order in onsets and codas, and plateaus are tolerated. See Rubach and Booij (1990a).

[8] The derivational analysis presented in this section follows, for the most part, Rubach and Booij (1990b) and Rubach (1996). For a critique of other analyses, see Rubach (1996).

[9] Transparency effects in Slavic voice assimilation were first analyzed in generative terms by Hayes (1984), who looked at Russian. The reader should be cautioned that the Russian data differ from the Polish data. Specifically, if Hayes is right, Russian does not exhibit the blocking effects discussed for Polish in (16) below. It is unlikely that Hayes's analysis of Russian could be used for Polish. First, as I point out below, Polish voice assimilation is sensitive to syllable structure. Second, [voice] plays a phonological role in Polish sonorants; see the discussion in connection with Initial Voice (39) below and note 31. In this chapter I focus on the prosodic status of extrasyllabic consonants, because, once this has been interpreted correctly, the spreading of [voice] should not present difficulty.

[10] I ignore feet as they play no role in the analysis of segmental phenomena in Polish.

uncontroversial assumption that Final Devoicing looks at phonological constituency, then the devoicing of //b// to [p] and //z// to [s] is accounted for.

The line of reasoning made explicit by Final Devoicing can be extended to word-internal clusters in (8) and (9). Also there we have a derivational stage at which prosodic structure has been erected by the regular rules, and extrasyllabic consonants remain unprosodified because they violate SSG. At this stage *mędrka*[11] 'crafty person' (gen.sg.) is represented as follows:

(11)

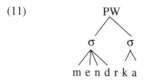

The segments that participate in Regressive Voice Assimilation, /d/ as an input and /k/ as the environment, share a common property: they are included in the prosodic structure. This situation parallels that of (10) in the sense that voice assimilation operates on prosodified segments. What remains mysterious is how [−voice] can spread from /k/ to /d/ across /r/.[12]

The spreading of [voice] takes place at the laryngeal tier. It is therefore there that /d/ and /k/ must be adjacent. This leads to the conclusion that /r/ should not have any representation at the laryngeal tier when voice assimilation takes effect.[13] That is, the desired representation of the cluster /drk/ is as follows:

(12)   d r k
       | |
       L   L
       | |
      +v   −v

How can we obtain this representation? An answer lies in the distinct role that [voice] plays in obstruents and in sonorants.

As is evident from the preceding discussion, Polish contrasts voiced and voiceless obstruents, for example, *bo* 'because'—*po* 'after'. Sonorants are different, because they are invariably voiced (but see below). This is a typical situation. It is accounted for by a universal default rule that assigns [+voice] to sonorants. The consequence of Sonorant Default is that sonorants are unspecified for [voice] in the underlying representation. Now we seem to have found a way of obtaining the representation in (12). What is required

---

[11] The letter *ę* represents a sequence of the vowel [e] plus a nasal consonant that shares the place of articulation with the following stop.

[12] Rubach (1996) has shown that [voice] must be regarded as binary rather than as privative.

[13] Here and below we shall look at [r] as an example, but the generalizations that refer to extrasyllabic *r* refer also to other extrasyllabic segments; see (7–9) above and (16) below.

is an assumption that Sonorant Default applies after Regressive Voice Assimilation. Then, /r/ is unspecified for [voice] and thus transparent.

However, close examination of this reasoning reveals an error in the analysis. If sonorants are unspecified for [voice] when Regressive Voice Assimilation applies, then not only the /r/ in /mendrka/ but also the sonorants in, for example, *barka* 'barge' are predicted to be transparent. Regressive Voice Assimilation would then devoice the /b/ under the influence of /k/, but this is incorrect. The correct generalization is that only the sonorants which have not been included into prosodic structure are transparent, e.g. the /r/ in /mendrka/ but not the /r/ and the /a/ in /barka/.[14] We conclude that Sonorant Default is sensitive to prosodic structure.

(13) Sonorant Default: Assign [+ voice] to prosodified sonorants

To summarize, the transparency of extrasyllabic consonants is accounted for by making two assumptions. First, Sonorant Default applies before Regressive Voice Assimilation but is unable to affect segments that have not been prosodified. Second, syllabification is governed by SSG and, consequently, not all segments can be syllabified. An outstanding question is how these segments are represented in surface structure. It is clear that they must ultimately be included into prosodic structure by an adjunction rule, but is it an adjunction to the coda, as in English, or to the onset, as in Slovak? Enlightening in the resolution of this dilemma are native-speaker intuitions about syllabification.[15]

Experimental evidence adduced by Rubach and Booij (1990*b*) shows that speakers are confused about the assignment of SSG offenders to syllables. These segments are perceived sometimes as belonging to the onset and sometimes as belonging to the coda. Such confusion can occur in the speech of a single informant. How can this be explained? One possibility is to assume that adjunction is optional; but then we would have to assume an overriding principle that one of the choices, adjunction to the onset or adjunction to the coda, must be selected. The point is that segments cannot be left unprosodified in surface representation. Another possibility afforded by DT is to assume two adjunction rules. One of them would be obligatory and the other optional. Then a segment adjoined first, for example, to the coda could subsequently be drawn into the onset. The confusion of native speakers with regard to syllabification might be explained as reflecting different derivational stages of prosodification. However, Rubach and Booij (1990*b*) do not find any of these accounts appealing, and suggest that extrasyllabic segments are adjoined directly to the phonological word node (PW). This is sufficient to save them from Stray

---

[14] Floating vowels (unvocalized yers) are also transparent; see note 17.

[15] I assume that, given several descriptively adequate options, it is preferable to choose the structure that is entirely consistent with native speaker intuitions.

Erasure. The confusion of native speakers is now clear, since SSG offenders do not belong to any syllable. The relevant adjunction rule is (14).

(14) Default Adjunction: Adjoin extrasyllabic consonants to PW

This rule derives the surface representation of /mendrka/ in (15).

(15)

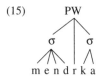

The assignment of [voice] to *r* is an open question. One might assume that Sonorant Default can reapply but, in the case of /mendrka/, it is blocked by the familiar 'no crossing of the lines' constraint. Indeed, the [r] in [mentrka] is voiceless. However, the facts of voicing in the instance of word-internal and word-final extrasyllabic segments are unclear and not well understood. They are obscured by stylistically conditioned tempo-sensitive variation (Wierzchowska, 1971; Rubach and Booij, 1990*b*). Briefly, [r] is normally voiceless in devoicing contexts; however, [l] may be but need not be. On the other hand, nasals are more often voiced than voiceless. There is no good understanding as to how these facts can be handled in a phonological analysis. The suggestion of Lombardi (1991), Bethin (1992), and Rubach (1996) is to relegate the devoicing of sonorants from phonology to the realm of phonetic implementation, a position that I shall also adopt here.[16]

The interest of looking at extrasyllabic consonants goes beyond transparency effects. An observation due to Rubach and Booij (1990*b*) and adopted subsequently by other authors is that word-initial sonorants are not transparent to voice assimilation. In contrast to (8b), voicing does not occur in phrases such as the following:

(16) rak rdzenia [k rdᶻ] 'spinal cord cancer', stek łgarstw [k wg] 'pack of lies', odgłos rżenia [s rž] 'sound of neighing', nawrót mżawki [t mž] 'return of drizzle', czas mgły [s mgw] 'the time of fog'

Following the logic adopted in the analysis of transparency effects, the blocking of Regressive Voice Assimilation in (16) must be ascribed to the lack of adjacency of the relevant nodes at the laryngeal tier. That is, it must be assumed that the consonant cluster of *rak rdzenia* 'spinal cord cancer' has

---

[16] Let me note that for all the instances discussed here, the prediction which is made is correct: extrasyllabic sonorants are devoiced in devoicing contexts, as in /mendrka/ → [mentrka] 'crafty person' (see above) and /krvi/ → [krfi] 'blood' (gen.sg.; see below). More generally, since no theory provides a complete account of the sonorant voicing facts, these facts, paradoxically, lose relevance as essential evidence.

the representation in (17) at the stage when Regressive Voice Assimilation applies.

(17)   k   r   d^z
        | | |
        L   L   L
        | | |
       −v   +v   +v

Regressive Voice Assimilation, an obstruent-to-obstruent rule, cannot apply because the laryngeal nodes of /d^z /, the environment, and /k/, the input, are not adjacent. Spreading is blocked by the 'no crossing of lines' constraint. The only remaining question is how to obtain the representation in (17). An answer is prompted by Sonorant Default.

Given that only prosodified sonorants are specified for [voice], it follows that the *r* in (17) must be prosodified. The required prosodification cannot be effected by Default Adjunction, since word-initial extrasyllabic consonants, as in (17), must be prosodified prior to Regressive Voice Assimilation, and Default Adjunction is ordered after Regressive Voice Assimilation. Rubach and Booij's (1990*b*) proposal is to introduce rule (18).

(18) Initial Adjunction: Adjoin a word-initial extrasyllabic consonant to PW.

Initial Adjunction is motivated independently of the voice transparency facts by two other generalizations. First, Polish restricts syllabification to the domain of words, as I clarify in (28) below. This restriction is understandable if we have rule (18) and if this rule is lexical rather than postlexical. Second, geminates (more exactly, pseudogeminates; see Rubach and Booij, 1990*b*) are permitted in two positions only: intervocalically and word-initially, as in *lasso* 'lasso', *flotylla* 'fleet', *ssać* 'suck', and *dżdżownica* [d^{ž}d^ž] 'earthworm'. Intervocalic geminates are to be expected, because they can be heterosyllabic. Word-initial geminates would be surprising if not for the fact that Polish has rule (18).

Rubach and Booij (1990*b*) point out that Initial Adjunction is a postcyclic lexical rule while Default Adjunction is postlexical. (This conclusion follows from the different domains of application: word level versus phrase level.) Regressive Voice Assimilation is also postlexical, because it applies across word boundaries. Now the ordering of Initial Adjunction before Regressive Voice Assimilation follows from the model of Lexical Phonology, in particular from the precedence of the lexical component over the postlexical component.

To summarize the discussion of extrasyllabic consonants, we look at the derivation of *mędrka* 'crafty person' (gen.sg.), *Piotr zawołał* 'Peter called', and *rak rdzenia* 'spinal cord cancer'. Note that in the postcyclic component each word is analyzed separately, as syntactic phrases have not been formed yet. The input structures are syllabified, which is an effect of continuous syllabification that begins operating in the cyclic component. For typographical simplicity, only the input structure is fully represented. Subsequent derivational stages have been simplified by leaving out the part of the representation that is not altered by a given rule.

(19)

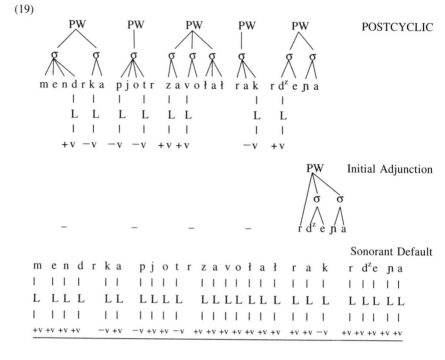

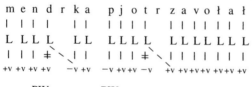

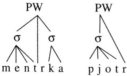

3. OPTIMALITY THEORY

Optimality Theory assumes that phonological generalizations are stated on output representation (Prince and Smolensky, 1993) or on the relationship between underlying representation and output representation (correspondence theory; McCarthy and Prince, 1995). This hypothesis conflicts directly with the analysis of extrasyllabic consonants in the preceding section. As is made clear by (19), the crux of the analysis is the assumption that the prosodification of extrasyllabic consonants proceeds in stages. Specifically, it is necessary to distinguish the stages before and after Regressive Voice Assimilation has applied. Word-initial extrasyllabic consonants are prosodified at an early stage (Initial Adjunction) and are therefore voiced (Sonorant Default). Word-medial and word-final SSG offenders are included into prosodic structure later (Default Adjunction). This explains why they have not undergone Sonorant Default and are therefore transparent to Regressive Voice Assimilation. The node to which extrasyllabic consonants are adjoined is the same for both Initial Adjunction and Default Adjunction: it is PW. The evidence for adjunction to PW comes from the behavior of word-medial consonants (native-speaker intuitions). The reasoning is then as follows. Since we know from the inspection of word-medial contexts that Polish favors adjunction to PW, it is natural to assume that consonants at word edges are also adjoined to PW. Challenging this assumption is the foundation for a reanalysis in terms of OT.

3.1 *Reanalysis*

In this section I demonstrate that OT affords a successful reanalysis of the facts considered in the preceding section. This reanalysis is more appealing than the original DT analysis, because it is more restrictive and follows from well-supported general constraints.

We know that extrasyllabic consonants in the word-initial position behave differently from those in other positions. If this difference cannot be ascribed to the difference in representation at various derivational stages (no such stages exist in OT), then it must be reflected in the output representation itself. A natural option is to assume that word-initial extrasyllabic consonants are adjoined to the syllable node while word-medial and word-final SSG offenders are linked to PW, as is the case in Derivational Theory. The output representations of the examples in (19) are therefore as follows:

(20) a.

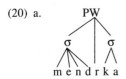 b.

The distinction between (20a) and (20b) makes sense only if it is of consequence for Sonorant Default. In particular, the [r] in (20b) must be specified for [voice], while the [r] in (20a) should not be. Sonorant Default, now an output constraint, must be restated.

(21) Sonorant Default (SONDEF): all and only syllabified sonorants are [+voice].

SONORANT DEFAULT has two functions (and hence should probably be broken down into two constraints). First, it mandates that all syllabified sonorants be specified as voiced. Second, it requires that unsyllabified sonorants may not be specified for voicing. Given these two functions, SONORANT DEFAULT produces the same configuration of specifications at the laryngeal tier as in (19). (The specification of [voice] on obstruents comes from the underlying representation.)

(22) a.

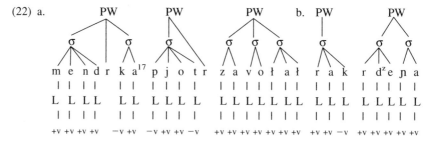

The *r* in (22a) is not part of the syllable and must therefore be unspecified for voicing. In contrast, the *r* in (22b) is syllabified and thus voiced. Constraints responsible for voice assimilation (that we do not discuss here) make sure that the outputs in (22a) have linked laryngeal nodes while the output in (22b) does not, exactly as in (19). The specification of [voice] on the extrasyllabic sonorants in (22a) is a matter of phonetic implementation, as is the case in the derivational account. The prediction with regard to the voicing of [r] in (22b) is the same in both analyses. More generally, all word-initial sonorants

---

[17] The underlying representation of *mędrk+a* 'crafty person' (gen.sg.) has a vowel after //r//. This vowel is the renowned Slavic yer. It surfaces phonetically in the nom.sg. *mędrek*. A standard analysis, due to Rubach (1986) and Kenstowicz and Rubach (1987), is to regard yers as floating melodic segments. In terms of representation, this means that yers have no X-slots (X-skeletal theory) or moras/root nodes (moraic theory). In some contexts, X-slots or moras are inserted by Yer Vocalization in DT or required by the respective constraints in OT. They are then syllabified as nuclei by regular syllabification rules/constraints. Vocalized yers, e.g. the [e] in *mędrek*, are obviously subject to Sonorant Default, because they are part of prosodic structure. The prediction is that they will block voice assimilation, which is correct. If Yer Vocalization is unable to apply, as in the gen.sg. *mędrk+a*, then yers remain floating melodies and are therefore invisible to syllabification rules. In consequence of this fact, they are not prosodified and escape Sonorant Default. We predict that unvocalized yers will be transparent to voice assimilation. This prediction is borne out. Underlying //mendrEk+a//, where *E* denotes a floating melody, surfaces as [mentrEka] or rather [mentrka] after Yer Deletion (Stray Erasure). I ignore unvocalized yers here, because they play no role in voice assimilation.

are predicted to be voiced, albeit for different reasons. In DT, this follows from the ordering of Initial Adjunction before Sonorant Default. In OT, the voicing of sonorants is a consequence of the output representation (adjunction to the syllable node) and the modification in the statement of Sonorant Default; compare (13) and (21).[18] The prediction is correct, as word-initial sonorants are always voiced, regardless of the context: *rtęć* 'mercury', *lśnić* 'shine', *mścić się* 'avenge'.

Now we return to the central question: how to guarantee that the representations in (22) are selected as optimal. (We shall ignore the constraints that account for voice assimilation.)

Syllabification is enforced in OT by the PARSE$_{SEGMENT}$ constraint.

(23) PARSE$_{SEG}$: Segments must be parsed into syllables (Prince and Smolensky, 1993).

This statement of PARSE$_{SEG}$ is inadequate for our purposes. It predicts the representation in (20b) but not the one in (20a). As has been amply demonstrated, not all segments are parsed into syllables; some segments must crucially be parsed directly into phonological words. Consequently, (23) must be relaxed to the extent that it should not specify the target node for parsing.

(24) PARSE$_{SEG}$: Segments must be parsed into prosodic structure.

The generalization that segments are normally parsed into syllables rather than into higher constituents is expressed by STRICT LAYER, a constraint which is based on the well known hierarchy of phonological constituents (Selkirk, 1978; Nespor and Vogel, 1986).

(25) STRICT LAYER: Segments-syllables-feet-phonological words, etc.

Selecting the candidates in (20a) as optimal is now a matter of constraint interaction. In (26) we suppress the linking due to Regressive Voice Assimilation (a set of constraints to this effect). The relevant instantiation of PARSE $_{SEG}$ is PARSE$_{CONS}$.
[See (26) on next pages]

A comparison of candidates (1) with (2), (3), and (4) leads to the conclusion that PARSE$_{CONS}$ and SSG must dominate STRICT LAYER. In candidate (5), SONORANT DEFAULT prohibits the assignment of [voice] to *r*, because *r* is not part of the syllable (recall the statement of SONORANT DEFAULT in (21) above).

Examples with final extrasyllabic sonorants are treated in the same way as //mendrka//: //pjotr zavołał// 'Peter called' is fully parallel to (26). Let us merely note that Final Devoicing in the prepausal position strengthens the

---

[18] The difference between OT and DT here is that OT *must* while DT *need not* ascribe the distinction between word-initial versus default adjunction to the difference in representation: adjunction to σ versus adjunction to PW. In DT the distinction between blocking effects (initially) and transparency effects (elsewhere) may be made derivationally, as shown in (19).

(26) //m e n d r k a//
$$\begin{array}{cc} | & | \\ L & L \\ | & | \\ +v & -v \end{array}$$

	PARSE$_{CONS}$	SONDEF	SSG	STRICT LAYER
(1) PW ☞ σ σ m e n d r k a | | | | | | L L L L L L | | | | | | +v +v +v +v −v +v				*
(2) PW σ σ m e n d r k a | | | | | | L L L L L L | | | | | | +v +v +v +v −v +v	*!			
(3) PW σ σ m e n d r k a | | | | | | | L L L L L L L | | | | | | | +v +v +v +v +v −v +v			*!	
(4) PW σ σ m e n d r k a | | | | | | | L L L L L L L | | | | | | | +v +v +v +v +v −v +v			*!	

(continues on next page)

(26) *continued*

	PARSE_{CONS}	SONDEF	SSG	STRICT LAYER
(5) PW σ σ m e n d r k a | | | | | | | L L L L L L L | | | | | | | +v +v +v +v +v −v +v		*!		*

conclusion that adjacency must be calculated at the laryngeal tier, as shown by the optimal candidate for *kandelabr* 'lamp'. (The effect of Final Devoicing has been suppressed.)

(27)

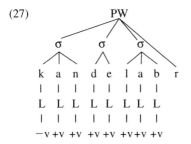

From the perspective of the root tier, //b//, phonetic [p], is not final in the phonological word, but its laryngeal node is final. If voice assimilation looks only at the laryngeal adjacency, as we suggest, then (27) satisfies the environment of Final Devoicing.

The prosodification of extrasyllabic consonants by the dominant PARSE_{CONS} raises the question of whether deletion, as a consequence of being unparsed, is at all possible in our analysis. Clearly, deletion is attested; for example, the *ć* of the stem *radość* 'joy' is deleted in the adjective *rados + n + y* 'joyful'. In order to obtain this result, the constraint banning *ć* in *rados + n + y* (whatever this constraint is)[19] must dominate PARSE_{CONS}. In sum, the prosodification of extrasyllabic consonants and deletion are not incompatible.

The selection of (20b) as the optimal candidate for *rdzenia* 'spinal cord' (gen.sg.) does not fall out from the system of constraints introduced thus far, and additional machinery is necessary. Fortunately, however, this machinery is

---

[19] This constraint prohibits certain clusters (here [çtᶜn] and is not related to SSG, since the syllabifications [ra.doç.tᶜnɨ] and [[ra.doçtᶜ.nɨ] are both well-formed in terms of sonority.

motivated independently of the voice assimilation facts (the blocking effects), as is demonstrated in (28).

In an ideal world, one could expect that the phrases in (28a) should be syllabified as in (28b) rather than as in (28c).

(28) a. choroba rdzenia [xoroba rdᶻeɲa] 'disease of the spinal cord'
     Piotr ufa [pjotr ufa] 'Peter trusts'

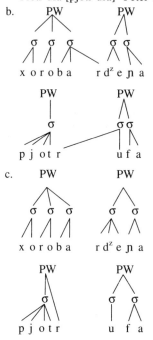

The representations in (28b) make perfect sense, since two universally very pervasive constraints are complied with: SSG in both examples and ONSET (syllables must have onsets) in *Piotr ufa*. Yet (28c) is correct. The generalization is simple: Polish does not permit syllabification across word boundaries (Kuryłowicz, 1952; Rubach and Booij, 1990*b*). In terms of OT, this generalization is expressed by alignment constraints which require that phonological and morphological constituents must coincide (McCarthy and Prince, 1994). For our purposes (word-initial adjunction), the appropriate constraint is ALIGN LEFT. McCarthy and Prince assume that this constraint aligns two constituents: phonological words and morphological stems. The facts of Polish require that the phonological constituent should be a syllable and not a phonological word.

(29) ALIGN LEFT (stem, σ)

The selection of σ rather than PW is made clear by candidates (1) and (2) for *rdzenia* 'spinal cord' (gen.sg.) in (30), on the next page. If PW were an

(30) // r dᶻ e ɲ a //
    |
    L
    |
   +v

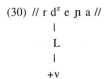

	PARSE_CONS	SONDEF	ALIGN L	SSG	STRICT LAYER
(1) PW — σ σ / r dᶻ e ɲ a / L L L L L / +v +v +v +v +v ☞				*	
(2) PW — σ σ / r dᶻ e ɲ a / L L L L / +v +v +v +v			*		*!
(3) PW — σ σ / r dᶻ e ɲ a / L L L L / +v +v +v +v	*		*!		
(4) PW — σ σ / r dᶻ e ɲ a / L L L L / +v +v +v +v		*		*!	

568   *Empirical Studies*

appropriate parameter, then candidate (2) would not violate ALIGN LEFT and would thus be optimal. Since word-initial sonorants must be voiced in order not to be transparent to voice assimilation, candidate (2) is not the correct representation.

To summarize, OT is successful in its handling of extrasyllabic consonants and the transparency/blocking effects *vis-à-vis* voice assimilation. In many ways, an OT analysis is more appealing than a derivational account, because it is able to generate the correct output from interaction of independently motivated simple generalizations (cf. Myers, Chapter 4 above). For example, adjunction to PW is seen as a result of PARSE$_{CONS}$ and SSG dominating STRICT LAYER, all of which are well-documented universal constraints. In contrast, the derivational analysis found in the literature writes this general information into a language specific rule: 'adjoin an extrasyllabic consonant to PW'. This way of handling the matter does not explain why the adjunction is not, for instance, to the phonological phrase node. An optimality answer is clear: violations should be minimal, and such an adjunction would incur an additional violation of STRICT LAYER by circumventing the PW node in addition to the syllable node.[20]

3.2. *Problematic onsets*

In this section we look at extrasyllabic consonants trapped in onsets. Their treatment is problematic in the current version of OT but not in DT. We conclude that OT should be enriched by permitting a residue of derivationalism—in other words, that OT should be replaced by DOT (Derivational Optimality Theory).

Difficulties with OT come to light when we consider sonorants that are trapped in word-initial onsets. Relevant here are the examples in (9) such as *krw + i* [krfi] 'blood' (gen.sg.).[21] The agreement in voicing between [k] and [f] is not accidental. The stem is derived from underlying //krEv//, where //E// denotes a yer, that is, a floating melodic segment (see footnote 17). The //v// is motivated by the alternation in *krew + n + y* [krev + n + i] 'relative' and the surface [f] in *krw + i* is an effect of Progressive Devoicing: /krv/ → [krf].[22] The yer //E// is not a problem.[23] As explained in note 17, unvocalized

---

[20] The difference between OT and DT here is that OT *requires* adjunction to the lowest available node while DT says nothing about it. In OT this requirement follows from the principle that violations (here of STRICT LAYER) should be minimized. There is no such principle in DT. Should it be added to DT, the difference between OT and DT for the cases under discussion would disappear.

[21] These examples illustrate the operation of Progressive Devoicing. However, it should be added that trapped sonorants in word-initial onsets occur also in cases that are traditionally analyzed in terms of Regressive Voice Assimilation such as *krtań* 'larynx' and *grdyk+a* 'Adam's apple'. From the point of view of transparency the problem is the same, regardless of whether the assimilation is progressive or regressive. Note: *kt-* and *gd-* are well-formed onsets in Polish; cf, *kto* 'who' and *gdy* 'when'; see also footnote 7.

[22] The fact that the assimilation is progressive rather than regressive is irrelevant for our purposes, because our focus is on transparency effects and not on the assimilation itself.

[23] Also, only some stems of the *krwi* type have yers.

yers are not prosodified. Consequently, Sonorant Default predicts that they are unspecified for [voice] and thus transparent. But, as I explain later, the transparency of //r// is problematic for OT.

DT has no difficulty dealing with *krwi* [krfi]. Recall that it ascribes laryngeal transparency to the fact that a consonant is not prosodified at the stage at which voice assimilation applies. The relevant representation is that in (31).

(31)

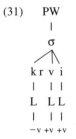

Deriving this representation is straightforward. The *k* is put into the onset by the regular syllabification rules. Alternatively, if we were to assume that the intervening *r* can block syllabification, then the *k* can be forced into the onset by Initial Adjunction if, drawing on the insight from OT we assume that it is an adjunction to the syllable rather than to the phonological word node.[24] After assimilation has taken effect, the *r* is prosodified into the syllable node because it is trapped in the onset.

(32)

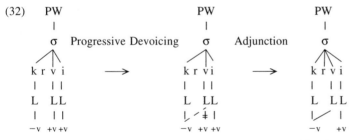

In OT, laryngeal transparency is ascribed to the prosodification of a consonant directly into PW. Therefore, to achieve the transparency, one would need the representation in (33).

---

[24] This is exactly the assumption that Bethin (1992) makes in her analysis of Polish syllabification in a derivational framework.

(33)   PW

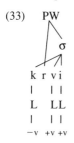

```
k r v i
|   | |
L  LL
|   | |
−v +v +v
```

In principle this representation is possible, because σ and PW are not on the same tier and, consequently, the 'no crossing of the lines' constraint is not violated.[25] However, it is difficult to maintain that (33) is desirable. If permitted, it seriously undermines the concept of the syllable and weakens the theory. Most researchers would assume that violations of STRICT LAYER should be restricted to edges of constituents, which calls for constraint (34):

(34) Constituent Contiguity (CONCONTIG): Split phonological constituents are not permitted.

This is related to the familiar contiguity constraint (e.g. Kiparsky, 1981; Levergood, 1984; Archangeli and Pulleyblank, 1994; McCarthy and Prince, 1993; Kenstowicz, 1994). The difference is that the required contiguity refers to prosodic constituency rather than to the melodic tier. That is, whether melodic segments are contiguous or not is irrelevant for (34). The instantiation of CONSTITUENT CONTIGUITY that is relevant to the exclusion of (33) is CONCONTIG$_{\text{syllable}}$: split syllables are not permitted.

As pointed out to me by Cheryl Zoll, an alternative to (33) is to permit defective syllables.

(35)   PW

```
σ | σ
|   | ∧
k r v i
|   | |
L  LL
|   | |
−v +v +v
```

This, however, is not much better than (33). First, it introduces into Polish phonology a theoretical construct—the defective syllable—that is otherwise totally unmotivated. Second, it is difficult to see what would enforce the creation of defective syllables, given the uncontroversial assumption that

---

[25] The tier distinction is precisely the reason why it is possible to speak about e.g. nucleus projection in rules ignoring consonants.

syllables must have nuclei. Notice that making STRICT LAYER dominant is not an option, because this would not permit the *r* in (35) to be prosodified into PW, and would thus miss the point.

An attempt to make SSG override the prohibition of defective syllables would damage our account of initial adjunction, since then not only the *k* in *krwi* 'blood' but also the *r* in *rdzenia* 'spinal cord' would erect a defective syllable. If this were the case, we would expect defective syllables to turn into fully-fledged syllables when an opportunity arises.[26] Such an opportunity is in fact provided by yers, the floating melodic segments explained in footnote 17. Some words with surface extrasyllabic consonants have yers in the underlying representation, e.g. *mch + u* [mx+u] 'moss' (gen.sg.). The underlying representation is //mEx + u// with a yer which is motivated by the alternation in the nom.sg. *mech* [mex]. The fact that the yer does not vocalize in [mx+u] is not understandable if *m* creates a defective syllable: *[mex+u] would have been a much better output. If defective syllables are not an option, as I suggest, then [mx + u] is the expected form. It is a consequence of ALIGN LEFTwhich pays no attention to whether a stem has an underlying yer, as in //mEx + u//, or not, as in //rd^{z}eɲ + a//.

A third possibility, linking both *k* and *r* to PW, is not attractive either.

(36)

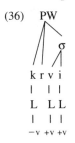

First, it is at odds with the generalization (well supported in Polish) that only syllabified segments can carry distinctive [voice]. In *krwi*, this is particularly cumbersome, since the [-voice] of *k* is actually the trigger of assimilation. Second, (36) is a violation of ALIGN LEFT (stem, σ). This by itself might not be a problem, because constraints are violable, but it is difficult to see what would enforce this violation.

In sum, OT is in trouble accounting for *krwi*. The predicted representation is (37).

---

[26] Along these lines, Piotrowski *et al.* (1992) argue that the vocalization of yers is a surface implementation of syllabic consonants.

(37)   PW

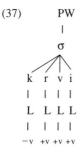

This representation is the effect of ALIGN LEFT, CONSTITUENT CONTI-GUITY, and SONORANT DEFAULT. But (37) is not good: with the *r* being syllabified and hence voiced, an account of Progressive Devoicing ($v \rightarrow f$) is impossible.

The fact that OT is unable to offer a convincing analysis of *krwi* is disturb-ing. Notice that the generalization is straightforward: non-initial extrasyllabic consonants are transparent. This generalization is reflected in *krwi*. Unlike in *rdzenia* 'spinal cord', the *r* in *krwi* is non-initial, just as in the case of *mędrka* 'crafty person'. Therefore it is natural that the *r*s in *krwi* and *mędrka* behave in the same way.

There is of course yet another analysis of *krwi*. Suppose evaluation of output candidates is carried out in two steps or at two levels (see chapters 8, 9, and, in particular, 16 and 17, all above). At level one, SSG dominates PARSE$_{CONS}$. Consider tableau (38) on the next page. Candidates (2) and (6) are correctly disqualified (they do not permit Progressive Devoicing; cf. the 'no crossing of lines' constraint). Candidate (5) is rejected, because it violates both SONOR-ANT DEFAULT and SSG. ALIGN LEFT (stem, σ) dismisses candidate (3), while CONSTITUENT CONTIGUITY argues against candidate (4). We thus arrive at (1) as the optimal output. Progressive Devoicing then takes effect (syllabified sonorants are not transparent, and must therefore include the value [+voice] at this stage).

The input to level two is the optimal output from level one, candidate (1) in (38). Faithfulness constraints make sure that any reversal of the Progressive Devoicing effects from level one is not possible. The crucial difference between levels one and two is the ranking of PARSE$_{CONS}$ and SSG: SSG >> PARSE$_{CONS}$ at level one, and PARSE$_{CONS}$ >> SSG at level two. Given the latter, the *r* is integrated into the onset. There is a violation of SONORANT DEFAULT (the *r* is syllabified and not voiced), but this is enforced by the 'no crossing of lines', an inviolable constraint on autosegmental linking. The ill-formed candidate (4) of (38) is excluded if CONSTITUENT CONTIGUITY outranks SONORANT DEFAULT. The optimal candidate is (5) from (38), but /k/ and /v/ share the laryngeal node, which is an effect of Progressive Devoi-cing at level one. This reasoning is summarized in tableau (39) on pp. 575–6.

(38) //k r v i//
```
     |   |
     L   L
     |   |
    −v   +v
```

	Align L	SonDef	ConContig	SSG	PARSE_CONS	Strict Layer
(1) PW ☞					*	
(2) PW		*!			*	
(3) PW	*!				*	*
(4) PW			*!			*

(continues on next page)

574   *Empirical Studies*

(38) *continued*

	Align L	SonDef	ConContig	SSG	PARSE_CONS	Strict Layer

(5)   PW
   |
   σ
 /|\\
k r v i
 | ||
 L LL
  | ||
−v +v+v
		*!		*		

(6)   PW
   |
   σ
 /|\\
k r v i
||||
LLLL
||||
−v+v +v+v
				*!		

Candidate (2) (or any other candidate in which the L nodes of //k// and //v// are not linked) violates Faithfulness with regard to Progressive Devoicing. Candidates (3), (4), and (5) are disqualified by No Crossing of Lines, PARSE_CONS, and CONSTITUENT CONTIGUITY, respectively. Candidate (5) is excluded by ALIGN LEFT and/or PARSE_CONS.

The two-level analysis of extrasyllabic consonants and their interaction with voice assimilation is appealing in the sense that it is set in terms of simple and widely recognized constraints and representations. However, it is difficult to accept from the point of view of OT, because it is based on the concept of steps or levels. These levels are derivational in the most classic understanding of the word, since they do not require any correlation to morphological constituency, as is the case in the stem versus stem-plus-affix levels of Axininca Campa in McCarthy and Prince (1993), or in the analysis of Booij and Clements in Chapters 8 and 9 above, respectively [Editor]. In correspondence theory (McCarthy and Prince, 1995), a recent variant of OT, a two-step analysis is completely untenable. This follows from the rejection of the principle of Containment requiring that unparsed structure be present in the output.[27] The consequence is that unparsed segments do not exist, because all unparsed information is immediately deleted. Thus, the optimal output in (38) would

[27] Containment prescribes that no structure is literally deleted in the output. Unparsed structure, i.e. the structure that is not linked to higher levels in the representation, is not realized phonetically.

(39)　PW

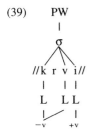

	Line Cross	ProgDev	Align L	ConContig	PARSE_CONS	SSG	SonDef	Strict Layer
(1) PW ☞						*	*	
(2) PW		*!				*	*	
(3) PW	*!					*		
(4) PW					*!			

(continues on next page)

(39) *continued*

	Line Cross	ProgDev	Align L	ConContig	PARSE$_{CONS}$	SSG	SonDef	Strict Layer
(5) PW σ k r v i | | | L LL ⌐/ | −v +v				*!				*
(6) PW σ k r v i | | | L LL ⌐/ | −v +v			*!		*			*

lose its *r* and the *r* could not be recovered at level two. The analysis would produce *[kfi] for the correct [krfi].

In sum, the correspondence theory of OT predicts that the analysis just outlined is impossible. Given this result, one is forced to look for further alternative treatments. Two new options are considered below.

One possibility is to assume the constraint in (40).[28]

(40) INITIAL VOICE: Word-initial sonorants must be voiced.

INITIAL VOICE yields the correct result: the *r* is required to be voiced in *rak rdzenia* [k rd^z] 'spinal cord cancer' but not in *krwi* [krfi] 'blood' (gen.sg.) where it is not word-initial. The facts of blocking (initially) and transparency (elsewhere) are accounted for.[29]

INITIAL VOICE would be a viable option if one could claim that it replaces the familiar generalization that sonorants are voiced (SONORANT DEFAULT). Word-initial sonorants would be voiced by (40). The voicing of sonorants in other positions might then be relegated to phonetic implementa-

---

[28] I would like to thank Michael Kenstowicz for drawing my attention to this possibility.

[29] Beckman (1995) in her analysis of vowel harmony in Shona suggests that word-initial syllables behave differently from other syllables. As pointed out to me by Michael Kenstowicz, the special behavior of word-initial extrasyllabic consonants in Polish might be related to Beckman's observation. This, however, does not solve our problem, as I explain below.

tion. SONORANT DEFAULT—more specifically, its clause mandating the voicing of sonorants—would not be a phonological generalization, which would produce a simpler system of phonological constraints. Unfortunately, this line of reasoning does not seem to be on the right track, as is demonstrated by the following two generalizations from Polish.

First, as mentioned in section 2, it is not true that only word-initial sonorants are non-transparent to voice assimilation. The generalization is that all syllabified sonorants, regardless of where they are in the word, are non-transparent. Thus, Regressive Voice Assimilation is blocked in *buty* 'shoes' and *burty* 'ship's sides' ([b] not [p]) as well as in *tuby* 'tubes' and *trudy* 'efforts' ([t] not [d]), which is understandable if SONORANT DEFAULT is a phonological constraint (the intervening sonorants are syllabified, hence voiced and non-transparent). Second, Obstruentization, a generalization that sonorants become obstruents in some contexts, yields invariably a voiced obstruent and the voicing of this obstruent is contrastive.[30] Thus, *kasz* + *e* [kaše] 'porridge' (nom.pl.) contrasts with *karz* + *e* [kaže] 'penalty' (dat.sg.). The latter has an underlying //r//, compare *kar* + *a* (nom.sg.). (The //r// changes into [ž] before front vowels; see Rubach (1984).) We conclude that Sonorant Default cannot be dispensed with.[31] But then postulating Initial Voice makes no sense, since we are back to the original dilemma: how to avoid syllabifying the *r* in *krwi* [krfi] 'blood' (gen.sg.) into the onset. (If *r* is syllabified, then it will be voiced and hence non-transparent, which is incorrect.)

There is yet another line of reasoning. Suppose we postulate (41) as a new constraint.

(41) TRAPPED SONORANT: Sonorants trapped in the onset cannot be voiced.

If (41) outranks SONORANT DEFAULT, then the *r* in *krwi* will not be voiced. It will therefore be transparent and, apparently, Progressive Devoicing can be accounted for: /krvi/ → [krfi].

The difficulty with TRAPPED SONORANT (as well as with IINITIAL VOICE) is that it states the problem rather than solves it. This is not satisfactory, since the point of the debate is not to state the problem but to derive the peculiar behavior of words such as *krwi* from an interaction of independent generalizations. DT achieves this goal by building its account on three different observations:

(42) a. Polish does not permit syllabification across word boundaries.
  b. Non-heterosyllabic geminate clusters are permitted only in the word-initial position: *ssać* 'suck'.
  c. Word-initial sonorants are non-transparent.

---

[30] This is a typical situation cross-linguistically, see Kenstowicz (1993).
[31] [voice] in sonorants is relevant for two other processes in Polish in addition to Obstruentization: Cracow Voicing and, historically, Raising. The former, specific to the Cracow dialect, voices obstruents before both syllabified and extrasyllabic sonorants across word boundaries (see e.g. Rubach, 1996). The latter raises //o// to [u] before voiced obstruents and sonorants (see e.g. Bethin, 1992).

These generalizations follow if we assume Initial Adjunction in addition to Default Adjunction. The behavior of *krwi* is then a consequence of derivation. The *r* in *krwi* is not subject to Initial Adjunction, because it is not at the beginning of the word. Therefore it remains unprosodified and unspecified for [voice]. Its transparency is predicted if Default Adjunction applies at a later derivational stage than Progressive Devoicing.

In OT the functions of Initial Adjunction and Default Adjunction are taken over without loss of generalization by ALIGN LEFT and PARSE$_{CONS}$, respectively. But the behavior of *krwi* is not a matter of interaction of generalizations. We need TRAPPED SONORANT as a separate constraint. The problem is that constraints such as TRAPPED SONORANT and INITIAL VOICE seem to be ad hoc stipulations. In terms of motivation, they are not even distantly comparable to constraints such as ALIGN LEFT which covers the three independent generalizations in (42). In addition, TRAPPED SONORANT is flawed for methodological reasons. Reference to the 'trapped segment' is in fact a reference to SSG ('trapped' means 'violating SSG'). Thus the effect of one constraint (SSG) is crucially written into the statement of another constraint (TRAPPED SONORANT). That is, TRAPPED SONORANT is not an independent generalization.[32]

The insights of OT and the descriptive adequacy of DT can be reconciled if we adopt the solution proposed in (38). Recall that it rests upon the assumption that OT evaluation is carried out in two steps. Then there is no need for ad hoc constraints. We obtain the correct result from the interaction of the constraints whose status is beyond doubt. But to permit this solution, the following two assumptions are necessary:

(i)   Some residue of serialism (stepwise evaluation) must be recognized as admissible, even when it is not obvious that the particular steps have to coincide with morphological domains.[33]

(ii) Containment or some such principle should be maintained. In particular, the assumption of correspondence OT that unparsed segments are automatically deleted must be abandoned. This is crucial, since unparsed segments must be able to survive into later levels or steps (recall the discussion in connection with (38)).

These assumptions incorporate into OT a derivational procedure of DT. We are thus looking at Derivational Optimality Theory (DOT).

---

[32] The same objection would be valid if TRAPPED SONORANT were to be generalized to all extrasyllabic sonorants.

[33] While it is true that the steps required by our analysis do not *have* to coincide with morphological domains, it is also true that they *may* be defined morphologically. In particular, as pointed out to me by Michael Kenstowicz, the first step shown in (38) could correspond to the word level (in the sense of Lexical Phonology) and the second step to the sentence level.

4. Conclusion

The assumption that generalizations must be stated on output forms makes OT more restrictive than DT, since less structure can be manipulated. The restriction to output forms leads to a highly articulated theory of representations, a point that has been illustrated by my analysis of transparency and blocking effects in voice assimilation. (Recall that the word-initial adjunction is to the syllable node while the default adjunction is to the PW node.)

The restrictiveness of OT leads to an analysis that is more explanatory than that of DT. With its principle that violations of constraints must be minimal, OT provides motivation for adjunction to the PW node in the instance of non-initial extrasyllabic consonants. Adjunction to higher nodes, for example to the phonological phrase node, would incur added violations of STRICT LAYER. Such an adjunction is predictably non-optimal. In a derivational account, the node to which adjunction is effected is no more than a stipulation.

The success of OT is overshadowed by the difficulties encountered with the analysis of sonorants trapped in onsets (Progressive Devoicing). A simple generalization that non-initial extrasyllabic sonorants are transparent cannot be expressed in OT without admitting odd representations that are otherwise not attested in the phonological system of Polish. There is, however, a straightforward solution to the difficulties encountered in OT: permit derivational evaluation. In sum, rather than DT or OT, we need DOT (Derivational Optimality Theory). It is clear, however, that the derivationalism of DOT should be minimized in order to keep the theory as restrictive as possible. A parallel to Lexical Phonology suggests itself: the fewer levels the better.

Acknowledgements

I would like to thank Juliette Blevins, Nick Clements, Michael Kenstowicz, Paddy Lyons, Doug Pulleyblank, Cathie Ringen, Iggy Roca, Cheryl Zoll, and the audiences at the University of Essex and in Cortona for discussion and inspiring comments. Needless to say, the responsibility for whatever errors there may be in this chapter is solely mine.

References

Archangeli, D., and Pulleyblank, D. (1994). *Grounded Phonology*. Cambridge, Mass.: MIT Press.

Beckman, J. N. (1995). 'Shona height harmony: markedness and positional identity', in J. N. Beckman, L. W. Dickey, and S. Urbanczyk (eds.), *Papers in Optimality Theory*, (University of Massachusetts Occasional Papers 18). Amherst: GLSA, 53–75.

Bethin, C. Y. (1992). *Polish Syllables: The Role of Prosody in Phonology and Morphology*. Columbus, Oh.: Slavica.

Booij, G. E., and Rubach, J. (1987). 'Postcyclic versus postlexical rules in Lexical Phonology', *Linguistic Inquiry* **18**: 1–44.

Fudge, E. C. (1969). 'Syllables', *Journal of Linguistics* **5**: 253–87.

Fujimura, O., and Lovins, J. (1978). 'Syllables as concatenative phonetic units', in A. Bell and J. Hooper (eds.), *Syllables and Segments*. New York: North-Holland.

Gussmann, E. (1992). 'Resyllabification and delinking: the case of Polish voicing', *Linguistic Inquiry* **23**: 29–56.

Halle, M., and Vergnaud, J.-R. (1980). 'Three-dimensional phonology', *Journal of Linguistic Research* **1**: 83–105.

Hayes, B. (1984). 'The phonetics and phonology of Russian voice assimilation', in M. Aronoff and R. T. Oehrle (eds.), *Language Sound Structure*. Cambridge, Mass.: MIT Press. 318–28.

Itô, J. (1986). 'The Syllable Theory in Prosodic Phonology'. Dissertation, University of Massachusetts, Amherst.

Jespersen, O. (1904). *Lehrbuch der Phonetik*. Leipzig: B. G. Teubner.

Kenstowicz, M. (1993). *Phonology in Generative Grammar*. Oxford: Blackwell.

———— (1994). 'Syllabification in Chukchee: a constraints-based analysis', Annual Meeting of the Formal Linguistics Society of Mid America **4**: 160–81.

———— and Rubach, J. (1987). 'The phonology of syllabic nuclei in Slovak', *Language* **63**: 463–97.

Kiparsky, P. (1981). 'Vowel Harmony'. MS, MIT.

Kuryłowicz, J. (1952). 'Uwagi o polskich grupach spółgłoskowych' (*Remarks about consonant clusters in Polish*), *Biuletyn Polskiego Towarzystwa Językoznawczego* **11**: 54–69 (in Polish).

Levergood, B. (1984). 'Rule-governed vowel harmony and the Strict Cycle', *North East Linguistic Society Proceedings* **14** (University of MAssachusetts, Amherst): 275–93.

Levin, J. (1985). 'A Metrical Theory of Syllabicity'. Dissertation, MIT.

Lombardi, L. (1991). 'Laryngeal Features and Laryngeal Neutralization'. Dissertation, University of Massachusetts, Amherst.

McCarthy, J. J., and Prince, A. S. (1993). 'Prosodic morphology: Constraint Interaction and Satisfaction'. MS, University of Massachusetts, Amherst, and Rutgers University.

———— ———— (1994). 'Generalized alignment', In G. E. Booij and J. van Marle (eds.), *Yearbook of Morphology 1993*. Dordrecht: Kluwer, 79–153.

———— ———— (1995). 'Faithfulness and Reduplicative Identity'. MS, University of Massachusetts, Amherst, and Rutgers University.

Nespor, M., and Vogel, I. (1986). *Prosodic Phonology*. Dordrecht: Foris.

Piotrowski, M., Roca, I., and Spencer, A. (1992). 'Polish yers and lexical syllabicity', *The Linguistic Review* **9**: 27–67.

Prince, A. S., and Smolensky, P. (1993). 'Optimality Theory: Constraint Interaction in Generative Grammar'. MS, Rutgers University and University of Colorado, Boulder.

Rubach, J. (1984). *Cyclic and Lexical Phonology: The Structure of Polish*. Dordrecht: Foris.

—— (1986). 'Abstract vowels in three-dimensional phonology: the yers', *The Linguistic Review* **5**: 247–80.

—— (1993). *The Lexical Phonology of Slovak*. Oxford: Clarendon Press.

—— (1996). 'Nonsyllabic analysis of voice assimilation in Polish'. *Linguistic Inquiry* **27**: 69–110.

—— and Booij, G. E. (1990*a*). 'Syllable structure assignment in Polish', *Phonology* **7**: 121–58.

—— —— (1990*b*). 'Edge of constituent effects in Polish', *Natural Language and Linguistic Theory* **8**: 427–63.

Selkirk, E. O. (1978). 'On prosodic structure and its relation to syntactic structure', in T. Fretheim (ed.), *Nordic Prosody, II*. Trondheim: Tapir, 111–40.

—— (1980). 'The role of prosodic categories in English word stress', *Linguistic Inquiry* **11**: 563–606.

Sievers, E. (1881). *Grundzüge der Phonetik*. Leipzig: Breitkopf & Hartel.

Steriade, D. (1982). 'Greek Prosodies and the Nature of Syllabification'. Dissertation, MIT.

Whitney, W. D. (1874). 'The relation of vowel and consonant', in Whitney, (ed.), *Oriental and Linguistic Studies*, 2nd series, New York: Scribner, Armstrong.

Wierzchowska, B. (1971). *Wymowa polska (Polish pronunciation)*. Warsaw: Państwowe Zakłady Wydawnictw Szkolnych.

Author Index

Language Index

Subject Index

(Constraint names are capitalized for ease of recognition; page numbers in bold identify constraint definitions; α is alphabetized as *a*, ŋ as *n*, σ as *s*, and *?* as *q*; operators and orthographic diacritics are ignored in the alphabetization)

600   Subject Index